Joseph's Temples

Kirtland Temple

Joseph's Temples

The Dynamic Relationship between Freemasonry and Mormonism

Michael W. Homer

THE UNIVERSITY OF UTAH PRESS
Salt Lake City

The Defiance House Man colophon is a registered trademark
of the University of Utah Press. It is based on a four-foot-tall Ancient
Puebloan pictograph (late PIII) near Glen Canyon, Utah.

LIBRARY OF CONGRESS CATALOGING-IN-PUBLICATION DATA
Homer, Michael W.
 Joseph's temples : the dynamic relationship between Freemasonry and Mormonism /
    Michael W. Homer.
     pages cm
 Includes bibliographical references and index.
 ISBN 978-1-60781-344-6 (cloth) -- ISBN 978-1-64769-212-4 (paperback) --
 ISBN 978-1-60781-346-0 (ebook)
 1. Church of Jesus Christ of Latter-day Saints--History. 2. Mormon Church--History.
 3. Freemasonry. 4. Freemasons. 5. Mormon temples. I. Title.
  BX8611.H68 2014
  289.309--dc23
                        2014007966

Some of the material in this work has previously been published in "Masonry
and Mormonism in Utah, 1847–1984," *Journal of Mormon History* 18, no. 2
(Fall 1992): 57–96; "'Similarity of Priesthood in Masonry': The Relationship
between Freemasonry and Mormonism," *Dialogue: A Journal of Mormon
Thought* 27, no. 3 (Fall 1994): 1–116; and "'Why Then Introduce Them into Our
Inner Temple?': The Masonic Influence on Mormon Denial of Priesthood
Ordination to African American Men," *The John Whitmer Historical
Association Journal* 26 (2006): 234–59.

Frontispiece: From Henry Howe, *Historical Collections of Ohio;
Containing a Collection of the Most Interesting Facts, Traditions, Biographical,
Sketches, Anecdotes, Etc. Relating to its General and Local History*
(Cincinnati: Published for the Author by Derby, Bradley & Co., 1848), 4.
Courtesy of Rick Grunder.

Contents

List of Illustrations

Acknowledgments

I have received valuable input from the following individuals: John R. Alley, Lavina Fielding Anderson, LeRoy Axland, Will Bagley, Clair Barrus, Gary Bergera, Martha Sonntag Bradley, John L. Brooke, Clint Bartholomew, Carter Charles, Clyde Forsberg, Robert A. Gilbert, Rick Grunder, Carmon Hardy, Mervin Hogan, Massimo Introvigne, Lyn Jacobs, Walter Jones, Tom Kimball, Lachlan MacKay, William MacKinnon, H. Michael Marquardt, Gary Maxwell, Connell O'Donovan, Gregory Prince, Michael Reed, Bernadette Rigal-Cellard, Blaine Simmons, Linda Thatcher, Gregory C. Thompson, and Richard Van Wagoner. Massimo Introvigne, Kent L. Walgren, and Arturo de Hoyas provided me with valuable information and analysis concerning this topic when I wrote "'Similarity of Priesthood in Masonry': The Relationship between Freemasonry and Mormonism."

I acknowledge the following institutions whose collections I have consulted while writing this work: J. Willard Marriott Library, Special Collections, University of Utah, Salt Lake City; Library of Congress, Washington, D.C.; Center for Studies on New Religions, Torino, Italy; Church History Library, the Church of Jesus Christ of Latter-day Saints, Salt Lake City; Grand Lodge Library, Grand Lodge of Utah, Salt Lake City; Library, United Grand Lodge of England, London. I also thank the British Library, London, England; Museum of the Grand Orient of France, Paris, France; the Grand Lodge of Ireland, Dublin, Ireland; Library of the Community of Christ, Independence, Missouri; Il Museo Egizio, Torino, Italy; Musée du Louvre, Paris, France; and the Egyptian Museum, Cairo, Egypt.

Introduction

Masonic scholars have complained that historians ignore the impact of freemasonry even though they should "cover the complete scope of all the fields which influenced or were influenced by freemasonry, and where freemasonry or freemasons played a role."[1] American Masons Arturo de Hoyos and Brent Morris agree that "academics have usually tended to discount Freemasonry and fraternalism, while Masons have often focused on...legendary beginnings (Egypt, Ancient Mysteries, Knights Templar, and so on)." The result has been, according to de Hoyos and Morris, "a dearth of research placing Freemasonry in its proper framework."[2]

Some of the same scholars have observed that Mormon historians in particular have neglected Masonic influences on their religion and rituals. De Hoyos has pointedly critiqued Mormons that rely on an "uncritical school" to "persuade members of the LDS Church [Church of Jesus Christ of Latter-day Saints] that Freemasonry has existed for thousands of years and that their *Temple Endowment Ritual* is an authentic restoration of ancient practices, rather than an unacknowledged 'borrowing from Freemasonry.'"[3] Similarly, two prominent British Masonic scholars concluded that Mormon historians refuse to address this topic because "Mormonism

---

1. Jan A. M. Snoek, "Researching Freemasonry: Where Are We?" *Journal for Research into Freemasonry and Fraternalism* 1:2 (2010): 242. British historian John Roberts lamented that historians have failed to study Freemasons' "influence as cultural agencies, as generators and transmitters of ideas and symbols, and of sources of attitudes and images." Ibid., 242–43. See also Pierre-Yves Beaurepaire, "Researching Freemasonry in the Twenty-first Century: Opportunities and Challenges," *Journal for Research into Freemasonry and Fraternalism* 1:2 (2010): 249–57; Natalie Bayer, "From a Legitimate Field of Research to an Accepted University-Taught Subject," *Journal for Research into Freemasonry and Fraternalism* 1:2 (2010): 258–64.
2. Arturo de Hoyos and S. Brent Morris, *Freemasonry in Context: History, Ritual, Controversy* (Lanham, MD: Lexington Books, 2004), viii.
3. Arturo de Hoyos, *The Cloud of Prejudice: A Study in Anti-Masonry* (Kila, MT: Kessinger Publishing Company, 1993), 75.

perpetuates and practices anti-Masonry—perhaps the only body to do so for reasons of self-preservation."[4]

Some non-Masonic historians have made similar statements. Mark C. Carnes has observed that: "The best history of the Mormon church, written by Mormons, skirts this issue. The authors refer to [Joseph] Smith's 'purported use of the Masonic ceremony in Mormon temple ordinances' and note that Mormons recognized that there were 'similarities as well as differences' in the rituals; there is no further elaboration."[5] But, as he noted, "Whether Smith stole the temple rites from Freemasonry, as the Masons claim, or received them as revelation from God is ultimately a question of faith," but it "cannot be disputed…that quasi-Masonic ritual figured prominently in the lives of most Mormon men."[6] Likewise, social historian Paul J. Rich concluded that: "Historians cannot afford to overlook the Masonic ingredient, which manifests itself in surprising ways" including the "pertinent case…of the world-wide Mormon movement," which "has an enormous debt to Freemasonry."[7]

Such criticisms provide a challenge to Mormon and non-Mormon historians to not only acknowledge the dynamic relationship between Freemasonry and Mormonism but to re-evaluate the implications of Smith's mistaken belief, shared by many of his contemporaries, that Freemasonry had ancient origins and that it could trace it rituals back to Solomon's Temple. This study will examine this dynamic relationship since the beginning of Mormonism until the present time.

The scope of parallels is much broader than the strains of anti-Masonry in the Book of Mormon or the similarities that have been noted between Masonic and Mormon temple rituals. There are likenesses between Masonry's Enochian legend and Smith's "gold plate" narrative, the Royal Arch High Priesthood and Smith's restoration of the High Priesthood, Masonry's and Mormonism's rites of washing and anointing, as well as Smith's retranslation of existing scriptures and his translation of ancient papyri and similar subjects in Freemasonry.

In order to provide a foundation for this discussion it is necessary to understand the rudiments of existing scholarship concerning the origins of Freemasonry in England, Ireland, and Scotland and its subsequent

---

4. John Hamill and R. A. Gilbert, *World Freemasonry, An Illustrated History* (London: Aquarian Press, 1991), 201. See also Henry W. Coil, *Conversations on Freemasonry* (Richmond, VA: Macoy Publishing and Masonic Supply Co., Inc., n.d.), 237–38.
5. Mark C. Carnes, *Secret Ritual and Manhood in Victorian America* (New Haven, CT: Yale University Press, 1989), 173n22.
6. Ibid., 6–7.
7. Paul J. Rich, *Chains of Empire: English Public Schools, Masonic Cabalism, Historical Causality, and Imperial Clubdom* (London: Regency Press, 1991), 137.

expansion and development on the Continent. The legends of Freemasonry, which are premised on the claim of ancient origins, differ significantly from its historical origins (which are still not agreed on) but which have been traced to medieval working guilds. The energetic evolution of Masonic high degrees, which introduced elaborations on scriptural narratives, adds an additional layer of complexity to Freemasonry and its connection with Mormonism.

The connection between Mormonism and Masonry began in New York and continued in Ohio, Missouri, Illinois, and Utah. Historian John L. Brooke has noted that eventually "Mormon commentary made the link with Freemasonry firm and inescapable."[8] Indeed, a catalogue of statements made by nineteenth-century LDS Church leaders demonstrates a solid belief that there was a connection between Masonry and Mormonism, particularly with respect to temple worship. In Nauvoo the connections were public and explicit as most of the Mormon hierarchy either became Masons or realigned themselves with it for the first time in more than a decade. Mormon leaders taught that Solomon's Temple was built "for the purpose of giving endowments" and had survived (in a degenerated form) in the rituals of Freemasonry.

Masons accordingly practiced an "apostate endowment" just as sectarians practiced "apostate religions" while Joseph Smith had restored the original ritual.[9] Apostle Heber C. Kimball quoted Smith as teaching that the LDS Church had "true Masonry" and that the "Masonry of today is taken from the apostasy which took place in the days of Solomon and David."[10] Smith's new temple ritual in Nauvoo, which was a radical elaboration of the earlier Kirtland endowment ceremony, was designed to bestow light, knowledge, and spiritual powers on Smith's inner circle and thereby enable them to eventually become exalted beings. It provided a synthesis of a number of eclectic and esoteric beliefs, such as baptism for the dead, access to the powers of heaven, the formulation of ways to bind those powers, and the creation of a highly ordered theocratic society.

Smith's organization of the Nauvoo Female Relief Society, which became connected with his expansive ideas concerning marriage, also contained a specter of Masonry. Smith attempted to teach the Mormon sisters to keep a secret through that society before he incorporated some of the

8. John L. Brooke, *The Refiner's Fire: The Making of Mormon Cosmology, 1644–1844* (Cambridge: Cambridge University Press, 1994), 252.

9. Brigham Young, "Remarks by President Brigham Young," *Journal of Discourses*, 26 vols. (Liverpool, England: Latter-day Saints' Bookseller's Depot, 1854–86), 18:303 (January 1, 1877).

10. Stanley B. Kimball, *Heber C. Kimball: Mormon Patriarch and Pioneer* (Urbana: University of Illinois Press, 1981), 84–85.

same women into temple rituals that included explicit vows of secrecy. Even Brigham Young's institutionalization and justification of a policy that prohibited blacks from holding priesthood powers and participating in Mormon temple rituals had parallels with American Masonic practices.

The dynamic connection between Masonry and Mormonism continued after the LDS Church transferred its headquarters to Salt Lake City. Non-Mormon merchants and soldiers organized Masonic lodges in Utah Territory and resolutely barred Mormons (even those who were already Masons) from participating because the church taught plural marriage. After the Mormons abandoned plural marriage, Utah Masons, believing that Smith had purloined Masonic rituals, argued that Mormons consequently were still ineligible to become Masons.

These developments took place during the same period when the Authentic School of Masonry was debunking the notion that Masonic rituals originated in antiquity. Thereafter, Mormon writers advanced revisionist theories concerning the origins of the endowment, which either denied or marginalized connections between Masonry and Mormonism. They may have believed that this approach promoted faith since it addressed the gap between Smith's teachings and the Authentic School of Masonry concerning the antiquity of Masonic rituals. Thereafter, a new generation of church leaders (who had never been Masons) airbrushed the connection out of church history even though many of their predecessors who knew and admired Smith had recognized and acknowledged the connection.

While most historians now acknowledge connections between Mormonism and Masonry, the current debate focuses on the significance and depth of these correspondences. Some historians contend that the goals and aspirations of Freemasonry and Mormonism were so radically different during the nineteenth century that any similarities in their rituals are superficial. While such arguments are faith-based and assume that the first Mormon was inspired, they discount the writings of early Mormon leaders and Masonic lecturers whose beliefs concerning the Craft contained many equivalents to both the spirit and form of Mormon beliefs and practices.

European Freemasonry

WHEN JOSEPH SMITH JR. (1805–1844) established the Church of Christ in 1830, the Grand Lodge of London was still a relatively young organization. In 1717 four London lodges organized a grand lodge and during the next century the institution of Freemasonry experienced dramatic growth in England, on the Continent, and in America. During this same period Masons embellished their legends, which claimed that the institution of Freemasonry could be traced to Adam, Enoch, and Noah and that Masonic rituals were descended from those practiced in Solomon's Temple. Masons also developed new "high degrees" that included the Master Masons Degree and the Royal Arch, which became core rituals.

Despite the relative youth of the Grand Lodge, Masonic historians have acknowledged that the origins of the institution of Freemasonry remain "one of the most debated, and debatable, subjects in the whole realm of historical inquiry." Frances Yates observed that "one has to distinguish between the legendary history of Freemasonry and the problem of when it actually began as an organized institution" and that "most books on Freemasonry confuse architecture in the Bible, legendary stories, the history of architecture in general, and the history of Freemasonry."[1]

OPERATIVE MASONRY

Some historians have concluded that modern Freemasonry can be traced to "the organization and practices, which have from time to time prevailed among medieval working masons." Operative masons formed Catholic brotherhoods in England, Scotland, and Ireland that observed a simple admission ceremony (at least in Scotland and England), which included a Christian invocation, the recitation of rules and regulations (eventually

1. Frances A. Yates, *The Rosicrucian Enlightenment* (London: Routledge & Kegan Paul, 1972), 209, 214.

called the Old Charges), as well as the administration of an oath sworn on the Bible to obey the rules and regulations and to be faithful to the monarch and the church.[2] At least 115 texts have been discovered that include Old Charges that were given to masons and contain a legendary history that had been developed by the fifteenth century.[3]

The earliest text, called the Regius Manuscript (c. 1390, also known as the Halliwell Manuscript), records that Euclid invented geometry in Egypt and that the knowledge of Masonry was preserved and "came into England" during the reign of King Athelstane. The Cooke Manuscript (c. 1410) revealed that Jabal, who was born into the seventh generation after Adam and was the son of Lamech, "was the first man that ever found geometry and Masonry." He was "Cain's master mason, and governor of all his works, when he made the city of Enock, that was the first city." Jabal's half-brother, Tubal Cain, "was the founder of smith's craft…that is to say, of iron, of brass, of gold, and of silver."[4]

The Cooke Manuscript recorded that Lamech, Jabal, and Tubal Cain preserved "the sciences that they [had] found on marble (that would not burn) and on latres (which would not sink) and these stones were preserved during Noah's flood. Pythagoras found one of the stones and Hermes found the other, many years after the flood," and "taught forth the sciences that they found therein written." Thereafter Abraham "taught the Egyptians the science of geometry" among whom was his clerk, Euclid. The Hebrews learned geometry in Egypt and afterward practiced it in Jerusalem where Solomon taught the craft. Finally, the science of geometry was brought to France and to England.[5]

These documents reflected inspiration from various sources, including the Bible, the writings of Josephus, the Hebrew Apocrypha, as well as the

2. See Wallace McLeod, "The Old Charges," in *The Collected "Prestonian Lectures,"* (London: Quartuor Coronati Lodge, 1986), 3:260–90.
3. See Wallace McLeod, *The Old Gothic Constitutions* (Bloomington, IL: The Masonic Book Club, 1985); *Anderson's Constitutions of 1738* (Bloomington, IL: The Masonic Book Club, 1978); William Preston, *Illustrations of Masonry*, 11th ed., 1801, reprinted with an introduction by Colin Dyer (Wellingborough: Aquarian Press, 1985); William Hutchinson, *The Spirit of Masonry* (London, 1775), reprinted with an introduction by Trevor Stewart (Wellingborough, UK: Aquarian Press, 1987); Thomas Smith Webb, *The Freemason's Monitor; or, Illustrations of Masonry* (New York: Southwick and Crooker, 1802); and George Oliver, *The Antiquities of Freemasonry; Comprising the Three Grand Periods of Masonry from the Creation of the World to the Dedication of King Solomon's Temple* (London: G. and W. B. Whittaker, 1823).
4. Douglas Knoop, G. P. Jones, and Douglas Hamer, *The Two Earliest Masonic Manuscripts* (Manchester, UK: Manchester University Press, 1938), 77. The Regius Manuscript may have been copied from earlier documents.
5. Knoop, Jones, and Hamer, *The Two Earliest Masonic Manuscripts*, 77.

classical tradition.[6] Historian David Stevenson has noted that these texts were "unusually elaborate" and that operative masonry "was to make a significant contribution to freemasonry through its emphasis on morality, its identification of the mason craft with geometry, and the importance it gave to Solomon's Temple and ancient Egypt."[7] These legends convinced Freemasons that their institution was ancient, and they continued to seek additional information concerning these founders (particularly Enoch, Abraham, and Solomon) as they developed their rituals.

By the mid-sixteenth century Scottish operative masons who completed their apprenticeships received a "mason's word," which they were bound by oath to keep secret. This word enabled them to recognize other members of the craft (and perhaps their assignments and pay grades) and prevented "cowans," nonmembers of the brotherhood, from obtaining unauthorized work. In England there is no evidence that operative masons used a mason's word as a form of recognition. Although Scottish masons only used a mason's word for a short time before non-Masons began joining the brotherhood or forming their own organizations, the word was eventually incorporated into the ritual of speculative Masonry.[8]

SPECULATIVE FREEMASONRY

There are at least seventeen Masonic documents that suggest that a speculative Masonic ritual, in which nonoperative gentlemen Masons who were drawn from the local gentry participated, existed as early as the mid-seventeenth century. Seven of these were published "from motives of curiosity, profit, or spite," and ten were prepared by Masons for personal use and to serve as *aides-mémoires*.[9] Some speculative lodges used Old Charges and the mason's word, which some Masonic historians believe establishes a link between "operative" and "speculative" Masonry. According to this theory

6. Douglas Knoop and G. P. Jones, *The Genesis of Freemasonry: An Account of the Rise and Development of Freemasonry in Its Operative, Accepted and Early Speculative Phases* (Manchester, UK: Manchester University Press, 1947), 65–66.
7. David Stevenson, *The Origins of Freemasonry: Scotland's Century, 1590–1710* (Cambridge: Cambridge University Press, 1988), 6.
8. See Harry Carr, *The Transition from Operative to Speculative Masonry* (N.P.: 1957); Douglas Knoop and G. P. Jones, *An Introduction to Freemasonry* (Manchester, UK: Manchester University Press, 1937); Douglas Knoop and G. P. Jones, *The Genesis of Freemasonry: An Account of the Rise and Development of Freemasonry in Its Operative, Accepted and Early Speculative Phases* (Manchester, UK: Manchester University Press, 1947); and Douglas Knoop and G. P. Jones, *A Short History of Freemasonry to 1730* (Manchester, UK: Manchester University Press, 1940).
9. Harry Carr, *An Analysis and Commentary of Samuel Prichard's* Masonry Dissected 1730 (Bloomington, IL: Masonic Book Club, 1977), 20–26.

nonmason gentlemen became honorary members of operative lodges because they were curious about the craft or wanted to socialize with masons
(hence "accepted"), or they were searching for esoteric secrets that they
hoped would be revealed in Masonic lodges (hence "speculative").[10]

Although not all Masonic scholars believe in this link theory, Jan Snoek
has suggested that operative masons should be referred to as "stone masons" while speculative Masons should be referred to as "gentlemen masons."[11] The difficulty of establishing such a link is that the brotherhoods
of operative masons were organized differently in Scotland and England.
Scottish masons bound themselves together as early as the sixteenth century in lodges where they governed their affairs and admitted new masons
into the craft. In England the operative masons, who formed guilds such as
the London Company of Masons, did not develop a lodge system until the
eighteenth century.[12] No one knows precisely why operative stonemasons
would admit nonguild members, or why they would agree to transform
their lodges into gentlemen's clubs, but one possible reason was because
they needed money. Historian Margaret Jacob has noted that "the Scottish
records as early as the 1650s show that the local guilds were in need of cash
and they began admitting non-masons who were relatives, or prominent
figures, with similar philosophical interests."[13]

In England, some operative lodges apparently accepted gentlemen (as
they had in Scotland) while other gentlemen decided to organize their own
lodges that did not include operative members and in which they adopted
the symbols and legends of stonemasons as allegorical teaching aids. But
some nonoperative lodges, which were controlled by gentlemen, occasionally accepted working masons who were members of an operative lodge and
bound themselves to assist them in times of need.

This combination of evolution and intervention led to the development
of a "mystical" form of speculative Masonry that was, in part, "a reaction to
Protestantism by providing a substitute for banished rituals."[14] Some of the
first documented "speculative Masons" were prominent and well-connected
gentlemen who were interested in Hermetic thought and esotericism. Her-

10. Hamill and Gilbert, *World Freemasonry*, 9–11; Knoop and Jones, *The Genesis of Freemasonry*, 41–46.
11. Snoek, "Researching Freemasonry," 236.
12. Knoop and Jones, *The Genesis of Freemasonry*, 11; Stevenson, *The Origins of Freemasonry*;
David Stevenson, *The First Freemasons: Scotland's Early Lodges and Their Members* (Aberdeen, KS: Aberdeen University Press, 1988).
13. Margaret Jacob, *The Origins of Freemasonry: Facts and Fictions* (Philadelphia: University
of Pennsylvania Press, 2006), 5.
14. See Stevenson, *The Origins of Freemasonry*, 120; Stevenson, *The First Freemasons*, 156–61;
Hamill and Gilbert, *World Freemasonry*, 9–17.

metica (Egyptian philosophical works) and the Kabbalah (a Jewish mystical system) emerged during the Renaissance and were premised on the notion that the universe could "be understood through revelation and purification."[15] Some believed that the Ancient Egyptians possessed "knowledge of the ancient world in its purest form" but that it had become "corrupted and distorted by the effete Greeks and parvenu Romans." They were convinced that "Egyptian scholars had deliberately locked up their profound knowledge in hieroglyphics," which were "the most profound of man-made symbols," and the "incomprehensibility of the hieroglyphics…served to stress how valuable that knowledge was."[16]

Masonic writer W. Kirk MacNulty has suggested that "the source of these Freemasons' interest in classical philosophy was their study of Renaissance philosophers."[17] David Stevenson, another Masonic scholar, has noted that Hermetic texts, which Renaissance gentlemen believed were written in Egypt eight centuries before Christ and foreshadowed his divine mission, but were actually written no earlier than the second century AD, emphasized "a spiritual quest whereby man could seek to distance himself from the material world and become imbued with divine power and virtues."[18] This "spiritual quest" was premised on the belief that "man could understand the world around him and would then be able to alter it, bending the powers of nature to his own ends."[19] It also advanced the notion that men could "ascend in consciousness from the physical world through the levels of the psychic/soul and the spirit and experience the Divine Presence while one is incarnate."[20] As such it provided a ladder up "to recover the divine power and perfection preserved by Adam before the Fall."[21]

ROSICRUCIAN ENLIGHTENMENT

This "new interest in the Hermetic tradition" influenced the development of a less widespread movement that has been called the "Rosicrucian Enlightenment."[22] Two Rosicrucian Manifestos, *Fama Fraternitatis* and *Confessio*

15. Stevenson, *The Origins of Freemasonry*, 79.
16. Ibid., 82–83.
17. W. Kirk MacNulty, *Freemasonry: Symbols, Secrets, Significance* (London: Thames & Hudson, Ltd., 2006), 45.
18. Stevenson, *The Origins of Freemasonry*, 83.
19. Ibid., 77, 84.
20. See MacNulty, *Freemasonry*, 44–45. MacNulty argues that "Freemasonry is a codification of that Hermetic/Kabbalistic tradition."
21. Brooke, *The Refiner's Fire*, 7. ("Adam was the manifestation of divine immortality," ibid, 8.)
22. MacNulty, *Freemasonry*, 45; Stevenson, *The Origins of Freemasonry*, 97.

Fraternitata, were published anonymously in 1614–1615 followed by a play, *The Chymical Wedding of Christian Rosenkreutz*, which was published in 1616. These documents claimed that the tomb of a mystic named Christian Rosenkreutz, who founded a secret brotherhood during the fifteenth century, was discovered that contained an altar covered with an engraved brass plate, books, and "looking-glasses of divers virtues." Rosenkreutz's remains were located beneath the altar and a parchment book (called I) was still in his hand "which next to our Bible is our greatest treasure, which ought to be delivered to the censure of the world."[23]

Frances Yates concluded in *The Rosicrucian Enlightenment* that Rosicrucian thought was a product of the seventeenth (not fifteenth) century and that it advocated "a great reformation" that would result in "'a great influx of truth and light' such as surrounded Adam in Paradise, and which God will allow before the end of the world" in order to bring about "a return to Adamic innocence."[24] The Rosicrucian documents invited interested souls to seek out the secret brotherhood and to become enlightened through a spiritual alchemy that regenerated and changed the soul.[25]

Yates argued that Protestant ministers and government agents invented the Rosicrucian myth for religious (anti-Catholic) and political (anti-Austrian) reasons. Nevertheless, some historians have speculated that Rosicrucian thought, which fueled rumors of lost ancient manuscripts, contributed to an increased interest in speculative Freemasonry.[26] Some gentlemen apparently believed that by joining a lodge bound by secret oath, with origins shrouded in mystery, they would obtain illumination concerning lost knowledge and ancient mysteries. They were anxious to obtain esoteric secrets and to advance a philosophical system of "building a better man in a better world" and adopted the tools and functions of the building trade as symbols and allegory.[27] They were also interested in architecture and geometry, and may have become persuaded that operative masons, who built cathedrals, castles, fortifications, and large estates, would share their knowledge concerning these subjects and that their lodges were good locations for intellectual exchanges.[28]

23. Yates, *The Rosicrucian Enlightenment*, 246–47.
24. Ibid., 48, 57.
25. Ibid., 61, 65.
26. Ibid., 48, 57. See also Brooke, *The Refiner's Fire*, 10–12.
27. Hamill and Gilbert, *World Freemasonry*, 15.
28. Yates, *The Rosicrucian Enlightenment*, 206–19. Yates notes: "Freemasonry combines an esoteric approach to religion with ethical teaching and emphasis on philanthropy, and in these ways follows the pattern of the R.C. [Rosicrucian] Brothers, but as A. E. Waite points out, it differs from that pattern in not being interested in reform of arts and sciences,

Sir Robert Moray (1608–1673), a founding member of the Royal Society who was interested in alchemy, was initiated in 1641 into a Scottish operative lodge that was working in northern England.[29] Elias Ashmole (1617–1692), another founding member of the Royal Society, an antiquarian book collector and a student of Hermeticism, alchemy, and Rosicrucianism, was initiated in a "casual Lodge" located in Warrington, Lancashire, England in 1646. The casual lodge that Ashmole joined consisted entirely of speculative masons. He either joined a new organization, which had never admitted operative Masons, or speculative masons had already taken control of an operative lodge. Dr. Robert Plot, who was the first keeper of the Asmolean Museum, wrote that "persons of the most eminent quality…did not disdain to be of this Fellowship."[30] Ashmole "copied out in his own hand the Rosicrucian manifestos adding to them a formal letter in his own hand admiring their aims and asking them to be allowed to join them."[31]

David Stevenson and other historians of Masonry have concluded that eventually these strands of esoteric Renaissance thought were spliced onto masonic legends.[32] Thereafter, "the myth of Egypt, Solomon's Temple, the Hermetic quest, the art of memory," were supplemented with a "secret order of invisible brethren, dedicated to seeking ultimate truths and to understanding the mysterious universe."[33] The rudimentary legends contained in the Halliwell, Cooke, and other Masonic manuscripts were symbolically reinterpreted and expanded to include new details about Noah's Ark and Solomon's Temple, including the story of Solomon's architect, Hiram Abiff.[34]

According to Stevenson there were "resemblances between Hermeticism and freemasonry which cannot be dismissed as mere coincidences." When gentlemen began to enter Freemasonry it coincided with "the Hermetic striving for enlightenment and spiritual rebirth of mankind, based on secret knowledge and secret societies or cults." This was not surprising given the Masonic Old Charges that made references to Euclid and Hermes

---

in scientific research, or in alchemy and magic, and in many other ways" (p. 218). See also Brooke, *The Refiner's Fire*, 17–19, 94 *et seq.*

29. Yates, *The Rosicrucian Enlightenment*, 209–19.

30. Ibid., 209–19; Stevenson, *The Origins of Freemasonry*, 98–105. Robert Plot, *Natural History of Staffordshire* (1686), 316, as quoted in Albert G. Mackey, *Encyclopedia of Freemasonry, A New and Revised Edition*, (New York: The Masonic History Company, 1920), 2:570. He also complained that Freemasonry's legendary history was "false and incoherent." Knoop and Jones, *A Short History of Freemasonry*, 76–77.

31. Yates, *The Rosicrucian Enlightenment*, 210.

32. Stevenson, *The Origins of Freemasonry*, 6; Stevenson, *The First Freemasons*, 8–9.

33. Stevenson, *The Origins of Freemasonry*, 85, 105.

34. Tobias Churton, *Freemasonry: The Reality* (Hersham, Surrey: Lewis Masonic, 2007), 384; Knoop, Jones, and Hamer, *The Two Earliest Masonic Manuscripts*, 77.

preserving Freemasonry in Egypt. Exploiting such connections, according to Stevenson, gave the Masonic craft a special status.[35]

Some Masonic writers have connected the Rosicrucian story concerning the discovery of a hidden tomb with the legends of Freemasonry. As noted earlier, the tomb contained an altar covered with an engraved brass plate, books, looking-glasses, and the remains of Rosenkreutz under the altar holding a parchment book.[36] The brass plate contained "figures and inscriptions, one of which is 'The whole Glory of God'" as well as information concerning the creation of the universe.[37] Thus, Rosicrucianism assisted the Masons in advancing the theme of loss and restoration of a primitive or pure body of knowledge accompanied by the persistent presence of an apostate version.

In addition, both movements valued secrecy. Stevenson has noted that even though the "secrecy associated with masonic lodges which emerged in seventeenth-century Scotland was partly a legacy of the Medieval past, of the craft keeping the 'mysteries' of its operative trade to itself," such secrecy was reinforced by the "common tendency to feel that the more exclusive knowledge was, the more valuable it must be" and because "the great secrets of the universe would be cheapened if revealed to all."[38] Thereafter speculative lodges gradually developed more esoteric rituals (which incorporated the "mason's word") that had significant similarities with rituals practiced by Rosicrucians and other hermeticists.[39]

THE PREMIER GRAND LODGE

Masonic historians have concluded that the transition from operative masonry to speculative Freemasonry was completed by the end of the seventeenth century.[40] By that time most gentlemen Masons had discovered that

35. Stevenson, *The Origins of Freemasonry*, 85.
36. Yates, *The Rosicrucian Enlightenment*, 246–47.
37. Churton, *Freemasonry*, 386–87; Brooke, *The Refiner's Fire*, 101. See also Webb, *The Freemason's Monitor*, 260; Hutchinson, *The Spirit of Masonry*, Appendix, 6–7.
38. Stevenson, *The Origins of Freemasonry*, 79.
39. See Yates, *The Rosicrucian Enlightenment*, 206–19. For an earlier version of the same argument, see Thomas De Quincey, "Historico-Critical Inquiry into the Origin of the Rosicrucians and the Freemasons," *London Magazine* (1824), reprinted in *Collected Works*, ed. David Masson (Edinburgh, 1890), 13:384–448, which relied heavily on a book by J. G. Buhle published in German in 1804. For Masonic responses, see Arthur Edward Waite, *A New Encyclopedia of Freemasonry* (London: William Rider and Son, 1921), 1:77, 181, and Waite, *The Real History of the Rosicrucians* (London: George Redway, 1887), 403–4; also Hamill and Gilbert, *World Freemasonry*, 28–35.
40. Jacob, *The Origins of Freemasonry*, 13.

operative masonry had little knowledge to impart, beyond the Old Charges concerning "enlightenment and the spiritual rebirth of mankind, based on secret knowledge and secret societies and cults." Thereafter, they became less interested in either esotericism or Christianity and emphasized the craft's teachings of morality, which were veiled in allegory and illustrated in symbols.

While operative masons were exclusively Christians, those who dominated speculative Freemasonry were deists, Jews, and students of the Enlightenment who eventually dispensed with the religious emphases of the earlier brotherhoods. Stevenson has noted that "the lodge system, combined with secrecy, ideals of loyalty and secret modes of recognition, had created an ideal organizational framework, into which members could put their own values and which they could adapt for their own uses." Protestants, who were suspicious of rituals and symbolism, responded to these changes by referring to Masons as "Evil-doers" and charged that "this devilish Sect of Men are Meeters in secret which swear against all without their Following."[41]

On June 24, 1717, speculative Masons from four lodges met at the Goose and Gridiron Ale House in St. Paul's Churchyard, where they organized what would eventually become the Grand Lodge of England. This new organization was controlled exclusively by gentlemen Masons and it became a bastion of Enlightenment deism.[42] This Premier Grand Lodge was independent of any other guild masons (including the London Company of Masons) and participant lodges gradually increased from four in 1717 to over seventy by 1730. The Grand Lodge began exercising control over as much territory as it could and insisted, according to Tobias Churton, "that a new lodge could be described as *regular* only if it had been created with permission of the grand master."[43]

In 1723 James Anderson (1679–1739), a Presbyterian minister and Freemason, published *Constitutions of Freemasons*, which summarized and elaborated the mythological history of Masonry as well as the Old Charges, which he referred to as "ancient landmarks." Thereafter *Constitutions* became the official version of such legends, history, and practices.[44] The landmarks included the requirement that a candidate for Freemasonry could not be "a stupid atheist." This was a deviation from the Old Charges

41. Stevenson, *The Origins of Freemasonry*, 7, 122.
42. Brooke, *The Refiner's Fire*, 95.
43. Churton, *Freemasonry*, 281. (Italics not in original).
44. James Anderson, *The Constitutions of Freemasons* (London, 1723). See Knoop and Jones, *A Short History of Freemasonry*, 26–38.

that were written when masons were Christian guild members. Some Masonic writers have concluded that Anderson's *Constitutions* effectively de-Christianized Masonry and afterward the Grand Lodge did not require belief in a Christian God,[45] but Alexander Piatigorsky has noted that there were "two streams of Masonic opinion at that time, specifically Christian and generally Deist," and that Anderson's *Constitutions* represented the latter while a book published the prior year—*The Old (or Robert's) Constitutions*—was representative of the Christian approach.[46]

The Old Charges also required Masons to be "good and true Men, free-born, and of mature and discreet Age, no Bondmen, no Women, no immoral or scandalous Men, but of good report." A Mason was required to be "a peaceable subject to the civil powers." Masons were judged on their own "personal merit," they were expected to "work honestly on working days, that they may live credibly on holy days," and while in the lodge they could not enter into "quarrels about religion, or Nations, or State policy."

Anderson's *Constitutions* endowed Masonry with historical legitimacy and social respectability. Anderson was the first Mason who referred to God as "the great Architect of the Universe,"[47] connected the Craft with "the chosen people of God" in the Old Testament, and asserted that primitive Freemasonry (Priesthood) had been taught and practiced since the creation of the world.[48] Most Freemasons believed that the Craft retained knowledge concerning the ancient mysteries that would have otherwise become lost or corrupted.[49]

Anderson's "History of Masonry," which was based on the Gothic Constitutions, traced the "Craft" from Adam to the building of Solomon's Temple and from there to contemporary times. According to *Constitutions*,

Adam taught his Sons Geometry, and the use of it, in the several Arts and Crafts convenient, at least for those early Times; for Cain, we find, built a city, which he called consecrated, or dedicated, after the name of his eldest son Enoch; and becoming the Prince of

45. Churton, *Freemasonry*, 319.
46. Alexander Piatigorsky, *Who's Afraid of Freemasons?* (New York: Barnes and Noble, 2005), 44–45.
47. Jean Calvin made the same comparison two centuries earlier. See Jean Calvin, *Instituto Christianae religionis* (Genevae, 1559). David Stevenson notes that the idea that "the universe was constructed by God according to mathematical principles was an ancient idea" and can be traced to Plato. During the Renaissance this concept was reintroduced by Pico della Mirandola, Johann Valentin Andreae, and Sir Thomas Browne. See Stevenson, *The Origins of Freemasonry*, 109.
48. Mackey, *An Encyclopaedia of Freemasonry*, 2:584.
49. Churton, *Freemasonry*, 277–79.

the one Half of Mankind, his posterity would imitate his royal Example in approving both the noble Science and the useful Art.... Noah, and his three sons, Japheth, Shem and Ham, all Masons true, brought with them over the Flood the Traditions and Arts of the Ante-deluvians, and amply communicated them to their growing Offspring.[50]

FULL CEREMONIES AND CATECHISMS

After the Premier Grand Lodge was organized, some of its members, including John Theopolis Desaguliers (1683–1744) and "other likeminded men, continued looking for a fresh model" that would result in "loosening of exclusive relations with Christianity." The new model became the story of Solomon's Temple, which was mentioned in the "Old Charges" and in early catechisms.[51] When a new third degree was developed from 1723 to 1725 the temple theme was paramount and facilitated a "spiritual quest for God's primal revelation" and for "ancient keys to divine knowledge" that had been lost.[52] When Samuel Prichard published an exposé in 1730 entitled *Masonry Dissected* he revealed "the full ceremonies and catechisms for the three Craft degrees" including the passwords for the various degrees.[53]

Afterward, Anderson published a second edition of *Constitutions* in which he acknowledged the newly developed three-degree ritual and slightly modified requirement for candidacy: "The Men made Masons must be Freeborn (or no Bondmen), of mature Age and of good Report, hail and sound, not deform'd or dismember'd at the Time of their making. But no Woman, no *Eunuch*." He claimed, for the first time, that the Grand Lodge had revived a prior practice of gathering lodges together for quarterly meetings when it was organized in 1717. Despite this claim there is no evidence that a Grand Lodge had previously existed or that such meetings had taken place.[54]

---

50. *Anderson's Constitutions of 1723*, 3.
51. Churton, *Freemasonry*, 72. Mackey notes that Masonic legend "assigns its origins equally to two other periods" upon which the rituals could have been developed, i.e., "the building of the Tower of Babel, when Nimrod was Grand Master, and to Egypt under the geometrician Euclid." Mackey, *The History of Freemasonry*, 1:163.
52. Churton, *Freemasonry*, 274–77.
53. John Hamill, *The Craft: A History of English Freemasonry* (Wellingborough, Eng.: Aquarian Press, 1986), 45. *Masonry Dissected* went through numerous printings during its first few weeks. Carr, *Samuel Prichard's Masonry Dissected*, 43.
54. Lewis Edwards concludes that the 1738 edition "followed the scriptures more closely" and that the working was less tentative. Edwards, "Anderson's Book of Constitutions of 1738," in *Anderson's Book of Constitutions of 1738, A Facsimile of the original text with*

Some Masonic writers have concluded that Anderson's revisions advanced a kind of "natural religion" that was consistent with Enlightenment thought, rather than revealed religion as taught by the Catholic Church.[55] Subsequent published exposés demonstrate that Masonic lodges continued to modify and embellish their rituals, and that there were variations in practices and many versions of the three degrees. The rituals provided candidates with knowledge as well as passwords and pass grips that would enable them to advance from spiritual darkness (the physical world) to increasingly higher levels of "individual consciousness and the Soul" and finally to a "level of consciousness that interfaces with the Spirit."[56] In each degree the candidates were given obligations of secrecy even though it soon became apparent that not every Mason complied with that requirement.

The three degrees (when fully developed) enabled initiates to take small steps, and to make progress by degrees, in order to ultimately attain perfection. The Entered Apprentice (the first degree) began his journey in Solomon's Temple where he was taught to use Jacob's ladder to ascend from spiritual darkness to consciousness. The candidate was compared to a "rough stone from which the perfect stone may be drawn" by "knocking chips off the disordered man on his path to (hopefully) perfection." He was also given pass grips and passwords, obligated himself to secrecy, and was introduced to various symbols, such as the square and compass.[57] The Fellow Craft (the second degree) continued his journey from darkness to illumination in Solomon's Temple where he was introduced into the middle chamber of the temple, where most of the ritual took place, and was shown the portal to the Holy of Holies.[58]

During the Master Mason, or third, degree, candidates were instructed that when Adam was expelled from the Garden of Eden, where he lived in God's presence, he became spiritually dead. This degree contained extra-Biblical details concerning Solomon's Temple and focused on the death of Hiram Abiff, the temple architect in Masonic legend, who is only briefly mentioned in the Bible. Abiff was murdered by three ruffians (Jubela, Jubelo, and Jubelum) during the construction of the temple because he refused to reveal temple secrets (the "Master's Word" or secret name of God)

---

commentaries by Lewis Edwards and W. J. Hughan (Bloomington, IL: The Masonic Book Club, 1978), 369, 395.

55. Churton, *Freemasonry*, 300–304.

56. McNulty, *Freemasonry*, 145.

57. Churton, *Freemasonry*, 15–16, 90.

58. Carnes, *Secret Ritual and Manhood*, 49. Town maintained that each candidate represented Adam in his "sincere desire to make advances in knowledge and virtue." See Salem Town, *A System of Speculative Masonry*, 2nd. ed. (Salem, NY: Dodd and Stevenson, 1822), 22–23, 67, 71–72.

that were thereafter lost.[59] The ruffians took his body outside the east gate of the temple and buried it on Mount Moriah.[60]

King Solomon sent twelve Fellowcraft Masons to find Abiff when he did not appear at the temple. When they found his grave they noted that the Master's Word was missing and they were unable to raise him from his grave by using grips from the first and second degrees. They finally lifted him from his grave by employing the grip of the third degree and the five points of fellowship. One ruffian was immediately apprehended, stabbed in the heart and head, and beheaded. The other ruffians fled to Gath but they were eventually tracked down and killed.[61]

During the ritual each candidate experienced death (spiritual death) and was raised by the five points of fellowship from the grave of darkness to a cradle of light, and thereafter became a new man. The candidate was taught that in order to regain consciousness and understand the real meaning of life it was necessary to be endowed with light, and with that endowment each Master Mason continued to build his spiritual temple in order to reestablish his presence with God.[62]

Master Masons were given additional tokens, signs, and substitute words for the lost Mason's word that would permit them to enter into a celestial lodge. Master Masons were introduced to new symbols, including the all-seeing eye and the beehive,[63] and learned that one of the symbols of

59. The construction of the Temple of Solomon (which took place between 958 BCE and 951 BCE) is mentioned in 2 Samuel, 1 Kings, and 1 Chronicles. Both of these books were written after the Assyrians captured Jerusalem in 586 BCE, the temple was destroyed, and the Jews were exiled in Babylon. The Masonic story of Hiram Abiff is much more detailed than the Biblical accounts. In the Bible "Huram" is identified as king of Tyre, who provided Solomon with "a cunning man" to help Solomon build his temple (2 Chronicles 2:13). Hiram, the "widow's son," is mentioned in I Kings 7:13–14 and 2 Chronicles 2:13–14 and 4:16, but the name "Hiram Abiff," or "Abiff," does not appear in the Old Testament. His cunning was required to construct two huge bronze pillars (Jachin and Boaz) at the entrance of the temple and the "Sea of Bronze" which was used by priests as an ablutions basin. According to some exposés, the signs, tokens, and words were used to distinguish the grades of masons and their wages. See Richard Carlile, *Manual of Freemasonry* (London: Wm. Reeves, n.d.), 49–50; David Bernard, *Light on Masonry: A Collection of all the Most Important Documents on the Subject of Speculative Free Masonry* (Utica, NY: William Williams, 1829), 94–95; Hutchinson, *The Spirit of Masonry*, 139; Wellins Calcott, *A Candid Disquisition of the Principles and Practices of the Most Ancient and Honorable Society of Free and Accepted Masons*, with an introduction by Wallace McLeod (Bloomington, Illinois: The Masonic Book Club, 1989), 123–24.
60. Mount Moriah was the location where Abraham was prepared to sacrifice his son Isaac. See 2 Chronicles 3:1.
61. See Ward, *Free Masonry* (New York, 1828), 1–5; Morgan, *Illustrations of Masonry*, 69–70; Bernard, *Light on Masonry*, 58–59.
62. Churton, *Freemasonry*, 42–43.
63. Carlile, *Manual of Freemasonry*, 49–50; Bernard, *Light on Masonry*, 61–74, 94–95;

Freemasonry is a virgin "weeping over a broken column, with a book open before her," which symbolizes the "unfinished state of the temple at the time of Hiram Abiff's murder."[64] In addition, this degree revealed "the grand hailing sign of distress," by which every Freemason in the future could seek assistance from other Masons when truly in distress.[65]

THE ANCIENTS

After the Premier Grand Lodge established its control of speculative Freemasonry in England, some lodges refused to admit Irish Masons because of their putative lower status. Some of those who were successful in gaining admission were shocked when they discovered that some English lodges had switched the passwords previously utilized in the first and second degrees to make it more difficult after Prichard published his exposé for non-Masons to surreptitiously gain admission into their rituals.[66] Eventually some of these Irish Masons formed their own lodges and in 1751 they organized a competing "Grand Lodge of Free and Accepted Masons according to the Old Institutions," and its members became known as the Ancients.[67]

In 1756 Laurence Dermott (1720–1791), who was the intellectual leader of the Ancients, published *Ahiman Rezon*, which was the Ancients' book of constitutions.[68] Dermott attacked the pretensions and authority of the Grand Lodge of England, which he successfully dubbed the Moderns, and claimed that it had not faithfully protected the "old institutions" of Freemasonry. In addition to objecting to changes in passwords, the Ancients noted "the omission of prayers, no longer celebrating the holy days of the saints John the Baptist and John the Evangelist, and the perception that the rituals of the Craft were being de-Christianized and replaced with deism."[69] They believed that after the Grand Lodge was organized, Freemasonry had "fallen away" from its primitive practices and was gripped by Enlightenment ideas.[70]

Hutchinson, *The Spirit of Masonry*, 139; Wellins Calcott, *Calcott's Masonry, with Considerate Additions and Improvements* (Philadelphia: Robert DeSilver, 1817), 123–24.

64. Morgan, *Illustrations of Masonry*, 78–103; Bernard, *Light on Masonry*, 61–74.

65. For an illustration, see Jabez Richardson, *Richardson's Monitor of Freemasonry* (New York: Lawrence Fitzgerald, 1860), 7.

66. Churton, *Freemasonry*, 28.

67. See Douglas Knoop and G. P. Jones, *The Genesis of Freemasonry* (Manchester: Manchester University Press, 1947); Neville Barker Cryer, *The Royal Arch Journey* (Hersham, Surrey: Lewis Masonic, 2009), 43–49; Churton, *Freemasonry*, 380–82.

68. See Laurence Dermott, *Ahiman Rezon* (London, 1756), facsimile reprint (Bloomington, IL: Masonic Book Club, 1975).

69. Mark Stavish, *Freemasonry: Rituals, Symbols and History of the Secret Society* (Woodbury, MN: Llewellyn Publications, 2007), 16.

70. For a summary of the conflict between the Moderns and Ancients, see Bernard K. Jones,

Although the Ancients claimed that they had restored the old forms that were modified by the Moderns, they also embraced a new degree known as the Royal Arch because they were convinced that it was the next logical step in the Hiramic legend outlined in the Master Masons Degree. The Royal Arch explained the circumstances under which "the pure Masonic tradition," including the Master's Word, was preserved and restored after Hiram Abiff was killed. It elaborated the story of Enoch, who spoke to God face to face and preserved the name of God on a gold plate that was buried in vaults located below the future site of Solomon's temple, and in the British Royal Arch the "mason's word" was rediscovered in these vaults when Zerubbabel rebuilt the temple.[71]

Dermott wrote that the Royal Arch degree, which emerged after the organization of the Grand Lodge, was "the root, heart, and marrow of Masonry."[72] The Royal Arch degree may have originated in Ireland, developed on the continent, been fabricated by Laurence Dermott, or taken from the third degree.[73] Although the Moderns initially rejected the Ancients' claim that the Royal Arch was part of ancient masonry and refused to include it in their rituals, they soon determined that they "were losing potential members to the Ancients," particularly those who were "attracted by the lure of a 'more ancient Masonry.'" As such, they signed a Charter of Compact that created a Grand and Royal Chapter of the Royal Arch of Jerusalem that enabled Moderns to become Royal Arch Masons. Even so, they did not consider it part of ancient Masonry or one of three degrees of Craft Masonry.[74]

HAUT GRADES

Shortly after the Grand Lodge was organized, the Craft quickly spread to continental Europe and throughout the British Empire.[75] In 1736 Scottish-born Andrew Michael Ramsay (1686–1743), a Jacobite living in exile in France, delivered a discourse at St. John's Lodge in Paris in which he

---

Freemasons' Guide and Compendium (N.p.: Dobby, 1956), 193–212. See also Harry Carr, ed., *Three Distinct Knocks and Jachin and Boaz* (Bloomington, IL: Masonic Book Club, 1981), 61–68; and Walter Sharman, "A look at the Hebraic terms and prayers used in Dermott," *AQC* 105 (1992), 49–68.

71. Knoop and Jones, *The Genesis of Freemasonry*, 286; Roy A. Wells, *Understanding Freemasonry* (London: Lewis Masonic, 1991), 8, 204; Roy A. Wells, *The Rise and Development of Organized Freemasonry* (London: Lewis Masonic, 1986), 151.

72. Dermott, *Ahiman Rezon*, 47–48.

73. Cryer, *The Royal Arch Journey*, 8.

74. This charter was signed in 1766. See Knoop and Jones, *The Genesis of Freemasonry*, 275–93; Cryer, *The Royal Arch Journey*, 8–24.

75. Grand lodges were organized in Ireland (1730), Scotland (1736), France (1738), and Germany (1741).

appealed to aristocrats, gentry, and bourgeoisie by deemphasizing the "operative stonemason origins" of Freemasonry and by emphasizing that the Craft could make "claim to very ancient and noble origins." Ramsay claimed that during the Crusades "many princes, lords, and citizens associated themselves and vowed to restore the temple of the Christians," and that they "agreed upon several ancient signs and symbolic words drawn from the well of religion in order to recognize themselves amongst the heathen and the Saracens." He also suggested that they intended to "unite Christians of all nationalities in one cofraternity." Thereafter, according to Ramsay, Masons "formed an intimate union with the Knights of St. John of Jerusalem." But Masonry was "founded in remote antiquity" and was "renewed in the Holy Land by our ancestors in order to recall the memory of the most sublime truths amidst the pleasures of society."[76]

When Ramsay requested Cardinal André-Hercule de Fleury (1653–1743), who was the Chief Minister to King Louis XV (1710–1774), to grant permission to publish his oration, he was rebuffed and the French King instead issued an edict that prohibited all of his subjects from becoming Freemasons. The French police were thereafter authorized to raid Masonic meeting places and the homes of Freemasons. In Paris, "Freemasonry was made Felony by law, and the brethren required the strictest obedience to the precepts and oaths of secrecy, or they fell into the hands of the civil authorities."[77] Shortly thereafter, Pope Clement XII (1652–1740) issued a Papal Bull in which he denounced Freemasonry and prohibited all Catholics from joining its lodges.[78]

These legal maneuvers did not retard the growth of French Freemasonry. Instead French Masons developed a number of high degrees (*haut grades*) including rituals concerning the Knights Templar. Some have suggested that Ramsay wrote, or at least inspired, these high degrees even though he did not mention Knights Templar during his oration.[79] But it is more

---

76. Andrew Michael Ramsay, "Discours Prononcé á la Réception des Fréres-Maçons. Par M. de Ramsay, grand Orateur de l'Ordre," in *Lettres de M. de V[oltaire] avec plusieurs pieces de differens auteurs*, La Haye, 47–70; G. Lamoine, "The Chevalier Ramsay's Oration, 1736–37: Early Masonry in France," *Ars Quatuor Coronatorum* 114 (2001), 226–37. See also Martin I. McGregor, "A Biographical Sketch of Chevalier Andrew Michael Ramsay, Including a full transcript of his oration of 1737, at http://www.freemasons-freemasonry.com/ramsay-biography-oration.html.

77. Henry Dana Ward, *The Anti-Masonic Review and Magazine* 2, no. 10 (October 1830): 293, 297. For a comprehensive discussion, see José A. Ferrer-Benimeli, *Les Archives Secrets du Vatican et la Franc-maçonnerie* (Paris: Dervy-Livres, 1989). See also Eugen Lennhoff, *The Freemasons: The History, Nature, Development and Secret of the Royal Art* (London: Methuen & Co., 1934), 66–69.

78. *In Eminenti Apostolatus Specula* (1738).

79. Ramsey apparently did make the Templar connection ("every Mason is a Knight

likely that the French adapted them from Karl Gotthelf, Baron von Hund's (1722–1776) Rite of Strict Observance, and Lambert de Lintot's (b. 1736) Rite of Seven Degrees. These rites taught that some Knights Templar survived the French purge and took refuge in Masonic guilds in England and Scotland where they continued as a secret society.[80]

In 1754 the Chevalier de Bonneville established a chapter known as the "Rite of Perfection," which worked these high degrees. The contents of these degrees were revealed in various French exposés, including *Les Plus Secrets Mystères des Hauts Grades de la Maçonnerie Dévoilés* (1766). That exposé contained descriptions of seven degrees (in addition to the three degrees of Craft Masonry) that elaborated the temple-building mythology. French Freemasons also developed several degrees, including the Knight King of the Rose Croix, which some claimed was descended from Rosicrucian sources but which were actually eighteenth-century rituals.

The expansion of Freemasonry to the continent and the creation of the *haut grades* coincided with "a revival of alchemical, Rosicrucian and Hermetic philosophy" on the continent.[81] The degrees that included hermetic strands eventually influenced Masonic lecturers and ritualists in England and America and advanced "the ultimate Masonic myth…the restoration of the paradisiacal power of Adam."[82]

ADOPTIVE RITES

Although Anderson's *Constitutions* prohibited the initiation of female members, some French lodges organized a system of separate adoptive lodges that included both men and women.[83] Janet Mackay Burke, a

Templar") in *The Philosophical Principles of Natural and Revealed Religion*, which was published posthumously in 1749.

80. For a summary of this, see Massimo Introvigne, *La Massoneria* (Leumann [Torino]: Elledici, 1997). Jan A. M. Snoek has reviewed new evidence which he believes supports the thesis that Ramsay founded the order. See "Researching Freemasonry," 239–42.

81. Churton, *Freemasonry*, 3.

82. Brooke, *The Refiner's Fire*, 101.

83. See Jan A. M. Snoek, "Introduction," in *Women's Agency and Rituals in Mixed and Female Masonic Orders*, Alexandra Heidle and Jan A. M. Snoek, eds. (Leiden: Brill, 2008), 4–7. For discussions of Adoptive Masonry in French, see Théodore Louis Tschoudy, *L'Etoile Flamboyante; Ou la Société des Francs-Maçons considerée sous tous les aspects* (Francfort: n.p., 1766); Claude Antoine Thory, *Annales orignis magni Galliarum Orientus ou Histoire de la fondation du Grand Orient de France*, 2 vol. (Paris, 1812); Jean Baptiste Pierre Julien Pyron, *Abregé historique de l'organisation en France des trente-trois degrés du Rite Ecossais Ancien et Accepté* (Paris, 1814); F.-T. B.-Clavel, *Histoire Pittoresque de la Franc-Maçonnerie et des Sociétés Secrètes Anciennes et Modernes*, 3d ed. (Paris: Pagnerre, 1844), 111–18; J.M. Ragon, *Rituel du grade de Compagnon* (Paris: Collignon, 1860); N. Deschamps, *Les Sociétés Secrètes et la Société ou Philosophie de l'historie contemporaine* (Paris: Oudin Frères and Avignon:

historian who studied this development, concluded that the French Grand
Master Count de Clermont produced the earliest surviving adoptive ritual
in 1763, which "appears to have been a prototype for all female rituals which
followed."[84]

But Masonic historian Jan Snoek has recently published a study in
which he speculates that these adoptive rituals were "clearly rooted" in
the rituals of the Harodim tradition that developed in England and were
introduced in France during the 1720s. These lodges initiated both men
and women and considered women to be regular Freemasons.[85] Snoek
has concluded that two French rituals, which were exposed in 1744 (*La
Franc-Maçonne ou Révélation des Mystères des Francs-Maçons* and *La Parfait
Maçon*), were part of this Harodim tradition.[86]

Harry Carr, who republished these exposés, had previously concluded
that they were not exposures of real rituals but instead smokescreens for
those that were. He noted that *La Franc-Maçonne* included three plates,
including one "depicting Adam and Eve under the Tree of Knowledge," but
that they are "only remotely relevant to the contents of the text and the
author has made no attempt to describe them or explain their presence."[87]
The *La Parfait Maçon* also included a woodcut of Adam and Eve being
tempted in the Garden, and its first degree is set in the Garden of Eden and
was described as "a sort of garden representing the Earthly paradise, with
the Tree of Knowledge of good & evil, around which are placed the figures
of Adam, Eve & the Serpent."[88]

Regardless of whether these French rituals were connected to Harodim
rites, Snoek has concluded that, based on their similar content, they were
modified and expanded to create an adoptive ritual. The first exposures of
a French adoptive ritual were published in London as *Women's Masonry, or
Masonry by Adoption*, in 1765 and in Paris as *Les quatre grades complets de*

Seguin Frères, 1881), 2:9–11. See also Michel Legris, "Les femmes dans la franc-maçonnerie,"
L'Express, 12 mai 1994, 34–38; Karen Benchetrit and Carina Louart, *La franc-maçonnerie
au féminin* (Paris: Belfond, 1994), and Dudley Wright, *Women and Freemasonry* (London:
William Rider & Son, 1922).
84. Janet Mackay Burke, "Sociability, Friendship and the Enlightenment among Women
Freemasons in Eighteenth-Century France," Ph.D. diss., Arizona State University, 1986, 229.
85. Jan A. M. Snoek, *Initiating Women in Freemasonry: The Adoptive Rite* (Leiden: Brill,
2012), 85, 120–23, 380. The Masonic order of the Strict Observance also contemplated
the establishment of a female branch. See Andreas Önnerfors, "*Maçonnerie des Dames*:
The Plans of the Strict Observance to Establish a Female Branch," in *Women's Agency and
Rituals*, 89–113.
86. Snoek, *Initiating Women in Freemasonry*, 25–34, 63–70.
87. Harry Carr, ed., *The Early French Exposures* (London: The Quatuor Coronati Lodge
No. 2076, 1971), 115, 117–52, 175–200.
88. Carr, *The Early French Exposures*, 175.

Illustration of Garden Scene in *Le Franc-Maçonne ou Révélation des Mystères des Francs-Maçons*. Published in Harry Carr, *The Early French Exposures*, 129.

l'Ordre de l'Adoption, ou la Maçonnerie des Dames in 1772.[89] Although the narratives of the three degrees of the adoptive rituals (Apprentisse, Compagnonne, and Maîtresse) were significantly different from the degrees of Craft Masonry that were exposed during the same period, they had significant similarities to the previous French exposures in *La Franc-Maçonne ou Révélation des Mystères des Francs-Maçons* and *Le Parfait Maçon*.

The adoptive rituals contained narratives that were based on stories contained in Genesis, including the Tower of Babel, Jacob's Ladder, Noah's Ark, and the Garden of Eden.[90] Snoek concluded that "the second degree [which narrates the story of Adam and Eve in the Garden of Eden] turns out to be the heart of the Adoption Rite."[91] During the ritual, the garden is filled with flowers and fruits, and there is an apple tree bearing fruit in the center of the lodge room and a serpent with an apple in its mouth.[92] The Master of the lodge tells the candidate to "receive the fruit from the tree which is in the midst [of the Garden of Eden]; as soon as you have tasted from it, you will become as one of us, knowing good and evil." According to Snoek, "this confirms that the Master plays here the role of God, and that he pronounces at this moment the divinity of Eve, played by the Candidate." But the ritual also emphasized the necessity for Eve and her other "companions" [the name of the degree] to exercise unrelenting discretion in the future and the candidates therefore took obligations of secrecy and the Master applied a paste called the "Seal of Taciturnity" with a trowel to the candidate's lips.[93]

The second degree ("The Fellow-Crafts Lodge") described in the London exposé, *Women's Masonry, or Masonry by Adoption*, included a dramatization of Eve's temptation in the Garden of Eden, "a garden of olives, watered by a river" which river represents the "rapidity of human passions, which are best curbed by becoming Masons and Masonesses," and the fruit of the "tree of Knowledge of good and evil."[94] In 1791 a second English translation, entitled *Free Masonry for the Ladies, or the Grand Secret*

89. See Snoek, *Initiating Women in Freemasonry*, 147. Other French exposures of the adoptive ritual include *La Maçonnerie des Femmes* (London: n.pub., 1774); *L'adoption ou la Maçonnerie des femmes en trois grades* (n.p., 1775); [Louis Guillemain de Saint Victor], *La vraie Maçonnerie d'Adoption* (London: Guillemain de Saint Victor, 1779), republished as *Le vraie Maçonnerie d'Adoption* (Philadelphia: Philarethe, 1787). See also Burke, *Sociability, Friendship, and the Enlightenment*, 218–58.
90. Snoek, *Initiating Women in Freemasonry*, 36.
91. Ibid., 62.
92. Ibid., 54.
93. Ibid., 40–41, 59. See also Henry Wilson Coil, *Coil's Masonic Encyclopedia* (New York: Macoy Publishing and Masonic Supply Co., 1961), 11, quoting Guillemain de St. Victor, *Le Vraie Maçonnerie d'Adoption* (Philadelphia: Philarethe, 1787).
94. *Women's Masonry or Masonry by Adoption. Explaining the Making of a Masoness, with the Form and Furniture of the Lodge. The Working of these Lectures, &c. with their Signs, Tokens,*

Discovered, was published in London and Dublin. It included a similar description of the second degree ("Companion") and referred to a candidate as the "Elected Lady," whose lips are anointed "with the seal of discretion."[95]

By 1774, after the number of female lodges had increased, the Grand Orient of France recognized them, took control of them, and promulgated rules and regulations under which the Master or Deputy Master of a regular male lodge presided over them and was "assisted by a female President."[96] Masonic writer Robert Gilbert has noted that the "structure and working Adoptive lodges resembled Craft lodges except that the female members were not permitted to work alone: each officer was accompanied by a mason who took a parallel office."[97] Thus, regardless of whether female initiates were originally real Masons, they were eventually "adopted" by regular male lodges and women were no longer considered Freemasons or allowed to attend regular male lodges.[98]

THREE GREAT EXPOUNDERS

Throughout the eighteenth century English Freemasons continued to modify and embellish the Craft's three-degree ritual,[99] and during the 1760s at least nine exposés were published in England.[100] The Craft degrees, which included tokens (pass grips), passwords, obligations of secrecy,

---

&c. Clearly Explained, By a Sister Mason (London: Printed for D. Hookham and D. Steel, 1765). R. A. Gilbert of Bristol, England, provided me with a photocopy of this pamphlet.

95. *Free Masonry of the Ladies, or the Grand Secret Discovered* (London: T. Wilkinson, ca. 1791), 25. This exposure was republished the following year as *Free Masonry of the Ladies, or the Grand Secret Disclosed* (London: Bew, 1792). See also John Yarker's translation of twelve degrees which appeared in *Collectanea* 1 (1937), Part 3, 145–242, and was republished in *Collectanea* (1978), 169–76. For a partial ritual, see *A.Q.C.* 12:37. Adoptive rituals were also published in Dutch, German, and Swedish. See Önnerfors, "*Maçonnerie des Dames*," in *Women's Agency and Rituals*, 111–13; Anton Van de Sande, "The 'Women's Question.' The Discussion, especially in the Nineteenth Century, about Opening membership of the Dutch Grand Lodge to Women," in *Women's Agency and Rituals*, 236–40.

96. Coil, *Coil's Masonic Encyclopedia*, 8.

97. R[obert] A. Gilbert, "'The Monstrous Regiment': Women and Freemasonry in the Nineteenth Century," *Ars Quatuor Coronatorum* 115 (2002): 156.

98. Fred L. Pick and G. Norman Knight, *The Freemason's Pocket Reference Book*, 3d rev. ed. (London: Frederick Muller, 1983), 22.

99. Concerning the gradual development of the ritual, see Knoop and Jones, *The Genesis of Freemasonry*, 274–75, 321–22. For a more recent treatment of this subject, see Stevenson, *The Origins of Freemasonry*.

100. See J. Burd, *A Master-key to Freemasonry* (London: n.p., 1760); W-O-V-n, *The Three Distinct Knocks* (London, 1760); Anonymous, *Jachin and Boaz* (London: n.p., 1762); Anonymous, *Hiram: The Grand Master-key to the Door of Both Ancient and Modern Free-masonry* (London, 1764); Anonymous, *Shibboleth* (London, 1765); W. Gordon, *Mystery of Freemasonry Explained* (London, 1777?); J. G., *Mahhabone* (Liverpool, 1766); Thomas Wilson,

and penalties for failing to keep those obligations, became more dynamic, refined, and complementary. The most influential exposures, *Three Distinct Knocks* (1760) and *Jachin and Boaz* (1762), were published without attribution and revealed that different lodges practiced variant forms of a dynamic ritual that included Christian prayers, which had not been mentioned in Prichard's exposé.[101] In addition, Arturo de Hoyas has noted that these exposés demonstrate that "only post-1760 rituals included separate obligations for the degrees, in conjunction with the penalties, tokens and words."[102]

Robin L. Carr and Louis L. Williams have concluded that following exposures the ritual was further modified and that "tiny bits" can be traced to "The Old Gothic Constitutions," "a good deal" from "The Early Masonic Catechisms," and "the largest amount, including many of the longer charges," from "the work of the so-called 'three great expounders' of the ritual."[103] These three expounders, Wellins Calcott (bap. 1726–1779?), William Hutchinson (1705–1777), and William Preston (1742–1818), polished the ritual into "a more attractive form, closer to what is familiar today" and "wrote longer charges and for the first time included something for the mind."[104] Their lectures emphasized that following Adam's expulsion from God's presence, God introduced "secret knowledge" to illuminate those who were worthy, and that Masonic rituals revealed such knowledge to aid men to return to God's presence.

In 1769 Calcott published *A Candid Disquisition of the Principles and Practices of the Most Ancient and Honorable Society of Free and Accepted Masons* in which he emphasized the legendary history of the Craft, that God revealed the sciences, law, and the royal art when Adam transgressed in the garden and that this secret knowledge was communicated to "the *worthy* only."[105] The workmen who built Solomon's temple "had certain modes of recognition, and a system of three degrees, and these were naturally passed on to their successors." Thus Masonry "became a regular and uniform *institution*" with the building of this temple.[106]

Solomon in All his Glory (London, 1766); and Charles Warren, *The Freemason Stripped Naked* (London, 1769).

101. Carr, *Three Distinct Knocks*, 1–2, 28–60; and A. C. F. Jackson, *English Masonic Exposures 1730–1760* (London: A. Lewis, 1986).
102. Correspondence from Arturo de Hoyas, November 22, 1993.
103. Calcott, *Candid Disquisition*, v.
104. Ibid., 1.
105. Ibid., 18.
106. Ibid., 8. The first quotation is from Calcott (as cited by McLeod) and the second is McLeod's summary of Calcott's text at pages 33–34.

Afterward, Solomon "contrive[d] a plan by *mechanical* and *practical allusions*, to instruct the craftsmen in the principles of the most *sublime speculative philosophy*, tending to the glory of God, and to secure to *them* temporal blessings *here*, and eternal life *hereafter*." The Craft had "*degrees of probation* and *injunctions of secrecy*."[107] Calcott included various charges that were delivered in Masonic lodges as well as "a prayer used at the empointing of a brother." This prayer was similar to one previously quoted by Dermott in *Ahiman Rezon* entitled "A Prayer used amongst the primitive Christian Masons."[108]

Both Preston's and Hutchinson's lectures, which also taught the antiquity of the Craft, were officially recognized by the Grand Lodge. Preston's *Illustrations of Masonry*, published in 1772, summarized his lectures, which explained the three degrees with clarity. Preston has been described as "the latest and greatest" of the men who "eventually took what was best in the other two [Calcott and Hutchinson] and consolidated it."[109] He became "the most important thinker in eighteenth century English Freemasonry," as evidenced by his system of lectures to modify and standardize the widely divergent rituals that were being practiced in English lodges.[110] His book was published in many subsequent editions, in England and America, and became a foundational work for later Masonic lecturers and commentators.[111]

Hutchinson, an attorney who was initiated into a Modern lodge in 1770, has been referred to as "the father of masonic symbolism." In 1775 he published *The Spirit of Masonry in Moral and Elucidatory Lectures*,[112] which has been described as "the first efficient attempt to explain the true philosophy of masonry, there represented as a Christian institution which should be open only to those who believe in the doctrine of the Holy Trinity."[113]

The great expounders did little to mollify the different perspectives in English Freemasonry concerning the Royal Arch, which were not resolved until decades later when the Moderns and Ancients formed a United Grand Lodge and agreed to define "Pure Antient Masonry" as consisting of the usual three degrees of Entered Apprentice, Fellow Craft, and Master

---

107. Ibid., 31–33.
108. Ibid., 22–23.
109. Carnes, *Secret Ritual and Manhood*, 48.
110. Colin Dyer, *William Preston and His Work* (London: Lewis Masonic, 1987), 236; Wells, *Understanding Freemasonry*, 8–9.
111. Hamill and Gilbert, *World Freemasonry*, 58. See also Robert Macoy, *General History, Cyclopedia and Dictionary of Freemasonry* (New York: Masonic Publishing Co., 1873), 326–29.
112. Hutchinson, *The Spirit of Masonry*, 139. See also Dyer, *Symbolism in Craft Freemasonry*, 236.
113. Knoop and Jones, *The Genesis of Freemasonry*, 7–8.

Mason, but expanded the last degree to include the Order of the Holy Royal Arch.[114] But the great expounders' emphasis on the Christian foundation of Masonry did become an important ingredient in American Freemasonry thought as it transitioned from a colonial to post-Revolutionary institution.

114. In 1813 Moderns and Ancients signed Articles of Union which created a Lodge of Reconciliation. This lodge recommended ceremonies and practices for a new United Grand Lodge of England. Hamill and Gilbert, *World Freemasonry*, 106. In 1816 the United Grand Lodge agreed on an Emulation Ritual which attempted to unify the rituals used in the various lodges. William Preston's lectures, as set forth in the *Syllabus Books*, included a description of the "periods of Creation," which continued to be given in connection with the new ritual. Dyer, *Symbolism in Craft Freemasonry*, 242–43. See *"Emulation" Working. The Lectures of the Three Degrees in Craft Masonry* (London: A. Lewis, 1899), 70–74; and *The Lectures of the Three Degrees in Craft Masonry* (London: Lewis Masonic, 1983), 108–12.

American Freemasonry

THE CRAFT WAS INTRODUCED to North America by English merchants and soldiers shortly after the London Grand Lodge was organized. By 1730 Benjamin Franklin had joined the Craft in Philadelphia, printed a notice that there were several active lodges in the city, and the following year published the first American edition of *Anderson's Constitutions*.[1] From 1730 to 1781 the Grand Lodge of London appointed thirty-six provincial grand masters to represent it in America. Daniel Coxe was the first provincial grand master for New York, New Jersey, and Pennsylvania, and in 1733 Henry Price became the provincial grand master for New England.[2] In 1734 Boston Lodge No. 126 became the first American lodge to appear on the list of English lodges, followed by Savannah/Province of Georgia Lodge No. 139 in 1736.[3]

Beginning in 1761 the Ancients appointed provincial grand masters and by the end of the Revolutionary War the Ancients Provincial Grand Lodge in Pennsylvania had authorized over fifty lodges to organize in

1. Before he became a Mason, Benjamin Franklin reprinted "The Mystery of Free-Masonry," in his *Pennsylvania Gazette* which was originally published in the London *Daily Journal*. There were also American editions of Prichard (1749), *Hiram* (1768), *Jachin and Boaz* (published in twenty editions from 1794 to 1828); Samuel Prichard, *Masonry Dissected* (n.p., 1749); Anonymous, *Hiram: on the Grand Master-Key to the Door of Both Ancient and Modern Free-Masonry* (New York: John Holt, 1768); and Anonymous, *Jachin and Boaz* (Boston: J. Bumstead for E. Larkin, 1794).
2. John Hamill, *The Craft: A History of English Freemasonry* (Wellingborough, England: Aquarian Press, 1986), 88. See also Coil, *Conversations on Freemasonry*, 99; Allen E. Roberts, *Freemasonry in American History* (Richmond, VA: Macoy Publishing and Masonic Supply, 1985), 12–13. Robert Gould claimed that two Masons immigrated to the province of "East Jersey" in 1682: one returned a year later, and one served as deputy-governor of the province, 1685–1690. There is no evidence that either of these Masons organized a lodge. See Robert F. Gould, *Gould History of Freemasonry Throughout the World* (New York: Charles Scribner's Sons, 1936), 6:1–2.
3. Roberts, *Freemasonry in American History*, 18–21, 23, 30.

North America and in the Caribbean.[4] In 1788 George Washington, who was initiated into Freemasonry in 1752 when he was a young man living in Fredericksburg, Virginia, was elected worshipful master of his lodge in Alexandria, Virginia, and four years later he laid the cornerstone of the new capitol building in full Masonic regalia. Steven Bullock has noted that "particularly in the years after President George Washington laid the cornerstone of the U.S. Capitol in 1792, the fraternity spread into nearly every locality in the country" and increased in "both numbers and prestige."[5]

American Masons began organizing their own grand lodges after the colonies broke away from their English king. In 1781 the first American grand lodge was organized in New York and by 1800 there were eleven grand lodges, 347 subordinate lodges, and 16,000 Freemasons.[6] In some states, such as Massachusetts, competing grand lodges were organized but they eventually worked out their differences. These grand lodges became new obediences or administrative organizations, which were independent of the two competing English grand lodges and claimed "exclusive jurisdiction" over all Masonic lodges that were organized within each state.

THE ILLUMINATI

As Freemasonry spread in America, it became the target of sectarian attacks by religious zealots who believed that it was connected to a secret European order known as the Order of the Illuminati. They alleged that the Illuminati had infiltrated into the high degrees and that Masonry, with its secret rituals and worldwide network, was a threat to the homeland and a hazard for Christianity. This conspiracy theory was an echo of claims that had been advanced by European writers shortly after the French Revolution and was premised on paranoia concerning a short-lived secret order that was inspired by Freemasonry and organized in Bavaria.[7]

In 1776 Adam Weishaupt (1748–1830), the dean of the law faculty at the University of Ingolstadt, established an "Order of the Illuminati" and constructed a legendary history that traced the organization's origins to Persia

4. Hamill, *The Craft*, 88. The Scottish Grand Lodge also appointed four Provincial Grand Masters but the Irish Grand Lodge did not establish lodges in America.
5. Steven C. Bullock, "Masons, Masonic History and Academic Scholarship," in de Hoyas and Morris, *Freemasonry in Context*, xii.
6. Ronald P. Formisano with Kathleen Smith Kutolowski, "Antimasonry and Masonry: The Genesis of Protest, 1826–1827," *American Quarterly* 29 (Summer 1977): 139, 143.
7. Concerning the Order of the Illuminati, see René Le Forestier, *Les Illuminés de Bavière et la franc-maçonnerie allemande* (Paris: Hachette, 1914; republished in Geneva: Slatkine-Megariotis Reprints, 1974), and Massimo Introvigne, *Gli Illuminati e il Priorato di Sion*, Casale Monferrato ([Alessandria]: Piemme, 2005). For an English summary see http://www.cesnur.org/2005/mi_illuminati_en.htm.

one thousand years earlier. He divided the order into various classes and degrees that practiced a quasi-Masonic ritual.[8] Weishaupt planned to utilize this new organization to overthrow the conservative Kingdom of Bavaria (which was dominated by the Roman Catholic Church) and to replace it with a liberal form of republican government.

In 1777, Weishaupt was initiated as a Freemason in Munich's "Zur Behutsamkeit" Lodge. He began recruiting heavily among its members and his organization soon had more than twenty-five hundred followers. In 1780 a prominent Freemason named Baron Adolf Franz Friedrich Ludwig von Knigge (1752–1796) joined Weishaupt's order and rewrote its rituals to more closely resemble Masonic ceremonies. But von Knigge eventually left the movement after losing a power struggle with Weishaupt.[9]

In 1784 the Elector of Bavaria issued an edict against secret societies after some former members of the Illuminati (including Professor Joseph Utzschneider) revealed Weishaupt's secret ambitions to the aristocracy. The following year the Bavarian monarch issued two additional edicts that prohibited all secret societies, including the Order of the Illuminati and Freemasonry, from operating within the kingdom. Soon thereafter the police seized documents that confirmed the Illuminati intended to overthrow the government and Weishaupt fled to Germany.

The government conducted additional inquiries following Weishaupt's departure to identify other members of the order who held teaching and government positions or were members of the military who were subsequently dismissed from their posts and even banished from Bavaria. The government eventually published many of the Illuminati's secret books, letters, and other records, issued a fourth edict, and aggressively took measures that effectively destroyed the order.[10]

---

8. Margaret Jacob notes that the Illuminati "self-consciously embraced secrecy in imitation of Masonic forms, but they did so with decidedly political agendas." Margaret C. Jacob, *Strangers Nowhere in the World: The Rise of Cosmopolitanism in Early Modern Europe* (Philadelphia: University of Pennsylvania Press, 2006), 100.

9. Masonic writer Henry W. Coil maintains that the Bavarian Illuminati were "not primarily Masonic, and evidently not founded by Masonic authority, though it pirated or paraphrased Masonic rituals and at one time or another had a number of prominent Freemasons in the group." Coil, *Coil's Masonic Encyclopedia*, 545. Others have reached opposite conclusions: Christopher McIntosh, *The Rose Cross and the Age of Reason* (Leiden: E. J. Brill, 1992); Jan Rachold, ed., *Quellen und Texte zur Aufklärungsideologie des Illuminatenorden (1776–1785)* (Berlin: Kademie, 1984).

10. See *Einige Originalschriften des Illuminaten Ordens* (Munich: A. Franz, 1787); and *Nachtrag von weitern Originalschriften*, 2 vols. (Munich: J. Lentner, 1787). The first work included documents outlining a proposal to allow women to join the secret order. For a discussion of mythology concerning the Illuminati, see Massimo Introvigne, *Gli Illuminati e el Priorato di Sion, La Vertità sulle due Società segrete del Codice da Vinci e di Angeli e Demoni* (Monferato, IT: Piemme, 2005).

During the French Revolution (1789–1799), English Congregationalist John Robison (1739–1805)[11] and French Jesuit Augustin Barruel (1741–1820)[12] published books that resurrected the Illuminati from its final resting place in Bavaria. Robison was a former Freemason, and Barruel was a Catholic abbot who took refuge in England; both claimed that after Weishaupt left Bavaria, the Illuminati "revived immediately, under another name, and in a different form."

Robison became interested in German Freemasonry and the Order of the Illuminati in 1795, after reading a German periodical, *Religions Begebenheiten*.[13] He noted that both politics and religion were discussed when he visited a lodge in France, and that "an organization [the Order of Illuminati] has been formed for the express purpose of rooting out all the religious establishments, and overturning all existing governments of Europe." He believed that although it "took its first rise among the Free Masons," it was "totally different from Freemasonry" and "rose naturally from the corruptions that had gradually crept into that fraternity."[14]

Robison claimed that the Illuminati encouraged its adepts to become initiated into the first degrees of Freemasonry and that if "his Superiors judge more favorably of him, he is drawn out of the general mass of Free Masons, and becomes *Illuminatus Minor*."[15] He believed the order had "taken so deep root that it still subsists without being detected and has spread into all the countries of Europe."[16] He asserted that members of the order took refuge in France, where they became the secret leaders of French Freemasonry, and helped foment the French Revolution and that the order ultimately accomplished its original goal of "revolution and the destruction of all authority, for the restoration of patriarchal life."[17]

Both authors were convinced that the Illuminati were continuing to conspire to overthrow all civil government and religion throughout the world, including in America. Barruel asserted that the Illuminati were a manifestation of Jacobinism, a radical and anticlerical faction in France that fomented the revolution. He lamented that these Jacobins taught "that all men were equal and free! In the name of their equality and disorganizing

11. John Robison, *Proofs of a Conspiracy against all the Religions and Governments of Europe carried on in the Secret Meetings of Freemasons, Illuminati and Reading Societies*, 4th ed. (London: Printed for T. Cadell Jun. and W. Davies and W. Creech, 1798).

12. Agustin Barruel, *Mémoires pour servir à l'histoire du Jacobinisme*, 5 vols. (Hamburg: P. Fauche, 1798–1799). The Italian edition was published the following year as *Memorie per servire alla storia del Giacobinismo*, 4 vol. (n.p.: n.p., 1800).

13. Robison, *Proofs of a Conspiracy*, 1.

14. Ibid., 1–17.

15. Ibid., 125–26.

16. Ibid., 15.

17. Waite, *A New Encyclopedia of Freemasonry*, 1:387.

liberty, they trampled underfoot the altar and the throne, they stimulated all nations to rebellion, and aimed at plunging them ultimately into the horrors of anarchy."[18]

The authors were familiar with the Illuminati documents that the Bavarian government had seized and published in 1786–1787. Robison revealed that these documents proved the Illuminati planned "a project for a sisterhood," and that the order believed that this female lodge "will be of great service, and procure us both much information and money, and will suit charmingly the taste of many of our truest members, who are lovers of the sex."[19] These lodges would consist of "two classes, the virtuous and the freer hearted (i.e. those who fly out of the common track of prudish manners); they must not know each other, and must be under the direction of men, but without knowing it. Proper books must be put into their hands, and such as teach them how to indulge their passions in secret."[20]

Robison's and Barruel's books were published in the United States during the so-called "Quasi War" (1798–1800) with France, which helped give their theories traction in America.[21] George Washington (1732–1799) "watched with dismay what he believed was the growing interference of the French government in American politics," and asserted that "the Republican party had become 'the French Party'" and that it was "'the curse of this country,' threatening the stability and independence of the United States."[22] He cautioned during his farewell address that "all obstructions to the execution of the laws, all combinations and associations, under whatever plausible character, with the real design to direct, control, counteract, or awe, the regular deliberations or actions of the constituted authorities, are

18. Barruel denounced Jacobinism, which was among the most radical groups in the French Revolution. It referred to a French Catholic religious order, the Jacobins, in whose convent the radical French Revolutionaries used to hold their meetings, and not to Scottish Jacobites who attempted to restore the Jacobite dynasty to the throne of Scotland (or England) and were members of French Masonic lodges.

19. Robison, *Proofs of a Conspiracy*, 138–39, 243–71. Robison visited female lodges (Loge de la Fidelite) in France.

20. Ibid., 138. William Preston responded to Robison's and Barruel's allegations concerning Freemasonry in the tenth edition of his *Illustrations of Masonry* which was published in 1801.

21. See Robison, *Proofs of a Conspiracy*, 3rd ed. (Philadelphia: Printed for T. Dobson, 1798); and 4th ed. (New York: G. Forman, 1798). Barruel was first translated into English by the Hon. Robert Clifford and published in London in 1798. See Abbé Augustin Barruel, *Memoirs Illustrating the History of Jacobinism* (London: T. Burton, 1798). The first American, and apparently only multivolume, edition of Barruel was published in 1799. A one-volume abridged edition was published as Abbé Augustin Barruel, *The Anti-Christian and Anti-Social Conspiracy* (Lancaster, PA: Joseph Ehrenfried, 1812). There were also contemporary newspaper accounts mentioning these works.

22. Gordon S. Wood, *Revolutionary Characters: What Made the Founders Different* (New York: Penguin Press, 2006), 61.

destructive of this fundamental principle, and of fatal tendency." Although Washington later reconfirmed his suspicions concerning "the doctrines of the *Illuminati* and the principles of Jacobinism," he "did not believe that the *lodges* of freemasons in *this* country had, as societies, endeavored to propagate the diabolical tenants of the former, or pernicious principles of the latter (if they are susceptible of separation)."[23]

After Washington left office, the French navy attempted to interrupt American trade with England by seizing commercial vessels, which reignited paranoia concerning the Illuminati and its connection with Freemasonry. During this crisis Congress enlarged the regular army, established an embargo on trade with France, and abrogated all treaties. John Adams (1735–1826) appointed Washington as "Lieutenant General and commander in Chief" of the United States military forces and established a navy department to prepare the country for war.[24]

In the midst of these events, Adams designated May 9, 1798, as a day for fasting and prayer and on that day Reverend Jedediah Morse (1761–1826), a fire-breathing Congregational minister in Charlestown, Massachusetts, delivered a sermon at New North Church in Boston in which he warned his congregation that the Illuminati were a real and continuing threat to the social and religious fabric of the new nation. Although Morse did not connect the Illuminati with Freemasons during this sermon, he eventually did in the published version. He alleged that the Illuminati were "a vile and pestiferous scion grafted on the stock of simple Masonry" and they had employed Masons as "secret conductors of their poisonous principles." In another sermon later that year, he tied the Illuminati threat to the United States conflict with France.[25]

---

23. See Worthington Chauncey Ford, ed., *The Writings of George Washington* (New York: G. P. Putnam's Sons, 1893), 19: 119–20. Despite this explanation, some seceding Masons insisted that Washington was a seceding Mason and that at least two Masonic congressmen (Andrew Jackson and Edward Livingston) voted against giving him thanks after his second term as president. See Joseph Ritner, *Vindication of General Washington from the stigma of adherence to Secret Societies* (Harrisburg: Printed by Theo. Fenn, 1837); and *Freemasonry on Trial: Masonic Attempt to Prevent by Law Public Initiations* (Chicago: Ezra A. Cook & Co., 1893). *The New England Anti-Masonic Almanac* (1831) included three letters the editors claim demonstrate that Washington agreed that both Jacobinism and the Illuminati had spread into the United States. See Rick Grunder, *Mormon Parallels: A Bibliographic Source* (LaFayette, NY: Rick Grunder Books, 2008), 1007.
24. See Gordon S. Wood, *Empire of Liberty: A History of the Early Republic, 1789–1815* (New York: Oxford University Press, 2009), 239–75.
25. Jedediah Morse, *A Sermon, Delivered at the New North Church in Boston* (Boston, 1798). When Morse published a sermon he delivered on Thanksgiving in Charlestown, Massachusetts, he included an appendix that correlated developments in the dispute between the United States and France with the continuing danger imposed by the Illuminati. See Morse,

Morse delivered another sermon on the national day of fast in April
1799 in which he charged that "it has long been suspected that *secret societies*...subversive of our religion and government, existed somewhere in
this country" and that several societies of Illuminati had been present in
the United States since 1786.[26] He claimed in tabloid style that there were
"no less than seventeen hundred of these Illuminati among us...in concert,
systematically conducting the plan of revolutionizing this country" and
published lists of members in America (who were Masons initiated into
the "high degrees" that were imported from France) including their ages,
residences, and occupations.[27] He concluded that "these societies have pre-
sumptuously assumed the forms of Masonry; but they are not of the order
of true and good Masons. They are imposters."[28]

During the same year John Cosens Ogden (1751–1800), an Episcopal
clergyman, wrote a pamphlet in which he asserted that the real Illuminati
in America were New England clergymen (Congregationalists, Methodists, and Baptists) and Federalists, that Protestant clergy in Connecticut,
led by Timothy Dwight, were attempting to control American society, and
that "diligent attention is needful. If this is neglected, our families, religion
and country will be destroyed by the Illuminati."[29] The growing acceptance
of Enlightenment ideas, the disestablishment of traditional Puritan institutions, the perception that secularism was eroding established religion,
as well as the tendency of many churchmen to see signs of an approaching
millennium, created a favorable environment among America's religious establishment for Robinson's and Barruel's conspiracy theories.

During this war of words, Congregationalists, Methodists, and Baptists
who had joined the Craft and were aligned with the Republicans denied
that Freemasonry was connected with any conspiracy or that it had deviated from its original religious orientation. The Reverend William Bentley accused the clergy "who ply the shuttle-cock of faith, with the dexterity

*A Sermon, Preached at Charlestown, November 29, 1798, on the Anniversary Thanksgiving in
Massachusetts* (Boston: Samuel Hall, 1799).
26. Jedediah Morse, *A Sermon, Exhibiting the Present Dangers, and Consequent Duties of the
Citizens of the United States of America* (New York: Printed and Sold by Cornelious Davis,
1799), 11 (emphasis in original).
27. Ibid., 24–32.
28. Ibid., 32.
29. [John Cosens Ogden], *View of the New-England Illuminati: Who are Indefatigably Engaged in DESTROYING THE RELIGION AND GOVERNMENT OF THE UNITED
STATES; Under a Feigned Regard for the Safety—and under an Impious abuse of True Religion,* 2nd ed. (Philadelphia: Printed for James Carey, 1799), 15. See Vernon L. Stauffer,
New England and the Bavarian Illuminati (New York: Columbia University Press, 1918),
348–54.

of expert gamesters, and have the art of making the multiple fly with its
feathers" of making false claims against Freemasonry without any evidence.
He wrote that we "must leave Robison to an inquisitive public…and forgive a worthy divine who has noticed the book, and has made our order
ridiculous."[30]

Reverend Thaddeus Mason Harris, the author of an important Masonic
commentary, made similar observations. "How much…are we surprised to
find opposers to an association whose law is peace, and whose disposition is
love," he wrote. "But, notwithstanding the ignorant mistake, and the preju-
diced censure the society, we are persuaded that its *real* character is too well
known, and its credit is too well supported, to be injured by their misrepre-
sentations, or destroyed by their invectives."[31]

These attacks and counterattacks, which were made in discourses and
published in pamphlets and newspapers, continued for several years, but
they began to moderate after Washington's highly publicized Masonic funeral. "It cannot be doubted," Vernon Stauffer has observed, "that American Freemasons, while sincere in their expressions of sorrow on account of
Washington's death, none the less found a peculiar comfort of soul in being
able *at such a time* to point to the fallen hero as *their* 'brother.'"[32] Adams
thereafter decided to negotiate when Alexander Hamilton secured a higher
commission in the new army and he eventually hammered out the Treaty
of Mortefontaine, which ended the Quasi War.[33] The treaty caused a major
fracture among the Federalists that resulted in Adams's defeat in the 1800
election.[34]

Even after the Quasi War ended there were periodic rumblings about
the Illuminati Masonic connection and some of its most controversial elements. In 1802 Reverend Seth Payson (1758–1820), a Congregational minister in Ringe, New Hampshire, wrote a book in which he included abstracts
from Barruel and Robison and reasserted that the Order of Illuminati was
still present in the United States and that its activities threatened the down-
fall of the American democracy and Christian religion.[35]

30. *A Charge delivered before the Morning Star Lodge, in Worcester, Massachusetts, upon the festival of Saint John the Baptist, June 25, A.L. 5798.* By the Rev. Brother William Bentley, of Salem, Massachusetts. Worcester, June, A.L. 5798, as quoted in Stauffer, *New England and the Bavarian Illuminati,* 326–27.
31. *Discourses, delivered on Public Occasions, Illustrating the Principles, Displaying the Tendency, and Vindicating the Design of Freemasonry.* By Thaddeus Mason Harris…Charlestown, Anno Lucis, 1801, as quoted in Stauffer, *New England the Bavarian Illuminati,* 327.
32. Stauffer, *New England and the Bavarian Illuminati,* 341.
33. Wood, *Revolutionary Characters,* 61–62, 138–39.
34. Joseph Wheelan, *Mr. Adams's Last Crusade* (New York: Public Affairs, 2008), 18, 23.
35. Seth Payson, *Proofs of the Real Existence, and Dangerous Tendency, of Illuminism.*

Payson repeated Robison's and Barruel's charges that the Illuminati planned "a project for a sisterhood" and presumed that the Illuminati had created rituals in which male initiates took sexual advantage of women with loose morals. Payson claimed that the Illuminati had attempted to establish such a lodge in Frankfurt, but that after the objective became known "it raised a terrible disturbance, and broke up the assembly."[36]

Although Payson's book had no lasting impact, the Illuminati conspiracy theory continued to be articulated by prominent pastors and other writers for the next three decades. In 1809 Ethan Smith (1762–1849), a New England Congregational minister, published *Dissertation on the Prophecies* in which he argued that the latter days had arrived and that Satanic plots, which included the Catholic Church and the Illuminati, threatened the stability of the United States and the rest of the world. "Secret societies," according to Smith, required "obedience to unknown leaders in those societies" and were intent on advancing "*atheism, anarchy, and licentiousness.*"[37]

But Smith was more cautious than Morse and did not claim that there was a connection between the Illuminati and Freemasonry. Instead he wrote that he did not intend "to reflect" negatively upon Freemasonry since "there is no institution among men, which is not capable of being abused to perverse purposes" and that "the most honorable among the Masonic Fraternity, have themselves sounded the alarm, and given notice of this horrid abuse of their order."[38]

Elias Boudinot (1740–1821), a prominent New Jersey politician who served as president of the Continental Congress, made much more specific allegations concerning the Illuminati in his *The Second Advent, or coming of the Messiah in Glory*. He claimed that the Illuminati used Freemasonry as a cover in the United States and that this was a sign of the approaching millennium and a threat to church and state.[39] He wrote that both Freemasonry and the Illuminati were "societies established for the express purpose of opposing and destroying the religion of Jesus Christ" and that even

---

Containing an Abstract of the Most Interesting Parts of what Dr. Robison and Abbe Barruel have published on this subject; with collateral proofs and general observations… (Charlestown [MA]: Printed by Samuel Etheridge, 1802). In 1812 Barruel's *Memoirs* was abridged and published as *The Antichristian and Antisocial Conspiracy* (Lancaster: Printed by Joseph Ehrenfried, 1812).

36. Payson, *Proofs of the Real Existence*, 124–25.

37. Ethan Smith, *A Dissertation on the Prophecies Relative to the AntiChrist and the Last Times; Exhibiting the Rise, Character, and Overthrow of the Terrible Power: and a Treatise on the Seven Apocalyptic Vials* (Charlestown [MA]: Samuel T. Armstrong, 1811), 116.

38. Smith, *A Dissertation on the Prophecies*, 14–15.

39. [Elias Boudinot], *The Second Advent, or coming of the Messiah in Glory* (Trenton, NJ: O. Fenton and S. Hutchinson, 1815).

after the Illuminati were "broke up" in Bavaria that it "soon rose with fresh vigour, under a new name."[40] He described how the Illuminati "established various lodges of ladies, whose moral principles they first totally perverted, by eradicating every former idea of chastity and virtue from their minds" and that Freemasonry provided cover for the adepts of the Illuminati.[41] He even repeated previously unfounded claims that there were lodges of the Illuminati in America.[42]

Finally, Josiah Priest (1788–1851), a self-educated New York harness maker, wrote *View of the Expected Millennium* in 1827 in which he claimed that "atheism…has been propagated under the auspices of a certain society, styled the Illuminati, which originated in France in the days of Jacobism, and has, in the most secret and subtle manner, accomplished the creation of many societies of the same kind in several countries, and even in America, covering themselves with the sacred cloak of Freemasonry."[43] Priest did not focus his criticism on Freemasonry but he did suggest that the Craft had been used, particularly in the high degrees, by those who had ulterior motives.[44]

THE YORK RITE

During the same period, American Masons completed the organization of a new American system under which grand lodges would be located in every state. By 1806 there was a grand lodge in each state and by the 1820s there were twenty-six grand lodges, three thousand constituent lodges, and between a hundred and a hundred fifty thousand Master Masons.[45] In New York State alone, which had the largest Masonic membership in the country, there were, according to one source, as many as five hundred lodges and twenty thousand members.[46]

40. Ibid., 354–55, 362.
41. Ibid., 364–65.
42. Ibid., 366–67.
43. Josiah Priest, *A View of the Expected Christian Millennium* (Albany: Loomis Press, 1827), 157–58.
44. Priest's book was republished in multiple editions from 1827 to 1831 and "represented the century's 'best selling' millenarian book to date." Such popularity, according to Lyn Jacobs, "suggests that millenarian thought had become an integral part of the general public consciousness." See Grunder, *Mormon Parallels*, 1318.
45. Goodman, *Towards a Christian Republic*, 3; Ronald P. Formisano and Kathleen Kutolowski, "Antimasonry and Masonry: The Genesis of Protest, 1826–1827," *American Quarterly* 29 (1977), 143n18; and *The Freemason's Library* (Baltimore, 1828), cited by Henry Dana Ward in *Freemasonry* (New York, 1828).
46. *A Report on the Abduction of William Morgan* (New York, Feb. 14, 1829). This number may be inflated since the *Freemason's Library* of approximately the same time listed 157 Masonic lodges in New York State. See also Henry Leonard Stillson, ed., *History of the Ancient*

American Masons also began to organize two rites (York Rite and Scottish Rite) that included the three degrees of Craft Masonry and high degrees containing more detailed versions of Masonic legends. American historian Mark Carnes has observed that the development of new rituals in America was more fluid and dynamic than in England.[47] "If a venerable and ancient Masonic tradition existed," writes Carnes, "no one could determine what it was." As a result, "American ritualists invented their own Masonic rituals or variants... [and] American Freemasonry took many forms, the legitimacy of each determined by the persuasiveness of its innovator."[48]

In 1797 American Mason Thomas Smith Webb (1771–1819) published *The Freemason's Monitor*, which adopted and truncated Preston's system of lectures and attempted to standardize American rituals.[49] Ironically, his *Monitor* became a standard textbook for lecturers and American rituals thereby more clearly reflected Preston's vision than the various form of rituals being practiced in England.[50] Webb's *Monitor*, other commentaries, and even British exposés provided Americans even on the frontier with ready access to Masonic legends and arguments concerning the antiquity of the Craft.

In 1798 Webb participated in the organization of a General Grand Chapter of Royal Arch Masons in Boston (when he became deputy general grand high priest) and helped develop the York Rite (which is also referred to as the American Rite), which was a confederation of three autonomous organizations of Master Masons who desired to receive additional degrees that explained the temple legend in greater detail.[51] These additional rituals were developed primarily in England, Ireland, and Scotland and included four capitular degrees conferred in Royal Arch chapters, two cryptic degrees conferred in Cryptic Masons councils, and three Knight Templar degrees (reserved for Christian Masons) conferred in Knight Templar commanderies.

---

and Honorable Fraternity of Free and Accepted Masons (Boston: Fraternity Publishing, 1910), 261; and James C. Odierne, *Opinions on Speculative Masonry* (Boston, 1830), 198.

47. Carnes, *Secret Ritual and Manhood*, 23.
48. Ibid., 23–24.
49. Webb, *The Freemason's Monitor*.
50. Coil, *Conversations on Freemasonry*, 99–200; Dyer, *William Preston and His Work*, 125, 128–29, 154.
51. See Henry Leonard Stillson, ed., *History of the Ancient and Honorable Fraternity of Free and Accepted Masons* (Boston: Fraternity Publishing Co., 1910), 640–41; Roberts, *Freemasonry in American History*, 222; Carnes, *Secret Ritual and Manhood*, 48. See also Coil, *Conversations on Freemasonry*, 99–100; and S. Brent Morris, "The Early Developments of the High Degrees," in Kent L. Walgren, *Freemasonry, Anti-Masonry and Illuminism in the United States, 1734–1850, A Bibliography* (Worcester, MA: American Antiquarian Society, 2003), lxxxii–lxxxviii.

THOMAS SMITH WEBB.

Thomas Smith Webb (1771–1819).

Webb's *Freemason's Monitor* described the four capitular degrees that were conferred in a Royal Arch chapter: Mark Master, Past Master, Most Excellent Master, and Royal Arch Mason, which was also known as the Holy Order of the Royal Arch. These chapters usually met in Craft lodges until a separate chapter hall could be built. Webb's book included a detailed summary of the legend of Enoch, which described how the Master's Word was preserved in vaults located beneath Solomon's Temple.[52]

---

52. For an Old Testament parallel to this legend, see Exodus 28:36–38: "And thou shalt make a plate of pure gold, and engrave upon it, like the engraving of a signet, HOLINESS TO THE LORD." Concerning the Royal Arch, see Bernard E. Jones, *Freemasons' Book of the Royal Arch* (London: George G. Harrap & Company Ltd., 1957).

Webb described how God showed Enoch, the same character who was taken up to Heaven in the Old Testament, a gold plate located in a mountain and told him: "'As thou art desirous to know my name, attend, and it shall be revealed unto thee.' Upon this, a mountain seemed to rise to the heavens, and Enoch was transferred to the top thereof, where he beheld a triangular plate of gold…upon which were some characters which he received a strict injunction never to pronounce."[53] Thereafter, Enoch was lowered into the vault, built an underground temple, and made a triangular plate of gold similar to the one he had been shown in his vision. He engraved "ineffable characters," or the true name of Deity on the plate and placed it on a triangular pedestal, and deposited it in the ninth arch of an underground temple he had built. Only Enoch knew where this treasure was located and the "right pronunciation of the great and sacred name."

To insure that the location would not be lost, Enoch placed a stone door over the cavern and built "two great pillars," one of brass to withstand water and one of marble to withstand fire. He placed a ball containing maps of the world and universe on top of the brass pillar that served as an instrument "for improving the mind and giving it the most distinct idea of any problem or proposition." Enoch was allowed to revisit this site (where the plate was deposited) once a year before his ultimate assumption into heaven.[54]

The American Royal Arch, which was patterned after the Irish Royal Arch, specified that Enoch's plate was eventually discovered while Solomon's Temple was being repaired during the reign of King Josiah (640–609 BCE). The ritual described how Master Masons, who were the true descendants of the lost tribes, gained access to the hidden vault from the northeast corner of the temple through a stone with an iron ring, which was determined to be the keystone of an arch. When this keystone was removed there was an aperture through which these temple workers discovered secret vaults below the temple. Here they discovered the Ark of the Covenant, which contained an "ancient looking book." This was the "book of the law—long lost, but now found. Holiness to the Lord."[55]

53. Webb, *The Freemason's Monitor*, 244–61.

54. Ibid. For other descriptions of Enoch's legend see Oliver, *The Antiquities of Freemasonry*, 88–92; Henry Andrew Francken, *Francken Manuscript, 1783* (Kila, MT: Kessinger Publishing Company, n.d.), 121–39. See also Arturo de Hoyos, "The Mystery of the Royal Arch Word," *Heredom* 2 (1993): 7–34, reprinted in de Hoyos and Morris, *Freemasonry in Context*, 209–30.

55. See Knoop and Jones, *The Genesis of Freemasonry*, 286; Wells, *Understanding Freemasonry*, 8, 204; Wells, *The Rise and Development of Organized Freemasonry*, 151. The scriptural references concerning Josiah's discovery of "the book of the law in the house of the LORD" are II Kings 22:8, 13; and II Chronicles 34: 8, 14–15, 18–19. According to Rabbinic tradition Josiah foresaw the destruction of the temple and therefore commanded temple workers to deposit the Ark of the Covenant in the vault. Oliver doubted the validity of this legend and

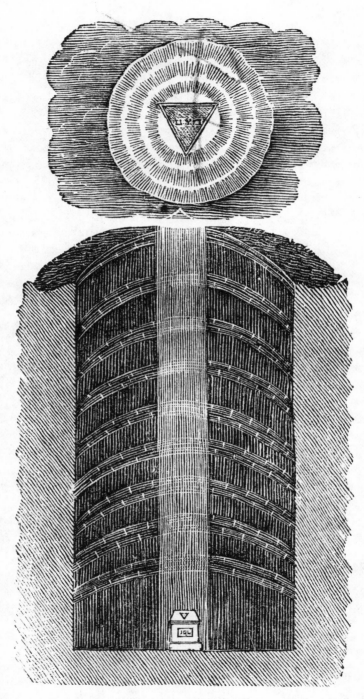

Illustration of Enoch's Plate and the underground vault where it was deposited.
Published in Jeremy L. Cross, *The True Masonic Chart, or Hieroglyphic Monitor*, 44.

A gold plate located on the Ark contained ineffable characters that contained a key word or the sacred name of God. According to the ritual, the "world is indebted to Masonry for the preservation of this sacred volume." The temple workers discovered "a key to the ineffable characters of this degree" through which they were able to translate "mysterious words in a triangular form."[56] The Royal Arch included instructions concerning this history while each candidate passed through the various veils in the temple. They were taught that since they had recovered the omnific word, which was originally communicated to Noah but which was lost shortly before the dedication of the Temple of Solomon, they were "endowed with every good and perfect gift." As such, "they could finally set about the work of rebuilding His temple." The Royal Arch Mason was assured that once the temple was completed, imitates would receive "eternal light and life."[57]

A Royal Arch chapter was presided over by a high priest, a king, and a scribe (or prophet). The presiding high priest wore clothing similar to those of a Hebrew priest, including a miter, upon which is inscribed "HOLINESS TO THE LORD," the motto of Royal Arch Masonry to "be engraven upon all our thoughts, words and actions," a shirt or tunic reaching to his feet, a robe, an ephod, and a breastplate. The Royal Arch rituals, which required nine or more high priests, were dedicated to, and included a history of, the Old Testament patriarch Melchizedek. The high priest officiated in a "tabernacle" with four veils, and an initiate was required to pass through these veils before being admitted into the Holy of Holies.[58]

---

suggested that Solomon built the vaults below his temple which was not known to Josiah or his immediate predecessors. See George Oliver, *The Historical Landmarks and other Evidences of Freemasonry Explained in a Series of Practical Lectures* (London, 1845–46), 2:436. The English Royal Arch ritual maintains that the gold plate was discovered seventy years after Solomon's Temple was destroyed. Zerubbabel led exiled Jews back to Jerusalem from Babylon to rebuild their temple after the Edict of Cyrus in 538 BCE. A Royal Arch chapter in England "represents the Tabernacle erected…near the ruins of King Solomon's Temple" after the Jewish return from captivity. Macoy, *General History*, 332–37, 367–68. See also Churton, *Freemasonry*, 26–27, 384–85.

56. Richardson, *Richardson's Monitor of Freemasonry*, 82; Duncan's *Masonic Ritual and Monitor*, 246–49. The Masonic monitors that included descriptions of the Royal Arch include: Webb, *The Freemason's Monitor* (1897), 153–80; Bradley, *Some of the Beauties of Free-Masonry* (Albany: G. J. Loomis & Co., 1821), 122–38; and Jeremy L. Cross, *The True Masonic Chart or Hieroglyphic Monitor* (New Haven, CT: John C. Gray, 1820), 103–20. Cross's description of the Royal Arch was replicated verbatim in many subsequently published monitors. The Royal Arch was described in more detail in the following anti-Masonic books: Avery Allyn, *A Ritual of Freemasonry* (Philadelphia: John Clarke, 1831), 118–43; Bernard, *Light on Masonry*, 124–44; Duncan, *Masonic Ritual and Monitor*, 217–65; and Richardson, *Richardson's Monitor of Freemasonry*, 66–83.

57. Carnes, *Secret Ritual and Manhood*, 39–49.

58. See John Sheville and James L. Gould, *Guide to the Royal Arch Chapter: A Complete Monitor for Royal Arch Masonry, etc. To Which Are Added Monitorial Instructions in the Holy*

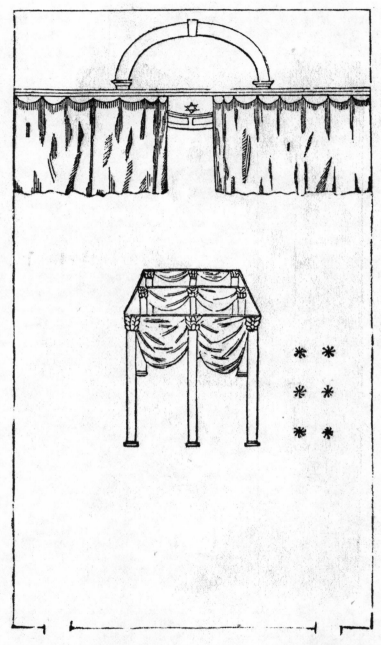

Illustration of a veil in Royal Arch chapter. Published in Jeremy L. Cross,
The True Masonic Chart, or Hieroglyphic Monitor, 30, 35.

Illustration of Royal Arch officers. Published in Jeremy L. Cross,
The True Masonic Chart, or Hieroglyphic Monitor, 31

In January 1799, the General Grand Chapter of Royal Arch Masons
approved a fifth honorary degree for high priests that was called the Holy
Order of High Priesthood, and Webb mentioned this new degree in the
second edition of *The Freemason's Monitor*, which was published in 1802.[59]
Royal Arch Masons who had received the four degrees of Royal Arch Masonry and had become high priests and presided over a Royal Arch chapter,
were eligible for this fifth honorary degree. The degree's symbol was Enoch's
plate of gold designed as a triple triangle.[60] During the ritual, which incorporated elements from other Masonic degrees including those practiced by
the exclusively Christian Knight Templars, high priests were consecrated
and anointed into the Holy Order of High Priesthood.[61]

Order of High Priesthood in Royal Arch Masonry, with the Ceremonies of the Order, by James
L. Gould (New York: Masonic Publishing and Manufacturing Co., 1868), 50–51, 132–208;
Edward T. Schultz, "The Order of High Priesthood," in Stillson, *History of the Ancient and
Honorable Fraternity*, 640–42; Macoy, *General History*, 50–51, 132–34, 212, 250, 303, 390–91,
458.

59. Thomas Smith Webb, *The Freemason's Monitor; or, Illustrations of Masonry* (New York:
Southwick and Crooker, 1802), 197–200. For other descriptions of the Holy Order, see Jeremy L. Cross, *The True Masonic Chart, or Hieroglyphic Monitor*, 2nd ed. (New Haven, CT:
John C. Gray, 1820), 129–66; and Joshua Bradley, *Some of the Beauties of Free-Masonry*, 2nd.
ed. (Albany: G. J. Loomis & Co., 1821), 231–71.

60. Macoy, *General History*, 168, 283; Sheville and Gould, *Guide to the Royal Arch Chapter*,
209, 212; Mackey, *An Encyclopaedia of Freemasonry*, 1:325–27; George W. Warvelle, *Observations on the Order of High Priesthood*, 2nd ed. (Chicago: J. C. Burmeister, 1915); Pick and
Knight, *The Freemason's Pocket Reference Book*, 144, 292.

61. See Warvelle, *Observations on the Order of High Priesthood*; Webb, *The Freemason's Monitor* (1802), 197–200; Pick and Knight, *The Freemason's Pocket Reference Book*, 144.

The York Rite also included two side degrees (Royal Master and Select Master) that were initially conferred by independent ritualists but that were eventually controlled, for the most part, by Cryptic Masons grand councils. These degrees provided additional details concerning the Mason's Word, which Enoch constructed before the Flood and was preserved in the crypts.

Finally, the York Rite eventually included Knight Templar degrees, which were conferred by Knight Templar encampments and which organized a grand encampment in 1816. These degrees were originally developed in Europe and were only conferred on Christian Masons. They included, like other rituals in the York Rite, legends concerning Solomon's Temple, except the last degree, the Order of the Temple, which enacted the story of crusading knights in the twelfth, thirteenth, and fourteenth centuries.

THE SCOTTISH RITE

The Scottish Rite, which included the Craft degrees and adapted degrees from the French *Haut Grades* and the Rite de Perfection, was organized during the same period as the York Rite.[62] The Haut Grades were introduced in America after 1761 when the Grand Lodge of France granted a patent to Etienne Morin to establish lodges throughout the world. In 1763 Morin introduced some of these degrees to Masons in the Caribbean, and four years later he authorized Henry Andrew Francken to establish a "Lodge of Perfection" in Albany, New York, which originally worked the three degrees of Craft Masonry and eleven additional degrees. But Francken copied the degrees and in 1771 he recorded twenty-three high degrees in addition to the three degrees of Craft Masonry.[63]

In May 1800 a Supreme Council of the Thirty-Third Degree, which was located in Charleston, South Carolina, announced that it controlled a thirty-three-degree system, which incorporated twenty-five degrees practiced in the Rite of Perfection as well as eight new degrees. Thirteen years later a second supreme council was created in New York City.

The Scottish Rite rituals included the legend of Enoch's plate that was recorded in the Francken manuscript. The Scottish Rite's thirteenth degree, the Knight of the Ninth Arch Degree (which is sometimes called the "Royal Arch of Solomon" or the "Royal Arch of Enoch") recounts the story

---

62. See Claude Guérillot, *La Genèse du Rite Écossais Ancien et Accepté* (Paris: Guy Trédaniel, 1993). See also Bernard, *Light on Masonry*, 253–72. For a comprehensive discussion of the Scottish Rite, see Arturo de Hoyos, *Scottish Rite Ritual, Monitor and Guide*, 2nd ed. (Washington D.C.: The Supreme Council, 33°, Southern Jurisdiction, 2009).

63. Francken made at least three copies of this twenty-five-degree rite which was an expansion of the fourteen-degree Rite of Perfection. See *Ars Quatuor Coronatorum* 89:208–10 [Transactions of the Quatuor Coronati Lodge No. 2076], hereafter cited as *AQC; AQC* 97:200–202; A. C. F. Jackson, *Rose Croix* (London: A. Lewis, 1987), 46–47.

of Enoch's Plate. Albert Mackey (1807–1881), who was the secretary general of the Scottish Rite's Supreme Council for the Southern District, noted that "though entirely different in its legend from the Royal Arch of the York and American Rites, its symbolic design is the same, for one common thought of a treasure lost and found pervades them all."[64] Albert Pike's (1809–1892) modifications to the Scottish Rite's thirty-three rituals retained all of the key elements of this degree.[65]

In the Scottish Rite, King Solomon sent three grand architects—Gibulum, Joabert, and Stolkyn—to search for ancient treasure near the site where his temple was being built. The architects entered Enoch's underground temple with nine arches through a trap door of stone, which is identified as the keystone of the highest arch. They descended into the temple three times where they discovered the gold plate which was engraved by Enoch and discovered the Master Mason's Word through the keystone.

These grand architects delivered the gold plate to Solomon who made them "knights of the ninth arch, afterwards called the Royal Arch." Solomon explained God's promise that "in fullness of time his name should be discovered, engraved upon a plate of gold; that they were bound to defend the sacred characters and that they were not at liberty to pronounce the sacred name." Solomon then took the gold plate into his temple through nine arches to deposit it in a place that he had originally named the "secret vault" but which he changed to "sacred vault." The Scottish Rite also included Knight of the Sun degree which, like the rituals of Adoptive Freemasonry, contained references to Adam, Eve, and their fall in the Garden of Eden.[66]

CHRISTIAN MASONRY

During the colonial period American Masons stressed the Craft's "universality and broad acceptability rather than its religious merits," but this "would change dramatically after the Revolution" when some American Freemasons began to identify the Craft with Christianity,[67] and, according

64. Mackey, *Encyclopedia of Freemasonry*, 41. See also Arturo de Hoyos, "The Mystery of the Royal Arch Word," *Heredom* 2 (1993), 7–34, reprinted in Hoyos and Morris, *Freemasonry in Context*, 209–30.

65. See Claude Guérillot, *La Rite de Perfection. Restitution des rituels taduits en anglais et copiés en 1783 par Henry Andrew Francken accompagnée de la tradution des textes statutaires* (Paris: Guy Trédaniel, 1993), 350–53; Francken, *Francken Manuscript, 1783*, 121–39.

66. Guerillot, *La Genèse du Rite Ecossais Ancien*. The Knight of the Sun Degree was originally the twenty-third degree of the Rite of Perfection. See Bernard, *Light on Masonry*, 253–72. Albert Pike made significant modifications to this degree which is now the twenty-eighth degree in Scottish Rite Freemasonry.

67. Stephen C. Bullock, *Revolutionary Brotherhood: Freemasonry and the Transformation of the American Social Order, 1730–1840* (Chapel Hill: University of North Carolina Press, 1996), 163.

to Mark Carnes, modified "Webb's rationalism and imposed on the most common American Rite sequence a more ominous conception of God."[68]

Steven Bullock has described this transition as a time when "a substantial number of Masonic brothers (and even non-Masons) came to see their order as not simply representing universal moral principles but as a unique order that fulfilled the purposes and proclaimed the truths of Christianity."[69] These brothers taught that Freemasonry was a "sacred institution," "a powerful auxiliary" and "handmaid" to religion. Christians who possessed "the secrets of Freemasonry" would be able "to unfold the mysteries of Godliness and Christianity." They believed that their rituals should in effect be reattached or at least blended into Christianity as both Masonry and Christianity continued their journey to prepare believers for the millennium.[70]

Salem Town (1779–1864), the grand chaplain of the Royal Arch Grand Chapter of New York, was one of the most ardent proponents of Christianizing Freemasonry. In 1818 he wrote *A System of Speculative Masonry* in which he argued that Freemasonry and Christianity were kindred spirits. He insisted that "ancient Masonry was, in a very important sense, ancient Christianity," that King Solomon organized and systematized speculative Freemasonry, which thereafter "flourished in Egypt," and that "speculative Masonry comprises those great and fundamental principles which constitute the very essence of the Christian system."[71]

Town described Masonry's first three degrees as Adam's journey from a "state of moral darkness" to a "pilgrimage state" in which he "is sometimes diverted from his Christian course."[72] He believed the Royal Arch ritual, which included the High Priesthood, included the "NAME which no man knoweth save he that receiveth it," and that an initiate "discovers his election to, and his glorified station in, the kingdom of his father," where "all the heavenly sojourners will be admitted within the veil of God's presence where they will become kings and priests before the throne of his glory for ever and ever."[73] Town concluded that eventually "when brotherly love shall abound...all shall practice what is now taught within the lodge and that "the great plan of human redemption" would be dramatized in the temple *"where every saint will be filled with the fullness of God forever and ever."*[74]

68. Carnes, *Secret Ritual and Manhood*, 49.
69. Bullock, *Revolutionary Brotherhood*, 163.
70. Ibid., 169, 171.
71. Town, *A System of Speculative Masonry*, 83, 90, 98, 103, 126–27, 145, 173–75, 178–79.
72. Ibid., 75–77.
73. Ibid., 73–81.
74. Ibid., 81– 82, 178–80.

Joshua Bradley (1778–1855), a Baptist minister and a Freemason, also believed in Freemasonry's essential Christian nature. He published *Some of the Beauties of Free-Masonry* because "some Christians feel injured when any of their relations, friends, and brethren join the lodges" and he wanted "to remove the objections which they bring against the order, that they may no longer disrespect a system that is founded in truth, and cannot be destroyed." He explained why Masons, whose principles were drawn from revelation, were required to maintain secrecy, and compared them to Immanuel "in rendering to all a suitable tribute of respect, and keep in their hearts these peculiarities which cannot in the present state of things be consistently revealed."

Bradley assured his readers that the obligations taken by Freemasons were "perfectly moral and compatible with the principles of Christianity, civil society, and good government." Nevertheless, he explained that Freemasonry accepted men of differing religious sentiments, as long as they believe in a supreme being, because "there must be one system formed by man in which the confusion of tongues, the rage of party, the fame of heroes, the distinctions of birth, nations, statesmen, kings, and ecclesiasticks should cease, and all meet on the level and greet each other as brethren."[75]

During this same period British Mason George Oliver (1782–1867) described the impact that Freemasonry would have on Christians seeking a more graphic pathway. He wrote that God (the great Architect) "was the founder of Masonry" and "sent forth his WORD, and called all things out of chaos into being."[76] He described the seven days of creation and God's instructions to Adam concerning Masonry. Adam "retained a perfect recollection of that speculative science which is now termed Masonry" after the first couple was driven from Paradise and that "one grand principle of antient Masonry was to preserve in men's minds the true knowledge of God." Primitive Masonry was preserved by Seth's descendants and "religion was the only foundation on which our order could be securely placed."[77]

Oliver extrapolated the Royal Arch legend, which was a crucial event in the preservation of primitive Freemasonry. Enoch engraved the "SACRED NAME OR WORD" or ineffable characters that he had seen in vision on

75. Bradley, *Some of the Beauties of Free-Masonry*, ii–xviii. Bradley also wrote an account of religious revivals, which included the area around Palmyra. See Joshua Bradley, *Accounts of Religious Revivals in Many Parts of the United States* (Albany: Printed by G.J. Loomis & Co., 1819). Anti-Masonic writers later noted that Bradley seceded from Freemasonry. See Ward, *Anti-Masonic Review*, I: 255.
76. George Oliver, *The Antiquities of Freemasonry* (London: G. and W. B. Whittaker, 1823), 28–32.
77. Ibid., 42–51.

George Oliver (1782–1867).

"a plate of Gold in the form of an equilateral triangle," which he placed in an underground temple that he constructed. He also "erected two great pillars...which contained the essence and end of Masonry" and "paid occasional visits to the temple" before he was translated into heaven. One of the pillars and the gold plate preserved the secrets of Masonry.[78]

Oliver believed that "following Solomon, pure, 'primitive' Masonry was a secret tradition, theoretically transmitted through the medieval guilds, whereas the spurious tradition survived as the pagan mysteries," and that the "Masonic orders founded in eighteenth-century France and Germany developed various versions of this theme of schism and transmission, creating a confusion of conflicting rites and degrees, each order in some way promising to be the true source of an 'antediluvian' purity."[79] Brooke concluded that Oliver believed that "the heart of all Masonic mythology" was centered on the "divine Adam in the Garden of Eden, 'in direct communication with God and the angels' and in 'a state of perfection.'"[80]

78. Ibid., 85–97.
79. Brooke, *The Refiner's Fire*, 165–66, quoting Oliver, *The Antiquities of Freemasonry*, 41–45.
80. Brooke, *The Refiner's Fire*, 165, quoting Oliver, *The Antiquities of Freemasonry*, 41–45.

These Masons maintained that Primitive Freemasonry withstood schisms and apostasy that had afflicted Christian denominations. Oliver asserted that Masonry "was coeval with true religion" and following the Christian revelation it was "purified from the defilements which it contracted by incorporation with false systems of worship, in every age, and amongst every people for many successive centuries."[81] Town also argued that the "glorious millennial period will soon be experienced in the church," that such renewal would "soon commence in the Masonic world," and that while "Christian churches are arising, trimming their lamps, and purifying their bodies" the Masonic "lodges are renewing their discipline, and pursuing such measures as shall more effectively promote the general good of mankind."[82] Thus, these American Masons were convinced that if Masonry restored its Christian soul, Ramsay's vision of all Christians becoming united in one cofraternity could be achieved.

THE MORGAN SCANDAL

Masonry's rapid expansion, and the attempts by some Masons to Christianize it, created severe tensions within the Craft. During the summer of 1826 John Glazier Stearns (1795–1874), a Baptist minister and Freemason, renounced Masonry and published *An Inquiry into the Nature and Tendency of Speculative Free-Masonry* in September of the same year. Stearns's book was not an exposé of Masonic rituals but instead an attack on the pretensions of Freemasonry, intended "to show, that Masonry and Christianity are Distinct Institutions, and that they never ought to be blended."[83]

Stearns, like many other Masons, assumed that the Craft (at least the first three degrees) had ancient origins, but he argued that it was practiced "among the wicked descendants of Ham," and that its degrees concerning the "High Priesthood" were a mockery. Stearns quoted liberally from Salem Town, particularly his narrative concerning Adam's fall and redemption, and he attacked Masonic claims that its rituals "save men, to conduct them to heaven, and bestow on them the rewards of a blessed immortality," and that it was "time to examine the claims of a society, which endangers the purity of our civil institutions."[84]

---

81. Oliver, *The Antiquities of Freemasonry*, 176–77.
82. Town, *A System of Speculative Masonry*, 174, 178–79.
83. John G. Stearns, *An Inquiry into the Nature and Tendency of Speculative Free-Masonry* (Utica, NY, 1826), 3.
84. Ibid., 3–4, 41, 96, 118–19. See also Grunder, *Mormon Parallels*, quoting Stearns, *An Inquiry*, 36–37, 43. I am indebted to Michael G. Reed who read a paper at the 2011 Mormon History Association entitled "The Mormon Endowment and the 'Christianization of Freemasonry'" in which he observed that Joseph Smith may have been influenced by Salem Town and his detractors including John Stearns and Henry Dana Ward.

William Morgan (1774–1826?). Published in
New England Anti-Masonic Almanac (1831).

During the same summer William Morgan (1774–1826) became a lightning rod in the increasingly vitriolic debate concerning the essential nature
of Freemasonry, and his disappearance was the initial catalyst for a national
anti-Masonic movement that eventually caused American Freemasonry to
experience "enormous membership losses."[85] Morgan, a professional brick
mason who lived in LeRoy, New York, claimed he was a Master Mason.
There are apparently no records that prove Morgan was initiated into Craft
Masonry, but he did become a Royal Arch Mason before he moved to Batavia, New York, where he joined Batavia Lodge and signed a petition seeking
permission to organize a Royal Arch chapter.[86]

---

85. Bullock, "Masons, Masonic History and Academic Scholarship," xii.
86. For a discussion of William Morgan, see Keith Muir, "The Morgan Affair and Its Effect
on Freemasonry," *AQC* 105 (1992): 217–34; Stanley Upton Mock, *The Morgan Episode in
American Free Masonry* (East Aurora, NY: Roycrofters, 1930); John C. Palmer, *The Morgan
Affair and Anti-Masonry* (Washington, DC: Masonic Service Association of the United
States, 1924); Rob Morris, *William Morgan: Or Political Anti-Masonry, its Rise, Growth
and Decadence* (New York: Robert McCoy, 1883); William L. Stone, *Letters on Masonry and
Anti-Masonry addressed to the Hon. John Quincy Adams* (New York: O. Halsted, 1832), 123–
297; Clarence O. Lewis, "The Morgan Affair," typescript, 1966, Niagara County Historical
Society and Lockport Public Library, Lockport, New York; John E. Thompson, *The Masons,
the Mormons, and the Morgan Incident* (Ames: Iowa Research Lodge No. 2 AF&AM, 1984).
Morgan claimed that it was "not an uncommon thing, by any means, for a chapter to confer
all four degrees in one night." Morgan, *Illustrations of Masonry*, 94.

But Morgan's name was removed from the petition and he was denied entrance into the chapter after it was organized, and he thereafter became a bitter enemy of Freemasonry and threatened to expose its rituals including the degrees of Royal Arch Masonry.[87] Arturo de Hoyas has noted that "both exposés (works intended for the public) and ritual guides (aids to the Fraternity) had been printed just shy of 100 years before Morgan's work." Nevertheless, Freemasons were incensed by Morgan's blatant disregard of his Masonic oaths of secrecy.[88]

Masons placed advertisements in local papers charging that Morgan was both a swindler and a danger to the Craft. Some Masons allegedly started a fire in the office of his publisher, David Cade Miller, and attempted, unsuccessfully, to seize Morgan's unpublished exposé.[89] On September 11, 1826, Morgan was arrested for a bad debt but local Masons discharged his debt, and when he was released the following day apparently abducted him and took him to a remote location near Fort Niagara. Thereafter, Morgan was never heard from again.[90]

In October Miller, the editor of the Batavia *Republican Advocate*, printed Morgan's exposé, which included only three degrees but very specific descriptions of signs, tokens, obligations, and penalties, under the ironic title of *Illustrations of Masonry by One of the Fraternity*, which was the same title William Preston used for his pro-Masonic work.[91]

This first American-born exposé eventually appeared in at least twenty-nine editions, which have survived, and one printer, perhaps recognizing

87. In 1812 an abridgment of Barruel's multivolume work concerning the Illuminati was published together with the British exposé of the Craft degrees (*Jachin and Boaz, or an Authentic Key to door of Freemasonry, Ancient and Modern*) in Lancaster, Pennsylvania, as *The Antichristian and Antisocial Conspiracy* (Lancaster: Joseph Ehrenfried, 1812).
88. Arturo de Hoyas, *Light on Masonry: The History and Rituals of America's Most Important Masonic Exposé* (Washington, DC: Scottish Rite Research Society, 2008), 24. Carlile, in his *Manual of Freemasonry*, claimed some credit for Morgan's exposé. In addition, the first exposé of so-called *haut grade* Masonry in America, written by Mary Hanlon, *Revelations of Masonry, Made by a Late Member of the Craft, in Four Parts* (New York, 1827), was a plagiarism, at least in part, of Carlile.
89. For an anti-Masonic perspective of the Morgan episode, see *Proceedings of United States Anti-Masonic Convention, held at Philadelphia, September 11, 1830* (New York: Skinner and Dewey, 1830); and Bernard, *Light on Masonry*. For a Masonic perspective, see Rob Morris, *William Morgan: Or Political Anti-Masonry, Its Rise, Growth, and Decadence* (New York: Robert McCoy, 1883). For a scholarly approach see William Preston Vaughn, *The Anti-Masonic Party in the United States 1826–1843* (Lexington: University Press of Kentucky, 1983).
90. See deposition of Mrs. Lucinda Morgan, in *A Narrative of the Facts and Circumstances Relating to the Kidnapping and Murder of William Morgan* (Batavia, NY: D. C. Miller, 1827).
91. Morgan, *Illustrations of Masonry*, 28–29. The Second or Fellow Craft Masons Degree in Morgan's exposé included a reference to the "undiscovered country, from whose bourne no traveler has returned." Morgan, *Illustrations of Masonry*, 49. Another variation of this Shakespearean phrase also appeared in the Book of Mormon three years later. See 2 Nephi 1:14.

the irony of the original title, changed it to *Masonry Unveiled.*[92] William
Preston Vaughn has described the initial reaction to Morgan's book as "intense but not hysterical" but the book was an important catalyst for the
development of a growing anti-Masonic movement.[93] Those who joined
this movement, which was initially a religious reaction followed by a political component, were dedicated to eliminating Freemasonry because
they believed it was conspiring to destroy civil government and Christian
religion.

"The Antimasonic fervor that swept the Burned-over District was enthusiastically evangelical," wrote Vaughn, "its advocates 'preaching' with
profound conviction, its written materials almost identical to missionary
tracts, and its literary style reminiscent of revivalist sermons." According to
Vaughn, "most of the evangelical Anti-masons [like those who attacked the
Illuminati thirty years earlier] appear to have been orthodox fundamentalists in religious orientation, possessing a strong dislike for the more 'liberal'
denominations such as Universalism and Unitarianism and worrying about
the rise of deism and rationalism in the United States."[94] Baptist, Presbyterian, and Methodist ministers became anti-Masonic leaders while Episco-
palian, Universalist, and Unitarian clergy chose not to secede or to stand
on the sidelines.

This religious anti-Masonic reaction did not intensify into a political
movement for more than a year after Morgan's disappearance. New York
governor DeWitt Clinton issued proclamations in September and October
in which he requested citizens to aid in apprehending Morgan's kidnappers.
Nevertheless, the first four men who were indicted in November and tried
in January were all given light sentences. In 1827 the New York legislature
considered but failed to pass a resolution that would have created a joint
committee to investigate William Morgan's "abduction, detention, and disposition." Instead, it enacted legislation to make kidnapping a felony, prohibited county sheriffs from summoning grand juries, and allowed town
supervisors to draft a list of prospective jurors.[95]

92. See Walgren, *Freemasonry, Anti-Masonry and Illuminism*, 513; and Grunder, *Mormon Parallels*, 951. See also William Morgan, *Masonry Unveiled, Containing a Full Exposition of the Secrets and Ceremonies of That "Ancient and Honorable" Institution, Freemasonry*. See also *Wayne Sentinel*, November 17, 1826.
93. I relied on William Preston Vaughn for this short description of the events which oc-
curred after the publication of Morgan's exposé. See William Preston Vaughn, *The Anti-Masonic Party in the United States, 1826–1843* (Lexington: University of Kentucky Press, 1983), 5.
94. Ibid., 21.
95. Ibid., 6.

Eventually only ten of the fifty-nine men who were indicted in connection with Morgan's disappearance were convicted.[96] Thurlow Weed (1797–1882), the editor of the *Rochester Telegraph*, was one of the first journalists in the country to publicize the Morgan scandal, which he believed constituted a political conspiracy. Weed's business partner, Robert Martin (who was a Mason), objected when Weed aggressively reported the story and used sensational headlines ("William Morgan was taken to Fort Niagara, murdered and thrown into the river!") and shortly thereafter they dissolved their partnership. In February 1828 Weed established the *Anti-Masonic Enquirer*, which became a leading anti-Masonic newspaper in New York, spread "anti-masonic hysteria" throughout the country, and catapulted Weed to political prominence.[97]

ANTI-MASONIC CONVENTION

The first convention of seceding Masons was held in LeRoy, New York, a year and a half after Morgan's disappearance.[98] Baptist minister David Bernard (1798–1876), recording secretary of the convention, noted that prior to this convention there were "but few [who] had the moral courage to openly dissent from the Masonic institution, and denounce it as wicked and dangerous."[99] Nevertheless, the convention was primarily a nonpolitical gathering organized to provide a religious response to Masonry, demand more indictments, and vigorously investigate the Craft.

The convention attracted approximately forty delegates, which included prominent businessmen, religious leaders, and publishers, such as David Cade Miller (William Morgan's publisher), Solomon Southwick (printer), and John G. Stearns and David Bernard (Baptist ministers). The attendees also included publisher William Wines Phelps (1792–1872) and William Morgan's lodge brother George Washington Harris (1780–1857), who both eventually converted to Mormonism.

96. Wheelan, *Mr. Adams's Last Crusade*, 86–87. See also Grunder, *Mormon Parallels*, 990–91, citing *A Narrative of the facts and circumstances relating to the Kidnapping of presumed murder of William Morgan* (Batavia, NY: Printed by D. C. Miller, Under the Direction of the Committees, 1826). Grunder observed that this report "cites eight instances of judges and other leading citizens commenting off-handedly that William Morgan ought to die for revealing the secrets of Freemasonry."
97. Grunder, *Mormon Parallels*, 1460–62.
98. Miller's preface to Morgan's exposé demonstrates that this issue arose immediately after Morgan disappeared. See Grunder, *Mormon Parallels*, 955; Vaughn, *The Anti-Masonic Party*, 27.
99. Bernard, *Light on Masonry*, 413.

The delegates met on February 19–20, March 6–7, and July 4–5, 1828, and listened to testimonials that Morgan's *Illustrations of Masonry* was accurate, voted that the obligations they had taken as Freemasons were not binding, and decided to publish a new exposé of the high degrees.[100] They attended sessions in which speakers attacked Freemasonry because of its secrecy and the "great danger" it posed "to our republican institutions."[101] William Phelps played a prominent role in these conventions and served on various committees, including those that prepared "the degrees of Free Masonry above that of Master," for publication and drafted a memorial to congress "to institute an enquiry into the facts respecting the incarceration of a free citizen in the arsenal of fort Niagara." He also prepared and circulated an invitation to seceding Masons to attend a meeting where a declaration of independence would be read and signed.[102]

On July 4, Phelps and Harris joined other anti-Masons who signed a "Declaration of Independence," which stated that "secret societies" were "dangerous to the government," and sought "to abolish the order of Free Masonry, and destroy its influence in our government."[103] Phelps also proposed a dinner toast to Morgan and referred to him as "the morning star of more light."[104]

100. Richard Carlile's *Manual of Freemasonry* (1825), was the first exposé of some of Freemasonry's high degrees. Beginning in 1825, this work was serialized in *The Republican* in London and partially reprinted in book form in 1831. Carlile claimed that his "exposure of Freemasonry in 1825 led to its exposure in the United States." See Richard Carlile, *Manual of Masonry, with an Introductory Key-stone to the Royal Arch* (London, 1831); Richard Carlile, *Manual of Freemasonry, in Three Parts, with an Explanatory Introduction to the Science, and a Free Translation of Some of the Sacred Scripture Names* (London, 1853).

101. *A Narrative of the Facts and Circumstances*; Bernard, *Light on Masonry*, 460–78. The new exposé was *A Revelation of Freemasonry* (Rochester: Weed & Heron, 1828), which was later incorporated into Bernard's *Light on Masonry*. Some delegates did not attend all of the sessions. For example, Bernard, Phelps, Southwick, and Stearns did not attend the March 6–7 gathering. See Bernard, *Light on Masonry*, 422.

102. Grunder, *Mormon Parallels*, 691–92.

103. Bernard, *Light on Masonry*, 413–17. *Light on Masonry* was published in six variant states in 1829.

104. *Republican Monitor* (Kazenovia, NY), July 15, 1828, 3. The phrase "morning star" appears in Revelation 2:28 and 22:16, and is reminiscent of the name Phelps chose for Mormonism's first newspaper, *The Evening and the Morning Star*. The convention is described in Bernard, *Light on Masonry*, 452–57, and in Mock, *The Morgan Episode*, 137–41. The high degrees were published in *A Revelation of Free Masonry as Published to the World by a Convention of Seceding Masons* (Rochester: The Lewiston Committee, 1828). The Lewiston Committee included Samuel Works, Frederick F. Backus, Frederick Whittlesey, and Thurlow Weed, who were businessmen and professionals in Rochester. The committee published exposures of degrees conferred in a Royal Arch Chapter, including Mark Master's Degree, Past Master's Degree, Most Excellent Master's Degree, and Royal Arch Degree, as well as exposés of Knights of the Red Cross, Knight Templar and Knight of Malta, Knights of the Christian Mark and Guards of the Conclave, Knight of the Holy Sepulchre, The Holy and

W. W. Phelps (1792–1872). Courtesy Special Collections,
J. Willard Marriott Library, University of Utah.

POLITICAL ANTI-MASONRY

While the first anti-Masonic convention held in LeRoy had a religious theme, politicians, such as Thurlow Weed and William Seward, gradually assumed "almost complete control" of the movement and attempted to propel it to national prominence.[105] In 1828 President John Quincy Adams (1767–1848), who was not a Freemason, was challenged a second time by Andrew Jackson (1767–1845), a Tennessee Freemason and a past grand master. Jackson's supporters were identified with Freemasonry and

Thrice Illustrious Order of the Cross called a Council, and Obligations of Thrice Illustrious Knights of the Cross. The committee obtained a transcript of the degrees, according to the "report of the publishing committee," through a pseudo-disciple of General Grand Lecturer of the United States Jeremy L. Cross, "who attended his Lectures until the entire degree was accurately written out." Ibid., v–vii. Cross denounced the claim as a fraud and declared that he never allowed his pupils to take notes. William O. Cummings, *A Bibliography of Freemasonry* (New York: Press of Henry Emmerson, 1963), 47. Vaughn concluded that the Lewiston Committee "quickly became the driving force of Antimasonry in western New York" and that it "memorialized the New York legislature, giving the facts about Morgan's abduction, explaining the difficulties of apprehending the guilty parties, asking that the kidnapping laws be strengthened, and requesting appointment of a special agent, unsympathetic to Masonic interests, to conduct the prosecutions and trials." Vaughan, *The Anti-Masonic Party*, 27.

105. Vaughn, *The Anti-Masonic Party*, 29.

his opponents rallied under the banner of anti-Masonry. Even Adams, who
did not adopt an anti-Masonic tone during his campaign, referred to the
Jackson-led Democratic Party as "The Combination." Despite the inclusion
of anti-Masonry in the campaign, Jackson beat Adams, providing an additional stimulus for the creation of an anti-Masonic party.[106]

ANTI-MASONIC PUBLICATIONS

Nevertheless, evangelical anti-Masons, who resented the influence of Masonry as their disestablished churches waned, continued to publish most
of the movement's influential books and were finally able to gain traction
against the institution they considered to be a pseudo- and false religion.[107]
Their publications advanced "the object of anti-masons," which according
to W. W. Phelps, was "to dissolve and demolish an institution, stained with
the blood of an innocent unoffending citizen of this 'free country.'"[108]

In 1829 Baptist minister David Bernard published *Light on Masonry*,
which became known as the "Bible of Antimasonry."[109] Bernard favored the
complete eradication of Freemasonry because he believed it had fallen away
from its well-intentioned designs and had become corrupt. He therefore
called upon former members of the Craft to assist him in his new mission:
"Brethren and companions, attired in your mourning robes, attend and let
us seal up the gates of our temple, for the profane have found means of pen-
etrating into them."[110]

Bernard urged that the elimination of Masonry would result in preserving "the rights and liberties of our country; promoting the glory of the Re-
deemer's kingdom; and saving souls from destruction." His book revealed
over forty Masonic degrees that supplemented Morgan's exposé of Craft
Masonry and the Lewiston Committee's exposé of the Royal Arch rituals.[111]

---

106. Wheelan, *Mr. Adams's Last Crusade*, 44, 55, 57. Two years later Adams was elected to the
United States House of Representatives and in 1831 he attended an anti-Masonic convention
in Faneuil Hall. The following year he flirted with becoming the anti-Masonic party's first
presidential candidate but William Wirt (1772–1834), who was the U.S. attorney general,
received the nomination but was outpolled by both Andrew Jackson (who won re-election)
and Henry Clay (1777–1852), the candidate of the National Republicans. Thereafter Adams
became a convinced anti-Mason and took an active role in the new party's politics. In 1833
the Massachusetts Antimasonic Party nominated Adams for governor but he was badly defeated. See Wheelan, *Mr. Adams's Last Crusade*, 86–87.
107. Carnes, *Secret Ritual and Manhood*, 24. See also Stone, *Letters on Masonry and Anti-
Masonry*, 388–97.
108. Grunder, *Mormon Parallels*, 1346, quoting *Republican Monitor*, September 16, 1828.
109. For the reference to Bernard's book as the "Bible of Antimasonry," see Vaughn, *The Anti-
Masonic Party*, 19–20.
110. Bernard, *Light on Masonry*, 379.
111. Ibid. In 1831 Avery Allyn published *A Ritual of Freemasonry* (Philadelphia: John Clarke,
1831) which added several important degrees not contained in *Light on Masonry*.

He wrote that he was justified in breaking his Masonic oaths because "moral obligation requires me to keep such secrets and such only as are calculated to promote God's glory and the best good of the community."[112]

ANTIQUITY OF THE CRAFT

Despite this aggressive rhetoric, many of Masonry's critics still believed that the institution had ancient origins. Bernard published an address made by an unnamed Mason who noted that Masonry "was formed at a very early age of the world" when it was necessary to have "a strong bond of union for the protection of its members.... However holy our mysteries may have been, the lodges are now profaned and sullied."[113] Similarly, Lebbeus Armstrong (1775–1860), a Presbyterian pastor and seceding Mason, told a Baptist congregation that while the Craft's claim to ancient origins "has not been satisfactorily proved to be wholly without foundation," that "when the Jews apostatized from God in after ages, and fell into abominable idolatry of the heathen, Masonry became just what the Prince of darkness would have it to be, a compound of jewish ceremonies and heathen rites."[114]

Cadwallader D. Colden (1769–1834), a prominent New York politician who renounced the Craft, also wrote that the three degrees of Craft Masonry "may claim some sort of antiquity" while the high degrees were "of very modern invention." He believed that the "modern institutions are no more branches of the Masonic system, than they are of the orders, whose titles they assume," but that despite these origins "it does no good that might not be accomplished by far better means. Its secrecy and extensive combinations are dangerous."[115]

Nevertheless, some anti-Masons, who believed in the antiquity of the Craft, believed that the Devil created Masonry or at least taught its principles. For example, Presbyterian minister Reuben Sanborn, who worked on a committee with W. W. Phelps at the LeRoy convention, wrote that the "principles of masonry are confessedly ancient. They can be traced back to the time when the first deceiver said, 'Ye shall not surely die'" and that "Freemasonry is a powerful combination of wicked men in league with the powers of darkness."[116]

Randolph Streeter maintained that Masonic principles "commenced with our first parents; and originated from that great grand master who

112. Bernard, *Light on Masonry*, iii, ix.
113. Grunder, *Mormon Parallels*, 229–231, quoting Bernard, *Light on Masonry*, 373–380.
114. Lebbeus Armstrong, *The Man of Sin Revealed, Or the Total Overthrow of the Institution of Freemasonry* (n.p., n.d.), quoted in Grunder, *Mormon Parallels*, 141.
115. Grunder, *Mormon Parallels*, 114, quoting *The Anti-Masonic Review and Magazine*, 172–78.
116. Ibid., 1350–54, quoting *Republican Monitor*, November 11 and 25, 1828.

appeared to them in the garden with a lie in his mouth."[117] Solomon Southwick advanced the same thesis during a speech when he concluded that
while Freemasonry could have originated anciently, he was certain that it
had become "wicked and worthless" and like "the serpent of Eden."[118]

Likewise, a "committee on the antiquity of Speculative Free Masonry,"
which met during the Antimasonic State Convention of Massachusetts
held in Boston's Faneuil Hall in 1829–1830, reported that several committee
members believed in the antiquity of the Craft but primarily on the basis
that "if antiquity could render crime respectable, murder was most illustrious, for it could trace its origin to the first born of the human race."[119]
Finally, a writer who signed his name "Luke De Faubourg," concluded that
the evil of the Craft could be traced from "the murder of Abel to the murder
of Morgan."[120]

THE RITUALS OF FREEMASONRY

Some anti-Masons adopted the same claims that had been hurled at the
Order of Illuminati three decades earlier. Bernard compared the goals of
Masonry with those of the Illuminati—"to abolish government and social
order and extinguish Christianity"[121] and Henry Dana Ward (1797–1884),
a seceding Mason who has been referred to as "antimasonry's most famous
'missionary,'" connected the Illuminati with high degrees of Freemasonry
and in particular with the Royal Arch.[122] Ward's *Free Masonry*, which was
published in 1828 and advertised in E. B. Grandin's *Wayne Sentinel*,[123] referred to Barruel's assertion that "the secret object of [Masonic] ceremony
is to re-establish religious liberty, and to exhibit all men equally priests and
pontiffs, to recall the brethren to natural religion, and to persuade them
that the religion of Moses, and of Christ, had violated religious liberty and
equality by the distinction of priests and laity."

Ward particularly ridiculed the legend of Enoch, as summarized in
Thomas Smith Webb's 1802 *Monitor*, and noted that "Free Masonry

117. Ibid., 1358–59, quoting *Republican Monitor*, April 14, 1829.
118. Ibid., 1684, quoting Solomon Southwick, *An Oration: Delivered, by Appointment, on the Fourth of July, AD 1828.*
119. Ibid., 125, citing *An Abstract of the Proceedings of the Anti-Masonic State Convention of Massachusetts* (Boston: John Marsh, 1830), 19–25.
120. "Luke de Faubourg," Letter III, July 4, 1828, in an unspecified issue of the Boston *Free Press*, as republished on the front page of the *Republican Monitor*, November 11, 1828. See also Grunder, *Mormon Parallels*, 1350–54, quoting *Republican Monitor*, November 11, 1828.
121. Bernard, *Light on Masonry*, x.
122. Vaughn, *The Anti-Masonic Party*, 72.
123. *The Wayne Sentinel* 6:25, whole no. 285 (Friday, March 13, 1829), p. [4].

pretends, that the *true and ineffable name* was deposited in each of these three temples" on Mount Moriah and that it was "'visible in the temple at the time St. Jerome flourished, written in the ancient Samaritan characters.'"[124] According to Ward, "This is the way with Masonic tradition, so exact, as even to remember the Samarian characters?" "But what *temple,*" asked the incredulous Ward, "was that? Enoch's subterranean cave fell in, after the erection of Solomon's; Solomon's was destroyed by Nebuchadnezzar; and the foundations of the second temple were ploughed up by Titus, AD 70."[125] He noted that the religious part of Masonic ritual included priests "vested in the ornaments of the priesthood, they offer bread and wine, according to the order of Melchisedec."[126]

Some anti-Masons were also anxious concerning the specter of female participation in masonic rituals. While the first English translation of an exposé of a French adoptive ritual was published in 1765 the first American exposé, *Illustration of the Four First Degrees of Female masonry, as practiced in Europe*, did not appear until 1827. Like those previously published in Europe, this American exposure included a description of the second degree that took place in the Garden of Eden.[127] Four years later Avery Allyn published *A Ritual of Freemasonry* in which he claimed that an androgynous ritual was practiced in America and that American female lodges conferred a degree entitled "Heroine of Jericho" "upon royal arch Masons, their wives and widows."[128]

This androgynous degree, which may have been developed between 1815 and 1820,[129] included women who took an oath to keep "the secrets of heroine of Jericho" and to "keep the secrets of a brother or sister heroine of Jericho." But Allyn believed that this ritual was "'got up' by those concerned in that Masonic outrage and by swearing their female relatives to conceal the same crimes, should they come to their knowledge, which they themselves, as royal arch Masons, felt bound to perpetrate, against the law of the land, upon the traitor Morgan."[130] During this same period, Master Masons

124. [Henry Dana Ward], *Freemasonry* (New York, 1828), 14–15, 18–19, 22, 28–29.

125. Ward, *Free Masonry*, 21.

126. Ibid., 292, quoting Augustin Barruel, *Memoirs, Illustrating the History of Jacobism* (Hartford and New York, 1799), 2:158.

127. *Illustration of the Four First Degrees of Female masonry, as practiced in Europe Illustration of the Four First Degrees of Female masonry, as practice in Europe* (Boston, 1827). This ritual was reproduced in de Hoyas, *Light on Masonry*, 167–98. R. A. Gilbert noted that *Observations on Freemasonry; with a Masonic Vision. Addressed, by a Lady in Worcester [Mrs. Crocker], to her Female Friend* (Worcester [MA.], 1798), was a simple Masonic apologia.

128. Allyn, *A Ritual of Freemasonry*, 172–77. The three degrees conferred on Heroines of Jericho were Master Masons' Daughter, True Kinsman, and Heroine of Jericho.

129. Coil, *Coil's Masonic Encyclopedia*, 13–14.

130. Allyn, *A Ritual of Freemasonry*, 175.

also practiced an androgynous ritual entitled "Mason's Wife," and the Royal Arch allegedly created another ritual entitled "Good Samaritan."[131]

These American female rituals were not intended to confer real Masonic degrees on women and instead provided a method "to associate in one common bond the worthy wives, widows, daughters, and sisters of Freemasons, so as to make their adoptive privileges available for all the purposes contemplated in Masonry; to secure to them the advantages of their claim in a moral, social, and charitable point of view, and from them the performance of corresponding duties."[132] Although some have claimed that they may have had some historical connection with French adoptive rituals, and were introduced to the colonies by French officers, they did not contain any narrative concerning the Garden of Eden, which Jan Snoek has concluded was the heart of those rituals.[133]

Most American anti-Masons were apparently unaware that American Masons had fostered limited female participation in very sterile but Masonic-like rituals that were in some respects reminiscent of the French system. David Bernard, attacking American Freemasonry's male exclusivity,

131. See *History of the Order of the Eastern Star* (N.p.: n.d.), 9. "Mason's Wife" was apparently published by William Leigh in *The Ladies of Masonry, or Hieroglyphic Monitor* (Louisville, KY, 1821).

132. Mackey, *Encyclopedia of Freemasonry*, 1:24–30.

133. There is disagreement concerning whether there is any connection between these rituals and the Eastern Star which was organized thirty years later. According to Jay Kinney, Rob Morris (1818–1888) and his wife received the "Heroine of Jericho" and "Martha's Daughter" degrees and described them as "poorly conceived, weakly wrought out, unimpressive." Jay Kinney, *The Masonic Myth* (New York: HarperOne, 2009), 75. Coil notes that the Eastern Star was "first suggested partly by the French Rite of Adoption and partly by several nineteenth century orders in the United States, which may also have been suggested by the French prototype" and has become the "largest and most successful of the androgynous orders anywhere in the world." Coil, *Coil's Masonic Encyclopedia*, 11–12. Nevertheless, Robert Gilbert insists that there is no strong evidence that "'female Freemasonry' of any kind existed in the United States of America before 1850, when Morris created a new ritual of Adoptive masonry which he named 'The Eastern Star.'" See R. A. Gilbert, "'The Monstrous Regiment': Women and Freemasonry in the Nineteenth Century," *Ars Quatuor Coronatorum* 115 (2002), 163–64; Mackey, *Encyclopedia of Freemasonry*, 1:24–30. Whatever its origins or inspiration, Morris created the "Eastern Star" in 1851 and in 1855 he revised and published the degrees of the ritual. In 1865 Robert Macoy "adapted [Eastern Star] to the System of Adoptive Masonry" and three years later organized it into chapters. A General Grand Chapter was established in 1876. Although Macoy claims that the adoptive rituals were as Masonic "as any degree outside the Symbolical Lodge [the first three degrees of Freemasonry]…and All degrees above the first three are Masonic only by adoption," he did not believe that women were entitled to receive the first three degrees of Craft Masonry on an equal basis with men. Macoy, *General History*, 78. In 1866, Albert Pike, who wrote the current version of Scottish Rite Freemasonry, drafted and published an androgynous ritual in *The Masonry of Adoption* which was, for the most part, a translation and enlargement of the French Adoptive Rite, including a Garden of Eden drama. Albert Pike, *The Masonry of Adoption* (n.p.: 1866).

noted that while "Masonry professes to bring men to heaven…it denies its blessings to a large majority of the human family." "All the *fair* part of creation, together with the old, young and poor, are exempted," he wrote. "How unlike the glorious gospel of the Son of God! In *this* there is no restriction of persons; the high and low, rich and poor, bond and free, male and female, are all one in Christ Jesus."[134] Similarily Solomon Southwick noted that women in America were spared "the orgies of a masonic lodge or a chapel, in the character of demons, of female furies, exciting conspirators, kidnappers and murderers."[135]

THE ILLUMINATI AND FREEMASONRY

Still, some anti-Masons advanced similar charges against American Masonry that were made concerning the Illuminati's "project for sisterhood" and its risqué rituals.[136] Ward wrote that these lodges would consist of two classes, the first "composed of virtuous women" and the second made up of "the wild, the giddy, and the voluptuous," that these lodges would be controlled by men even though most participants would believe that they were directed by women, and that their purpose would be to provide men the ability of "secretly gratifying their passions."[137] Ward warned that adoptive rituals were "the only form of Freemasonry yet to be introduced into this country"[138] and that "we may expect it; and it is good to see how it appears at home, that we may know how to receive it coming abroad."[139]

But not all anti-Masons were convinced that there was a tight bond between the Illuminati and Masonry. In 1829 Ethan Smith, who wrote about the Illuminati and Masonry twenty years earlier, attended an anti-Masonic convention in Boston's Faneuil Hall, where he was appointed to chair a committee "to inquire how far Free Masonry and French Illuminism are connected." Although Smith's report, which was published in the proceedings of the convention, reflected many of the myths that were popularized by Barruel and Robison, his conclusions were not significantly different from those he made twenty years earlier. His committee distinguished between the Illuminati in Europe and the average Freemason: "When honest Masons, of the lower degrees, (who had not gone up to the higher secrets of infidelity and anarchy, and had not known their designs,) learned the use

134. Bernard, *Light on Masonry*, 62 (emphasis in original).
135. Southwick, *An Oration*, 47–48, as quoted in Grunder, *Mormon Parallels*, 1688.
136. Ward, *Free Masonry*, 368.
137. Ibid., 369, quoting Barruel, *Memoirs*, 24.
138. Ward, *Free Masonry*, 371–77. See also Ward, *Antimasonic Review*, 2:303–4.
139. Ward, *Free Masonry*, 255–56.

thus made of their Masonic order," wrote Smith, "they closed their temple, and fled!"

Smith's committee concluded "that a distinction should be made between Masonry, and Masons in the lower degrees," and that American Illuminism, as in Europe, "was most secretly planted by the side of Speculative Masonry, and led (in a way unknown to Masons in the first degrees) to gross infidelity and licentiousness; so it has been in our nation." The committee concluded that "while we utterly condemn the former, as having been found capable, both in Europe and America, of becoming a cover of Illuminism...we ought to feel a tender concern for many of our fellow citizens, in the lower degrees of Masonry, who have been led to unite in their present connection, with no deigns of promoting the horrid aims of Illuminism."[140]

The anti-Masonic movement lasted less than a decade and was ultimately unsuccessful in its avowed goal of completely destroying the Craft. But it did cause enormous damage to the previously revered institution. The number of active American Masons decreased dramatically from 100,000 in 1826 to less than 40,000 in 1835. The number of lodges communicating with the Grand Lodge of New York, one of the strongest in the nation, fell from 480 in 1826 to 82 a decade later.[141] But the anti-Masons' political aspirations were never realized on a national scale.

In 1832 Jackson was re-elected and his closest competitor, Henry Clay, was also a past grand master (from Kentucky) while William Wirt, the candidate of the Anti-Masonic Party, came in fourth place in the electoral college and only won the seven electoral votes of Vermont.[142] Thus, by 1836 William Seward, Thurlow Weed, and other prominent anti-Masons had abandoned the cause of anti-Masonry and became committed to the newly formed Whig Party, which was focused on the issue of slavery.[143] Thereafter, the Freemasons who had survived the ten-year onslaught on their institution began to rebuild the Craft and attempted to restore its former social and political status.

---

140. Addenda, *An Abstract of the Proceedings of the Anti-Masonic State Convention of Massachusetts, Held in Faneuil Hall, Boston, Dec. 30 and 31, 1829, and Jan. 1, 1830* (Boston: John Marsh, Jan. 1830), 29–32.

141. Vaughn, *The Anti-Masonic Party*, 187. Formisano notes that there were 11 Grand Lodges, 347 subordinate lodges, and 16,000 American Masons; that in 1820 New York alone had 300 subordinate lodges and 15,000 Masons; and that by 1825 the state had 450 lodges and 20,000 members. See Ronald P. Formisano, *American Populist Movements from the Revolution to the 1850s* (Chapel Hill: University of North Carolina Press, 2008), 95–96.

142. Jackson won with 219 votes, Clay had 49, John Floyd captured South Carolina's 11 votes, and Wirt received seven.

143. Wheelan, *Mr. Adams's Last Crusade*, 86–87. In the election of 1836 Martin Van Buren was elected with 170 electoral votes but four Whig candidates (split by region) received 124 electoral votes.

The Rise of Mormonism

JOSEPH SMITH AND HIS FAMILY resided in the Burned-Over District of New York State during the Second Great Awakening and the opening events of the anti-Masonic movement.[1] The newspapers in the Burned-Over District, including the *Wayne Sentinel*, which was published in Palmyra, reported about many of the events associated with the Second Great Awakening and the developments during the Morgan scandal. It is likely that the future Mormon prophet became increasingly familiar with many of the nuances of restoration religion as well as the philosophical underpinnings and legends of Freemasonry during this period.

Freemasons believed that their legends concerning Enoch, Melchizedek, Solomon, and Hiram Abiff included extrapolations of the Bible and other helpful aids to understand the true nature of God and the best possible way to return to His presence. Smith's writings, translations, and revelations contained the markers of not only Christianity but also Masonry and anti-Masonry and demonstrate that he studied the Bible, Christian churches, and Freemasonry in order to understand the characteristics of the primitive church.

1. See Whitney R. Cross, *The Burned Over District: The Social and Intellectual History of Enthusiastic Religion in Western New York, 1800–1850* (Ithaca: Cornell University Press, 1950); and Paul E. Johnson, *A Shopkeeper's Millennium: Society and Revivals in Rochester, New York, 1815–1837* (New York: Hill and Wang, 1978). Several of the most important religious revivalists during the Second Great Awakening were Master Masons, including Charles Grandison Finney (1792–1875) and Lorenzo Dow (1777–1834). Finney described his association with the Craft in C[harles] G. Finney, *The Character, Claims, and Practical Workings of Freemasonry* (Cincinnati: Western Tract and Book Society, 1869), and his epiphany seven years later in Charles Grandison Finney, *Memoirs of Charles G. Finney* (New York: A. S. Barnes and Co., 1876), 13–23. Dow was initiated in 1824, and thereafter became a Master Mason, a high priest in the Royal Arch, and a Knight Templar. Dow remained an enthusiastic member of the Freemasonry, even after the disappearance of William Morgan, and continued to believe that it was an ancient institution, which preserved scripture, and that there was a "*chain* and a harmony in the institution" which was organized before the appearance of any creeds. Lorenzo Dow, *Biography and Miscellany* (Norwich, CT, 1834), 137, 159–60.

SMITH'S VISIONS

Smith became convinced that Christian sects had become corrupt and that authentic Christianity could only be restored through heavenly intervention. In 1832 he recorded two celestial visions he had received during the 1820s that he considered the beginning of his prophetic calling.[2] Although there were eventually at least nine different versions of his "first vision," the official account, which was written in 1839, begins with Smith's reading of the Epistle of St. James (James 1:5), which instructs seekers to "ask of God." Smith took these instructions seriously and "retired to the woods to make the attempt."[3]

In a grove of trees Smith sought divine guidance concerning which church to join, and after initially struggling with "some power which entirely overcame me...as to bind my tongue so that I could not speak," he exerted all his powers to call upon God. He recalled: "I saw a pillar [of] light exactly over my head above the brightness of the sun, which descended gradually until it fell upon me." Within the light he saw "two personages," God the Father and Jesus Christ, who told him not to join any church "for they were all wrong...that all their creeds were an abomination in his sight" and "that those professors were all corrupt." Thereafter, Smith refused to join any church even though he was ridiculed by both ministers and laypersons when he recounted his story.[4]

2. The chronology of these events remains controversial. Peter Bauder claimed that he spoke to Smith in October 1830, when Smith was translating the Old Testament, and that during their discussion—which took place over a twenty-four-hour period—Smith "could give me no Christian experience," which some have interpreted as evidence that Smith had not yet received a heavenly manifestation. See Peter Bauder, *The Kingdom of the Gospel of Jesus Christ* (Canajoharie, NY: Printed by A. H. Calhoun, 1834), 36, quoted in Dan Vogel, ed., *Early Mormon Documents* (Salt Lake City: Signature Books, 1996–2003), 1:16–18. See also Fawn M. Brodie, *No Man Knows My History: The Life of Joseph Smith the Mormon Prophet* (New York: Vintage Books, 1995), 16–27; H. Michael Marquardt and Wesley P. Walters, *Inventing Mormonism, Tradition and the Historical Record* (Salt Lake City: Smith Research Associates, 1994), 15–41; and Grunder, *Mormon Parallels*, entry 42. Nevertheless, Joseph Smith Sr. had previously received at least seven visions. See Trevan G. Hatch, *Visions, Manifestations and Miracles of the Restoration* (Orem, UT: Granite Publishing, 2008), 15–33, 69–70, 75.
3. James 1:5, "If any of you lack wisdom, let him ask of God, that giveth to all men liberally, and upbraideth not; and it shall be given."
4. The earliest version of this account was written in 1832. Karen Lynn Davidson et al., eds., *The Joseph Smith Papers, Histories, vol. 1, Joseph Smith Histories, 1832–1844* (Salt Lake City: Church Historian's Press, 2012), 10–16. Oliver Cowdery later wrote that the vision took place in Joseph's fifteenth year. He modified the date to Smith's seventeenth year "or down to the year 1823." Ibid., 52, 56. See also Richard L. Saunders, ed., *Dale Morgan on the Mormons: Collected Works, Part 2, 1949–1970* (Norman, OK: The Arthur H. Clark Company, 2013),

Some historians are convinced that Smith's earliest Mormon narratives, including those relating to this first vision, contain Masonic parallels. Clyde Forsberg has argued that Smith's first vision had a "Masonic insignia" because he referred to the same scripture (James 1:5) that is utilized in the Knight Templar Degree, and this detail was mentioned by Webb in his *The Freemason's Monitor*, the same book that summarized the legend of Enoch's plate. Forsberg also compared Carnes's discussion of Finney's epiphany with the details of Smith's account.[5] While John-Charles Duffy and others have criticized Forsberg's connection of Smith's first vision with Masonic folklore, because it is either too exotic or overreaching, it is important to consider that the first account of this event was written several years after the Book of Mormon was published, which contained more obvious markers of Freemasonry.[6]

The other celestial encounter that Smith first recorded in 1832 contained more vivid Masonic parallels.[7] The official account of Smith's second vision,

92n3; and Dean Jessee, "The Early Accounts of Joseph Smith's First Vision," *BYU Studies* 9 (Spring 1969): 275–94.

5. Forsberg, *Equal Rites*, 57–66, and Carnes, *Secret Ritual and Manhood*, 69–72. Mark Carnes has concluded Finney's theophany was "similar in certain respects to the Master Mason Degree." "Much as the initiate," according to Carnes, Finney "circumambulated the temple…[and]…set himself in motion to find places to pray, traveling first to a 'kind of closet' in the woods and going later into a back room in his home. Masons, after journeying around the lodge, searched for their departed master, Hiram Abiff; Finney received as revelation a passage of scripture [Jeremiah 20:12] containing a similar quest: 'Then shall ye seek me and find me, when ye shall reach for me with all your heart.'" Carnes, *Secret Ritual and Manhood*, 69–72.

6. John-Charles Duffy, "Clyde Forsberg's *Equal Rites* and the Exoticizing of Mormonism," *Dialogue: A Journal of Mormon Thought* 39:1 (Spring 2006): 4–34.

7. Smith's first account of this second vision was recorded in 1832 in an autobiographical narrative. Dean C. Jessee, ed., *The Papers of Joseph Smith* (Salt Lake City: Deseret Book Company, 1989–1992), 2:7–9, quoting *MS. Joseph Smith Letterbook 1*. In this account Smith referred to an unidentified angel who appeared to him "three times in one night and once on the next day" in 1823 and that he obtained the plates in 1827 after marrying Emma Hale. In 1835 Oliver Cowdery wrote and published another account in a church newspaper *Messenger and Advocate* which also referred to an unidentified heavenly messenger but makes no reference to the number of appearances made by the angel or when Smith obtained the plates. Oliver Cowdery, "Letter IV to W. W. Phelps," *Latter Day Saints' Messenger and Advocate* 1, no. 5 (February 1835): 78–80, cited in Jessee, *The Papers of Joseph Smith* 1:50–52. Another account written in 1835 referred to an unidentified angel, three nocturnal visitations, one visitation the following day; that Smith visited the site one year after the original visit as well as three years later; and that he finally received the plates four years after first being shown the site. Joseph Smith, "Sketch Book for the use of Joseph Smith, Jr.," Journal, September 1835–April 1836, quoted in Dean C. Jessee, Mark Ashurst-McGee, and Richard L. Jensen, eds., *The Joseph Smith Papers, Journals Volume 1: 1832–1834* (Salt Lake City: The Church Historian's Press, 2008), 1:88–89. The official account, which was recorded in 1839 by James Mulholland in the *Manuscript History of the Church*, identifies the angel who

written in 1839, described an angel who appeared to him in his bedroom
and told him that "God had a work for me to do" and that "there was a book
deposited, written upon gold plates, giving an account of the former inhabitants of this continent, and the source from whence they sprang." The angel
told Smith that "the fullness of the everlasting Gospel was contained in it,
as delivered by the Savior to the ancient inhabitants," and that "there were
two stones in silver bows—and these stones fastened to a breastplate, constituted what is called the Urim and Thummim," deposited with the plates
"for the purpose of translating the book."

Smith recalled that the angel appeared to him three times during the
same night, and once the following morning, before he went to a hill (later
referred to as Cumorah) that was located a short distance from his home.
He pried a large rock loose and located the stone box containing the gold
plates, Urim and Thummim, and the breastplate. But the angel did not allow him to remove these objects from the hill or to translate them but instead instructed the young prophet to return to the hill one year later and
continue to do so until he was ready to receive the plates.

Smith recovered the contents of the buried box on September 22, 1827,
and began dictating a translation of the characters to Martin Harris, Emma
Smith, and Oliver Cowdery. He translated the characters that were engraved on the gold plates by using the Urim and Thummim as well as other
"seer stones" that he had located in other excavations.[8] When Smith finished translating the plates he returned them to the angel, but one Mormon
writer has noted that the angel continued to tutor Smith during at least
twenty subsequent encounters.[9]

---

appeared three times during the night and once the following morning as an ancient American prophet named Nephi, that Smith returned to the site each year, and that he eventually
received the gold plates four years after the angel first appeared to him. Jessee, *The Papers of
Joseph Smith* 1:276–82, quoting *Joseph Smith History*, vol. A-1. In 1842 the official account
was published in two church publications. *Times and Seasons*, 3: 749, 753 (April 1, 1842);
and *Millennial Star*, 3: 53, 71 (August 1842). This account was published in the first edition
of The Pearl of Great Price in 1851 and in Lucy Mack Smith's *Biographical Sketches of Joseph
Smith the Prophet* in 1853. But Orson Pratt, who published Lucy Mack Smith's account,
included a footnote that the angel described was actually Moroni, and he cited references
to the Doctrine and Covenants, sec. L, par. 2, which was published in 1835 (now Doctrine
and Covenants 27:5); *Elders' Journal* I1: 28, 129; *History of Joseph Smith* under year 1838; and
Deseret News, vol. 3, no. 10. See Lucy Mack Smith's, *Biographical Sketches of Joseph Smith the
Prophet*, (Liverpool, 1853), 79. The official account, subsequently republished in The Pearl of
Great Price (1878) and canonized (1880), correctly identified the angel as Moroni.
8. See Van Wagoner, *Sidney Rigdon*, 56. For a speculative analysis concerning the origins of
the name Cumorah, see Ronald V. Huggins, "From Captain Kidd's Treasure Ghost to the
Angel Moroni: Changing *Dramatis Personae* in Early Mormonism," *Dialogue: A Journal of
Mormon Thought* 36 (Winter 2003). See also, D[aniel] P[ierce] Thompson, *May Martin:
Money Diggers. A Green Mountain Tale* (Montpelier, VT: E. P. Walton and Son, 1835).
9. Hatch, *Visions, Manifestations and Miracles*, 96.

ENOCH'S PLATE

Smith's accounts concerning the gold plates contained parallels to the Masonic Royal Arch, the Rite de Perfection, and Rosicrucianism. Smith's recovery of the plates in an underground vault and the events leading to his translation were reminiscent of the Royal Arch legend, summarized by Thomas Smith Webb and George Oliver, in which Enoch received a vision of a gold plate containing the lost name of God and later engraved the plate and hid it in an underground vault. Thereafter, he was allowed to visit the site once a year until he was translated into heaven, and the plate remained undisturbed until Solomon's Temple was constructed above the vault. During the temple's construction Hiram Abiff was killed (which was described in the Master Masons Degree), and the Master's Word was lost and replaced with a substituted word. But Solomon eventually discovered Enoch's gold plate within nine secret vaults and the Master's Word was restored.

Royal Arch Masons referred to the restoration of Enoch's plate, with the word of God, as the keystone of Freemasonry since it contained "a key to the ineffable characters of this degree" through which they are able to translate "mysterious words in a triangular form."[10] Henry Dana Ward and other anti-Masons vigorously attacked Webb's description of this legend and noted sarcastically that God's promise that the "true word…should be found 'engraved upon a plate of gold'" and the "particulars of the wonderful discovery of Enoch's triangular plate of gold, will be food for admiration."[11]

After Smith began his mission to restore primitive Christianity, he was referred to as Enoch in at least five of his revelations. Like his namesake he received a vision concerning gold plates and was allowed to visit the site where they were located once a year for four years before he removed them from the vault and translated them.[12] In Masonic legend the word engraved

10. Webb, *The Freemason's Monitor*, 244–61. For Masonic references to the restoration of the Master's Word as the "keystone," see Churton, *Freemasonry*, 27, 391.

11. Ward, *Free-Masonry*, 13–22, 28–29.

12. There were at least five early references to Smith as Enoch. D&C (1835), secs. 75, 86, 93, 96, and 98. The reference has been eliminated in modern editions. See D&C (1981), secs. 78, 82, 92, 96, and 104. Jack Adamson notes that Smith was the same age when he organized the Church of Christ in 1830 as Enoch was when he received the Melchizedek priesthood. See D&C (1981), 107:48. He also noted similarities between the gold plate that "became part of the collection of sacred objects in the temple: the gold plate, the breastplate of the high priest of Israel and the Urim and Thummim" and the gold plates that Smith translated, a parallel between the two pillars (marble and brass) that were placed above Enoch's secret cavern (the marble pillar contained the history of the treasure engraved in Egyptian hieroglyphics and the brass pillar had a ball on top of it with maps of the world and universe) and the ball which guided Lehi and his family out of the wilderness and across the ocean to America. He also compares Hiram Abiff's murder by three ruffians and Smith's account that

on the gold plate was literally God's name whereas in Mormonism the gold plates were engraved with God's word or teachings.

Smith's recovery of the plates, where they had been deposited by a prophet hundreds of years earlier, and his discovery that God's word was engraved on them, was reminiscent of Masonic lore concerning Solomon's discovery of Enoch's plate below the keystone of his underground temple. Just as Freemasons referred to the restoration of Enoch's plate as the keystone of Freemasonry, Smith stated that the Book of Mormon, which restored God's word to his generation, was the "keystone of our religion."[13]

Smith eventually prepared a sample of the characters he discovered on the plates (now known as the Anton Manuscript) and dispatched his trusted mentor, Martin Harris, to show the characters to Charles Anthon (1797–1867), a classical scholar at Columbia University in New York. According to Harris, Anthon identified the characters as Egyptian, Chaldaic, Assyriac, and Arabic.[14] David John Buerger has speculated that the characters on the Anthon Manuscript were based on a Masonic alphabet that was revealed in Royal Arch chapters and that the languages Anthon identified in Harris's account were similar to those mentioned in the Royal Arch degree.[15] In that ritual the Masons Word (the Grand Omnific Royal Arch Word) is the name of deity in three languages: Chaldeac, Hebrew, and Syriac, which were written anciently utilizing "ineffable characters."[16]

These Masonic elements in Smith's description of his second vision were noted by Jonathan Blanchard (1811–1892), an evangelical pastor who was a protégé of Charles Finney, founded Wheaton College (1860), organized the National Christian Association (1868) to reinvigorate the anti-Masonic movement, and wrote an exposé of an irregular Masonic ritual.[17] Blanchard concluded that there was a "striking resemblance" between Smith's account

---

he was accosted three times while he was recovering the plates. See Adamson, "The Treasure of the Widow's Son," 5, 7, 9–10. See also Bushman, *Rough Stone Rolling*, 140, 287.

13. See Joseph Smith Jr., et al., *History of the Church of Jesus Christ of Latter-day Saints*, ed. B. H. Roberts (Salt Lake City: Deseret News Press, 1902–1932), 4:461 (November 28, 1841). The history is based upon Wilford Woodruff's Journal; see Scott G. Kenny, ed., *Wilford Woodruff's Journal, 1833–1898* (Midvale, UT: Signature Books, 1983–1985), 2:139. For references concerning the origin of the Gold plates see Book of Mormon, Ether 2, 3, 15.

14. The first reference to "Reformed Egyptian" was set forth in Mormon 9:32. See Vogel, *Early Mormon Documents* 1:70. Anthon later denied he had identified the characters and said they were a hoax. E. D. Howe, *Mormonism Unvailed* (Painesville, OH, 1834), 269–74.

15. See David John Buerger, "A Preliminary Approach to Linguistic Aspects of the Anthon Transcript," Unpublished manuscript prepared for a BYU Semester Project, 1978, pp. 6–8.

16. See Bernard, *Light on Masonry*, 138–39; Richardson, *Monitor of Freemasonry*, 79–80.

17. Jonathan Blanchard, *Scotch Rite Masonry Illustrated*, 2 vols. (1887–1888; reprint ed., Chicago: Ezra A. Cook, 1925). Blanchard's exposé was of an irregular ritual (Henry C. Atwood's Supreme Council of the Sovereign and Independent State of New York) which was patterned after the Scottish Rite. De Hoyos, *The Cloud of Prejudice*. For a discussion

of finding gold plates and the Royal Arch legend concerning Enoch's gold plate, but he was apparently more upset that Royal Arch Masonry "has convinced thousands that their gold plate, like those of the Mormon, has revealed truth outside of and beyond the Bible. And the popularity and power of the falsehood, in both cases, depend on the multitudes who believe the lie and pay for it."[18]

Despite these suggestions, most Mormon historians have focused only on Biblical precedents (which were the sources for the Masonic legends) and ignored the Masonic connection between Enoch's and Smith's gold plates. For example, Jan Shipps concluded that Smith's discovery of the gold plates was an echo of "the priests' discovery in the recesses of the temple [during King Josiah's reign] of a book said to have been written by Moses."[19] But John-Charles Duffy has acknowledged that even though he prefers "to seek biblical origins for Mormon motifs before looking to extra biblical sources," he has concluded that "compared to Josiah's temple scroll, I find the Masonic golden plate a more satisfying, because more similar, prototype for Smith's plates."[20]

THE BOOK OF MORMON

Smith's translation of the golden plates, like the legends of Freemasonry, included supplementary information about persons mentioned in the Bible and introduced new characters into religious history. The Book of Mormon recorded that Lehi, the patriarch of a Jewish family, was commanded by God to leave Jerusalem just prior to the Babylonians' destruction of Solomon's Temple in 586 BCE. Before their departure Lehi instructed his sons to seize Brass Plates with Egyptian engravings which included a record of the Jews to the reign of Zedekiah (the five books of Moses and the Book of Isaiah) as well as his family's genealogy. Afterward, the family constructed a ship that transported them to America.

Lehi preserved these records and kept his own diary until he died. Thereafter, his son Nephi succeeded him and continued to engrave a spiritual and secular history on small and large plates of ore. The plates Nephi engraved included copies of some of the scriptures that were brought from Jerusalem as well as an abridgment of his father's record. These plates were preserved and updated by succeeding generations. In addition, Lehi's

of Blanchard, see Clyde S. Kilby, *Minority of One: The Biography of Jonathan Blanchard* (Grand Rapids, MI: Wm B. Eerdmans, 1959); Carnes, *Secret Ritual and Manhood*, 72–80.
18. Blanchard, *Scotch Rite Masonry Illustrated*, 1:288–90.
19. Jan Shipps, *Mormonism: The Story of a New Religious Tradition* (Urbana: University of Illinois Press, 1987), 58.
20. Duffy, "Clyde Forsberg's *Equal Rites*," 27n20.

descendants discovered twenty-four plates that were buried by the Jaredites, a dead civilization whose ancestors had immigrated to America in approximately 2200 BCE after they participated in the unsuccessful attempt to build the anti-temple Tower of Babel.

The Book of Mormon recorded that the descendants of Lehi eventually separated into two tribes and that those with the blood lines of Nephi, the faithful son, were white while those of another son named Laman, who was not faithful, became dark and were the ancestors of the American Indians.[21] Nephi built a temple in America "after the manner of the temple of Solomon," his descendants taught within a temple,[22] God wrote on the temple wall with his finger, and Christ visited the American continent after his resurrection and appeared to multitudes gathered around the temple.[23]

The Nephites and Lamanites remained bitter enemies for most of the book and both groups became permeated by secret societies. Eventually Mormon, who was one of Nephi's descendants, abridged large plates (which contained a secular history) into a record engraved on gold plates, and combined it with small plates. Before Mormon died he entrusted these plates to his son Moroni who finished the record, incorporated a portion of the twenty-four plates that had been recorded by the Jaredites, and then buried them in the Hill Cumorah for future generations (400 CE).

The Book of Mormon is reminiscent of the theses advanced by Ethan Smith, Elias Boudinot, and Josiah Priest, the same authors who warned Smith's generation about the presence of Illuminati in America, who wrote that a portion of the Lost Ten Tribes had migrated to America and that their descendants were the American Indians.[24] Salem Town, the Royal Arch Mason who conflated ancient Masonry and ancient Christianity, published a lecture in 1812 in which he speculated that American Indians were descendants of ancient Israelites who had come to America around 600 BCE and that "Masonry has existed amongst the ten tribes of our North American Indians."[25]

21. The Book of Mormon contains a passage stating that "the skins of the Lamanites were dark, according to the mark which was set upon their fathers" (Alma 3:6). The righteous seed and the wicked seed alternate between the Nephites and Lamanites. Eventually some Lamanites, who were initially cursed with dark skin, were able to become white through their righteousness.
22. II Nephi, 5:16; Jacob 1:17, 2:2, 11; Mosiah 1:18; Alma 16:13.
23. Alma 10:2; III Nephi 11:1.
24. Elias Boudinot, *A Star in the West; or, a Humble Attempt to Discover the Long Lost Tribes of Israel* (Trenton, 1816); Ethan Smith, *View of the Hebrews; or the Tribes of Israel in America* (Poultney, VT, 1823); [Josiah Priest], *The Wonders of Nature and Providence Displayed* (Albany, 1825). For a discussion of these and other sources, see Dan Vogel, *Indian Origins and the Book of Mormon* (Salt Lake City: Signature Books, 1986).
25. Salem Town, *The Probable Origin and Dissemination of Ancient Masonry, Amongst the*

In fact, Alexander Campbell (1788–1866), one of the founders of an alternative Christian restoration movement often called Campbellite, concluded shortly after reading the Book of Mormon that Smith's translation was permeated with contemporary political and social issues.[26] Among those issues was the origin of the American Indians. Mormon writer Terryl Givens has concluded that the "pervasive appeal of the mystery of Amerindian origins only made the Book of Mormon's case more compelling since it claimed to provide a historical, rather than speculative solution to the conundrum."[27] Laurie F. Maffly-Kipp, who is a student of Mormonism, noted that the Book of Mormon not only identified the origin of the American Indians, it "wove together two of the most widespread theories of American Indian origins [immigration of Jews to America after the Tower of Babel and at the destruction of Solomon's Temple] and also provided an explanation of how their migrations had taken place."[28]

But Campbell's principal complaint was that the prophet Moroni "laments the prevalency of free masonry in the times when his Book should be dug up out of the earth," and that the book "decides all the great controversies…and even the question of Freemasonry."[29] Other contemporary observers also believed they detected this same issue in the book. Eber D. Howe, an Ohio newspaper publisher, concluded that "the Nephites are represented as being Anti-Masons and Christians, which carries with it some evidence that the writer foresaw the politics of New York in 1828–29, or that the work was revised at or about that time."[30] Jason Whitman, a Unitarian minister, concluded that "it is well known that, in many minds, there is a strong feeling of opposition to the institution of Masonry. All such find something in the Book of Mormon to meet their views…thus there are, in the book itself, artful adaptations to the known prejudices of the community."[31]

Various Nations (1812), 16–19. I am indebted to Michael G. Reed for pointing out this publication which includes Town's beliefs concerning the origins of the American Indians and that they practiced Freemasonry after they arrived on the American continent.

26. Alexander Campbell, "Delusions," *Millennial Harbinger* 2 (February 7, 1831): 90, 93.

27. Terryl L. Givens, *The Book of Mormon: A Very Short History* (Oxford, Oxford University Press, 2009), 116.

28. Laurie F. Maffly-Kipp, introduction, The Book of Mormon (New York: Penguin Books, 2008), viii–xi, xv–xxii.

29. Campbell, "Delusions," 90, 93.

30. Howe, *Mormonism Unvailed*, 81.

31. Jason Whitman, "The Book of Mormon," *The Unitarian* 1 (January 1, 1834): 47–48. British traveler Edward Strut Abdy (1790–1846) also noted that the book "alludes most unequivocally to the free-masons." Edward Strut Abdy, *Journal of a residence and tour in the United States of North America, from April, 1833 to October, 1834* (London: J. Murray, 1835), 55–56. Methodist minister (and sometime mesmerist) La Roy Sunderland (1802–1885)

The book's passages that attracted the attention of these writers revealed that Nephi's descendants were destroyed by secret societies that had satanic origins and whose objectives were to obtain and maintain power.[32] The Book of Mormon seemed to criticize what Margaret C. Jacob has recently called "the Masonic form" of "secret passwords, gestures, rituals and signs."[33] Moroni, who eventually appeared to Joseph Smith as a resurrected personage, warned future generations, presumably those who eventually read Smith's translation, about these "secret combinations" that were "built up by the devil." He prophesied that "whatever nation shall uphold such secret combinations, to get power and gain, until they shall spread over the nation, behold, they shall be destroyed," and that "the Lord commandeth you, when ye shall see these things come among you that ye shall awaken to a sense of your awful situation, because of this secret combination which shall be among you; or woe be unto it, because of the blood of them who have been slain; for they cry from the dust for vengeance upon it, and also upon those who built it up."[34]

Mormon apologists and critics continue to debate the meaning and implications of these passages about "secret combinations."[35] Givens and other apologists have pointed out that "Moroni wrote to his future readers, 'Jesus Christ has shown you unto me, and I know your doing' (Mormon

found "frequent allussians [sic] in [the Book of Mormon] to Freemasonry…under the names of 'secret societies,' 'dreadful oaths' and 'secret combination.'" La Roy Sunderland, *Mormonism Exposed and Refuted* (New York: Pieray & Reed, 1838), 46.

32. Helaman 6:21–30; Ether 8:22–26; Helaman 2:5–11, 8:22–26; Ether 11:15, 22, 13:18, 14:8–10.

33. Margaret C. Jacob, *Strangers Nowhere in the World: The Rise of Cosmopolitanism in Early Modern Europe* (Philadelphia: University of Pennsylvania Press, 2006), 96. See Ether 10:33.

34. Ether, 8:22–26.

35. Dan Vogel, "'Mormonism's Anti-Masonick Bible,'" *John Whitmer Historical Association Journal* 9 (1989): 17–30. Dan Peterson challenged Vogel's interpretation in his "Notes on 'Gadianton Freemasonry,'" in *Warfare and the Book of Mormon*, ed. Steven D. Ricks and William J. Hamblin (Salt Lake City: Deseret Book Co.; Provo, UT: Foundation for Ancient Research and Mormon Studies, 1990), 174–224. See also Richard L. Bushman, *Joseph Smith and the Beginnings of Mormonism* (Urbana: University of Illinois Press, 1984), 128–31; Blake T. Ostler, "The Book of Mormon as a Modern Expansion of An Ancient Source," *Dialogue: A Journal of Mormon Thought* 20 (Spring 1987): 73–76; Quinn, *Early Mormonism and the Magic World View*, 160–65. See also Kevin Christensen, "Review of Dan Vogel, *Indian Origins and the Book of Mormon*," *Review of Books on the Book of Mormon* (Provo, UT: Foundation for Ancient Research and Mormon Studies, 1990), 2:222n18; and Matthew Roper, "Review of Jerald and Sandra Tanner, *Mormonism: Shadow or Reality*," *Review of Books on the Book of Mormon* (Provo, UT: Foundation for Ancient Research and Mormon Studies, 1992), 4:184–85. More recent attempts to interpret the meaning of these "secret combinations" point to prophecies of contemporary satanic ritual abuse. See Massimo Introvigne, "A Rumor of Devils," delivered at 1994 Mormon History Association, Park City, Utah. [www.cesnur.org]

8:35)." As such, "the text's ability to engage and clarify contemporary debates" to Mormon readers is "a crucial feature of its inspired nature," and "its prescience was evidence of divine foresight."[36] But John-Charles Duffy has observed that most orthodox Mormons continue to reject any such connection between the Book of Mormon and Freemasonry because "anti-Masonic readings tend to assume that Smith is the author of the Book of Mormon (rather than the translator of an ancient record by the power of God); and since contemporary Mormons are not inclined to regard Masonry as a satanic conspiracy, they are naturally loath to believe that their scripture presents it as such."[37]

Consistent with Duffy's observation, Daniel Peterson, a Brigham Young University professor, contends that "one of the major difficulties" of accepting the notion that the Book of Mormon reflected contemporary debates concerning Freemasonry is that "one must see Joseph Smith as a vocal and committed anti-Mason in 1830 who then, only twelve years later, enthusiastically joined the Masons and, as some would have it, borrowed the most sacred rituals of his religion from them."[38] Peterson's observation is a serious barrier to considering the Book of Mormon passages as reflecting anti-Masonic sentiment.

But another possible reading of these passages is that the Book of Mormon's "secret combinations" referred to the Illuminati rather than Freemasonry. John Thompson has noted that many residing in the "burned-over district," where nineteenth-century anti-Masonry was born, "were really transplanted New Englanders who had been listening to anti-Masonic and anti-Illuminati sermons and speeches for years."[39] Dan Vogel has concluded that "the political anti-Masonry of the late 1820s and early 1830s was simply a revival of the Illuminati agitation that had already occurred in New England."[40]

36. Givens, *The Book of Mormon: A Very Short Introduction*, 116. See also Vogel, "Echoes of Freemasonry," 307–8.

37. Duffy, "Clyde Forsberg's *Equal Rites*," 7.

38. Peterson, "Notes on 'Gadianton Masonry,'" 181–82, 200, as quoted in Dan Vogel, "Echoes of Anti-Masonry: A Rejoinder to Critics of the Anti-Masonic Thesis," in Dan Vogel and Brent Lee Metcalfe, *American Apocrypha, Essays on the Book of Mormon* (Salt Lake City: Signature Books, 2002), 297.

39. John E. Thompson, *The Masons, the Mormons and the Morgan Incident* (Ames, IA: Iowa Research Lodge No. 2 AF&AM, 1984).

40. Vogel, "Echoes of Anti-Masonry," 291–93. William Preston Vaughn agrees: "The rhetoric and ideology of nineteenth-century Antimasonry was an expansion of that found in the seventeenth- and eighteenth-century publications and the propaganda of 1797–1799." Vaughn, *The Anti-Masonic Party in the United States*, 14. See also Paul Goodman, *Towards a Christian Republic: Antimasonry and the Great Transition in New England, 1826–1836* (New York: Oxford University Press, 1988), 5, 21.

As previously discussed, the critics of Freemasonry, from Jedediah Morse to Ethan Smith, were extremely careful to distinguish between "honest Masons, of the lower degrees" and the Illuminati who they claimed controlled some of Masonry's high degrees that had French pedigrees. They argued that "Illuminism was most secretly planted by the side of Speculative Masonry, and led (and unknown to Masons in the first degrees) to gross infidelity and licentiousness."[41] Thus, the Book of Mormon may have targeted the "Illuminati" or "spurious Freemasons" rather than regular Craft members.

Smith recognized very early during his ministry that not all Masons were "good Masons," but there is little evidence that he ever believed that all Masons were inherently evil. Although the Mormon prophet may have been concerned about the excesses of Freemasonry when it pursued political agendas or deviated from the Craft's original purpose, he never advocated (like the anti-Masons) the complete eradication of Freemasonry, even during the bitterest days of the anti-Masonic movement, and he did not request that any of his inner circle secede from the movement.

Another response to Peterson's dilemma is that Smith was not bound by a closed canon as he continued to piece together his new Mormon matrix and that he may have changed his mind concerning Freemasonry just as he did about polygamy.[42] In fact, Dan Vogel speculates that Smith changed his views about Freemasonry shortly after he published the Book of Mormon.[43]

NEGOTIATING PRINTING AND BINDING

After Smith completed his translation of the gold plates, he approached Egbert B. Grandin (1806–1845), who owned the *Wayne Sentinel* in Palmyra, New York, to request that he publish the Book of Mormon.[44] Grandin

41. Addenda, *An Abstract of the Proceedings*, 29–32. These types of "bastard" organizations were particularly distrusted because of their "secrecy within secrecy" and because they employed "secrecy to prevent detection" and to "vie with conventional ones for the loyalties of citizens." See Jacob, *Strangers Nowhere in the World*, 106–7; 114.
42. Carmon Hardy has observed that while "The Book of Mormon condemns polygamy as a 'wicked practice' and was 'abominable before me, saith the Lord,'" Smith may have come to a new understanding concerning polygamy while he was retranslating the Old Testament. B. Carmon Hardy, *Doing the Works of Abraham, Mormon Polygamy, Its Origin, Practice, and Demise* (Norman, OK: The Arthur H. Clark Company, 2007), 33–34, 33n2. These Book of Mormon passages are located in Jacob 1:15, 2:23–35, 3:5; Mosiah 11:2; Ether 10:5. In fact, there was an escape clause in the Book of Mormon which provided that God could command men to practice polygamy in order to "raise up seed unto me" (Jacob 2:30).
43. See Dan Vogel, "Mormonism's Anti-Masonick Bible," 27–29.
44. Pomeroy Tucker remembered that Oliver Cowdery accompanied Smith and Harris to Grandin's office when they made their initial proposal that Grandin publish the Book of

seemed like a natural choice. He had previously published contemporary accounts of men who received visions of Christ that all denominations had become corrupt.[45] He had also flirted with anti-Masonry, but by the time Smith approached him he had become "disenchanted with political antimasonry."[46] In 1829 he wrote an editorial in which he stated that he detected "the old 'cloven foot' of *Federalism*" in the anti-Masonic movement, and that it should be called "ANTI-MASONIC FEDERALISM."

Grandin acknowledged that "we sympathize with those original and honest anti-masons who became so from the love of liberty—from a veneration of liberty—from a devotion to the peace and good order of society," and that "it is on such principles, we could be willing to remain anti-masons." But he emphasized that "we will not, we cannot, be so blinded to the sacredness of the cause, as to assent to its prostitution to political purposes—to foster bankrupts in honor and honesty, into high and responsible offices: we do not wish to see it profaned, by being connected with low and base motives."[47]

Grandin initially declined to print Smith's manuscript. Harris also approached Jonathan Hadley, the proprietor of the anti-Masonic *Palmyra Freeman*, to publish the new work. Even though Harris was apparently a subscriber to Hadley's newspaper, the Palmyra printer refused to consider the undertaking and even threatened to "expose him and the whole Mormon gang."[48] Smith and Harris thereafter traveled to Rochester, twenty-five miles from Palmyra, where they spoke on two separate occasions to Thurlow Weed, the publisher of the *Anti-Masonic Inquirer* who had become a political heavyweight in the New York Anti-Masonic Party.[49]

Weed also declined to print the book (even though Harris repeated his offer to pledge his farm as security) but he apparently suggested that they approach Elihu F. Marshall (1794–1840), who owned a Rochester printing

Mormon. See Pomeroy Tucker, *Origin, Rise, and Progress of Mormonism* (New York: D. Appleton & Co., 1867), 51–52.

45. See, for example, "Remarkable Vision and Revelation; as seen by Asa Wild, of Amsterdam, New York," *Wayne Sentinel* 1: 4 (October 22, 1823).

46. Grunder, *Mormon Parallels*, 1838.

47. *Wayne Sentinel* 6:25; whole no. 285 (Friday, March 13, 1829), p. [3], column 3. See also Bullock, *Revolutionary Brotherhood*, 303.

48. Jonathan A. Hadley, "Origin of Mormonism," *Wayne County Whig* 3:51 (September 14, 1842).

49. See Vaughn, *The Anti-Masonic Party*, 26. Weed later wrote that he had "been governed through the 'Anti-masonic excitement' by a sincere desire, first, to vindicate the violated laws of my country, and next, to arrest the great power and dangerous influences of 'secret societies.'" See Thurlow Weed, *The Facts Stated* (Chicago: National Christian Association, 1882), 14.

business, and make the same proposal.[50] Marshall, according to Pomeroy
Tucker, agreed to publish the book and "gave his terms for the printing and
binding of the book, with his acceptance of the proffered mode of security
for the payment."[51]

When Smith and Harris returned to Palmyra, they informed Grandin
that they had made a deal with Marshall and thereafter the Palmyra printer
agreed to print five thousand copies on the same terms—that is, for three
thousand dollars if Harris agreed to mortgage his farm as security for the
printing costs. This arrangement with a Palmyra printer allowed Smith to
examine the proof-sheets almost daily and thereby "be saved much incon-
venience and cost of travel."[52]

But Grandin demanded that the deal be modified, and that he be paid
in full, when a group of Palmyra citizens organized a boycott while the book
was still being published. After this, Harris, who was prodded by revelation,
sold his farm and paid Grandin the full costs of printing.[53] On March 26,
1830, the *Wayne Sentinel* announced that the Book of Mormon had been
printed and could be purchased. Even though Smith was listed as the book's
author, there is no question that he never suggested that the Book of Mormon was a romance, similar to Ethan Smith's tome, but that it was instead
an actual history of an ancient people who lived on the American continent. In fact, the book included the testimonies of three men (including
Martin Harris) who testified that they were visited by an angel who showed
them the plates before they were returned and the testimony of eight others
who swore that they had also seen the plates.

SECRET CHAMBERS

After the Book of Mormon was published, Smith organized the Church of
Christ (later known as the Church of Jesus Christ of Latter-day Saints), in
Manchester, New York. Thereafter, he received revelations that occasionally
referred to secret combinations, warned of enemies in "secret chambers,"[54]
and instructed members to "flee to the west...in consequence of that which
is coming on earth, and of secret combinations."[55] But none of these reve-

---

50. Marshall was a Quaker and the author of *A Spelling Book of the English Language; or the
American Tutor's Assistant. Intended Particularly for the Use of 'Common Schools.' The Pronunciation Being Adapted to the Much Approved Principles of J. Walker* (1821).

51. Tucker, *Origin, Rise, and Progress of*, 52.

52. Ibid., 52.

53. *Book of Commandments*, ch. 16, pp. 40–41. See also Brodie, *No Man Knows My History*,
81–82.

54. D&C 38: 12–13, 28–29, 32 (January 2, 1831).

55. D&C 42:64 (February 9, 1831).

lations, which were directed to the contemporary church, specifically mentioned Freemasonry and Smith still did not prohibit church members from participating in Freemasonry.

During the fall and winter of 1830, Joseph and his mother, Lucy Mack Smith (1775–1856), made statements that have been interpreted as anti-Masonic. Alexander McIntyre (1792–1859), the Smith family physician and a Freemason attempted to collect a debt from Hyrum Smith (1800–1844), who was Joseph's brother and a member of the same Masonic lodge as McIntyre. Lucy recalled that Joseph received a revelation that Hyrum should leave Manchester and go to Colesville because his "enemies were combining in secret chambers to take away his life."[56] She lamented that when McIntyre's representatives approached her, "Hyrum was flying from his home, and why I knew not; and that the secret combinations of his enemies were not yet fully developed."[57]

In December 1830 Joseph sent a letter to Hyrum to warn him that McIntyre was attempting to find him: "Beware of the freemasons, McIntyre heard that you were in Manchester and he got out a warrant and went to your father's to distress the family but [Samuel] Harrison [another Smith brother] overheard their talk and they said that they cared not for the debt, if only they could obtain your body. They were there in carriages. Therefore beware of the Freemasons."[58] But Lucy's memoirs and Joseph's letter were just as likely intended as warnings against specific freemasons, who were attempting to collect a debt, as they were condemnations of the entire institution.

Despite the parallels between Joseph Smith's story concerning the origins of Mormonism and Masonic legend, and anti-Masonic references in Smith's revelations, only a handful of Freemasons or apparent anti-Masons joined the Church of Christ in New York. Hyrum Smith, who was initiated in Mount Moriah Lodge No. 112 in Palmyra, Ontario County, New York, during the 1820s, was the only founding member of the church who was a Freemason. Mervin B. Hogan, a twentieth-century Mormon Mason, claimed that Joseph Smith Sr. (1771–1840), who was Joseph and Hyrum's father, was a Mason but there is no compelling evidence to support his assertion.[59] There was a man named Joseph Smith who was initiated, passed, and raised in Ontario Lodge No. 23, Canandaigua, Ontario County, New

56. Vogel, *Early Mormon Documents* 1:426, quoting from Smith, 158.
57. Ibid., 1:432–33 (quoting from Lucy Mack Smith).
58. Ibid., 1:22. See also 3:171–72, 426; Record of Nauvoo Lodge, December 30, 1841; Lucy Mack Smith History, 1844–1845, bk. 4, [3]–[4]; Lucy Mack Smith History, 1845, 183–84.
59. See Mervin B. Hogan, "The Two Joseph Smith's Masonic Experiences" (self-published paper), Jan. 17, 1987, 10–11. Record of Nauvoo Lodge, December 30, 1841; Lucy Mack Smith History, 1844–1845, bk. 4, [3]–[4]; Lucy Mack Smith History, 1845, 183–84.

York, between December 26, 1817, and May 17, 1818, but the 1820 census includes eight men with the name of "Joseph Smith" including a "Joseph Smith, Jr.", who lived in Ontario County.[60] It is unlikely that Joseph Sr. would have joined Ontario Lodge in Canandaigua, which was located approximately nine miles from Palmyra, especially when one considers that his son Hyrum joined Mount Moriah Lodge No. 112, which was located much closer to the Smith farm.[61]

In addition, no contemporary observer, including Joseph Smith Jr., Hyrum Smith, or Lucy Mack Smith, mentioned that Joseph Sr. was a Freemason. When Joseph Sr. was imprisoned in Canandaigua for an unpaid debt (in the same jail where William Morgan was incarcerated four years earlier), he met Eli Bruce (1793–1832), the former sheriff of Niagara County, New York, who was serving time in connection with Morgan's disappearance. Smith told Bruce that he had been commissioned "by God to baptize and preach this new doctrine" and that the "Bible is much abridged and deficient; that soon the Divine will is to be made known to all, as written in the *new* Bible, or *Book of* Mormon." Although they had a "long talk," which both Bruce and Lucy Mack memorialized, neither one mentioned that Joseph Sr. was a Freemason.[62]

There is evidence that at least one founding member of the church in New York participated in anti-Masonic activities. In 1827 Martin Harris attended a Wayne County anti-Masonic convention in Palmyra, New York, and was appointed to the Palmyra committee of vigilance,[63] but there is no

60. Vogel notes that Hogan did not consider that the census evidence showed there were many Joseph Smiths in the area, that Smith never claimed to be a Mason, or that Ontario Lodge No. 23 was not the closest lodge to his home. See Vogel, *Early Mormon Documents* 3:452–56.
61. Records of the Grand Lodge of Free and Accepted Masons of the State of New York, Chancellor Livingston Library, New York.
62. Rob Morris, *The Masonic Martyr: The Biography of Eli Bruce* (Louisville, KY: Morris & Konsarrat, 1861), 266–67; and Lucy Mack Smith, *Biographical Sketches of Joseph Smith, the Prophet, and His Progenitors for Many Generations* (Liverpool: S.W. Richards, 1853), 162, 164–65. Lucy Smith did not mention Bruce by name but acknowledged that while Joseph Smith Sr. was incarcerated in Canandaigua as "an imprisoned debtor," he visited with a "man committed for murder" who was "confined in the same dungeon." See also John E. Thompson, "The Patriarch and the Martyr: Joseph Smith, Senior and Eli Bruce in Canandaigua (N.Y.) Jail," *The Philalethes* (April 1983); John E. Thompson, "The Patriarch and the Martyr: Joseph Smith, Senior and Eli Bruce in Canandaigua (N.Y.) Jail," *Restoration* 5 (October 1986): 22; and H. Michael Marquardt and Wesley P. Walters, *Inventing Mormonism: Tradition and the Historical Record* (San Francisco: Smith Research Associates, 1994), 137.
63. *Wayne Sentinel*, Oct. 5, 1827, Palmyra, New York. The convention adopted the following resolution: "Resolved. That we conceive it a dereliction of our duty to give suffrages for any office within the gift of the people to a freemason who has not publicly renounced the institution and principles of freemasonry, or to any person who approbates the institution or treats with levity, or attempts to palliate or screen the hor[r]id transaction relative to

evidence that Harris participated in any other anti-Masonic activity in New York.[64] Some writers have claimed that Joseph Smith Sr. (or perhaps Joseph Jr.) flirted with anti-Masonry based on an 1826 petition that appeared in the anti-Masonic newspaper *Seneca Farmer and Waterloo Advertiser*, and in various other area newspapers (including E. B. Grandin's *Wayne Sentinel*) to solicit "Christian humanitarian concern" and "offer assistance to Morgan's unfortunate wife." Although one of the signatories was a "J. Smith," that person was more likely a citizen of Batavia (and perhaps a former Mason) rather than one of the Smiths who later embraced Mormonism.[65]

The notion that the Smith family was involved in the anti-Masonic movement is further undermined when one considers that at least three Masons, who knew the Smith family intimately and authored anti-Mormon accounts, failed to connect them with anti-Masonry. Neither Pomeroy Tucker (1802–1870), the foreman in E. B. Grandin's printing shop where the Book of Mormon was published,[66] Abner Cole (1783–1835), who published excerpts from the Book of Mormon under the pseudonym of Obediah Dogberry in the *Palmyra Reflector*,[67] (both of whom were Hyrum Smith's lodge brothers in Mount Moriah Lodge No. 112), nor Orsamus Turner (1801–1855), who, like Eli Bruce, was incarcerated in connection with Morgan's abduction, claimed that Joseph Smith Jr. or any member of his family was an anti-Mason.[68]

---

the abduction of William Morgan." See also Richard Lloyd Anderson, "Martin Harris, the Honorable New York Farmer," *Improvement Era* 72 (Feb. 1969): 20.

64. Emer Harris, Martin's brother, was a Freemason during this period. See remarks Emer Harris gave April 6, 1856. Utah Stake General Minutes, General Record 9629, ser. 11, vol. 10 (1855–60), 268–70, Church History Library.

65. See Reed Durham, "Is There No Help for the Widow's Son?" *Mormon Miscellaneous* 1 (October 1975): 11–16. Mervin Hogan quoted this portion of Durham's speech in Mervin B. Hogan, "The Two Joseph Smith's Masonic Experiences," January 17, 1987, 13. Robert N. Hullinger noted that "the letter was signed by a committee of ten men, one of whom signed himself 'Ja's Smith' (probably James), but the letter was reproduced in many papers and in some it was signed simply as 'J. Smith.' This is doubtful since the committee was formed by residents of Batavia." Robert N. Hullinger, *Joseph Smith's Response to Skepticism*, 113n28. See also John E. Becker, *A History of Freemasonry in Waterloo, New York, 1817–1942* (Waterloo, NY: Seneca Lodge No. 113, F. & A. M., 1942), 22–23.

66. Tucker, *Origin, Rise, and Progress of Mormonism*.

67. Cole wrote, "We understand that the Anti-Masons have declared war against the Gold Bible.—Oh! How impious." *The Reflector* 1 (September 23, 1829): 14. Cole, who was raised a Master Mason in Mount Moriah Lodge No. 112 on June 24, 1815, published the first extracts from and commentary about the Book of Mormon in *The Reflector*, January 2, 1830. Arthur de Hoyos provided the information concerning Cole's Masonic membership, who obtained it from Kathleen M. Haley, assistant librarian, Grand Lodge of State of New York (Letter, October 21, 1992).

68. Orsamus Turner, *History of the Pioneer Settlement of Phelps and Gorham's Purchase* (Rochester, NY: William Alling, 1851); Rob Morris, *William Morgan: or political Anti-Masonry, its Rise, Growth and Decadence* (New York, 1883), 191–92, 206, 209, 224, 228.

THE OHIO MARKET

In September and October 1830 the prophet called Oliver Cowdery, Parley P. Pratt (1807–1857), Peter Whitmer Jr., and Ziba Peterson to "go unto the Lamanites and preach my gospel."[69] They signed a "Missionaries Covenant" to accept this assignment and to locate a temple site in Missouri and distributed copies of the Book of Mormon to prove that the true church had been restored.[70] In November, these missionaries arrived in Mentor, Ohio, where they contacted Sidney Rigdon (1793–1876), a Reformed Baptist minister who had recently broken with Alexander Campbell. Pratt, who was a former Campbellite minister and had been associated with Rigdon's splinter "Campbellite congregation," presented Rigdon with a copy of the Book of Mormon. Rigdon read the book, was baptized, and shortly thereafter converted more than one hundred of his own congregation.[71]

In December Smith dictated several revelations in New York that declared that Christ would "suddenly come to my temple" and that those who embraced the restored gospel were to "be endowed with power from on high."[72] Smith's temple revelations had Biblical antecedents reaching back to the Temple of Solomon, which was constructed to provide God with an earthy abode. In addition, the Book of Mormon contained scattered references to a temple in the new world that was patterned after Solomon's Temple.[73]

But some have noted that Smith's revelation was arguably reminiscent of Royal Arch rituals that contained the legend concerning Enoch's gold plate, which included instructions to rebuild the temple after the discovery of the lost word inscribed on the gold plate. Smith received his own temple

---

69. See D&C 28:8; 30:5–6; 32:1, 3. Brooke connected Pratt with Masonry in his description of his vision in the fall of 1830 in which a cloud appeared as "a Masonic square and compass, which he interpreted as a 'marvelous...sign of the coming of the Son of Man.'" Brooke, *The Refiner's Fire*, 61, citing Parley P. Pratt, *Autobiography of Parley P. Pratt* (New York, 1874), 45–46. Pratt did not identify the square or compass specifically as "Masonic," but he did write that he was "wrapt in deep meditations" on various subjects including "the important revelations of the Book of Mormon." See Parley P. Pratt, *Autobiography of Parley P. Pratt*, Third Ed. (Salt Lake City: Deseret Book Company, 1938), 43–44.
70. Vogel, *Early Mormon Documents*, 3:504–6.
71. See Bushman, *Rough Stone Rolling*, 123–24. John Brooke notes that Rigdon "had Masonic connections" since his cousin Thomas was a Royal Arch Mason. He relies on Masonic registers to support this conclusion. See Brooke, *The Refiner's Fire*, 195, 375n36.
72. D&C 36:8 (December 1830); "Revelations. Revelation Given, January 1831," *The Evening and the Morning Star* 1, no. 8 (January 1833): 6; D&C 38:32 (January 2, 1831). Richard Bushman believes that these revelations eventually led to the development of the endowment temple rituals. Richard Lyman Bushman, *Joseph Smith: Rough Stone Rolling* (New York: Alfred A. Knopf, 2005), 159.
73. II Nephi 5:16.

revelations shortly after the lost word from his gold plates was translated and published.[74] During the same month, Rigdon traveled to New York where he met the prophet who shortly thereafter recorded revelations in which the Lord instructed church members to move to Ohio.[75]

ANTI-MASON MORMONS

Eventually, two very prominent New York anti-Masons joined Smith's new church.[76] William Wines Phelps and George Washington Harris may have been attracted because they believed that Mormonism was an anti-Masonic religion.[77] Phelps was a newspaper man who was well known by such luminaries as Thurlow Weed and David Bernard. In October 1827 R. M. Bloomer, one of the owners (with Orsamus B. Clark) of *The Lake Light*, an anti-Masonic newspaper in Trumansburgh, Tompkins County, New York, announced that they had hired Phelps, who was the founding editor of the *Western Courier* in Cortland, New York.

The following January Phelps published his "renunciation" of Freemasonry in which he asserted that "secret societies [were] incompatible with the principles and derogatory to the constitution of a free government" and for this reason he decided to "renounce the self-organized institution of free masonry."[78] In February Phelps attended the first anti-Masonic convention held in LeRoy, New York, where he became acquainted with many of the

---

74. Carnes discussed the Royal Arch Degree which includes these instructions. Carnes, *Secret Ritual and Manhood*, 42–48. See also Allyn, *A Ritual of Freemasonry*, 117–43.

75. D&C 37; 38:31–32.

76. There were other anti-Masons, such as Martin Harris and Ezra Booth, who joined Smith's movement. Ezra Booth was a Methodist minister who was baptized in Kirtland and served as a missionary for a short time before renouncing the church. Ephraim Wood, "To the Methodists of Portage County," *Boston Masonic Mirror*, New Series, vol. 2, no. 47 (May 21, 1831): 372. I am indebted to Dan Vogel and Mike Marquardt for the reference to Ezra Booth.

77. Concerning Phelps, see Andrew Jenson, *Latter-day Saint Biographical Encyclopedia* (Salt Lake City: Andrew Jenson Historical Co., 1901–1936), 3:692–97; Walter D. Bown, "The Versatile W. W. Phelps: Mormon Writer, Educator, and Pioneer" (M.A. Thesis, Brigham Young University, 1958); Samuel Brown, "The Translator and Ghostwriter: Joseph Smith and W. W. Phelps," *Journal of Mormon History* 34, no. 1 (Winter 2008): 26–62; Samuel Brown, "William Phelps's Paracletes, An Early Witness to Joseph Smith's Divine Anthropology," *International Journal of Mormon Studies* 2, no. 1 (2009): 62–82.

78. See "Renunciation," *The Seneca Farmer, and Waterloo Advertiser* 5:28 (February 6, 1828), quoting the *National Observer* and taken from *The Lake Light*. When Phelps renounced Masonry he announced he would "answer any question relative to the secret, that I may be acquainted with—for in the language of the learned Dr. Paley 'an obligation from which a man can discharge himself by his own act, is no obligation at all.' 'The guilt therefore,' if any there be in denouncing the system of speculative free masonry 'lie in *making* not in breaking' the Masonic oaths." Ibid.

future leaders of the anti-Masonic movement. In May, Bloomer dissolved his publishing partnership with Clark and joined with Phelps to establish the *Ontario Phoenix* in Canandaigua, Ontario County, where legal proceedings concerning Morgan's disappearance had taken place.[79] In July, Phelps utilized his newspaper's platform and joined 103 delegates who signed the convention's Declaration of Independence.

In 1830 Phelps became involved in anti-Masonic politics, attended conventions to nominate candidates for the New York State Assembly, and advocated for the "Anti-Masonic Ticket."[80] The pro-Masonic *Geneva Gazette* ridiculed Phelps's participation in politics: "[Phelps] spake furiously after this sort: Let me maul him; let me douse him with five columns of clear Phoenix grit, as I doused them fellers that called me 'deserter.'"[81]

Although the *Ontario Phoenix* editorial page teased the *Ontario Repository* because it "hung out a splendid sign of the 'Book of Mormon,'"[82] Phelps purchased a copy of the Book of Mormon in April.[83] In December he met the Mormon prophet and later reported that as soon as he met him he "was willing to acknowledge [him] as a prophet of the Lord." But when he corresponded with fellow anti-Mason E. D. Howe, he only acknowledged that he had read the Book of Mormon and that he had "nothing by which we can positively detect it as an imposition." He confirmed that he had met church leaders and tactfully reported that Joseph Smith's "knowledge of divine things…has astonished many," that Martin Harris was "a wealthy farmer, but of small literary accomplishments," and that he had a ten-hour conversation with "a man from your state, named Sidney Rigdon, and he declared it was true, and he knew it by the power of the Holy Ghost."[84]

Three months later while Phelps was "comparing the 'Book of Mormon' with the Bible," he was served with a warrant by an anti-Mason for a debt that he had apparently not repaid. He later claimed that his creditors were Presbyterian traders who were "keeping me from joining the Mormons."[85]

79. Phelps, and R. M. Bloomer (his coeditor of *The Lake Light*) established the *Ontario Phoenix* on April 28, 1829, in Canandaigua, New York. See Milton W. Hamilton, *Anti-Masonic Newspapers, 1826–1834* (Portland, ME: Southworth-Authoesen Press, 1939), 82. See also "Notice," *The Geneva Gazette and Mercantile Advertiser* 19:36 (May 7, 1836) (Geneva, Ontario County, New York).
80. "Notice," *Ontario Phoenix* (July 28, 1830); "Voice of the People," *Ontario Phoenix* (September 1, 1830); "Voice of the People," *Ontario Phoenix* (September 15, 1830).
81. "Book of Chronicles," *Supplement to the Geneva Gazette* (November 1, 1830).
82. "Voice of the People," *Ontario Phoenix* (September 15, 1830). See also *Ontario Phoenix* (April 16, 1831).
83. See "Letter No. 6," *Messenger and Advocate* 1 (April 1835): 96–97; *Deseret News* 10 (April 11, 1860): 45, 48.
84. E. D. Howe, *Mormonism Unvailed*, 273–74.
85. "Letter No. 6," *Messenger and Advocate* 1 (April 1835): 96–97.

He was incarcerated in Lyons, Wayne County, New York, for thirty days and he wrote a bitter account of these events that was published by Masonic newspapers. Phelps called his accusers "pretended anti-masons" and he sarcastically inquired whether their actions reflected "the principles of anti-masonry."[86]

In May 1831 the anti-Masonic *Ithaca Journal & General Advertiser* gleefully reported that Phelps had been "kidnapped by his brethren of the same principle" and that he was "a very intelligent Mormonite." The paper made light of Morgan's murder, five years after his disappearance, and sarcastically suggested that the "freemen of Old Ontario" should "restore [Phelps] to his wife, or else to Morganize him as speedily as possible."[87] During the same month, Phelps resigned as editor of the *Ontario Phoenix* but he continued to be a committed anti-Mason and insisted that "secret societies and 'all combinations' must be resisted by the virtuous force of public opinion."[88]

When Phelps was released from jail, he traveled to Ohio where he reconnected with the Mormon prophet and shortly thereafter Smith told him that he was "called and chosen" and that he should be baptized, ordained an elder, and "preach repentance and remission of sins."[89] Phelps's baptism was widely reported in the New York anti-Masonic press. The *Niagara Courier* revealed that Phelps "has joined himself to the Mormonites, and been ordained an elder of those fanatics." The article went on to state that "Mr. Phelps once before in his life made a mistake. He joined himself to the Masonic imposture! But he had the good sense to quit that well-organized band of ruffians and cut-throats—and we doubt not, when reason shall have resumed her place in his mind, he will also abandon the equally false, yet far more innocent, association with which is he now joined."[90] But the anti-Masonic *Ithaca Journal & General Advertiser* observed that Phelps

---

86. See letter of W. W. Phelps, "Retribution," *The Wayne Sentinel* 8 (May 13, 1831): 3, which was originally published in *The Geneva Gazette and Mercantile Advertiser* 22 (May 11, 1831): 2. Throughout this period Phelps attacked *The Wayne Sentinel* (which he considered a Masonic newspaper) and its editor, E. B. Grandin (whom he considered a tool). *The Countryman* reported on September 28, 1830, that [E. B. Grandin] "not the *editor* of the Sentinel, but a mere tool in the hands of Palmyra masons." *The Countryman* 1 (November 9, 1830): 2. The same newspaper noted on November 9, 1830, that the *Sentinel* issued another paper, *The Reflector*, which was described as "a satirical, obscene little paper" as well as "the infamous, catch-penny work, entitled the "Book of Mormon," or as it is generally called, the "Golden Bible." *The Countryman* 1 (November 9, 1830).
87. "Anti-Masonick Kidnapping!!!" *Ithaca Journal & General Advertiser* XIV: 42 (May 18, 1831).
88. See *Ontario Phoenix* 4 (May 4, 1831); 4 (May 11, 1831): 2; and 4 (May 25, 1831).
89. D&C 55:1–2 (June 1831).
90. *Niagara Courier* (August 30, 1831). The newspaper was reacting to more general reports of Phelps's conversion. See *Onondaga Register* (August 10, 1831); *Syracuse Gazette* (August 10, 1831); *Ontario Repository* 29: 1473 (July 20, 1831): 3.

was "much more consistent than many other anti-Masonick editors: he has chosen a *religion* which corresponds admirably with his *politicks*."[91]

George Washington Harris, the other prominent New York anti-Mason who joined Mormonism, was not an intellectual like Phelps, but he was perhaps just as well known because of his connection with William Morgan. He was a Freemason for almost twenty years before he was expelled from Batavia Lodge No. 433 on August 15, 1826, "for the enormous depravity of his masonic conduct" which was apparently warning Morgan "that the Batavia Lodge was making arrangements to destroy him." The lodge also published notice of his expulsion and a "Notice and Caution" that he was a "*swindler* and a *dangerous* man."[92]

William and Lucinda Morgan (1801–c. 1860) and their two children resided above Harris's silversmith shop and after Morgan's disappearance his dependents became Harris's wards.[93] In 1827 Harris accompanied Lucinda to Carlton, New York, to attend an inquest to identify a body that washed up on the south shore of Lake Ontario. They both identified Morgan's remains, which were confirmed by a unanimous jury, and the body was taken to Batavia where it was buried "with great (Antimasonic) pomp and ceremony."[94] But within a year another inquest determined that the body was actually that of Timothy Munroe of Canada and it was thereafter disinterred with much less fanfare.

Harris continued to care for Morgan's family and on at least one occasion it was reported that he presented Lucinda with a contribution from an anti-Masonic benefactor.[95] While anti-Masons continued to believe

91. *Ithaca Journal & General Advertiser* 15:4 (August 24, 1831).

92. See *Masonic Mirror and Mechanic's Intelligencer* 2 (September 2, 1826): 290. The *Republican Advocate* published a story three years after Morgan's disappearance, which was taken from an article published in the *Batavia Times* (a Masonic newspaper in Batavia, New York) about three weeks before Morgan was kidnapped, which explained why Harris was expelled "for the enormous depravity of his masonic conduct." *Republican Advocate* 19:986 (December 31, 1830): 2.

93. George W. Harris, *"Deposition": A Narrative of the Facts and Circumstances Relating to the Kidnapping and Murder of William Morgan* (Batavia, NY: D. C. Miller, 1827); Morris, *William Morgan*, 258–59. See also *A Supplementary Report of the Committee Appointed to Ascertain the Fate of Captain William Morgan* (Rochester, NY: Printed for the Committee by Edwin Scranton, 1827).

94. Vaughn, *The Antimasonic Party*, 9. For Harris's testimony at the inquest, see *Supplementary Report*, 6–7, quoted in Grunder, *Mormon Parallels*, 1746. Grunder has published portions of a letter in which Lucinda Morgan states that she "*cannot* be mistaken" in her identification of Morgan's body. See Grunder, *Mormon Parallels*, 1746–47.

95. In January 1830 Harris presented Lucinda with a fifty-dollar contribution. See letter written by Lucinda Morgan to Frederick A. Sumner dated February 1, 1830, and published in the anti-Masonic newspaper *The Countryman* 1 (March 2, 1830): 2, in Lyons, New York, and reprinted in the *Boston Free Press*. See also Grunder, *Mormon Parallels*, 98, citing *Yates*

that members of the Craft murdered Morgan, the Masons fostered rumors that Morgan had abandoned his family and his project to publish an exposé and that he had escaped to Europe.[96] In 1830, four years after Morgan's disappearance, Harris and Lucinda were married in Batavia[97] and four years later they encountered Mormon apostle Orson Pratt (1811–1881) in Terre Haute, Indiana, where they were baptized and became ardent followers of Joseph Smith.

It is difficult to ascertain whether the Masons and anti-Masons who joined Mormonism connected the church's teachings with their prior experiences with the Craft. Nevertheless, it is possible that they continued to believe in the concept of a primitive Masonry and in Masonic legends associated with Solomon's Temple. John Brooke has observed that Joseph Smith "bore contradictory feelings about Freemasonry" since he "condemned the spurious tradition, while embracing the pure tradition."[98] Similarly, Clyde Forsberg has concluded that both Masons and anti-Masons were attracted to the Book of Mormon precisely because it attacked both "Masonry for the grisly murder of Morgan" and "Evangelical Anti-Masonry…for grandstanding and political avarice."[99]

Mormonism eventually offered these men, who were, in the words of John Brooke, "open to a new way into the 'ancient mysteries,'" an alternative method to re-Christianize the Craft and return it to its historical roots.[100]

Republican 6:12 (Penn-Yan, New York, February 24, 1830); *Anti-Masonic Telegraph* (February 24, 1830); and *Chautauqua Phoenix* 2 (March 10, 1830), 2.

96. John L. Emery claimed that he was present when Henry L. Valence confessed on his deathbed in 1848 that Morgan was drowned in the Niagara River and that Valence compared himself with Cain after he had participated in the murder. See Henry L. Valence, *Confessions of the Murder of William Morgan* (Dayton, OH: W.J. Shuey, 1869). Charles Grandison Finney published excerpts from this deathbed confession in *The Character, Claims and Practical Workings of Freemasonry*. Thurlow Weed also claimed on his deathbed that John Whitney (who was one of the defendants convicted of conspiracy in connection with Morgan's disappearance) confessed to the murder in 1861. Rob Morris published a conflicting statement made by Whitney. See Morris, *William Morgan*.

97. Harris and Morgan were married on November 23, 1830. See "Married," *Spirit of the Times & People's Press* 1 (November 30, 1830): 3, Batavia, NY. See also "Married," *Rochester Daily Advertiser* 5 (whole no. 1249; November 27, 1830), Rochester, NY, (quoted and reproduced in Grunder, *Mormon Parallels*, 1746); and Morris, *William Morgan*, 276–78. Rob Morris wrote, tongue in cheek, that the *American Masonic Record* was relieved when she remarried, writing that "Anti-Masonry is no more!" and gloating, "This celebrated woman who, like Niobe, was all tears and affliction, whose hand was ever held forth to receive contributions from the sympathetic Anti-Masons, who vowed eternal widowhood, pains and penance, is married! Is married, and, tell it not in Gath, is married to a Mason!" Ibid., 277.

98. Brooke, *The Refiner's Fire*, 168–69.

99. Forsberg, *Equal Rites*, 73.

100. Brooke, *The Refiner's Fire*, 168–69.

Smith and his followers, like other "anti-Mason Masons" (a term coined
by Rick Grunder), "claimed that it was not 'ancient' Freemasonry that disturbed them, but its excesses and misuse by wicked adherents in modern
times."[101] Smith continued to introduce ideas and concepts that would
harken back to Freemasonry but that were presented in a new and fresh
context.[102]

101. Rick Grunder has concluded that "antimasons of Joseph Smith's day were no less varied
and independent in their thinking than are adherents to various religious and political parties today." He notes that while "most of them agreed with later evidence and scholarship
that Freemasonry is simply not a continuation of some ancient system of ritual begun in the
temple of Solomon and perpetuated to the modern era…there were also many antimasons
who thought otherwise." See Grunder, *Parallels*, 217–32.
102. Rick Grunder, "More Parallels: A Survey of Little-Known Sources of Mormon History,"
(unpublished paper presented at the Sunstone Symposium, Salt Lake City, Utah, September
1987).

Joseph's First Temple

IN FEBRUARY 1831 the prophet revealed that the Saints should flee from the East "in consequence of that which is coming on the earth and of secret combinations" and that they would eventually be gathered in the New Jerusalem. The revelation informed the church that the location of this gathering spot would be revealed "in my own due time."[1] Shortly thereafter Smith led his new church to Ohio, which was initially intended to be a "way station" until the "the city of the New Jerusalem" was identified and constructed.[2] In Ohio, Smith continued to retranslate the Bible, "giving some more extended information upon the scriptures," and studied extrabiblical sources.[3] His new revelations commanded church members to "sanctify yourselves and ye shall be endowed with power, that ye may give even as I have spoken"[4] and to schedule a church conference where the Lord promised to "pour out my spirit upon them in the day that they assemble themselves together."[5]

1. D&C 42:8–9, 62–66.
2. See Mark Ashurst-McGee, "Zion in America: The Origins of Mormon Constitutionalism," *Journal of Mormon History* 38, no. 3 (Summer 2012): 92, for the reference to "way station."
3. *History of the Church*, 1:132.
4. "Extract of a Revelation given February, 1831," *The Evening and the Morning Star* 1:5 (October 1832), 34; D&C 43:16. These revelations were reminiscent of the Pentecost experience by Christ's disciples as recorded in Acts 2:1–6.
5. "History of Joseph Smith," *Times and Seasons* 5:1 (January 1, 1844), 385. In May Smith informed Ezra Thayer, by revelation, that Thayer would "be ordained unto power from on high" at the assembly. Joseph Smith Revelation, May 1831, in "Kirtland Revelation Book," 91–92; See H. Michael Marquardt, *The Joseph Smith Revelations, Text and Commentary* (Salt Lake City: Signature Books, 1999), 135. Greg Prince has located several newspaper articles referring to this pending conference. See Gregory A. Prince, "The Development of the Latter-day Saint Doctrine of 'Endowment,' 1831–1844 (Mss. January 1990), citing *Western Courier* (Ravenna, Ohio), May 26, 1831, reprinted in *St. Louis Times* 3: 105 (July 9, 1831), 2. See also, Gregory A. Prince, *Having Authority: The Origins and Development of Priesthood during the Ministry of Joseph Smith* (Independence, Mo.: Independence Press, 1993); and *Power from on High: The Development of Mormon Priesthood* (Salt Lake City: Signature Books, 1995).

ANTI-MASONIC BIBLE

When the Mormons moved to Ohio, Martin Harris "was in serious hock to pay for the printing of the Book of Mormon" and he "carried multiple copies around personally, concerned that they were not selling as well as he apparently had hoped."[6] When Harris arrived in Painesville, *The Telegraph*, a weekly newspaper published by Eber D. Howe, reported that he "planted himself in the bar-room of the hotel" where "he commenced reading and explaining the Mormon hoax...curiosity soon drew around thirty or forty spectators, and all who presumed to question his blasphemous pretentions, were pronounced infidels." *The Telegraph* recorded that when Harris was asked to leave, he told the crowd that "all who believed the new bible would *see Christ* within fifteen years and all who did not would absolutely be destroyed and dam'd."[7]

The *Geauga Gazette*, a competing newspaper that was published in the same village, reported that "Martin Harris, one of the first Mormon prophets, arrived in the village last Sunday on his way to the 'Holy Land,'" and provided an additional detail concerning Harris's barroom encounter: Harris "publickly declared that the 'Golden Bible' is the Anti-masonick Bible."[8] The *Gazette* asserted that "it is a singular truth that everyone of its followers, so far as we are able to ascertain are antimasons."[9] But neither *The Telegraph*, which was an anti-Masonic paper that frequently reported on the movement and published articles from other newspapers including W. W. Phelps' *Ontario Phoenix* and Ward's *Anti-Masonic Review*, nor its editor E. D. Howe, who was himself a fervent anti-Mason who attended Ohio's first anti-Masonic convention, believed that Mormons were anti-Masons.

The *Telegraph* criticized its "neighbor-in-law" for claiming "that Mor-

6. Grunder, *Mormon Parallels*, 223–24.
7. *The Telegraph* 2:39 (March 15, 1831).
8. *The Geauga Gazette* (Painesville, Ohio) (March 15, 1831), reprinted in *The Ohio Star* (Ravenna, Ohio), 2:12 (March 24, 1831). On March 29, 2008, Gregory C. Thompson, director of special collections at the J. Willard Marriott Library, University of Utah, and the author examined the March 15, 1831, issue of the *Geauga Gazette* in the Library of Congress and confirmed that Dale Morgan's transcription of the entry, which is included in the Special Collections of the J. Willard Marriott Library, is accurate. Nevertheless, the Library of Congress's index of newspapers incorrectly identifies the *Geauga Gazette* as the *Georgia Gazette*. The *Ohio Star* issue of March 24, 1831, which quotes the *Geauga Gazette*, does not include the Harris quotation. Dan Vogel cites the *Geauga Gazette* (May 1, 1832) as a reference for the Book of Mormon being referred to as anti-Masonic. See Dan Vogel, "Mormonism's 'Anti-Masonic Bible,'" *The John Whitmer Historical Association Journal* 9 (1989): 17–30. See also Max H. Parkin, *Conflict at Kirtland* (Salt Lake City, 1966), 23; and Richard S. Van Wagoner, *Mormon Polygamy: A History*, 2nd. ed. (Salt Lake City: Signature Books, 1992), 119.
9. E. D. Howe apparently disagreed with this reference in the March 22, 1831, issue of *The Telegraph*.

monism is the Antimasonic religion, because *all* who have embraced it are antimasons."[10] It concluded that "some 'zealous masons' and several 'republican jacks' have beset Jo Smith for 'more light,'" and that "the Mormon bible was printed and sent forth to the world, from a Masonic printing office, under a masonic, or some other injunction of secrecy."[11] The paper claimed that "You may also discover a striking resemblance between masonry and Mormonism," and wrote that the similarities included claims "to have a very ancient origin, and so possess some wonderful secrets that the world cannot have without submitting to the prescribed ceremonies, and appropriating a portion or all of their property as common stock. The secrets of masonry are kept from the world by blasphemous oaths, under a penalty of death—the secrets of mormonism by making the candidate *believe* that it will be violating the 'express command of Heaven,' and the penalty is the eternal displeasure of God, and all 'worthy and well qualified' mormons."[12]

This skirmish between *The Telegraph* and *The Geauga Gazette* demonstrates that Mormonism was already caught up in contemporary debates concerning Freemasonry, soon after it arrived in Ohio.[13] If Harris actually called the Book of Mormon "the "Anti-Masonic Bible" as reported, he probably knew that the moniker was used in connection with Bernard's *Light on Masonry.* The physical appearance of the Book of Mormon resembled Bernard's book: the binding was similar, it contained the same number of pages, and was copyrighted in the same office.[14] Howe's counterassertion, that Grandin's newspaper was a Masonic organ, was completely unfounded. But he was closer to the mark when he suggested that some Masons had joined Smith's church. Those new converts included Newel K. Whitney (1795–1850), who was initiated, passed, and raised in Meridian Orb Lodge

10. Howe wrote, after attending an anti-Masonic convention in July 1830, that anti-Masonry was "beginning to stand erect and…the great state of Ohio in due time, will show herself a powerful auxiliary in the present warfare against Freemasonry." See Grunder, *Mormon Parallels*, 135–36.
11. *The Telegraph* (Painesville, Ohio), 2d. Series II (March 22, 1831): 40. Thurlow Weed, the editor of the anti-Masonic *Rochester Telegraph* who refused to publish The Book of Mormon, referred to E. B. Grandin as a Mason. See Thurlow Weed, *Life of Thurlow Weed*, ed. Harriet A. Weed (Boston: Houghton Miflin and Co., 1883), 358–59.
12. *The Telegraph* (Painesville, Ohio), 2d. Series II (March 22, 1831): 40.
13. Since this exchange took place in a barroom where patrons (perhaps including Martin Harris and the reporters) were imbibing, one should consider David Wondrich's observation that "drinking places are particularly resistive to narrative" and that "a good deal of the testimony about what transpired in bars comes from people who had been drinking when they witnessed it" which "causes a certain imprecision in the data." See David Wondrich, "The All-American Place," *The Wall Street Journal* (July 9–10, 2011), C7, reviewing Christine Sismondo, *America Walks into a Bar* (Oxford: Oxford University Press, 2011).
14. See Grunder, *Mormon Parallels*, 224.

No. 10, Painesville, Lake County, Ohio, and Heber C. Kimball (1801–1868), who was raised a Master Mason in 1823 in Victor Lodge No. 303, Victor, Ontario County, New York.[15]

It seems likely that Mormon Masons like Hyrum Smith, Whitney, and Kimball were aware of the intense anti-Masonic feelings that existed in both New York and Ohio, but they did not secede after Morgan's abduction or after they joined the Mormons. Kimball was prepared to become a Royal Arch Mason—he signed a petition to organize a chapter in Victor, New York—before his lodge was destroyed in a fire.[16] He recalled, after he became a Mormon, that he was driven from his home five times by mobs because he was a Mason and "I have been as true as an angel from the heavens to the covenants I made in the lodge at Victor."[17] Perhaps persecution for honorable beliefs was a foretaste, for some, of the anti-Mormon feeling that would soon be unleashed over secret temple rituals and plural marriage.

Despite these conversions, most observers in Ohio eventually associated Mormonism with anti-Masonry because of specific passages in the Book of Mormon about secret combinations. Howe gradually evolved from an anti-Mason to an anti-Mormon after his wife and daughter converted to Mormonism and he published Alexander Campbell's negative review of the Book of Mormon. Several years later Howe acquired some affidavits from Philastus Hurlbut that he published in his own anti-Mormon book entitled *Mormonism Unvailed*.[18] Ironically, Howe may have chosen the title because at least one printer of William Morgan's anti-masonic exposé changed the original title of his pamphlet *Illustrations of Masonry* to *Masonry Unveiled*.[19]

THE HIGH PRIESTHOOD

In June 1831 Joseph Smith presided over a church conference in Ohio where the revelation concerning the endowment was fulfilled. Parley Pratt (a former Campbellite minister and protégé of Sidney Rigdon) reported that fifty elders attended a conference and that Smith and seventeen other men were "ordained" "to the High Priesthood after the order of the Son of God, which is after the Order of Melchisedek" and that "this was the first occasion in which this priesthood had been revealed and conferred

15. For a short history of Heber C. Kimball's experiences in Freemasonry, see Orson F. Whitney, *Life of Heber C. Kimball* (Salt Lake City: Published by the Kimball Family, 1888), 26–28. See also *Latter Day Saints' Millennial Star* 26 (July 23, 1864): 471–72.

16. *Millennial Star* 26 (July 23, 1864): 471–72.

17. Whitney, *Life of Heber C. Kimball*, 26–27.

18. Howe, *Mormonism Unvailed*, 81.

19. See Morgan, *Masonry Unveiled, Containing a Full Exposition of the Secrets and Ceremonies of That "Ancient and Honorable" Institution, Freemasonry*. See Walgren, *Freemasonry, Anti-Masonry and Illuminism*, 513.

upon the Elders in this dispensation."[20] The restoration of the high priesthood was accompanied by personal religious experiences and Smith recorded that "the Lord displayed his power in a manner that could not be mistaken." "The man of sin was revealed," Smith wrote, "and the authority of the Melchisedec priesthood was manifested, and conferred for the first time upon several of the elders."[21] Other participants confirmed that the "endowment" consisted of "the same power as the ancient apostles," that there were visions of God and Jesus Christ, and that "the spirit of God was made manifest to the heeling [sic] of the sick, casting out devils, speaking in unknown tongues, discerning of spirits, and prophesying with mighty power."[22]

When Smith restored the High Priesthood he undoubtedly received much inspiration from reading and translating the Bible. His translation of Genesis extrapolates the biblical account (which refers to Melchizedek as "the priest of the most high God")[23] and reveals Melchizedek as a "high priest after the order of the covenant which God made with Enoch." Smith's translation also reveals Melchizedek as "one being ordained after this order and calling" and as "a Priest of this order," who was given "power by faith to break Mountains to divide the seas to dry up waters [sic] to turn them out of their course and to put at defiance the armies of nations to divide the earth to break every band to stand in the presence of God to do all things according to his will according to his command subdue principalities and powers and by this by the will of the Son of God."[24]

The Book of Hebrews refers to those who "come out of the loins of Abraham" as "a priest forever after the order of Melchizedek"[25] and the Book of Mormon refers to "the holy order of this High Priesthood" and that Melchizedek "was also a High Priest after this same order."[26] There are

20. *Journal History*, June 3, 1831. See also Pratt, *Autobiography*, 68 (1976 edition); Quinn, *Early Mormonism and the Magic World View*, 223.

21. "History of Joseph Smith," *Times and Seasons* 5:3 (February 1, 1844), 416. Concerning the "sin of man" see Grunder, *Mormon Parallels*, 144.

22. See, e.g., Levi Ward Hancock Diary, June 4, 1831; and Levi Ward Hancock, 1854 Autobiography, Church History Library, pp. 88–94. See also Lyman Wight to Wilford Woodruff, August 24, 1857, Church History Library; Newell Knight Autobiographical Sketch, Church History Library; Jared Carter Journal, *Journal History* (June 8, 1831), Church History Library; and Ezra Booth to Rev. Ira Eddy (September 1831), in E. D. Howe, *Mormonism Unvailed*, 180–90. Prince notes that this event was reported in the press. See *Painsville Telegraph* (June 14, 1831) and *Niles Weekly Register* (July 16, 1831).

23. Genesis 14:18.

24. Old Testament Manuscript 1, pp. 32–34 (Ca. February 9 thru March [6–7] 1831, Archives of the Community of Christ, Independence, Missouri). Not in King James Version. Added after Genesis 14:24. The scribe was Sidney Rigdon.

25. Hebrews 7:1–6. See also I Kings 5:16; 9:23; and 6:1, 38 for parallels.

26. See Book of Mormon [1830], 260. These references were originally in Alma, chapters 9 and 10, but are now set forth in Alma 13:6–16. One reference which originally read "the

also biblical passages that record ritual washing and the Lord's Supper.[27] Smith later emphasized that "the order of the High-priesthood is that they have power given them to seal up the Saints unto eternal life. And it was the privilege of every Elder present to be ordained to the High priesthood."[28] This was an important development and, according to Mormon historian Greg Prince, "the first recorded association of endowment (specifically, the exercise of High Priesthood) and afterlife,"[29] and that this first Kirtland endowment was part of the "restoration of all things" and that its "ancient antecedent" was Christ's charge to his apostles, following his resurrection, to "tarry ye in the city of Jerusalem, until ye be endued with power from on high."[30] When Smith and other men who experienced the endowment encountered sincere investigators they "seeled [sic] them up into Eternal life."[31]

Prince has noted that those who became members of the order, and participated in the endowment, described it as "a pentecost consisting of revelation, prophecy, vision, healing, casting out of evil spirits, speaking in unknown tongues, and according to one witness, an unsuccessful attempt to raise a dead child."[32] Nevertheless, the meaning of being "sealed unto eternal life" remained ambiguous until the emerging doctrine of salvation was placed in a clearer context.

The following year Smith was ordained president of the High Priesthood.[33] He held the highest position in the church and revealed that those who were "priests of the Most High, after the order of Melchizedek, which was after the order of Enoch, which was after the order of the Only Begotten Son" were members of the church of the First Born, members of the general assembly of the church of Enoch, "gods, even the sons of God," and "shall dwell in the presence of God and his Christ forever and ever."[34]

---

holy order of this High Priesthood" now reads "the holy order, or this high priesthood." See Alma 13:10.

27. Foot washing was practiced in the Old Testament. See Genesis 18:4; 19:2; 24:32; 43:24; I Samuel 25:41.

28. Donald Q. Cannon and Lyndon W. Cook, *Far West Record: Minutes of the Church of Jesus Christ of Latter-day Saints* (Salt Lake City: Deseret Book Company, 1983), 20–21 (October 25, 1831).

29. Prince, "The Development of the Latter-day Saints Doctrine of 'Endowment,'" 11; Prince, *Having Authority*, 40–42; and Prince, *Power from on High*, 157–58.

30. Luke 24:46–49. See Prince, "The Development of the Latter-day Saints Doctrine of 'Endowment,'" 10.

31. Reynolds Cahoon Diary (November 9–26, 1831), Church History Library; Dean C. Jessee, "Joseph Knight's 'Early History of Mormonism,'" *BYU Studies* 17:1 (Autumn 1976), 39; Orson Pratt Diary, August 26, 1833; September 8, 1833.

32. Prince, *Power from on High*, 18.

33. Cannon and Cook, *Far West Record*, April 26, 1832, p. 44.

34. D&C 76:57–62.

While Smith was inspired by the Bible when he restored the high priesthood, there are also parallels between Smith's high priesthood and Royal
Arch Masonry.[35] In 1818 Royal Arch Masons in Ohio organized a Council of High Priests, which was one of the earliest. Both Lorenzo Dow, a
primitive gospeler, and Newel K. Whitney, an early Ohio convert to Mormonism, were members of the Ohio Royal Arch.[36] When Smith translated
Biblical passages about Enoch and Melchizedek, he may have already been
convinced that Masonic rituals contained a remnant of ceremonies that
were practiced in Solomon's Temple and that he was called to restore the
original ritual through revelation. Whitney and other Mason Mormons
(including W. W. Phelps) were undoubtedly aware that the high priesthood
had both biblical and Masonic antecedents.

This Mormon high priesthood was different from what later became
known as the Melchizedek Priesthood since there were initially two kinds
of elders, those who held the high priesthood and those who did not, and
only those who held the high priesthood were permitted to receive the
endowment just as only those who became high priests in Royal Arch
Masonry were eligible to become members of the Holy Order of High
Priesthood.[37]

Jeremy Cross (1783–1861), who was a student of Thomas Smith Webb,
recorded a Masonic prayer, given during the installation of a high priest in
the Order of High Priesthood, which exhorts the "Almighty and Supreme
High Priest of heaven and earth," that the officers of the chapter "be endowed with wisdom."[38] The ritual included scriptural passages that refer to
"Melchisedek, king of Salem, [that he] brought forth bread and wine: and
he was the priest of the Most High God. And he blessed him [Abraham],
and said, Blessed be Abram of the Most High God" (Genesis 14:12–24);
and Abraham is told that "Thou art a priest for ever, after the order of
Melchisedek" (Hebrews 7:1–6).[39]

These aspects of the Royal Arch were well briefed in anti-Masonic publications. John Stearns, who quoted Salem Town liberally, ridiculed the Royal
Arch's High Priesthood because it "has no connection with ancient masonry," and argued that the "title high priest, as worn by them is mockery."[40]

35. Webb, *The Freemason's Monitor* (1808), 173–76.
36. Mackey, *Encyclopaedia of Freemasonry*, 1:327. For an early newspaper reference to the
Royal Arch's high priesthood in Ohio, see "Masonic," *Norwalk* (Ohio) *Reporter and Huron
Advertiser*, February 9, 1828, [2].
37. Smith did not establish the office of high priest until he had conferred the high priesthood on selected elders. See Prince, *Power from on High*, 19–21, 71–72; Cannon and Cook,
Far West Record, 8.
38. Cross, *The True Masonic Chart*, 135.
39. Ibid., 130–33.
40. Stearns, *An Inquiry*, 30–32, 40, 64–66, 153.

In 1828 a group of ministers opposed to Freemasonry met in Livonia, New York, and passed a resolution that church members should not have any association with Freemasonry "because it confers the office of High Priest upon those who are not called of God as was Aaron, and because its high priesthood is said to be after the order of Melchisedick, when Christ is the only priest after that order."[41]

Anti-Mason Randolph Streeter objected that Masonry had instituted and maintained an "unholy priesthood" and that "it is said...that Melchisedec is King of righteousness and peace" but that there was no peace realized by this "Masonic priesthood."[42] Beriah B. Hotchkin, the editor of the anti-Masonic *LeRoy Gazette*, also argued that Masonry disguised itself to appear "like the priests of the Lord.... The mitre inscribed with '*Holiness to the Lord*,' was upon her head; the breast plate, the *Urim and Thummim*, were upon her breast," and that she made her members "masters, kings, priests, sovereigns," and "gave them a mystic key to unlock the door and enter the sanctorum of 'mystery, BABYLON THE GREAT, *the mother of harlots and of the abominations of the earth!*'"[43]

Henry Dana Ward's *The Anti-Masonic Review and Magazine* also noted in its first issue that Masonry deceives the public when "it claims a divine origin; presents itself on the same immutable foundation with divine revelation; and offers a guide to eternal happiness. For this it imitates the celebration of the Christian sacraments; impiously dedicates Masonic priests to Jehovah, after the order of Melchisedec; and professes to have and to teach the only true pronunciation of the name of the Almighty."[44] Ward quoted Salem Town's thesis liberally in his book *Free-Masonry* and attacked "the Heavenly Order of the Masonic Degrees."[45]

THE ZION TEMPLE

In July 1831 Smith traveled to Missouri where he received a revelation confirming that Independence, Missouri, was "the land of promise, and the place for the city of Zion," and as "the center place and a spot for the

41. *Republican Monitor* (Cazenovia, New York), November 25, 1828, p. 4, citied in Grunder, *Mormon Parallels*, 1364.
42. Grunder, *Mormon Parallels*, 1359.
43. Ibid., 1355–57. See Revelation 17:5.
44. Grunder, *Mormon Parallels*, 108–9, quoting *The Anti-Masonic Review and Magazine* 1 (December 1828): 24.
45. Ward, *Free-Masonry*, 200–1. For additional critiques of Masonry's high priesthood, see "Moral and Religious," *Western Intelligencer*, November 1, 1828, 17; "Freemasonry," *Religious Examiner*, February 1831, 48.

temple."[46] He received additional revelations during the next several weeks that specified that the New Jerusalem would become the permanent head-quarters of the church and a gathering place for all church members.[47] From 1831 to 1833 more than twelve hundred Latter-day Saints moved to Jackson County, which was consecrated by Smith as a gathering place and where he planned to construct the New Jerusalem with a temple at its center.

W. W. Phelps became the editor of the first Mormon periodical, *The Evening and Morning Star*, which was published in Missouri.[48] Beginning in June 1832 he published extracts from the Book of Mormon warning against "secret abominations,"[49] and reported concerning Smith's ongoing translations of the Book of Genesis, which revealed new information concerning the prophet Enoch. He wrote that "as the public seem somewhat astonished, that we, among all the light of this century, should have 'sacred records which have slept for ages' to publish, it is our duty to say, that we shall take an extract from The Prophecy of Enoch, for our second or third number."[50] During this same period, the Mormon prophet identified himself with Enoch who, according to Masonic legend, built the first temple on Mount Moriah.[51]

But in December 1832 Smith received a revelation commanding him to "establish a house, even a house of prayer, a house of fasting, a house of faith, a house of learning, a house of glory, a house of order, a house of God" in Kirtland, Ohio.[52] The structure was described as a place for "the presidency of the school of the prophets for their instruction in all things, even for the officers of the church, or in other words, those who are called to the ministry in the church, beginning at the high priests, even down to the

46. D&C 57:2–3. (July 20, 1831).

47. D&C 58–62. (August 1, 1831 to August 13, 1831). During his mission to the Lamanites the previous October, Oliver Cowdery wrote that he would be in search of the location to build the New Jerusalem temple. *Journal History*, October 17, 1830.

48. In June 1831 Smith instructed Phelps to travel to Jackson County, Missouri, to assist Oliver Cowdery in "the work of printing, and of selecting and writing books for schools in this church." D&C 55:4. In July Phelps was called as the church printer and Oliver Cowdery was selected as his assistant. D&C 57:11–13 (July 20, 1831).

49. "From the Book of Mormon," *The Evening and the Morning Star* 1: 1 (June 1832): 8.

50. "To Agents and the Public," *The Evening and the Morning Star* 1:1 (June 1832): 6. Phelps also noted that "Jude spake of this prophet in the 14th verse of his epistle. There are too many books mentioned and missing in the Bible, for any one to query about more sacred records."

51. "Extract from the Prophecy of Enoch," *The Evening and the Morning Star* 1:3 (August 1832): 2–3. See also *History of the Church* 1:133–39.

52. D&C 88:117–19, 136–39. This revelation was received over at least three days from December 27–28, 1832, to January 3, 1833. *The Evening and the Morning Star* 1:10 (March 1833), 78.

deacons."[53] But while the revelation did not identify the building as a temple (reserving that distinction for Zion), it did indicate that the Lord would visit the School of the Prophets that would take place there.[54]

This new "School of the Prophets" was organized and began to meet before the commencement of construction on the new structure.[55] On January 23–24, 1833, Smith addressed this new "conference," which was held in the upper room of his home, and introduced a new purification ritual that had parallels to the Royal Arch's Order of High Priesthood. The school's minutes reflect that "after much speaking praying and singing, all done in Tongues," Smith "proceeded to washing hands faces and feet in the name of the Lord as commanded of God each one washing his own after which the president girded himself with a towel and again washed the feet of all the Elders wiping them with the towel."[56]

During this ceremony Joseph Smith Sr. blessed his son and pronounced that "he should continue in his Priests office until Christ come." Frederick G. Williams (1787–1842), one of Smith's scribes and confidantes, washed Smith's feet and then the elders washed each other's feet. Smith told the assembled elders that they "were all clean from the blood of this generation but that those among them who should sin willfully after they were thus cleansed and sealed up unto eternal life should be given over to the buffetings of Satan until the day of redemption." They then "partook of the Lords supper" and did "eat and drank and were filled then sang a hymn and went out."[57]

When high priests met in Kirtland in May 1833, they voted to seek subscriptions to build "a school house for the purpose of accommodating the Elders who should come in to receive their education for the ministry

53. D&C 88:127.
54. See Correspondence from Joseph Smith to W. W. Phelps, January 11, 1833, in Dean C. Jessee, ed., *The Personal Writings of Joseph Smith* (Salt Lake City: Deseret Book; Provo, Utah: Brigham Young University Press, 2002), 293. Prince notes that the Doctrine and Covenants 88:138–41 instructed that the Saints would "cleanse your hands and your feet before me, that I may make you clean," but that this portion of the revelation was "most probably written after the washing of feet conducted at the School of the Prophets on 23–24 January." Prince, *Power from on High*, 20n65. Generally the Kirtland structure was referred to as the "House of the Lord" and not as a temple. See Richard S. Van Wagoner, *The Complete Discourses of Brigham Young* (Salt Lake City: Smith-Pettit Foundation, 2009), 1:11 (November 17, 1839).
55. The School of the Prophets had an Old Testament counterpart. "And Saul sent messengers to take David, and when they saw the company of the prophets prophesying, and Samuel standing as appointed over them, the Spirit of God was upon the messengers of Saul and they also prophesied" (1 Sam. 19:20). Some Masonic writers claimed that such schools were established "to counteract the progress of the Spurious Freemasonry which was introduced unto Palestine before his time." Oliver, *Historical Landmarks* 2:373–74.
56. Kirtland Council Minutes (January 23, 1833).
57. Ibid.; Zebedee Coltrin Diary (January 24, 1833), Church History Library; Lucy Mack Smith Manuscript, 162–63.

according to a revelation given on that subject March 8, 1833." But the prophet rejected this initiative and instead revealed the partial "pattern" for the Kirtland House of the Lord.[58] This revelation used explicit terminology associated with Solomon's Temple and provided that the structure's inner court (that is, the interior of the structure) would be fifty-five feet by sixty-five feet, that there would be two floors, an upper court and a lower court. The house would be "dedicated unto the Lord from the foundation thereof, according to the order of the priesthood" and "ye shall not suffer any unclean thing to come in unto it; and my glory shall be there, and my presence shall be there."[59]

Although Smith's first endowment given in Kirtland to the Order of High Priesthood did not take place inside a temple, he gradually strengthened the connection between endowment and temple. In June 1833 he revealed that he was rebuked in a revelation because he had delayed the construction of the house of God in Kirtland where God would "endow those whom I have chosen with power from on high."[60] Shortly thereafter Smith presided over a ceremony in which ground was broken and the first stone hauled. On July 23 the High Priesthood laid the cornerstones "after the order of the Holy Priesthood."[61]

Nevertheless, church leaders still maintained that "Zion is the place where the temple will be built, and the people gathered"[62] and continued to plan for the plat of Zion.[63] The plat for this "New Jerusalem" contained twenty-four temples, including a two-story rectangular structure facing east

---

58. Kirtland Council Minutes (May 4, 1833). Levi W. Hancock wrote that the prophet rejected a proposal to build a house of worship because "the Lord would not except [*sic*] it, and gave a command to build a temple." Levi W. Hancock Autobiography, Church History Library.

59. D&C 94:1–9 (May 6, 1834); *History of the Church* 1:346–47. For a description of Solomon's Temple, see 1 Kings 6:23–28, 7:13–14, 28–50; 2 Kings 6:31–32. See also William J. Hamblin and David Rolph Seely, *Solomon's Temple: Myth and History* (London: Thames & Hudson, 2007). Karen Armstrong notes that since a "temple had to be a copy of the god's heavenly home…the plans of a temple had to be revealed, as they were to David, so that the dimensions and furnishings of the god's home in the world above could be accurately reproduced on earth." Karen Armstrong, *Jerusalem: One City, Three Faiths* (New York: Ballantine Books, 1997), 45.

60. D&C 95 (Revelation, June 1, 1833).

61. *History of the Church* 1:353–56, 400. The Masonic ceremony of laying a cornerstone consisted of testing and choosing a stone that was perfectly square on the surface and a perfect cube in its solid contents (representing the testing of initiates), which is dragged by a rope to the proper location in the northeast corner (which location symbolized the meeting of darkness and light and the progression of initiates toward immortality and eternal life) where it was set apart by pouring wine, corn, and oil on its surface (just as men who did work in the temple would be set apart). See Mackey, *Encyclopedia of Freemasonry* 1:178–79.

62. Orson Hyde and Hyrum Smith, "From a Conference of Twelve High Priests, to the Bishop, his Council, and the Inhabitants of Zion," in *History of the Church* 1:320.

63. See C. Mark Hamilton, *Nineteenth-Century Mormon Architecture & City Planning* (New York: Oxford University Press, 1995), 34–37.

with pulpits on both the east and west ends of the house.[64] But during the summer of 1833 the Saints in Missouri began to experience intense persecution and most of them were forced to abandon their homes in Jackson County by the end of the year.

Smith's revelations still confirmed that Zion "shall not be moved out of her place, notwithstanding her children are scattered" and that "there is none other place appointed; neither shall there be any other place appointed than that which I have appointed, for the work of gathering of my saints."[65] To underscore his dedication to Zion, Smith organized an expedition in May 1834 known as Zion's Camp, which marched to Missouri. There he called three high priests—David Whitmer, W. W. Phelps, and John Whitmer—to the Presidency of the Church in Zion, and he called other high priests to a High Council.

During the expedition Oliver Cowdery wrote a letter to John F. Boynton that the Lord had promised to "endow his servants…on the condition that they build him a house; and that if the house is not built the Elders will not be endowed with power." He described the endowment as an event that would include "fire more gloriously and marvelously than at Pentecost, because the work to be performed in the last days is greater than in that day."[66] One non-Mormon observed that "God directed them there and there alone to build up his holy temple for the gathering of the scattered tribes of Israel."[67]

Ultimately, the expedition failed to reach Jackson County due to the threats of mobs and Missouri's failure to provide militia protection. This was a watershed event for the Mormon prophet. Although he continued to equate Jackson County with Zion, he recognized that the church would need to remain in Kirtland for longer than he had anticipated. But he also taught that the church would eventually return to Missouri and later stated that Missouri was literally the site where some events recorded in the Old Testament had actually taken place.[68]

---

64. *History of the Church* 1:358.

65. D&C 101:17, 20 (December 16, 1833).

66. Oliver Cowdery (for Sidney Rigdon and Newel K. Whitney) to John F. Boynton, May 6, 1834, in Oliver Cowdery Letterbook, 45–46, Huntington Library.

67. J. C. Chauncey to "Dear Sir," *Liberty, Clay County*, June 17, 1834, f1 P31, Community of Christ Library-Archives, Independence, Missouri.

68. When Smith returned to Missouri in 1838 he taught that it was "the land where Adam dwelt" (D&C 117:8) and the "place where Adam shall come to visit his people" (D&C 116). Jessee, *Papers of Joseph Smith* 2:244–45. After Brigham Young succeeded Smith he repeated his predecessor's teaching concerning this subject. Kenney, *Wilford Woodruff's Journal* 5:33 (March 15, 1857) and 7:129; Van Wagoner, *The Complete Discourses of Brigham Young* 3:1744 (February 2, 1861), quoting *Brigham Young's Office Journal*, 204 (same date). See Brook Wilensky-Lanford, *Searching for the Garden of Eden* (New York: Grove Press, 2011) for other speculations concerning the location of the Garden of Eden.

PURIFICATION RITUALS

During Smith's return journey to Ohio, he recorded a revelation (known as the Fishing River Revelation) that confirmed that the long-promised endowment would take place in Kirtland rather than Jackson County: "It is expedient in me that the first elders of my church should receive their endowment from on high, in my house, which I have commanded to be built unto my name in the land of Kirtland."[69] Smith instructed his followers to delay their return to Jackson County until the Kirtland structure was completed and where church missionaries could be endowed.[70] The Mormon prophet also instructed the newly installed Quorum of the Twelve Apostles (most of whom were veterans of Zion's Camp) to "tarry at Kirtland until you are endowed with power from on high."[71]

Thereafter, Smith increasingly focused on the construction of the House of the Lord in Kirtland and introduced new purification ordinances to the High Priesthood to prepare them for the Pentecost-like spiritual outpouring that would take place during a solemn assembly in that structure.[72] These rituals included washings and anointings, which had Biblical antecedents and which were referenced in Royal Arch rituals. In October 1835 he told the Twelve that they would "attend to the ordinence [*sic*] of the washing of the feet and to prepare their hearts in all humility for an endowment with power from on high."[73]

69. D&C 105:33; "History of Joseph Smith," in *Times and Seasons* 6:22 (February 1, 1846), 1104–5. Smith met with a council of high priests to choose those who would be "the first elders to receive their endowment," and wrote a letter to the high council informing it that it could select additional elders to receive this ritual. Kimball, "Extracts from H. C. Kimball's Journal," *Times and Seasons* 6 (February 15, 1845): 804–5. Kimball recounted this same experience after arriving in Utah. Kimball, "Our Duties to God Paramount to all other obligations—Danger of Speculation," *Journal of Discourses*, 10:76–77 (October 2, 1862). See also *History of the Church* 2:112–13. Joseph Smith to Lyman Wight, Edward Partridge, John Corrill, Isaac Morley, and Others of the High Council, August 16, 1834, quoted in Jessee, *The Personal Writings of Joseph Smith*, 329. Prince notes that although there is no record that any additional elders were chosen, even the first elders who were chosen were not given any particular priority when the endowment was given two years later. Prince, *Power from on High* 16.
70. D&C 105 (Revelation of June 22, 1834). This revelation was first included in the 1844 edition of the Doctrine and Covenants as section 102.
71. *History of the Church* 2:197. Edward Partridge wrote a letter on August 31, 1833, in which he discussed the endowment given during the day of Pentecost and Christ's injunction to his apostles to tarry in Jerusalem to obtain the endowment. See "Dear Friends and Neighbors," *Messenger and Advocate* 1:4 (January 1835), 59–60. Oliver Cowdery reminded the Mormon authorities that they could not fulfill their missions until they were endowed. Kirtland High Council Minutes, February 21, 1835.
72. Hamilton, *Nineteenth-Century Mormon Architecture*, 34–37.
73. *History of the Church* 2:287; Jessee, *Personal Writings of Joseph Smith*, 61; Jessee, Ashurst-McGee, and Jensen, eds., *Journals 1: 1832–1839*, 68 (October 5, 1835).

In November he received a revelation that reminded the apostles that they "must all humble themselves before Me, before they will be accounted worthy to receive an endowment to go forth in my name unto all nations,"[74] and he told quorum members that "the ordinance of washing of feet" had not yet been restored "as it was in the days of the Saviour," but that it would be restored, and an endowment given, in a Solemn Assembly to be held in the House of the Lord. During the endowment those who were prepared would "abide the presence of the Saviour" and would see him.[75]

On January 16, 1836, Oliver Cowdery, John Corrill, and Martin Harris met the prophet at his home where a new ritual was introduced. Cowdery recorded that "after pure water was prepared, [we] called upon the Lord and proceeded to wash each other's bodies, and bath the same with whiskey, perfumed with cinnamon. This we did that we might be clearn [sic] before the Lord for the Sabbath, confessing our sins and covenanting to be faithful to God." Cowdery noted that "while performing this washing unto the Lord with solemnity, our minds were filled with many reflections upon the propriety of the same, and how the priests anciently used to wash before administering before the Lord."[76]

Thereafter, Smith and other church leaders continued to participate in the purification rituals and experience spiritual manifestations. On January 21, the apostles anointed each other's heads with oil, which they had previously consecrated, and they then "sealed" the anointings. Joseph Smith Sr. anointed his son and then sealed upon him "the blessings of Moses, to lead Israel in the latter days, even as [M]oses led him in days of old...[and]...the blessings of Abraham Isaac and Jacob." Smith reported, after the completion of these ordinances, that he saw visions of the Celestial Kingdom and celestial personages, including Adam, Abraham, and Michael, and received a revelation that "all who have died with[out] knowledge of this gospel, who would have received it, if they had been permitted to tarry, shall be heirs of the celestial kingdom of God." The "angels ministered," and "the power of the highest rested upon, us." It was also reported that some even "saw the face of the Saviour."[77]

The following day Smith performed washings, anointings, and sealings of the Twelve Apostles and the Presidency of the Seventy during a meeting

74. *History of the Church* 2:83 (November 3, 1835).

75. Ibid., 2:97, 99 (November 12, 1835).

76. Oliver Cowdery's Kirtland, Ohio, "Sketch Book," in Leonard Arrington, "Oliver Cowdery's Kirtland, Ohio, 'Sketch Book,'" *BYU Studies* 12:4 (1972): 416.

77. Ibid., 167–68, 170 (January 21, 1836); Arrington, "Sketch Book," 414. The revelation of the Celestial Kingdom is recorded in D&C 137. See also account in "Kirtland, Ohio, March 27th, 1836," *Messenger and Advocate* 2:6 (March 1836): 274–81, which was written by Oliver Cowdery. See Arrington, "Sketch Book," 9 (March 27, 1836).

that lasted until two a.m., and he recorded that "the gift of toungs [*sic*], fell upon us in mighty pour [*sic*], angels mingled their voices with ours, while their presence was in our midst, and unseasing prasis [*sic*] swelled our bosoms for the space of half an hour."[78]

These ordinances were repeated for the next two months, in preparation for the dedication of the Kirtland House of the Lord, and an ever-widening group of elders experienced the spiritual manifestations associated with them.[79] Stephen Post reported that on January 28 "there was a considerable of an outpouring of the spirit of the Lord many spoke in tongues, some saw visions and angels, many angels were in the room."[80] Oliver Cowdery wrote that during a meeting on February 6 there were "visions, many prophesied, and many spoke in tongues."[81] During this same period there continued to be ordinations to the High Priesthood.[82]

The purification rituals that Smith introduced in Kirtland, and that were later associated with the Nauvoo Temple, had both Biblical and Masonic antecedents. Some Masonic high degrees included "washing the hands, and sometimes the whole body" as a symbol of internal purification as well as anointing and the giving of a new name.[83] Some commentators have suggested that Thomas Smith Webb incorporated portions of these rituals, including the Knight Templar degree, when he introduced the Order of High Priesthood.[84] The Knight Templar ritual, as worked in the Baldwyn Encampment (ca. 1780), reportedly included anointing of body parts followed by the giving of a new name. The candidate was presented with a shield "in defense and protection of Virtue and Innocence and in distress, and of the Noble cause" and ceremonial robes that the candidate is instructed "never to be forgotten or laid aside."[85]

78. Jessee, Ashurst-McGee, and Jensen, *Journals 1: 1832–1839*, 172 (January 22, 1836).
79. Ibid., 171–72, 174–75, 181–82 (January 22 and 28, and February 6, 1836); Arrington, "Sketch Book," 5–9; *History of the Church* 2:287, 308, 379–82, 391–92; Jessee, *Personal Writings of Joseph Smith*, 88, 110, 174–77, 186–87; *Kirtland Elder's Quorum Record, 1836–1841*, 3–18. See also *Journal of Discourses* 2:31. Smith may not have introduced the ceremony in secret if he had adopted a broad interpretation of the Book of Mormon language concerning secret combinations. *History of the Church* 2:379–82, 286–88, 391–92.
80. Stephen Post Journal, January 28, 1836.
81. Arrington, "Sketch Book," 7 (February 6, 1836).
82. Stephen Post Journal, February 13, 1836.
83. Mackey, *Encyclopedia of Freemasonry* 1:454. The College of Priests Masons of the Red Cross of Constantine in England anointed a priest after the Order of Melchizedek with Holy Oil in the "Knight Priest" degree in the rite of Fratres Lucis (ca. 1780), Fratres Lucis, *Collectanea* 1 (1937), reprinted (1978), 142–43.
84. Stillson, *History of the Ancient and Honorable Fraternity*, 641.
85. I am indebted to Art de Hoyos for this connection. For a cryptic reference to this parallel, see Salem Town, *A System of Speculative Freemasonry*, 76. Jonathan Blanchard's exposure of an irregular ritual, the Grand Pontiff Degree, also contained references to anointing. Blanchard, *Scotch Rite Masonry Illustrated* 1:288–90.

Clyde Forsberg has speculated that there were connections between the Knight Templar or Christian degrees and Joseph Smith's goal to bridge the gap between "Ancients, or Royal Arch Masons, and their orthodox counterparts, dubbed Moderns but calling themselves Craft Masons" and in the process essentially reestablishing Christian Masonry.[86]

THE TEMPLE DEDICATION

Mark Hamilton has noted that although the architectural drawings for the Kirtland temple do not survive, they resembled surviving exterior drawings of the temple in Independence, Missouri, which "contemplated a structure with two and a half stories and two interior courts that were reached from a vestibule entrance" and an attic.[87] While neither Hamilton nor Laurel Andrews, who studied the architectural design of Mormon temples, noted any Masonic influences in the Kirtland temple, Clyde Forsberg argues that there are a number of Masonic design features on the inside and outside of the building.[88]

Although the Kirtland temple was constructed from east to west like Masonic temples (and the Temple of Solomon), this was common for many Catholic churches and other religious structures. Although Smith was certainly aware that Freemasons believed their temples preserved the rituals from Solomon's Temple, most lodges met in rented structures that were not dedicated exclusively to the Craft. Thus, it is unlikely that Smith sought or received inspiration from any existing Masonic structure for the design of the temple's exterior. But when he visited New York City (with Royal Arch Mason Newel K. Whitney) in October 1832, he could have observed several churches that were similar in appearance to the Kirtland temple's ultimate as-built appearance.[89]

Forsberg's argument concerning the interior space being reminiscent of a Masonic temple is more convincing. The temple's two main floors were

86. Forsberg, *Equal Rites*, 127–35.
87. Hamilton, *Nineteenth-Century Mormon Architecture*, 37. See also Laurel Andrews, *The Early Temples of the Mormons* (Albany: State University of New York Press, 1978), 32–33.
88. Clyde R. Forsberg, "Kirtland through the Christian-Masonic, Neo-Hebraic, Neo-Pagan Looking Glass: Architecture, Ritual, Gender, and Race," *The John Whitmer Historical Association Journal* 30 (2010): 176–205.
89. Jessee, *Personal Writings of Joseph Smith*, 287. During Smith's visit to Manhattan, the city's infrastructure extended to Union Square (16th Street and Fourth Avenue) and Fifth Avenue ended at 23rd Street. Smith's lodgings were located within easy walking distance from Mariner's Temple Baptist Church (3 Henry Street) and the Sea and Land Church (61 Henry Street, now the First Chinese Presbyterian Church). Smith also visited Albany and Boston during the same trip. D&C 84:114; *New England Christian Herald*, November 7, 1832. See H. Michael Marquardt, "Notes on the Document," *Signature Books Keepsake, No. 5* (Salt Lake City: Signature Books, 2010).

Kirtland Temple. Courtesy Utah State Historical Society.

referred to as a lower court and an upper court. The lower court was fitted with pews and was for general worship. The pulpits on the west side of the lower court were used by the Melchizedek Priesthood when it officiated and the pulpits on the east side were used by the Aaronic Priesthood when it officiated.[90] In a Master Masons Lodge the worshipful master sits and presides on the east end, with the treasurer to his right and the secretary to his left, and on the west end the senior warden (the second line officer) sits with the junior deacon to his right and the marshal to his left. The Kirtland temple had a lectern with three rows of pulpits (with three pulpits in each row) at each end. The upper court was not completed at the time of the dedication but both the lower court and the upper court were designed to be divided into smaller rooms or compartments when veils, which were mounted on the ceilings, were lowered to the floor. The structure's attic was partitioned into ten offices that were used by Smith and other church leaders.

Eliza R. Snow (1804–1887) described the lower court in which "each [row of pulpits] had curtains hanging from the ceiling overhead down to the top of the pulpit, which could be rolled up or down at pleasure, and when dropped down would completely exclude those within the apartment [those on the pulpit] from the sight of all others." These "curtains or veils hanging from the ceiling" could also be lowered "overhead down to

90. See Andrews, *Early Temples*, 46–51. Pulpits were eventually constructed in the upper court as well. The division of priesthood into Aaronic and Melchisedec was revealed in 1835 while the House of the Lord was being constructed. See D&C 107.

Interior of Kirtland Temple. Courtesy Community of Christ Archives.

the floor, so that the house could be used for different purposes."[91] These veils were not only reminiscent of Moses' tabernacle and Solomon's temple where deity could commune with His earthly oracles in the "holy of holies" but also a Royal Arch Chapter where the room where the ritual of the Royal Arch took place was separated by veils as candidates progressed from one stage to another.

On March 27, 1836, Smith dedicated the House of the Lord (as it was designated above the east entrance) during a ceremony that was attended by male priesthood holders, sisters, and lay members.[92] Even before the congregation entered the lower court, Smith dedicated and consecrated the pulpits. More than one thousand men and women were eventually seated in the pews before an additional eight hundred, who could not be accommodated, were informed that the same dedication ceremony would be repeated four days later.

During the dedication Joseph Smith Jr. was joined by Sidney Rigdon, Frederick G. Williams, Joseph Smith Sr., William W. Phelps, Hyrum Smith, David Whitmer, Oliver Cowdery, John Whitmer, the president of the high priests, his counselors, and two choristers on the west end of the building behind the pulpits of the Melchizedek Priesthood. The twelve apostles, the president of the elders, his counselors, his clerk, the High Council of Kirtland, and Warren Cowdery and Warren Parrish, who served as scribes, also sat in the west end. The pulpits on the east end, which were reserved for the Aaronic Priesthood, were occupied by the bishop of Kirtland and his

91. Eliza R. Snow Smith, *Biography and Family Record of Lorenzo Snow* (Salt Lake City, 1884), 12; Laurel Andrews, *Early Temples*, 47.
92. Jessee, Ashurst-McGee, and Jensen, *Journals 1: 1832–1839*, 200–211 (March 27, 1836).

counselors, the bishop of Zion and his counselors, the president of priests and his counselors, the presidents of teachers and his counselors, the president of deacons and his counselors, the High Council of Zion, the seven presidents of the Seventies, and one chorister.[93]

Sidney Rigdon read Psalms 96 ("Song of Praise") and 54 ("A Prayer for Protection from Enemies"), the choir sang, and Rigdon read from Matthew 8:18–20.[94] The congregation sustained church officers, including Joseph Smith as "prophet and seer."[95] The Mormon prophet delivered the dedicatory prayer that Sidney Rigdon, Oliver Cowdery, Warren Cowdery, and Warren Parrish had assisted in writing. Smith prayed that "the anointings of thy ministers be sealed upon them with power from on high. Let it be fulfilled upon them as upon those on the day of Pentecost [*sic*]; let the gift of tongues be poured out upon thy people, even cloven tongues as of fire, and the interpretation thereof. And let thy house be filled, as with a rushing mighty wind, with thy glory." He concluded the dedication by asking that "thine anointed ones be clothed with salvation, and thy Saints shout aloud with joy" and bear "testimony of the administering of angels."[96]

Rigdon offered a prayer and "led the way followed by the whole congregation acknowledging the Lord anointed: Hosanna! Hosanna! Hosanna to God & the Lamb Amen! amen! & Amen!" Stephen Post wrote that "this was done three times making 9 hosanna & 9 amens." Thereafter the sacrament, of bread and wine, was administered to the congregation.[97] While the sacrament was being administered Joseph Smith, Hyrum Smith, Oliver Cowdery, and Carlos Smith all testified concerning the truth of the restoration. Frederick G. Williams arose and testified that while Rigdon was reading the Psalms, an angel entered and sat between him and Joseph Smith Sr. David Whitmer said he saw angels.[98] Nancy Tracy also confirmed that "Heavenly Beings appeared to many" and that she "felt that it was heaven on earth."[99]

93. *History of the Church* 2:411.

94. "When Jesus saw the crowd around him, he gave orders to cross to the other side of the lake. Then a teacher of the law came to him and said, 'Teacher I will follow you wherever you go.' Jesus replied 'Foxes have holes and birds of the air have nests, but the Son of Man has no place to lay his head.'"

95. Arrington, *Kirtland Sketch Book*, 9 (March 19, 1836).

96. D&C 109:1–80; *History of the Church* 2:420–26; Jessee, Ashurst-McGee, and Jensen, *Journals 1: 1832–1839*, 207, 210.

97. Stephen Post Journal, March 27, 1836, Church History Library.

98. Smith recorded that the congregation sang "The Spirit of God Like a Fire is Burning" (written by W. W. Phelps) and that the chorus (in which the word "Hosanna" is used two times) was repeated six times during the song. See *History of the Church* 2:427.

99. Jill Mulvay Derr, Janath Russell Cannon, and Maureen Ursenbach Beecher, *Women of Covenant: The Story of the Relief Society* (Salt Lake City: Deseret Book, 1992), 16.

RESTORATION OF ALL THINGS

While women were permitted to attend the dedication of the temple, and witnessed these spiritual manifestations, the purification rituals were reserved for male priesthood holders.[100] Smith asked "official members" (i.e., those who had been ordained) to return to the Lord's House that evening so that "quorums [could be instructed] respecting the ordinance of washing of feet."[101] Oliver Cowdery reported that 316 "officers of the church" attended this meeting, and Stephen Post recorded that Smith "showed us the order of dedicating a house of God anciently: this evening was designed as a continuation of our pentecost" and also claimed that "Angels of God came into the room, cloven tongues rested upon some of the servants of the Lord like unto fire, & they spake with tongues & prophesied."[102]

George A. Smith, the prophet's cousin, "arose and began to prophesy, when a noise was heard like a sound of a rushing mighty wind, which filled the Temple,…many began to speak in tongues and prophesy; others saw glorious visions; and I [Joseph Smith] beheld the Temple was filled with angels." At this same time there was "a bright light like a pillar of fire resting upon the temple."[103] Cowdery recorded that "the Spirit was poured out—I saw the glory of God like a great cloud, come down and rest upon the house, and fill the same like a mighty rushing wind. I also saw cloven tongues, like as of fire rest upon many (for there were 316 present,) while they spake with other tongues and prophesied."[104]

Two days after the temple dedication the church leadership washed each other's feet, presumably in the upper court, to prepare themselves to introduce the ritual of washing of feet to church elders who were not present during the temple's dedication. When the leaders completed this ritual they "partook of the bread and wine" and the "Holy S[p]irit rested down upon us and we continued in the Lords house all night prophesying and giving glory to God."[105]

The following day approximately three hundred men, who had been ordained to the High Priesthood, "met in the House of the Lord to attend to the last ordinance of the endowment viz. the ordinance of the washing of

100. See Benjamin F. Johnson, *My Life's Review* (n.p. n.d.), 23. But Aaronic priesthood holders were also eligible. See Edward Partridge Journal, January 26, 1836, March 29, 1836.
101. Jessee, Ashurst-McGee, and Jensen, *Journals 1: 1832–1839*, 211.
102. Stephen Post Journal, March 27, 1836.
103. *History of the Church* 2:428; Edward Partridge Diary, March 27, 1836; Oliver Cowdery Diary, March 27, 1836.
104. Arrington, *Kirtland Sketch Book*, 9 (March 27, 1836)
105. See Jessee, Ashurst-McGee, and Jensen, *Journals 1: 1832–1839*, 212–16 (March 29–30, 1836).

the feet."[106] Smith "called the House to order" as "tubs, water, and towels were prepared" and bread and wine were brought to the house ("sufficient to make our hearts glad") for use in the sacrament.

Smith revealed a new covenant that eventually became a staple of Mormon temple rituals. He told the High Priesthood that "if any more of our brethren are slain or driven from their lands in Missouri by the mob that we will give ourselves no rest until we are avenged of our enemies [*sic*] to the uttermost." He recorded that this "covenant was sealed unanimously by a hosanna and Amen." Smith then announced that he had "completed the organization of the Church, and we had passed through all the necessary ceremonies" and that the brethren were permitted to depart for their missions to Zion and to other locations. Following this announcement Smith was exhausted and requested the Twelve Apostles to preside during the remainder of the meeting.[107]

Smith later wrote that during the evening and well into the following morning "the brethren continued exhorting, prophesying and speaking in tongues" and that "the Saviour made his appearance to some, while angels ministered unto others, and it was a penticost [*sic*] and enduement [*sic*] indeed, long to be remembered." He also rejoiced that "the sound shall go forth from this place into all the world, and the occurrences of this day shall be handed down upon the pages of sacred history to all generations, as the day of Pentecost, so shall this day be numbered and celebrated as a year of Jubilee and time of rejoicing to the saints of the most high God."[108]

Smith and Cowdery received a vision of Jesus Christ during a Sunday service held one week after the dedication and attended by a thousand (male and female) parishioners. During this meeting a veil was dropped in front of the pulpits during this manifestation and the congregation could not see the heavenly manifestations. Smith and Cowdery recorded that they were told by the Lord that "the hearts of thousands and tens of thousands shall greatly rejoice in consequence of the blessings which shall be

---

106. Stephen Post Journal, March 30, 1836, LDS Church History Library.

107. *History of the Church* 2:410–33; Jessee, Ashurst-McGee, and Jensen, *Journals 1: 1832–1839*, 213–15. Additional washings, anointings, and washing of feet were performed on April 3–6, 1837. *History of the Church* 2:410–33, 475–77; Jessee, *Personal Writings of Joseph Smith*, 145, 182–84. Although this ordinance was performed by Jesus for his apostles at the Last Supper (see John 13:4–6), it is now apparently reserved only for the second anointing.

108. Jessee, Ashurst-McGee, and Jensen, *Journals 1: 1832–1839*, 215–16. Brigham Young later recalled that Truman Angell and he witnessed "a Circle of about 40 persons dressed in white robes & caps in the upper Story of the Temple.... There was no person in that room at the time that was mortal yet the room was filled with light & many personages did appear Clothed in white & frequently went to windows and looked out So that the Brethren in the street Could see them plainly." Kenney, *Wilford Woodruff's Journal* 5:120 (November 8, 1857).

poured out, and the endowment with which my servants have already been endowed and shall hereafter be endowed." Moses appeared and "committed unto them the Keys of the gathering of Israel," Elias appeared and "committed the dispensation of the gospel of Abraham," and Elijah appeared to "turn the hearts of the Fathers to the children, and the children to the fathers, lest the whole earth be smitten with a curse" and consigned to Smith and Cowdery "the Keys of this dispensation."[109] Post later wrote when "the house was divided into four parts by the curtains & they [the Brethren] prophesied, spake and sang in tongues in each room. We fasted until even when we partook of bread & wine in commemoration of the marriage supper of the Lamb."[110]

Wilford Woodruff, John Taylor, and other priesthood holders who were not in attendance at the first Solemn Assembly also received the purification ordinances and their endowments after the temple was dedicated.[111] When Woodruff received his endowment in 1837 he recorded "the events of each day of the endowment…for the benefit of the generation to come." On the first day Woodruff received his first complete washing "from head to foot in soap & watter [sic]" in the upper rooms of the temple followed by "clear water in perfumed spirits." Later he "spent the evening with several Elders in Prayer before God & the Power of God rested upon us." The next day Woodruff was again in the "upper part" of the temple where he was washed in preparation for his anointing. During his anointing various blessings were pronounced and then his anointing was sealed. Woodruff remained in the temple during the entire evening "in prayer & fasting before God."

Woodruff attended a "solemn assembly" two days after being anointed and sealed, which he described as "something similar to the Pentecost that St. Paul speak [sic] of at Jerusalem." He met with members of the High Priesthood in the "upper part of the house" where the First Presidency "confirmed & sealed upon our heads all the blessings of our ordination, anointing, & Patricarchal [sic] with a seal in the presence of God & the Lamb & holy angels that they should all be fulfilled upon our heads than not one jot or tittle should fail & the seal was confirmed upon our heads with a shout of all the anointed with uplifted hand to heaven."

109. Jessee, Ashurst-McGee, and Jensen, *Journals 1: 1832–1839*, 222; D&C Sec. 110. See also David John Buerger, "'The Fullness of the Priesthood': The Second Anointing in Latter-day Saint Theology and Practice," *Dialogue: A Journal of Mormon Thought* 16 (Spring 1983): 15–16.
110. Stephen Post Journal, March 30, 1836, LDS Church History Library.
111. See *History of the Church* 2:475–77; Charles C. Rich Diary, Vol. 5, Ms 889, Church History Library; "Kirtland Elder's Quorum Record," March 29, 1837; Kenney, *Wilford Woodruff's Journal*, April 3, 1837. In fact there were a few endowments given until 1839. See Manuscript History of Brigham Young, November 17, 1839.

Woodruff "joined the congregation of the Saints in the lower court" after he received his endowment where "the veils were closed & each apartment commenced the duties of the day." These duties included the washing of the feet of the anointed. After this was completed the veils, which divided the room into four parts, were lifted, but the pulpits remained still veiled and the presidency addressed the congregation from that location and there was speaking in tongues and other spiritual manifestations.[112]

John Taylor, who was baptized after the first Solemn Assembly, received his endowment after he was ordained an apostle and called to serve a mission in England. He visited Kirtland in 1838 after Smith, Rigdon, and other church members had left the state in the wake of the Kirtland Bank failure. He was greeted by Brigham Young, Heber C. Kimball, and George A. Smith and then anointed before he experienced the same type of spiritual manifestations that others had before him.[113]

MASONIC CONNECTIONS

Mormon historian Ken Godfrey has observed that "the number of Mormons in the church, together with Joseph Smith's close association with [W. W.] Phelps, suggests the possibility that the Prophet and other Mormons may have been acquainted with some aspects of the Masonic ceremony before they settled in Illinois."[114] John Brooke expanded the possibility of "Masonic influence at Kirtland" by noting that such influence is perceptible in Smith's revelations, which include "detail about priesthoods

---

112. Kenney, *Wilford Woodruff's Journal*, April 3 to April 6, 1837. Before Woodruff received his endowment he studied Rev. Royal Robbins, *Outlines of ancient and modern history on a new plan, Embracing biographical notices of illustrious persons, and general views of the geography, customs and society of ancient nations*, 2 vols. (Hartford: Edward Hopkins, 1830). Robbins divided the six-thousand-year history of the world into ten periods and focused, although not exclusively, on Biblical events. He discussed the iniquity of Cain, Ham, and Canaan, the virtue of Enoch, the flood, the tower of Babel, the life of Abraham, and the building of Solomon's Temple. Woodruff commented in his journal that Robbins's book "strikes the reflecting mind with deep sensibility to contemplate the scenery of the rise progress decline & fall of the Nations and the kingdoms of the earth from the days of ADAM untill 1837 years after Christ.... And it is equally interesting to contemplate the day that is now at hand & hath already began in fulfillment of Ancient prophets in bringing the Church of Christ out of the wilderness in establishing Israel upon those lands by a Theocratical government in fulfillment of the covenants God made with Abram Isaac & Jacob." Kenney, *Wilford Woodruff's Journal* 1:127–36 (April 2–6, 1837). Subsequent editions of Robbins's popular work were published in 1834, 1835, 1836, 1837, and thereafter.
113. David John Buerger, *The Mysteries of Godliness: A History of Mormon Temple Worship* (San Francisco: Smith Research Associates, 1994), 34.
114. See Kenneth W. Godfrey, "Joseph Smith and the Masons," *Journal of the Illinois State Historical Society* 64 (Spring 1971): 82.

and temples, and a new language of sealing, binding, purity, and 'fullness' becoming more and more pronounced."[115]

While Brooke and Forsberg have opened up a serious discussion concerning connections during the Kirtland period, they have also been criticized for exaggerating such influences. John-Charles Duffy observed that many Mormon reviewers criticized John Brooke's *The Refiner's Fire* because he "had overlooked parallels to the Bible and Christian tradition that offered more instructive analogues to Mormon belief and practice" and that "hermetic connections before the Nauvoo period are weak or poorly documented."[116]

While biblical connections are primary, it is also possible that Smith and other Mormons often understood the same scriptures through a Masonic lens. When Smith introduced the high priesthood, purification rituals, and temple worship, all of these innovations had both Biblical and Masonic antecedents and he emphasized that he was restoring all of these practices from the primitive church. If Smith was inspired by Freemasonry in Kirtland he would have recognized that Masonic legends and rituals were elaborations of Biblical history and that Masons claimed that their rituals were descended from Solomon's Temple. Stephen Post, who participated in the Kirtland endowment, wrote in 1836, "Now having attended through the endowment I could form an idea of the endowment anciently for God's ordinances change not."[117]

But while Smith initially believed that the high priesthood had "passed through all the necessary ceremonies" associated with the Kirtland endowment, he later extrapolated the ritual to take on an even more recognizable Masonic flavor. He expanded the Kirtland ritual (which was limited to the preparatory ordinances of washings and anointings) to include the taking of oaths as well as passwords and signs.[118] Those developments, which would take place in Nauvoo, would provide even more transparent evidence that Smith believed that Freemasonry retained some elements of the primitive church that he could restore to its pristine condition.

115. Brooke, *The Refiner's Fire*, 207, 379n90.
116. Duffy, "Clyde Forsberg's *Equal Rites*," 13, 16.
117. Stephen Post Journal, March 30, 1836.
118. "[W]e had no basement in it, nor a font" for performing baptisms for the dead, Brigham Young later recalled, "nor preparations to give endowments for the living or the dead." Van Wagoner, *Complete Discourses* 5:3101, quoting Brigham Young, "Dedication of the St. George Temple," *Journal of Discourses* 18:303 (January 1, 1877).

Pharaoh's Curse

JOSEPH SMITH'S THINKING about the status of African Americans evolved throughout his prophetic career and to some extent reflected the attitudes of his contemporaries who questioned the morality of slavery but were not prepared to welcome African American men and women into their homes, churches, or clubs. Smith's attitudes concerning race were probably also influenced by the legends and policies of American Freemasonry. Masons believed that Africans were descended from Cain and Ham and that they had perverted pure Freemasonry and established a spurious form of the Craft. More significantly, American Freemasons developed policies that prohibited anyone with African descent from joining their lodges, participating in their rituals, or visiting their temples.

MASONIC LEGENDS

Masonry's exclusionary policies were eventually connected to its legendary history and old charges. James Anderson's *Constitutions* recounts a fanciful history in which Adam was the first Mason and both Cain and Ham—whom he, like many of his contemporaries, identified with the African race—were also members of the Craft. A rival society, known as the Khaibarites, teased the Freemasons about this legend in verse:

> Hence Cain was for the Craft renown'd,
> And mighty Nimrod was a Mason.
> Cain founded not his City fair,
> Till mark'd for murthering of Abel:
>
> Cain was their Head before the Flood,
> And Ham the first Grand Master after.

No Ham accurs'd or Vagrant Cain,
In the *Grand Khaibar* can you see,
No Nimrod with Ambition vain
E'er tainted this Society.[1]

Laurence Dermott, the intellectual leader of the ancients, who may have been aware of these criticisms, purged both Cain and Ham from pure Masonry. His modified history concluded that "Cain and the builders of his city were strangers to the secret mystery of Masonry, that there were but four Masons in the world when the deluge happened; that one of the four, even the second son of Noah, was not a master of the art."[2] Dermott may have been influenced by Chevalier Andrew Michael Ramsay, who taught that there was a distinction between primitive and spurious Freemasonry and advanced a two-race theory.

"The legends and truths which were transmitted pure through the race of Seth, were altered and corrupted by that of Cain," according to Albert Mackey, a nineteenth-century Masonic writer, and "this schism from the pure and original source has been designated by the name of the Spurious Freemasonry." After the flood, according to this theory, "Ham [who] had been long familiar with the corruptions of the system of Cain...propagated the worst features of both systems among his descendants."[3] Some Masons believed that Primitive Freemasonry was almost completely perverted when the Tower of Babel was constructed, but that the Master's Word was preserved in the vaults below Solomon's Temple, which was so important in the restoration of pure Masonry.[4]

1. Douglas Knoop, G. P. Jones, and Douglas Hamer, *Early Masonic Pamphlets* (Manchester: Manchester University Press, 1945), 186–87. Anderson's legendary history enabled the critics of Freemasonry (including seceding Masons) to ridicule the Craft by claiming that it "originated among the wicked descendants of Ham." Stearns, *An Inquiry*, 36–37. Knoop and Jones note that Anderson's history "provoked...sarcastic references from Dermott in *Ahiman Rezon*." Knoop and Jones, *A Short History of Freemasonry*, 76–77.
2. Dermott, *Ahiman Rezon*, xiv. *See also* Laurence Dermott, *The Constitution of Free-Masonry, or Ahiman Rezon* (London: T. Harper Jr., 1807), v; and Laurence Dermott, *Ahiman Rezon, or a help to all that are or would be Free and Accepted Masons* (Philadelphia: Leon Hyneman, 1855), 11.
3. See Albert Mackey, *A Lexicon of Freemasonry* (London: Griffin, 1873), 323 (entry on "Spurious Freemasonry"); and Mackey, *An Encyclopedia of Freemasonry* 2:584, 706–8.
4. Mackey wrote that Ramsay advanced his two-race theory in *Philosophical Principles of Natural and Revealed Religion unfolded in Geometrical Order*, which was published posthumously in 1749. See Mackey, *An Encyclopedia of Freemasonry* 2:584, 706–8. See Brooke, *The Refiner's Fire*, 206, concerning Ramsay's posthumous book which included passages concerning "ethereal fluid," "two creations (spiritual and material), and of the scriptural basis of a doctrine of spiritual preexistence." See also Andrew Michael Ramsay, *The Philosophical Principles of Natural and Revealed Religion* Part Second (Glasgow, 1749), 8–15, 215–99.

William Hutchinson, who was a Modern, may have adopted this modified history. "Through the endowments of memory," he wrote, "Adam would necessarily teach to his family the sciences which he had comprehended in Eden," which included the "first stage of masonry" and "originated in the mind of Adam." While Masonry "descended pure through the antediluvian ages," Hutchinson wrote that "the family of Cain (who bore the seal of the curse on his forehead) was given up to ignorance" and even though Masonry was "taught by Ham, and from him, amidst corruptions of mankind, flowed unpolluted and unstained with idolatry to these our times," his posterity "forsook the doctrines of their predecessor...and worshipped the Sun, which was regarded in the first ages after the delouge [*sic*], as the Type or Emblem of the Divinity."[5]

Masonic historian Bernard Jones has noted that "the Old Charges [which required Freemasons to be "freeborn"] were written in full consciousness of the existence of feudal serfdom" during a time when there were certainly no Masons of African descent in England.[6] But another English Masonic writer, Colin Dyer, has observed more convincingly that Anderson's *Constitutions*, which required that "men made Masons must be Freeborn, or no Bondmen,"[7] was written when "servitude and slavery were still in existence...[and] that masonry has always been restricted to men who were free—and until 1848 the qualification in England was actually to have been *born* free."[8] When Masonry was established in America there were broader implications and more severe consequences for Anderson's requirement that Masons be "freeborn" and for Dermott's removal of Cain and Ham from the history of ancient Freemasonry.

AFRICAN LODGE

In 1775 Regimental Lodge No. 441, a regular military lodge listed on the Irish Registry and located near Boston, initiated, passed, and raised fifteen free African American volunteers.[9] Several months later, when the military

5. Hutchinson, *The Spirit of Masonry*, xx, xxii, 6–7, 9, 11, 169–70.
6. See Jones, *Freemasons' Guide and Compendium*, 152–58; and Knoop and Jones, *A Short History of Freemasonry*, 26–38, 76–77.
7. *Anderson's Constitutions of 1723, with Introduction by Bro. Lionel Vibert* (Washington, D.C.: The Masonic Service Association of the United States, 1924), 51.
8. Colin Dyer, *Symbolism in Craft Masonry* (London: Lewis Masonic, 1983), 10.
9. Gordon Wood has observed that "finding African Americans among the New England troops in 1775 was an eye-opening experience for [Washington], and he began advocating the recruitment of free blacks into the Continental army.... [T]hrough the years of the war Washington had led a racially integrated army composed of as many as five thousand African American soldiers." Gordon S. Wood, *Revolutionary Characters: What Made the Founders Different* (New York: Penguin Press, 2006), 39. But David McCullough concluded that

Lodge left the area after the outbreak of the Revolutionary War, these African American Masons were apparently granted permission to meet, form processions, and conduct funerals but they were no longer members of a lodge and they could not confer degrees.[10] Prince Hall (1735?–1807), who was a former slave, was the leader of these African American Freemasons.

During the American Revolution Massachusetts Masonic lodges began organizing independent obediences, and in 1782 most of the lodges that had been granted warrants by the Scottish Provincial Grand Lodge organized the Massachusetts Grand Lodge. Nevertheless, one lodge, St. Andrews Lodge, refused to join the newly formed Grand Lodge and remained in the registry of Scottish Grand Lodge until 1809. In 1790 the lodges that the English Provincial Grand Lodge (Moderns) had organized the competing St. John's Grand Lodge and elected their own grand master.[11]

Prince Hall and his African brethren met as Masons during this period of reorganization and actively encouraged Bostonians to provide educational benefits to African Americans. In addition, according to later historical accounts, the lodge "petitioned the Grand Lodge of Massachusetts for a charter" and "although the petition appeared in proper form, it was rejected; the cause of which sprang from that difference which color has established." Thereafter, the Masons of African Lodge voted to "petition to foreigners for what is denied us at home."[12]

In 1784 Prince Hall sent two letters to Brother Moddy, a Mason in London, requesting his assistance in obtaining a warrant to establish a lodge. The English Grand Lodge (Moderns) issued a warrant during the same year—the last warrant it issued to American Masons—but the document did not arrive in Boston until 1787.[13] Thereafter Prince Hall's lodge was inscribed upon the register of the Grand Lodge of England as African Lodge

---

Washington, "like most southerners" initially issued orders that "Negroes" were not to be enlisted but that he soon reversed this order because "new recruits [were] urgently needed and numbers of free blacks wanting to serve." David McCullough, *1776* (New York, Simon & Schuster Paperbacks, 2005), 36–37.

10. For the history of Prince Hall Masonry, see William Alan Muraskin, *Middle-Class Blacks in a White Society: Prince Hall Freemasonry in America* (Berkeley: University of California Press, 1975); and Loretta J. Williams, *Black Freemasonry and Middle-Class Realities* (Columbia: University of Missouri Press, 1980). See also J. G. Findel, *History of Freemasonry*, 2nd ed. (Philadelphia: J. B. Lippincott, 1869), 356–58; William H. Upton, "Prince Hall's Letter Book," *Ars Quatuor Coronatorum* XIII (1900): 54–65; Donn A. Cass, *Negro Freemasonry and Segregation* (Chicago: Ezra A. Cook Publications, Inc., 1957), 20–30; and George Draffen, "Prince Hall Freemasonry," *Ars Quatuor Coronatorum* 89 (1976): 70–91.

11. Bullock, *Revolutionary Brotherhood*, 115–21.

12. Lewis Hayden, *Caste Among Masons: Address Before Prince Hall Grand Lodge of Free and Accepted Masons of the State of Massachusetts at the Festival of St. John the Evangelist, December 27, 1865*, 2nd ed. (Boston: Printed by Edward S. Coombs & Company, 1866), 22.

13. George Draffen, "Prince Hall Freemasonry."

No. 459. On May 2, 1787, the *Massachusetts Sentinel* reported that the lodge had received its warrant, soon thereafter it was regularly organized, Prince Hall was installed as Master, and the lodge began to initiate new Masons who were for the most part African Americans.[14]

Shortly thereafter several press reports were published that lampooned Freemasons for their apparent association with African Americans. The *Massachusetts Sentinel* published a poem in May 1787 that touted that "ev'n Afric's sons—ill-fated race!/Now feel its genial heart;/With charter'd rights, from England's Duke,/The Sable Lodges meet."[15] The following year the *Columbian Magazine* published a verse that parodied a Mason's oration delivered in African Lodge. The author described the lodge room, which displayed "a representation of the antediluvian city built by Cain, and on the other of Noah's Ark" as well as the orator's speech in which he claimed that "Cain was the first mason," that Ham was "our second founder," and that "men may be masons, tho' not free."[16]

Even though African Lodge had a charter from regular Masons in England, the white Masons who controlled Massachusetts Masonry refused to recognize the lodge or to grant its members visitation rights in their lodges.[17] In 1792, Massachusetts Grand Lodge and St. John's Grand Lodge merged to form one united Grand Lodge of Massachusetts.[18] Although the new grand lodge invited other lodges that were chartered by English Moderns to join their new coalition, the new obedience "never once invited the black Lodge No. 459 to do so."[19] Despite the Grand Lodge's rejection of African Lodge, it still had its English charter, a valid claim of Masonic

14. *Proceedings of the Grand Lodge of the F.A. & H.F. of F.A.M. of the Commonwealth of Massachusetts, March 9–December 27, 1870* (Boston, 1871), 41.

15. "Masonry," *Massachusetts Sentinel*, May 5, 1787, cited in Laurie F. Maffly-Kipp, *Setting Down the Sacred Past: African-American Race Histories* (Cambridge: The Belknap Press of Harvard University Press, 2010), 31.

16. "The African Lodge, An Oration delivered before the Grand Master, Wardens and Brethren of the most Ancient and venerable Lodge of African Masons," *Columbian Magazine* 2:8 (August 1788): 467, reprinted in *The New England Mason* 2:11 (November 1875): 543–49.

17. In 1791 *Fleets' Almanac* published a list of Masonic lodges in Boston and stated that "there is also a regular African Lodge in Boston." *Fleets' Pocket Almanack for the Year of Our Lord 1792* (Boston: T. & J. Fleet, 1791), 94–95. It was listed as a lodge under the jurisdiction of St. Andrews Grand Lodge which Thomas Smith Webb wrote was made up of Ancients, chartered by the Grand Lodge of Scotland, and remained independent of the competing grand lodges when they unified. See Webb, *The Freemason's Monitor*, 196–206.

18. In 1792 *Fleets' Pocket Almanack* reported the unification of the two competing grand lodges and that "the African Lodge in Boston, meet the first Tuesday in every month at the Golden Fleece." *Fleets' Pocket Almanack for the Year of Our Lord 1793* (Boston: T. & J. Fleet, 1792), 80–82.

19. William Upton, *Negro Masonry* (Cambridge, MA: The M.W. Prince Hall Grand Lodge, 1902), 52, 138.

regularity that "still corresponded with London as if it were a subordinate lodge." But during this same period it began to exercise some of the prerogatives normally reserved for a grand lodge.[20]

In 1797 African Lodge granted permits to African American Masons residing in Providence, Rhode Island, and Philadelphia, Pennsylvania, who complained that they could not obtain warrants from any grand lodge.[21] Peter Mantore, one of the black Masons in Philadelphia, explained that "white Masons have refused to grant us a Dispensation, fearing that black men living in Virginia would get to be Masons too."[22]

In 1808, shortly after Prince Hall died, African Lodge changed its name to Most Worshipful Prince Hall Lodge and its representatives met with the lodges that had been organized in Philadelphia and Providence and organized the African Grand Lodge, which was later changed to Prince Hall Grand Lodge.[23] Five years later, when the competing "Moderns" and "Antients" in London agreed to unify (which was made easier since their respective Grand Masters were biological brothers), the United Grand Lodge erased African Lodge from its list of lodges and the Prince Hall Masons lost their connection with the English Masons who had granted their warrant.[24]

The United Grand Lodge of England also erased the Craft's legendary history from its book of constitutions, apparently because the Moderns and Ancients could not reconcile their conflicting versions that appeared in Anderson's *Constitutions* and Dermott's *Ahiman Rezon*.[25] But Massachusetts' Masons continued to subscribe to the Ancients' legendary history,

20. Christopher Haffner, *Regularity of Origin* (Hong Kong: The Paul Chater Lodge and Lodge Cosmopolitan, n.d. [1986]), 54. According to Haffner, African Lodge "started referring to itself as 'African Grand Lodge'" during this period and that "it seems that really it was trying to act as a Provincial Grand Lodge." See also Christopher Haffner, *Workman Unashamed: The Testimony of a Christian Freemason* (London: Lewis Masonic, 1989), 23–27. According to George Draffen, African Lodge continued to communicate with the Grand Lodge of England (Moderns) until 1797. During that year African Lodge's number was changed to African Lodge No. 370. See Draffen, "Prince Hall Freemasonry," 77–78; and Wells, *The Rise and Development of Organized Masonry*, 146–47.

21. Cass, *Negro Freemasonry and Segregation*, 139; Upton, *Negro Freemasonry*, 11–12.

22. Joanna Brooks, *American Lazarus: Religion and the Rise of African-American and Native American Literatures* (Oxford: Oxford University Press, 2003), 140.

23. Upton, *Negro Freemasonry*, 134–35.

24. From 1792 to 1813 the Massachusetts' press referred to African Lodge as a regular lodge. See *Fleets' Pocket Almanack* for 1794, 1795, 1796, and 1797; *Fleets' Register and Pocket Almanac* for 1798, 1799, and 1800; and *The Massachusetts Register and United States Calendar* for the years 1801 through 1813. In 1813 African Lodge was also mentioned, with other Boston lodges, in *The Gentleman's Pocket Register, and Free-Mason's Annual Anthology, for the Year of Our Lord 1813* (Boston: Charles Williams, 1813), 209–49, but it was not mentioned in either *The Massachusetts Register* or *The Gentleman's Pocket Register* after the English Ancients and Moderns were unified in 1813.

25. Pick and Knight, *The Pocket History of Freemasonry*, 106.

and David Vinton's *The Masonic Minstrel*, which was published in 1816, confirmed that "Cain and the builders of his city were strangers to the secret mystery of masonry" and that Ham "was not a master of the art."[26]

In 1827 Prince Hall Grand Lodge, which developed its own independent lodge system after being rebuffed by white lodges, declared that it was "free and independent of other lodges" including the Grand Lodge in London.[27] They later claimed that they "imitated our white brethren in declaring our independence, in the hope and belief that we should receive succor and support from them."[28] Thus, at the dawn of the American anti-Masonic movement, Prince Hall Freemasonry declared itself independent from the American grand lodges that had refused to recognize the regularity of Prince Hall Freemasonry or to initiate African Americans into their own regular lodges. Walker Lewis (1798–1856), one of the Prince Hall Masons who signed this declaration, would eventually join the LDS Church.[29]

LEGALISMS, LEGENDS, AND RACISM

Massachusetts Masons justified their policy of not recognizing African Lodge, excluding black Masons visitation rights, and refusing to initiate blacks into their lodges by resorting to legalistic arguments that their lodge (and later grand lodge) were not properly created under Masonic law and that men of African descent were not freeborn, and were therefore ineligible under Masonry's ancient landmarks.[30] The argument that African Lodge was not legally constituted was originally premised on the claim that the "Modern" Grand Lodge in London, which chartered African Lodge, had "invaded" the jurisdiction of the Massachusetts Grand Lodge and that the charter was therefore invalid and that lodges could not be chartered by

26. David Vinton, *The Masonic Minstrel* (Dedham, MA: H. Mann and Co., 1816), 337. Knoop and Jones have noted that "the views of the two Grand Lodges on the subject were so divergent that the historical section was omitted when the sixth edition of the *Book of Constitutions* [was published in 1815] and that it has been omitted from all subsequent editions." Knoop and Jones, *A Short History of Freemasonry*, 77.
27. Mark A. Tabbert, *American Freemasons* (New York: New York University Press, 2005), 64. The complete declaration is set forth in *Proceedings of Grand Lodge of Massachusetts (1870)*, 41–42.
28. Hayden, *Caste among Masons*, 55. For a discussion of American Freemasonry's transition from control by English, Scottish, and Irish grand lodges to the American system under which each state had a grand lodge, see Bullock, *Revolutionary Brotherhood*, 114–21.
29. Concerning Walker Lewis, see Connell O'Donovan, "The Mormon Priesthood Ban and Elder Q. Walker Lewis: 'An example for his more whiter brethren to follow,'" *The John Whitmer Historical Association Journal* 26 (2006): 47–99.
30. Paul Goodman has concluded that American Masons assumed that all free blacks had been rendered unfit for membership in the Order by experience of servitude." Goodman, *Towards a Christian Republic*, 12.

or recognize a foreign grand lodge. The grand lodge's earliest written policy that impacted African Lodge was written in 1797 and simply stated that the grand lodge would "not hold communication with, or admit as visitors, any Masons, residing in this State, who hold authority under, and acknowledge the supremacy of, any foreign Grand Lodge."[31] When African Lodge began to refer to itself as a grand lodge, the Massachusetts Grand Lodge claimed that this was contrary to the emerging practice of exclusive jurisdiction under which two grand lodges cannot exist in the same state.[32]

The Massachusetts Grand Lodge, like most American obediences, was an "Ancient" body that accepted Dermott's version of Masonic legends and also utilized these legends to support its exclusion of black men. They argued that all men of African descent, even those who were born free or were emancipated, were cursed and were therefore incapable of meeting the Masonic requirement of being freeborn.

Prince Hall and his followers challenged this legendary history by advancing Anderson's history, which supported their claims to the "ancient rights to the order."[33] In 1789 John Marrant (1755–1791), an African American Methodist preacher who was initiated in African Lodge, asserted that both Cain and Ham had been prominent Masons, that Cain studied architecture, arts, and sciences, and that he built a city on the east of Eden. He claimed that Ham's son introduced Masonry into Egypt, where his descendants built the Sphinx and other monuments, and that they eventually helped build the Tabernacle and Temple in Jerusalem. He concluded that since those Masons "were of different nations, and different colours, yet they were in perfect harmony among themselves," that "men of all nations and languages, or sects of religion, are admitted and received as members."[34]

Prince Hall made similar remarks to his lodge in 1792 and 1797 that reinforced Marrant's thesis that Africans were prominent participants in ancient Masonry. He emphasized that Jethro, an Ethiopian, had tutored Moses, that the Queen of Sheba has discussed "points of Masonry" with Solomon in his temple, and that Africans helped protect the temple in Jerusalem and eventually became members of the Knights of Malta. He concluded, based on this rich history, that if Massachusetts Masons failed to recognize African Lodge as "a charter'd lodge" or to "give the right hand

---

31. *Proceedings of the Grand Lodge of Massachusetts (1870)*, 37.
32. For an explanation of exclusive jurisdiction, see *Proceedings of the Grand Lodge of Massachusetts (1870)*, 24; Upton, *Negro Freemasonry*, 69–75.
33. Brooks, *American Lazarus*, 121–26.
34. See "A Sermon Preached on the 24th Day of June 1789," in *"Face Zion Forward": First Writers of the Black Atlantic, 1785–1798*, edited and introduced by Joanna Brooks and John Saillant (Boston: Northeastern University Press, 2002), 77–92. See also Brooks, *American Lazarus*, 87–113; and Maffly-Kipp, *Setting Down the Sacred Past*, 33–35.

of affection and friendship to whom it justly belongs let their colour and complexion be what it will," they were in violation of "Solomon's creed."[35]

The Grand Lodge rejected Prince Hall's version of Masonic legends and instead remained convinced by Dermott's theory. Nevertheless, despite the grand lodge's legalistic and legend-bound justifications, the Massachusetts exclusionary policy was primarily based on racial prejudice. Masonic historian Lynn Dumenil has explained that the Craft's commitment to equality prevented them from addressing "the order's de facto racial exclusion"[36] and that there were therefore "few racial overtones in white Masons' explanation for their policy. Nevertheless, some white Masons periodically acknowledged this motivation."[37]

In 1795 John Elliott, a white Massachusetts Freemason, wrote to American clergyman and historian Jeremy Belknap (1744–1798) that "the African Lodge though possessing a charter from England, meet by themselves; and white masons not more skilled in geometry, will not acknowledge them.... The truth is, they are *ashamed* of being on *equality* with blacks."[38] Another white Mason, Samuel Dexter (who admitted he had attended lodge for more than twenty-five years), told Belknap that he did not know "whether

35. See "A Charge Delivered to the Brethren of the African Lodge on the 25th of June 1792," in Brooks and Saillant, *"Face Zion Forward,* 191–98; "A Charge, Delivered to the African Lodge June 24, 1797 at Menotomy," in Brooks and Saillant, *"Face Zion Forward* 199–208. See also Brooks, *American Lazarus,* 115–50, and Maffly-Kipp, *Setting Down the Sacred Past,* 35–37.
36. Lynn Dumenil, *Freemasonry and American Culture, 1880–1930* (Princeton: Princeton University Press, 1984), 10. Dumenil concludes that although "racism and anti-Semitism existed in Masonic circles" that "little or no racism appeared in the Masonic press or official transactions. Masonic leaders' desire to be consistent with Masonic principles constituted the major impediment to overt racism. Central to Masonic ideology, of course, was the belief in the equality of man." Dumenil, *Freemasonry and American Culture,* 123.
37. Upton (*Negro Masonry,* 32) notes that "race prejudice is, and always has been, the real *fons et origo* of the opposition to our negro brethren" and "[b]ut for that, African Lodge No. 459 would have been as eagerly urged to come into the Grand Lodge formed in Massachusetts in 1792 as was St. Andrew's Lodge." The policy set in Massachusetts soon spread to other jurisdictions. In 1827 a committee of the Grand Lodge of Vermont recommended that a lodge made up of black Freemasons should not be granted a charter. See *Journal of the Most Worshipful Grand Lodge of Vermont* (Montpelier: Geo. W. Hill, 1827). Similarly, Masons noted after the Morgan affair that a black lodge that was organized in Philadelphia in 1796 could not obtain a charter and was therefore considered clandestine. *Reason versus Prejudice, Morgan Refuted* (Philadelphia: R. Desilber, 1828), 25. In 1831 the Grand Lodge of Maryland investigated whether masons were visiting black lodges and resolved to suspend or expel those who did. See *Proceedings of the R.W.G. Lodge of Maryland* (Baltimore, 1831).
38. "Belknap Papers II," *Collections of the Massachusetts Historical Society,* 5th series (Boston, 1877), 3:383. Belknap quoted Elliott in his response to an inquiry made by George Tucker, a Virginian, concerning the history of slavery and race relations in Massachusetts. See "Queries Respecting the Slavery and Emancipation of Negroes in Massachusetts," *Collections of the Massachusetts Historical Society, for the year 1795* (Boston: Printed by Samuel Hall, 1795; Reprinted by John H. Eastburn, 1835), 209–11.

they [African American Freemasons] modestly decline mixing with whites in public processions of the fraternity, or whether they occasionally desire admittance as visiting brothers at other lodges" but that "they cannot be denied without violating the design of the institution."[39]

During the same decade that Joseph Smith translated the Book of Mormon, George Oliver (1781–1861), a British Mason and Anglican pastor, explained the connection between the legendary history of Cain and Ham and the falling away and restoration of Freemasonry. In 1823 Oliver wrote that Masonry was introduced by God in the Garden of Eden, but that "the evil spirit of darkness…succeeded in working up the malevolent passions in the heart of Cain, until he apostatized from Masonry, and slew his brother Abel." Thereafter Cain was cursed and "his race forsook every good and laudable pursuit, along with Masonry, and degenerated into every species of impurity and wickedness" and "Masonry was at length wholly given up by this race." Ham, according to Oliver, also "renounced the worship of the true God" after his "unnatural conduct" brought forth "his father's curse," and he "began to practice the corrupted and spurious system of Masonry which Cain had introduced."[40]

According to Oliver, primitive Masonry was preserved by Adam's descendants through Seth who became Grand Master when Adam died.[41] After Seth's death Enoch became the Grand Master and preserved the most essential elements of the Craft, including the sacred name or word, on a gold plate that he buried on Mount Moriah, and placed two pillars above ground, one of which could withstand fire and the other water, which contained the principles of the Craft. After Enoch, Lamech became grand master, and his successor Noah continued to practice "primitive" Freemasonry after the flood, and Ham's descendants, and others who were alienated from the Old Testament prophets, practiced counterfeit forms of Freemasonry.

After the dispersion that occurred after the destruction of the Tower of Babel (c. 2200 BCE), a degraded form of Freemasonry was incorporated into the pagan mysteries. Oliver wrote that there were numerous examples of a falling away and restoration of true Masonry before the Christian era. Melchizedek instructed Abraham (1800 BCE) who became a "perfect master of the art" before he was called to "restore the true worship along with the purity of Masonry." Moses (c. 1300–1150 BCE), who "had been initiated

39. "Belknap Papers II," 3:387.
40. Oliver, *The Antiquities of Free-Masonry*, 46–51, 132–35. Oliver noted that Lamech, who was one of Cain's descendants, "introduced the evil of bigamy; and the effects of his example increased to such a degree, that before the flood, there existed amongst his posterity an indiscriminate community of wives, as well as a bestial intercourse with each other" (51). See also Oliver, *Historical Landmarks*; Mackey, *An Encyclopaedia of Freemasonry* 2:584, 706–8; and Mackey, *A Lexicon of Freemasonry*, 323 (entry on "Spurious Freemasonry").
41. Oliver, *The Antiquities of Free-Masonry*, 42–51.

into the spurious Freemasonry of the Egyptians," was mentored by Jethro who "communicated to him, as the last and best endowment he could bestow, the sublime secrets of Masonry." Solomon eventually introduced a Masonic ritual in his temple (c. 967 BCE) that was preserved until the creation of the Grand Lodge of London.[42]

During the same decade, American anti-Masons noted that English Moderns and Ancients (before their union) had advanced divergent legends concerning Cain and Ham. Henry Dana Ward wrote that "There is a discrepance [*sic*] in the traditions respecting Ham," that the Moderns taught "the first stage of Masonry was originated in the mind of Adam, descended pure through the antediluvian ages, was afterwards taught by Ham, and from him flowed, unpolluted and unstained with idolatry, to those of our times," whereas the Ancients taught that Ham "was not a master of the art," i.e., Ham was not "a master Mason."[43]

John G. Stearns argued, based on the Moderns' teachings that the Phoenicians and Egyptians were the descendants of Ham, that through "these filthy Canaanites and Egyptians the world has received the mysteries of Masonry" and that "it must appear with a high degree of certainty, that the ancient and honorable institution of freemasonry, originated among the wicked descendants of Ham."[44]

MASTER MAHON

Shortly after Joseph Smith organized the Mormon Church, he introduced teachings and revelations concerning race that have common elements with Masonic legends. In 1830 and 1831, the Mormon prophet announced that he had discovered remnants of the Book of Enoch, while he was translating the Book of Genesis, which confirmed that Enoch received a revelation in

42. Ibid., 1–130. Twenty-two years later Oliver discussed the dichotomy between "primitive freemasonry" and "spurious freemasonry." See Oliver, *Historical Landmarks*, 1:41–64. For a discussion of the "Oliverian theory," see Albert Gallatin Mackey, *The History of Freemasonry* (New York: The Masonic History Company, 1898), 143–50; and Mackey, *An Encyclopaedia of Freemasonry* 2:584, 706–8.
43. Ward, *Free Masonry*, 27. Ward quoted Hutchinson, *The Spirit of Masonry*, 169–70 ("Masonry…was originated in the mind of ADAM…was afterwards taught by HAM"), which is consistent with James Anderson's version of the legend. But Hutchinson also wrote that "the family of Cain (who bore the seal of the curse on his forehead) was given up to ignorance" (p. 7) and that the posterity of Ham forsook the doctrines of their predecessor" (p. 11). Ward cited Dermott, *Ahiman Rezon*, 13, and Vinton's *The Masonic Minstrel*, 337, for the Ancients' perspective.
44. Stearns, *An Inquiry*, 36–37. In 1828 a Masonic newspaper reported that anti-Mason Solomon Southwick delivered an oration in 1828 in which he claimed that "Masonry was the sole cause of introducing sin into our world, in the Garden of Eden!!!!" *American Masonic Record and Albany Saturday Magazine* 2:27 (August 2, 1828): 215. See Grunder, *Mormon Parallels*, 1629.

which he "beheld the residue of the people which were the sons of Adam; and they were a mixture of all the seed of Adam save it was the seed of Cain, for the seed of Cain were black, and had not place among them."[45]

Smith's translation of Enoch's record revealed that Satan and Cain entered into a secret alliance and that Cain proclaimed, "Truly I am Mahon, the master of this great secret, that I may murder and get great gain. Wherefore Cain was called Master Mahon, and he glorified in his wickedness."[46] Thereafter, Cain's evil descendant Lamech "entered into a covenant with Satan after the manner of Cain wherein he became Master Mahan of that great secret which was administered unto Cain by Satan."[47] Lamech killed Irad (the son of Enoch) "for the oath's sake" because he revealed portions of "that great secret which was administered unto Cain by Satan" and "there was a secret combination, and their works were in the dark, and they knew every man his brother."[48] Smith's translation revealed that "Canaan shall be his servant and a vail of darkness shall cover him that he shall be known among all men," and that "there was a blackness come upon all the children of Canaan, that they were despised among all people."[49]

45. Old Testament Manuscript 1, p. 16 (hereafter OT MS); JST Genesis 7:29, LDS Moses 7:22: "save it were the seed of Cain, for the seed of Cain were black, and had not place among them" (Joseph Smith Translation, Community of Christ Library-Archives). This translation appeared in "Extract from the Prophecy of Enoch," *The Evening and the Morning Star* 1 (August 1832): 2, and was consistent with Alexander Campbell's teachings that Ham's curse "which yet cleaves to that people; or rather the destiny of that branch of Noah's family, was at that time, sketched in a few words—Ham imports, as Dr. Hales affirms, *'burnt, or black.'*" "Ancient Historical Sketches. From the Millennial Harbinger," *The Telegraph* (July 19, 1831). See also Thomas Mann, *A Picture of Woonsocket* (n.p.: Printed for the Author, 1835), 23–24 ("View the negro in all his relations, and…does he not…seem rather to establish the opinion expressed by some of the most learned Commentators on the Bible, in relation to his color, to the curse pronounced on Cain for his transgression? And has he not the indelible mark of blackness stamped on his visage?"), as cited in Grunder, *Mormon Parallels*, 900. For a discussion of Cain and Freemasonry, see Vogel, "Echoes of Anti-Masonry," 288–90, 296.
46. OT MS 1, 9 (ca. June 1830). See Moses 5:31. This verse is not in the King James Bible. This translation was transcribed by Oliver Cowdery who spelled the word "Mahon" with the letter "o" which was changed to an "a" in later transcriptions and publications.
47. OT MS 1, 10 (ca. October 21, 1830). Moses 5:49. This verse is not in the King James Bible. This translation was transcribed by John Whitmer who spelled "Mahan" with an "a" rather than an "o". See also OT MS 2, 12–13, which was also transcribed around May 8 through April, 1831, by Whitmer who copied the previous transcription of the word "Mahon" made by Cowdery but who spelled it with an "a."
48. Moses 5: 49–51; Genesis 5:35–37 JST.
49. OT MS 1, 25, JST Genesis 9:30 (does not appear in the King James Bible or LDS Moses): "Canaan shall be his servant and a vail of darkness shall cover him that he shall be known among all men." The last reference, Old Testament Manuscript 1, 15; JST Genesis 7:10, LDS Moses 7:8: "There was a blackness come upon all the children of Canaan, that they were despised among all people," appeared in "Extract from the Prophecy of Enoch," *The Evening and the Morning Star* 1 (August 1832): 2, and "Olden Time," *The Evening and the Morning Star* 1 (April 1833): 5. John Brooke noted in *Refiner's Fire* that "the pure Masonic tradition was preserved from the Flood by Enoch, who buried the mysteries in his arched vault before

While the Bible mentions that a "mark" was placed on Cain it does not connect that curse with either skin color or with slavery. Similarly, Noah's curse of Canaan to be "a slave of slaves...to his brothers" is often extended to his father Ham but there is no connection between that curse and skin color.[50] David Goldenberg has pointed out that despite this paucity in the Biblical record to suggest such an explicit connection with such dire circumstances, this dual curse had made "its most harmful appearance in America" and had become "the ideological cornerstone for the justification of Black slavery."[51]

Goldenberg also noted that following Joseph Smith's translation of Enoch's record, "Cain's blackness became part of Mormon theology."[52] That translation contained the markers of the two-seed tradition advanced by George Oliver who maintained that Cain and Ham were spurious Masons who had injected evil into Masonry and that the descendants of Enoch and Melchizedek, who were righteous men, preserved primitive Freemasonry.[53] In Smith's revelation, Cain's alliance with the Devil earned him the title "Master Mahan" (perhaps referring to a master of a spurious Masonic lodge) and he thereafter created secret oaths and combinations.

SLAVERY AND ABOLITIONISM

When W. W. Phelps settled in Independence, Missouri, to edit *The Evening and the Morning Star* (the first Mormon periodical), he observed that African Americans were "descendants of Ham"[54] and dispatched a letter to the

---

being taken bodily up to heaven, and by Noah, who alone with his family was saved from the Flood." Eventually, after "Noah's son Ham became the new progenitor of spurious, Cainite Masonry...a debased tradition of pure Masonry was passed down from Noah to Solomon, to be revitalized with the discovery of Enoch's buried plates in the arched vault." Brooke, *The Refiner's Fire*, 165.

50. Winthrop D. Jordan, *White over Black, American Attitudes toward the Negro, 1550–1812* (Chapel Hill: University of North Carolina Press, 1968), 54. See Goldenberg, *The Curse of Ham*, 168–82, and Stephen R. Haynes, *Noah's Curse: The Biblical Justification of American Slavery* (Oxford: Oxford University Press, 2002).

51. David M. Goldenberg, *The Curse of Ham: Race and Slavery in Early Judaism, Christianity, and Islam* (Princeton: Princeton University Press, 2003), 175–77.

52. Goldenberg, *The Curse of Ham*, 178. See Lester E. Bush Jr., "Mormonism's Negro Doctrine: An Historical Overview," *Dialogue* 8:1 (Spring 1973): 21; Newell G. Bringhurst, *Saints, Slaves and Blacks: The Changing Place of Black People within Mormonism* (Westport, CT: Greenwood Press, 1981), for a discussion concerning Smith's changing views concerning race. Bringhurst argues in his essay "Four American Prophets Confront Slavery" that Joseph Smith took a strong antislavery position in the Book of Mormon.

53. A two-seed tradition was introduced in the Book of Mormon in which the descendants of Nephi, who were white, followed God's commandments while the descendants of Laman, who were dark skinned, followed a different path.

54. *Manuscript History* Book A-1:129 (July 1831). Phelps wrote this in the Manuscript

anti-Masonic newspaper *Ontario Phoenix* (without revealing that he had converted to Mormonism) to notify his former colleagues that "no danger need be feared from *secret societies*, or any other," in Jackson County. He also observed that "the people are proverbially idle or lazy, and mostly ignorant; reckoning no body equal to themselves in many respects, and as it is a slave holding state, Japeth will make Canaan serve him, while he dwells in the tents of Shem."[55]

Phelps would soon learn that Missouri slaveholders were very sensitive about the immigration of free blacks into their state because they feared they might foment unrest among the slave population. In fact the United States Congress postponed Missouri's entry as a state from 1820 to 1821 because it initially proposed a constitution that would have prevented all free blacks (whether citizens or not) from entering the state. By 1832 there were more than thirty thousand African slaves living in the state and no free blacks residing in Jackson County.

During the same year Joseph Smith received a revelation confirming that "slaves shall rise up against their masters, who shall be marshaled and disciplined for war."[56] Even though this revelation was not published it may have contributed to distrust of the Mormons. A Presbyterian preacher and slaveholder then circulated rumors that Mormons were attempting to convince "the blacks to become disobedient and leave, or rise in a rebellion against their masters." The Mormon settlers denied these charges and attempted to calm the fears of slaveholders by promising to "bring to justice every person who might, to their knowledge, violate the law of the land by stirring up the blacks."[57]

In 1833 Phelps readdressed the issue in an article he published in *The Evening and Morning Star* entitled "Free People of Color," which outlined

History (which is in his handwriting) but it was not published in the *Times and Seasons* until March 1, 1844. The phrase "descendents of Ham" was originally edited out of the "History of Joseph Smith," *Times and* Seasons (1 March 1844): 448, but when B. H. Roberts published the first volume of his *History of the Church* in 1902 he restored that phrase. See Smith, *History of the Church* 1:191.

55. "Extract of a Letter from the late Editor of this Paper," *Ontario Phoenix* 4:19 (September 7, 1831).

56. The revelation was first published in The Pearl of Great Price in 1851. It was later included in the 1876 edition of the Doctrine and Covenants. See D&C 87:4. Brigham Young noted in 1860 that the "revelation was reserved at that time" from the compilation of revelations made in 1835. "It was not wisdom to publish it to the world, and it remained in the private escritoire. Brother Joseph had that revelation concerning this nation at a time when the brethren were reflecting and reasoning with regard to African slavery on this continent, and the slavery of the children of men throughout the world." *Journal of Discourses* 8:58 (May 20, 1860).

57. *The Evening and the Morning Star* [Kirtland, Ohio], 2 (January 1834): 122.

the legal requirement that free blacks were required to be citizens of another state to be eligible to settle in Missouri. He cautioned his fellow churchmen concerning the gathering of African Americans to Missouri but noted, "So long as we have no special rule in the church, as to people of color, let prudence guide." He wrote that "slaves are real estate in this and other states, and wisdom would dictate great care among the branches of the church of Christ, on this subject."[58]

Phelps published a separate article in the same issue, entitled "The Elders Stationed in Zion to the Churches Abroad" which made reference to the Missouri statute and warned, "Great care should be taken on this point. The saints must shun every appearance of evil. As to slaves we have nothing to say." He then inexplicably concluded that "in connection with the wonderful events of this age, much is doing towards abolishing slavery, and colonizing the blacks, in Africa."[59] It is not surprising that local citizens, who did not trust Yankee Mormons, interpreted Phelps's editorial as a thinly veiled invitation for free blacks who had joined the LDS Church to immigrate to Missouri. They drafted a list of grievances against the church that included allegations that the Mormons had reneged on their previous agreement to refrain from "tampering with our slaves, and endeavoring to sow dissentions and raise seditions amongst them." They claimed that Phelps's articles sought to insure that "the introduction of such a caste [free blacks] amongst us would corrupt our blacks, and instigate them to bloodshed."[60]

When Phelps became aware that he had struck a hornet's nest he published an "extra," which he distributed as a handbill, in which he claimed that he had been "misunderstood" and "that our intention was not only to stop free people of color from emigrating to this state, but to prevent them from being admitted as members of the Church." He contended instead that "we are opposed to have free people of color admitted into the state; and we say, that none will be admitted into the Church; for we are determined to obey the laws and constitutions of our country."

In addition to this clarification, Phelps again inexplicably republished the same prediction he made in the prior issue that "much is doing towards abolishing slavery."[61] The local citizens were still not satisfied and accused

58. "Free People of Color," *The Evening and the Morning Star* 2 (July 1833): 109.
59. Ibid., 111.
60. Smith, *History of the Church*, 1:375.
61. "Extra," *The Evening and the Morning Star*, reprinted in *Times and Seasons* 6:818. See also Smith, *History of the Church*, 1:378–79. B. H. Roberts, in his notes to *History of the Church*, pointedly states that Phelps "goes too far when he says that no free people of color 'will be admitted into the Church.' Such was never the doctrine or policy of the Church." Ibid., 379. He also writes that "the Church had formulated no doctrine or policy with reference to slaves or free people of color; and in formulating his [Phelps's] judgment of this matter

the Mormons of providing free blacks with "all the necessary directions and cautions to enable the free blacks, on their arrival here to claim and exercise their rights of citizenship" and "that a considerable number of this degraded class were only waiting this information before they set out on their journey."[62] The Missouri citizens therefore demanded that the Mormons leave Jackson County. When the Mormons refused, a mob intervened and destroyed the press of *The Evening and the Morning Star*.

After this, most Mormons in Jackson County moved to other settlements in either Missouri or Ohio. Even in Ohio Smith and other church members remained extremely cautious when they made public statements concerning slavery or the civil rights of free blacks. When *The Evening and the Morning Star* recommenced publication, under the editorship of Oliver Cowdery in Kirtland, it denied "the charge, that the slaves in [Jackson] county were ever tampered with by it, or at any time persuaded to be refactory, or taught in any respect whatever, that it was not right and just that they should remain peaceable servants."[63]

After Phelps's inept handling of the crisis in Jackson County, he became a member of a three-man stake presidency in Clay County, Missouri, and wrote a letter to Oliver Cowdery in which he insisted that African Americans had black skin because they were cursed. He observed that "God causes the saints, or people that fall away from his church to be cursed in time, with a *black skin!* Was or was not Cain, being marked, obliged to inherit the curse, he and his children forever?" Cain's curse, according to Phelps, continued after the flood because "Ham, like other sons of God, might break the rule of God, by marrying out of the church [had]...a Canaanite wife, whereby some of the *black seed* was preserved through the flood." "From Cain's officiating at the altar," he continued, "I have no doubt that he was a high priest after the holy order of God, and he, for being overcome by Satan, when he had such great light, was marked and sent to a land of out-casts, to live by his own inventions, and the assistance of the evil one."[64]

Shortly thereafter the church adopted a policy of "governments and laws in general" (under which the gospel would be preached "to the nations of the earth" in order to "warn the righteous to save themselves from the

the reader must remember that the statement about not admitting such people into the Church is merely the view at that time of the editor of the *Star*, and by no means represents the policy of the Church." Ibid.

62. Warren A. Jennings, "Factors in the Destruction of the Mormon Press," *Utah Historical Quarterly* 35 (Winter 1967): 70.

63. Oliver Cowdery, "The Outrage in Jackson County, Missouri," *The Evening and the Morning Star* 2:16 (January 1834): 122. The monthly would be renamed the *Latter-day Saint Messenger and Advocate* later that year.

64. *Latter Day Saints Messenger and Advocate* 1 (March 1835): 82 (italics in original).

corruption of the world") that provided guidance to missionaries in the South. "We do not believe it right to interfere with bond-servants, neither preach the gospel to, nor baptize them," the policy stated, "contrary to the will and wish of their masters, nor to meddle with, or influence them in the least to cause them to be dissatisfied with their situations in this life, thereby jeopardizing the lives of men." Any such interference, according to the policy, would be "unlawful and unjust, and dangerous to the peace of every Government allowing human beings to be held in servitude."[65]

During this period Smith published two letters that confirmed that he believed that the gospel was intended for all men, bond and free, and explained in greater detail the church policy concerning servants. Smith denied charges that "in preaching the doctrine of gathering, we break up families, and give license for men to leave their families; women their husbands; children their parents, and slaves their masters, thereby deranging the order, and breaking up the harmony and peace of society." He assured the elders that the mission of the church was to preach "both to old and young, rich and poor, bond and free" in a proper manner.[66]

The Mormon prophet directed elders to obtain permission from the master of the house to preach the gospel to family and servants and taught that "when he enters into a house to salute the master of that house, and if he gain his consent, then he may preach to all that are in that house...his family, his wife, and his servants, his man-servants, or his maid servants, or his slaves." Smith also taught that "if he gain not his consent let him go not unto his slaves or servants" and that if a slave master did not permit missionaries to enter, "the responsibility be upon the master of that house, and the consequences thereof."[67]

Based on these developments it is not surprising that when several abolitionists sent correspondence to the *Northern Times*, a Kirtland newspaper edited by Frederick G. Williams, the editor informed his readers that he would not publish communications advocating abolitionism: "We are opposed to abolitionism, and whatever is calculated to disturb the peace and harmony of our constitution and country. Abolition does hardly belong to law or religion, politics or gospel, according to our idea on the subject."[68]

---

65. This policy, which was adopted on August 17, 1835, was published in the Doctrine and Covenants. D&C, sec. 102, 253–54 (Kirtland, Ohio, 1835,currently D&C 134:12). See also Smith, *History of the Church* 2: 247–49.

66. Joseph Smith, "To the elders of the Church of Latter Day Saints," *Latter Day Saints' Messenger and Advocate* (September 1835), 1:180–81.

67. Joseph Smith, "To the elders of the Church of Latter Day Saints," *Latter Day Saints' Messenger and Advocate* (November 1835), 2:210–11. See Jessee, *Personal Writings of Joseph Smith*, 371, 378–79.

68. *Northern Times* (Kirtland, Ohio), October 9, 1835, p. 2.

THE WRITINGS OF ABRAHAM

While Joseph Smith was thinking about the nuances of race, he purchased four mummies (including papyri inscribed with Egyptian hieroglyphics) that had been looted approximately fifteen years earlier in Egypt.[69] The mummies were discovered in Thebes by Bernardino Drovetti (1776–1852), the French consul general in Alexandria from 1803 to 1814 and again from 1820 to 1829,[70] who employed a group of men (known as the "La Banda Drovetti") to recover artifacts, mummies, and papyri in Egypt.[71] When Antonio Giovanni Pietro Lebolo (1781–1830), a member of Drovetti's band, returned to Piedmont he had at least eleven mummies that he later consigned to Albano Oblasser in Trieste, Italy.[72]

69. Egyptian hieroglyphics were first developed in 3500 BCE and were used until around 300 CE. The discovery of the Rosetta Stone, during Napoleon's Egyptian campaign at the end of the 1700s, enabled scholars to finally discover the key to translating Egyptian hieroglyphics. Jean-François Champollion (1790–1832), known as "the Founder and 'Father' of Egyptology," studied wax copies of the Rosetta Stone. The remnant contained a decree written in three scripts, hieroglyphs (found on most Egyptian documents), Demotic (a script used by literate Egyptians), and Greek (the language used by the government). Champollion studied the Greek script to translate the hieroglyphs. In 1824 he published his *Précis du système hiéroglyphique des anciens Égyptiens* which became the foundation of modern Egyptology. See Warren R. Dawson and Eric P. Uphill, *Who Was Who in Egyptology*, 2nd rev. ed. (London: The Egypt Exploration Society, 1972), 58–60.
70. Drovetti has been connected with members of a secret Masonic "Egyptian" society. See Luigi Arnaldi, ed., *Carte segrete e atti ufficiali della polizia austriaca in Italia* (Capolago, Italy: Tipografia Helvetica, 1851), 1:117–21. See also Dawson and Uphill, *Who Was Who in Egyptology*, 90; Ronald T. Ridley, *Napoleon's Proconsul in Egypt: The Life and Times of Bernardino Drovetti* (London: The Rubicon Press, n.d.); Alessandro Bongioanni and Riccardo Grazzi, *Torino L'Egitto e L'Oriente fra Storia e Leggenda* (Torino: Libreria L'Angolo Manzoni Editrice, 1994), 23–28; H. Donl Peterson, *The Story of the Book of Abraham: Mummies, Manuscripts, and Mormonism* (Salt Lake City: Deseret Book Company, 1995), 68. Drovetti's collection was an important foundation for the Egyptian Museum in Torino. Champollion visited Torino in 1824 (the same year he published *Précis du système hiéroglyphique des anciens Égyptiens*) to study the House of Savoy's holdings which were acquired from Drovetti. See Jean-François Champollion, *Lettres relatives au Musée Royale de Turin* (Paris, 1824–1826).
71. Drovetti's band included Antonio Giovanni Pietro Lebolo, Frédéric Cailliaud (1787–1869), Jacques "Riffo" Rifaud (1786– c. 1845), and Giuseppe Rosignani. Dawson writes that Lebolo was particularly hostile toward Belzoni and with Rosignani he attempted to intimidate or kill him. See, Dawson and Uphill, *Who Was Who in Egyptology*, 166.
72. For information concerning Lebolo see, Dawson and Uphill, *Who Was Who in Egyptology*, 166; Dan C. Jorgensen, "New Facts on the Life and History of Giovanni Pietro Antonio Lebolo," (Unpublished paper, October 1976); H. Donl Peterson, *The Pearl of Great Price: A History and Commentary* (Salt Lake City: Deseret Book Company, 1987), 36–46; H. Donl Peterson, "Antonio Lebolo: Excavator of the Book of Abraham," *Brigham Young University Studies* 31 (Summer 1991), 5–25; H. Donl Peterson, *The Story of the Book of Abraham*; Marco Zatterin, "Lebolo e le mummie del Profeta: Come furono scoperti i papiri dei mormoni," *La Stampa* (17 luglio 2000), 9. Jorgensen examined Lobolo's birth record (January 22, 1781, in

When Lebolo died in 1830 the consigned items had not been sold and his wife and four surviving children inherited his estate. In October 1833 Lebolo's eldest son, Pietro (who lived in Trieste), executed a special power of attorney in which he authorized Francesco Bertola, an Italian veterinarian living in Philadelphia, to claim the eleven mummies that Oblasser had shipped to New York. But before Pietro even executed this power of attorney the mummies had apparently arrived in New York and were claimed by Michael H. Chandler (1797–1866).

Beginning in April 1833 Chandler published notices and advertisements in Philadelphia newspapers announcing an exhibition of Egyptian mummies at the Masonic Hall (and later at the Arcade). The announcements noted that the mummies had been discovered by Antonio Lebolo and Chevalier Drovetti and that the exhibit included the testimonials of at least seven doctors who attested that the artifacts were probably at least three thousand years old.

Chandler sold at least two mummies in Philadelphia and organized additional exhibitions in Harrisburg, Baltimore, and Cleveland, where at least five more mummies were sold.[73] In June 1835 he displayed four mummies in Kirtland and told Joseph Smith that he was Antonio Lebolo's nephew. Smith agreed to purchase the mummies and papyri for $2,400 and shortly thereafter he recorded that "much to our joy [we] found that some of the rolls contained the writings of Abraham, and another the writings of Joseph of Egypt."[74]

Smith's translation revealed that Abraham had come into the possession of "the records of the fathers, even the patriarchs" and that he made his record "for the benefit of my posterity that shall come after me."[75] Abraham revealed that he "became a rightful heir, a High Priest, holding the

---

Castellamonte), his death record (February 19, 1830, in Castellamonte), the death certificate of his first wife (Maria Lebolo on November 7, 1821, in Castellamonte) and the baptismal record and marriage certificate of his second wife (Anna Maria Darfour in Venice on June 12, 1824). Anna Maria, who is also referred to as "Donna Africana," was Drovetti's slave. Drovetti apparently gave Anna Maria to Lebolo and they became lovers. Jorgensen found evidence that "Ant. Lebolo, neg[oziante]. Da Venezia" arrived in Trieste in April 1823. See "Arrivi in Trieste," *L'Osservatore Triestinto*, No. 48 (April 24, 1823). Peterson discovered several other notices which mentioned that Lebolo was in Trieste in October 1822, that his future wife and her two children (perhaps Lebolo's) were enrolled at the Istituto Catecumeni and that Lebolo sold portions of his collection to the Vatican Museum in Rome and the Kunsthistoriches Museum in Vienna. Peterson, *The Book of Abraham*, 63–70.
73. Peterson, *The Story of the Book of Abraham*, 89–118.
74. *History of the Church* 2:235–38.
75. Book of Abraham, 1:31. The portion of Smith's translation which took place in Kirtland (some of which he dictated to Warren Parrish) eventually became Book of Abraham 1:1 to 2:18.

right belonging to the fathers"; that "the race which preserved the curse in the land of [Egypt]" came through Ham; and that the "king of Egypt was a descendant from the loins of Ham, and was a partaker of the blood of the Canaanites by birth." This priesthood curse, which was not mentioned in the Bible, infected the Pharaoh who was "cursed…as pertaining to the Priesthood" because he was descended from "lineage by which he could not have the right of Priesthood."[76] Thereafter Ham's curse, which had previously been connected by Smith with race and servitude, became associated with a third consequence, which provided that Ham's descendants were not eligible to be ordained to the priesthood.

John Brooke noted in *Refiner's Fire* that George Oliver's two-seed theory was premised on Ramsay's "idea of ancient Masonic schisms," and that "its parallels—and probably its roots—[are found] in earlier Judaic, hermetic, and sectarian thought." This theory distinguished between primitive Freemasonry (which was preserved after the Flood by Noah and his righteous descendants) and spurious Freemasonry (which was practiced by Africans who descended from Cain, Ham, and Canaan). He concluded that "there is very good evidence that the two-seed tradition, specifically in its Masonic manifestation, played a significant role in Joseph Smith's later thinking." The evidence that Brooke cites is Smith's translation of the Book of Genesis in which Enoch is shown "the seed of Adam" and "the seed of Cain" as well as Smith's "restoration of the hermetic promise of a pure Gnostic Freemasonry."[77]

Smith's translation of the papyri revealed more primitive doctrines and practices that were consistent with Masonic legends. In particular, the new information concerning priesthood revealed in the Book of Abraham was reminiscent of Laurence Dermott's and George Oliver's speculations concerning those who were true Masons in the Old Testament and contradicted Prince Hall Masons' perspective concerning the important role that black Africans played in the development of Freemasonry in Egypt.[78]

Smith's search for hidden knowledge in Egyptian symbols was consistent with the aspirations of Freemasons and other esoteric groups. Erik Iversen has noted that "the growing myth about an idealized Egypt, the original home of all mystic and occult knowledge," was particularly popular "among the various occult sects and societies of the seventeenth and eighteenth centuries, among Freemasons and Rosicrucians." These societies desired "to obtain perfection by means of a secret knowledge of an esoteric

76. The description of Pharaoh's curse is in *Book of Abraham* 1:21–27.
77. Brooke, *The Refiner's Fire*, 166.
78. Stevenson, *The Origins of Freemasonry*, 82–83.

truth, manifest in allegorical symbols, the true meaning of which was gradually revealed to the initiate as he passed through the rites of the various
degrees."

Some Masons believed that this secret knowledge, which was first discovered by Egyptians, was embedded in hieroglyphic symbols and that such
symbols preserved an "unbroken chain of tradition."[79] When the science of
geometry was brought to France and to England and the French adapted
portions of Egyptian legends during Napoleon's Egyptian campaign, it
became a catalyst for modern Egyptian archeology and helped promote
"Egyptomania."[80] Afterward, some Freemasons secretly converted to what
they believed was the genuine Egyptian religion.[81]

The Masonic fascination with Abraham spanned the history of the
Craft and may have influenced Smith when he translated the papyri. According to the fifteenth-century Cooke Manuscript, Abraham "taught the
Egyptians [including his clerk, Euclid] the science of geometry." The Hebrews learned geometry in Egypt and thereafter practiced it in Jerusalem
where Solomon taught the craft. They believed that the Egyptians "taught
their principles through allegory and symbolism," that they "concealed their
ideas under the cover of hieroglyphics," and that there was a direct link between ancient Egyptians and Masonic rituals.[82]

Thomas Smith Webb, who wrote during the nineteenth century,
claimed that "the usages and customs of Masons" corresponded with those
of Egyptian philosophers who had concealed "their particular tenants, and
principle of polity, under hieroglyphical figures; and expressed their notions of government by signs and symbols, which they committed to their
Magi alone, who were bound by oath not to reveal them."[83]

79. Erik Iversen, *The Myth of Egypt and Its Hieroglypics in European Tradition* (Princeton:
Princeton University Press, 1993), 59–60, 77, 95–96, 121.

80. Knoop, Jones, and Hamer, *The Two Earliest Masonic Manuscripts*, 77. See also Mackey,
The History of Freemasonry, 154.

81. In 1835 James Fellows noted in his introduction to *An Exposition of the Mysteries, or Religious Dogmas and Customs* that if he had taken notice of a work cited by Barruel, "he would
probably have been saved much trouble in the prosecution of this research.—'We recommend,' says he, 'to our reader to peruse the treatise of a most learned and zealous mason, dedicated *Demen die es Verstehen*, or *To those who can understand.*' He leaves no stone unturned
throughout antiquity to prove the identity of the ancient mysteries of Eleusis, of the Jews,
of the Druids, and the Egyptians, with those of freemasonry." See Fellows, *An Exposition of
the Mysteries, or Religious Dogmas and Customs* (New York: Printed for the Author, 1835),
ix. Mackey discusses "the theory that ascribes the origin of Freemasonry as a secret society to
the Pagan Mysteries" in his *The History of Freemasonry*, 174–98.

82. See Calcott, *A Candid Disquisition* [1989], 26, 113; Preston, *Illustrations of Masonry*,
55–56.

83. Webb, *The Freemason's Monitor* (1818), 51–52.

Thus, when Webb introduced the Holy Order of High Priesthood he included the story of Abraham, who many Masons believed was the founder of Masonry, and his encounter with Melchizedek, who promised Abraham, "Thou art a priest forever, after the order of Melchisedec."[84] Similarly, Salem Town emphasized that Abraham was called of God, "became a most eminent Christian, and a distinguished instructor in the principles of Christianity, and the art of geometry or Masonry." According to Town, "the great plan of redemption began to be published to our first parents immediately after their apostasy" and through Abraham's "lineal descendants the church was preserved from one generation to another, till the advent of the promised Messiah."[85]

CIVIL RIGHTS

During this same period Joseph Smith Jr. wrote a letter (perhaps with Phelps's assistance), after an abolitionist spoke in Kirtland, in which he reconfirmed that Mormons were not sympathetic. He observed that some church members had criticized Mormons in the South "and are ready to withdraw the hand of fellowship because they will not renounce the principle of slavery and raise their voice against everything of the kind," but acknowledged that "if slavery is an evil" then the people of the slave states would be in a better position to "learn this fact" and in "prescribing a remedy."

Smith concluded that most Northerners "are not interested in the freedom of the slaves, any other than upon the mere principles of human rights and of the gospel, and we are ready to admit that these are men of piety who reside in the South, who are immediately concerned, and until they complain, and call for assistance, why not cease their clamor, and no further urge the slave to acts of murder, and the master to vigorous discipline, rendering both miserable." He concluded, "I do not believe that the people of the North have any more right to say that the South *shall not* hold slaves, than the South have to say the North *shall*."

But Smith did acknowledge that slavery was mentioned in the Bible and that Noah's curse of Ham's offspring was literally fulfilled by the South in "holding the sons of Ham in servitude." Smith wrote, "I can say that the curse is not yet taken off the sons of Canaan, neither will be until it is affected by as great power as caused it to come: and the people who interfere the least with the decrees and purposes of God in this matter, will come under the least condemnation before him." He also pointed out that

84. Ibid., 150.
85. See Town, *A System of Speculative Freemasonry*, 119, 171–73.

Abraham had servants and that Paul instructed servants to be obedient to their masters.

The Mormon prophet instructed traveling elders to "search the book of Covenants," which was published the previous year, "in which you will see the belief of the church concerning masters and servants." "We have no right to interfere," Smith emphasized, "with slaves contrary to the mind and will of their masters. In fact, it would be much better and more prudent, not to preach at all to slaves, until after their masters are converted." He concluded by expressing his hope "that no one who is authorized from this church to preach the gospel, will so far depart from the scripture as to be found stirring up strife and sedition against our brethren of the South."[86]

Warren Parrish, who was a scribe for Smith when he translated the papyri, and Oliver Cowdery, who transcribed portions of the gold plates, wrote scathing criticisms of abolitionism in the same issue of the *Latter Day Saints' Messenger and Advocate*. Parrish noted that the founding fathers took into "consideration the general good of this republic and deemed it expedient to guarantee to the Southern States the right of holding slaves." Such slavery was justified, according to Parrish, because of Ham's curse and the curse would remain in effect "until He, who pronounced it shall order it otherwise." He further predicted, "And all the abolition societies that now or ever will be, cannot cause one jot or tittle of the prophecy to fail."

Cowdery's editorial entitled "The Abolitionists" concluded that slavery was recognized by the founders of the nation and in the Bible, and the South was entitled to practice slavery and protect their property rights. He stressed that African Americans were cursed in the Bible: "There is a strange mysteriousness over the face of the scripture with regard to servitude. The fourth son of Ham was cursed by Noah, and to this day we may look upon the fulfillment of that singular thing." He acknowledged that "When it will be removed we know not, and where he now remains in bondage, remain he must till the hand of God interposes. As to this nation his fate is inevitably sealed, so long as this form of government exists."[87]

But Cowdery was convinced that if slaves were emancipated the North would be "overrun with paupers, and a reckless mass of human beings, uncultivated, untaught, and unaccustomed to provide for themselves the

---

86. *Latter Day Saints' Messenger and Advocate* 2 (April 1836): 289–91; *The Essential Joseph Smith* (Salt Lake City: Signature Books, 1995), 85–90. He also cited Genesis 8:25–27. Concerning W. W. Phelps ghostwriting on behalf of Smith, see Samuel L. Brown, "The Translator and the Ghostwriter, Joseph Smith and William W. Phelps," in Stephen C. Taysom, ed., *Dimensions of Faith, A Mormon Studies Reader* (Salt Lake City: Signature Books, 2011), 259–96.
87. "The Abolitionists," *Messenger and Advocate* 2 (April 1836): 301.

necessities of life—*endangering the chastity of every female who might by chance be found in our streets*—our prisons filled with convicts, and the hang-man wearied with executing the functions of his office." He queried: "Must we open our houses, unfold our arms, and bid these degraded and degrading sons of Canaan, *a hearty welcome and a free admittance to all we possess!*" Cowdery's fears reflected those of many Americans who did not believe that emancipated African Americans should be allowed to integrate into white society. "The notion of amalgamation is devilish!" he wrote, "And insensible to feeling must be the heart, and low indeed must be the mind, that would consent for a moment, to see his fair daughter, his sister, or perhaps, his bosom companion in the embrace of a NEGRO!"

Cowdery's warning concerning the consequences of emancipation, that black men would compromise white women's chastity, provided an additional rationale for excluding them from white social circles and even encouraged some to advocate colonization of all blacks to a location outside the United States. Neither Smith, Parrish, nor Cowdery distinguished between black slaves, who they believed were cursed, degraded, and apparently ineligible for full civil rights, and free blacks who had obtained such rights in a limited number of Northern states and who were eligible to be baptized.

Despite these strong racist statements, the citizens of Clay County, Missouri, demanded that Mormon settlers leave because, among other reasons, "they are non-slave holders, and opposed to slavery; which in this particular period, when abolitionism has reared its deformed and haggard visage in our land, is well calculated to excite deep and abiding prejudices."[88] Most Mormons recognized that they were outnumbered and since the local citizens had offered them time to sell their land, they agreed to leave the county.

That same year, Elijah Abel (1810—1884), a free African American who had been baptized in 1832, was ordained to the office of Seventy.[89] As a member of the Mormon priesthood, Abel was "a duly licensed minister of the Gospel" and he was washed and anointed in the Kirtland Temple.[90] The prophet's father, Joseph Sr., blessed Abel, confirmed that he had been "ordained an Elder and anointed to secure thee against the power of the destroyer," and promised him, "Thou shalt be made equal to thy brethren

88. "Public Meeting," *Messenger and Advocate* 2 (August 1836): 353–54.
89. General Record of the Seventies Book A. Meeting of December 20, 1836, Church History Library. For a listing of Abel's license, see *Messenger and Advocate* 4 (June 1836): 335.
90. General Record of the Seventies Book A, Meeting of December 20, 1836, Church History Library.

and thy soul be white in eternity and thy robes glittering: thou shalt receive these blessings because of the covenants of thy fathers."[91] Abel's ordination was later viewed as an aberration by those who claimed that African Americans were inherently ineligible for the priesthood.

91. Patriarchal Blessing of Elijah Abel given by Patriarch Joseph Smith Sr., circa May 1836. Patriarchal Blessing Book 1:49. See H. Michael Marquardt, *Early Patriarchal Blessings of the Church of Jesus Christ of Latter-day Saints* (Salt Lake City: The Smith-Pettit Foundation, 2007), 99. This promise was similar to that given to the Lamanites in the Book of Mormon who were told that they would become "white and delightsome" if they lived a pure life (2 Nephi 30:6). In 1879 Zebedee Coltrin (1804–1887) claimed that "in the washing and anointing of Bro. Abel at Kirtland, I anointed him, and while I had my hands upon his head, I never had such unpleasant feelings in my life—and I said I never would again anoint another person who had Negro blood in him, unless I was commanded by the Prophet to do so." See L. John Nuttall Diary, May 31, 1879, Harold B. Lee Library, Brigham Young University; Bush, "Mormonism's Negro Doctrine," 52n29. Brooke, *The Refiner's Fire*, 211. Zebedee Coltrin's testimony is the only piece of evidence which supports the thesis that Joseph Smith had already determined that African Americans could not be ordained. But Coltrin's testimony is inconsistent with Smith's seeming acquiescence of Elijah Abel's ordination and Brigham Young's first statement that "blood" was not determinative of the rights to ordination.

6

Mormon Freemasonry

IN JANUARY 1838 JOSEPH SMITH left Kirtland and settled in Far West, Missouri, where he and his family resided for at least three months with the famous anti-Mason George W. Harris and his wife, Lucinda Morgan Harris.[1] The Harrises had joined the church four years earlier and George was a member of the high council that "participated in the excommunication of Oliver Cowdery (the principal scribe and one of the Three Witnesses of the Book of Mormon) in part because Cowdery had apparently accused the Mormon prophet of committing adultery with Fanny Alger."[2] Given Harris's position in the church council, and the action it took, it is ironic that some Mormon historians have suggested that Smith, during this same period, was courting Lucinda, and that she may have become his plural wife.[3]

During Smith's short sojourn in Missouri he rebuked some of his closest associates and even excommunicated a few—including Cowdery and

1. Susan Ward Easton Black, *Membership of the Church of Jesus Christ of Latter-day Saints* (Provo: Religious Studies Center, Brigham Young University, 1986), 21:40; Elden J. Watson, comp., *The Orson Pratt's Journals* (Salt Lake City: Compiler, 1975), 44.
2. See Grunder, *Mormon Parallels*, 1747, citing Cannon and Cook, *Far West Record*, 162–71. Although some historians maintain that Smith had a relationship with Fanny Alger in Ohio, there is no consensus that she was actually considered a plural wife. George D. Smith discusses Joseph Smith's relationship with Alger, which apparently lasted for three years, in *Nauvoo Polygamy... "but we called it celestial marriage,"* (Salt Lake City: Signature Books, 2008), 38–45. Smith did state in Kirtland that he had the right to marry persons "by the authority of the holy Priesthood and the Gentile law has no power to call me to an account for it. It is my religious priviledge [*sic*], and the congress of the United States has no power to make a law that would abridge the rights of my religion." "Sketch of the Life of Newell Knight," 6, fd. 2, draft #1, Church History Library, as quoted and cited in D. Michael Quinn, *The Mormon Hierarchy, Origins of Power* (Salt Lake City: Signature Books, 1994), 88, 326. Nevertheless, this statement was given in the context of his calling to perform marriages as a minister and not necessarily to marry multiple wives.
3. See Todd Compton, *In Sacred Loneliness: The Plural Wives of Joseph Smith* (Salt Lake City: Signature Books, 1997), 49. In Nauvoo, Harris became a member of the high council and the couple lived across the street from Smith and his family. D&C 124:131–32; Donna Hill, *Joseph Smith, the First Mormon* (Garden City, NY: Doubleday, 1977), 227; Brodie, *No Man Knows My History*, 436–37.

W. W. Phelps who he believed were too openly critical of his authority. In July he told another close associate, Newel K. Whitney, to "be ashamed of the Nicolaitane band," which was made up of church dissenters, because of "their secret abominations."[4] In November Smith and Rigdon were arrested and spent the next five months incarcerated in Liberty, Missouri. While there, Smith wrote about the "impropriety of the organization of bands or companies by covenant or oaths[,] by penalties or secrecies.... Pure friendships always become weakened the very moment you undertake to make it stronger by penal oaths and secrecy." Smith's Missouri statements concerning "secret abominations" and "organization of bands" did not refer directly to Freemasonry but instead to secret organizations within Mormonism, including the Danites.[5]

In April 1839 Smith and Rigdon escaped and crossed the Mississippi River to Illinois, where Smith organized a new city and made plans to construct a large temple and introduce a more elaborate endowment. In Illinois Smith joined the Masonic Craft and told his followers that its ritual was an apostate form of an endowment that was introduced in Solomon's Temple. While the Kirtland endowment was limited to priesthood holders and emphasized purification rituals and personal spiritual experiences, the Nauvoo endowment would be expanded to include more explicit Masonic elements, including obligations of secrecy, and it would eventually be open to men and women.

THE GRAND LODGE OF ILLINOIS

When the Mormons settled in Illinois, American Freemasonry was beginning to experience growth for the first time since the Morgan episode. On December 29, 1839, four Illinois lodges (which beginning in 1835 received charters from Grand Lodges that, unlike the Grand Lodge of Illinois, had survived the anti-Masonic onslaught) met in Jacksonville to discuss the prospect of organizing a new grand lodge.[6] They met again on January 26

4. D&C 117: 11 (July 8, 1838).
5. Dean C. Jessee, ed., *Personal Writings of Joseph Smith*, 405–6; Vogel, *Early Mormon Documents*, 3:452–56. See also *Times and Seasons* 1:9 (July 1840): 133.
6. The Grand Lodge of Illinois was originally organized in 1822 by eight Illinois lodges (which surrendered their charters to the grand lodges that had conferred them before obtaining new charters from the newly organized grand lodge) and met until 1827 when, according to Reynolds, "the Grand Lodge went down, and with it, its constitution." John C. Reynolds, *History of the M[ost]. W[orshipful]. Grand Lodge of Illinois, Ancient, Free, and Accepted Masons, From the Organization of the first Lodge within the limits of the State, up to and including 1850* (Springfield: H. G. Reynolds Jr., 1869), 74–77, 101. Beginning in August 1835 there was a gradual revival of Freemasonry in Illinois. Bodley Lodge (Quincy) received a dispensation from the Grand Lodge of Kentucky in 1835 and a charter in 1836. This was

and decided to hold a convention the following April to determine "the place for the permanent location of the Grand Lodge, the officers elected, and the Grand Lodge finally constituted."[7] On April 6, the same day the Mormons commemorated their tenth anniversary, six Illinois lodges met together, adopted a constitution and bylaws, and organized the Grand Lodge of Illinois.

Abraham Jonas (1801–1864), past grand master of the Grand Lodge of Kentucky and master of Columbus Lodge, was elected grand master *in absentia*, while James Adams (1783–1843), past grand secretary of the Grand Lodge of Illinois and past master of Springfield Lodge, was elected deputy grand master.[8] Thereafter, Jonas appointed Meredith Helm (1802–1866) as grand marshal. Thereafter the six lodges that organized the grand lodge received new charters and the grand lodge scheduled the first annual communication (or annual meeting) to take place the following October in Jacksonville.[9]

Deputy Grand Master James Adams, who would later become a close friend of Joseph Smith, was born in Simsbury Township, Hartford County, Connecticut, married Harriet Denton (1787–1844), and moved to New York where they had five children. He was initiated into Freemasonry in Washington Lodge No. 220 (Orange County), became a justice of the peace (Lysander Township), served in various infantry regiments of the New York State Militia where he eventually attained the rank of brigadier general, was a member of the New York State Bar, and was commissioner of roads for the Westmoreland and Sodus Bay Turnpike Company.

But in 1818 the district attorney in Oswego County indicted Adams for forging and backdating a deed and after posting bail he avoided trial by leaving Oswego County and moved to Baldwinsville (Onondaga County)

---

followed by Franklin Lodge (Alton) which was organized in 1836; Equality Lodge (Equality) in 1837; Harmony Lodge (Jacksonville) in 1838; Temperance Lodge (Vandolia) in 1838; Springfield Lodge (Springfield) in 1839; Far West Lodge (Far West) in 1839; Mount Moriah Lodge (Hillsboro) in 1839; and Columbus Lodge (Columbus) in 1839. See Reynolds, *History of the M. W. Grand Lodge of Illinois*, 108–31.

7. Ibid., 130–31.

8. *The Proceedings of the Grand Lodge of Illinois, from its Organization in 1840–1850 Inclusive* (Freeport: Journal Reprint, 1892), 1–5. *History of the Church* 4:20. The lodges represented were Springfield Lodge (Springfield), Bodley Lodge (Quincy), Columbus Lodge (Columbus), Equality Lodge (Equality), Far West Lodge (Far West), and Harmony Lodge (Jacksonville).

9. Hogan notes that Jonas was not present when he was elected on April 6 and for that reason the installation of grand lodge officers was postponed until April 28. Nevertheless, Jonas was still not present at that meeting and he was therefore installed as the grand master by proxy. See Mervin B. Hogan, "Mormonism and Freemasonry: The Illinois Episode," *The Little Masonic Library* 2 (1977): 311. This article was reprinted as Mervin B. Hogan, *Mormonism and Masonry: The Illinois Episode* (Salt Lake City: Third Century Graphics, 1980).

where he clerked in a mercantile enterprise. In 1821 he moved to Springfield, Illinois, where he set up a law practice, was appointed Sangamon County justice of the peace, and was confirmed as Sangamon County probate judge.[10] He also joined Sangamon Lodge No. 9 and acted as grand secretary *pro tem* during one meeting of the Grand Lodge of Illinois.[11]

In 1834 Adams ran (as a nonpartisan candidate) for governor of Illinois, was defeated, and continued to serve as probate judge.[12] In 1837 the Illinois State Legislature passed a bill requiring Adams to stand for election to retain his judgeship. Adams ran as a Democrat and was challenged by Whig candidate Anson G. Henry who was a close friend of Abraham Lincoln.[13] During the campaign Lincoln wrote letters to the *Sangamo Journal* (a Whig newspaper in Springfield) in which he disclosed that Adams had been indicted in Oswego County, New York, and accused him of fraud concerning the transfer of two other land parcels in Springfield.[14] In addition, Lincoln may have written six letters (which were signed by "Sampson's Ghost") to the same newspaper, attempting to goad Adams to respond to Lincoln's allegations.[15] Two days before the election, Lincoln distributed handbills that republished his allegations and Adams finally published a denial, won the election, and retained his position as probate judge.[16]

In 1839 Adams was elected the first master of the newly organized Springfield Lodge and represented it in the meetings held that year to

10. I have relied on the following articles for background concerning James Adams: Kent L. Walgren, "James Adams: Early Springfield Mormon and Freemason," *Journal of the Illinois State Historical Society* 75:2 (Summer 1982): 121–36; Wayne C. Temple, "James Adams and Abraham Lincoln," *Illinois Lodge of Research* 16 (September 2007): 8; Susan Easton Black, "James Adams of Springfield, Illinois: The Link Between Abraham Lincoln and Joseph Smith," *Mormon Historical Studies* 10 (Spring 2009): 33–49.

11. Reynolds, *History of the M. W. Grand Lodge of Illinois*, 79, 83.

12. Mervin Hogan believes that Adams was secretly baptized in 1836 when he was visiting Missouri. He relies on a letter he received from W. Wallace Smith, president of the Reorganized Church of Jesus Christ of Latter Day Saints, on September 22, 1969. Hogan, *Mormonism and Freemasonry*, 311. Walgren concludes that Adams was not baptized until 1840. Walgren, "James Adams," 127n29.

13. See Paul M. Angle, *Here I Have Lived: A History of Lincoln's Springfield, 1821–1865* (Chicago: Abraham Lincoln Book Shop, 1971), 151.

14. See *Sangamo Journal*, November 18, 1837, p. 2, and November 25, 1837, p. 1.

15. See *Sangamo Journal*, Sampson's Ghost, "To the Editor of the Journal," *Sangamo Journal*, June 17 and 24, July 8, 15, 22, and 29, 1837.

16. "To the Voters of Sangamo County," *Sangamo Journal*, August 19, 1837, p. 2; and Walgren, "James Adams," 124–25. One Mason has argued that Abraham Lincoln may not have become a Mason because of his dislike of Adams arising out of this incident. Paul Bessel, "Abraham Lincoln and Freemasonry," Paper written in September 1994, in possession of author. Concerning Lincoln's authorship of the letters and handbill, Bessel cites R. V. Havlik, "Is This of Your Own Free Will and Accord," *Lincoln Herald* (Fall 1985), 67–68; and Wayne C. Temple, "An Aftermath of 'Sampson's Ghost': A New Lincoln Document," *Lincoln Herald* (Summer 1989): 42–47.

organize a new grand lodge in Illinois. Adams was apparently the only Mason attending those meetings who had participated in the first Illinois Grand Lodge before it was deconstructed during the Morgan debacle.[17] In November Adams met Joseph Smith when the Mormon prophet was in Springfield and, according to Smith's account, Adams "took me home with him, and treated me like a father."[18] Shortly thereafter, Adams was baptized and became a member of the Mormon Church but he apparently requested that his membership status be kept confidential.[19]

NAUVOO MASONS

During this same period Smith developed a close relationship with another Freemason named John Cook Bennett (1804–1867) who also resided in Springfield. In 1826 Bennett was initiated into Freemasonry in Belmont Lodge No. 16, St. Clairsville, Ohio, but he did not secede from the Craft when the Morgan affair exploded over the next several years.[20] He eventually became a member of Pickaway Lodge No. 23 in Circleville, Ohio (1828–1829), and of Friendship Lodge No. 89 in Barnesville, Ohio (1830–1832), and was elected as grand chaplain of the Grand Lodge of Ohio.[21] He was selected as chaplain because he had been a Methodist preacher and a follower of Alexander Campbell for a short period; he had met Joseph Smith and Sidney Rigdon before he left Ohio in 1838.[22]

In July 1840, while he was serving as the quartermaster general of the Illinois State Militia,[23] Bennett wrote at least three letters to Smith in which he expressed his interest in the Nauvoo Saints.[24] In August Smith responded to Bennett's first letter and invited him to Nauvoo, and when Bennett received the response he raced to the city at a time when Brigham Young, and most of the other church apostles, were serving missions in England. During the same month Smith's father died, and perhaps this void was part

17. Hogan, *Mormonism and Freemasonry*, 309.

18. Walgren, "James Adams," 121–136; Hogan, *Mormonism and Freemasonry*, 311; *History of the Church* 4:20.

19. Black, "James Adams of Springfield, Illinois," 39–41.

20. See Andrew F. Smith, *Saintly Scoundrel: The Life and Times of Dr. John Cook Bennett* (Urbana: University of Illinois Press, 1997).

21. Mervin B. Hogan, "John Cook Bennett and Pickaway Lodge No. 23," October 12, 1983, 9–10 (J. Willard Marriott Library, University of Utah), 2–3.

22. Smith, *Saintly Scoundrel*, 56. See also Jan Shipps and John W. Welch, eds., *The Journals of William E. McLellin, 1831–1836* (Provo: BYU Studies, Brigham Young University, 1994), 69.

23. Bennett wrote letters to Smith and Rigdon on July 25, 27, and 30. *History of the Church* 4:168–70, 172. As quartermaster general, Bennett was in charge of supplies for the state militia.

24. Smith, *Saintly Scoundrel*, 57.

John C. Bennett (1804–1867). Published in
John C. Bennett, *History of the Saints*.

of the reason Smith was smitten by the Illinois quartermaster's congenial personality and seeming political influence. He invited Bennett to lodge at the Homestead House and Bennett lived there for at least eight months. In early October, Bennett's rising status became evident when Smith invited him to address the church's general conference "at some length" and asked him to help secure a city charter.[25]

During the same month the newly organized Illinois Grand Lodge held its first annual communication in Jacksonville. The meeting was attended by representatives of Bodley Lodge (Quincy), Harmony Lodge (Jacksonville), Springfield Lodge (Springfield), and Columbus Lodge (Columbus), which represented ninety-nine Masons in Illinois' subordinate lodges. During this meeting the grand lodge officially installed Jonas as grand master, Adams as deputy grand master, and Stephen A. Douglas as grand orator.[26]

In December Bennett and other representatives of the church traveled to Springfield and successfully secured a city charter for Nauvoo from the state legislature that granted corporate city status. The fledgling city was only one of six Illinois cities to obtain a charter, which authorized Nauvoo

25. *History of the Church* 4:177–79.
26. Douglas eventually declined and did not serve in the grand lodge.

to establish not only a city government but also a city militia (referred to as the Nauvoo Legion), a municipal court, and even a university.

In January 1841 Smith referred to Bennett as one of the "principal men in Illinois, who have listened to the doctrines we promulgate, have become obedient to the faith, and are rejoicing in the same."[27] During the same month Smith received a revelation to build another temple, and Bennett was specifically enlisted to help "in sending my word to the kings and people of the earth, and stand by...Joseph Smith, in the hour of affliction, and its reward shall not fail, if he receive counsel."[28] Thereafter Bennett was quickly rewarded for his services, and with Smith's backing he was elected as Nauvoo's first mayor and as major general of the Nauvoo Legion.[29] Finally, on April 8, Smith called Bennett as assistant church president and by that time he had effectively circumscribed Sidney Rigdon, who was in poor health, as the Mormon president's chief confidante.

Meanwhile James Adams also gradually established a close bond with the Mormon prophet. In 1840 Smith appointed him as a trustee of the new university, and during the same year he was baptized (for the dead) on behalf of his grandmother, father, and uncle in the Mississippi River. In 1841 Hyrum Smith gave him a patriarchal blessing and Adams performed an additional eighty-three baptisms for the dead, including a baptism for President John Adams and for the two men whom Lincoln had claimed Adams swindled when he took title to their property after they died.[30]

Nevertheless, Adams's influence among his fellow Freemasons was waning. In April 1841, when members of Springfield Lodge accused him of meddling in their affairs, the deputy grand master promised its members "that in future he would refrain altogether from taking part in the ordinary business of the Lodge"[31] and he did not attend any other Masonic meetings (either at lodge or grand lodge). Instead, he became increasingly involved in politics (he was reelected Sangamon County probate justice by thirty-eight votes) and committed to Joseph Smith and Mormonism.

In June 1841 Bennett and other Mormon Masons sent a communication to Bodley Lodge No. 1 (Quincy) to inform them that they wished to organize a Masonic lodge in Nauvoo and "asking [Bodley] Lodge to recommend to the Grand Lodge of the State certain individuals whose names

27. *History of the Church*, 4:270.
28. Ibid., 4:275–76.
29. Robert Bruce Flanders, *Nauvoo: Kingdom on the Mississippi* (Urbana: University of Illinois Press, 1965), 101; *History of the Church* 4:309.
30. Black, "James Adams of Springfield, Illinois," 40–41.
31. Walgren, "James Adams," 127, quoting Reynolds, *History of the M. W. Grand Lodge of Illinois*, 153–54.

are therein contained to be appointed Master and Wardens of a Lodge to be established at said city." On June 28 Bodley Lodge reviewed this communication "from John C. Bennett and others, of the city of Nauvoo," and declined since "as these persons were unknown to this Lodge as Masons, it was thought prudent not to do so."[32]

Bodley Lodge's response only mentioned John C. Bennett and failed to reference other prominent Nauvoo Masons, including Past Masters Asahel Perry, Daniel S. Miles, and Hezekiah Peck, as well as Hyrum Smith, Heber C. Kimball, Newel K. Whitney, George Miller, John D. Parker, and Lucius N. Scovil. However, that does not suggest the Lodge's response was directed primarily at Bennett or that its members believed that Bennett was a bad man. In fact, Bodley Lodge's response was not particularly surprising since the Mormons had only been in Illinois for a brief period and it is unlikely that any of the Nauvoo Masons had been members of another Illinois lodge or had even visited Quincy Lodge prior to making the request.[33]

In October, when the Illinois Grand Lodge held its annual communication, Jonas was reelected grand master but Adams was replaced by Meredith Helm who, like Adams, was past master of Springfield Lodge. In fact, Adams did not attend Grand Lodge because he was in Nauvoo attending Church General Conference.[34] There were only about 131 members in the constituent lodges that sent representatives to the meeting, and Jonas emphasized that he wanted to build up Masonry in Illinois while at the same time following the Craft's rules and regulations.

During the communication the Illinois Grand Lodge criticized Springfield Lodge because it advanced candidates too rapidly: "In several instances, [it] received the petition and initiated the candidate on the same

32. Reynolds, *History of the M. W. Grand Lodge of Illinois*, 152, quoting *Records of Bodley Lodge, No. 1, Quincy, Illinois*, June 28, 1841. See also James J. Tyler, *John Cook Bennett* (n.p., n.d.). Albert G. Mackey notes that "the recommendation of a neighboring lodge is the general usage of the craft, and is intended to certify to the superior authority, on the very best evidence that can be obtained, namely, of an adjacent lodge, that the new lodge will be productive of no injury to the Order." Albert G. Mackey, *The Principles of Masonic Law: A Treatise of the Constitutional Laws, Usages and Landmarks of Freemasonry* (New York: Jno. W. Leonard & Co., 1856), 79–80.

33. See Hogan, *Mormonism and Masonry*, 303. Susan Black observes that Adams "encouraged Lucius N. Scovil and other Freemasons in Nauvoo to submit a request in June 1841 for a lodge to Masonic leaders in Springfield." See Black, "James Adams of Springfield, Illinois," 48n55. Godfrey concludes that the petition "was apparently signed by all the known Masons in the church." See Kenneth W. Godfrey, "Joseph Smith and the Masons," *Journal of the Illinois State Historical Society* 64 (Spring 1971): 83.

34. During this visit to Nauvoo, Adams received his patriarchal blessing. His absence from grand lodge demonstrates his dissatisfaction with Illinois Masonry. See Walgren, "James Adams," 127. See also *History of the Church* 4:20n.

evening; and also have passed and raised candidates at the same setting of
the lodge—which course of work the majority of your committee believe to
be in violation of the spirit of Masonry." Macon Lodge was also criticized
for the same practice.[35]

The Mormon Masons, who were rebuffed by Bodley Lodge, eventually
persuaded Columbus Lodge (which was Grand Master Jonas's lodge) to
recommend them to the grand master.[36] They petitioned the grand master
and stated that they were Master Masons who had been members of a regular lodge before settling in Nauvoo and identified their proposed master
and wardens and where they would meet.[37] The grand master was entitled
to authorize such Freemasons, who were recommended by a working lodge,
to form a lodge and work "under dispensation." While a lodge organized
under dispensation was authorized to "make Masons," it was only considered a temporary lodge and was not "admitted into the register of lodges"
until it received a warrant (charter) from the Grand Lodge.[38]

Prior to October 1841 Grand Master Jonas had issued only one dispensation (to Masons residing in Macon), but shortly after Grand Lodge
adjourned he granted seven additional dispensations authorizing Masons
to organize lodges in Virginia, Vermillionville, Rushville, Shawneetown,
Peoria, and Nauvoo (all in Illinois), as well as one in Montrose (Iowa Territory) that was also organized by Mormon Masons.[39] The dispensation authorizing the Mormon Masons to organize Nauvoo Lodge was executed
by Jonas on October 15 and provided that "when duly formed and opened"
the lodge was authorized "to enter, pass, and raise to the Sublime Degree
of Master Mason, all such as may be so congregated, entered, passed, and
raised in due time."[40]

35. *Proceedings of the Grand Lodge*, 22.
36. Mervin Hogan published the dispensation in *Founding Minutes of Nauvoo Lodge, U.D.*
(Des Moines: Research Lodge No. 2, 1971), 3. Hogan published the original minute book as
Founding Minutes of Nauvoo Lodge, U.D., and portions of a second minute book as *The Of-
ficial Minutes of Nauvoo Lodge, U.D.* The complete minutes (from the second minute book)
are located in the Church History Library and are referred to herein as *Record of Nauvoo
Lodge.* Hogan believed that "Jonas appeared in two Masonic roles, as Master and Grand
Master. As Worshipful Master of Columbus Lodge No. 6 he recommended the 'sundry
Brethren of Hancock County' to Jonas the Most Worshipful Master." Hogan, "Mormon
Involvement with Freemasonry on the Illinois and Iowa Frontier between 1840 and 1846"
(n.p., n.d.). See also Kenneth W. Godfrey, "Freemasonry in Nauvoo," in Daniel H. Ludlow,
ed., *Encyclopedia of Mormonism* (New York: Macmillan, 1992), 2:527–28. Although Jonas
was not the Master of Columbus Lodge when the dispensation was granted, he may have
requested his fellow lodge members to support his initiative.
37. For a reference to this procedure, see Mackey, *The Principles of Masonic Law*, 77–78.
38. See Ibid., 37–41, 48, 93.
39. *Proceedings of the Grand Lodge*, 52; Reynolds, *History of the M. W. Grand Lodge of Illinois*, 184.
40. Hogan, *Founding Minutes*, 3.

Illustration of Lodge of Entered Apprentice, Fellow Craft and Master Mason.
Published in Avery Allyn, *A Ritual of Freemasonry*, 27.

ORGANIZING THE LODGE

During this same period Smith began to emphasize the need to keep secrets, and vowed that he could keep a secret until doomsday.[41] On December 29, 1841, eighteen Mormon Masons met in Hyrum Smith's office to organize Nauvoo Lodge. George D. Miller was elected master (the presiding officer of the lodge), with Hyrum Smith as senior warden *pro tem* (the second officer), Lucius Scovil as junior warden (the third officer), and John C. Bennett as secretary. These officers all represented that they were Master Masons in good standing and listed their prior lodges. Miller was initiated in Widow's Son No. 60 in Virginia, Smith in Mount Moriah No. 112 in New York, Scovil in Morning Star No. 83 in Ohio, and Bennett in Friendship Lodge No. 89 of Ohio.

The following day the lodge adopted bylaws requiring the master to cause "the usages of masonry, to be duly observed." These Masonic usages included compliance with the ancient landmarks under which petitioners were required to meet moral (belief in deity), physical (no deformations), intellectual (neither a fool nor idiot), and political (freeborn) standards.[42] These usages also required the lodge to give notice of petitions, to wait until the next regular meeting before balloting, to examine each petitioner's character, to vote separately on each candidate, to require unanimous approval, and not to confer more than two degrees on any candidate at one communication.[43]

Joseph Smith, Sidney Rigdon, and forty other Mormons petitioned Nauvoo Lodge for membership during the same meeting and their petitions were referred to a committee of investigation.[44] In January 1842 Nauvoo Lodge began holding regular meetings on the first and third Thursdays of each month. Shortly after Nauvoo Lodge was organized, Smith wrote that this was the "day in which the God of heaven has begun to restore the ancient order of his kingdom." He also wrote that God had begun to manifest "those things which have been, and those things which the ancient prophets and wise men desired to see but died without beholding them."[45]

41. *History of the Church* 4:479 (December 19, 1841).
42. Mackey, *The Principles of Masonic Law*, 157–86.
43. Ibid., 114–15, 187–201.
44. See Hogan, *Founding Minutes*, 11–13. For a complete list of those initiated into Masonry in Nauvoo, see Mervin B. Hogan, *The Official Minutes of Nauvoo Lodge* (Des Moines: Research Lodge No. 2, 1974); and Mervin B. Hogan, *The Vital Statistics of Nauvoo Lodge* (Des Moines: Research Lodge No. 2, 1976).
45. *History of the Church* 4:492; 2 *RLDS History of the Church* 2:568–69; *Millennial Star* 19:21–22.

On February 3 the lodge's committee of investigation reported favorably concerning those who had petitioned the lodge for membership, including Smith and Rigdon, and when ballots were taken all were found clear.[46] On February 17 the lodge voted that the grand master would install the lodge the following month, Bennett was appointed marshal and the Quorum of Twelve were invited to join in the procession. On March 15 Grand Master Jonas installed Nauvoo Lodge at a grove near the temple site. Masons from various lodges in Illinois visited Nauvoo Lodge during this installation and were generally pleased with the proceedings.[47] During the installation Joseph Smith acted as chaplain and the lodge formally adopted its bylaws and submitted them to the grand lodge. Jonas gave an address and confirmed the lodge's principal officers.

Jonas also delivered a letter that authorized "the Brethren of Nauvoo Lodge under dispensation to receive the petitions of Joseph Smith and Sidney Rigdon—and act on the same instant [*sic*]—and should the ballot be unanimous in favor of said Smith and Rigdon at a full meeting of said Nauvoo Lodge—then and in that case—the said lodge is authorized to confer the three degrees of ancient York Masonry on the said Joseph Smith and Sidney Rigdon—as speedily as the nature of the case will permit." But Jonas also wrote that the lodge could not violate "any of the ancient landmarks of the order" and that it could not act "contrary to their provisions of their By-laws."[48]

Apparently Jonas was alarmed because Nauvoo Lodge had already violated such landmarks when it accepted petitions and balloted on fifty-seven candidates before it was officially installed. Mervin Hogan has speculated that Jonas may have instructed the lodge to begin a new minute book and to record that these petitions were not voted on until the installation of the lodge.[49] In fact, the lodge did create a new minute book, which has since been recovered from the foundation of the Nauvoo Lodge, that removed references to the December 30, 1841, petitions of Smith and Rigdon, the February 3, 1842, ballots to approve those petitions, and all the other petitions that were received and voted on by the lodge before it was installed.[50]

The new official minutes recorded that on March 15 Smith's and Rigdon's petitions to be initiated as Entered Apprentices were approved and they were initiated as Entered Apprentices on the same day. The new

46. Hogan, *Founding Minutes*, 8, 10.
47. *History of the Church* 4:565.
48. Letter of Abraham Jonas to Nauvoo Lodge, March 15, 1842, Record of Nauvoo Lodge, Church History Library.
49. Hogan, *Official Minutes*, 4–5.
50. Compare Hogan, *Founding Minutes*, 8–11, and Hogan, *Official Minutes*, 16–20.

Joseph Smith's Masonic apron. Photographed by Val Brinkerhoff.
Courtesy Community of Christ Archives.

minutes also recorded that on the next day ballots were taken for Smith and
Rigdon to be passed as Fellowcrafts and raised as Master Masons and that
Jonas passed and raised them during a ceremony referred to as being made
"Masons at sight."[51] This means that Smith and Rigdon were not required
to demonstrate that they were proficient in the Entered Apprentice ritual
(which they had received the previous day) before receiving the Fellowcraft
degree and that they were not required to be proficient in the Fellow Craft
ritual before receiving the Master Mason degree.

During these rituals Smith and Rigdon were given signs, due-grips, due-
guards, pass-grips, words, passwords, and obligations of secrecy of those degrees. The Master Mason degree contained references that would become
familiar to Mormons, including the "all-seeing eye, whom the sun, moon
and stars obey," the bee-hive as "an emblem of industry," the five points of
fellowship, and the grand hailing sign of distress.[52] On March 17 Nauvoo
Lodge received other petitions that had apparently also been previously approved. In addition, Smith assisted in the organization of the Female Relief
Society on the same day, in the same second-story room in his red brick
store where he was initiated, passed, and raised.

51. *History of the Church* 4:550, 566; Hogan, *Founding Minutes*, 11–14; and Hogan, *Official
Minutes*, 21–23.
52. Grunder, *Mormon Parallels*, 960–64.

A VERY BAD MAN

Bennett continued to enjoy Smith's confidence following the installation of Nauvoo Lodge. The March 15, 1842, edition of *Times and Seasons* reported that Smith recognized Bennett as "respected brother" and Bennett referred to Smith as "esteemed friend."[53] Two weeks later the periodical published a letter written by Bennett's mother in which she congratulated her son "for the prosperity of your *church*, as I trust you are building on the rock of *Christ Jesus*, which is a sure foundation, and nothing will be suffered to prevail against it." On April 15 it noted that "Gen. Bennett Pres't. pro tem" had addressed the congregation at a Special Conference.

But on May 3 Grand Master Jonas sent a communication to Master George Miller that complicated Bennett's position with the prophet. Jonas informed Miller that he had received a letter written by a fellow Mason who severely criticized both James Adams and John C. Bennett. "I am informed that a lodge either has been or is about to be started in Nauvoo by the Mormons," the author wrote. "If either Gen. Bennett or Gen. Adams be concerned in it is the more to be regretted." He wrote that Adams's "character now among us (Springfield) is very far from being enviable" and that "Bennett is an expelled Mason having been expelled some time ago from a lodge at Fairfield Ohio—I have this from Dr. King of Decatur, who is very worthy mason, and was a member of the said lodge at Fairfield at the time of Bennett's expulsion." Jonas also advised Miller that Bennett, who claimed to be a bachelor, was actually married to a woman in Ohio. Jonas warned Miller that "irregularities are taking place in your lodge which I shall look to you to correct" and that "your lodge must be aware that you are regarded by some with some mistrust and therefore it is requisite that the strictest attention be paid to the ancient landmarks." He noted that he had sent a letter to "my correspondent [Deputy Grand Master Helm] to obtain all the evidence in the case and if true Gen. Bennett must be a very bad man."[54]

On May 7 Miller read Jonas's communication to a special meeting of Nauvoo Lodge, which took place at five a.m. and was attended by Joseph Smith, Bennett, and other high-ranking church members.[55] That same evening the Nauvoo Legion conducted a sham battle that was attended by most church authorities and a few guests including Stephen A. Douglas.

53. "Correspondence," *Times and Seasons* 3:10 (March 15, 1842), 724–25. Both letters were also printed in *The Wasp* 1 (May 28, 1842).
54. Letter from Abraham Jonas to George Miller, May 4, 1842, Record of Nauvoo Lodge, Church History Library.
55. Record of Nauvoo Lodge, May 7, 1842, Church History Library.

Following this event Smith invited the legion's officers (including Bennett) to dinner. When Willard Richards wrote an account of this battle almost three years later, he claimed that Smith believed that Bennett had planned to kill him during the battle and that this caused the final rupture between the two church leaders. Nevertheless, the manuscript history of Nauvoo Legion makes no reference to Smith's suspicions and this episode was not mentioned in any of the charges and countercharges that were exchanged after Bennett left Nauvoo.[56]

Jonas's surprising revelation that Bennett was an expelled Mason and that the professed bachelor was still married to a woman in Ohio was the more likely catalyst for Bennett's rapid fall from grace. Although it is unlikely that these revelations alone would have totally destroyed his relationship with Smith, the Mormon prophet must have been furious when Bennett justified his prior pretense, that he was a bachelor, by comparing his conduct with that of Smith who was also a married man who courted women.[57] In addition, Smith had worked hard to establish good relations with Jonas and other Illinois Masons, and Bennett's breaches of confidence concerning his private life (particularly the still secret practice of plural marriage) were undoubtedly viewed as particularly disloyal.

On May 9, Willard Richards replaced Bennett as secretary *pro tem* of Nauvoo Lodge and two days later the Mormon prophet, Hyrum Smith, and William Law determined that Bennett should be disfellowshipped. Although Bennett's church discipline was apparently approved by most members of the Twelve Apostles, and by the church's bishops, it was not immediately published and Bennett later claimed that Orson Pratt refused to sign the notice and that three of the other apostles' names were forged.[58]

56. See *History of the Church* 5:4; and Smith, *Saintly Scoundrel*, 85–86. Richard E. Bennett, Susan Easton Black, and Donald Q. Cannon narrate the events, as written by Willard Richards, but also note that on June 3 Bennett was congratulated by the Nauvoo Legion "for the able discharge of his duty since the foundation of the Legion" and that "the timing of this court is curious, for Bennett had orchestrated a sham battle on May 7." See Richard E. Bennett, Susan Easton Black, and Donald Q. Cannon, *The Nauvoo Legion in Illinois: A History of the Mormon Militia, 1841–1846* (Norman: The Arthur H. Clark Company, 2010), 157, 175–77.
57. *History of the Church* 4:287, 293, 295–96, 341, 502; 5: 3–5; Flanders, *Nauvoo: Kingdom on the Mississippi*, 112.
58. Smith's *History of the Church* (5:76) noted that William Law approved Bennett's disfellowship on May 11 and that he informed Bennett about the decision. Bennett later claimed that the signatures of three apostles (including Lyman Wight) were forged and that Orson Pratt refused to sign it. In fact, Willard Richards apparently wrote the signatures of John Page (who was in Pittsburgh when the document was dated), William Smith, and George A. Smith, as well as Orson Pratt. But Pratt's name was later crossed out and it appears that Lyman Wight did sign his own name. See John C. Bennett, *The History of the Saints; or, an Exposé of Joe Smith and Mormonism* (Boston: Leland & Whiting, 1842), 41.

On May 17 Joseph King responded to Helm's inquiry concerning Bennett's expulsion from Pickaway Lodge in Ohio and informed him that "soon after I was raised to the sublime degree of a master mason Bro. Patterson preferred charges against him [Bennett] in Pickaway Lodge from which he was expelled," and that he had spoken again with Patterson "who says it is consistent with his recollection."[59]

On the same day Smith instructed James Sloan (1792–1886), the general church clerk and recorder, to permit Bennett "to withdraw his name from the Church Record, if he desires to do so, and this with the best of feelings towards you and General Bennett." When Bennett submitted his resignation as mayor of Nauvoo, he signed an affidavit before Daniel H. Wells (1814–1891) in which he stated that Smith "never did teach to me in private that an illegal, illicit intercourse with females, was under any circumstances justifiable."[60]

On May 19 the Nauvoo City Council unanimously passed a resolution in which the "Council tender a vote of thanks to General John C. Bennett, for his great zeal in having good and wholesome laws adopted for the government of this city; and for the faithful discharge of his duty while Mayor of the same."[61] During the same meeting Bennett apparently confirmed that Smith had never "given me authority to hold illicit intercourse with women" and that he wished to "be restored to full confidence, fellowship, and my former standing in the Church."[62] Nevertheless, Bennett was notified six days later that he had been disfellowshipped by the First Presidency, Twelve, and bishops and that a notice would be published. But Smith recorded that the notice was not printed after Bennett pleaded to "spare him from the paper, for his mother's sake."[63]

---

59. Letter from Joseph King to Meredith Helm, May 17, 1842, Record of Nauvoo Lodge, Church History Library.

60. A copy of Smith's note to Sloan is located in the Joseph Smith Collection, Letters Sent, Box 2, fd. 5, Church History Library; but it was not published in either *The Wasp* or in *Times and Seasons* and it is not mentioned in *History of the Church*. Bennett mentioned the letter in the *Sangamo Journal*, July 8, 1842, and his affidavit was published several times and is mentioned in *History of the Church* 5:11, 38, 73; Danel W. Bachman, "A Study of the Mormon Practice of Plural Marriage before the Death of Joseph Smith" (master's thesis, Purdue University, 1975), 228. See also Bennett, *The History of the Saints*, 40–41.

61. This resolution was passed on May 19 and published in *The Wasp* two days later (May 21, 1842), 3.

62. *History of the Church* 5:13. The portion of the *History of the Church* which records these events was written after Smith's murder. It records that on May 19 Joseph Smith wrote that "John C. Bennett having discovered that his whoredoms and abominations were fast coming to light, and that the indignation of an insulted and abused people were rising rapidly against him, thought best to make a virtue of necessity, and try to make it appear that he was innocent, by resigning his office of Mayor, which the council most gladly accepted" (*History of the Church*, 5:12).

63. Ibid., 5:18.

On May 19 Thomas Grover (1807–1887), relying on Grand Master Jonas's May 4 communication, filed charges against Bennett in Nauvoo Lodge. Shortly thereafter the lodge began to investigate these allegations. Smith's history claims that Bennett acknowledged, during a meeting of Nauvoo Lodge on May 26, that he was guilty of "wicked and licentious conduct" [perhaps with Catherine Warren] and that he "cried like a child, and begged that he might be spared," and that Smith responded and "plead for mercy for him."[64] Nevertheless, the Nauvoo Lodge minutes do not record, or make any veiled reference, to this event.[65] In fact, on June 2 the lodge reviewed Grand Master Jonas's communication concerning Bennett but declined to act because there was "no evidence appearing to substantiate the charge." Instead, the lodge voted to postpone the investigation until its next regular meeting and to inform the grand master of the same.[66]

The lodge's postponement is not surprising when one considers that Bennett continued to publicly support the Mormon prophet and may have believed that Smith would eventually restore his membership as he had previously done in other cases involving church authorities. On June 14 Bennett wrote a letter to *The Wasp* (which was published on June 18) in which he defended Smith from attacks that were published in the *Sangamo Journal*. But during the same week the *Times and Seasons* finally published a notice that "members of the First Presidency of the church of Jesus Christ of Latter Day Saints, withdraw the hand of fellowship from General John C. Bennett, as a christian, he having labored with from time to time, to persuade him to amend his conduct, apparently to no good effect."[67]

Meanwhile Nauvoo Lodge met on June 16 (attended by Joseph Smith, Bennett, Wilford Woodruff, John Taylor, and others) where several letters were reviewed that seemingly confirmed that Bennett had been expelled from his lodge in Ohio. But even though "those communications satisfied

---

64. See Jessee, *Papers of Joseph Smith* 2: 387–88, and *History of the Church* 5:18–19 (May 26, 1842). On May 25 George Miller brought charges against Catherine Warren "for unchaste and unvirtuous conduct with John C. Bennett and others." She confessed to the charges "stating that they taught the doctrine that it was right to have free intercourse with women and that the heads of the Church also taught and practiced it, which things caused her to be led away, thinking it to be right—but becoming convinced that it was not right and learning that the heads of the church did not believe nor practice such things, she was willing to confess her sins and did repent before God for what she had done and desired earnestly that the Council would forgive her, and covenanted that she would hence forth do so no more." Following this confession "she was restored to fellowship by the unanimous vote of the Council." *The Nauvoo High Council Minute Book*, May 25, 1842, Church History Library. See also John S. Dinger, ed., *The Nauvoo City and High Council Minutes* (Salt Lake City: Signature Books, 2011), 417–18.
65. Record of Nauvoo Lodge, Church History Library, May 26, 1842.
66. Ibid., June 2, 1842.
67. "Notice," *Times and Seasons* 3:18 (June 15, 1842).

the minds of a majority of the brethren of the reality of his being an expelled Mason," the lodge still failed to act because Bennett produced "various documents from men of high standing in society in the neighborhood of Willoughby, and some from brethren of the Fraternity in the same neighborhood dated about the time bro Patterson says he was expelled showing the high estimation in which he was held by those gentlemen." Bennett also produced a document that referred "expressly to a communication from bro. Patterson to him, dated sometime about a year ago, breathing the most friendly feelings, and in the strongest language soliciting the continuance of former friendship." He told the lodge "that if he had been so expelled he never had been informed of the circumstances until the same was read in a communication from Grand Master A. Jonas dated May 4th." Following Bennett's explanation Nauvoo Lodge voted to postpone further proceedings until its next regular meeting, to request copies of Pickaway Lodge minutes, and to inform the grand master of the current status.[68]

The following day Willard Richards, as secretary *pro tem* of Nauvoo Lodge, wrote to Jonas to inform him that his letter "was read to the lodge which satisfied the minds of a majority of the brethren of the reality of Bennett's expulsion and was regarded as sufficient evidence of the fact." But Richards also reported that "in consequence of his [Bennett's] presenting various documents from men of high standing in society," which included "brethren of the fraternity in the same neighborhood," and "a communication from bro Patterson to him," and Bennett's own claim that he knew nothing about the expulsion, the lodge decided to postpone any action concerning Bennett pending further information and instructions.[69]

Meanwhile the Mormon prophet became increasingly frustrated by rumors Bennett was spreading concerning the practice of plural marriage. On June 18 the Mormon hierarchy finally excommunicated their former colleague and Smith publicly denounced him. According to Wilford Woodruff, he "spoke his mind in great plainness," during a public meeting

68. Record of Nauvoo Lodge, June 16, 1842, Church History Library. Erastus Webb, Bennett's uncle, wrote one of the letters. See *Sangamo Journal* (July 15, 1842); minutes also quoted in Hogan, "The Confrontation of Grand Master Abraham Jonas and John Cook Bennett at Nauvoo," 11. *History of the Church* references under this same date that Nauvoo Lodge published a notice signed by George Miller that Bennett had "palmed himself upon the fraternity as a regular mason, in good standing: and satisfactory testimony having been produced before said lodge, that he, said Bennett, was an expelled mason, we therefore publish to all the masonic world the above facts that he, the said Bennett, may not impose himself again upon the fraternity of masons." *History of the Church* 5:32 (June 16, 1842). There is no reference to this published notice in the lodge minutes on this date, which were kept by Willard Richards, but the notice did appear in *The Wasp* on June 25, 1842, with other material submitted by Joseph Smith.
69. Letter from Willard Richards to Abraham Jonas, June 17, 1842, Record of Nauvoo Lodge, Church History Library.

held near the temple site, "concerning the iniquity & wickedness of Gen John Cook Bennett, & exposed him before the public."[70] Three days later Willard Richards reported to Jonas that Bennett had left Nauvoo and informed the grand master, for the first time, that even before Jonas informed Miller that Bennett was an expelled Mason, "we were busily engaged in ferreting out evidence concerning his [Bennett's] conduct here in our city, as charges had been preferred against him, to the effect he was a wicked, adulterous character." Richards asserted that Bennett had "taught and solemnly affirmed" to various females that Smith and others were teaching and practicing loose sexual morals and that "the hand of fellowship was withdrawn" because of his "wicked conduct."[71]

On June 24 Sidney Rigdon delivered an address to Nauvoo Lodge during the St. Johns Day celebration. The communication was attended by Grand Master Jonas who later "ordered the Sec'y pro tem [Willard Richards] to read all the communications touching the case of Dr John C. Bennett, which was accordingly done."[72] During the same day Smith wrote a letter to Governor Carlin explaining Bennett's illicit activities and claimed for the first time that he had discovered in July 1841 that Bennett had a wife and children in Ohio. He also charged that Bennett was an adulterer, that he had seduced women in Nauvoo, and that even though Bennett had told others that Smith sanctioned and practiced "promiscuous intercourse," he had ultimately admitted, under oath, that Smith had "never taught him that illicit intercourse with females was under any circumstances justifiable." Smith also confirmed that Bennett had "seen fit to leave Nauvoo, and that very abruptly."[73]

Smith wrote a full explanation of the Bennett affair that was published in the June 25 issue of *The Wasp* and the July 1 issue of the *Times and Seasons*.[74] The letter, which was written "to the Church of Jesus Christ of Latter Day Saints, and to all the honorable part of the community," contained

70. Kenney, *Wilford Woodruff's Journal* 2:179 (June 18, 1842). See also *History of the Church* 5:34–35 (June 18, 1842). Bennett acknowledged that he was excommunicated on this date. See *Sangamo Journal*, July 8, 1842.

71. Letter from Willard Richards to Abraham Jonas, June 21, 1842, Record of Nauvoo Lodge, Church History Library.

72. While Jonas accepted Nauvoo Lodge's invitation, Bodley Lodge declined. See Record of Nauvoo Lodge, Church History Library, June 24, 1842; *History of the Church* 5:42 (June 24, 1842).

73. *History of the Church* 5:42 (June 24, 1842)

74. "To the Church of Jesus Christ of Latter Day Saints, and to all the Honorable part of community," *Times and Seasons* 3: 17 (July 1, 1842). Bachman, *A Study in the Mormon Practice of Plural Marriage*, 223; Flanders, *Nauvoo: Kingdom on the Mississippi*, 262; *The History of the Reorganized Church of Jesus Christ of Latter Day Saints* (Independence: Herald House, 1967), 2:585.

various flashbacks in which he revealed that he knew as early as 1840 that Bennett was a married man, that as soon as he learned about Bennett's family in Ohio he counseled him not to associate with women in Nauvoo, but that Bennett failed to follow his counsel and had seduced numerous Mormon women.[75] The Mormon prophet also revealed that he first learned about Bennett's marital status from "a person of respectable character" shortly after Bennett arrived in Nauvoo, who informed him that Bennett "had a wife and two or three children in McConnelsville, Morgan County, Ohio." Despite Bennett's marital status Smith charged that he "began to keep company with a young lady" in Nauvoo, and that even after Smith had discouraged him from doing so he nevertheless began to teach other unsuspecting women "that promiscuous intercourse between the sexes, was doctrine believed in by the Latter-Day Saints, and that there was no harm in it."

The Wasp published a March 2, 1841, letter, written by Miller to Smith, in which Miller confirmed that Bennett abandoned his wife and children in Marietta, Ohio. The Mormon prophet revealed for the first time that Hyrum Smith and William Law, in a letter dated June 15, 1841 (and delivered during the early part of July), reported that Bennett "had a wife and children living, and that she had left him because of his ill-treatment towards her," and that Bennett "did not attempt to deny [it]; but candidly acknowledged as fact."[76] *The Wasp* also republished Bennett's affidavit in which he denied "that General Joseph Smith has given me authority to hold illicit intercourse with women," his similar statement made to the Nauvoo City Council, and Miller's notice, as master of Nauvoo Lodge, that when the Nauvoo Lodge determined that Bennett was an expelled Mason, they expelled him from their own lodge in order that he "may not again impose himself upon the fraternity of Masons."[77]

Smith's letter about Bennett's marital status, his seduction of women, and his acknowledgment that Smith did not teach "promiscuous intercourse," left out the important details that Smith was privately practicing plural marriage, courting women, and teaching that he had a celestial mandate to do so. In addition, Smith's assertion that he knew about Bennett's

75. "To the Church of Jesus Christ of Latter Day Saints, and to all the honorable part of the community," *The Wasp* 1 (June 25, 1842); *Times and Seasons* 3 (July 1, 1842): 839–42; Flanders, *Nauvoo: Kingdom on the Mississippi*, 266; Bachman, *A Study in the Mormon Practice of Plural Marriage*, 232. These revelations, some of which were also included in Smith's letter to Governor Carlin, should be treated cautiously and evaluated in the context of the ugly, bare-knuckles fight that was beginning to unfold.
76. *The Wasp* 1:11 (June 25, 1842). See also Bachman, *A Study in the Mormon Practice of Plural Marriage*, 223.
77. Joseph Smith, "Important Facts Relative to…John C. Bennett," *Times and Seasons* 3:17 (1 July 1842): 839–43.

marriage shortly after he arrived in Nauvoo in 1840, that he received two
letters confirming this in 1841, and that he confronted Bennett about it
shortly thereafter, should be treated with caution. The chronology seems inconsistent with the confidence that Smith placed in Bennett when he supported him in the first mayoral election in Nauvoo and when he appointed
him as chancellor of the University of the City of Nauvoo and as assistant
church president. Smith upheld Bennett as a "respected brother" until at
least April 1842, and George Miller also supported Bennett's appointment
as secretary of Nauvoo Lodge more than a year after Smith claimed that
Miller was aware that Bennett had left a wife and children in Ohio.[78]

Meanwhile, Nauvoo Lodge continued to function and initiate Masons
throughout this period and it soon became the largest lodge in Illinois. Ken
Godfrey has noted there were only 480 Masons in the other twelve Illinois
lodges and that Nauvoo Lodge, during the first five months of its existence,
had "six times as many initiations and elevations from all the other lodges
in the state combined." He has also noted that this "seems to have aroused
jealousy, and rumors circulated that Mormons were becoming Masons so as
to completely dominate the Masonic organization of the state."[79]

HISTORY OF THE SAINTS

Bennett began publishing his sensationalist insider's view of Mormonism
not long after Smith's letter was published in *The Wasp* and *Times and Seasons*. Between July 8 and September 2, 1842, he wrote letters to the *Sangamo
Journal* in Springfield in which he claimed that Smith had successfully convinced women in Nauvoo to become his plural wives. He charged that while
Smith had successfully seduced several Master Masons' wives he failed with
several other women, including Nancy Rigdon who was the daughter of
one of his counselors.[80] He also challenged his disfellowshipping (claiming it contained forged signatures); alleged that Smith sold property to his

78. Miller detested Bennett in Nauvoo and continued to criticize him even after they both
had left the main branch of Mormonism and became, for a time, followers of James Strang.
In 1855 Miller asserted in a letter to the *Northern Islander* that "John C. Bennet[t], [is] one
of the most corrupt of corrupted men, having been severely reproved for his corruptions and
false teachings, set out to get revenge for being so harshly dealt by.—He wrote and published
a series of exposures of Mormon corruptions, as he was pleased to call them, and by his falsehoods procured another requisition by the Gov. of Missouri, upon the Governor of Illinois,
for the expatriation of Joseph Smith, as accessory before the fact to an attempt to commit
murder on the body of Ex. Gov. Lilburn W. Boggs." George Miller to "Dear Brother," June
26, 1855, in "Correspondence," *Northern Islander* 5 (August 16, 1855): 4 (Saint James, Beaver
Island).
79. Godfrey, "Joseph Smith and the Masons," 85.
80. The letters were published (with the date they were written in parentheses) as follows:

closest associates before filing a petition for bankruptcy; maintained that he was coerced to sign the affidavit concerning Smith's teachings; and claimed that Smith had prophesied the death of Missouri governor Lilburn Boggs. He also wrote about the Female Relief Society and the exclusive quorum founded in 1842 known as the Holy Order (which he referred to as Order Lodge).

Bennett also made allegations concerning Nauvoo Lodge that would have very serious consequences. In his June 27 letter (published on July 8) he promised to "expose [Smith's] actings and doings in Nauvoo Lodge, U.D. when none but the Mormon *brethren* were present;—that he (Joe Smith) and five others, were entered, passed, and raised, before the Lodge was installed by the Grand Master; and that they all passed through a second time afterwards, with the exception of one, who is now abroad; and many other like irregularities, and departures from the ancient land-marks." Bennett repeated this claim (that six Mormons were "initiated, passed and raised, before the installation of the Lodge") in his July 4 letter (published on July 15) and identified them as "Joseph Smith, John Snyder, Brigham Young, Peter Haws, Willard Richards, and one other."

Bennett alleged that Nauvoo Lodge's minute book, which recorded these initiations, "was sealed up, and a new one commenced—the second was sealed up, and a third commenced—and then a new record book procured and such parts copied as they were willing should go out to the Grand Lodge—and such only." Finally, in his July 15 letter (published on July 22), he claimed that the lodge did not conduct separate ballots for each of the candidates ("sixty three persons were balloted for *in one ballot*") and that "three entered, three passed, and *four* raised, in one day, and the records made to appear as only *three* were raised by ante-dating one." He urged that "their dispensation should be immediately withdrawn, and a charter refused, and Miller and Joe expelled."[81] Although Abraham Lincoln observed that Bennett's letters "are making some little stir here, but not very great,"[82] his correspondence apparently had a much greater impact on Illinois Freemasons.

On July 7 Nauvoo Lodge passed a resolution that it was "fully satisfied that John C. Bennett, is an expelled mason, and that his name be stricken

July 8 (June 27); July 15 (July 2); July 15 (July 4); July 22 (July 15); August 19 (July 23); August 19 (August 3); and September 2 (July 30).
81. See *Sangamo Journal*, July 8, 15, and 22, 1842. See also Smith, *Saintly Scoundrel*, 100–104.
82. Bachman, *A Study of the Mormon Practice of Plural Marriage*, 255, quoting Roy P. Balser, ed., *The Collected Works of Abraham Lincoln* (New Brunswick, NJ: Rutgers University Press, 1953), 291–92.

from the rolls; and that this lodge regards him as totally unworthy [of] the fellowship, or regard, of all good and honorable men or masons."[83] Meanwhile, Bodley Lodge, which had refused to vouch for Nauvoo's Masons, met in a special communication on July 16 where it voted to recommend to the grand master to suspend Nauvoo Lodge's dispensation. It apparently relied on Bennett's claim, which was published the previous day, that there were irregularities in the number of Masons who had joined Nauvoo Lodge.[84] The lodge requested that the Grand Lodge investigate the "manner the officers of the Nauvoo Lodge, U.D. were installed" and by what authority the grand master purported to initiate, pass, and raise Joseph Smith and Sidney Rigdon "at one and the same time."[85]

Bodley Lodge apparently believed that Nauvoo Lodge was violating Masonic policy by conferring too many degrees at each communication and that the candidates were not proficient in the initial degrees (Apprentice or Fellow Craft) before being passed or raised to the next degrees (Fellow Craft or Master Mason). Jonas responded favorably to Bodley Lodge's recommendation and ordered that Nauvoo Lodge suspend its work beginning on July 30 until the next annual communication in October but he did not specify why the work was being suspended.[86] Nevertheless, Jonas was not satisfied with Nauvoo Lodge's rationale for expelling Bennett, i.e., that he was an expelled Mason, and he delivered a letter to the lodge (apparently before he suspended its work) in which he instructed "that whether Bennett had previously been expelled or not it was our duty to expel him for his conduct here."[87]

On August 4 Nauvoo Lodge read Jonas's letter concerning Bennett during its regular communication, and four days later it passed another resolution to expel Bennett from the lodge for his conduct in Illinois, i.e., seduction, adultery, lying, perjury, embezzlement, and illicit intercourse with a Master Mason's wife.[88] Shortly thereafter, Joseph Smith, with the

83. Record of Nauvoo Lodge, Church History Library, July 7, 1842.

84. Reynolds, *History of the M. W. Grand Lodge of Illinois*, 174–75.

85. Ibid., 175. Mackey notes that a grand master has "the power to 'make Masons at sight.'" Mackey, *The Principles of Masonic Law*, 44.

86. Record of Nauvoo Lodge, Church History Library, August 11, 1842. Albert Mackey later noted that "no lodge shall make more than five new brothers at one time" and that "no candidate shall be permitted to receive more than one degree on the same day" or additional degrees less than "four weeks his receiving previous degrees." Mackey, *The Principles of Masonic Law*, 217, 228. Hogan has claimed that Jonas had authorized Nauvoo Lodge to obligate nine men each day as long as no more than three were obligated at one meeting and that it was authorized to meet three times each day six times a week.

87. Record of Nauvoo Lodge, Church History Library, August 4, 1842.

88. Ibid., August 8, 1842. Jonas may have suspected that the allegations concerning Bennett's expulsion from Pickaway Lodge in Ohio were doubtful, but he was certain that there was a basis for expelling him more quickly based on his conduct in Illinois.

assistance of James Adams and other Mormon Masons, organized the Rising Sun Lodge in Montrose, Iowa, in order to continue to work the rituals of Freemasonry.[89]

During the same month Bennett delivered a series of speeches during a lecture tour that began in New York City and continued to Boston and Salem. In October his *History of the Saints* (which was an embellished collection of his letters written to the *Sangamo Journal*) was published in Boston. The book contained forty-five pages of affidavits affirming his good character (including his uncle's letter stating that he would be welcome to visit Pickaway Lodge) and the same number of pages containing affidavits attacking Joseph Smith's character. Bennett also stretched his own credibility when he claimed that he never believed in Mormonism's truth claims.

Ironically, Bennett's most believable passage related to his Masonic membership in Ohio. The minutes of Pickaway Lodge No. 23, located in Circleville, Ohio, confirm his claim that he was not expelled. He was a member of that lodge from October 22, 1828, until August 12, 1829, and during most of that period he was senior deacon of the lodge. The minutes also note that he requested a "diploma," which meant that the lodge acknowledged that he was leaving in good standing. Thereafter, Bennett became a member of Friendship Lodge No. 89 in Barnesville, Ohio, which was the lodge he listed when he was signed as one of the organizers of Nauvoo Lodge.

The real background for Bennett's problems with some Masons in Ohio was much more nuanced than alleged in Nauvoo. George A. Patterson (who like Bennett was a Protestant minister and had served as grand chaplain for the Grand Lodge of Ohio) filed charges against Bennett (more than four years after Bennett demitted from Pickaway Lodge) for lying, selling diplomas, submitting petitions to the legislature with forged signatures, "gambling and preaching," submitting false plats, and falsely professing to be an officer of the U.S. Army. But Pickaway Lodge never acted on these charges, presumably because Bennett was no longer a member. When Patterson left the lodge two years later in good standing, the matter became moot. Thus, the statement of Dr. Eustus Webb (who was Bennett's uncle and a member of Pickaway Lodge) that Bennett was not expelled was apparently true.[90]

---

89. *History of the Church* 5:85.
90. Bennett, *The History of the Saints*, 48. Hogan, who reviewed a report from a past master of Pickaway Lodge, concluded that "in all fairness to Bennett, it appears he had some justification to claim before Nauvoo Lodge that his status with Pickaway Lodge No. 23 was not clear to him." Hogan, "John Cook Bennett and Pickaway Lodge No. 23"; Hogan, "Mormonism and Freemasonry on the Midwest Frontier," Unpublished ms. in Church History Library.

TOO MANY MASONS

On September 29, 1842, George Miller sent a letter to Jonas to inform him that he was disappointed that the grand master had suspended the lodge's dispensation and that the reasons given (that "we made too many masons," and that Miller "had published Bennett's expulsion") were excuses and not the real reason, which was "our religious tenants." He wrote that there was nothing in the ancient landmarks that prohibited "so many made, provided they all had the necessary qualifications" and he insisted that he had published Bennett's expulsion to minimize the possibility that Bennett might "palm himself upon other lodges." He concluded that "after twenty five years (I trust respectable) standing as a member of the fraternity," he had never previously known of any example when a religious test was used to disqualify a Masonic lodge.[91]

Nevertheless, Miller requested Lucius Scovil (1806–1889) and Henry Sherwood (1785–1862) to represent Nauvoo Lodge at the grand lodge's annual communication. Since Nauvoo Lodge had operated under a dispensation (rather than a charter), it had never been admitted into the registry of lodges and had no voting rights. When Scovil and Sherwood arrived at the annual communication they were requested to pay Nauvoo Lodge's dues and submit a return that revealed that Nauvoo Lodge had 243 Master Masons, four Fellow Crafts, and nine Entered Apprentices.[92] This rapid growth of the Mormons' lodge, which was highlighted by Bennett, was the primary cause for tension between Nauvoo Lodge and the rest of the lodges in Illinois. Bennett's other allegations, that Smith created "spurious" rituals that were practiced in "Order Lodge" and in the Female Relief Society, were not even mentioned. Instead, the Illinois lodges represented in Grand Lodge believed that Nauvoo Lodge was advancing candidates too rapidly and questioned the accuracy of the lodge's books and records.

Sherwood reported that "G[rand] M[aster] Jonas made a flaming speech in behalf of the N[auvoo] Lodge saying they were the fairest books and papers that had been brought from any Lodge to the Grand Lodge, and said he went and installed it, and found the people as peaceable, quiet and genteel as any people he was ever among in his life, and he verily believed

91. Letter from George Miller to Abraham Jonas, September 29, 1842, Record of Nauvoo Lodge, Church History Library.
92. After Grand Master Jonas installed the lodge it initiated 286 candidates, passed 276 Fellow Craft, and raised 272 Master Masons. Hogan, *Vital Statistics*, 16. Hogan notes that the "membership of 243 Master Masons reported in the 1842 Return of the Lodge was due to the extensive practice of granting demits freely when requested; even shortly after having been raised." Ibid.

that if they were not Mormons, the Lodge would stand the highest of any Lodge, that had come to that Grand Lodge." Sherwood argued "that he had been long of the opinion it was by reason of being Mormons that we were kept at arm's length" and complained about Quincy Lodge's prior refusal "to recommend us to the G[rand] L[odge] and said they could not recommend us by reason of 'an unacquaintance with us as masons and other things' that I supposed the other things meant Mormonism."[93]

Hiram D. Rogers of Bodley Lodge [Quincy] denied the charge that his lodge was biased against the Mormons and claimed that it had refused to recommend Nauvoo Lodge because its members knew that John C. Bennett was an expelled member. He asserted that after Bennett "was expelled from the Nauvoo Lodge he went to Hannibal Lodge and made the complaints who informed the Quincy Lodge who informed this G[rand] L[odge]." Sherwood observed that "in consequence 'of the credible information' of this expelled member J.C.B. they served the injunction believing an expelled member in preference to G.M. Jonas and called upon the G.M. to appoint a committee to go to Nauvoo and examine books."[94]

Sherwood reported that "the Grand Lodge appointed a committee of 3 to examine them [books and papers] and after several days examination reported them all fair, but recommended that the Grand Lodge should

93. H[enry] G. Sherwood, "H. G. Sherwood, 1839–1844," Church History Library, [1854], CR 100 396. Although Hogan published Sherwood's holographic report to demonstrate that the grand lodge misrepresented events that occurred during the 1843 communication, the grand lodge proceedings record that Sherwood and Jonas were in attendance in 1842, and there is no record that either one of them were in attendance in 1843. Furthermore, Sherwood's account describes events that took place during the 1842 annual communication, rather than a year later, including references to John C. Bennett's disclosures. Sherwood had a dispute with Hyrum Smith in April 1843 and four months later he declined to serve as master of Nye Lodge. See *The Nauvoo Diaries of William Clayton, 1842–1846, Abridged* (Salt Lake City, 2010), 11–12 (April 25, 1843); and Record of Nauvoo Lodge, Church History Library, July 29 and August 10, 1843. Kent Walgren observes that Sherwood's account "suggests that the only reason the Mormon lodges were disenfranchised was prejudice against Mormonism" but that it "ignores the influence of John C. Bennett's disclosures in the Springfield, Illinois *Sangamo Journal*…charging the Mormon-dominated Nauvoo Lodge with irregularities, including Joseph Smith's being made a Master Mason before the Lodge was installed and having sexual intercourse with the wives of other Master Masons." See Kent L. Walgren, "Fast and Loose Masonry," *Dialogue: A Journal of Mormon Thought* 18:3 (Fall 1985): 173.
94. Sherwood, "H. G. Sherwood, 1839–1844." Sherwood's account is confusing since it refers to both Bodley Lodge's refusal to recommend Nauvoo Lodge for a dispensation in 1841 and to its request made a year later to suspend the dispensation of the lodge. It is unlikely that anyone in Bodley Lodge believed or suspected that Bennett was an expelled Mason as early as 1841, but Quincy Masons apparently did rely on his allegations concerning the organization of Nauvoo Lodge in 1841–1842 when it requested that the lodge's dispensation be suspended.

suspend the N.L. [Nauvoo Lodge] another year *for fear there might be some-thing wrong.*"[95] In fact, the grand lodge passed a resolution to establish a committee "to examine the original minutes of Nauvoo, and diligently inquire into any irregularity or misconduct alleged to have been committed by said lodge, and to examine persons and papers connected with the subject, and report the facts to the M.W. Grand Master."

The resolution stated that the grand master could, upon receipt of the committee's report, continue the suspension of the lodge or reinstate its dispensation. Meredith Helm, who succeeded Jonas as grand master during the communication, appointed Jonathan Nye, W. B. Warren, and Hiram N. Rogers to conduct the investigation. During the same communication the grand lodge granted a charter to Rising Sun Lodge, the Mormon lodge that Joseph Smith helped organize in Montrose, Iowa.[96]

The report of Nye and Warren, which was completed within a month, concluded that the "principal charges which had been made against the lodge your committee found groundless" but that there were irregularities such as "balloting for more than one applicant at one and the same time" and "an applicant of at least doubtful character [perhaps Bennett] was received on a promise of reformation and restitution." Despite these irregularities the committee recommended that the lodge be allowed to continue to work if it did not repeat these offenses.[97] Although the committee was probably aware that Bennett had alleged that Smith created at least two clandestine rituals (Order Lodge and the Female Relief Society), it did not mention these claims in its report.

RECOMMENCE THE WORK

On November 2 Grand Master Helm accepted the committee's recommendation and reinstated Nauvoo Lodge's dispensation.[98] Thereafter Joseph Smith continued to attend lodge meetings and used Masonic terminology

95. Ibid. See also Hogan, "Mormonism and Freemasonry," 280–83, quoting from "H.G. Sherwood's statements, 1843, October 8th," recorded by Thomas Bullock, Church History Library.
96. *Proceedings of the Grand Lodge of Illinois from Its Organization in 1980–1850 Inclusive* (Freeport, IL: Journal Reprint, 1892), 59–60; Reynolds, *History of the M. W. Grand Lodge of Illinois*, 174. The official proceedings do not list Hiram N. Rogers but Sherwood's account does.
97. *Proceedings of the Grand Lodge of Illinois*, 70–72; Reynolds, *History of the M. W. Grand Lodge of Illinois*, 172–73. Sherwood noted that "Col. Warren invited Sherwood to go with him to the Lodge at Montrose as it was all right and clear with the N[auvoo] Lodge they accordingly went together, and sat in the L[odge] there." Sherwood, "H.G. Sherwood, 1839–1844."
98. *Proceedings of the Grand Lodge of Illinois*, 71–72; Reynolds, *History of the M. W. Grand Lodge of Illinois*, 172–73; Hogan, *Official Minutes*, 134.

to describe himself (notably, in a reference to the Entered Apprentice ritual, as "a rough stone [on which] the sound of the hammer and chisel was never heard"), encouraged confidentiality, and made references to lost rituals.[99] On November 10 Nauvoo Lodge met and elected Hyrum Smith to succeed George Miller as master, Lucius Scovil as senior warden, Samuel Rolfe as junior warden, William Felshaw as treasurer, and William Clayton as secretary.[100] When Rolfe and Felshaw declined, they were replaced by Noah Rogers and James Sloan.

Shortly thereafter Nauvoo Lodge voted to divide itself into three separate lodges because of its increasing membership and decided Henry Sherwood would become master of Nye Lodge and that Samuel Rolfe would become master of Hiram (later renamed Helm) Lodge.[101] In addition, Mormon Masons were participating in two other lodges in Iowa that were connected with the Illinois Grand Lodge. Eagle Lodge was located in Keokuk, Iowa, and was working under dispensation while Rising Sun Lodge in Montrose, Iowa, was working under a charter.[102] While the growth of Nauvoo Lodge was disturbing to the other Illinois lodges, the creation of new lodges (one of which was a voting participant in grand lodge) would become even more threatening to those who controlled the grand lodge.

On June 24, 1843, Worshipful Master Hyrum Smith laid the cornerstone for the Masonic temple in Nauvoo with great fanfare. The ceremony

99. See Bushman, *Rough Stone Rolling*, vi, and Grunder, *Mormon Parallels*, 958. Smith made these comparisons in May and June, 1843. Bennett's exposé prompted Missouri state officials to renew their attempts to extradite Smith to put him on trial for the attempted assassination of former governor Lilburn Boggs. See Thomas Ford, *A History of Illinois* (Chicago: S. C. Griggs & Co., 1854), 315–17. James Adams encouraged Smith to appear in United States District Court in Springfield even though the trial could have taken place in Nauvoo Municipal Court. James Adams to Joseph Smith, December 17, 1842, *History of the Church* 5:206. See also Walgren, "James Adams," 133–35. During Smith's trial, which lasted for seven days in December 1842–January 1843, he resided at Adams's home. *History of the Church* 5:216–20. See also Ford, *A History of Illinois*, 315–17. When the charges were dismissed, Smith returned to Nauvoo and established an increasingly close personal and business relationship with Adams and on one occasion in May even "prayed that James Adams might be delivered from his enemies." *History of the Church* 5:412. See also Black, "James Adams of Springfield, Illinois," 42.
100. Record of Nauvoo Lodge, November 10 and 17, 1842, Church History Library.
101. Ibid., November 19 and 23, 1842.
102. Reynolds, *History of the M. W. Grand Lodge of Illinois*, 192–93, 226; *Proceedings of the Grand Lodge of Illinois*, 120–21. Horace Eldredge (1816–1888) wrote during the summer of 1843 that he and George Watt (1812–1881) went "to Jacksonville and Springfield to obtain a couple of new dispensations for Masonic Lodges in Nauvoo which the officers of the grand body refused to grant unto us." Horace S. Eldredge Journal, Church History Library. Godfrey cites Eldredge at p. 89 but assumes that this occurred in 1844. Mervin Hogan has written about discussions that occurred in Nauvoo Lodge concerning the division of the lodge into three separate lodges. See Mervin Hogan, "Grand Master Jonathan Nye and Nauvoo Lodge," (November 1983), 10–22.

was attended by eight officers and 107 members of Nauvoo Lodge as well
as forty-three visiting Masons from other Illinois lodges. During this ceremony the second set of lodge minutes was placed in the cornerstone and
Apostle John Taylor delivered the oration.[103] During this same period,
James Adams, who had moved to Nauvoo and was elected Hancock County
probate justice of the peace, died of cholera before he took office[104] and was
buried, with full Masonic honors, in Nauvoo. During October general conference the Mormon prophet stated that Adams "is now one of the spirits of
the just men made perfect; and, if revealed, must be revealed in fire; and the
glory could not be endured." He also mused, perhaps referring to Adams's
conflicts with his fellow Freemasons, that "it should appear strange that so
good and so great a man was hated.... Wherever light shone, it stirred up
darkness. Truth and error, good and evil cannot be reconciled. Judge Adams
had some enemies, but such a man ought not to have had one."[105]

NEW IRREGULARITIES

Shortly after Smith gave his eulogy for Adams, the Grand Lodge of Illinois held its next annual communication, and the committee on returns
and work reported that irregularities remained in the "abstract returns" of
Nauvoo Lodge and claimed that the "lodge has failed to bring their record
before the committee, which to some of your committee at least, is a matter
of surprise, knowing as they do the severe lesson the said lodge was taught at
the last Grand Communication." The greatest irregularity, according to the
committee, was the lodge's "disposition to accumulate and gather members
without regard to character, and to push them on through the 2nd and 3rd
degrees before they can be possibly skilled in the 1st or 2nd."

The committee's real concern was more likely that Nauvoo Lodge had
initiated 187, passed 177, and raised 159 men from November 11, 1842, to
September 26, 1843.[106] Although the lodge initiated fewer men during this
period than it had from March 15, 1842, until August of the same year, when
Grand Master Jonas enjoined the lodge from further activity, the number of
initiates was still much greater than the 67 men who were initiated in all the
other Illinois lodges during the same period.[107] The grand lodge members

103. Record of Nauvoo Lodge, Church History Library, February 16, 1843. See also Hogan,
"The Erection and Dedication of the Nauvoo Masonic Temple" (unpublished manuscript,
Dec. 27, 1976), 3–6.
104. See Black, "James Adams of Springfield, Illinois," 42–43. See also "Obituary," *Times and
Seasons* 4: 18 (August 1, 1843), 287.
105. *History of the Church* 6:50–52.
106. Hogan, *Vital Statistics*, 16.
107. Ibid. Hogan believes that the 1842 returns actually understates Nauvoo Lodge's work
from March to August of that year.

were undoubtedly aware that Mormon Masons were initiating Masons in at least five lodges and that this growth threatened the balance of power among the Illinois lodges.

Thus, it is not surprising that the same Masons who were concerned in October 1842 about the rapid growth of Nauvoo Lodge were even more alarmed one year later when five Mormon lodges (not just one) were experiencing such extraordinary growth. Many members of the Illinois Craft were convinced that Mormons bent rules, "overstepped the bounds of prudence,"[108] and developed a "well-founded fear that within a short time the Mormon Lodges, if allowed to continue, would become more numerous than all others in the jurisdiction, and thus be able to control the Grand Lodge."[109]

The committee on returns and work observed in its report that other "Masons of eminence who have visited the lodge at Nauvoo" had provided them with the basis to "believe that they [Nauvoo Masons] put on their best dress when they appear before this Grand Lodge." The committee made similar representations concerning irregular practices in Helm and Nye Lodges and concluded that the work of Rising Sun Lodge was irregular and that it was "at a great loss to know what course to recommend in relation...to Keokuk Lodge."[110]

The grand lodge elected Alexander Dunlap as grand master who, unlike his predecessor, did not appoint a special committee to evaluate the practices of the Mormon lodges but instead relied upon the standing committee's report. Thus, when the committee offered resolutions to suspend the charter of Rising Sun Lodge and to revoke the dispensations of Nauvoo, Helm, Nye, and Keokuk Lodges, they "were called up and fully discussed, when on motion, they were unanimously adopted." Following the vote Past Grand Master Helm asked to be excused from the meeting. He may have objected to the new grand master's procedure of calling for a vote before a full investigation and undoubtedly recognized that the Mormon lodges had been disenfranchised, after he was replaced, because of their rapidly expanding numbers.[111]

108. Joseph E. Morcombe, "Masonry and Mormonism: A Record and a Study of Events in Illinois and Iowa Transpiring between the Years 1840 and 1846," *New Age* 2 (1905): 451.
109. Joseph E. Morcombe, "Masonry and Mormonism," *Masonic Standard* 11 (Sept. 1, 1906): 6.
110. *Proceedings of the Grand Lodge of Illinois*, 95–97. The committee noted that it was "aware that there is no by-law of this Grand Lodge to prevent this; nor are they sure that any length of probation would in all cases insure skill; but they feel certain that the ancient landmarks of the order require that the lodge should know that the candidate is well skilled in one degree, before he is advanced to another." Ibid., 95.
111. Ibid., 95–97. *History of the M. W. Grand Lodge of Illinois*, 199–200. Albert Mackey later claimed that Nauvoo Lodge was "guilty of passing the candidate through the second and

On November 2, 1843, Nauvoo Lodge met to discuss the grand lodge's decision. During this meeting Master Hyrum Smith "proceeded to call the attention of the Lodge to the ungenerous and in his estimation the unmasonic treatment of the Grand Lodge toward us as a lodge, and considered that we should be justified masonically by the Grand Lodge of the United States in resuming our work until we had the privilege of presenting a memorial and an appeal from the decision of the Grand Lodge of Illinois to a higher tribunal." The lodge then voted unanimously to continue to meet and work as a lodge and thereafter continued to make Masons with the same rapidity as it had previously. [112] Mormon Masons (particularly Master Lucius Scovil) also insisted, during this period of uncertainty, that the lodge complete the construction of the Masonic temple.

In January 1844 Grand Master Dunlap sent a communication to Nauvoo Lodge to demand that its "Dispensation, Jewels, Books & Papers" be returned and "forbidding us to meet any more as a Lodge of free and accepted Masons." Hyrum Smith responded that Nauvoo Lodge would "appeal to the next General Grand Convention, and also that we should refuse to give up our Dispensation, Books, Jewels &c or take any notice of the injunction until we could have our cause adjusted by the Convention."[113]

During the same month, the Mormon prophet asked W. W. Phelps, Mormonism's most celebrated anti-Mason who was not a member of Nauvoo Lodge, to read his appeal to the Vermont Freemasons (the "Brave Green Mountain Boys") to the select Quorum of the Anointed, also known as the Holy Order.[114] The appeal included a specific reference to Vermont Freemasons ("the fraternity of brethren, who are bound by kindred ties, to assist a brother in distress…to extend the boon of benevolence and protection, in avenging the Lord of His enemies, as if a Solomon, a Hiram, a St. John, or a Washington raised his hands before a wondering world, and exclaimed, 'My life for his!'") and requested their assistance in holding the citizens of Missouri accountable for the wrongs they had committed against the church. The appeal also suggested that Illinois Masons were cooperating in attempts to extradite the Mormon prophet to Missouri rather than trying to protect him.[115]

---

third degrees, before he could possibly be skilled in the proceeding degrees" and for that reason the lodge's dispensation was revoked. Mackey, *The Principles of Masonic Law*, 219–20.
112. Record of Nauvoo Lodge, November 2, 1843, Church History Library.
113. Ibid., January 4, 1844.
114. Devery S. Anderson and Gary James Bergera, eds., *Joseph Smith's Quorum of the Anointed 1842–1845: A Documentary History* (Salt Lake City: Signature Books, 2005), xxix, 19–22, 25–27, 41–42; Buerger, *The Mysteries of Godliness*, 60–63; Andrew F. Ehat, "Joseph Smith's Introduction of Temple Ordinances and the 1844 Mormon Succession Question" (M.A. thesis, Brigham Young University, 1981), 101.
115. *History of the Church* 6:90–91. W. W. Phelps was excommunicated in 1838 and again in

In February, Thomas C. Sharp (1818–1894), editor of the *Warsaw Signal* and one of Mormonism's most bitter critics, published a letter that he claimed he received from Strafford, Orange County, Vermont, which purported to answer Smith's appeal to the Masonic fraternity. "We consider the Masonic institution disgraced by establishing a lodge in Nauvoo," the letter stated, "and we will never own as a brother of the fraternity one who we believe to be guilty of violating every law of civil society." The letter predicted that "a Solomon, a Hiram, a St. John or a Washington would never raise their hands before a wondering world and say my life for his, in reference to Joe Smith or any of your clan, no: not by a long way Joe." Instead, Freemasons "would say to you in true Roman style, procul. O procell este profane! (off be, be off ye profane.)"[116]

Despite the rejection of the Illinois Grand Lodge and perhaps Vermont Freemasons, Master Hyrum Smith and the Mormon Masons followed through with plans to dedicate their newly constructed Masonic temple. William Weeks (1813–1900), who was the architect of the Masonic lodge (as well as the Nauvoo Temple), included details in his design of the lodge that included an all-seeing eye (on the tympanum of the pediment) as well as a female figure (perhaps Fama) over the dome, which were not retained on the completed structure. Instead, the final structure was much more simple and devoid of Masonic symbols. The dedication, which took place on April 5, was attended by fifty-one Masons from other lodges, most of whom were either Mormon Masons or members of lodges located outside of Illinois.

Erastus Snow delivered a discourse concerning the "beauties and benefits of the institution" and Joseph Smith also spoke. During the dedication, "the oppression and ill treatment of the Grand Lodge" was mentioned, which provoked "a feeling of holy indignation," but the celebration did not focus on the lodge's legal status.[117] Another speaker at the dedication was William G. Goforth, a non-Mormon member of St. Clair Lodge No. 24, which provoked the grand lodge to send a communication of complaint to his St. Clair Lodge. Although the lodge formed a committee to investigate

1839 but was reinstated in 1840. Despite his well-known Masonic pedigree, Phelps did not rejoin Masonry and was not involved in the Nauvoo Lodge. *History of the Church* 4:164.
116. See Annette P. Hampshire, "Thomas Sharp and Anti-Mormon Sentiment in Illinois, 1842–1845," *Journal of Illinois Historical Society* 72 (May 1979), 84–89. The respondent, if he was a Mason, may have been even angrier if he had known that the appeal was written by Phelps, one of America's most famous seceding Masons. See also Vogel, *Early Mormon Documents* 1:595–98, concerning this response.
117. Record of Nauvoo Lodge, April 5, 1844, Church History Library; Reynolds, *History of the M. W. Grand Lodge of Illinois*, 244; *History of the Church* 6:287; Kenney, *Wilford Woodruff's Journal* 2:373; Hogan, "Erection and Dedication," 13.

the charge that one of its members had associated with "clandestine Masons of Nauvoo," there is no evidence that Goforth was ever disciplined.[118]

O LORD MY GOD

Despite the poisoned relationship that developed between Illinois Masons and Mormons, the catalyst for Smith's death had at least as much to do with internal dissent in the church as it did with relations with outsiders. Nevertheless, when a mob that included Freemasons killed Joseph and his brother Hyrum on June 27, 1844, it created an even more hostile relationship between Mormon Masons and their Gentile brothers, and the narration of the killings was permeated with Masonic language. Joseph and Hyrum were both shot multiple times and Joseph was apparently shot again while he attempted to leap out of the window. These events were witnessed by Willard Richards, who was not injured, and by John Taylor, who survived after being hit by three balls. Richards identified sixteen members of the mob and others identified many more.[119]

On July 1 the Nauvoo City Council voted to seek "private revenge on the assassinators of General Joseph Smith," and three days later Justice of the Peace Aaron Johnson interviewed William M. Daniels, who said he was an eyewitness, who identified Jacob Davis, Thomas Sharp, and Levi Williams as principal participants in the murders. Daniels testified that he "saw Joseph Smith leap from the window of the jail, and that one of the company picked him up and placed him against the well curb, and several shot him, Colonel Williams exclaiming, 'Shoot him! Damn him! Shoot him!'"[120]

On July 15 the *Times and Seasons* published an unsigned editorial confirming that both Joseph and Hyrum "were both Masons in good standing," that they were "shot to death, while, with uplifted hands they gave such signs of distress as would have commanded the interposition and benevolence of Savages or Pagans," and that "Joseph's last exclamation was 'O Lord my God!'" which is the first few words of the Masonic distress call.[121] The

118. Reynolds, *History of the M. W. Grand Lodge of Illinois*, 254–57. See also Hogan, "Erection and Dedication," 13, who confirms that the lodge minutes enumerate ten officers and 318 members of Nauvoo Lodge, and 51 Masonic visitors.

119. *History of the Church* 7:142–46.

120. Ibid., 7:162–63.

121. "The Murder," *Times and Seasons* 5:13 (July 15, 1844), 584–86. Roberts republished this editorial in *History of the Church* 7: 186–89. This article may have been written by Richards, who was a Master Mason and served as secretary pro tem of Nauvoo Lodge, following John C. Bennett's removal from that office. The factual account set forth in the editorial (as well as in the Doctrine and Covenants) is very similar to Richards's signed account except for the reference to Joseph Smith making the Masonic distress call before his death. It is possible that Richards was assisted by the famous anti-Mason W. W. Phelps, who delivered the

editorial criticized Masons in the mob for failing to recognize their fellow Mason's plea for help: "Ye brethren of 'the mystic tie' what think ye! Where is our good Master Joseph and Hyrum? Is there a pagan, heathen, or savage nation on the globe that would not be moved on this great occasion, as the trees of the forest are moved by a mighty wind?"[122]

The *Times and Seasons* editorial undoubtedly relied on the recollections of Richards and Taylor, who were present when the murders took place, but neither apostle referred to the Masonic distress call in their accounts concerning those tragic events. Richards mentioned that Joseph's last words were "O Lord my God!" but he did not identify it as the distress call and these words were also included in the account published in the 1844 edition of the Doctrine and Covenants.[123] Taylor wrote his account after the Mormons had settled in Salt Lake City, apparently after Richards died, but it was not published until 1861.[124] He wrote that "the last words I ever heard [Smith] speak on earth" were "that's right Brother Taylor; parry them off as well as you can" as "I parried [the mob's guns] off with my stick, giving them another direction." Although he did not specifically state that Joseph and Hyrum gave Masonic distress calls, he mentioned Richards "elevating his hands two or three times, [while] he exclaimed, 'O Lord, my God, spare thy servants.'"[125]

On August 5 the Mormons gained complete control of the Hancock County Commission during county elections. Minor Deming, who believed that two to three hundred people were involved in the murders, was elected sheriff. This made it much more likely that those who were complicit in the murders of the Mormon prophet and patriarch would be tried.

---

funeral sermon on July 28 when the bodies of Joseph and Hyrum arrived in Nauvoo and who wrote the poem "Praise to the Man," which expressed similar worshipful sentiments toward the Mormon prophet and which eventually became a popular Mormon hymn.

122. "The Murder," *Times and Seasons* 5 (July 15, 1844), 585. Masons were defensive on this issue. The Vermonters who responded to Joseph Smith's "Appeal to the Green Mountain Boys" articulated a rationale for failing to come to the assistance of a fellow Mason in distress and Albert Mackey (although not referring specifically to Smith's case) wrote that Masons entitled to relief "must be in distress," "must be worthy," and "the assistance is not to be beyond the ability of the giver." Mackey, *The Principles of Masonic Law*, 267–69.

123. See Willard Richards, "Two Minutes in Jail," *Nauvoo Neighbor* 2:13 (July 24, 1844), 3; and Willard Richards, "Two Minutes in Jail," *Times and Seasons* 5:14 (August 1, 1844), 598–99. B. H. Roberts republished Richards's account in *History of the Church* 6:619–21. D&C, Section 121, 444–45. This section has been renumbered and is currently section 135.

124. Richard F. Burton, *The City of the Saints and across the Rocky Mountains to California* (London: Longman, Green, Longman, and Roberts, 1861), 625–67; Richard F. Burton, *The City of the Saints and across the Rocky Mountains to California* (New York: Harper & Brothers, Publishers, 1862), 517–47. This account was republished in Daniel Tyler, *A Concise History of the Mormon Battalion in the Mexican War, 1846–1847* (Salt Lake City, 1881), 10–64, and by Roberts in *History of the Church* 7: 53–125.

125. Burton, *The City of the Saints*, 653–54 (1861).

Thereafter, John Taylor published William Daniels's *A Correct Account of the Murder of Generals Joseph and Hyrum Smith at Carthage on the 27th day of June, 1844*, which was ghost-written by Lyman Littlefield and was an elaboration of Daniels's earlier affidavit, which contained Masonic markers.

Daniels claimed that he was present outside the Carthage jail when the Mormon prophet was killed. He wrote that Smith "exclaimed, three or four times, '*O Lord My God!!!*'" before he jumped from the second-story window to pavement below. He stated that a member of the mob "set President Smith against the south side of the well-curb, that was situated a few feet from the jail," and that when Smith began to stir, four members of the militia fired on him and the man who dragged him to the well drew his bowie knife to cut off the prophet's head. But before he could complete his down stroke, a pillar of light appeared from heaven and caused the prophet's assassins to flee.[126]

This exaggerated account contains parallels to the mythology associated with the murder of Hiram Abiff. According to Masonic legend, Abiff was killed by fellow Masons because he possessed hidden knowledge (the Master Mason's word) that they were trying to extract from him before the completion of the temple. Similarly, Smith possessed an ancient record, which other men attempted to steal, and restored the "Master's Word which, like Abiff's word, would eventually be revealed in a temple that he was constructing."[127] The temple workers who investigated Hiram Abiff's death followed his blood trail to a well north of Solomon's temple. They "concluded that H. A. had been killed there and perhaps flung in the well," and noted "the appearance of a Luminous light or meteor standing over the well."[128]

There is a Masonic legend that a well near the temple dried up after Hiram Abiff's murder. At least one observer also reported that Smith was wearing a talisman, inscribed with the name of God, at the time of his

126. William Daniels, *A Correct Account of the Murder of Generals Joseph and Hyrum Smith at Carthage on the 27th day of June, 1844* (Nauvoo, IL: J. Taylor, 1845). Nauvoo Mason Lyman O. Littlefield (1819–1888) ghost-wrote the volume for Daniels who was a prosecution witness during the murder trial. All persons who wished to order the pamphlet were directed to Littlefield and he later admitted that the "account given by Wm. M. Daniels... was written out carefully" by him and he quoted liberally from it in his own account of the martyrdom. Lyman O. Littlefield, *The Martyrs; The Sketch of the lives and a full account of the martyrdom of Joseph and Hyrum Smith* (Salt Lake City: Juvenile Instructor Office, 1882), 71. Daniels's version of events, including that a "man with a bowie knife raised his hand to cut off Joseph's head" and that a "vivid flash of lightning caused his arm to fall powerless," was later published in a Deseret Sunday school catechism by the church in 1882. See *Questions and Answers on the Life and Mission of the Prophet Joseph Smith* (Salt Lake City: Juvenile Instructor Office, 1882), 51.
127. For a discussion of the "theme of the stolen manuscript," see Grunder, *Mormon Parallels*, 1144–45.
128. Perfect Master Degree, 1783 Franken Ms.

death.[129] Although that talisman was not Masonic it is at least reminiscent of the Hiram Abiff story. Those who investigated his death also discovered a jewel that Abiff had apparently cast into the well when he was attacked by the ruffians.[130] The jewel, in some rituals, was a talisman with the name of God in Hebrew inscribed within two interlaced triangles forming a six-pointed star, which is a Masonic symbol for the perfect Godhead.[131]

The official accounts of Smith's murder are also reminiscent of narratives concerning William Morgan's disappearance. Lebbeus Armstrong, a Presbyterian minister who seceded from the Craft, noted that "under the direction of Divine Providence, William Morgan was an instrument of commencing the work. At the risk, and eventual loss of his life, he seized the mask of disguise, which has so long concealed the real character of Free-masonry; and, rending, he broke the Masonic enchantment."[132] Another seceder named Solomon Southwick delivered an oration in 1828 in which he quoted Morgan as saying, "I will go to Canandaigua…and meet my accusers face to face, and prove my innocence: I have nothing to fear from such a charge." Southwick then observed, "How little did he foresee, that he was then going, like a lamb to the slaughter, to part for ever from all that he held dear on earth—wife, children, friends, the cheering sun-beam, and the refreshing shade, the blooming groves and the green fields of his country, and the holy altars of his God!"[133]

129. Quinn, *Early Mormonism and the Magic World View*, 65–66. In an affidavit written in 1938 Charles Bidamon, stepson of Emma Smith, testified: "I have many times heard her [Emma Smith] say, when being interviewed, and showing the piece, that it was in the Prophet's pocket when he was martyred at Carthage, Illinois." Ibid.
130. In some rituals it was found on Hiram's body.
131. Arturo de Hoyos pointed out the parallels between Hiram Abiff and Joseph Smith (as described in Nels Lundwall's *Fate of the Persecutors of the Prophet Joseph Smith*), including the pillar of light, the well, and the possession of talismans. Although Daniels was not a Mason his ghost-writer, Lyman O. Littlefield, was a Master Mason. See also Hogan, *Official Minutes*, 79; Eugene E. Hinman, Ray V. Denslow, and Charles C. Hunt, *A History of the Cryptic Rite*, 2 vols. (Cedar Rapids, IA, 1931), 1:177 (the signet referred to in this book is apparently from George Oliver's *Rite de Bouillon* which, according to Hamill, is a fraud. See, Hamill, *The Craft*, 21–22).
132. See Lebbeus Armstrong, *The Man of Sin Revealed* (Waterford, NY?: J. C. Johnson, 1829?), 46, quoted in Grunder, *Mormon Parallels*, 152. Smith may have been influenced by the Antimasonic Party when he decided to run as a third-party candidate for president of the United States. William Wirt was the first viable third-party candidate who ran on the Antimasonic Party ticket in 1832. Wirt garnered seven electoral votes by winning in Smith's home state of Vermont. Smith was killed before the election in 1844, but some have speculated that he was positioned to be competitive in New York. See Robert S. Wicks and Fred R. Foister, *Junius and Julius: Presidential Politics and the Assassination of the First Mormon Prophet* (Logan: Utah State University Press, 2005).
133. See Grunder, *Mormon Parallels*, 1690, quoting Solomon Southwick, *An Oration* (Albany: Webster and Wood, 1828), 34. This was also cited in the *New England Anti-Masonic Almanac for…1831*. See Grunder, *Mormon Parallels*, 1009.

After his death, the *Times and Seasons* reported Joseph Smith saying, several days before his death, "I am going like a lamb to the slaughter: but I am calm as a summer's morning: I have a conscience void of offence toward God, and toward all men: I shall die innocent."[134] This statement was later modified in the Doctrine and Covenants (section 111, paragraph 4) to: "I am going like a lamb to the slaughter; but I am calm as a summer's morning; I have a conscience void of offence, towards God, and towards all men—I SHALL DIE INNOCENT, AND IT SHALL YET BE SAID OF ME, HE WAS MURDERED IN COLD BLOOD."[135] The *History of the Church*, which was based on an 1854 manuscript, included the phrase "my blood shall cry from the ground for vengeance."[136]

Finally, several decades after Smith's murder, a newspaper account was published claiming that Dr. B. W. Richmond was present in Nauvoo in June 1844. Richmond stated that he met Lucinda Morgan (William Morgan's widow and by some accounts Joseph Smith's plural wife) several days before Smith was killed and that he noticed she had a copy of "Stearns on Masonry" that contained a likeness of William Morgan and that after Smith died he saw her again "standing at the head of Joseph Smith's body [in the Mansion House], her face covered, and her whole frame convulsed with weeping."[137] The Master Mason degree, as summarized by William Morgan, recounted that Abiff's body was buried under the holy of holies in King Solomon's Temple, which was marked by a monument with an inscription that included: "A virgin weeping over a broken column, with a book open before her," and that the inscription symbolizes the "unfinished state of the temple" at the time of Hiram Abiff's murder.[138] Although Lucinda was certainly not a virgin when Joseph was murdered, she may have wept for him and for the unfinished state of his second temple.

134. *Times and Seasons* 5 [July 15, 1844]: 585.
135. D&C sec. 111, para. 4 (1844, now D&C 135:4).
136. The LDS *History of the Church* (which reflected a manuscript compiled in 1854) recorded that Joseph Smith said on June 24, 1844: "I am going like a lamb to the slaughter, but I am calm as a summer's morning. I have a conscience void of offense toward God and toward all men. If they take my life I shall die an innocent man, and my blood shall cry from the ground for vengeance, and it shall be said of me 'He was murdered in cold blood!'" *History of the Church* 6:555. See also Brigham Young, "Knowledge, Correctly Applied, the True Source of Wealth and Power, etc.," *Journal of Discourses* 10:184.
137. "The Prophet's Death," *Deseret News*, Nov. 27, 1875, pp. 2–3, attributed to an article previously published in the *Chicago Tribune*. Rick Grunder has noted that Stearns's book was published prior to William Morgan's exposé, that it did not have an engraving of Morgan even after it was expanded after Morgan's abduction, but that Bernard's *Light on Masonry* did. See Grunder, *Mormon Parallels*, 1708–9 [Entry 416].
138. Morgan, *Illustrations of Masonry*, 98. For an example of this imagery, see Cross, *The True Masonic Chart*, 18.

Illustration of weeping Mason widow. Published in Jeremy L. Cross,
The True Masonic Chart, or Hieroglyphic Monitor, 18.

SEVERING ALL RELATIONS

Shortly after the Carthage murders, Past Grand Master Helm—who was apparently upset when the grand lodge disenfranchised Mormon Masons—advised Springfield Lodge that he had "resigned from Masonry."[139] Then in October 1844 the Grand Lodge of Illinois severed all relations with Nauvoo, Helm, and Nye Lodges because those lodges refused to surrender their dispensations. The grand lodge also voted to declare the work of the Mormon lodges clandestine and suspended their members from the privileges of Masonry. It also appointed a committee to review the work of Eagle Lodge that determined that its dispensation should not be renewed.[140]

During the same month nine men were indicted for the Smith brothers' murders but only five of them were arrested and tried. Mark Aldrich, a Master Mason who visited Nauvoo Lodge in January 1842, was the only Mason indicted.[141] He was a member of Warsaw Lodge, which was organized in 1843.[142] Three of the other defendants (Thomas Sharp, Levi Williams, and Jacob C. Davis) were initiated, passed, and raised as Master Masons in Warsaw Lodge after they were indicted.[143] In May 1845 these men were tried and acquitted by a jury. During the trial O. H. Browning, one of the defendants' attorneys, questioned William Daniels's credibility when he testified concerning the embellishments he had included in his published account and in particular the appearance of a light when the Mormon prophet was lying beside the well.[144]

On June 15 Aldrich was elected master of his lodge[145] and the following October the Grand Lodge of Illinois voted to investigate Warsaw Lodge's decision to initiate, pass, and raise men who were under criminal indictment.[146] The lodge responded that an "indictment was no evidence of crime," that the indictments had "been procured by the testimony of perjured witnesses who had been suborned by the Mormons," and that the applicants'

139. Hogan, *Mormonism and Masonry*, 316.

140. Reynolds, *History of the M. W. Grand Lodge of Illinois*, 232, 228, 261.

141. See Hogan, *Founding Minutes*, 9 (January 3, 1842); Hogan, *Official Minutes*, 17 (January 3, 1842).

142. Mormon Masons attended the first meeting of Warsaw Lodge. See Reynolds, *History of the M. W. Grand Lodge of Illinois*, 218–19.

143. Ibid., 350–52. See also Dallin H. Oaks and Marvin S. Hill, *Carthage Conspiracy: The Trial of the Accused Assassins of Joseph Smith* (Urbana: University of Illinois Press, 1975), 66–67.

144. B. H. Roberts later wrote that "it is unfortunate that this affiant [William Daniels] did not keep his subsequent statements at trial within the limits of this affidavit as he would have then been a much more efficient witness at the subsequent trial."

145. Reynolds, *History of the M. W. Grand Lodge of Illinois*, 315 (June 25, 1845).

146. *Proceedings of the Grand Lodge*, 178; Reynolds, *History of the M. W. Grand Lodge of Illinois*, 305–6.

standing in the community had actually improved after they were indicted "from the fact that they had been particularly selected as the victims of Mormon vengeance."[147]

Thereafter Grand Master Walker reported to the grand lodge that the lodge committed an "error of the head and not of the heart; that all the harm has been done; the men have been since tried by the laws of their country and a jury of their peers, and acquitted."[148] Such a response is reminiscent of the attitude of some New York Freemasons who continued to protect Craft members who were implicated in the disappearance of William Morgan, which led to the fracture of the Masonic movement and the disappearance of many Masonic lodges as well as every lodge chartered by the original Grand Lodge of Illinois.[149]

Nevertheless, despite the Illinois Craft's myopic attitude toward Mormon Masons, the Nauvoo Lodge ignored the grand lodge's withdrawal of recognition and continued to initiate new members. On December 5, 1844, Brigham Young nominated Lucius Scovil to become master of Nauvoo Lodge and Shadrach Roundy as senior warden. George A. Smith, the martyred prophet's cousin, was nominated as junior warden and all the nominees were unanimously elected.[150] On December 19 Nauvoo Lodge discussed its relationship with the Grand Lodge of Illinois and the possibility that the Mormon lodges could "call a convention of the several lodges thus oppressed and form a Grand Lodge." George A. Smith made a motion that a committee be formed to discuss the matter further and Master Scovil appointed himself, Newel K. Whitney, George Miller, John G. Parker, and Asahel Perry to the committee.[151] Eventually, however, Scovil decided that it was not "good policy to form a Grand Lodge."[152]

On April 10, 1845, Heber C. Kimball, who was Brigham Young's closest confidante, instructed Worshipful Master Lucius Scovil to "stop making Masons, only as time shall permit," and to transform the Masonic hall

---

147. Reynolds, *History of the M. W. Grand Lodge of Illinois*, 350–52. See also Joseph E. Morcombe, *History of the Grand Lodge of Iowa A.F. & M.* (Cedar Rapids: Grand Lodge of Iowa, 1910), 1:164–65. See also *Masonic Voice—Review* (May 1909): 152. When Warsaw Lodge later surrendered its charter, it was reported that the reason was because it lacked the proper space in which to conduct its work. Reynolds, *History of the M. W. Grand Lodge of Illinois*, 395.

148. *Proceedings of the Grand Lodge*, 337n; Hogan, "Freemasonry and the Lynching at Carthage Jail," 16–17.

149. Oaks and Hill have suggested that Warsaw Lodge eventually surrendered its charter in 1846 because of these events rather than the reason given—that "the members of Warsaw Lodge No. 21 have no suitable room to work in." See Oaks and Hill, *Carthage Conspiracy*, 395; and Reynolds, *History of the M. W. Grand Lodge of Illinois*, 395.

150. Hogan, *Official Minutes*, December 5, 1844.

151. Ibid., December 19, 1844.

152. Ibid., January 2, 1845.

into a printing office. Despite these instructions, Scovil continued to make Masons even after the Nauvoo temple was dedicated. The Nauvoo Lodge met until February 1846, which coincided with Scovil's mission call to England.[153] By the end of 1845 the five Mormon lodges had raised more than 1,366 Master Masons while all the other Illinois lodges combined had less than 800. Thus, Mormon lodge activity continued at nearly the same pace, during the year and a half following Smith's death, as it had during his lifetime.[154] Thereafter Mormon participation in Freemasonry came to an abrupt end when Brigham Young led the Saints to the Great Basin and the relationship between the Craft and the LDS Church was completely unraveled.

153. Stanley B. Kimball, ed., *On the Potter's Wheel: The Diaries of Heber C. Kimball* (Salt Lake City: Signature Books in Association with Smith Research Associates, 1987), 103 (April 10, 1845).
154. Reed C. Durham Jr., "Is There No Help for the Widow's Son?" *Mormon Miscellaneous* 1 (Oct. 1975): 17; and Hogan, *Official Minutes*, 49–81. See also Hogan, *Vital Statistics*, 16. Hogan calculates that Nauvoo Lodge received 369 petitions between November 2, 1843, and August 1, 1844, and 439 petitions from August 15, 1844, and September 15, 1845.

The Female Relief Society

WHILE MORMON FREEMASONS were in the process of organizing Nauvoo Lodge, Joseph Smith authorized the formation of a female benevolent society. Eliza R. Snow (1804–1887), who would eventually become one of Smith's plural wives, approached the prophet and requested that he approve a constitution and bylaws that she had drafted for such a society. She envisioned a society that would furnish clothes and materials to men working on the temple, but Smith did not approve the documents she proposed. Although he acknowledged that they "were the best he had ever seen," he preferred to "organize the women under the priesthood after the pattern of the priesthood."[1]

THERE IS NOTHING PRIVATE

Smith organized the Female Relief Society of Nauvoo on March 17, 1842 (just two days after he was initiated into Freemasonry), in the same "Lodge Room" where the Nauvoo Lodge held its meeting, above his red brick store on Water Street. Willard Richards, who was the recording secretary for a portion of the first meeting of the society, noted that he found a scrap of paper "lying on an open Bible in the room appropriated by the Society... at its first meeting" that was probably used during Masonic initiations. The scrap contained the following Masonic prayer: "O, Lord! help our widows, and fatherless children! So mote it be. Amen. With the *sword* and the *word* of *truth*, defend thou them. So mote it be. Amen."[2]

1. Sarah M. Kimball, "Auto-biography," *Woman's Exponent* (September 1, 1883), 51.
2. The words "written on a scrap" were written below Richard's notation and above the frontispiece. Those words may have been added later, either by Richards or by the Eliza R. Snow who was the Relief Society's secretary. "A Book of Records. Containing the Proceedings of the Female Relief Society of Nauvoo," (March 17, 1842–March 16, 1844), LDS Church History Library (hereafter "A Book of Records"), 1.

When Smith addressed the Relief Society he used Masonic terminology and taught its members that among the most important lessons they needed to learn was the Masonic skill of being able to keep a secret. He hoped that the Relief Society would help prepare Mormon women for the temple endowment, which the Mormon prophet revealed several weeks later, and he wanted to protect the secrecy of the ever-growing practice that he was beginning to disclose to his closest associates.

During the first meeting it became apparent that the new organization would not be a typical female benevolent society. Smith addressed the twenty charter members, nine of whom, according to Jill Derr, Janath Cannon, and Maureen Ursenbach Beecher, "were already, or soon would be, partakers in the newly reinstituted Old Testament practice [of plural marriage], five of them as plural wives to the Prophet Joseph himself."[3] Smith told the society that they constituted a "Society of Sisters [that] might provoke the brethren to good works in looking to the wants of the poor—searching after objects of charity, and in administering to their wants to assist; by correcting the morals and strengthening the virtues of the female community, and save the Elders the trouble of rebuking; that they may give their time to other duties &c. in their public teaching."[4] Thereafter Eliza Snow observed "that the popular Institutions of the day should not be our guide—that as daughters of Zion, we should set an example for all the world, rather than confine ourselves to the course which had been heretofore pursued."[5]

The women selected Emma Smith, the prophet's wife, as the society's first president, Sarah Cleveland (who would soon become one of Smith's plural wives) and Elizabeth Ann Whitney (1800–1882), the mother of another future Smith wife, as her counselors. Smith reminded the sisters that his wife had been designated an "Elect Lady" in an 1830 revelation and that "she was ordain'd at the time the Revelation was given, to expound the scriptures to all; and to teach the female part of [the] community."[6] He also told them that the revelation was fulfilled when the society elected her as its president.[7] Thereafter Apostle John Taylor confirmed "all the blessings

3. Derr, Cannon, and Beecher, *Women of Covenant*, 60.
4. "A Book of Records," March 17, 1842, 1.
5. Ibid., 1–2.
6. D&C, 25: 3. The precise instruction was: "And thou shalt be ordained under his hand to expound the scriptures, and to exhort the church, according as it shall be given thee by my spirit" (25:7).
7. *History of the Church*, 4:552–53; D&C, Sec. 25. The revelation instructed him to "hearken unto the voice of the Lord your God" and informed his wife Emma that "thou art an elect lady, whom I have called." After receiving this revelation, Emma was "ordained" to "the office of thy calling." D&C, 25:1, 3, 5, 7. 2 John 1:1 reads: "The elder unto the elect lady and her children, whom I love in the truth; and not I only, but also all they that have known the

which had been confer'd" on Emma and he ordained her counselors to their offices.[8]

MORAL SURVEILLANCE

When Smith organized the Relief Society he had already married, or been sealed to, at least six women in addition to his legal wife, Emma.[9] He began to reveal the principle of plural marriage to his most trusted followers, including the Twelve Apostles who had returned from missions to England the previous summer, and he encouraged them to embrace the practice. Among those who knew about the still-secret teaching were John C. Bennett, Joseph Noble, Brigham Young, Heber C. Kimball, Reynolds Cahoon, and Vinson Knight. These men, with the exception of Bennett, became some of the most enthusiastic participants in Nauvoo polygamy.[10]

Thus the society, which was initially conceived as a benevolent society, became dedicated to what Carmon Hardy has described as "moral surveillance."[11] Joseph counseled the society to "keep all your doings within your own bosoms, and hold all characters sacred," and it provided a forum to detect and shield the church from gossip. In particular, the society was intended to protect Joseph and the church hierarchy from rumors that the prophet was teaching the doctrine of plural marriage or that he was having sexual relations with multiple women.[12]

On March 24 Emma initially advised the sisters that "there is nothing private" in their deliberations. But, during the same meeting, a discussion

truth." Although "elect lady" is a title that appears in the Bible (2 John 1:1), it was also the name of a degree in the French Adoptive Rite. It would also be used as the name of the fifth degree in the ritual of the Eastern Star beginning in the 1850s. For Masonic applications of the term, see Coil, *Coil's Masonic Encyclopedia*, 9; Macoy, *General History*, 123, 130; *Order of the Eastern Star: An Instructive Manual on the Organization and Government of Chapters of the Order with Ceremonies and Ritual*, arranged by F. A. Bell (Chicago: Ezra A. Cook Publications, 1948), 20–22, 88–93.

8. "A Book of Records," March 17, 1842, 1–2; *History of the Church*, 4:552–53.

9. Smith began taking plural wives in Nauvoo beginning with Louisa Beaman on April 5, 1841. For "intellectual origins of polygamy" before Nauvoo, see Lawrence Foster, *Religion and Sexuality: The Shakers, the Mormons, and the Oneida Community* (Urbana: University of Illinois Press, 1984), 130–39; B. Carmon Hardy, *Solemn Covenant: The Mormon Polygamous Passage* (Urbana: University of Illinois Press, 1992), 5–6.

10. Smith, *Nauvoo Polygamy*, 259–64.

11. Hardy, *Doing the Works of Abraham*, 54.

12. "A Book of Records," March 17, 1842, 11–12. During the first meeting Sarah Kingsley Cleveland, one of Emma Smith's counselors who became one of her husband's plural wives the following year, noted that "we should not regard the idle speech of our enemies." Emma Smith said during the same meeting that "the members should deal frankly with each other—to watch over the morals and be very careful of the character and reputation—of the members of the Institution &c."

took place concerning "Clarissa Marvel [who] was accus'd of scandalous falsehoods on the character of Prest. Joseph Smith." Emma told the sisters that she hoped they could "adopt some plan to bring her to repentance." Emma also said that it was their duty "to look into the morals of each other" and that she hoped that Clarissa Marvel "might be reform'd." A committee was then formed to visit and discuss these matters with Sister Marvel, and thereafter Emma told the sisters that their discussions "should be kept among the members" and that she hoped "all would feel themselves bound to observe this rule."[13]

During its third meeting, on March 30, Joseph Smith told the society that he was concerned it was growing "too fast" and he suggested that it "should go into a close examination of every candidate" and that "the society should grow up by degrees." He was much more concerned about the growth of the society than he was about the growth of Nauvoo Lodge. He emphasized that "one principal object of the Institution was to purge out iniquity" and that "the Society should move according to the ancient Priesthood, hence there should be a select Society separate from all the evils of the world, choice virtuous and holy." To accomplish this object, Smith said that "he was going to make of this Society, a kingdom of priests as in Enoch's day—as in Paul's day." Thereafter the sisters voted to continue to investigate the claims made against Clarissa Marvel.[14]

At the same meeting Emma Smith read an "article" to the sisters "which would test that ability of the members in keeping secrets."[15] Although the article was vague, it referred to rumors circulating in Nauvoo (during the period when John C. Bennett was quickly losing his standing in the church and in Freemasonry) that Smith had authorized men to have extramarital relations with women. The authors refused to name the culprit(s) who were spreading these rumors because they were concerned that "there may be some among you who are not sufficiently skill'd in Masonry as to keep a secret." They also noted that "this epistle be had as a private matter in your Society, and then we shall learn whether you are good masons."

Joseph Smith, Brigham Young, Hyrum Smith, Heber C. Kimball, Willard Richards, and Vinson Knight addressed the article to Emma and they all signed it. They inquired whether the society could "be trusted with some important matters," in order to "prevent iniquitous characters from carrying their iniquity into effect; such as, for instance, a man who may be

13. Ibid., March 24, 1842, 17–18.
14. For a discussion of the Clarissa Marvel episode, see Linda King Newell and Valeen Tippetts Avery, *Mormon Enigma: Emma Hale Smith, Prophet's Wife, Elect Lady, Polygamy's Eve* (New York: Doubleday, 1984), 108–10.
15. "A Book of Records," March 30, 1842, 22–25. The article referred to is recorded on pp. 86–89.

aspiring after power and authority, and yet without principle, regardless of God, man, or the devil, or the interest or welfare of man, or the virtue or innocence of woman." Such men, according to the article, "say they have authority from Joseph, or the First Presidency, or any other Presidency of the Church" to carry such iniquity into effect. "You may be inform'd," the authors assured the women of the Relief Society, "that no such authority ever has, ever can, or ever will be given to any man, and if any man has been guilty of any such thing, let him be treated with utter contempt, and let the curse of God fall on his head." Nevertheless, "some unprincipled men," the article warned, "whose names we will not mention at present, have been guilty of such crimes." Although Smith had previously warned society members to keep confidences, this was his first instruction to them to sharpen their Masonic skills and to keep their discussions secret as good Masons.

The minutes also included a statement signed by Clarissa Marvel in which she affirmed that she had never "seen or heard anything improper or unvirtuous of the conduct or conversation of either President Smith or Mrs. Agnes Smith," who rumors said had married one another.[16]

On April 14 Sarah Cleveland told the society that Clarissa Marvel had recanted her prior gossip and that her case "should be a warning, how we hear and how we speak." She also cautioned the sisters "against speaking evil of Prest. J. Smith and his companion" and "express'd her fears that the Lord would cut off those who will not take counsel &c." During the same meeting Emma Smith reported that "the disagreeable business of searching out those who were iniquitous, seem'd to fall on her."[17]

DELIVERING THE KEYS

The membership of the Relief Society, which originally consisted of a select group of "priestesses," exploded after a few meetings. The society accepted, like Nauvoo Lodge, most of those who applied for membership even after Joseph cautioned that it control its growth.[18] By the time the Relief Society met for the sixth time on April 28, there were 229 members. During that

16. Ibid., September 8, 1842, 86–89 (recording of an epistle read to the society on March 30, 1842). On January 6, 1842, Brigham Young referred to an encounter in the lodge room between Joseph Smith and Agnes Coolbrith Smith, who was the widow of Joseph's brother, Don Carlos Smith, which some have interpreted as evidence that Smith and his former sister-in-law were sealed on that date. "Brigham Young Journal," January 6, 1842, Brigham Young Papers, Church History Library. See also S. Dilworth Young, *"Here is Brigham..." Brigham Young...the years to 1844* (Salt Lake City: Bookcraft, 1964), 307.

17. "A Book of Records," April 14, 1842, 26.

18. Smith cautioned the society on at least three occasions (March 30, April 28, and June 9, 1842) to control its growth.

meeting the prophet spoke to the society "respecting the Priesthood." He informed the sisters that "the church is not now organiz'd in its proper order, and cannot be until the Temple is completed." He assured them that women could heal the sick but that if they "have faith to heal the sick, let all hold their tongues, and let everything roll on."[19]

Smith "spoke of delivering the keys to this Society and the church," and that "the keys of the kingdom are about to be given to them." But he also warned them, in Masonic terminology, that they "need not be fearing men for their deeds, but let the weight of innocence be felt; which is more mighty than a millstone hung around the neck." He ended his discourse with words whose meaning have been debated ever since: "I now turn the key to you in the name of God and this Society shall rejoice and knowledge and intelligence shall flow down from this time—this is the beginning of better days to this Society."[20]

Mormon historian Andrew F. Ehat has concluded that the "key" that Smith turned over to the Relief Society was the same key that he received during the endowment.[21] On May 1 Joseph defined "the keys of the kingdom" and the "keys" to a general church audience as "certain signs & words by which false spirits & personages may be detected from true—which cannot be revealed to the Elders till the Temple is completed."[22] Other LDS historians have concluded that this key "would serve as schoolmaster in preparing women toward the great end of sanctification and eternal life in God's presence." This sanctification would be accomplished "through the authority and ordinances of the Melchizedek Priesthood, particularly temple ordinances," and the Relief Society was commissioned to prepare women for its ordinances.[23]

On May 13 the Relief Society approved more than 176 new members, almost doubling its size.[24] Both Emma Smith and her husband continued to exhort the sisters to expose the sins "practiced by some in authority, pretending to be sanction'd by Prest. Smith."[25] These warnings were intended

19. "A Book of Records," April 28, 1842, 35–39.
20. Ibid., 40. Derr, Cannon, and Beecher note that when the Quorum of the Twelve Apostles wrote the history of the church in 1855, it edited the wording in the original minutes, "I now turn the key to you," to read "I now turn the key in your behalf." Derr, Cannon, and Beecher, *Women of Covenant*, 49.
21. Ehat, "Joseph Smith's Introduction of Temple Ordinances," 30–33.
22. Andrew H. Hedges, Alex D. Smith, and Richard Lloyd Anderson, eds., *Journals, Volume 2: December 1841–April 1843* (Salt Lake City: Church Historian's Press, 2011), 53 (May 1, 1842).
23. Derr, Cannon, and Beecher, *Women of Covenant*, 41, 48, 46.
24. "A Book of Records," May 13, 1842, 43–46.
25. Ibid., May 19, 1842, 48. For the most complete listing of Relief Society members, see Maurine Carr Ward, "'This Institution Is a Good One': The Female Relief Society of

to counter John C. Bennett's statements, made shortly after Meredith Helm notified Nauvoo Lodge that Bennett was married and an expelled Mason, that Smith taught and practiced plural marriage. Although Smith had married plural wives he had not authorized Bennett to reveal that practice to the general church membership or to outsiders. In fact, Smith had assured his wife, and most of the church hierarchy, that he had not taught, authorized, or practiced the doctrine of plural marriage. "It was a nightmare for Joseph," writes Mormon historian Richard Bushman, "to have his carefully regulated celestial marriages debased into a device for seducing the unsuspecting."[26] Smith was therefore forced to take extreme measures to quell the rumors by attacking Bennett's own moral turpitude.

On May 26 Joseph Smith addressed the Relief Society and advised it "to put a double watch over the tongue," and that "no organiz'd body can exist without this at all." Without mentioning Bennett's name he warned the sisters that "the tongue is an unruly member—hold your tongues about things of no moment—a little tale will set the world on fire," and that "the truth on the guilty should not be told openly—Strange as this may seem, yet this is policy."

The prophet told the sisters, referring to Bennett, "We must use precaution in bringing sinners to justice lest in exposing these heinous sins, we draw the indignation of a gentile world upon us (and to their imagination justly too)." Finally, he said that although "I do not want to cloak iniquity," he nevertheless did not want to do "more hurt than good with your tongues." Being discreet and doing the work of God was, according to the Mormon prophet, "the grand key words for the Society to act upon." Emma concluded the meeting by noting that "all idle rumor and idle talk must be laid aside yet sin must not be covered" and that she "wanted none in this Society who had violated the laws of nature."[27]

By May 27 the society had grown so large that it began holding meetings outdoors in an area known as the grove. It approved 178 new members, bringing the total membership to almost six hundred. Both Joseph Smith and his trusted associate Newel K. Whitney attended this meeting. Whitney addressed the sisters and assured them that "without the female all things cannot be restor'd to the earth—it takes all to restore the Priesthood." He asserted that it was "the intent of the Society" to usher in this restoration "in connection with those husbands that are found worthy." But he also advised them to "throw the vail of charity over failings," that he was

Nauvoo, March 17, 1842, to March 16, 1844," *Mormon Historical Studies* 3, no. 2 (Fall 2002): 87–203.

26. See Bushman, *Rough Stone Rolling*, 460.

27. "A Book of Records," May 26, 1842, 51–53.

striving "to bridle my tongue," that he had "of late decreed to set a double watch on my tongue," and, undoubtedly referring to the new endowment, he promised them that there were blessings "to be confer'd as soon as our hearts are prepared to receive them."[28]

When the society met on June 9, it had 779 members. The Mormon prophet told the sisters that the purpose of their organization was "not only to relieve the poor but to save souls" and he continued to counsel them about maintaining secrecy.[29] By this time Joseph had undoubtedly decided that he would either have to admit publicly that he and others had taken plural wives or create a more select female "order" to preserve the secret.[30] As such, it would be necessary to keep secrets not only from the outside world but, ironically, from most of the society he had created, in large part to stimulate the practice of polygamy and to keep it secret at the same time. Since only the inner core of the society knew the secret, and it was never openly discussed in the group's meetings, double meanings and confusing messages were inevitable.[31]

THE MORMON INQUISITION

On June 15 the *Times and Seasons* published the First Presidency's notice that Bennett had been disfellowshipped, and within two weeks the ex-mayor left Nauvoo. In July Smith was incensed when Bennett began publishing letters in the *Sangamo Journal* alleging that Smith had made romantic overtures to Nancy Rigdon, the daughter of Sidney Rigdon, his counselor (Nancy was apparently present at the first meeting of the society but her name was struck from the minutes) and to Sarah Pratt, the wife of Orson Pratt, one of his apostles.[32] Thereafter Sarah Cleveland requested members to record their observations concerning Bennett's character.[33]

On July 30 Bennett wrote a letter to the *Louisville Journal* (which was published in the *Sangamo Journal* on September 2) alleging that Smith "has a secret lodge of women" that he called "The Mormon Inquisition, and Seraglio." According to Bennett this lodge conducted a ritual that included

28. Ibid., May 27, 1842, 58–60.
29. Ibid., June 9, 1842, 63.
30. Newell and Avery, *Mormon Enigma*, 116.
31. Ibid., 114–16.
32. Smith thereafter accused Bennett of seducing Sister Pratt. See Bushman, *Rough Stone Rolling*, 466–68. For a chronological history of Smith's marriages see Todd Compton, *In Sacred Loneliness, The Plural Wives of Joseph Smith* (Salt Lake City: Signature Books, 1997). Concerning Smith's teaching concerning polygamy see Hardy, *Doing the Works of Abraham*.
33. "A Book of Records," n.d., 69–71 (twelfth meeting undated, occurred in June or July 1842). Throughout much of that summer Smith went into hiding to avoid arrest in connection with the attempted murder of the ex-governor of Missouri, Lilburn Boggs.

anointings, investments, oaths, ceremonies, lectures and "the GRAND FINALE." He promised to give a complete description of this female lodge in his soon-to-be-published exposé.[34] Bennett later claimed in *The History of the Saints* that Joseph was inspired by "institutions on the eastern continent"—including polygamists such as King Solomon and other monarchs from the orient and Africa—for the "idea of his more extensive and elaborate system."[35] Bennett claimed that this "seraglio" was organized into a grand lodge that was "systematically divided into three distinct orders, or degrees."[36]

The first degree, the Cyprian Saints, consisted of women who were selected by Relief Society sisters—"who are ever upon their watch for victims" from among those who had "lapsed from the straight path of virtue, without the sanction or knowledge of the Prophet." The Relief Society brought these women before "the Inquisition," which forced them to confess their crimes, pronounced them a "Cyprian," and excluded them from "any further connection with the Relief Society." Their names were given to "trustworthy members of the church" for their "licentious purposes," and they were "set apart and appropriated to the gratification of the vilest appetites of the brutal Priests and Elders of the Mormon Church."[37]

The second degree, the Chambered Sisters of Charity, consisted of women "who indulge their sensual propensities, without restraint, whether married or single, by the express permission of the Prophet." When a Mormon elder became "enamored" with a woman, and the feeling was reciprocated (regardless of whether either was married) they could obtain permission from Joseph Smith to become "conjugal helpmates." This order, according to Bennett, was "much more numerous than the Cyprian Saints" because of "the greater respectability of their order."[38]

The "third and highest order" was the Consecratees of the Cloister, or Cloistered Saints, which "are set apart and consecrated to the use and benefit of particular individuals as select, spiritual wives" and are therefore considered "the special favorites of Heaven, and the most honorable among the daughters of Jacob."[39] Members of the Cloistered Saints and their suitors could "love a husband or wife, already united...according to the laws of the

34. Bennett, *The History of the Saints*, 217.
35. Ibid., 218.
36. Ibid., 220. Francis Higbee wrote a letter to the *Warsaw Signal* two years after the appearance of Bennett's book in which he described the forthcoming inaugural issue of the *Nauvoo Expositor*, which would include an exposé of the "Mormon Seraglio a[nd] Nauvoo Harem." Klaus J. Hansen, *Quest for Empire: The Political Kingdom of God and the Council of Fifty in Mormon History* (Lansing: Michigan State University Press, 1967), 157.
37. Bennett, *The History of the Saints*, 221.
38. Ibid., 222.
39. Ibid., 223.

land," and if the union was approved by the prophet a marriage ceremony would take place and they would "consider themselves as united in spiritual marriage."[40]

While the society minutes confirm that Smith wanted to quell rumors concerning polygamy, and that the members of the Relief Society were encouraged to keep their proceedings secret, they do not support Bennett's notion that an exotic ritual was ever contemplated. But it is not surprising that Bennett claimed it was. British Freemasons had long predicted that the inclusion of women in their institution would cause their enemies to accuse them of immoral activities. Furthermore, Bennett was aware that Smith had already married multiple wives before he formed the Holy Order and that he was obsessed with keeping this practice secret.[41]

Smith's former confidant probably suspected that since the new female society was organized in the same lodge room where the Nauvoo Masonic Lodge met, Smith intended to obligate women, who were aware that plural marriages were being performed, to keep the practice secret by requiring them to take oaths during Masonic-like rituals.[42] But Bennett did not create his descriptions of the "Seraglio" out of thin air. He modified and elaborated descriptions that Augustin Barruel and John Robison had sketched forty years earlier concerning the Illuminati's planned establishment of "Female Lodges of the Illuminees," which Barruel had claimed separated virtuous women from "the wild, the giddy, and the voluptuous," and would permit men to "secretly gratify their passions."[43]

Bennett was probably also familiar with a revelation given on April 7, 1842, a month before his removal from the church hierarchy and his resignation from city government, concerning the political Kingdom of God, better known as the Council of Fifty, and connected the goals of the Illuminati (as represented by Barruel, Robison, and others) and the aspirations of

40. Ibid., 224.
41. See Foster, *Religion and Sexuality*, 171–73.
42. Bennett initially compared what he referred to as Order Lodge (Holy Order) to a female ritual practiced in New York by "Matthias" as reported in *New York Herald*, July 26, 1842, morning ed., 2, col. 4. Bennett wrote: "The initiatory proceedings at Joe's Order Lodge resemble those practiced by Matthias at Pearson's home; only his members were females, and they danced round a store, while Matthias anointed them. But perhaps, after all, Joe Smith has a secret lodge of women. We shall see." Bennett, *The History of the Saints*, 217. Matthias visited Joseph Smith in Kirtland in November 1835, who told him "that his doctrine was of the devil, that he was in reality in possession of a wicked a depraved spirit" and that "his god was the devil." *History of the Church*, 2:307. For contemporary accounts of Matthias, a self-proclaimed prophet, see W. E. Drake, *Robert Matthews, Defendant, The Prophet! A Full and Accurate Report of the Judicial Proceedings* (1834); William L. Stone, *Matthias and His Impostures* (New York: Harper & Brothers, 1835); G. Vale, *Fanaticism: Its Sources and Influence* (New York, 1835); and S. B. Emmons, *Philosophy of Popular Superstitions* (Boston, 1853).
43. Ward, *Free Masonry*, 369, quoting Barruel, *Memoirs*, 24.

the Council of Fifty (the government of the Kingdom of God "from which all law emanates, for the rule, government & controle [*sic*] of all Nations Kingdoms & toungs [*sic*] and People under the Whole Heavens").

Klaus Hansen has noted that both institutions had quasi-Masonic rituals with robes and secret signs and that the revelation concerning the Council of Fifty—like the establishment of the Relief Society and the organization of the Holy Order—was received shortly after the organization of Nauvoo Lodge. Nevertheless, Hansen admits that he could not determine if "there existed any direct connection between the government of the kingdom of God and Freemasonry."[44]

Finally, two years after he published his *History of the Saints*, Bennett claimed that Joseph Smith received a revelation on April 7, 1841, in which Bennett was commanded to establish an "Order of the Illuminati" after Smith died and in 1846 he organized such a group after joining James Strang, who claimed to be Smith's successor, in Voree, Wisconsin, where Strang became the Imperial Primate and Bennett the General-in-Chief of the Illuminati.[45]

THE PEACE MAKER

On August 21, 1842, Smith reported to the society that he "had whip'd out all of Bennett's host," reminded the society to "hold your tongues," and observed that it "has taken the most active part in my welfare against my enemies." He also mentioned the endowment, which he had still not

44. See Hansen, *Quest for Empire*, 52–66. David B. Clark has suggested that the "Halcyon Order" referred to by Bennett may have "formed the basis of the Council of Fifty." Clark, "Sidney Rigdon's Rights of Succession," *Restoration* 6 (April 1987): 10n21. The Council of Fifty, Minutes, dated April 10 and 21, 1880, suggest that revelation on the Council of Fifty was given on April 7, 1842, but even this date has been questioned, since the Council of Fifty did not first meet until March 10, 1844, almost two years after the 1842 revelation and Bennett's departure from Nauvoo. Nevertheless, Foster, *Religion and Sexuality*, 172–73, has speculated that Bennett "simply invented" the "Order of the Illuminati" and the terms "Cyprian Saints," "Chambered Sisters of Charity," and "Cloistered Saints," while at the same time giving credence to Bennett's allegations that "three distinct orders or degrees" existed in the Mormon marriage system.
45. Hansen, *Quest for Empire*, 54–55. Milo M. Quaiffe, *The Kingdom of Saint James: A Narrative of the Mormons* (New Haven, CT: Yale University Press, 1930), 49–50; Roger Van Noord, *King of Beaver Island: The Life and Assassination of James Jesse Strang* (Urbana: University of Illinois Press, 1988), 60–65. This revelation was apparently published in Sidney Rigdon's *Messenger and Advocate* and then reprinted by Parley P. Pratt in *The Prophet*, May 10, 1845, where Pratt called it a "Base Attempt at Imposition," a "counterfeit" and "bungling…attempt at feigned Revelation." For information concerning this revelation, see D. Michael Quinn, "The Mormon Succession Crisis of 1844," *BYU Studies* 16 (Winter 1976), 192n15; Thomas J. Gregory, "Sidney Rigdon: Post Nauvoo," *BYU Studies* 21 (Winter 1981), 63n70; Ehat, "Joseph Smith's Introduction of Temple Ordinances," 220–24, 292; Clark, "Sidney Rigdon's Rights of Succession," 9–10.

introduced to any of the sisters.[46] One week later he advised them again
to "hold your tongues, and the least harm will be done."[47] On September
28, 1842, when the society held its last meeting of that year, it had more
than one thousand members.[48] Nineteen of these women signed a petition, which was published in *Times and Seasons* on October 1, in which
they declared that "we know of no system of marriage being practiced in the
church...save the one contained in the Book of Doctrine and Covenants,
and we give this certificate to the public to show that J. C. Bennett's 'secret
wife system' is a disclosure of his own make."[49]

Despite these careful denials, Udney Hay Jacob (1781–1860) published
*An extract, from a manuscript entitled: The Peace Maker. Or the doctrines
of the Millennium* at Joseph Smith's print shop, in which he advocated the
practice of polygamy.[50] The pamphlet connected the marriage system with
the Relief Society and argued that it would be restored before the millennium. Lawrence Foster has suggested that Smith authorized Jacob, even
though he did not convert to Mormonism until the following year, to publish the pamphlet as a trial balloon to determine the general church membership's reaction to plural marriage.[51]

The reaction was apparently not good. Smith published a notice in the
October 1 issue of the *Times and Seasons* in which he stated that he had
not reviewed the pamphlet before it was published and that "I should not
have printed it; not that I am opposed to any man enjoying his privileges;
but I do not wish to have my name associated with the authors, in such an
unmeaning rigamarole of nonsense, folly, and trash."[52] After the Mormon
prophet published this repudiation, it did not divert him from his clandestine advancement of polygamy.[53]

In fact, during the Relief Society's first year of existence Smith married
at least fifteen additional plural wives, ten of whom were members of the

46. "A Book of Records," August 31, 1842, 80–81.
47. Ibid., August 31, 1842.
48. Ibid., September 28, 1842, 85.
49. *Times and Seasons* 3, no. 23 (October 1, 1842): 940.
50. Udney Hay Jacob, *An extract, from a manuscript entitled The Peacemaker. Or the doctrines of the millennium: being a treatise on religion and jurisprudence. Or a new system of
religion and politicks* (Nauvoo, IL: J. Smith, Printer, 1842).
51. Foster, *Religion and Sexuality*, 174–77.
52. See *Times and Seasons* 4, no. 2 (December 1, 1842). The pamphlet also advocated the
restoration of patriarchal authority and a "Biblical standard" of divorce.
53. Louis J. Kern, *An Ordered Love* (Chapel Hill: The University of North Carolina Press,
1981), 358n3. See also Hardy, *Solemn Covenant*, 7–8; Lawrence Foster, "A Little-Known
Defense of Polygamy from the Mormon Press in 1842," *Dialogue: A Journal of Mormon
Thought* 9 (Winter 1974): 21–34; and Kenneth W. Godfrey, "A New Look at the Alleged
Little-Known Discourse by Joseph Smith," *BYU Studies* 9 (Autumn 1968): 339–50.

society, including Sarah Cleveland, the first counselor, Eliza R. Snow, the secretary, and Elvira Cowles, the treasurer.[54] By the end of March 1843, Smith had twenty-two wives (including Emma), and fifteen of them were members of the Relief Society. Of these fifteen, twelve had joined during the first two meetings and four held the society's most important leadership positions. Bennett and others alleged that Joseph attempted to seduce Nancy Rigdon, another charter member of the society, but that she rebuffed him.[55] In addition, at least ten of Joseph's associates in the church hierarchy entered into the principle during this period, including Brigham Young, Heber C. Kimball, Reynolds Cahoon, Willard Richards, Thomas Bullock (1816–1885), and William D. Huntington.[56]

After Bennett accused Smith of ordering the murder of former Missouri governor Lilburn Boggs, the Mormon prophet spent much of his time in hiding to avoid extradition and he did not marry any additional plural wives from August 1842 to February 1843. As a result, neither Joseph nor Emma attended any of the fourteen meetings of the Relief Society held in 1843 and the society grew at a much slower pace after Bennett's book was published. Nevertheless the society did have more than a thousand members and the sisters, like their Masonic husbands, decided to divide their organization into smaller groups. Emma's counselors presided at these meetings, and the organization, no longer exclusive, seemed to concentrate its efforts on supporting the temple-building effort and providing a social outlet for the city's women.[57] In August, Reynolds Cahoon, stated that "the Order of the

54. See Andrew Jenson, "Plural Marriage," *Historical Record* 4, nos. 3–5 (May 1887): 219–34; Fawn M. Brodie, *No Man Knows My History: The Life of Joseph Smith, the Mormon Prophet*, 2d ed. rev. (New York: Alfred A. Knopf, 1971); Bachman, "A Study of the Mormon Practice of Plural Marriage"; Todd Compton, *In Sacred Loneliness*; George D. Smith, "Nauvoo Roots of Mormon Polygamy, 1841–46: A Preliminary Demographic Report," *Dialogue: A Journal of Mormon Thought* 27, no. 1 (Spring 1994): 1–72; and George D. Smith, *Nauvoo Polygamy*. Although these authors do not agree on the precise numbers and identity of Joseph Smith's plural wives, they all list Cleveland, Snow, and Cowles. Bachman's list includes women from Jenson and Brodie even though the evidence for some is weak. But Bachman criticizes Jenson for including Cleveland despite "little supporting evidence" for it. Bachman, "A Study of the Mormon Practice," 108. George D. Smith lists the plural wives of church officials, discusses the secrecy associated with the practice, and cites examples of precautions taken by the participants. George D. Smith, "Nauvoo Roots of Mormon Polygamy," 26–28; and George D. Smith, *Nauvoo Polygamy*, 573–656. See also Foster, *Religion and Sexuality*, 153, concerning other women who refused Joseph's overtures to marriage.

55. See *History of the Church* 5:134–36; Bennett, *History of the Saints*, 243–45; Jessee, *Personal Writings of Joseph Smith*, 537–40.

56. Smith, "Nauvoo Roots of Mormon Polygamy," 13–14.

57. By July there were almost twelve hundred members of the Relief Society. "A Book of Records," n.d.

Priesthood is not complete without [the Relief Society]" and that it was "rais[e]d by the Lord to prepare us for the great blessings which are for us in the House of the Lord in the Temple."[58] Shortly thereafter women began to participate in the endowment ritual.

THE VOICE OF INNOCENCE

After women were initiated into the Holy Order (those who were initiated into the endowment ritual) there was a dramatic decrease in the activities and influence of the Relief Society. The only meetings held in 1844 took place on March 9 and March 16 when the Relief Society held "four over-flowing meetings" in Smith's red brick store. Emma attended these meetings to encourage support for her husband who continued to be accused of im-morality. The society addressed "John C. Bennett's 'spiritual wife system'" as well as "the envenomed slander of O[rsimus] F. Botswick, that he could 'take a half bushel of meal, obtain his vile purpose, and get what accommo-dation he wanted with almost any woman in the city.'"[59]

During these meetings "The Voice of Innocence," which was written by W. W. Phelps and signed by Emma Smith, was read to the sisters. The pamphlet contained a preamble condemning Botswick, who had been fined fifty dollars by the Nauvoo Municipal Court in February for slandering Hyrum Smith.[60] It urged that "the whole virtuous female population of the city, with one voice, declare that the Seducer of female chastity, the Slan-derer of Female Character or the Defamer of the Character of the Heads of the Church…shall have no place in our houses, in our affections or in our society." The society unanimously approved several resolutions that were intended to support the church leadership. The first resolution proposed that "Joseph Smith, the Mayor of the city, be tendered our thanks for the able and manly manner in which he defended injured innocence in the late trial of O. P. Botswick for slandering President Hyrum Smith, and almost all the women of the city."[61]

58. Derr, Cannon, and Beecher, *Women of Covenant*, 50.
59. See "Virtue Will Triumph," *Nauvoo Neighbor* 1:47 (March 20, 1844), p. 2. "The Voice of Innocence from Nauvoo" was read to "four overflowing meetings" of the Relief Society on March 9 and March 16. On May 26 Smith publicly stated that he could "only find one" wife, thus continuing his public denials of plural marriage. He seems to have been making a legalistic argument, relying on a revelation of July 12, 1843, which not only sanctioned polygamy but differentiated it from adultery. *History of the Church* 5:504–5. See also Foster, *Religion and Sexuality*, 163. On June 7 William Law characterized polygamy as adultery in the *Nauvoo Expositor*.
60. *History of the Church* 6:225.
61. "A Book of Records," March 9, 1844, 123. Joseph expressed displeasure with this doc-ument on May 26: "I never had any fuss with these men until that Female Relief Society brought out the paper against adulterers and adulteresses." *History of the Church* 6:411.

The women also approved a resolution that they would "raise our voices and hands against John C. Bennett's 'spiritual wife system' as a scheme of profligates to seduce women; and they that harp upon it, wish to make it popular for the convenience of their own cupidity; wherefore, while the marriage bed, undefiled is honorable, let polygamy, bigamy, fornication[,] adultery, and prostitution, be drowned out of the hearts of honest men to drop it in the gulf of fallen nature, 'where the worm dieth not and the fire is not quenched!' and let all the saints say Amen!"

During the same meeting Emma advised her society to abide by the teachings of the Book of Mormon and Doctrine and Covenants, which she apparently believed mandated monogamy. She also reread an epistle, that was originally read to the society on March 30, 1842, in which the church leadership denied that it permitted any practices that would jeopardize "the virtue or innocence of woman" and advised the Relief Society to keep the epistle "as a private matter in your society, and then we shall learn whether you are good masons."[62]

Emma's reliance on Mormon scripture and the church epistle was not a very good defense against allegations that her husband and other members of the hierarchy were taking plural wives. Although the Doctrine and Covenants included a section that responded to allegations that Mormons were polygamists with the church's teaching that "one man should have one wife; and one woman, but one husband," the Book of Mormon's prohibition of the practice, which referred to polygamy as "abominable" (Jacob 2:24–29), provided that God could nevertheless command the practice in order to "raise up seed unto me" (Jacob 2:30). As such, Emma's defense failed to address the issue of whether the church's teaching that "one man should have one wife" was still applicable or whether God had commanded her husband and other church leaders to "raise up seed unto me."[63]

---

62. "A Book of Records," March 16, 1844, 125.

63. The Book of Mormon references concerning polygamy included Jacob 2:24, 27 ("Behold, David and Solomon truly had many wives and concubines, which thing was abominable before me, saith the Lord.... For there shall not any man among you have save it be one wife; and concubines he shall have none."); Jacob 2:30 (God could command the practice in order to "raise up seed unto me."); Mosiah 11:2 ("For behold, he did not keep the commandments of God, but he did walk after the desires of his own heart. And he had many wives and concubines."); Ether 10:5 ("And it came to pass that Riplakish did not do that which was right in the sight of the Lord, for he did have many wives and concubines."). The references in the 1835 edition of the Doctrine and Covenants included section 13:7 ("Thou shalt love thy wife with all thy heart, and shall cleave unto her and none else"), which was a revelation received in February 1831, originally published in the *Book of Commandments* (64:22) and remains in D&C 42:22 section 65:3 ("It is lawful that he should have one wife, and they twain shall be one flesh", recorded in March 1831, originally published in *Book of Commandments* 52:17 and remains in D&C 49:16). The most direct passage, which specifically contrasted monogamy and polygamy, was section 101 which acknowledged that since "this church of Christ has been reproached with the crime of fornication, and polygamy: we declare that we believe, that one man should have one wife; and one woman, but one husband" (D&C 101).

With respect to her reliance on the epistle, the Mormon historians who wrote a history of the Relief Society note that it endorsed "old established morals & virtues & scriptural laws," but that it was "so general as to be easily misconstrued" and seemed "to confirm monogamy as the order of the kingdom." They go on to say that the statement, "'We wish to keep the commandments of God in all things, as given directly from heav'n to us, living by every word that proceeded out of the mouth of the Lord,' suggests that the Saints would not reject polygamy when the Prophet had received a revelation."[64] Similarly, the authors of Emma Smith's biography believe that she was well aware that her husband was practicing plural marriage and that she "reaffirmed the traditional Christian standards of marriage, using Joseph's public denials of polygamy, the March 1842 letter, and later the 'Voice of Innocence' to give every woman present a valid reason for avoiding plural marriage."[65]

Although it remains unclear how much Emma really knew, the reality was much different than what she implied to her society. Carmon Hardy has pointed out the irony that Joseph married some of the leading members of a society whose president was a "staunch enemy" of plural marriage and which "sought to be an implement for suppressing evils like bigamy and adultery."[66] In fact, the prophet married at least twenty-two women during the second year of the society (between April 1843 and June 1844), though only three of them were members of the Relief Society. [67] During this same period nineteen additional men, including William Clayton, Orson Hyde, Parley P. Pratt, James Adams, Amasa Lyman, Hyrum Smith, John Taylor, and Erastus Snow, married their first plural wives. Ironically, very few of Smith's and his associates' new wives were affiliated with the society, even though the society was initially envisioned as a proving ground for such marriages and admission into the Holy Order.[68]

When Joseph Smith was killed in June 1844, at least thirty men had accepted the principle of plural marriage and were married to approximately eighty-four women. Emma Smith, and perhaps as many as forty-three other women, became the "widows" of Joseph Smith.[69] Shortly thereafter,

64. Derr, Cannon, and Beecher, *Women of Covenant*, 61–62.
65. Newell and Avery, *Mormon Enigma*, 106–18, 134–37, 147; and Linda King Newell, "Emma Hale Smith and the Polygamy Question," *John Whitmer Historical Association Journal* 4 (1984): 3–15.
66. Hardy, *Solemn Covenant*, 8–9.
67. Smith, *Nauvoo Polygamy*, 223–24.
68. Francis Higbee wrote a letter to the *Warsaw Signal* in which he described the forthcoming inaugural issue of the *Nauvoo Expositor* which would include an exposé of the "Mormon Seraglio a[nd] Nauvoo Harem." Hansen, *Quest for Empire*, 157.
69. Smith, "Nauvoo Roots of Mormon Polygamy," 13–15.

Brigham Young discontinued the Relief Society, which had 1,341 members, to avoid disharmony in the church. When most of the Saints moved westward, Emma Smith remained in Nauvoo where she continued to oppose the practice of plural marriage.[70] The Relief Society did not meet again until it was reorganized in Utah in 1866. It is notable that when the society was reorganized one of its principal purposes was to provide a forum for Mormon women to testify to the world that Joseph Smith had restored plural marriage, that they were plural wives, and that they were very happy in that role.

PROVOKE THE BRETHREN

Some Mormon historians emphasize that the Relief Society's original purpose was to "relieve the poor," "to save souls," to "provoke the brethren to good works in looking to the wants of the poor—searching after objects of charity, and in administering to their wants to assist; by correcting the morals and strengthening the virtues of the female community, and save the Elders the trouble of rebuking; that they may give their time to other duties, &c. in their public teaching." They note that because the primary "appeal of the society was spiritual," other "acts of charity followed inevitably."[71]

These historians suggest that "the inclusion of women within the structure of the church organization reflected the divine pattern of the perfect union of man and woman."[72] This enabled women in the church to share the blessings of the priesthood by relieving the poor, assisting in the construction of the temple, performing baptisms for the dead, and ultimately receiving priesthood endowments.[73] The first members of the Relief Society were handpicked, through family and personal connections, and its members were considered unquestionably loyal to Joseph Smith and the church.[74]

---

70. Derr, Cannon, and Beecher, *Women of Covenant*, 62–63. See also Newell and Avery, *Mormon Enigma*, 175.

71. Derr, Cannon, and Beecher, *Women of Covenant*, 30, 36, 37. Although the authors insist that *Women of Covenant* is not an "official" history of the society, it is published by the church-owned Deseret Book, and the authors acknowledge that it was reviewed by church authorities prior to publication (xii). Derr and Beecher were employed by BYU at the Joseph Fielding Smith Institute for Latter-day History. Cannon was a former counselor in Barbara Bradshaw Smith's Relief Society general presidency. An official history was previously published in 1966. *History of the Relief Society 1842–1966* (Salt Lake City: General Board of the Relief Society, 1966). See also Mary Stovall Richards, "Review of Three Books on Women," *BYU Studies* 33, no. 4 (1993): 794.

72. Derr, Cannon, and Beecher, *Women of Covenant*, 50.

73. Ibid., 50–56.

74. Lawrence Foster, *Women, Family, and Utopia: Communal Experiments of the Shakers, the Oneida Community, and the Mormons* (Syracuse, NY: Syracuse University Press, 1991), 138.

Nevertheless, Smith's remarks to the Relief Society reveal the organization was not simply another benevolent organization. It was created as part of "the restoration of all things" and within it "women assumed a new and significant place within church ordinances and organization."[75] Some church writers have concluded that when Smith told the society that he had conferred a key on them, this "opened to women their place and responsibility in the organization of the church" and constituted "authority to minister to the spiritual welfare and salvation of the female members of the church."[76]

The society helped prepare its members for the temple by providing money and materials for the structure, by accepting a norm of secrecy, by obeying the prophet's teachings, and by affirmatively contradicting any allegations against his character, including rumors that he had taken plural wives.[77] Because of this connection with the priesthood, and its role of preparing women for the temple, the society had a dimension that other benevolent societies lacked, even those connected with religious congregations.[78]

75. Peggy Pascoe argues that the society was "like other nineteenth century women's organizations" and was purposed "primarily in charitable activities." Even if Mormon women had "moral influence" with church leaders, they were unable to transform it into "authority" as exercised by the male hierarchy. Despite Joseph Smith's statement that he had turned "keys" to the society, "Mormon women were expected to remain subordinate to the all-male priesthood." Pascoe found evidence for this subordinate position in the society's gradual loss of control over its finances and programs to the male hierarchy during the twentieth century. See Peggy Pascoe, "A History of Two Stories," *Dialogue: A Journal of Mormon Thought* 27, no. 2 (Summer 1994): 239, 241. Roger D. Launius, "The 'New Social History' and the 'New Mormon History': Reflection on Recent Trends," *Dialogue: A Journal of Mormon Thought* 27, no. 1 (Spring 1994): 125, goes further in arguing that Joseph Smith "was never interested in equality, regardless of gender."
76. Carol Cornwall Madsen, "Mormon Women and the Temple," in *Sisters in Spirit: Mormon Women in Historical and Cultural Perspective*, ed. Maureen Ursenbach Beecher and Lavina Fielding Anderson (Urbana: University of Illinois Press, 1987), 83–85.
77. For the Nauvoo Relief Society's role in preparing its members for temple ceremonies, see minutes, June 16, July 15, and August 13, 1843. Counsel on obeying Joseph Smith appears in entries for March 30, 1842, August 13, 1843, and March 9 and 16, 1844. Its decisive action to counter attacks on Joseph Smith and others are recorded in entries for March 24 and 30, 1842 (Clarissa Marvel); April 14, 1842 (Emma Smith's comment about "the disagreeable business of searching out those that were iniquitous"); April 28, May 19, June 23, August 4 and 31, 1842 (Joseph Smith's praise of the Relief Society for taking "the most active part in my welfare against my enemies"), and March 9 and 16, 1844.
78. The authors of *Women of Covenant* concluded that although the Female Relief Society was organized "under the Priesthood after the pattern of the Priesthood," that no priesthood was conferred on the presidency of the new society when they were "ordained" to their positions. Like the priesthood quorums, the society operated "under the direction of the Melchizedek Priesthood," but the authority given by Joseph to prepare the women for sanctification did not constitute priesthood. Female members were authorized to lay on hands to heal the sick "according to revelation" but not by priesthood power. Among the proof-texts they cite to support this conclusion are an 1880 statement of John Taylor, a 1906 statement made by Bathsheba W. Smith and Emmeline B. Wells, as well as a 1958 statement

KEEP A SECRET

Nevertheless, the timing of the Relief Society's organization, so soon after the installation of Nauvoo Lodge, and Smith's use of Masonic terminology during its meetings, suggests that the Mormon prophet also expected the society to construct a wall of secrecy concerning the emerging practice of plural marriage. He may have believed that the Relief Society was an important experiment to determine if one of the important elements of Masonry—protecting institutional secrets from outsiders—could be adapted in a religious society without a ritual to enforce the obligation.

Although Smith told members of the Relief Society on March 17, 1842, to prepare for the endowment, they were not allowed to participate for another eighteen months. During the Relief Society's first year, Joseph attended at least nine of its seventeen meetings while Emma attended at least eleven. The instructions Smith gave about secrecy, which he believed was one of the purposes of Freemasonry, were not mere generalities unrelated to current events in Nauvoo.[79] Kent L. Walgren has noted: "Freemasonry provided instruction in the art of secrecy, a desirable commodity for an organization in which plural marriages were being contracted.... It is probably not coincidental that concurrent with his initiation into Freemasonry Smith... established the Female Relief Society of Nauvoo, which also seems to have had the aim of institutionalizing secrecy."[80]

In this sense John C. Bennett's claim that there was a connection between Freemasonry and the Relief Society may have had some validity insofar as both were focused on maintaining secrecy. Larry Foster has observed

---

of Joseph Fielding Smith. Derr, Cannon, and Beecher, *Women of Covenant*, 27, 29, 48–49. Taylor said, "The ordination then given did not mean the conferring of the Priesthood upon those sisters yet the sisters hold a portion of the Priesthood in connection with their husbands." "R[elief]. S[ociety]. Reports," *Woman's Exponent* 9:7 (Sept. 1, 1880): 53.

79. *History of the Church*, 6:59; Kenney, *Wilford Woodruff's Journal* 5:418 (January 22, 1860); *Journal of Discourses* 5:133 (August 2, 1857). Ironically, secrecy was an aspect of Masonry which was attacked by the clergy and which contemporary observers claimed was the target of Book of Mormon references to "secret combinations." See Bernard, *Light on Masonry*, ix–x; See, for example, La Roy Sunderland, *Mormonism Exposed and Refuted* (New York: Piercy & Reed, 1838), 46; and Jason Whitman, "Notices of Books, The Book of Mormon," *The Unitarian* 1 (Jan. 1, 1834): 47.

80. Walgren, "James Adams," 131–32. As evidence, Walgren quoted Smith's several references to Masonry and secrecy in his epistle of March 30, 1842, to the Relief Society. See also Cheryl L. Bruno, "Keeping a Secret: Freemasonry, Polygamy, and the Nauvoo Relief Society, 1842–44," *The Journal of Mormon History* 39, no. 4 (Fall 2013): 158–81. Bruno suggests that some Relief Society sisters had been initiated into androgynous Masonic degrees and that Smith may have initially contemplated introducing such a ritual to the female society. For another study on Mormonism and secrecy, see Jean-François Mayer, "Du Secret dans le mormonisme," *Politica Hermetica* 5 (1991): 14–30. Klaus J. Hansen, *Quest for Empire*, 56, also notes the connection between Freemasonry and the secrecy associated with the practice of plural marriage.

that the practice of plural marriage in Nauvoo "obviously necessitated some means of maintaining strict secrecy and determining who had first-hand knowledge of the new practices from those who did not. Some form of secret society thus was a pragmatic necessity."[81]

When Joseph Smith lectured to the society in October 1843, he stressed that "the secret of masonry is to keep a secret."[82] Nevertheless, despite these teachings it remained extremely difficult to maintain such obedience and secrecy, especially as the Relief Society continued to grow. After select women were admitted into the Holy Order the Relief Society became less important and it was eventually abandoned by the church. Thereafter Smith ritually obligated them to keep their activities a secret, including the practice of plural marriage.

81. Foster, *Religion and Sexuality*, 304n64.
82. *History of the Church* 6:59 (October 15, 1843).

The Holy Order

JOSEPH SMITH INTRODUCED a new endowment to his closest followers within six weeks after he was initiated into Freemasonry and had organized the Female Relief Society. Although he initially believed that the Kirtland Temple endowment constituted a full restoration of an ancient temple ceremony, he revealed an even more elaborate ritual in Nauvoo. While the participants in the Kirtland endowment were able to commune with God on earth after being ritually purified, those who were endowed in Nauvoo were given instructions that would enable them to return to God's presence after they died and eventually become gods themselves.

The new endowment, which was modified throughout the Nauvoo period, included not only the initiatory rites that were practiced in the Kirtland Temple but also a creation drama, degrees of elevation, symbolic clothing, secret means of recognition, obligations, and penalties, as well as symbols the saints had never used before. Smith also introduced new rituals of baptism for the dead (which enabled descendants to perform the essential ordinance of baptism as proxies on behalf of their ancestors), celestial marriage (through which men could be sealed to their wives), and a "second anointing" (in which men holding the Melchizedek priesthood and their wives were virtually guaranteed that their "calling and election would be made sure" and that they would become exalted as gods).

A HOUSE OF PRAYER

Smith's belief that Masonic rituals contained remnants of biblical ceremonies, and that he could restore them to their former pristine condition, became most apparent when he introduced a more elaborate endowment to the Holy Order in Nauvoo. In July 1840 Smith said, "I obligate myself to build as great a temple as ever Solomon did, if the church will back me up."[1] He believed that he was called to build a temple and to restore the ritual that was practiced in the Old Testament. The First Presidency issued a circular in August stating that "the time has now come, when it is necessary to erect a house of prayer, a house of order, a house for the worship of our God, where the ordinances can be attended to agreeably to His divine will,"[2] and the Mormon prophet announced that "persons of all languages, and of every tongue, and of every color;...shall with us worship the Lord of Hosts in his holy temple."[3]

Smith received a revelation two months later that promised, "I will show unto my servant Joseph all things pertaining to this house, and the priesthood thereof, and the place whereupon it shall rest."[4] In October church members approved the construction of a temple[5] and the following January Smith received another revelation, consistent with these promises, to "build a house to my [the Lord's] name, for the Most High to dwell therein." "For there is not a place found on earth," the revelation stated, "that he may come to and restore again that which was lost unto you, or which he hath taken away, even the fullness of the priesthood." The communication revealed that Saints would participate in ordinances in the new temple "which have been kept hid from before the foundation of the world, things that pertain to the dispensation of the fullness of times."[6]

Nevertheless, the ordinances mentioned in this revelation were reminiscent of those that Smith introduced in Kirtland:

Therefore, verily I say unto you, that your anointings, and your washings...and your solemn assemblies, and your memorials for your sacrifices by the sons of Levi, and for your oracles in your most holy places wherein you receive conversations, and your statutes and judgments, from the beginning of revelations and foundation of Zion, and for the glory, honor, and endowment of all her municipals,

1. Dean C. Jessee, "Joseph Smith's July 19, 1840, Discourse," *BYU Studies* 19, no. 3: 393–94. This discourse was reported by Martha Jane Knowlton.
2. "An Address by the First Presidency to the Church, August 31, 1840," *History of the Church* 4:186.
3. "Report from the Presidency," *Times and Seasons*, 1:12: 188. See also *History of the Church* 4:213. During the same period Nauvoo City Council passed an *Act to Incorporate the City of Nauvoo* that provided only for "free white male" voting rights. *History of the Church* 4:241.
4. D&C 124:42.
5. "Minutes of General Conference, October 3, 1840, *Times and Seasons* 1:12 (October 1840): 184–88. During this same period Smith purchased four acres for the construction of the temple. See Glen M. Leonard, *Nauvoo: A Place of Peace, A People of Promise* (Salt Lake City: Deseret Book, 2002), 235–43.
6. *History of the Church* 4:274. See D&C 124:27–28, 41.

are ordained by the ordinance of my holy house which my people are always commanded to build unto my holy name.[7]

But the revelation also mentioned the ordinance of baptism for the dead: "For a baptismal font there is not upon the earth that they, my saints, may be baptized for those who are dead."[8] Smith taught that this ordinance, by which dead men and women could be baptized by living proxies, was taught in the primitive church and that it was part of the restoration of all things. He explained that when the Apostle Paul wrote to the Corinthians, "Else what shall they do which are baptized for the dead, if the dead rise not at all? Why are they then baptized for the dead?" that he was referring to baptism for the dead.[9] The purpose of the proxy baptisms was to afford those who had died without knowledge of the gospel the opportunity to accept it in the next life and be saved.[10]

During a ceremony on April 6, 1841, the initial cornerstone for Joseph's second temple was set in place.[11] Thereafter, William Weeks, the architect of the Masonic Lodge, was asked by the Mormon prophet to prepare drawings for the new temple.[12] Weeks's plans included a baptismal font that was reminiscent of Old Testament descriptions of the "molten sea," a purification vessel located outside of Solomon's Temple. Although baptism for the dead (like the endowment) was introduced before the temple was completed (the baptisms took place in the Mississippi River until October 1841), they were required to be performed in a temporary wooden vessel in the temple's basement beginning in November when it was completed and dedicated.[13]

Baptism for the dead was the first Mormon temple ordinance in which women were allowed to participate. Brigham Young later noted that

7. D&C 124:39.
8. Ibid., 124:29.
9. I Corinthians 15:29.
10. See M. Guy Bishop, "'What Has Become of Our Fathers?': Baptism for the Dead at Nauvoo," *Dialogue: A Journal of Mormon Thought* 23 (Summer 1990): 85–97; D&C 124:55.
11. The description of the laying of the four cornerstones is set forth in *History of the Church* 4:326–31. Joseph Smith laid the southeast cornerstone first, followed by the southwest, northwest, and northeast. This was unlike Masonic ceremonies in which the northeast cornerstone was laid first.
12. Weeks was born on Martha's Vineyard, Massachusetts, and came from a family of designers, builders, and craftsmen. For more information concerning Weeks, see Marjorie Hopkins Bennion, "The Rediscovery of William Weeks' Nauvoo Temple Drawings," *Mormon Historical Studies* 3:1 (Spring 2002): 73–90; J. Earl Arrington, "William Weeks, Architect of the Nauvoo Temple," *BYU Studies* 19, no. 3 (Spring 1979): 337–59. Unless otherwise noted, I relied on Bennion's article for information concerning Weeks.
13. Smith's inspiration for the baptismal font was the "molten sea" described in 2 Chronicles 4:2 and 1 Kings 7:23. That vessel was located in front of Solomon's Temple.

"women were baptized for men and men for women."[14] One contemporary Masonic writer (citing Exodus 38:8) claimed that the Egyptian "brazen sea," which was used to purify with water, and was adopted by Moses and Solomon after him, was the model for French adoptive lodges.[15] As such this Masonic model for including women in temple rituals may have influenced Smith's decision to include them in the restored rituals he introduced in Nauvoo.

During this same period the Twelve Apostles issued an epistle instructing the Saints that ordinances "which have been hid for ages" would be revealed in the temple. Given these developments it is not surprising that Smith mentioned during a meeting of the Twelve Apostles on December 19, 1841, that it was important to keep secrets and that he could keep a secret until doomsday.[16]

THE GRAND KEY

On January 6, 1842, Smith recorded in his journal that the Saints were building a temple and that this was part of the "Last Days; A day in which the God of heaven has begun to restore the ancient order of his Kingdom unto his servants & his people: a day in which all things are concurring together to bring about the compl[e]tion of the fullness of the gospel, a fullness of the dispensation of Dispensations even the fullness of Times." Smith also recorded that the church would "prepare the earth for the return of his [Jehovah's] glory, even a celestial glory; and a kingdom of Priests & Kings to God & the Lamb forever, on Mount Zion."[17]

Meanwhile, Smith was completing the translation of Egyptian papyri that he had purchased in Kirtland. As previously noted, Thomas Smith Webb had taught Royal Arch Masons that "the usages and customs of Masons" corresponded with those of Egyptian philosophers who had concealed "their particular tenants, and principle of polity, under hieroglyphical figures; and expressed their notions of government by signs and symbols, which they committed to their Magi alone, who were bound by oath not to reveal them."[18] In 1835 Smith had discovered some of these

14. Van Wagoner, *Complete Discourses* 2993 (August 31, 1873); Brigham Young, "Discourse by Brigham Young," *Journal of Discourses* 16: 165–66.

15. F. M. Reghellini noted that "the women of the tribe of Levi, who passed the night watching at the door of the tabernacle, presented to Moses their mirrors, which were of brass or silver, to make the brazen sea. Hence the lodges of Adoption." See F. M. R[eghellini], *Esprit du Dogme de la Franche-Maçonnerie* (Bruxelle: H. Tarlier, 1825), 39, quoted in Ward, *Free Masonry*, 255.

16. *History of the Church* 4:479 (December 19, 1841). This epistle repeated the language of the January 19, 1841, revelation.

17. Hedges, Smith, and Anderson, *Journals* 2:26 (January 6, 1842).

18. Webb, *The Freemason's Monitor*, 51–52.

tenets and principles, particularly Pharaoh's curse, when he translated the first part of the papyri.[19]

The portion of the papyri that Smith translated in Nauvoo included Facsimile No. 2 and his explanation of its various figures.[20] In March he published the completed translation as the "Book of Abraham" in the *Times and Seasons* in two installments. The second installment, which included the explanation of Facsimile No. 2 and contained the markers of Mormon temple worship, was published after Smith was initiated into Freemasonry.[21] The words that became associated with temple worship included "the grand Key-words of the Holy Priesthood, as revealed to Adam in the Garden of Eden as also to Seth, Noah, Moses, Abraham, and all to whom the priesthood was revealed"; "the grand Key, or, in other words, the governing power"; "the grand Key-words of the Priesthood"; and "writings that cannot be revealed unto the world; but is to be had in the Holy Temple of God."[22] Within days after the "Book of Abraham" was published, Smith preached in the grove near the temple site that "there are certain key words and signs belonging to the priesthood."[23]

Despite these developments, Hyrum Smith (who had been a Master Mason for more than fifteen years) believed that the Nauvoo endowment

19. See, Book of Abraham 1:1–2:18. The reference to the curse is contained in 1:21–27.
20. See ibid., 2:19–5:21.
21. See "Book of Abraham," *Times and Seasons* 3:9 (March 1, 1842): 705, and "Book of Abraham," *Times and Seasons* 3:10 (March 15, 1842).
22. Joseph Smith was inspired by Revelation 2:17 ("To him that overcometh will I give to eat of the hidden manna, and will give him a white stone, and in the stone a new name written which no man knoweth saving he that receiveth it") to speak concerning this key-word. He noted, "And a white stone is given to each of those who come into the celestial kingdom, whereon is a new name written, which no man knoweth save he that receiveth it. The new name is the key-word" (D&C 130:11). See also *History of the Church* 5:323–25. Apostle Charles C. Rich explained in February 1878, "Joseph tells us that this new name is a key-word, which can only be obtained through the endowments. This is one of the keys and blessings that will be bestowed upon the Saints in these last days, for which we should be very thankful." Charles C. Rich, "Blessing the Result of Obedience to Law," *Journal of Discourses* 19:249 (February 10, 1878).
23. *History of the Church* 4:555 (March 20, 1842). Mormon historian Andrew Ehat has argued that "Joseph's publication of the Book of Abraham two months before the endowment ordinances were first given included allusions to both rituals—the endowment and Freemasonry." The facsimiles in that book, he writes, include Abraham seeking angelic intervention after receiving his endowment, Adam receiving "the Grand Key-words of the Holy Priesthood" in the Garden of Eden, and "God sitting upon his Throne" revealing the same "grand Key-words of the Priesthood" to the ancients. Ehat, "Joseph Smith's Introduction of Temple Ceremonies," 43–44. Based on this evidence some Mormons have concluded that Smith's translation of papyri, which were discovered in Egypt and published as the Book of Abraham, contained "most of the temple ordinances." See H. Donl Peterson, *The Pearl of Great Price: A History and Commentary* (Salt Lake City: Deseret Book Co., 1987), 38–39. See also Hugh Nibley, "The Early Christian Prayer Circle," *Brigham Young University Studies* 19 (Fall 1978): 41–78; and Hugh Nibley, *The Message of the Joseph Smith Papyri: An Egyptian Endowment* (Salt Lake City: Deseret Book, 1975), 4–5.

would be very similar to the Kirtland endowment and was apparently unaware of his brother's plan to inject Masonic-like ritual into the ceremony.
During a special church conference that took place less than a month before
the new endowment was introduced, Hyrum "spoke concerning the elders
who went forth to preach from Kirtland, and were afterwards called in for
the washing and anointing at the dedication of the House." He asserted
that, in comparison, "those who go now will be called in also, when this
Temple is about to be dedicated, and will then be endowed to go forth with
mighty power having the same anointing, that all may go forth and have the
same power."[24]

Smith hinted, shortly after Hyrum's statement, that the new endowment would include much more than washings, anointings, and sealings,
in preparation for an outpouring of the spirit that he introduced in Kirtland. On May 1 he linked his prior observations concerning keywords with
the new endowment. He preached that there are "certain signs & words by
which false spirits & personages may be detected from true—which cannot
be revealed to the Elders till the Temple is completed.... [T]he elders must
know them all to be endued with power.... No one can truly say he knows
God until he has handled something, & this can only be in the holiest of
Holies."[25]

Joseph's statement suggests that he believed that the restoration of key-
words, which were utilized in Masonic ritual, was an essential part of the
new endowment. Joseph intended to restore the keywords and other portions of the Masonic ritual into an entirely new ritual whose purpose was
to create a framework for eternal salvation and exaltation. A later apostle
observed that "the way and manner in which the ordinances have to be performed have been determined in the eternal world, and unless you comply
with the requirements and obey the law, you cannot obtain the keys, and
without the keys you cannot pass the angels and the Gods in the eternal
world."[26]

A NEW ENDOWMENT

When Smith organized the Holy Order he introduced it to a new endowment that included not only washings and anointings, similar to those introduced in Kirtland, but also to a much more elaborate ritual. On May 3
Smith asked Lucius Scovil, a Master Mason who was involved in the

24. Hyrum Smith, General Conference address, April 7, 1842, in *Times & Seasons* 3(12):763
(April 15, 1842); *History of the Church* 4:585.
25. Hedges, Smith, and Anderson, *Journals* 2:53 (May 1, 1842).
26. See Charles C. Rich, "Blessing the Result of Obedience to Law," *Journal of Discourses*
19:253 (February 10, 1878).

construction of a Masonic hall, and several others, "to work and fit up" the upper room of the red brick store "preparatory to giving endowments to a few Elders that he might give unto them all the keys of power pertaining to the A[a]ronic and Melchisedec Priesthoods." Scovil and the others prepared the room to represent "the interior of a temple as much as the circumstance would permit." They separated it into five stages or compartments by using canvas partitions. The compartments represented the Creation, the Garden of Eden, the earth after Adam and Eve's expulsion, the present day world, and finally a veil through which they would pass into a celestial room. The participants in the endowment would be instructed in each of these compartments where they were endowed with knowledge and receive keywords and other gestures.[27]

On May 4 Smith introduced the new endowment to nine men on the second floor of his red brick store. His preliminary presentation was similar to the careful process he followed in Kirtland where he introduced washings and anointings to a select few in the upper room of the temple. Unlike Kirtland, however, all of the Nauvoo initiates, whom Smith referred to as the Quorum of the Anointed or Holy Order, were Master Masons. Five quorum members had become Freemasons before they became Mormons (Hyrum Smith, Heber C. Kimball, Newell K. Whitney, George Miller, and James Adams)[28] while the other five (Joseph Smith, Brigham Young,[29]

---

27. Lucius N. Scovil[le], Letter to the Editor dated [February] 2, 1884, "The Higher Ordinances," *Deseret News Semi-Weekly*, February 15, 1884, 2, as quoted in Anderson and Bergera, *Joseph Smith's Quorum of the Anointed*, 2. The others mentioned by Scovil included Shadrak Roundy, Noah Rogers, Dimick B. Huntington, and Daniel Cairns. He also wrote that Hosea Stout may have been involved as well. Lisle Brown notes that "the storage room also served for meetings of the Nauvoo Female Relief Society, the Nauvoo Masonic Lodge, the Nauvoo Legion, the Nauvoo Seminary, the Anointed Quorum [Holy Order], and various priesthood councils; it also offered a space for drama and talent productions, religious lectures, political speeches, and a classroom." Lisle G. Brown, "'Temple Pro Tempore': The Salt Lake City Endowment House," *Journal of Mormon History* 34 (Fall 2008): 2.
28. B. H. Roberts, *A Comprehensive History of the Church of Jesus Christ of Latter-day Saints, Century I* (Salt Lake City: Church of Jesus Christ of Latter-day Saints, 1930), 2:135–36 (hereafter cited as *Comprehensive History*); *Complainants Abstract of Pleading in Evidence in the Circuit Court of the United States, Western District of Missouri, Western Division at Kansas City, the Reorganized Church of Jesus Christ of the Latter-day Saints, Complainant, vs. The Church of Christ at Independence, Missouri* (Lamoni, IA: Herald House, 1893), 299. When the Holy Order first met, Miller was master of Nauvoo Lodge, Hyrum Smith was senior warden, Whitney was treasurer, and Kimball was junior deacon.
29. Some have claimed that Young was a Freemason before joining the church. See Kenneth W. Godfrey, "Joseph Smith and the Masons," *Journal of the Illinois State Historical Society* 64 (Spring 1971): 81–82; Leonard J. Arrington, *Brigham Young: American Moses* (New York: Alfred A. Knopf, 1985), 89; James J. Tyler, "John Cook Bennett, Colorful Freemason of the Early Nineteenth Century," reprint from *Proceedings of the Grand Lodge of Ohio* (n.p., 1947), 8. Nevertheless, Young was not a charter member of Nauvoo Lodge and was initiated, passed, and raised in April 1842. See Hogan, *Official Minutes*.

William Law, Willard Richards, and William Marks) were initiated, passed, and raised in the Nauvoo Lodge.

Smith taught that the Holy Order "instituted the ancient order of things for the first time in these latter days," and he "instruct[ed] them in the principles and order of the Priesthood, attending to washings, anointings, endowments and the communication of keywords."[30] On the first day Joseph initiated and endowed all of the members of the Holy Order except for his brother Hyrum. The following day the eight members of the Holy Order, whom Smith had endowed, participated in the initiation of the two Smith brothers.[31]

The Nauvoo endowment ritual began with the same initiatory ordinances (washing, anointing, and sealing) that were introduced in Kirtland. Brigham Young recalled that the initiates were "washed and anointed, had our garments placed upon us, and received our new name" in a "little side room."[32] The little side room was Joseph Smith's business office, which adjoined the larger room in which the more elaborate portions of the endowment took place.[33]

The Holy Order proceeded to the larger room following these initiatory rites that he had "divided up…the best that he could, hung up the veil, marked it." Brigham Young recalled that Smith gave them "instructions as we passed along from one department to another, giving us signs, tokens, penalties with the Key words pertaining to those signs."[34] These signs, tokens, and keys were part of "the Aaronic Priesthood, and so on to the highest order of the Melchisedek Priesthood, setting forth the order pertaining to the Ancient of days & all those plans and principles by which any one is enabled to secure the fullness of those blessings which has been prepared for the church of the firstborn, and come up into and abide in the presence of Eloheim [God] in the eternal worlds."[35]

30. *History of the Church* 5:1–2.
31. Ibid., 5:2–3; Brigham Young, "Manuscript History," 116, Church History Library.
32. "Those first Elders [in Kirtland]…" Brigham Young noted, "received a portion of their first endowments, or we might say more clearly, some of the first, or introductory, or initiatory ordinances, preparatory to an endowment." He also taught that "the preparatory ordinances there administered, though accompanied by the ministration of angels, and the presence of the Lord Jesus, were but a faint similitude of the ordinances of the House of the Lord in their fullness," and that many church members who received the endowment in Kirtland "thought that they had received all, and knew as much as God" but eventually "they have apostatized, and gone to hell." *Journal of Discourses* 2:31.
33. See L. John Nuttall, Diary, February 7, 1877, L. Tom Perry Special Collections, Harold B. Lee Library, Brigham Young University, Provo, Utah. See also Anderson and Bergera, *Joseph Smith's Quorum of the Anointed*, xxii.
34. Nuttall, Diary, February 1, 1877, cited in Van Wagoner, *Complete Discourses*, 3104.
35. *History of the Church* 5:1–2.

At the conclusion of the new endowment, Smith told Brigham Young that "this is not arranged right but we have done the best we could under the circumstances in which we are placed, and I wish you to take this matter in hand and organize and systematize all these ceremonies with the signs, tokens, penalties and key words." Young recalled, "I did so, and each time I got something more, so that when we went through the temple at Nauvoo I understood and knew how to place them there. We had our ceremonies pretty correct."[36] When the endowment was finally introduced in the Nauvoo Temple it included a ritual drama that took place in separate areas and related the story of the creation, the fall of man, and mankind's eternal progression to celestial realms.

ORDER LODGE

The Holy Order, or at least some of its members, met four times from May until September 1842, where the group may have commenced forming a prayer circle (also known as the true order of prayer), which was a shorted version of the endowment, where they exchanged the signs, tokens, and passwords, and received lectures concerning church doctrine.[37] During these meetings Smith instructed those who attended that during "the dispensation of the fullness of times" there would be "a whole and complete and perfect union, and welding together of dispensations, and keys, and powers, and glories." This would include a restoration of all that had been "revealed from the days of Adam even to the present time" as well as "those things which never have been revealed from the foundation of the world, but have been kept hid from the wise and prudent." "Let the sun, moon, and the morning stars," proclaimed Smith, "sing together, and let all the sons of God shout for joy…and let us present in his holy temple, when it is finished a book containing the record of our dead, which shall be worthy of all acceptation."[38]

Shortly after Smith organized the Holy Order, John C. Bennett referred to it as "Order Lodge" and connected the new order with the practice of plural marriage.[39] Bennett appealed to William Marks (who was a member of the Holy Order) as well as to Sidney Rigdon and Orson Pratt (who were not) to assist him in exposing Smith and his new endowment. In July 1842

36. Nuttall, Diary, February 7, 1877, quoted in Van Wagoner, *Complete Discourses*, 3104.
37. D. Michael Quinn, "Latter-day Saint Prayer Circles," *Brigham Young University Studies* 19 (Fall 1978), 82–90. Quinn notes that "although the order of prayer may have been instituted as early as 1842, the organization of a prayer circle was not complete until 1843" p. 82.
38. D&C 128:18, 23–24.
39. Bennett, *History of the Saints*, 272–78.

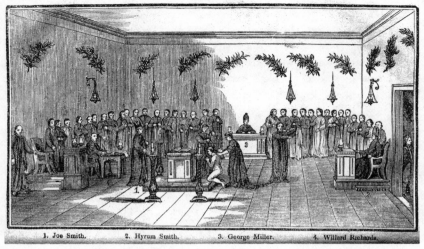

ORDER LODGE.

1. Joe Smith.   2. Hyrum Smith.   3. George Miller.   4. Willard Richards.

Illustration of Order Lodge. Published in John C. Bennett, *History of the Saints*, 273.

he published scathing attacks in the *Sangamo Journal*, which were collected and expanded in *The History of the Saints*.[40] Bennett had fallen out of favor with Smith within a few days after the Holy Order met, and his description is not a firsthand account or an exposure of the ceremony.[41] Nevertheless, Smith's former confidante undoubtedly understood the general purpose of the new endowment and its connection with Freemasonry. Bennett charged that Smith "pretends that God has revealed to him the *real Master's word* which is here given to the candidate" and that "Order Lodge" was part of Joseph's "mission for the 'restoration of the ancient order of things.'"[42]

40. John C. Bennett, "Joe's Holy Lodge called 'Order,'" *Sangamo Journal* (July 15, 1842).
41. Richard S. Van Wagoner, *Mormon Polygamy: A History*, 2nd ed. (Salt Lake City: Signature Books, 1992), 29–30. See Andrew F. Smith, *Saintly Scoundrel: The Life and Times of Dr. John Cook Bennett* (Urbana: University of Illinois Press, 1997). When the *Warsaw Signal* attacked Bennett, the Mormon press came to his defense. See "The Warsaw Signal," *Times and Seasons* 2 (June 1, 1841): 431–32. Nevertheless, three members of the Holy Order—Hyrum Smith, William Law, and George Miller—later claimed that they distrusted Bennett for more than a year prior to his disaffection. *Affidavits and Certificates, Disproving the Statements and Affidavits Contained in John C. Bennett's Letters* (Nauvoo, Ill., Aug. 31, 1842), reprinted in part in *History of the Church* 5:67–88; *Times and Seasons* 3 (July 1, 1842): 839–42. B. H. Roberts speculates that Smith and Bennett's relationship broke down on May 7, 1842 but Bennett's exclusion from the Holy Order suggests that on May 4 he was no longer in the inner circle. See Roberts, *Comprehensive History*, 2:140–47; *History of the Church* 5:4.
42. Bennett, *History of the Saints*, 276. Bennett briefly wrote about "Order Lodge" in a letter dated June 27 and published in the *Sangamo Journal* on July 8, and in a letter dated July 4 and published in the same newspaper on July 15, 1842.

His account, which inspired future exposés after the endowment was introduced in the Nauvoo Temple, emphasized the secrecy of the ceremony and revealed that there were oaths, covenants, penalties, and special garments related to priesthood power. Bennett claimed that candidates were "blindfolded" and "stripped naked," which was an obvious attempt to suggest that Smith had plagiarized a great portion of this ritual from Masonry. He also asserted that members of the Holy Order took an oath to "overturn the Constitution of the United States."

Bennett's book included a plate reminiscent of illustrations published in Masonic exposés, which portrayed candidates who were blindfolded and stripped to the waist taking the oaths of an Entered Apprentice, Fellow Craft, and Master Mason.[43] Bennett's plate, which represented the room where the endowment took place, had acacia hanging on the walls (a Masonic symbol of immortality), furniture which was reminiscent of a Masonic lodge, and the presiding officers of the lodge (Joseph Smith, Hyrum Smith, and George Miller) wearing miters.[44]

Devery Anderson and Gary Bergera have noted that Bennett's exposé put Smith in the awkward position of having to denounce the allegations while at the same time "remaining committed to the doctrines he had been teaching."[45] He did both, as demonstrated by the fact that from January to September 1842 he may have been sealed to as many as thirteen additional wives,[46] curtailed the activities of the Holy Order from September 1842 until May 1843, and gradually introduced the emerging doctrine of plural marriage to additional members of the Holy Order. Ironically, Brigham Young (and not Smith's brother) was one of his first disciples to be converted to the doctrine of plural marriage.[47] Smith undoubtedly felt confident that his

43. For examples of these illustrations, see Edward Giddins, *The New England Anti-Masonic Almanac, for the Year of Our Lord 1829* (Boston: Anti-Masonic Free Press, 1829); Giddins, *The Anti-Masonic Almanac, for the Year of the Christian Era 1829* (Rochester NY: E. Scranton, 1829); Giddins, *The New England Anti-Masonic Almanac for the year of Our Lord 1831* (Boston: John Marsh & Co., 1831). A caption in the 1831 *Almanac* reads: "A 'Poor Blind Candidate' receiving his obligation; or the true form of initiating a member to the secret arts and mysteries of Freemasonry." For subsequently published illustrations, see Malcolm C. Duncan, *Masonic Ritual and Monitor; or, Guide to the Three Degrees of the Ancient York Rite and to the Degrees of Mark Master, Past Master, Most Excellent Master, and the Royal Master* (New York: L. Fitzgerald, 1866), 33, 64, 94.

44. Bennett, *History of the Saints*, 273.

45. Anderson and Bergera, *Joseph Smith's Quorum of the Anointed*, xxv.

46. These included Agnes Coolbrith Smith, Lucinda Morgan, Sylvia Sessions Lyon, Mary Rollins, Patty Sessions, Sarah Kingsley, Elizabeth Davis, Marinda Nancy Johnson, Delcena Diadamia Johnson, Eliza R. Snow, Sarah Rapson, Sarah Ann Whitney, and Martha McBride. Smith, *Nauvoo Polygamy*, 87–157.

47. See "Mary Elizabeth Lightner, Address at Brigham Young University, April 14, 1905,"

most trusted confidantes in church leadership would accept the practice
and be bound by obligations of secrecy,[48] and apparently introduced the
principle to some to test their loyalty.[49]

When Hyrum confronted Brigham Young in May 1843 concerning plural marriage, the senior apostle refused to confirm that Smith was teaching the principle until the prophet's brother agreed to "never say another
word against Joseph, and his doings, and the doctrines he is preaching to
the people." When Hyrum agreed to this condition, Young acknowledged
the doctrine and Hyrum "bowed to it and wept like a child, and said, 'God
be praised.'"[50] Thereafter Hyrum took on an increasingly prominent role in
the church and eventually became his brother's heir apparent.[51]

SEALING WOMEN TO MEN

On May 26 Smith reconstituted the Holy Order after Hyrum accepted
the practice of plural marriage. During the initial meeting of the quorum,
seven members, including Hyrum Smith, James Adams, Newel K. Whitney,
Brigham Young, Heber C. Kimball, Willard Richards, and William Law,
were re-endowed.[52] The order continued to meet in a prayer circle where
they exchanged signs, tokens, and passwords, and listened to lectures concerning church doctrine.[53] Although Smith apparently did not acknowledge the practice of plural marriage to the entire assembled quorum, he did
gradually reveal it to selected individual quorum members.[54]

When the Holy Order met two days later Smith was re-endowed and he
revealed the ordinance of sealing of men to their wives. During the meeting

typescript, Special Collections, Harold B. Lee Library, Brigham Young University, Provo,
Utah, 1–3.

48. Bachman, "A Study of the Mormon Practice of Plural Marriage," 179–80.

49. See Ehat, "Joseph Smith's Introduction of Temple Ordinances," 74–75. This sealing ritual was also a restoration of an ancient ritual (see D&C, sec. 132) and some church leaders
even taught that Jesus was married. See Brigham Young, "Discourse by Brigham Young,"
Journal of Discourses 11:328 (February 10, 1867); Brigham Young, "Discourse by Brigham
Young," *Journal of Discourses* 13:309 (November 13, 1870).

50. Brigham Young, cited in Van Wagoner, *Complete Discourses*, 2383 (Oct. 8, 1866).

51. Hyrum Smith embraced the doctrine because it provided a rationale to explain how
his first wife, who predeceased him, and his second wife, who was still living, could both be
sealed to him for eternity. See Anderson and Bergera, *Joseph Smith's Quorum of the Anointed*,
17–18.

52. Neither William Marks nor George Miller attended this meeting. See ibid., 17–19.

53. Quinn, "Latter-day Saint Prayer Circles"; Quinn, *The Mormon Hierarchy: Origins of
Power*, 494; Anderson and Bergera, *Joseph Smith's Quorum of the Anointed*, 17–19; Scott H.
Faulring, *An American Prophet's Record: The Diaries and Journals of Joseph Smith* (Salt Lake
City: Signature Books, 1987), 381 (May 26, 1843).

54. Newell and Avery, *Mormon Enigma*, 140, 161–62, 172; and Anderson and Bergera, *Joseph
Smith's Quorum of the Anointed*, xxv–xxviii.

Smith was sealed to his first and only legal wife, Emma, and James Adams was sealed to his wife, Harriet.[55] Brigham Young, Hyrum Smith, and Willard Richards were each sealed the following day to their legal spouses.[56] Although Joseph had been sealed to many plural wives before these sealings took place, this was the first time he had authorized men and women who had been legally married to be sealed for eternity.

Some historians have concluded that Emma could not have been sealed to Joseph unless she had previously accepted the principle of plural marriage. Anderson and Bergera argue that "she would have had to reconcile herself to the doctrine, a requirement of all hoping to receive the ordinance [of eternal marriage]."[57] In fact, several of Joseph's plural wives later claimed that Emma accepted the practice and was present when they were sealed to the prophet. Despite these statements it is difficult to determine what Emma actually knew about the emerging practice of plural marriage, and whether she ever embraced it, particularly because Emma vehemently denied the practice to the Relief Society and virtually everyone who was involved in the practice shaded the truth.

In addition, Emma denied to the end of her life that she either knew about or accepted her husband's revelations concerning plural marriage. Shortly after she died on April 30, 1879, the Reorganized Church of Jesus Christ of Latter Day Saints (which was organized by her son Joseph Smith III, who claimed to be his father's legitimate successor) published the "Last Testimony of Sister Emma" in the *Saints' Advocate* and the *Saints' Herald*. The article included her representation made to her son Joseph that "there were some rumors of something of that sort [concerning a revelation on plural marriage] which I asked my husband. He assured me that all there was of it was, that, in a chat about plural wives, he had said, 'Well such a system might possibly be, if everybody was agreed to it, and would behave as they should; but they would not; and besides, it was contrary to the will of heaven.'"[58]

The Mormon Church–owned *Deseret News* responded with published statements the same year, which were assembled by Hyrum Smith's son Joseph Fielding, to demonstrate that Joseph Smith Jr. taught and practiced plural marriage and that Emma knew about the practice and accepted it. Two of the statements were made by Emily Dow Partridge (1824–1899) and

55. Quinn, *The Mormon Hierarchy: Origins of Power*, 495.
56. Anderson and Bergera, *Joseph Smith's Quorum of the Anointed*, 21–22.
57. Ibid., xxvii, xxviin42, 19n6. See also Walgren, "James Adams," 132–33; Ehat, "Joseph Smith's Introduction of Temple Ordinances," 74–75; Lyndon W. Cook, *William Law* (Orem, UT: Grandin Book, 1996), 27n84.
58. Newell and Avery, *Mormon Enigma*, 301, quoting *Saints' Advocate* 2, no. 4 (Oct. 1879): 49–52; *Saints' Herald* 26 (Oct. 1, 1879): 289–90.

Eliza Maria Partridge (1820–1886) who claimed that Judge James Adams sealed them to the prophet on May 11, 1843, in the presence of Emma.[59] Emily acknowledged that Heber C. Kimball initially sealed them to Joseph in March 1843, without Emma's knowledge or consent, but that Emma gave Joseph permission, two months later, to take plural wives if she "could select her husband's wives" and she chose Emily and Eliza. Emma apparently did not know that they had already been sealed to Smith and, according to Emily, "to save family trouble Brother Joseph thought it best to have another ceremony performed."[60]

Eliza Roxcy Snow (1804–1887), who was sealed to Smith, Lovina Walker (Joseph F. Smith's sister), and William Clayton (Joseph Smith's clerk) also claimed they had personal knowledge that Emma knew about plural marriage and agreed that Joseph could take additional wives.[61] In 1887 William Law, who withdrew from the church primarily because of Smith's teaching concerning plural marriage, stated that he believed Emma "was his [Joseph's] full accomplice" and that she "complained about Joseph's living with the L[awrence] girls, but not very violently." He said that Emma told him, "I guess I have to submit [to plural marriage]" and "Joe and I have settled our troubles on an equal basis."[62]

59. On May 1, 1869, Emily Dow Partridge Young signed two affidavits. The first stated that Heber C. Kimball sealed her and her sister to Smith in March 1843, while the second stated that James Adams sealed them to Smith again on May 11, 1843, in Emma's presence. Emily's second affidavit was published in "Joseph the Seer's Plural Marriages," *Deseret Evening News*, October 18, 1879, 2. Her sister Eliza M. Partridge Lyman signed an affidavit on July 1, 1869, in which she stated that "she was married or Sealed to Joseph Smith…by James Adams a high-priest…in the presence of Emma (Hale) Smith and Emily Dow Partridge." *Deseret Evening News*, October 18, 1879, 2. See also *Historical Record* 6:3–5 (May 1887), 223.

60. Emily Dow Partridge Young, "Incidents of Early Life of Emily Dow Partridge," Type-script, Special Collections, J. Willard Marriott Library, 4–5; "Autobiography of Emily D. P. Young," *Women's Exponent* 14 (August 1, 1885), 37–38; and *Historical Record* 6:3–5 (May 1887), 240. On March 19, 1892, Emily was deposed and reconfirmed that Emma had consented to her marriage to Smith. See H. Michael Marquardt, "Emily Dow Partridge Smith Young on the Witness Stand: Recollections of a Plural Wife," *Journal of Mormon History* 34:3 (Summer 2008): 119–23. See also Anderson and Bergera, *Quorum of the Anointed*, xxvii, 19; and Compton, *In Sacred Loneliness*, 314–16.

61. Lovina Walker's affidavit concerning Emma's acquiescence to her husband's plural marriages to the Partridge sisters and the Lawrence sisters was dated June 16, 1869, while Clayton's statement was dated February 16, 1874. The affidavits of Snow and Walker, which were originally published in the *Deseret Evening News* on October 18 and 22, 1879, to counter Emma's "Last Testimony," were republished in the *Historical Record* 6:3–5 (May 1887), 223–24. Clayton's statement was also published in the *Historical Record* 6:3–5 (May 1887), 224–26. See also Joseph F. Smith Jr., *Blood Atonement and the Origin of Plural Marriage* (Independence, MO: Zion's Printing and Publishing Co., 1905), 73; Compton, *In Sacred Loneliness*, 458.

62. See Lyndon W. Cook, *William Law, Biographical Essay, Nauvoo Diary, Correspondence, Interview* (Orem, UT: Grandin Book Company, 1994), 120–27, quoting Interview by Wilhelm Wyl, *The Daily Tribune* (Shullsburg, Wisconsin), July 31, 1887. Other sources suggest

William Clayton's account (written in 1874) concerning the Mormon prophet's revelation about plural marriage (which was dictated and transcribed on July 12, 1843) recounted that Hyrum read the revelation to Emma to "convince her of its truth" but that she rejected it and shortly thereafter convinced her husband to discard it. Clayton does not claim that Emma had previously embraced the principle, but he did state that she was "cognizant of the fact of some [Eliza Partridge, Emily Partridge, Sarah Ann Whitney, Helen Kimball, and Flora Woodworth], if not all, of these being his wives, and she generally treated them kindly."[63]

All of these accounts were written decades after Joseph's marriages took place and all of the authors (except Law) were partisans in the dispute between the descendants of Joseph Smith, who remained in Nauvoo and denied that Joseph taught or practiced polygamy, and the followers of Brigham Young, who argued that they were the legitimate successors of Smith prophetic authority and that he taught them the doctrine of plural marriage. Even if Emma suspected or knew about her husband's plural relationships, which she undoubtedly did, or agreed that he could be sealed to other women, which is more nuanced, it is unlikely that she knew he had been sealed to at least sixteen other women before he was sealed to her.

Furthermore, if Emma witnessed the sealing ceremony that Emily and Eliza Partridge described, she may not have understood or accepted the full implications of plural marriage including the sexual component.[64] Thus, while it is difficult to fully accept Emma's statements that she did not know

---

that Emma confronted Joseph concerning plural marriage. See George D. Smith, ed., *An Intimate Chronicle: The Journals of William Clayton* (Salt Lake City: Signature Books and Smith Research Associates, 1991), 108 (June 23, 1843), 110 (July 12, 13, and 15, 1843), 118 (August 23, 1843). William McLellin described a conversation he had with Emma Smith in 1847 in which he claims that Emma acknowledged that she confronted her husband about his relationships with other women while the church was still located in Kirtland, Ohio. See Letters of William E. McLellin to Joseph Smith III, January 10, 1861, and July 1872, Community of Christ Archives. See Stan Larson and Samuel J. Passey, eds., *The William E. McLellin Papers, 1854–1880* (Salt Lake City: Signature Books, 2007), 440–44, 483–95. Larry Foster suggests that John Bennett's revelations may have encouraged Emma's suspicions about her husband's teachings concerning plural marriage. Foster, *Religion and Sexuality*, 169–74.

63. *Historical Record* 6:3–5 (May 1887), 224–26. See also Smith, *An Intimate Chronicle*, 110 (July 12, 1843); and D&C, section 132. This revelation required the first wife to approve of the marriage. D&C, 132:24. Orson Pratt revealed the contents of this ceremony in the church periodical *The Seer*, which was published in Washington, D.C. See Orson Pratt, "Celestial Marriage," *The Seer* 1:2 (February 1853): 31. See also Hardy, *Doing the Works of Abraham*, 58–61.

64. Lucy Kimball suggested that Emma gave Joseph permission to marry at least four women and that "she was well aware that he associated with them as wives within the meaning of all that word implies. This is proven by the fact, that she herself on several occasions, kept guard at the door to prevent disinterested persons from intruding, when these ladies were in the house." See "Lucy Kimball's Testimony," *Historical Record* 6:3–5 (May 1887), 229–30.

her husband had extramarital relationships, it is more problematic to determine whether she fully embraced the practice before she received her endowment and was sealed to the prophet.

Nevertheless, some Mormon historians are surprisingly harsh in their assessment of Emma's attitude toward plural marriage when one considers that her rejection of the practice is consistent with the current LDS position. They claim that Emma brought "dissent into the inner circles of the church" and that her actions, "like the highly publicized dissent of other prominent Saints in Nauvoo, threatened the essential order and unity without which the church could not survive."[65]

In July or August 1843 Hyrum delivered a copy of the marriage revelation to William Law (a member of the First Presidency who had defended the prophet against John C. Bennett's salacious allegations that Smith was guilty of taking multiple wives) and to the Nauvoo High Council, which included William Marks.[66] Law and Marks (who were both charter members of the Holy Order) bitterly rejected the practice. Law must have been particularly shell-shocked when the prophet finally admitted that he condoned the taking of plural wives and was thereafter removed from the First Presidency.[67] During the same period James Adams became ill and died while he was preparing to relocate to Nauvoo. Thus, Joseph lost two of his most vocal supporters who had advised him during the hard slog against Bennett's numerous allegations.[68]

---

65. Derr, Cannon, and Beecher, *Women of Covenant*, 62.
66. See "Thomas Grover's Testimony" and "David Fullmer's Testimony," in *Historical Record* 6:3–5 (May 1887), 226–27.
67. "Law Interview," March 30, 1887, p. 6; "1885 Affidavit of William Law," Charles Augustus Shook, *The True Origins of Mormon Polygamy* (Cincinnati: The Standard Publishing Company, 1914), 126. For a discussion of William Law's disaffection, see Lyndon W. Cook, "William Law, Nauvoo Dissenter," *BYU Studies* 22:1 (Winter 1982), 47–72. Law became Smith's second counselor (in place of Hyrum Smith) in January 1841. See D&C, 124:91; *Times and Seasons* 1 (February 1, 1841): 310.
68. James Adams was elected as a Hancock County probate judge and was preparing to move his family to Nauvoo when he died unexpectedly in Springfield on August 11, 1843. He was buried in Nauvoo with Masonic honors and during October conference Joseph Smith eulogized him, noting, "I anointed him to the patriarchal power—to receive the keys of knowledge and power, by revelation to himself." *History of the Church* 6:50–52. See also Walgren, "James Adams," 133–35. Although Adams died before Joseph Smith introduced the second anointing, Smith stated during his October general conference eulogy that "Patriarch Adams is now one of the spirits of the just men made perfect; and, if revealed now, must be revealed in fire; and the glory could not be endured." He noted that Adams "has had revelations concerning his departure, and has gone to a more important work. When men are prepared, they are better off to go hence. Brother Adams has gone to open up a more effectual door for the dead." See *History of the Church* 6:50–52.

SECOND ANOINTING

On September 28, 1843, Smith introduced a new, two-part ritual to the Holy Order that he called the second anointing. Smith's diary, which was written by Willard Richards, records that "Baurah Ale [Joseph Smith] was by common consent, & unanimous voice chosen president of the quorum, & anointed & orda[ined] to the highest and holiest order of the priesthood (& companion)."[69] One of Smith's other scribes, William Clayton, recorded that on October 19, 1843, Smith told him that Emma "had been anointed & he [Smith] also had been a[nointed] K[ing]."[70] Thus, Emma, the Elect Lady who was the first president of the Relief Society, became the first female member admitted to the Holy Order and received both the first and second endowments, even though she had rejected the plural marriage revelation. This provides some evidence that the prophet's wife was not required to accept the plural marriage revelation (as other members of the order apparently were) in order to be sealed to her husband.

Shortly after Emma became the first woman admitted into the Holy Order, other women were initiated into the order (who were married to other male members of the order) and Joseph endowed, anointed, and sealed them to their husbands. Those who received the second anointing had their feet washed, were anointed as priests and kings, priestesses and queens, and their exaltation and promise of eternal life (which they received during the first endowment) was sealed upon them. They were given the "sure word of prophecy," which confirmed that the eternal life and exaltation and their calling was "made sure."[71] George A. Smith later observed that the Mormon prophet instructed the Holy Order that "but one King and Priest could

---

69. Joseph Smith, Journal, Sept. 28, 1843, Church History Library. Wilford Woodruff did not write Emma's name in his journal. He recorded that "President Joseph Smith received his second Anointing this day." See Kenney, *Wilford Woodruff's Journal* 2:313 (September 28, 1843). Emma was not listed as an attendee (See *History of the Church* 6:39; and Kenney, *Wilford Woodruff's Journal* 2:313) even though later entries list wives being present. See "Manuscript History of Brigham Young," 154–59 (October 22, 1843–January 28, 1844). See also Faulring, *An American Prophet's Record*, 418, 425, 426, 440–42, 444–45. For other references to the second anointing see Kenney, *Wilford Woodruff's Journal* 2:340–41, 344, 346, 354. Quinn specifically states that the word "companion" refers to Joseph's companion, Emma, who was ordained as a queen and priestess. Quinn, "Latter-day Saint Prayer Circles," 85–86.

70. See Smith, *An Intimate Chronicle*, 122 (October 19, 1843).

71. See David John Buerger, "'The Fullness of the Priesthood': The Second Anointing in Latter-day Saint Theology and Practice," *Dialogue: A Journal of Mormon Thought* 16 (Spring 1983): 10–44. See also Joseph Smith, Journal, Church History Library (Sept. 28, 1843); Smith, *An Intimate Chronicle*, 202n5.

be anointed at one meeting in a private room dedicated by permission to anoint in."[72] During the anointing "the Administrator should anoint the man A King & Priest unto the most High God. Then he should Anoint his wife or wives Queens or Priestesses unto her husband."[73]

On November 22 Brigham Young and his wife Mary Ann received their second anointing and Smith instructed Young to confer the ordinance on other members of the Twelve.[74] Orson Hyde later wrote that Smith told those who received this anointing that "'To us were committed the Keys of the Kingdom, and every gift, key and power, that Joseph ever had,' confirmed upon our heads by an anointing."[75] Throughout Joseph's lifetime, the Holy Order grew much more slowly and deliberately than the Female Relief Society or the Nauvoo Masonic Lodge. By the end of 1843 there were only thirty-eight members of the Holy Order—twenty men and eighteen women, while only fifteen quorum members received their second anointing and seventeen couples were married for eternity.[76]

BUILD UP THE TEMPLE

Meanwhile, William Weeks continued to work on drawings for the Nauvoo Temple even as it was being built on a hill facing the Mississippi River. In April 1843 Smith, who supervised Weeks's work on the temples, gave him a certificate to carry out his designs that specifically provided that "no person or persons shall interfere with him or his plans in the building of the Temple."[77] Weeks's interior design included two levels: "the first floor exhibited the double-ended arrangement of three rows of pulpits to seat the two priesthoods" while the attic "contained a long central room with

72. Kenney, *Wilford Woodruff's Journal* 5: 139–40 (December 18, 1857).

73. Ibid., 6:307–9 (December 26, 1866). Brigham Young explained that "the Lord will say unto you, you shall never fall; your salvation is sealed unto you; and you are sealed unto eternal life and salvation, through your integrity." Brigham Young, "Exchange of Feeling and Sentiment Produces Mutual Confidence," *Journal of Discourses* 4:372 (June 28, 1857). He also taught that "[t]he only men who become Gods, even sons of God, are those who enter into polygamy." Brigham Young, "Delegate Hooper—Beneficial Effects of Polygamy—Final Redemption of Cain," *Journal of Discourses* 11:269 (August 19, 1866). See also Joseph F. Smith, "Plural Marriage—For the Righteous Only—Obedience Imperative—Blessings Resulting, *Journal of Discourses* 20:28–29 (July 7, 1878); Wilford Woodruff, "Object of Meeting Together," *Journal of Discourses* 24: 243–44 (July 20, 1883).

74. Joseph Smith, Journal, LDS Church History Library (November 22, 1843); Anderson and Bergera, *Joseph Smith's Quorum of the Anointed*, 38.

75. Orson Hyde to Ebenezer Robinson, September 19, 1844, Davis City, Iowa, as cited in *The Return* 2 (April 1890): 253.

76. Anderson and Bergera, *Joseph Smith's Quorum of the Anointed*, xxx.

77. *History of the Church* 5:353; 6:196–97.

twelve side chambers."[78] Lisle Brown has noted that the design of Joseph's second temple "mirrored the Kirtland Temple—two large meeting halls on the ground and second floors, and attic office rooms, as well as a finished basement."[79]

In February 1844 the Mormon prophet instructed Weeks to include circular windows in the design even though Weeks told him that "windows in the broad side of a building were a violation of all known rules of architecture, and contended that they should be semicircular." But Smith insisted and told Weeks, "I wish you to carry out *my* designs. I have seen in vision the splendid appearance of that building illuminated, and will have it built according to the pattern shown me."[80]

Weeks's exterior plans included "an immense tower (four stories) over the façade immediately behind the pediment" and an "ashlar surface" that included sunstones, moonstones, and starstones. The temple's tower would be capped by a flying angel that would serve as a weather vane, dressed in temple clothes (a cap, robe, and slippers) holding a book in its right hand and a trumpet in its left.[81] While such weather vanes were common in New England, Weeks's angelic design included obvious Masonic symbols (a square and compass) as well as a Rosicrucian burning heart on the base below the flying angel.[82]

---

78. Laurel B. Andrew has noted that "it would seem more accurate to call Weeks a builder rather than an architect." For a description of Weeks's various drawings for the temple, see Laurel B. Andrew, *The Early Temples of the Mormons: The Architecture of the Millennial Kingdom in the American West* (Albany: State University of New York Press, 1978), 55–96.

79. Lisle G. Brown, "'Temple Pro Tempore': The Salt Lake City Endowment House," *Journal of Mormon History* 34 (Fall 2008), 1–3. See also William Weeks, Transverse drawing of the Nauvoo Temple, undated, William Weeks Papers, Church History Library; and Don C. Colvin, *Nauvoo Temple: A Temple of Faith* (American Fork, UT: Covenant Communications, 2002), 168–69.

80. *History of the Church* 6:197 (February 5, 1844).

81. Trevan Hatch concludes that "Joseph Smith came to know later in life that the apparel worn by Moroni on this occasion resembled ancient temple vestments." Hatch, *Visions, Manifestations and Miracles*, 101, 123n21.

82. These images, including the burning heart, were utilized by Jeremy L. Cross, in his *The True Masonic Chart*. Although Mackey has noted in his *Encyclopedia of Freemasonry* that "there is no such symbol [as a burning heart] in the [Masonic] ritual," he acknowledged that "the theory that every man who becomes a Mason must first be prepared in his heart was advanced among the earliest lectures of the last century" and that "there is a legend in some of the high degrees and in continental Masonry, that the heart of Hiram Abiff was deposited in an urn and placed on a monument near the holy of holies." See Mackey, *Encyclopedia of Freemasonry* 1:320. Lance Owens noted that the burning heart was utilized by Rosicrucians as an emblem and that Orson Pratt used the image of a heart encasing an all-seeing eye on the masthead of *The Seer*, which he published in Washington, D.C., from January 1853 to June 1854 and in Liverpool from June 1854 to July 1854. Lance Owens, "Joseph Smith and the Kabbalah," 148.

Nauvoo Temple. Courtesy Utah State Historical Society.

Neither Smith nor Weeks named the flying angel who would appear atop the Nauvoo Temple, and Perrigrine Sessions, who was present when Weeks's flying angel was placed on the temple, wrote only that it was "an angel in his priestly robes with a Book of Mormon in one hand and a trumpet in the other which is over laid with gold leaf." [83] There were many angels who could have inspired Weeks's own vision of a flying angel. The Bible and Mormon scriptures included many angels (some of whom blew trumpets) who warned of apocalyptic events and proclaimed new revelations. [84] Smith revealed in 1831 that Moroni, who informed him about gold plates that were buried in the Hill Cumorah, was the same angel that John the Revelator described flying "in the midst of heaven, having the everlasting gospel." [85]

In addition, Christian art included hundreds of images of trumpet-blowing angels. Some of the most famous examples, which were based on the angels described in the Book of Revelation, include Giotto's La Cappella degli Scrovegni in Padova (c. 1305), the Western Rose Window in the

---

83. Perregrine Sessions Journal, quoted in Leonard, *Nauvoo*, 254.

84. For a detailed discussion of Egyptian, Greek, Roman, and Biblical references to trumpets see Gerhard Kittel and Gerhard Friedrich, eds., *Theological Dictionary of the New Testament* (Grand Rapids, MI: William F. Eerdman Publishing Company, 1973), 7:71–88. The sound of a trumpet was associated with new revelations or warnings. Hosea 5:7–9; Daniel 3:15; Matthew 24:31; 1 Corinthians 15:51–52; Revelations, chapters 8–11. The Bible also refers to the "trumpet blast heard on Rosh Hashanah...to symbolically 'awaken' God's children from a 'spiritual slumber,'" Isaiah 42:11; 44:23; Jeremiah 31:7; 1 Corinthians 15:46, and to accompany the gathering of Israel. Isaiah 27:13. Friedrich notes that 120 priests blew trumpets at the dedication of Solomon's Temple (2 Corinthians 5:12, 7:6), and when the foundation of the new temple was completed the priests also blew trumpets (Ezra 3:10). The Book of Mormon (Mosiah 26:25; Mormon 9:13) and Doctrine and Covenants (D&C 24:12; 29:13; 29:26; 43:25; 45:45; 49:23; 77:12; 88:92, 98–110; 109:75) also mention trumpet-blowing angels. See Hatch, *Visions, Manifestations and Miracles*, 116.

85. Revelations 14:6 refers to "another angel fly[ing] in the midst of heaven, having the everlasting gospel to preach to them that dwell on the earth, and to every nation, and kindred, and tongue, and people." John Taylor recorded that he saw a vision before he converted to Mormonism of "an angel in the heavens, holding a trumpet to his mouth, sounding a message to the nations," B. H. Roberts, *The Life of John Taylor* (Salt Lake City: George Q. Cannon & Sons, 1892), 27–28. In 1831 Joseph Smith published a revelation stating, "I have sent forth mine angel...flying through the midst of heaven, having the everlasting gospel, who hath appeared unto some and hath committed it unto man, who shall appear unto many that dwell on the earth. And this gospel shall be preached unto every nation, and kindred, and tongue, and people." (D&C, 133: 36–37). Although Moroni appeared to Smith on at least twenty occasions (see Hatch, *Visions, Manifestations and Miracles*, 96), he was also visited by other heavenly messengers who imparted new revelations including God the Father, Jesus Christ, Adam, Noah, Seth, Enos, Cainan, Mahalaleel, Jared, Enoch, Methuselah, Abraham, Jacob, Joseph, Moses, Elijah, Elias, John the Baptist, Paul, Peter, James, and John. See Hatch, *Visions, Manifestations and Miracles*, 139, 146–52. See also D&C 27:5–18; 76: 21, 57; 107: 53; 128: 21; *Journal of Discourses* 17:374.

Detail of flying angel on Nauvoo Temple. Courtesy H. Michael Marquardt.

Sainte-Chapelle in Paris (1485–1491), and Michelangelo *Buonarotti's Final Judgment* in the Sistine Chapel in Vatican City (1535–1541).[86]

Greek and Roman mythology included a trumpet-blowing angel named Fama (Fame).[87] Fama was incorporated into the Rosicrucian text *The Chymical Wedding of Christian Rosencreutz*, which "opens with a personification of Fame, sounding her trumpet call." The text recorded that she "bore a golden trumpet whereon a Name was engraved which the narrator [Chris-

86. La Cappella degli Scrovegni (like the Sistine Chapel) was constructed with similar dimensions to those of Solomon's Temple. It contained at least nine frescoes with temple themes, some of which have trumpet-blowing angels. See Jules Lubbock, *Storytelling in Christian Art from Giotto to Donatello* (New Haven: Yale University Press, 2006), 53. Other examples of trumpet-blowing angels include a painting by Jusepe de Ribera (1591–1652) that has an angel of judgment blowing a trumpet while appearing to St. Jerome in 1626 (which currently resides at Capodimonte in Napoli); interiors of Roman churches: La Chiesa di San Antonio dei Portoghesi; La Chiesa di Santa Maddalena; La Chiesa di Santa Maria di Montesanto, La Basilica di San Marco (carved above a monument to Francesco Erizzo c. 1700), the Galleria Borghese (on the ceiling of the entrance hall); and the interiors of other churches: La Chiesa Scalzi in Venezia, the Palais du Louvre (in the Galerie D'Apollon) in Paris, and the Cattedrale di San Giovanni in Torino (carved above the Royal Tribune in 1775). There are also images of trumpet-blowing angels located on the Uffizzi in Firenze; the Arc de Triomphe in Paris; St. Patrick's Room in Dublin Castle; and on a bas-relief that is below the peristyle above the central door of the Paris Pantheon.

87. Fama was the Roman Goddess of Rumor (known as Pheme in Greek mythology) who had wings, multiple tongues, eyes, and ears, and who blew a trumpet to inform the world that she was prepared to reveal information from the gods.

tian Rosenkreutz] could read but dared not reveal" in her right hand while "in her left hand she had a bundle of letters in all languages which she was to carry into all countries. Her large wings were covered with eyes, as she mounted aloft she gave a mighty blast of her trumpet."[88]

There were also images of trumpet-blowing angels (inspired by the Greek and Roman model) located in the United States that could have caught Weeks's attention. Antonio Capellano designed an image of Washington being crowned by Peace and Fame (with trumpet), which was carved on a relief above the east-central portico in the interior of the U.S. Capitol (1827), and the Washington Benevolent Society published a similar image of George Washington being crowned by Fame.[89]

During the April 1844 general conference, Hyrum Smith encouraged church members to complete the Nauvoo Temple where endowments would be performed. Both Hyrum and Brigham Young urged church members to "build up the Temple" where they would "get your washings, anointings, and endowments."[90] Hyrum said, "I cannot make a comparison between the House of God and anything now in existence. Great things are to grow out of that house. There is a great and mighty power to grow out of it. There is an endowment. Knowledge is power. We want knowledge."[91] He also assured the sisters that they would "have a seat in that house" and in Masonic terminology said that "we are designated by the All-seeing Eye to do good, not to stoop to anything low."[92]

On April 8 Hyrum Smith publicly discussed rumors concerning the practice of plural marriage, and while he did not admit that the practice was authorized he did acknowledge that he had been sealed to two women. "No spiritual wife doctrine ever originated with me," he said, but he also explained that Joseph taught him that his first wife, who had died, could be sealed to him for eternity and that this would not prevent his second wife from being sealed to him as well. He rejoiced that "the Lord has given to Joseph the power to seal on earth and in heaven those who are found worthy; having the spirit of Elijah and Elias he has power to seal with a Seal that shall never be broken, and it shall be in force in the morn of the resurrection." "Talk about Spiritual wives," Hyrum said, "one that is dead and

---

88. See Yates, *The Rosicrucian Enlightenment*, 60–61. Bernardo Strozzi (1581–1644) painted "A Personification of Fama" in 1635–1636. This painting represents the Roman goddess with both a golden trumpet (honorable fame) and a wooden wind instrument (infamy), and is located in the National Gallery in London.
89. See *Constantino Brumindi, Artist of the Capitol* (Washington, DC: U.S. Government Printing Office, 1998), 128. See also Grunder, *Mormon Parallels*, Entry 408, p. 1681.
90. *History of the Church* 6:321–22. For Hyrum Smith's address, see ibid., 6:298–301.
91. Ibid., 6:298–99.
92. Ibid., 6:299.

gone is spiritual." Nevertheless, the prophet's brother warned that "every great and good principle should be taught to the Saints, but some must not be taught to the world; until they are prepared to receive them; it would be like casting pearls before swine. No man must attempt to preach them."[93]

As the temple neared completion the Holy Order met as a prayer circle in Joseph Smith's mansion house and red brick store as well as Brigham Young's home.[94] In May, Smith hosted Josiah Quincy (1802–1882) and Charles Francis Adams (1807–1886) at the mansion house, which was designed with its own Masonic symbolism.[95] According to Quincy, the Mormon prophet asked the Brahmin cousins rhetorically, reminiscent of Justinian's statement after the completion of the Hagia Sophia in Constantinople, whether he was not "greater than Solomon who built a Temple with the treasures of his father David and with the assistance of Huram, King of Tyre?" Smith then answered his own question: "Joseph Smith has built his Temple with no one to aid him in the work."[96]

"FALSE AND DAMNABLE DOCTRINE"

William Law (a charter member of the Holy Order) tried to convince the prophet to abandon plural marriage, and at one point placed "his arms around the neck of the Prophet, [and] was pleading with him to withdraw the doctrine of plural marriage." Law predicted that if Smith "would abandon the doctrine 'Mormonism' would, in fifty or one hundred years,

---

93. *Manuscript History of the Church*, Book E-1, 1986–88 (April 8, 1844).

94. Quinn, "Latter-day Saint Prayer Circles," 85.

95. The rainwater conductor heads were designed in 1842 with images of the sun, moon, and stars (see illustrations 19 and 20). Quincy became mayor of Boston and Charles Francis Adams was a member of the Massachusetts Legislature and later was appointed as Lincoln's minister to England during the Civil War.

96. Josiah Quincy, *Figures of the Past* (Boston: Roberts Brothers, 1883), 390. When the Hagia Sophia was completed in 537 BCE the emperor exclaimed, "Solomon I have surpassed thee." Other structures that were later built with dimensions similar to Solomon's Temple included the Capella degli Scrovegni (Padova) (c. 1305), the Sistine Chapel (1477–1480) and the Capella Paolina (Palazzo Quirinale) (1617). When Pope Sixtus IV (1414–1484) authorized the reconstruction of the Sistine Chapel in Rome, he apparently believed that the chapel would replace the temple that had been destroyed in Jerusalem just as the Roman Catholic Church had succeeded Judaism as the keeper of the temple. Nevertheless, Jules Lubbock has argued that "most, if not all, synagogues and churches follow the proportions of the [Solomon's] Temple closely." Jules Lubbock, *Storytelling in Christian Art from Giotto to Donatello* (New Haven: Yale University Press, 2006), 53n28, 306n23; and Richard Krautheimer notes that for a medieval church to be described as an imitation or copy of a prototype it was not necessary for all the precise features or measurements of the original to be observed, only a "selective transfer" of architectural elements or measurements was required. See Richard Krautheimer, "Introduction to an 'Iconography of Medieval Architecture,'" *Journal of the Warburg and Courtauld Institutes*, 5 (1942): 1–33.

Illustration of Masonic symbols. Published in Jeremy Cross,
The True Masonic Chart, or Hieroglyphic Monitor.

Mansion House in Nauvoo. Courtesy of Community of Christ Archives.

dominate the Christian world. Mr Law pleaded for this...with tears stream-
ing from his eyes." But Smith refused to reverse his course "for God had
commanded him to teach it, and condemnation would come upon him if
he was not obedient to the commandment."[97]

Nevertheless, there is a very cryptic minute entry suggesting that Smith
may have sealed Law to his wife, Jane, even after he rejected plural marriage.[98] Smith may have believed that if he agreed to the sealing, the Laws
might eventually be attracted to the doctrine when they recognized that it
was interconnected with their own eternal relationship.[99] But, just as there
is conflicting evidence concerning whether Emma Smith accepted the practice of plural marriage, it is questionable whether the Laws were sealed in
exchange for reconsidering Smith's marriage revelation.

Ultimately, Brigham Young presided over the tribunal that excommunicated Law and thirty-one other male members.[100] The Holy Order met
more than twenty times during January and February of 1844, but it only
met eleven times from March through June. In May Joseph Smith initiated
five additional men into the order, including Sidney Rigdon, his longstanding counselor and mentor, as well as his brother William.[101] William later

97. "Joseph W. McMurrin's interview with Richard S. Law," *Improvement Era* 6 (May 1903):
507–10.
98. "Joseph acknowledged—& sealed William wife." See Cook, "William Law, Nauvoo
Dissenter," 65n82. See also Minutes of Quorum of Twelve, April 18, 1844.
99. Jane Law (wife of William Law) was among those who were admitted into the Holy
Order. She was admitted sometime prior to October 1, 1843. See Faulring, *An American
Prophet's Record*, 417 (October 1, 1843).
100. Diary of William Law, April 21, 1844; *Nauvoo Expositor*, June 7, 1844, p. 2.
101. Rigdon was initiated, passed, and raised in Freemasonry on the same day as the prophet

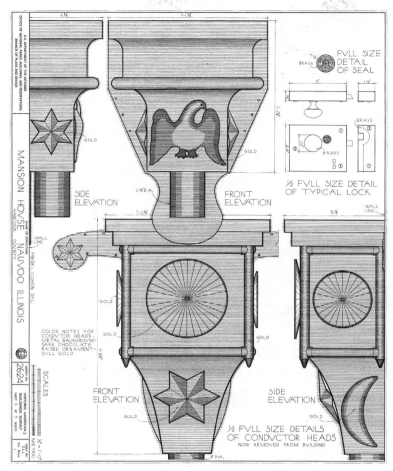

Detail of rainwater conductor heads on Nauvoo Mansion House.
Courtesy Community of Christ.

wrote a vague account of his initiation that mentions only the initiatory rites and makes no mention of Masonic parallels.[102]

During this same period Smith organized a Council of Fifty (which included all of the apostles and many of the male members of the Holy Order)

but he was not invited to join the Holy Order until more than two years after it was organized. After Law was excommunicated Smith invited Rigdon, John P. Greene (May 11), Almon Babbitt (May 12), William Smith (May 12), and Lyman Wight (May 14) to join the Holy Order. See Anderson and Bergera, *Joseph Smith's Quorum of the Anointed*, 75–77.

102. See William Smith, "General Epistle of Wm. Smith to all the Church: Startling developments, Saints take warning," in William Smith letters—1845, MS 601, Church History Library. Will Bagley has concluded that this undated manuscript was written on November 14, 1845. See Bagley, *Scoundrel's Tale*, 98. I am indebted to Connell O'Donovan for providing a copy of this manuscript, his transcription, and Bagley's reference to its date of creation.

that was described by one member as the "outer wall or government around the inner temple of priesthood." Smith assured the Council of Fifty, as he had the Holy Order, that they were commissioned to carry out his work after his death.[103]

Smith also continued to encourage a select group of men, including Joseph Andrew Kelting, who was a lawyer and sheriff in Hancock County, to take plural wives. Kelting later recalled that when he asked Smith if he was practicing plural marriage, Smith refused to answer since "it might militate against you as an officer as well as against us." Kelting responded that "whatever you tell me as your friend is safe; I came here upon the square (and we were both Masons) it shall never injure you in any shape." Smith then told him that "I did moot plural marriage," that he received a revelation on the subject, and that he had more than one wife.[104]

Meanwhile, William Law assisted in the organization of the True Church of Jesus Christ of Latter Day Saints and with six other men (Wilson Law, Charles Ivins, Francis M. Higbee, Chaucey Higbee, Robert D. Foster, and Charles A. Foster) published the first and only issue of the *Nauvoo Expositor*. The newspaper published many of the same allegations against Smith's moral character that John C. Bennett had previously advanced in the *Sangamo Journal*. The newspaper claimed that "many females in foreign climes" were being "induced, by the sound of the Gospel," to travel to Nauvoo "that she should be his (Joseph's) Spiritual wife," and concluded that "it is difficult—perhaps impossible—to describe the wretchedness of the females in this place."

The *Expositor* challenged the "false and damnable doctrine" that had been introduced into the church, including "plurality of Gods," "the plurality of wives, for time and eternity," and "the doctrine of unconditional sealing up to eternal life, against all crimes except that of shedding [*sic*] innocent blood, by a perversion of their priestly authority." It alleged that the Mormon marriage ceremony included a vow to "never divulge what is revealed to them, with a penalty of death attached, that God Almighty has revealed it to him, that she should be his (Joseph's) Spiritual wife."

The editors took aim at the very organizations (the Holy Order and Freemasonry) that they had previously embraced. They criticized "all secret societies, and combinations under penal oaths and obligations (professing

103. Faulring, *An American Prophet's Record*, 458–59; Klaus J. Hansen, *Quest for Empire: The Political Kingdom of God and the Council of Fifty in Mormon History* (Lansing: Michigan State University Press, 1967), 72–89.

104. Joseph Andrew Ketling recorded two affidavits on this subject: the first on March 1, 1894, and the second (from which the quoted material is taken) on September 11, 1903. See Smith, *Nauvoo Polygamy*, 241–59, 474–78. Smith lists various affidavits concerning plural marriage, which are located in the LDS Church History Library.

to be organized for religious purposes,)" and concluded that they were "anti-Christian, hypocritical and corrupt." In short, the editors did not acknowledge "any man as king or law-giver to the church; for Christ is our only king and law-giver."[105]

Although the Mormon prophet undoubtedly felt betrayed by Law, who had supported him during the Bennett affair, the former counselor had never accepted plural marriage and, unlike Bennett, apparently had no moral shortcomings.[106] Smith, who had been tentative when Bennett betrayed him, struck back immediately after the publication of the newspaper and claimed that Law was an adulterer and a liar. On June 8, the Nauvoo City Council, which was presided over by seceding Mason George Washington Harris, passed a resolution declaring the *Nauvoo Expositor* a public nuisance and authorized the mayor "to cause said printing establishment and papers to be removed without delay in such manner as he shall direct." On May 10 Smith signed an order commanding that the city marshal, John P. Greene, to destroy the press and the paper.[107]

After Greene carried out Smith's order, the publishers of the *Expositor* filed a complaint with the justice of the peace in Carthage (the seat of Hancock County) who charged Smith, the city council, and city marshal with riot. The city council thereafter declared martial law to prevent arrest. Nevertheless, the charged parties appeared before the justice on June 24, after Governor Thomas Ford guaranteed their safety, and the justice dismissed the pending charges. Both Joseph and Hyrum, however, were charged with treason and bound over for trial. On June 25, Joseph and Hyrum were incarcerated in Carthage Jail, where they awaited trial on this new charge, and both John Taylor and Willard Richards joined them to offer their moral support.

Before Smith was killed at Carthage, he had introduced the endowment to thirty-seven men and thirty-two women in a little over two years.[108] The

---

105. "Preamble," *Nauvoo Expositor*, June 7, 1844. The publishers did not describe the endowment ceremony but their complaints concerning secret societies, "man as king," and "unconditional sealing up" are references to the endowment ritual.

106. Although Smith apparently accused Law of being an adulterer, there is no evidence to support this claim. See Cook, "William Law, Nauvoo Dissenter," 65n82.

107. *Nauvoo Neighbor* 2 (June 19, 1844); "History of Joseph Smith" *Deseret News*, September 23, 1857, pp. 225–26; *History of the Church* 6: 434–48. The minutes recorded that "Mayor [Joseph Smith] said he had never preached the revelation [July 12, 1843] in private; but he had in public. Had not taught it to the anointed in the church in private, which statement many present confirmed; that on inquiring concerning the passage on the resurrection concerning 'they neither marry nor are given in marriage,' &c., he received for answer 'Man in this life must marry in view of eternity, otherwise must remain as angels, or be single in heaven.'" *History of the Church*, 6:442.

108. See Anderson and Bergera, *Joseph Smith's Quorum of the Anointed*, 75–77; Quinn, "Latter-day Saint Prayer Circles," 84.

men who joined this Holy Order, or Quorum of the Anointed (with the exception of three), were Masons while the women were all members of the Relief Society and either the first wife or a plural wife of a male member, including at least five of Smith's plural wives. Approximately 33 percent of these men (twenty-seven) were polygamists while about 17 percent of the initiated women were plural wives.[109] Yet only 57 percent of the polygamists in Nauvoo were members of the quorum and 58 percent of the quorum (male and female) were polygamists.[110]

When the Holy Order met shortly after Smith's death, it voted to temporarily discontinue its prayer circles. But less than six months later the quorum began to meet again, formed prayer circles and exchanged signs, tokens, and passwords, and Brigham Young began to initiate new members. Young was careful to keep activities of the Holy Order secret and the ritual under wraps, and when William Clayton's wife and three other women were initiated on December 22, 1844, Young noted that "we have to use the greatest care and caution and dare not let it be known that we meet."[111]

109. Quinn, "Latter-day Saint Prayer Circles," 88. The only men who were not Masons were Orson Pratt, Almon W. Babbitt, and ex-Mason W. W. Phelps.
110. D. Michael Quinn, "Mormon Women Have Had the Priesthood since 1843," in *Women and Authority, Re-emerging Mormon Feminism*, ed. Maxine Hanks, 365–409 (Salt Lake City: Signature Books, 1992). Quinn does not include Phebe Waltrous as a member of the Endowment Council and calls Marinda Nancy Hyde "a special case" since, although she was Joseph Smith's plural wife, she "participated with her husband Orson in the Holy Order." Quinn, "Latter-day Saint Prayer Circles," 87–88. Smith's plural wives in the Holy Order included Elizabeth Durfee, Phebe Waltrous, Fanny Murray, Agnes Coolbrith, and Marinda N. Hyde.
111. Smith, *An Intimate Chronicle*, 153.

Joseph's Second Temple

JOSEPH SMITH PLANNED to introduce the endowment to all worthy church members as soon as the temple in Nauvoo was completed, and Brigham Young fulfilled this pledge after Smith was killed. The select group that received the endowment prior to the completion of the temple was a relatively small number compared to the fourteen hundred who had been initiated into Nauvoo Lodge and other Mormon Masonic lodges and the thirteen hundred women who had joined the Female Relief Society.[1] But the endowment that Smith and Young developed was even more conducive to large numbers since it was a condensed ritual that the initiates could experience in a few hours compared to the multiple Masonic rites that required months and even years to complete.

HOSANNA! HOSANNA! HOSANNA!

Young continued to build the temple even though he recognized that the church might eventually be forced to evacuate the City of Joseph.[2] The *Times and Seasons* reported on January 15, 1845, that the wooden baptismal font (which rested on wooden oxen) in the basement of the temple had been removed and would be replaced by a font "of hewn stone." The new font would include "stone steps and an iron railing" that would "stand upon twelve oxen, which will be cast of iron or brass, or perhaps hewn stone."[3]

1. See Anderson and Bergera, *Joseph Smith's Quorum of the Anointed*, xxxviii. See also Devery S. Anderson and Gary James Bergera, eds., *The Nauvoo Endowment Companies, 1845–1846: A Documentary History* (Salt Lake City: Signature Books, 2005).
2. *History of the Church* 7:314. On January 26, 1845, Brigham Young "proposed to the quorum to finish off the upper story of the temple in which they could receive their washings and anointings instead of undertaking a building [High Priests Hall] from the commencement: this proposition was received by unanimous vote." See *History of the Church* 7:364.
3. "An Epistle of the Twelve, to the Church of Jesus Christ of Latter Day Saints in all the World," *Times and Seasons* 6 (January 15, 1845): 779.

On May 24 Young presided when the capstone was placed on the temple and he told priesthood authorities, who were the only invitees at this event, that "the last stone is laid upon the Temple and I pray the Almighty in the name of Jesus to defend us in this place, and sustain us until the Temple is finished and we have all got our endowments." Following Young's remarks those who attended the ceremony shouted "Hosanna! Hosanna! Hosanna! To God and the Lamb! Amen! Amen! and Amen!" and repeated it a second and third time. "So let it be," Young concluded, "thou Lord Almighty."[4]

On June 27 the Holy Order met at Willard Richards's home on the first anniversary of Joseph Smith's assassination and Heber C. Kimball recorded that, while assembled in their circle, the group prayed "that God would curs[e] those that had spilt thare B[l]ood and all those that persecute the Saints. O Lord I thank Thy holy name that Thou dost hear Thy servants and bring trouble on them."[5] Although this prayer was similar to a passage in the Book of Revelation that called upon God to avenge the deaths "of those who had been slain for the word of God,"[6] and an oath Freemasons made to avenge the death of Hiram Abiff and to take vengeance on those who betray the secrets of Freemasonry,[7] its most important antecedent was a covenant that Smith revealed in the Kirtland Temple concerning Missouri mobs. Thereafter this covenant became part of the endowment ritual and remained one of its most controversial elements for almost a century.[8]

In October five thousand church members attended a general conference that was held on the main level of the unfinished temple, where Brigham Young revealed to the church that the temple would be completed regardless of whether the church remained in Nauvoo.[9] During the next two months construction workers focused their efforts on the attic, where the endowment would be introduced, and the basement where the baptismal font was located and baptisms for the dead would be performed.[10]

4. "The Nauvoo Temple," *Historical Record* 8:4–6 (June 1889), 870.

5. Kimball, *On the Potter's Wheel*, 125.

6. See Revelation 6:9–10 for the biblical antecedent. "When he opened the fifth seal, I saw under the altar the lost souls of those who had been slain for the word of God and for the witness they had born. They cried out with a loud voice, 'O Sovereign Lord, how holy and true, how long before you will judge and avenge our blood on those who dwell on the earth?'"

7. See Bernard, *Light on Masonry*, 196–99 concerning the Masonic oath. The beheading of the third ruffian and the pledge to revenge his death was recounted in the Elected Knights of Nine Degree. See also 1783 Francken, Manuscript, Archives of the Supreme Council, 33°, Northern Jurisdiction, Lexington, Massachusetts, published by Kessinger Publishing Company; and Guérillot, *La Rite de Perfection*.

8. See Jessee, Ashurst-McGee, and Jensen, *Journals*, 215 (March 30, 1836), concerning the origin of this covenant in Kirtland.

9. *History of the Church* 7:456–77.

10. Ibid., 7:463–64.

Richard Bushman has observed that the design of the temple did not include an "elaboration of function." In fact, Weeks's plans "provided distinctive space for only one temple ordinance, baptisms for the dead."[11] Kimball recorded that canvas partitions were used to divide the interior attic space into six separate rooms (creation, garden, telestial, terrestrial, veil, and celestial rooms) "for the convenience of the Holy Priesthood." W. W. Phelps brought cedar trees into the garden room and other endowed priesthood holders completed three temple altars and placed the old veil, from Joseph Smith's red brick store, and a new veil in the temple's veil room. The celestial room was decorated with maps, portraits, and "looking glasses [mirrors]." Two other rooms were used as preparation rooms where washing and anointing would take place.[12]

On November 30 Young dedicated the unfinished attic of Joseph's second temple in anticipation of the introduction of the endowment.[13] This dedication, unlike the meeting that took place in Kirtland, was not open to all church members. "No ones admitted," wrote Heber C. Kimball, "only those that had received the Preasthood." He continued, "We clothed our selves for prair and council.... We offered up the Signs of the Holy Priesthood...B. Young being Mouth offered up the dedacation of the Hall and small rooms." Kimball's reference to "priesthood" suggests that only members of the Holy Order were invited to participate in these prayer circles that were formed at the dedication.[14]

Before the endowment was introduced to the general church membership in the temple, the Holy Order consisted of forty-two men and forty-eight women.[15] On December 7 Brigham Young met with the Order in the temple attic, where all were dressed in temple clothes to view the various rooms and then "pute up the Veil and choe [show] the Order of it." Thereafter they listened to speeches, sang hymns, and partook of the sacrament.[16] Three days later Young began to introduce the endowment to the general church membership.

11. Bushman, *Rough Stone Rolling*, 448.
12. Cross includes interior drawings of a Royal Arch temple, including veils, altars, and temple clothing. Cross, *The True Masonic Chart*.
13. Anderson and Bergera, *Joseph Smith's Quorum of the Anointed*, 185–90.
14. Kimball, *On the Potter's Wheel*, 154 (November 30, 1845).
15. Anderson and Bergera, *Joseph Smith's Quorum of the Anointed*, xxxviii. During 1845 there was a dramatic increase in the number of female and polygamous members in the Holy Order when twenty-one additional members were initiated.
16. Kimball, *On the Potter's Wheel*, 156–68. For a description of the temple attic, see Smith, *An Intimate Chronicle*, 204–6. See also Joseph Fielding, as quoted by Andrew F. Ehat, "'They Might Have Known that He Was Not a Fallen Prophet': The Nauvoo Journal of Joseph Fielding," *BYU Studies* 19:2 (Winter 1979): 158.

Both Heber C. Kimball and William Clayton recorded their observations during this period, which provide the earliest details concerning
the contents of the Nauvoo Temple endowment. Young and other church
leaders met with "all those who could clothe themselves in the garments
of the Priesthood" prior to the commencement of the endowment ritual
and instructed them concerning "the principles of the Holy Priesthood,"
the temple garment and the protection it would provide, as well as the obligation of secrecy.

Young pointedly told those who would receive their endowments: "If
any brother divulges any thing we shall cut him off. We shall not be with
you long."[17] Young instructed those who had received their endowments
"to cease talking about what you see and hear in this place. No man or
woman has a right to mention a word of the appearance of this building in
the least; nor to give the signs and tokens except when assembled together,
according to the order of the priesthood, which is in an upper room." He
assured them that "there are not a dozen persons that can give the signs and
tokens correct, and the reason is that person would run to that vail, one of
the most sacred places on the face of the earth, that had not understood the
right manner of giving the signs and tokens."[18]

NAUVOO TEMPLE RITUALS

Between December 10, 1845, and February of the following year, 5,634
members received their endowments including more than three thousand
women.[19] Young later observed that "we had our ceremonies pretty correct"
at the time the new ritual effectively superseded those previously introduced in the Kirtland Temple and before the temple was completed in
Nauvoo.[20] The Kirtland Temple rituals promised and produced angels and
visions to those who purified themselves, while the Nauvoo ritual was a
much more formal drama that endowed initiates with knowledge, a new
name, and passwords that would permit their entry into heaven.

Kimball's and Clayton's journals recorded that the temple endowment
consisted of four primary elements: initiatory rites including washings and
anointings; a dramatic presentation that included a recitation of Biblical
history; communication of keys pertaining to the Aaronic and Melchisedek

17. Smith, *An Intimate Chronicle*, 220–29.
18. Ibid., 239.
19. Anderson and Bergera, *Joseph Smith's Quorum of the Anointed*, xxxviii. See also Anderson and Bergera, *Nauvoo Endowment Companies*; Quinn, "Latter-day Saint Prayer Circles,"
93; Ehat, "'They Might Have Known,'" 97–98; Buerger, "'The Fullness of the Priesthood,'"
25n48; John K. Edmonds, *Through Temple Doors* (Salt Lake City: Bookcraft, 1978), 72.
20. L. John Nuttall, Diary, February 7, 1877, Special Collections, Lee Library.

Priesthoods; and tests of knowledge in preparation for passing through the temple veil.[21] These elements were retained and institutionalized during the next one hundred fifty years.[22]

These early statements (supplemented by Brigham's later observations) confirm that each initiate was washed and anointed, clothed in an under-garment and robes, and received a new name before advancing through the various stages of the endowment drama.[23] Clayton recorded that male initiates played the role of Adam and female initiates the role of Eve while church officials (the first temple workers) played the other roles (Elohim [God], Jehovah [Jesus], Michael, and the Devil).[24] The drama described the creation of the world, and like some French adoptive rituals recounted the biblical accounts of the Garden of Eden where Adam and Eve conversed with God, the fall and expulsion, and God's instructions concerning the way they could again be reunited with him.[25]

During the endowment church members received signs, tokens, and passwords that enabled them to progress from one room to another and endowed them with knowledge to "gain your eternal exaltation in spite of earth and hell." As the initiates progressed to new states or degrees in the temple, they agreed to obligations of obedience, chastity, and secrecy, which were accompanied by penalties if they failed to meet their obligations.[26] Young later explained that when a member took obligations, "it is a sign which you make in token of your covenant with God and with one another, and it is for you to perform your vows. When you raise your hands to heaven

---

21. *History of the Church* 5:2.
22. For a summary of the endowment written by church authorities during the early twentieth century, see James E. Talmage, *The House of the Lord* (Salt Lake City: Deseret News, 1912), 99–101; John A. Widtsoe, "Temple Worship," *Utah Genealogical and Historical Magazine* 12 (April 1921), 58.
23. Concerning the temple garments, see Smith, *An Intimate Chronicle*, 217, 219–21, 229, 231, 232, 238, 242–43.
24. Ibid., 203n10 ("At that time the roles of Adam and Eve were taken by those being initiated, while an officiating elder took the role of the serpent [Satan]"). It was also necessary for church officials to take other roles such as Elohim, Jehovah, and Michael. On December 13 three new characters (Peter, James, and John) were added to the drama that conducted initiates "though the Telestial and Terrestrial kingdom administering the charges and tokens in each and conducts them to the veil where they are received by Eloheem and after talking with him by words and tokens are admitted by him into the Celestial Kingdom." Ibid., 210.
25. Heber C. Kimball later spoke about "Father Adam" and the Garden of Eden, which he said was in Jackson County, Missouri, and then added: "I might say much more upon this subject, but I will ask, has it not been imitated before you in your holy endowments so that you might understand how things were in the beginning of creation and cultivation of this earth?" Heber C. Kimball, "Advancement of the Saints," *Journal of Discourses* 10:25 (June 27, 1863).
26. Brigham Young, *Journal of Discourses* 2:31 (April 6, 1853); Nuttall, Diary, February 7, 1877. See also Van Wagoner, *Complete Discourses* 4:3104–5.

and let them fall and then pass on with your covenants unfulfilled, you will be cursed."[27]

The final stage of the endowment consisted of a prayer circle, which was a summary of the entire ritual. The initiates were given instructions concerning the "true order of prayer" to enable them to "pass beyond the veil" to the celestial room, which represented the very presence of God. They were conducted through the veil where they "offered up the signs of the Holy Priesthood, and offered up prayers" upon "the five points of fellowship" into the celestial room where initiates could continue to converse concerning their redemption and exaltation.[28]

Young instructed members of the Holy Order, who had previously received their endowment, that they were required to be washed, anointed and re-endowed in the new temple. Both W. W. Phelps, who was endowed during Joseph Smith's lifetime, and his fellow anti-Mason, George Washington Harris, who was not, were endowed in the Nauvoo Temple. Young also introduced other rituals that the first Mormon prophet had bestowed on the Holy Order. These rituals included marriage sealings, sealings of parents and children, and a second anointing. In addition, the Nauvoo Temple included some vicarious ordinances for the dead, including baptisms for the dead and marriage sealings of living men and women to deceased men and women.[29] In Nauvoo there were no vicarious endowments for the dead and no children were sealed to their deceased parents.[30]

Perhaps the most notable vicarious ritual performed in Nauvoo involved the widow of William Morgan. Lucinda Morgan Harris was endowed on December 12, 1845, and received her second anointing the following month. These ceremonies were witnessed by Orson Pratt who had taught and converted the Harrises twelve years earlier. Brigham Young performed the marriage of George Washington Harris and Lucinda for time and then sealed Lucinda to Joseph Smith for eternity with Harris acting as proxy for Smith.[31]

Although some historians have speculated that Smith and Lucinda were romantically involved in Missouri, there is no record that they were sealed during Smith's lifetime. Martha Taysom has speculated that if Smith did

27. Brigham Young, "Irrigation—Every Saint Should Labor for the Interest of the Community—It is the Lord that Gives the Increase—Etc.," *Journal of Discourses* 3:332 (June 8, 1856).
28. Smith, *An Intimate Chronicle*, 204, 208, 214–16, 218, 234, 247.
29. Gordon I. Irving, "The Law of Adoption: One Phase of the Development of the Mormon Concept of Salvation, 1830–1900," *BYU Studies* 14 (Spring 1974): 291–314; Kenney, *Wilford Woodruff's Journal* 2:340–41.
30. Van Wagoner, *Complete Discourses* 5:2998–99, quoting *Journal of Discourses* 16:185–89.
31. See Lisle G. Brown, *Nauvoo Sealings, Adoptions and Anointings: A Comprehensive Register of Persons Receiving LDS Temple Ordinances, 1841–1846* (Salt Lake City: The Smith-Pettit Foundation, 2006), 130, 282.

take her as a plural wife and the missing Morgan was still alive, "Lucinda may have had three living husbands in the early 1840s, something almost unheard of in nineteenth-century America." Although this was not the model for the Mormon marriage system, there were multiple contemporary examples of Mormon polyandry among the church hierarchy.[32] Nevertheless Harris and Lucinda separated within a decade after they were sealed, and in 1856 Lucinda sued her second legal husband for divorce in Pottawatomie County, Iowa. She later joined the Catholic Sisters of Charity rather than marry a fourth husband.[33]

Young spent most of his time in the temple while these rituals were introduced, where he "presided and dictated the ordinances and also took an active part in nearly every instance except when entirely overcome by fatigue through his constant labors to forward the work."[34] "I have given myself up entirely to the work of the Lord in the Temple night and day," Young wrote, "not taking more than four hours sleep, upon an average, per day, and going home but once a week."[35] Young told those who served in the temple that "when persons come into this house and receive the tokens, and signs and the keywords, they have got all they have worked for in building this house."[36] He followed up several months later with, "We should build more temples, and have fuller opportunities to receive the blessings of the Lord, as soon as the saints were prepared to receive them."[37]

Young directed W. W. Phelps to draft "Rules of Order" to maintain decorum in the temple. The rules provided instructions for those who were in the temple for the first time as well as for those who had already been endowed.[38] Some who assisted in maintaining decorum used Masonic terminology, as some sisters had during meetings of the Relief Society, while working in the temple. John D. Lee, who was a temple recorder, noted that when he arrived at the "the door of the outer court which I found tyled within by an officer I having the proper implements of that degree gained admittance through the outer and inner courts which opened and led to the sacred departments."[39]

32. See Martha Taysom, "Is There No Help for the Widow? The Strange Life of Lucinda Pendleton Morgan Harris," (Unpublished paper presented at the Mormon History Association, Lamoni, Iowa, May 1993), 5.

33. See Morris, *William Morgan*, 278–79. Concerning Lucinda Morgan Harris's adventures in Mormonism, see Compton, *In Sacred Loneliness*, 43–70.

34. Smith, *An Intimate Chronicle*, 209.

35. *History of the Church* 7:567.

36. Smith, *An Intimate Chronicle*, 234.

37. *History of the Church* 7:579.

38. Smith, *An Intimate Chronicle*, 211–12.

39. John D. Lee, Diary, December 16, 1845, Harold B. Lee Special Collections, as quoted in Anderson and Bergera, *Nauvoo Endowment Companies*, 55.

On January 14, 1846, Young sent an epistle to advise church members that temple construction, which continued while endowments were given, had "progressed very rapidly since the death of our Prophet and Patriarch… that the capitals of the columns were all on" and that stonecutters would soon "proceed to cut the stone for and erect a font of hewn stone."[40] On January 30 the flying angel designed by William Weeks was placed above the temple's tower[41] and two weeks later Truman Angell (Brigham Young's brother-in-law) was appointed as the new architect of the temple and charged with the task of completing the upper and lower stories of the structure.[42]

On April 30 Joseph Young (Brigham's older brother) dedicated the temple during a private ceremony. According to James Talmage, "The semi-private character of the dedication was due to the thought that possibly there would be interference in a public ceremony, so active was the spirit of intolerance and persecution."[43] Although Orson Hyde dedicated the structure the following day during a public ceremony, neither dedication was comparable to the dedication of Joseph's first temple a decade earlier when heavenly manifestations were witnessed.

TEMPLE EXPOSÉS

The first exposés of the endowment were written and published shortly after the dedication of the new temple. Although these exposures did not specifically link the endowment to Masonic rituals, they did disclose the same elements privately described by church officials, that had parallels in Masonic rites. These included signs, tokens, and obligations as well as an oath to avenge the death of Joseph Smith. They also mentioned other rituals, such as marriage sealings, that were introduced in the temple. The material set forth in these exposés was repeated in many other published descriptions of the endowment during the next sixty years and became grist

---

40. *History of the Church* 7:357–58.
41. Derr, Cannon, and Beecher, *Women of Covenant*, 64.
42. See Bennion, "The Rediscovery of William Weeks' Nauvoo Temple Drawings," 78. See also William Weeks's appointment of Truman Angell architect, February 13, 1846, holograph, Church History Library. This appointment apparently contains a holographic notation made by Brigham Young which states: "I wish Br. T. O. Angel to carry out the designs of the Temple and Nauvoo House." See Bennion, "The Rediscovery of William Weeks' Nauvoo Temple Drawings," 90n22. Nevertheless, Angell claimed in 1884 that Weeks had "deserted and left for the East, thereby taking himself from the duties of said office, which position I hold to this day." Beatrice B. Malouf, comp., *Pioneer Buildings of Early Utah* (Salt Lake City: Daughters of Utah Pioneers, 1991), 118.
43. James E. Talmage, *The House of the Lord* (Salt Lake City: The Deseret News, 1912), 134.

in the campaign to pressure the church to abandon plural marriage and to affirm its absolute allegiance to the United States.[44]

The first exposure was written under the assumed name of "Emeline" and published in the *Warsaw* (Illinois) *Signal*.[45] The author stated that she wanted to counter claims made in an earlier issue of the same newspaper (February 18, 1846) that participants in the endowment were "in a state of nudity throughout the ceremony."[46] She denied that the endowment took place in such a state, except for an initial washing and anointing where only women were present; and that no indecency took place between men and women since the sexes were segregated during the ceremony. But she claimed that church authorities were "the most debased wretches" and the endowment was "nothing less than fearful blasphemy." While she did not remember many of the details of the ceremony, she described the rooms and characters in the drama, as well as the fact that there were oaths, obligations, and penalties.

Increase McGee Van Dusen and his wife, Maria, wrote the second exposé.[47] Shortly after attending temple, the Van Dusens rejected the leadership of Brigham Young and joined James J. Strang in Voree, Wisconsin, who also claimed to be Joseph Smith's successor. Some of Strang's earliest followers included John C. Bennett, William Marks (Nauvoo Stake president and charter member of the Holy Order), George Miller (the first worshipful grand master of Nauvoo Lodge and a charter member of the Holy Order), Apostle William Smith (the prophet's brother), and another apostle, John Page.

44. See David John Buerger, "Chronological Annotated Bibliography of Publications Giving the Mormon Temple Ceremony in Full or in Part" (1987, Marriott Library, University of Utah). In contrast, very little information concerning the second anointing is available since it has never been extended to the general church membership. For a brief exposé of the second endowment by a disaffected Mormon, see Mrs. T. B. H. [Fanny] Stenhouse, *"Tell it All": The Story of a Life's Experience in Mormonism* (Hartford, CT: A. D. Worthington & Co., 1874), 514–18. See also Buerger, "'The Fullness of the Priesthood'"; Buerger, *The Mystery of Godliness*; and Levi S. Peterson, "My Mother's House," *Dialogue: A Journal of Mormon Thought* 44 (Fall 1991): 79–88.
45. Emeline [pseudonym], "Mormon endowments," *Warsaw Signal* 3:2 (April 15, 1846), 2.
46. "Ceremony of the endowment," *Warsaw Signal* 2:42 (February 18, 1846), 2.
47. Increase McGee V. D. and Maria, his wife, *The Mormon Endowment: A Secret Drama, or Conspiracy, in the Nauvoo-Temple in 1846* (Syracuse, NY: N. M. D. Lathrop, 1847). See Craig L. Foster, "From Temple Mormon to Anti-Mormon: The Ambivalent Odyssey of Increase Van Dusen," *Dialogue: A Journal of Mormon Thought* 27, no. 3 (Fall 1994): 275–88. The Van Dusens had worked for several years on the temple before being endowed and writing their exposé. Larry Draper notes that although the couple's name is spelled Van Dusen, Increase signed his name on at least one occasion with the spelling Van Deusen. Flake and Draper, *A Mormon Bibliography: The Life of James Jesse Strang*, 2nd ed. (Urbana: University of Illinois Press, 1988), 2:487.

While Van Dusen served a mission to New York, he coauthored, with his wife, his recollections of the Nauvoo endowment. Strang criticized Van Dusen for violating his temple oaths and eventually excommunicated him after he claimed to receive a revelation. Thereafter, the Van Dusen temple exposé was modified with increasingly salacious and shocking details and was republished at least twenty-two times between 1847 and 1864. Nevertheless, the Van Dusens continued to believe that Joseph Smith was a prophet and even included Smith's account of his first vision in various editions. The early editions also included a letter claiming to be Smith's appointment of Strang as his successor. Since the Van Dusens did not know what fellow Strangites Bennett, Marks, Miller, and William Smith knew, they asserted that both the "spiritual wife doctrine" and the endowment were introduced by the "Imposter B. Young."[48] The Van Dusen exposure did not specifically mention Freemasonry but it did (beginning in the second edition) divide the endowment into seven degrees that correlated to the number of degrees conferred in a Master Masons lodge and a Royal Arch chapter.[49]

The exposé described the rooms, the substance of the endowment, as well as the oaths, tokens, signs, and penalties, and claimed that initiates were required to kneel at an altar where they took an oath "that we will avenge the blood of Joseph Smith on this Nation, and teach our children the same."[50] This oath was amended in some editions to read: "We will, from this time henceforth and forever, use our influence to murder this nation, and teach it to our posterity and all that we have influence over, in return for their killing the Prophet Joseph."[51] The Van Dusen exposure transformed the prayer, which Heber Kimball had recorded, asking the Lord to curse those who had persecuted and spilt blood, into an actual oath taken during the ritual. This exposé was widely quoted in many subsequent anti-Mormon writings.[52]

48. Van Dusen, *The Mormon Endowment*. See also Correspondence, Increase Van Dusen to James J. Strang, June 18, 1849, James J. Strang Papers, Yale University, New Haven, Connecticut, as quoted in Foster, "From Temple Mormon to Anti-Mormon," 276–77. See Van Noord, *Assassination of a Michigan King* (Provo, UT: Religious Studies Center, Brigham Young University, 2004), 84–87, concerning Van Dusen's adherence to Strangism.
49. Other authors claimed to expose the seven degrees of Freemasonry. See Malcolm C. Duncan, *Masonic Ritual and Monitor; or, Guide to the Three Degrees of the Ancient York Rite and to the Degrees of Mark Master, Past Master, Most Excellent Master, and the Royal Master* (New York: L. Fitzgerald, 1866).
50. Van Dusen, *The Mormon Endowment*, 9.
51. I. McGee Van Dusen and Maria, his wife, *A Dialogue Between Adam and Eve, the Lord and the Devil, called the Endowment*, (Albany: Printed by C. Kilmer, 1847), 12.
52. John Thomas, *Sketch of the Rise, Progress, and Dispersion of the Mormons* (London: Arthur Hall & Co., 1848). Foster cites other London publications that refer to the Van Dusen

Catherine Lewis, who was endowed on December 22, 1845, wrote a third exposé, which was published in 1848 and appeared in at least one subsequent edition.[53] Lewis's account included a description of the various stages of the ritual, references to signs, penalties, and new name, and to an oath requiring initiates to "avenge my brother's blood in every possible way." Lewis was an unmarried woman and her narrative more clearly linked the endowment with the practice of "plurality of wives."

Lewis wrote that men and women went through the temple ceremony as companions and that one was not considered to have received the "full endowment" unless a woman was sealed to a man as her husband and families were sealed to apostles as children. She also claimed that Heber and Vilate Kimball approached her several times to inquire whether she would become Kimball's plural wife. Because of these and other exposures, the endowment became connected with plural marriage and an oath to avenge the death of Joseph Smith.

CONNECTIONS BETWEEN MASONRY AND MORMONISM

Many nineteenth-century Mormons who were serious students of Freemasonry believed that the endowment was a restoration of the ritual introduced in Solomon's Temple that had been partially preserved by the Craft. The Mormon prophet was apparently quite transparent with his inner circle concerning these connections.[54] Willard Richards (1804–1854), who was Smith's scribe and an apostle, wrote to his brother Levi on the same day that

work: John Bowes, *Mormonism Exposed* (London: E. Ward, [ca. 1850]); and T. W. P. Taylder, *Twenty Reasons for Rejecting Mormonism* (London: Partridge & Co., 1857). Thomas White apparently lifted the Van Dusen exposure even though he claimed that he had witnessed Joseph Smith participating in the endowment in the Nauvoo Temple and that there were seven degrees in that ritual. [Thomas White], *Authentic History of Remarkable Persons, Who Have Attracted Public Attention in Various Parts of the World; Including a Full Exposure of the Iniquities of the Pretended Prophet Joe Smith, and the Seven Degrees of the Mormon Temple, and an Account of the Frauds Practiced by Matthias the Prophet, and Other Religious Imposters* (New York: Wilson and Company, 1849); also reprinted as Thomas White, *The Mormon Mysteries: Being an Exposition of the Ceremonies of "The Endowment" and the Seven Degrees of the Temple* (New York: Edmund K. Knowlton, 1851).
53. Catherine Lewis, *Narrative of Some of the Proceedings of the Mormons, etc.* (Lynn, MA: Author, 1848).
54. Rick Grunder has observed that many people, "when the Book of Mormon was dictated—believed Freemasonry to be ancient in origin," which included "some former Masons…[who]…still believed in the essential form and precepts of some supposedly ancient Freemasonry." Notable Mormon Masons (Hyrum Smith, Heber C. Kimball, and Newel Whitney) and anti-Masons (W. W. Phelps and George Washington Harris) continued to believe in the antiquity of the Craft and were convinced that similarities between the endowment and Masonic ritual could be explained because Smith restored the original ancient ritual. Grunder, *Mormon Parallels*, 118–19, 229.

Smith and Rigdon were initiated as Entered Apprentices, the first degree of Craft Masonry, that "Masonry had its origin in the Priesthood. A hint to the wise is sufficient."[55]

James Cummings, another Nauvoo Mason, made a similar disclosure to his family (which was recorded many years later) that when Smith was initiated into Freemasonry he "seemed to understand some of the features of the [Masonic] ceremonies better than any mason, and made explanations that rendered them much more beautiful and full of meaning." Cummings's grandson believed that "it was evident to [Cummings] that [Smith] knew more of what was given in the Temple of Solomon than did the masons who claim that their ceremonies originated there."[56]

The Mormon prophet gave a sermon on March 20, 1842, less than one week after his initiation into Freemasonry, in which he revealed that there are "certain key words & signs belonging to the priesthood which must be observed in order to obtain the Blessings."[57] Less than six weeks later, while he was preparing to introduce the endowment to the Holy Order, Smith revealed that the signs and words to detect false spirits and personages would not be revealed until the temple was completed. There were signs in heaven,

55. Willard Richards to Levi Richards, March 7–25, 1842, as cited in Joseph Grant Stevenson, *Richards Family History* (Provo, UT: Stevenson's Genealogical Center, 1991), 3:90.
56. Horace Cummings, "Autobiography of Horace Cummings," Ms 1575, L. Tom Perry Special Collections, Harold B. Lee Library, Brigham Young University, Provo, Utah, p. C1-3, cited as "History of Horace Cummings," in Kenneth W. Godfrey, "Causes of Mormon Non-Mormon Conflict in Hancock County, Illinois, 1839–1846" (PhD diss., Brigham Young University, 1967), 86. Although James Cummings apparently told this story to his son, it was not recorded until Horace Cummings, his grandson, wrote his autobiography. A portion of Cummings "Autobiography" was published in the *Juvenile Instructor* in August 1929. In that version Horace Cummings wrote, "One of the first incidents recorded which greatly impressed my mind and which make a useful lesson was related by my father. His parents, who had a large family, lived in Nauvoo, and were quite intimate with the Prophet Joseph. In fact, his father, being a Master Mason, officiated in conducting the Prophet through all the degrees of Masonry. In doing this the Prophet explained many things about the rite that even Masons do not pretend to understand but which he made most clear and beautiful." See Horace Cummings, "True Leaves from My Journal," *Juvenile Instructor* 6 (August 1929), 440–41. On March 17 Cummings petitioned for membership in Nauvoo Lodge which was approved on April 7. See Hogan, *Founding Minutes*, 14–15. Hogan criticized Godfrey for citing Cummings, perhaps a little too enthusiastically. See Hogan, *Mormonism and Freemasonry*, 274–78. He notes that on March 15 Jonas presided over the installation of the lodge and that Cummings was a visitor. He notes that there is no indication in the lodge minutes that Cummings participated in the initiation and that he is not even listed as being present on the following day when both Smith and Rigdon were made Fellowcrafts and Master Masons on sight. He suggested that if Smith had made the comments quoted by Cummings's grandson, it would have been recorded in the minutes and that the prophet "had the advantage of some fifteen years' lead time in his study and command of Masonry." Hogan, *Mormonism and Freemasonry*, 278.
57. Kenney, *Wilford Woodruff's Journal* 2:162 (March 20, 1842); *History of the Church* 4:555.

earth, and hell, Smith said, that elders must know to be endowed with power. Although the Devil knows many signs he did not know the sign of Jesus: "No one can truly say he knows God until he has handled something. & this can only be in the holiest of Holies."[58]

During the same month Smith introduced the endowment to the Holy Order, he told the officers of the Nauvoo Masonic Lodge, "I have done what King Solomon King Hiram & Hiram Abiff could not do[:] I have set up the Kingdom no more to be thrown down forever nor never to be given to another people."[59] Smith was apparently very specific when he discussed the connection with members of the Holy Order. Although these initiates believed that Smith had received the endowment through revelation, they also acknowledged privately that there were parallels in the Masonic ritual. Heber C. Kimball, a charter member of the Holy Order, wrote a letter to his fellow apostle Parley Pratt six weeks after he received his endowment, stating that Smith taught that there was "similarity of preast Hood [sic] in Masonary [sic]" and that Freemasonry was "taken from [the] preasthood [sic] but has become degenerated [sic]."[60]

Similarly, Joseph Fielding (Hyrum Smith's brother-in-law), wrote shortly after joining the Holy Order in December 1843 that "many have joined the masonic Institution" and "this seems to have been a Stepping Stone or Preparation for something else, the true Origin of Masonry, this I have also seen and rejoice in it."[61] Benjamin F. Johnson (1818–1905), who married William and Lucinda Morgan's daughter and received his endowment in the Nauvoo Temple, wrote in April 1843 that Smith "gave me such ideas pertaining to endowments as he thought proper," and assured him that "Freemasonry, as at present, was the apostate endowments, as sectarian religion was the apostate religion."[62]

Even those who believed that the Mormon prophet had pilfered portions of Masonic rituals repeated Smith's thesis concerning the connection

---

58. Hedges, Smith, and Anderson, *Journals* 2:53 (May 1, 1842); *History of the Church* 4:608. See also Flanders, *Nauvoo: Kingdom on the Mississippi*, 192.
59. Dimick B. Huntington, Undated Statement, May Brown Firmage Papers, L. Tom Perry Special Collections, Harold B. Lee Library, Brigham Young University, Provo, Utah, quoted in Anderson and Bergera, *Joseph Smith's Quorum of the Anointed*, 3–4.
60. Heber C. Kimball to Parley P. Pratt, June 17, 1842, Parley P. Pratt Papers, Church History Library.
61. Ehat, "The Nauvoo Journal of Joseph Fielding," 145, 147.
62. Benjamin F. Johnson, Papers 1852–1911, MS 1289, p. 92. Church History Library. See also *My Life's Review* (Independence, MO: Zion's Printing and Publishing Co., 1947), 61, 96. Johnson's statement is consistent with the other contemporary observations, even though it was written many years after the events described. Johnson wrote that Smith "showed me his garments and explained that they were such as the Lord made for Adam from skins." Ibid., 96.

between Masonic ritual and the endowment. John C. Bennett, a Nauvoo Mason and confidante of Smith, publicized the Masonic connection in his letters to the *Sangamo Journal* and in his *History of the Saints*, while Oliver H. Olney, who was not a Mason, gossiped that: "We have of late had an institution Amongst us set up By a man from a distance Said to be Masonry in its best state.... They say threw [*sic*] it to obtain The fullness of the P[riest]hood That I say they have lost because of their unlawful works." Like Bennett, Olney concluded that the ancient prophets had "lived as being masons" and that the Saints were encouraged by the establishment of a lodge to "think soon to arise to perfection & some few secrets They have obtained."[63]

THE CRAFT

The Mormon Masons who were initiated into the Holy Order undoubtedly recognized the connections between Craft Masonry and the endowment. The Craft rituals and the endowment included the use of aprons, key words, a new name, the five points of fellowship, signs, tokens (grips), obligations, and penalties, as well as the familiar symbols of square, compass, all-seeing eye, clasping hands, and the sun, moon, and stars.[64] While there

63. *History of the Church* 4:552; *Times and Seasons*, 3 (1 April 1842): 747–48; Oliver Olney, "On the commencement of Nauvoo Masonic Lodge," April 6, 1842; Oliver H. Olney Papers, Yale Collection of Western Americana, Beinecke Rare Book and Manuscript Library, Yale University, New Haven, Connecticut. See also Oliver Olney, *The Absurdities of Mormonism Portrayed*, 1843, summarized in the *Stanley Snow Ivins Collection*, and "Papers of Oliver Olney," Library of the Utah State Historical Society in Salt Lake City, Utah. Olney also wrote, "This master Mason instructed them In many good things He said there were certain degrees For the Fair sex of the land They soon met in union A lodge to form but changed the name That they mite [*sic*] be distinguished From the Lodge of the men" (ibid.). On March 17, 1842, Olny was stripped of his license to preach after John C. Bennett accused him of "setting himself up as a prophet & revelator in the Church." See Nauvoo High Council Minutes, March 17, 1842, LDS Church History Library.

64. For references to signs, tokens, obligations, penalties, prayer circle, veil, and apron, see generally Bernard, *Light on Masonry*. For specific references to the veil, see Bernard, *Light on Masonry*, 124–43; Cross, *The True Masonic Chart*, 30, 35. The reference to an apron as a fig leaf in the Bible has been used as a justification for the Masonic apron. See Dyer, *Symbolism in Craft Masonry*, 47–49; George Oliver, *Signs and Symbols Illustrated and Explained, in a course of Twelve Lectures on Freemasonry* (London: Sherwood, Gilbert, and Piper, 1837), 205. "Freemasons were able," according to Tobias Churton, "to decorate their apron as preferred" (Churton, *Freemasonry*, 10). The Marquis de Lafayette, who visited Masonic lodges during the American Revolution, owned an apron with leaves (Hamill and Gilbert, *World Freemasonry*, 102); and Stephen A. Douglas, an Illinois Mason when Joseph Smith was initiated into the Craft, is pictured wearing an apron with leaves in an 1840s painting which hangs in the Masonic Temple in Springfield, Illinois. See Wayne C. Temple, *Stephen A. Douglas, Freemason* (Bloomington, IL: Masonic Book Club and Illinois Lodge of Research, 1982). The first aprons used in the temple endowment consisted of "sheep skin made to the

were multiple Masonic degrees that were presented on separate occasions, the endowment's four stages—which included two levels for the Aaronic priesthood and two levels for the Melchizedek priesthood—took place in one ceremony. Arturo de Hoyas has noted that "only post-1760 rituals included separate obligations for the degrees, in conjunction with the penalties, tokens and words" and that the Mormon endowment, which had separate obligations and penalties after each stage, was consistent with these revisions in English and American Masonic rituals.[65]

During the endowment the initiates received a word that enabled them to enter into a celestial room. This was similar to the Master Mason degree that taught initiates that after Hiram Abiff's murder the Master Mason's word (called the "Ineffable Word") was lost and that it was necessary to use a substituted word. Smith's version of the five points of fellowship, where this word was revealed, was consistent with William Preston's eighteenth-century revision of the Masonic five points of fellowship adopted by Thomas Smith Webb and other American ritualists.[66]

At least two members of the Quorum of the Twelve Apostles, Heber C. Kimball and Wilford Woodruff, owned Masonic exposés that they may have used as *aides-mémoires* for the Craft degrees or to become familiar with high degrees.[67]

Masonic writers, such as William Hutchinson, referred to Masonic rites as "endowments,"[68] which provided Masons with light and knowledge to help prepare them for entry into a celestial lodge.[69] Many Freemasons were

---

order and by the direction of Joseph Smith" on which fig leaves were painted. See Oliver B. Huntington Journal, 51, Oliver Huntington Collection, L. Tom Perry Special Collections, Harold B. Lee Library, Brigham Young University. The aprons that eventually were used in the Mormon endowment consisted of green silk with nine fig leaves (presumably symbolizing the first nine members of the Holy Order) stitched in brown silk. See *Salt Lake Tribune*, September 28, 1879, 4. For a reference to the prayer circle, see Bernard, *Light on Masonry*, 125–26.

65. Correspondence from Art de Hoyas, November 22, 1993. De Hoyas notes that "the Nauvoo endowment ceremony resembles the state of Masonic ritual in Joseph Smith's time" and thus it "is similar to the latest forms of Freemasonry, not the earliest."

66. The Masonic five points of fellowship is utilized in the Master Mason degree when Masons assist a candidate while being raised from the dead or from darkness to illumination. These five points originally consisted of the hand, the foot, the knee, the breast, and the back until William Preston and Thomas Smith Webb introduced a modification which substituted the mouth and ear for the hand. Mackey, *Encyclopedia of Freemasonry* 2:572–73.

67. See Kenney, *Wilford Woodruff's Journal* 2:545 (May 9, 1845): "I spent the day at Clithore at Sister Duckworth copying a work from an account of the 5 first degrees upon Masonery"; and Helen Mar Whitney, "Scenes in Nauvoo, and Incidents from H. C. Kimball's Journal," *Woman's Exponent* 12 (July 15, 1883): 26, "I remember once when but a young girl, of getting a glimpse of the outside of the Morgan's book, Exposing Masonry, but which my father [Heber C. Kimball] always kept locked up."

68. Hutchinson, *The Spirit of Masonry*, 6, 177.

69. Calcott, *Calcott's Masonry*, 123.

convinced that their rituals were "drawn from revelation," and that "ancient Masonry, since the time of Solomon, has been handed down, in all essential points, in perfect conformity to the rights and ceremonies then established."[70] They believed that their temples were allegories for a "celestial lodge," and that the temple ritual would prepare them for their eventual entry into that lodge.[71]

But the connection extended beyond form and symbols into the Christian spirit of the Craft. Brigham Young, who continued to develop the endowment after he was initiated into the Holy Order, owned a copy of Joshua Bradley's *Some of the Beauties of Freemasonry* in which the Baptist minister argued that Masonry was essentially a Christian institution that prepared men for celestial glory.[72]

Some American Masons believed that Masonic rituals provided a pathway for salvation and even hinted at exaltation. Masonic writer Albert Mackey wrote that the Master Masons degree "is intended by symbolical representations to teach the resurrection from death, and the divine dogma of eternal life."[73] The lodge consisted of "practical allusions to instruct the craftsmen…tending to the glory of God, and to secure to them temporal blessings here, and eternal life hereafter."[74]

Master Masons were taught that after death "the Son of Righteousness shall descend, and send forth his angels to collect our ransomed dust; then

70. Bradley, *Some of the Beauties of Freemasonry*, xii; Town, *A System of Speculative Masonry*, 165.

71. Calcott, *Calcott's Masonry*, 123. American Freemason Salem Town wrote that "the principles which constitute the foundation of the Masonic Institution, were known to the ancient wise men and father, from time immemorial" and that such principles were systematized and the Institution of Freemasonry, including its rituals, was founded by Solomon. Thereafter, Freemasonry spread throughout the world and even flourished in Egypt. Town, *A System of Speculative Masonry*, 97–98, 93–103, 126–27. See also Webb, *The Freemason's Monitor*, 7. See also Rev. Cheever T. Felch, *An Address Delivered Before Mount Carmel Lodge at Lynn, June 1821* (Boston, n.d.), 7. (Freemasonry provided "eternal and invariable principles of natural religion" by which men could pattern their conduct.) Wellins Calcott, whose book was widely read in America, also believed in the Craft's antiquity, that it was "derived from the Almighty Creator to Adam, its principles ever since have been and still are most sacredly preserved and inviolably concealed." He wrote that Masons, "foreseeing the great abuses which their exalted mysteries might sustain, if generally made known, [had] determined to confine the knowledge of them only to the select Brethren." He also wrote that despite the decay and corruption of the world, the basic truths of Masonry were preserved from generation to generation. Calcott, *Calcott's Masonry*, 111–16.

72. Brigham Young's copy of Bradley's *Some of the Beauties of Freemasonry* is currently located at the Daughters of Utah Pioneers Museum in Salt Lake City. Bradley suggested that Masons should pray to go "from this earthly tabernacle to the heavenly temple above; there, among thy jewels, may we appear in thy glory for ever and ever." Bradley, *Some of the Beauties of Freemasonry*, 168.

73. See Mackey, *The History of Freemasonry*, 1:151–65, 198. See also Robert Freke Gould, *The History of Freemasonry*, 4 vols. (New York: John C. Yorston & Co., 1885–1889).

74. Calcott, *Calcott's Masonry*, 123.

if we are found worthy, by his pass-word, we shall enter into the celestial lodge above where the Supreme Architect of the Universe presides, where we shall see the King in the beauty of holiness, and with him enter into an endless eternity."[75] They were raised by the five points of fellowship from the grave of darkness to a cradle of light, and became new men. Thereafter they continued to build their spiritual temple in order to reestablish their presence with God.[76]

THE ROYAL ARCH

There were also recognizable connections between Mormon legends and Royal Arch legends and rituals. Although Smith was not a Royal Arch Mason, he may have been familiar with the Royal Arch through Newell K. Whitney, a Royal Arch Mason who was one of his closest advisors,[77] or by reading treatises such as Webb's *Freemason's Monitor*[78] or a wide variety of anti-Masonic literature.[79] The likelihood of the Mormon prophet's acquaintance with the Royal Arch is heightened when one considers that he developed an Adamic alphabet similar to a Royal Arch cipher;[80] one of

75. Morgan, *Illustrations of Masonry*, 93; Bernard, *Light on Masonry*, 84. For a Masonic oration making reference to this same imagery, see Thomas Cary, *An Oration Pronounced Before the Right Worshipful Master and Brethren of St. Peter's at the Episcopal Church in Newburyport, on the Festival of St. John the Baptist, Celebrated June 24th, 5801* (n.p.: From the Press of Brother Angier March, n.d.): "[W]hen this frail fabric shall be dissolved, and the SUPREME ARCHITECT shall summon his laborers to receive their reward, to the condescending Saviour we will listen for the pass word, which shall admit us to his father's temple, a house not made with hands, eternal in the heavens."

76. Churton, *Freemasonry*, 42–43.

77. Some have claimed that there were other members of the Royal Arch in Smith's inner circle. Forsberg relied on John Brooke when he suggested that Oliver Cowdery may have become a Royal Arch Mason before the Morgan affair, but there is no evidence that Cowdery was ever initiated into the Craft or received any of the high degrees. Forsberg, *Equal Rites*, 45. The first Royal Arch chapter in Illinois (Springfield Chapter No. 1) was granted a dispensation on July 20, 1841, and a charter on September 17, 1841. *Memorial Volume of the Seventy-Fifth Anniversary of the Grand Royal Arch Chapter of the State of Illinois* (Springfield, IL: Phillips Bros., 1924), 10–14. There is no evidence that James Adams, who was both a Mormon and a Mason, was connected with Springfield's Royal Arch chapter because chapter records prior to 1850 were destroyed in a fire. See *Illinois Masonic Directory* (Springfield, 1953), 6. Sheville and Gould, *Guide to the Royal Arch Chapter*, 131–32.

78. Webb, *The Freemason's Monitor*, A2; Bradley, *Some of the Beauties of Freemasonry*.

79. The Royal Arch cipher was exposed, and described as the "key to the ineffable characters," in the report of the Lewiston Committee in *A Revelation of Freemasonry*, 60; and in Bernard, *Light on Masonry*, 138.

80. See Clinton Bartholomew, Mormon History Association Presentation, St. George, Utah, May 2011. Bartholomew compares the Royal Arch cipher to Smith's "A Sample of pure language." See also Robin Scott Jensen, Robert J. Woodford, and Steven C. Harper, eds., *Revelations and Translations, Manuscript Revelation Books* (Salt Lake City: Church Historian's Press, 2009), 264–65; W. W. Phelps' "Specimen," Correspondence of W. W. Phelps to Sally Phelps, May 26, 1835, W. W. Phelps Papers, L. Tom Perry Special Collections,

MAH-HAH-BONE.

HUMANITY LODGE,

MORGAN CHAPTER,

And Niagara Encampment.

IMPORTANT QUERIES.

Who kidnapped Capt Wm. Morgan from his wife and infant children, and after keeping him in confinement in Fort Niagara several days, inhumanly murdered him, and sunk his body in Niagara river, for disclosing the secrets of masonry?

Who, after murdering the husband, sport with the feelings of the bereaved widow, and expose their savage and fiendlike dispositions, by assailing her fair reputation, and resorting to every trick and artifice that malignity could invent, to disgrace her in the eyes of the public?

Let masons answer these queries & tremble for the result.

This is a Key to the Masonic Alphabet as given in the lodges.

a b c d e f g h i j k l m n o p q r s t u v

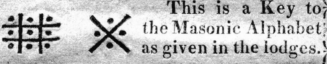

w x y z   [Serious Truths.]

WORTHY OF RECOLLECTION.

Remember the 5th of March 1770—Americans!
Remember the 11th of Sept. 1826—Masonic Assassins!
Remember the next Election—Freemen! and
Remember the Martyr Morgan—but above all
Remember the rights and privileges—secured to us by the Constitution.

Illustration of the key to the Masonic alphabet.
Published in *The Anti-Masonic Almanack, For the Year 1828*.

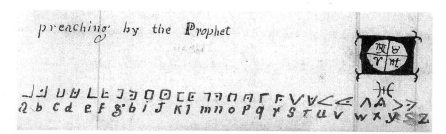

Cipher utilized by Oliver Huntington. Courtesy H. Michael Marquardt.

his apostles (Heber C. Kimball) apparently repeated Smith's use of Royal Arch terminology when he described the endowment as "priesthood"; and several of the prophet's followers (Brigham Young, Oliver Huntington, and Samuel Richards) utilized a Royal Arch cipher in secret communications.[81]

The Royal Arch legend of Enoch, and his preparation of a gold plate, provided not only a connection between the loss and restoration of gold plates containing the word of God (which took place during the reign of King Josiah), but also background for the restoration of the Master's Word in the American ritual that was reminiscent of Smith's restoration of a "key word" in the Mormon endowment. In addition, Royal Arch rituals, unlike Craft degrees, included washings and anointings, garments, priestly robes, a new name, the restoration of the key word, and the concept of exaltation. The veil, which was also part of the Royal Arch ritual, became a symbolic

Harold B. Lee Library, Brigham Young University, Provo, Utah; and the Egyptian Alphabet Notebooks which were prepared in connection with the translation of the Egyptian papyri in H. Michael Marquardt, comp., *The Joseph Smith Egyptian Papers* (Cullman, AL: Printing Service, 1981). Smith's "Sample" only included Adamic pronunciations while Phelps's "Specimen" and the Egyptian Alphabet included pronunciations and symbols.

81. On January 6, 1842, Young recorded in his diary, using this cipher, that "I was taken into the Lodge J. Smith was Agness." Brigham Young Journal, Brigham Young Papers, Church History Library. See also S. Dilworth Young, *"Here is Brigham…": Brigham Young, the Years to 1844* (Salt Lake City: Bookcraft, 1964), 307. Some historians have concluded that Young's cipher recorded the secret sealing of the Mormon prophet to Agnes Coolbrith Smith, who was the widow of his brother Don Carlos Smith who died on August 7, 1841. Smith recorded on the same date in his journal (but not in cipher) that "the God of heaven has begun to restore the ancient order of his kingdom" and to manifest "those things which have been, and those things which the ancient prophets and wise men desired to see but died without beholding them." *History of the Church* 4:492; *RLDS History of the Church* 2:568-69; *Millennial Star* 19:21–22. Art de Hoyas has suggested that the word "was" was an acronym for "washed, anointed, sealed" or "wedded and sealed." See *Mormon History Association Newsletter*, no. 102 (Summer 1996): 9. See also "Secret Codes in Early Mormon History," *Mormon Heritage*, no. 2 (January 1986): 5–6. Both Oliver Huntington and Samuel W. Richards utilized the same cipher. See Oliver Huntington Journal, January 21, 1844; Correspondence of Samuel W. Richards to Brigham Young, Brigham Young Collection, Church History Library, Salt Lake City, Utah, partially reproduced in paper presented by Ardis E. Parshall, MHA Presentation, Caspar, Wyoming, 2006.

gate through which candidates were required to pass before being allowed
to enter into celestial space.[82]

There were other elements of the Royal Arch rituals that were reminiscent of the form and substance of the ritual Smith introduced to the Holy
Order. A Royal Arch chapter was presided over by a "high priest" who was
eligible to be exalted in the Anointed Order of High Priesthood or Holy
Order of High Priesthood.[83] The Order of Anointed High Priest, "Order
of High Priests," or "Holy Order of High Priesthood," included the consecration and anointing after the Order of Melchizedek in a chapter of Royal
Arch Masons with assistance in "ample form" of not less than nine.[84] Thus
Masons were anointed, had hands laid upon their heads, and were set apart
for the office of high priest in the Holy Order of High Priesthood.[85]

The Royal Arch ritual contained language suggesting that enlightenment would lead to exaltation.[86] High Priests of the Royal Arch were "exalted" into the Order of High Priesthood and the grand high priest, in his

82. Some early participants in the endowment believed that the veil was "in imitation of
the one in Solomon's Temple" and that the temple garment represented the "white stone"
or new name given to each candidate. See *Salt Lake Daily Tribune*, September 28, 1879, 4;
Thomas White, *The Mormon Mysteries; Being an Exposition of the Ceremonies of "The Endowment" and the Seven Degrees of the Temple* (New York: Edmund K. Knowlton, 1851), 7.
83. Thomas Smith Webb mentioned this degree in the 1802 edition of *The Freemason's
Monitor; or, Illustrations of Masonry*, 2d ed. (New York: Southwick and Crooker, 1802),
197–200. More substantive descriptions appear in Cross, *The True Masonic Chart*, 129–66.
Joshua Bradley also discussed the Holy Order in *Some of the Beauties of Freemasonry*, 231–
71. Cross's description of the "High Priesthood" was replicated verbatim in many subsequently published monitors, including Cornelius Moore, *The Craftsman, and Freemason's
Guide*, 2d. ed. (Cincinnati, OH: J. Ernst, 1848), 160–93; Rev. K. J. Stewart, *The Freemason's
Manual; A Companion for the Initiated through all the degrees of Freemasonry*, new ed. rev.
(Philadelphia: E. H. Butler & Co., 1853), 155–86; Z. A. Davis, *The Freemason's Monitor; Containing a Delineation of the Fundamental Principles of Freemasonry*, new ed. rev. and enl.
(Philadelphia: Clark and Hesser, 1854), 237–64; and Charles W. Moore, *The New Masonic
Trestle-Board*, stereotype ed. (Boston: Charles W. Moore, 1856), 52–69. See also Mackey,
A Lexicon of Freemasonry; Sheville and Gould, *Guide to the Royal Arch Chapter*, 209–29;
Mackey, *An Encyclopedia of Freemasonry* 1:325–27; and Warvelle, *Observations on the Order
of High Priesthood*. Anti-Masonic descriptions are found in Stearns, *An Inquiry*, 64–66; and
in Ward's *Antimasonic Review* 2:290.
84. See Warvelle, *Observations on the Order of High Priesthood*; Webb, *The Freemason's
Monitor*, 197–200; Pick and Knight, *The Freemason's Pocket Reference Book*, 144.
85. A Royal Arch chapter required the participation of nine Master Masons. See Sheville
and Gould, *Guide to the Royal Arch Chapter*, 212; and Pick and Knight, *The Freemason's
Pocket Reference Book*, 144. Although Joseph Smith selected nine Master Masons as the initial members of the Holy Order, there were actually ten men endowed. Heber C. Kimball
wrote that he was endowed "in company with nine others." Kimball, *On the Potter's Wheel*,
55; *History of the Church* 5:2–3. I am indebted to Richard S. Van Wagoner for pointing out
the connection between Royal Arch Masonry and the endowment.
86. Macoy observes that "it is a grievous error to suppose [signs] to be the essence of the system" and that "signs, tokens, and words do not constitute Freemasonry." See Macoy, *General
History*, 667, 686.

address to the Order of High Priesthood, expressed his hope that the "*chapter* become *beautiful* as the *temple, peaceful* as the *ark,* and *sacred* as its *most holy place.*" He also asked that "you be endowed with every good and perfect gift, while *traveling* the *rugged path* of life, and finally be *admitted within the veil* of heaven to the full enjoyment of life eternal."[87] The candidate passed through four veils to be "admitted within the veil of God's presence, where they will become kings and priests before the throne of his glory for ever and ever."[88]

Finally, the endowment's restoration theme was reminiscent of the Royal Arch's theme that its ritual restored the lost word. The Royal Arch revealed how the Master's word was restored,[89] and Masons were taught that one "who has worthily attained the sublime degree of *Master Mason,* has done well; but he ought not to stop; he has not the key; nor can he get it until he has ascended the pinnacle of the Masonic fabric, the ROYAL ARCH."[90] Many American Masons believed that the Royal Arch was "indescribably more august, sublime, and important than all which precede it, and is the summit and perfection of ancient Masonry."[91]

ADOPTIVE MASONRY

There were also connections between the endowment and some adoptive rituals. When Joseph Smith was initiated, passed, and raised as an Entered Apprentice, Fellow Craft, and Master Mason, he became part of an exclusive male fraternity.[92] When he became a Mason he promised that he

87. Cross, *The True Masonic Chart*, 155.

88. Town, *A System of Speculative Masonry*, 76, as cited in Ward, Free *Masonry*. See Grunder, *Mormon Parallels*, 1842.

89. Bernard, *Light on Masonry*, 124–44. William Morgan, who some claim was never initiated into Craft Masonry but who did indisputably participate in a Royal Arch chapter, claimed that it was "not an uncommon thing, by any means, for a chapter to confer all four degrees in one night." Morgan, *Illustrations of Masonry*, 94.

90. Ward, *The Anti-Masonic Review*, 1:202, quoting *Hardie's Monitor*, 2nd ed., 163.

91. Stone, *Letters on Masonry and Anti-Masonry*, 43; Macoy, *General History*, 332, 502–3; Sheville and Gould, *Guide to the Royal Arch Chapter*, 131–32.

92. *Anderson's Constitutions* required that candidates "must be good and true Men...no Women" (p. 51). British Masons have debated the exclusion of women from their lodges. In 1785 George Smith defended the exclusionary policy: the Craft's exclusion of women was not unique—women were also excluded from the clergy, universities, and many professions. Freemasonry began when women were not "so enlightened as in the present age." Women were also allegedly not adept at keeping secrets; and including women would subject the Craft to "Calumy and reproach" and to allegations of lurid activities which accompany the association of the sexes in secret rituals. See George Smith, *The Use and Abuse of Free-Masonry* (London, 1783), 349–66 (the quotations are from pp. 351, 352.) For more recent arguments on excluding women, see Carr, *The Early French Exposures*, 174; Macoy, *General History*, 394; and J. S. M. Ward, *Freemasonry: Its Aims and Ideals* (London: William Rider & Son, 1923), 115–45. Although British Masons have never seriously considered changing their

would never allow a woman to be initiated into his lodge.[93] Those who recognized the connection between Masonic rituals and the endowment that
Smith introduced may have expected that the Holy Order, which began
as a group of Master Masons, would retain its male-only exclusivity.[94] But
Smith promised the Female Relief Society that women would eventually be
allowed to participate in the Holy Order and he refrained from introducing
a female ritual to the Relief Society.

Although Mormon Masons recognized that there were parallels between the endowment and the rituals of Craft and Royal Arch rituals, they
were probably not aware that there were also connections between the
Mormon ritual and some of the ceremonies of adoptive Masonry. In particular, the endowment's Garden of Eden drama was reminiscent of female
adoptive rituals, which originated in France. The adoptive ritual, which was
published in English as early as 1765 followed by the first American exposé
in 1827,[95] mirrored earlier French exposés which included a second degree
recounting the story of Eve's temptation in the Garden of Eden with an
apple plucked and presented by a figure representing Satan.[96] Arturo de
Hoyas has noted that "the lodge room has a painting of the Garden of

exclusionary policy, some women have apparently been mistakenly initiated into regular
lodges. One woman was admitted to a lodge in Ireland in the eighteenth century, either by
accident or to bind her to keep a ritual secret she had surreptitiously observed in her father's
house. Ward, *Free Masonry*, 115. Other women have also been initiated in England, France,
Hungary, the United States, and Mexico under similar circumstances. Coil, *Coil's Masonic
Encyclopedia*, 15.
93. See Godfrey, "Joseph Smith and the Masons," 84. Godfrey relied on a document entitled "Description of the Ceremonies Used in Opening the Nauvoo Lodge of Entered
Apprentice Masons" (n.p., n.d.). Although he acknowledged that "it is probable that the
document is not authentic," he noted that the vows are nevertheless "not atypical" (ibid.,
84n17). For a typical oath given in connection with the Master Mason degree in New York
state before the Morgan disappearance, which included a promise not to initiate women,
see William Morgan, *Illustrations of Masonry* (Rochester, NY, 1827), 68; Bernard, *Light on
Masonry*, 62; Stone, *Letters on Masonry and Anti-Masonry*, Appendix.
94. Roberts, *A Comprehensive History of the Church*, 2:135–36.
95. *Illustration of the Four First Degrees of Female masonry, as practiced in Europe* (Boston,
1827). This ritual is reprinted in de Hoyas, *Light on Masonry*, 167–98. Cheryl L. Bruno
suggests that some Relief Society sisters had been initiated into androgynous degrees and
that Smith may have initially contemplated introducing such a ritual to the female society.
Bruno, "Keeping a Secret," 158–81.
96. See Janet Mackay Burke, "Sociability, Friendship and the Enlightenment among Women
Freemasons in Eighteenth-Century France," PhD diss., Arizona State University, 1986,
232–33, 245–47, 272–74. For examples of French androgynous rites which included references to the Creation, see *La Maçonnerie des Femmes* (London: n.p., 1774); *L'adoption ou la
Maçonnerie des femmes en trois grades* (n.c.: n.p., 1775); [Louis Guillemain de Saint Victor],
La vraie Maçonnerie d'Adoption (London: Guillemain de Saint Victor, 1779); and "Rite of
Adoption," *Collectanea* 1 (1937; reprinted 1978), 169–76.

Eden…the candidate ('sister') is apparently veiled…she is also called 'Elected Lady'…she is anointed on the lips, is presented with apple and told 'you will become as one of us.'"[97]

WOMEN AND PRIESTHOOD

Jan A. M. Snoek has noted that adoptive rites have been "slightingly described as only a toy for the girls to keep them quiet."[98] More recently, however, he has concluded that females who were initiated into adoptive lodges, at least until the Grand Orient of France took control of them in 1774, became Freemasons just as much as the men who were initiated into the same lodges.[99] Nevertheless, when these lodges were recognized by the Grand Lodge of France in 1774, they became exclusively female and thereafter women were excluded from the Craft lodges and could not become Master Masons.[100] But Margaret Jacob argues that the "records from the eighteenth century are largely inconclusive as to the actual role women played, although clearly the evidence points in the direction of an idealization of gender relations at a time when women's inequality was legally enforced and morally expected."[101]

If Smith intended that men and women should be included in the same ritual on an equal basis, similar to what Snoek believes was the intention of the original French adoptive lodges, he may have believed that endowed women received priesthood. On the other hand, if the Mormon prophet (or his successors) intended that women be adopted into the Holy Order primarily to subject them to the same obligations as their husbands, similar to what Allyn alleged was the purpose of the American androgynous rituals that were introduced during the 1820s, then the model may be more

---

97. Correspondence from Arturo de Hoyos to Michael W. Homer dated June 27, 1994. In addition to these parallels there was at least one other subtle connection noted by anti-Mason Henry Dana Ward between adoptive Masonry and the endowment. He noted that Freemasons believed that the Old Testament description of the Brazen Sea (which was used by priests to purify themselves) provided a model for French "lodges of Adoption." Smith planned and built a similar structure in the basement of the Nauvoo Temple that was eventually used as a font for baptisms for the dead. Ward, *Free Masonry*, 255–56. Ward quoted F. M. Reghellini's *Esprit du Dogme de la Franche-Maçonnerie* (Bruxelles: H. Tarlier, 1825), 39, for the Masonic connection between the brazen sea and the lodges of adoption.
98. Snoek, "Researching Freemasonry," 245.
99. Snoek, *Initiating Women in Freemasonry*, 83–86, 380.
100. Ibid., 121–24, 380.
101. Margaret C. Jacob, "Book Review of Alexandra Heidle and Jan A. M. Snoek, eds., *Women's Agency and Rituals in Mixed and Female Masonic Orders*," in *Journal for Research into Masonry and Fraternalism* 1:2 (2010): 266–67.

similar to the French adoptive rituals practiced after 1774.[102] Given Smith's
well-known tendency to break down traditional barriers, and sporadic
statements made by LDS Church authorities during the nineteenth century, it is worth considering whether Smith's possible use of adoptive rituals
as a model for the endowment may offer any suggestions concerning his
motivation.

The evidence that has been cited to support the thesis that Smith intended endowed women to be given the priesthood includes Smith's declaration to the Female Relief Society that it "should move according to the
ancient Priesthood," that it would be "a kingdom of priests as in Enoch's
day—as in Paul's day," and that he conferred "the keys of the kingdom" on
the society.[103] During this same period Willard Richards sent a letter to his
wife Jennetta Richards (1817–1845) in which he reconfirmed, "I have written you from time to time. The priesthood is for the Sisters as well as the
brethren. The blessings which await you are without bou[n]ds."[104]

Some Mormon women did feel empowered by Smith's decision to include them in the same ritual as men, where they took most of the same
obligations as their husbands, and they understandably believed that the

102. Smith's androgynous ritual anticipated Le Droit Humain (which was founded in France
by Georges Martin and Maria Deraismes) and Co-Masonry (which was sponsored by the
Theosophical Society) which were androgynous rites introduced decades after Smith incorporated women into the Holy Order. In Co-Masonry women receive the first three degrees
of Craft Masonry and both males and females are full members of the lodge. But Le Droit
Humain and Co-Masonry are not recognized as regular by any grand lodge. Although the
Grand Lodge of London and the grand lodges in the United States tolerate organizations
which adopt women they still regard such organizations which initiate women as Masons
as clandestine.
103. Heber C. Kimball, Letter to Parley P. Pratt, June 17, 1842, Parley P. Pratt Papers, Church
History Library. See also Brigham Young's diary entries concerning endowed women whom
he described as being "taken into the order of the priesthood" and "admitted in to the highest order Preasthood"; William Clayton's diary entry in 1844 in which he noted that Jane
Bicknell Young was endowed and received "into the Quorum of the Priesthood"; Kimball's
diary entry in December 1845 that included the names of the men and women who had
received their endowments before the deaths of Joseph and Hyrum Smith who he designated as "members of the Holy Order of the Holy Preasthood," as well as the appointment
of W. W. Phelps and Parley P. Pratt "to instruct the brethren and sisters…more fully into
the nature and importance of the blessings and powers of the Holy Priesthood they had
received." See also D. Michael Quinn, "Response," Sunstone 6, no. 5 (September/October
1981): 26–27. Margaret M. Toscano, "The Missing Rib: The Forgotten Place of Queens and
Priestesses in the Establishment of Zion," Sunstone 10, no. 7 (July 1985): 17–22; Linda King
Newell, "The Historical Relationship of Mormon Women and Priesthood," Dialogue: A
Journal of Mormon Thought 18 (Fall 1985): 21–32. D. Michael Quinn, "Mormon Women
Have Had the Priesthood since 1843," in Women and Authority, Re-emerging Mormon Feminism, ed. Maxine Hanks (Salt Lake City: Signature Books, 1992), 365–409.
104. Correspondence from Willard Richards to Jennetta Richards, undated but sent with
another letter dated February 16, 1842, LDS Church History Library.

endowment created a new partnership between men and women.[105] Mormon women "occupy a more important position than is occupied by any other women on earth," Eliza R. Snow wrote, "associated as they are, with apostles and prophets inspired by the living God—with them sharing in the gifts and powers of the holy Priesthood."[106]

Michael Quinn quoted Smith's journal that he gave "a lecture on the pries[t]hood shewing [sic] how the Sisters would come in possession of the privileges & blessings & gifts of the priesthood & that the signs should follow them"[107] and that Mormon women were also given patriarchal blessings in which they were told that they had received the Priesthood.[108] Furthermore, they were allowed to perform healing ordinances, through the laying on of hands, which was done by virtue of the priesthood and "not simply ministrations of faith."[109] Because of such evidence Edward W. Tullidge (1829–1894) described the woman's role in the temple as that of "a Mason, of the Hebraic order, whose Grand Master is the God of Israel and whose anointer is the Holy Ghost." He concluded that each Mormon woman received a portion of the Priesthood, and that as "a high priestess she blessed with the laying on of hands!"[110]

105. Carol Madsen noted that a process "began when Joseph Smith turned the key to women" in the Relief Society through which an "equitable" relationship between men and women, which existed before Adam's fall, would be restored. For Madsen, the inclusion of sisters in these rituals "had particular significance to women" since it "opened up a new concept of spiritual participation relating to the 'privileges, blessings and gifts of the priesthood' which not only enhanced their position in the church, but offered limitless potential in the hereafter." She concluded that "women were as essential to the restoration of all things as were men and both would experience the promised blessings of the temple ordinances." Carol Cornwall Madsen, "Mormon Women and the Temple," in *Sisters in Spirit: Mormon Women in Historical and Cultural Perspective*, ed. Maureen Ursenbach Beecher and Lavina Fielding Anderson (Urbana: University of Illinois Press, 1987), 83–85.
106. Derr, Cannon, and Beecher, *Women of Covenant*, 56, quoting E. R. S., "Position and Duties," *Women's Exponent* 3 (July 15, 1874): 28.
107. Quinn, "Mormon Women Have Had the Priesthood since 1843," 366.
108. These include Hyrum Smith's patriarchal blessing to Leonora Cannon Taylor in 1843 in which he promised her that she would "be blesst [sic] with your portion of the Priesthood" and various blessings given by church patriarch John Smith. In 1845 John Smith promised Maria Turnbow that she "would receive an Endowment in the Lord's house [and] be clothed with the Power of the Holy Priesthood"; Louisa C. Jackson that she was a "lawful heir to the Priesthood" and that she would be endowed and possess the priesthood "in common with thy companion"; "a women whose husband was a non-Mormon" had "a right to the Priesthood by inheritance"; and that "the Priesthood in its fullness" would be conferred on Mehitable Duty. Joseph Young (Brigham Young's brother) conferred a blessing on Zina Young (Brigham's daughter) in 1878 concerning "the blessings and power according to the holy Melchizedek Priesthood you received in your Endowments." See Quinn, "Mormon Women Have Had the Priesthood," 366–71.
109. Quinn, "Mormon Women Have Had the Priesthood," 366.
110. Edward W. Tullidge, *The Women of Mormondom* (New York: n.p., 1877), 23, 29.

While this evidence (particularly Smith's statements) is consistent with the priesthood thesis, it must be evaluated in the context of other contemporary statements.[111] Some church leaders gave patriarchal blessings during this same period that suggest endowed women were dependent upon their husband's priesthood. On January 31, 1844, Hyrum Smith gave a patriarchal blessing to Sarah Forstner Zundel in which he said, "You shall be blessed in common with your Husband and shall receive all the blessings of the priesthood that are sealed upon his head, even the seal of the covenant."[112] In addition, Michael Quinn notes that John Smith's blessing to Emily Jacob on January 26, 1846, concluded that "a woman can have but little power in the Priesthood without a man."[113]

Furthermore, the thesis that Mormon women performed healing ordinances by virtue of their priesthood and "not simply as an act of faith" is complicated by the fact that they were allowed to perform such ordinances even before they were endowed. They were allowed to "lay hands" on the sick in Kirtland where no woman received her endowments,[114] and they were also allowed to do so in Nauvoo before any woman received her endowments. The prophet used the terms "ordained," "set apart," and "administer in that authority which is conferr'd on them" when he instructed the Relief Society about laying on hands for healing purposes.[115] "There could be no more sin in any female laying hands on the sick than in wetting the

111. In 1980 Linda King Newell and Valeen Tippetts Avery distinguished between female ordination and male priesthood but conceded four years later that Joseph's "words were ambiguous concerning the women's relationship to priesthood authority and [that] the issue would be questioned in the future." Linda King Newell and Valeen Tippetts Avery, "'Sweet Counsel and Seas of Tribulation': The Righteous Life of the Women in Kirtland," *BYU Studies* 20, no. 2 (Winter 1980): 158, 161; and Newell and Avery, *Mormon Enigma*, 111. But in 1985, Newell struggled to differentiate women's authority and priesthood. Newell, "The Historical Relationship of Mormon Women and the Priesthood," 21–32. Lynn Matthews Anderson later criticized the distinction as being "legalistic" and "hairsplitting." She argued that during the nineteenth century male and female blessings were acts "contingent on faith" whether or not done by priesthood authority. But she acknowledged that while Quinn's evidence may be "compelling," it "cannot unequivocally support the conclusion the title ["Mormon Women Have Had the Priesthood since 1843"] proclaims." Lynn Matthews Anderson, "Review of *Women and Authority: Reemerging Mormon Feminism*," *John Whitmer Historical Association Journal* 13 (1993): 115–18. Mary Stovall Richards has commented on Joseph's words, which have been interpreted as promising the priesthood to women, and concluded that the prophet's famous statement that he had turned "the key" over to the society "does not have a simple or clear historical meaning." But she still wondered about "the relationship between conferred priesthood, the blessings of the temple endowment, and the gifts of the spirit." Richards, "Review of Three Books on Women," 791–801.
112. See H. Michael Marquardt, comp., *Early Patriarchal Blessings of the Church of Jesus Christ of Latter-day Saints* (Salt Lake City: The Smith-Pettit Foundation, 2007), 226.
113. Quinn, "Mormon Women Have Had the Priesthood," 399n43.
114. Patriarchal blessing given to Edna Rogers by Joseph Smith Sr., as cited in Carol Lynn Pearson, *Daughters of Light* (Salt Lake City: Bookcraft, 1973), 65.
115. Relief Society, Minutes, April 28, 1842.

face with water," he told the sisters, and "that it is no sin for any body to do it that has faith, or if the sick has faith to be heal'd by the administration." He also told them, without invoking the priesthood, that females had the right to lay on hands "according to revelation."[116]

Nevertheless, even if Smith intended that Mormon women who participated in the endowment receive the priesthood, it is clear that his successors had very different ideas.[117] In March 1845 Brigham Young told a group of Seventies that "sister[s]...have no right to meddle in the affairs of the kingdom of God.... [They] never can hold the Priesthood apart from their husbands."[118] Thereafter, the church authorities reconfirmed that "the priesthood is on your husbands."[119] The LDS hierarchy established a new

116. On August 14, 1843, after the organization of the Holy Order but before women were included in it, Reynolds Cahoon told the society that one of its functions was "to look after the sick," that this responsibility was "according to the Order of God connected with the Priesthood," and that if the society did not perform this function "the Order of the Priesthood is not complete." Ibid., August 13, 1843.

117. This current view is similar to Catholic teachings. Pope John Paul II wrote in an apostolic letter that "the Church has no capacity to confer the ordination of Priesthood on women." See Giovanni Paolo II, "Sull'ordinazione sacerdotale da riservarsi soltanto agli uomini," (Vatican City: Libreria Editrice Vaticana, 1994); *Catechism of the Catholic Church* (Vatican City: Libreria Editrice Vaticana, 1994; English edition in cooperation with William H. Sadier, 1577). However, the Roman Catholic Church does employ a dual definition of "priesthood," teaching that all baptized Christians, including women, have a "common priesthood," but that this is only a metaphorical "priesthood" which should not be confused with the "ministerial" priesthood reserved for (male only) ordained ministers. Nevertheless, laypersons (male and female) are entitled to share, through the "common priesthood," in the spiritual benefits of the ministerial priesthood reserved to the male clergy.

118. Seventies Record, March 9, 1845, as quoted in Newell, "The Historical Relationship of Mormon Women and Priesthood," 27. Richards wondered "if Brigham Young's October 29, 1843, description of women's receiving their endowments as being 'taken into the order of the priesthood' meant the same as receiving the priesthood." Young's statement eighteen months later that women do not hold the priesthood apart from their husbands is some evidence of the limited meaning of his earlier statement unless he had changed his mind. Richards, "Review of Three Books on Women," 801.

119. July 12, 1857, *Journal of Discourses*, 5:31. John Taylor reaffirmed in 1880 as the church's presiding officer, regarding the ordination of the Relief Society presidency in 1842: "It is not the calling of these sisters to hold the Priesthood, only in connection with their husbands, they being one with their husbands." *Journal of Discourses* 21:367–68 (August 8, 1880). Similar statements were made by Joseph F. Smith in 1907, in the *Relief Society Bulletin* in 1914, and by other General Authorities in the twentieth century. Joseph F. Smith, "Questions and Answers," *Improvement Era* 10 (February 1907): 308; *Relief Society Bulletin* 1 (February 1914): 1–3; James E. Talmage, "The Eternity of Sex," *Young Woman's Journal* 25 (October 1914): 602–3; Rudger Clawson, *Conference Reports*, April 1921, 24–25; Charles W. Penrose, ibid., 198; Heber J. Grant, Charles W. Penrose, and Anthony W. Ivins, October 5, 1922, *Messages of the First Presidency*, compiled by James R. Clark, (Salt Lake City: Bookcraft, 1965–1975), 5:216; Stephen L. Richards, *Conference Reports*, October 5, 1952, 99–100. More recently, Spencer W. Kimball told the press in June 1978, "We pray to God to reveal his mind and we always will, but we don't expect any revelation regarding women and the priesthood." "Kimball Says No Women in Priesthood," *Salt Lake Tribune*, June 13, 1978, D-1.

policy under which sisters could not participate in prayer circles in the absence of their husbands and eventually they were not permitted to attend at all.[120]

Based on this evidence Richard P. Howard, a member of the Community of Christ, which now ordains women to its priesthood, concluded that although "there is no record of women serving in Aaronic or Melchisedec offices in the *public church*, at Nauvoo," that they were given priesthood, or "private ecclesiastical orders," in a private church."[121] Smith's reference to a "Kingdom of Priests" was, according to Howard, a "metaphor to embellish" the roles of a few selected women in the private church but that it is "hazardous" to argue that Joseph intended to ordain women to the priesthood in the public church based on that terminology.[122]

Nevertheless, Howard believes that some women were perhaps deceived into believing that they were "secretly" ordained to the priesthood so that they would accept plural marriage. Similarly, Greg Prince has noted that despite suggestive rhetoric Mormon women did not perform priesthood functions relating to ordinations, baptisms, confirmations, administering the sacrament, marrying couples, or serving on missions.

WOMEN AND SECRECY

Thus, although women became "priestesses" in a temple context, there were additional, and perhaps more practical, reasons they were admitted into the Holy Order.[123] The Masonic theme of male authority, female transgression and the "companion" role of women, was arguably something that fit Joseph Smith's plan to protect the secrecy of plural marriage. Although Relief Society sisters were frequently reminded by the Mormon leadership about the importance of keeping secrets, the society never placed its members under a ritual obligation to maintain secrecy. During its short existence the society failed to extinguish rumors concerning the Mormon prophet's practice of plural marriages and such rumors increasingly dominated its proceedings. The Mormon prophet eventually initiated selected sisters into the Holy Order where they were ritually obligated to keep secrets, in part because the Relief Society had failed in that part of its mission.

120. Quinn, "Latter-day Saint Prayer Circles," 88–89.
121. Richard P. Howard, "What Sort of Priesthood for Women at Nauvoo?" *John Whitmer Historical Association Journal* 13 (1993): 20, 29. Howard, the RLDS Church Historian, published this statement after the church president introduced a revelation authorizing priesthood ordination for women in his Community of Christ (formerly Reorganized Church of Jesus Christ of Latter Day Saints) and after the first women were so ordained.
122. Ibid., 24, 28–30.
123. Prince, *Power from on High*, 204.

After Smith was murdered, the church hierarchy expressed concern about the ability of women to keep the endowment a secret. In December 1845, Heber C. Kimball made a motion, while the church hierarchy was introducing the endowment to the general church membership, "that no man tell his wife what he has seen," and then "alluded to the stories in circulation that several persons had been killed on their way through the ordinances, and that men and women were stripped naked here."[124]

During this same period four General Authorities gave speeches concerning the danger of revealing secrets to women. "I am subject to my God," announced Heber C. Kimball, "my wife is in subjection to me," and God "did not make the man for the woman; but the woman for the man." Kimball also reminded those assembled that "females were not received when we first received the Holy Order," and "spoke of the Necessity of Women being in subjection to husbands." Kimball recalled that "females were not received when we first received the Holy Order" and confirmed that "men apostatized, being led by their wives—if any such cases occur again—no more women will be admitted."[125] He noted that Joseph taught that "a wife must obey a righteous husband" to be worthy to receive her endowment.[126]

Amasa Lyman taught that a man "has covenanted to keep the law of God, and the woman to obey her husband," and George A. Smith counseled that a "woman ought to be in subjection to the man, be careful to guard against loud laughter, against whispering, levity, talebearing." Finally, Brigham Young concluded that "the man must love his God and the woman must love her husband."[127] Thereafter, these church leaders, whose role models were the Old Testament prophets who were patriarchs, polygamists, and temple builders, would insist that women were not entitled to be ordained to priesthood.

124. Smith, *An Intimate Chronicle*, 240.
125. Newell and Avery, *Mormon Enigma*, 140, quoting Heber C. Kimball, December 21, 1845, found in William Clayton, Diary, kept for Heber C. Kimball. See also Anderson and Bergera, *Joseph Smith's Quorum of the Anointed*, 25n15.
126. Quoted in Newell and Avery, *Mormon Enigma*, 140.
127. Quoted in Smith, *An Intimate Chronicle*, 222, 227, 225–26, 239. Apostle James E. Talmage tacitly recognized women's subordination when he wrote, in 1914, that when women leave "the frailties and imperfections of mortality…behind," they will be glorified and "recompensed in rich measure for all the injustice that womanhood has endured in mortality." Talmage, "The Eternity of Sex," 602–3.

Brigham's Temples

WHEN BRIGHAM YOUNG led the Saints to the Great Salt Lake Valley it was still part of Mexico. Young did not request a city charter or any other form of recognition but instead established a theocracy. In March 1849, after the United States obtained the territory by treaty, the Mormon leadership established a provisional State of Deseret that included executive, legislative, and judicial branches, and petitioned the United States Congress for statehood.[1] Ironically, William Smith (1811–1893), the first Mormon prophet's younger brother, wrote a "remonstrance" in opposition to Deseret's petition in which he asserted that the temple ritual included oaths that were disloyal to the United States.

Smith claimed that "1,500 Salt Lake Mormons" had taken such an oath in the Nauvoo Temple to "avenge the blood of Joseph Smith on this nation" and that they pledged to "carry out hostilities against this nation."[2] Smith did not mention that he had been endowed and instead conflated John Bennett's claim that the Holy Order took oaths to "overturn the constitution of the United States" with the Van Dusens' assertions that initiates took an oath of vengeance on the nation that was significantly different from the prayer recorded by Heber Kimball that invoked the Lord's curse on violent persecutors.

It is unlikely William Smith knew that Young recommended performing the endowment the same year in makeshift locations. On July 21, 1849, Young, together with six apostles and three presidents of the Seventy, ascended Ensign Peak at six o'clock in the morning where he "consecrated the

1. See Dale L. Morgan, *State of Deseret* (Logan: Utah State University Press and Utah Historical Society, 1987); and William MacKinnon, "'Like Splitting a Man up His Back Bone': The Territorial Dismemberment of Utah, 1850–1896," *Utah Historical Quarterly* 71: 2 (Spring 2003): 100–24.
2. William Smith, *Remonstrance of William Smith et al., of Covington, Kentucky, against the Admission of Deseret into the Union.* 31st Cong., 1st sess., House Misc. Doc. 43, Serial 581, 1849, 1–2.

Hill for the erection of a standard thereon a place of prayer."[3] Young prayed that this standard "should be glorious in the eyes of all its beholders, that no unholy thing might come here, that thy servants may come here to offer up their prayers and obtain the ministration of angels."[4] Addison Pratt was then washed and anointed by Young, Charles C. Rich, and Erastus Snow and received his endowment.[5]

UTAH TERRITORY

In 1850 the U.S. Congress ignored Deseret's petition for statehood and instead voted to approve California as a free state and to create territorial forms of government in what was now officially named Utah, and New Mexico, both of which had the option of adopting slavery.[6] Millard Fillmore (1800–1874), who became president when Zachary Taylor died in July 1850, appointed Brigham Young the first governor of Utah Territory.[7] In December 1850 the General Assembly of the State of Deseret met for the last time in the newly constructed Council Hall before news reached Salt Lake City that Utah Territory had been created and that Young had been appointed governor.

In January 1851 Young learned from press reports that Fillmore had appointed him governor. On February 3 Daniel H. Wells, chief justice of the State of Deseret, administered the oath of office to him before the arrival of Fillmore's other appointees. Young instructed Thomas Bullock, his church clerk, to take a census of the territory, in order to apportion districts for the Legislative Assembly, which would have a Council and House of Representatives, and issued a proclamation on July 1 announcing the apportionment and directing that "an election be held in the respective precincts throughout the Territory on the first Monday in August next, in accordance with the existing laws of the provisional government of Deseret regulating elections, passed by the General Assembly November 12, 1849."[8]

3. Franklin D. Richards Journal, MS 1215, Box 1, Vol. 9, February 20, 1849–November 6, 1849, Church History Library, Selected Collections, Vol. 1, DVD 34.
4. Addison Pratt Family Papers, Endowment Record, Utah State University, Coll Mss 228b, Box 1, fd 23, Minutes, July 21, 1849.
5. Ibid. Addison Pratt had been called as a missionary to the Society Islands. See also *History of the Church* 7:iii; Roberts, *Comprehensive History* 3:386; and Andrew Jenson, *Church Chronology*, 38. See also Brown, "'Temple Pro Tempore,'" 4.
6. John J. Flynn, "Federalism and Viable State Government—The History of Utah's Constitution," *Utah Law Review* 1966: 311–25; Brad C. Smith, "Comment, Be No More Children: An Analysis of *Article I, Section 4 of the Utah Constitution*," *Utah Law Review* 1992: 1431, 1444. This legislation took effect on September 9, 1851.
7. Fillmore appointed Young on September 28, 1850.
8. *Latter-day Saints in Utah. Opinion of Z. Snow, Judge of the Supreme Court of the United*

When Fillmore's other appointees, Justices Lemuel Brandenberry and
Perry Brochus, Territorial Secretary Broughton Harris, and Indian Agent
Henry Day, arrived in the territory later that summer they were immediately alarmed by what they considered Young's autocratic actions. Young
had already been sworn in as governor, the census had been taken, and elections were scheduled. Brandenberry, who was the first to arrive, challenged
Daniel H. Wells's authority to administer the oath of office to Governor
Young. Harris complained that the census was flawed because Young's proclamation was executed before his arrival and lacked his seal. He also refused
to deliver twenty-four thousand dollars in gold that had been appropriated
by the U.S. Congress for the construction of a statehouse.

On September 8 Justice Brochus, who was the last official to arrive
in the territory, spoke to an audience assembled in a temporary meeting
place called the Bowery, in which he requested that the Mormons donate
a block of stone for the Washington Monument. The construction of the
monument, which would eventually become an Egyptian-style obelisk, had
commenced four years earlier with full Masonic ceremony. During the same
speech Brochus challenged Wells's assertion that the federal government
had taken advantage of the Latter-day Saints during the Mexican War when
it enlisted the Mormon Battalion and what he considered other antigov-
ernment rhetoric. But Brochus's fatal error, according to Brigham Young,
occurred when he "directed a portion of his discourse towards the ladies…
and…strongly recommended them to become virtuous."

Young delivered a strong rebuke and provided examples of federal persecution. He said that "if I permit discussion to arise here, there may be either
a pulling of hair or a cutting of throats," and that "by silence [the federal
government] gave sanction to the lawless proceedings" that had been per-
petrated against the Mormons. Because of this silence "hundreds of women
and children have been laid in the tomb prematurely…and their blood cries
to the Father for vengeance against those who caused or consented to their
death." But, he also admitted, "I love the government and the constitution
of the United States, but I do not love the damned rascals who administer
the government." Following his remarks Young sent a written invitation to
Brochus to return to the Bowery the following Sunday in order to apolo-
gize. When Brochus refused, Young sent him three additional letters repeating the same request.[9]

States for the Territory of Utah, upon the official course of His Excellency Gov. Brigham Young
(Liverpool: F. D. Richards, 1852), 5–12.
9. See Norman H. Furniss, The Mormon Conflict, 1850–1859 (New Haven: Yale University
Press, 1960), 21–29. Brochus was probably unaware that Brigham Young had claimed as early
as 1847 that "damned President Polk" had concocted a plan "to destroy the Saints by forcing

On September 18 Young certified the election results and called upon the legislature to meet at the Council House three days later.[10] On September 22 the Territorial Council and House of Representatives met for the first time in the Council House. The thirteen-member council elected Willard Richards as its president pro tem, and the house, with its twenty-six members, elected W. W. Phelps, the famous anti-Mason, as its speaker. The legislature eventually adopted all the laws of the provisional state government, which were signed by Governor Young.[11]

On September 28 Brochus, Brandenberry, Harris, and U.S. Indian Agent Henry Day departed the territory with the twenty-four thousand dollars in gold. Young wrote a letter to President Fillmore explaining his position and attacking the judges and secretary. He also wrote a letter to Brochus in which he confirmed his prior statements.[12] The departing officials wrote letters to the Fillmore Administration in which they responded to Young's claim that Fillmore's predecessor was rotting in Hell, accused the Mormons of being disloyal, accused Young of presiding over a theocracy, and criticized his attempts to circumvent the territorial secretary to obtain the federal gold.[13]

Justice Zerrubabel Snow, a Mormon convert and the only judge who did not leave the territory, ruled after the departure of Brandenberry and Brochus that Young's actions in connection with the census and elections were legal and valid. Thereafter Fillmore made no further appointments to the Utah judiciary and the territorial government operated for nearly two years without two of its three federal judges and without a territorial secretary.[14]

PREPARATIONS FOR THE TEMPLE

In 1851 the Mormon hierarchy organized prayer circles, which included worthy members but apparently not women, that were held each evening.[15] In April of the following year Young told an audience in the tabernacle (which replaced the Bowery) that even though there was no temple in the territory, God would recognize endowments given "on these mountains"

them to raise the battalion." See Matthew J. Grow, *"Liberty to the Downtrodden": Thomas L. Kane, Romantic Reformer* (New Haven: Yale University Press, 2009), 53–54.

10. *Journal History*, LDS Church History Library, September 8, 1851.

11. See David L. Bigler, *Forgotten Kingdom: The Mormon Theocracy in the American West, 1847–1896* (Spokane, WA: The Arthur H. Clark Company, 1998), 56–60.

12. See *Journal History*, September 19, 20, 21, 28, 29, and 30.

13. Furniss, *The Mormon Conflict*, 28–30.

14. *Opinion of Z. Snow*, 5–12.

15. Quinn, "Latter-day Saint Prayer Circles," 90.

and "all Hell could not prevail against them." Young announced that he had a vision of the temple "as plainly as if it was in reality before me. I have never looked upon that ground, but the vision of it was there. I see it as plainly as if it was in reality before me. Wait until it is done."[16]

Young then informed the church that "we make preparations to commence the temple in the spring of 1853" where the entire endowment ceremony could be performed. His announcement confirmed that his predecessor's initial idea, that there would be only one temple in Jackson County, had been modified and that the church would continue to construct temples throughout the "stakes of Zion." The Mormon prophet advised the congregation that the temple, unlike the temples in Kirtland and Nauvoo, would be used exclusively for giving endowments and related ordinances and not "for the assembly of the people, and for the public worship of God."[17]

In August Young institutionalized the practice of plural marriage and acknowledged the legitimacy of Joseph Smith's revelation and teachings on that subject. He requested Apostle Orson Pratt to deliver an oration in the tabernacle to explain that polygamy was previously practiced by Old Testament patriarchs, such as Solomon, that those who practiced the principle were chosen in the preexistence (as opposed to "Hottentots, the African negroes, the idolatrous Hindoos, or any of the other fallen nations"), and that Elijah restored "the sealing keys of power" in the Kirtland Temple "at the time of the endowments in that house." After the restoration of this power celestial marriages were performed, remained valid for eternity, and the Saints became part of "a kingdom of Kings and Priests, a kingdom unto Himself, or in other words, a kingdom of Gods."[18]

When Young announced plans for a temple he had already made arrangements for endowments to be given on the second floor of the Council House. The following October Young observed that endowments in the Council House were "given merely by permission, as we have not a house in

16. Fred C. Collier, ed., *The Teachings of President Brigham Young* (Salt Lake City: Collier's Publishing Company, 1987), 3:74.
17. See Brigham Young, "The Temple Corner Stones—The Apostleship, &c.," *Journal of Discourses* 1:131–37; "Discourse delivered by President B. Young," (April 8, 1852), *Millennial Star* 16: 310–12, 324–28 (May 20, 27, 1854); Collier, *The Teachings of President Brigham Young*, 3:71–84 (reported by George D. Watt); *Deseret News* 2:46, no. 12 (April 17, 1852); Kenney, *Wilford Woodruff's Journal* 4:123–25. In 1856 Truman Angell recorded that when "Young mentioned to the Saints in the Valley that the Salt Lake Temple would have six towers, he also added he hoped none would apostatize because he was having six towers built and Joseph only had one." Beatrice B. Malouf, *Pioneer Buildings of Early Utah* (Salt Lake City: Daughters of Utah Pioneers, 1991), 122.
18. Orson Pratt, "Celestial Marriage," *Journal of Discourses* 1:53–66 (August 29, 1852). The LDS hierarchy did not publish the 1843 revelation on plural marriage, or remove Doctrine and Covenants section 101 which mandated monogamous marriages, until 1876.

Illustration of Salt Lake Temple from original drawings.
Courtesy Utah State Historical Society.

which to officiate in these ordinances of salvation" but that "we do not give all the endowments, neither can we, legally, until we build a temple."[19] The room where the endowments were given was divided into temporary spaces, using white screens, which corresponded to the same divisions (Initiation

19. See "Remarks made by Brigham Young" (October 6, 1852), *Millennial Star* 15:129–33, 149–52, 385–90; *Deseret News* 2:98, no. 25 (October 16, 1852); 2:104, no. 26 (November 6, 1852), quoted in Collier, *The Teachings of President Brigham Young*, 133–37.

Details of Salt Lake Temple symbols from original drawings.
Courtesy H. Michael Marquardt.

Room, Creation Room, World Room, Celestial Room, etc.) that had been used in the attic of the Nauvoo Temple. Although Young taught that the endowments given in the Council House were valid, he also cautioned that everyone (including those who were endowed in the Nauvoo Temple) would be required to be re-endowed when the new temple was completed.[20]

Church architect Truman Angell prepared drawings for a new temple that resembled a gothic-style castle with battlements, six pointed towers, and two flying angels (reminiscent of Weeks's Nauvoo weathervane) that would be placed atop the central towers on the east and west sides of the building. The plans also included graphic Masonic symbols on the exterior of the structure, including earthstones, moonstones, sunstones, cloudstones, starstones (six-sided stars known in Masonry as the seal of Solomon), the Big Dipper, ritualistic hand grips, an all-seeing eye, and interlocking squares and compasses.[21]

20. Brown, "'Temple Pro Tempore,'" 4–5.
21. See Andrews, *The Early Temples*, 119–32, 142–45.

Angell's plans provided for a twelve-foot outer wall to segregate and provide a buffer for the ten-acre temple site from the rest of the city and that created an outer courtyard for the projected temple. Young insisted that he would "not build a temple nor…commence to put one piece of hewn stone upon the foundation, or plane a board or stick of timber for that building, until the Temple is fenced."[22] Not surprisingly, this wall was completed decades before the structure itself and today remains the most striking and perhaps unattractive part of Temple Square. Some have argued that the wall should be removed ("tear down that wall"), since it obscures the structures located on Temple Square. But others believe that the wall evokes the Temple of Solomon, which included inner and outer courts, serves as an initial veil between the temple grounds and the outside world, and protects the quiet and sacred courtyard outside the temple structure.

MENTIONS OF MASONRY

During these early territorial days Mormon Masons remained surprisingly loyal to the Craft. Young wore a Masonic pin while sitting for a photograph[23] and his closest friend in the hierarchy, Heber C. Kimball, rejoiced that "I have been as true as an angel from the heavens to the covenants I made in the lodge at Victor."[24] The church also held "Masonic Schools"[25] and continued to use and display Masonic symbols on church buildings, cooperatives, grave markers, newspaper mastheads, hotels, residences, coins, logos, and seals.[26] During the same period Young told the First Presidency that "Hyrum believed that Masonry wo[ul]d save them—but it was masonry that killed them—you will find in the sequel that the Lord has ordered it so."[27]

The second Mormon prophet believed that Freemasonry was a perversion of a primitive ritual that he had restored to its fullness. That the

22. Brigham Young, "Spiritual Gifts—Hell—The Spirit World—The Elders of the Nations—The Lamanites—The Temple," *Journal of Discourses* 2:144 (December 3, 1854).

23. Young had several photographs taken wearing a Masonic pin. See *The City of the Saints in Picture and Story* (Salt Lake City: Deseret News, 1906), p. 34; and Douglas F. Tobler and Nelson B. Wadsworth, *The History of the Mormons in Photographs* (New York: St. Martin's Press, 1989), 10. Frederick Hawkins Piercy published a steel engraving made from this photograph which was published in 1853. Ibid., 11, 23.

24. Orson F. Whitney, *Life of Heber C. Kimball, An Apostle* (Salt Lake City: Published by the Kimball Family, 1888), 27.

25. See, e.g., Juanita Brooks, ed., *On the Mormon Frontier: The Diary of Hosea Stout*, 2 vols. (Salt Lake City: University of Utah Press, 1964), 2:415, 423.

26. Allen D. Roberts, "Where Are the All-Seeing Eyes? The Origin, Use and Decline of Early Mormon Symbolism," *Sunstone* 4 (May–June 1979): 22–37.

27. "Minutes of the First Presidency," January 26, 1850, Church History Library.

Brigham Young (1801–1877) with Masonic device.
Courtesy Utah State History.

hierarchy continued to make this claim is demonstrated by recollections made by a number of travelers who visited the territory. The first such account was written by John W. Gunnison, a member of the Stansbury expedition, who spent many months among the Mormons in 1849 and 1850.

Gunnison's recollections were published in a posthumous volume in which he recounted that the church had "working signs" and that "Masonry was originally of the church, and one of its favored institutions, to advance the members to their spiritual functions." He noted, "It had become perverted from its designs, and was restored to its true work by Joseph, who gave again, by angelic assistance, the key-words of the several degrees that had been lost." Mormons told him, Gunnison wrote, that "when [Smith] entered the lodges of Illinois, he could work right ahead of the promoted; for which, through envy, the Nauvoo lodge was excommunicated, on account of its ignorance of the greatest truths and benefits of Masonry."[28]

THE FOURTH GOD-SANCTIONED TEMPLE

In February 1853 Young dedicated the site where the temple would be built, and the following April he presided over the laying and dedication of the cornerstones. Young decided to lay the chief cornerstone on the southeast

28. John W. Gunnison, *The Mormons, or Latter-day Saints, in the Valley of the Great Salt Lake* (Philadelphia: Lippincott, Grambo & Co., 1852), 59–60.

corner, even though it was customary to place it at the northeast corner, "because *there* is the most *light*." The First Presidency laid that first stone, followed by the presiding bishop who laid the southwest stone, the high priests and elders who laid the northwest stone, and the Twelve Apostles who laid the northeast stone. This, according to Young, was done in the "perfect form and order" of the priesthood even if it deviated from the order followed in Masonry.[29]

During this dedication Brigham Young observed that the Salt Lake Temple would be the fourth God-sanctioned temple that had ever been constructed. He noted that although Solomon and Smith had received revelations, commandments, and patterns to construct their temples, the endowment was not given in its fullness in any of these prior structures located in Jerusalem, Kirtland, and Nauvoo. This was because of persecution, mobocracy, and murder which, in the case of Solomon, resulted in the loss of the key word and, in the case of the Mormons in Kirtland and Nauvoo, frustrated the full development of the endowment.

Even in Nauvoo, Young said, "Many received a small portion of their endowment, but we know of no one who received it in its fullness." Young confirmed "all those ordinances in the House of the Lord, which are necessary for you, after you have departed this life, to enable you to walk back to the presence of the Father, passing the angels who stand as sentinels, being enable to give them the key words, the signs and tokens, pertaining to the Holy Priesthood, and gain your exaltation in spite of earth and hell." He also promised them that the enemies of the church could not again destroy the Holy Priesthood "by *killing* a few" since many thousands had been entrusted with key words, signs, and tokens.[30]

The following year Young told a congregation assembled in the tabernacle that the Mormon priesthood is received in the temple endowment and is "the principle of salvation, a perfect system of government, of laws and ordinances, by which we can be prepared to pass from one gate to another, and from one sentinel to another, until we go into the presence of our Father and God." He assured them that "if we are successful, and are blessed and preserved...we shall probably commence two or three more [temples], and so on as fast as the work requires, for the express purpose of redeeming our dead." He asked, "What are we trying to build a temple for?" and

29. Brigham Young, "The Temple Corner Stones—The Apostleship, &c.," *Journal of Discourses* 1:131–37 (April 6, 1853).
30. Brigham Young, "Necessity of Building Temples—The Endowment," *Journal of Discourses* 2:31–32 (April 6, 1853). Young didn't mention that temples were also referred to in the Book of Mormon. See 2 Nephi 5:16: "And I Nephi, did build a temple, and I did construct it after the manner of the temple of Solomon save it were not built of so many precious things."

answered that "when I get a revelation that some of my progenitors lived and died without the blessings of the gospel," he would "go and be baptized, confirmed, washed, and anointed, and go through all the ordinances and endowments, that their way be opened to the celestial kingdom."[31]

In May 1855 the church hierarchy dedicated an Endowment House that, although not a temple, was called "The House of the Lord."[32] The two-story adobe structure's exterior was plain and more reminiscent of Smith's red brick store than either the Kirtland or Nauvoo temples. But the interior was more elaborate than those temples, or even the Council House, and included some important innovations. The interior had permanent rooms (reception room, initiatory room, garden room, world room, prayer circle room, instruction room, celestial room, and sealing room) rather than a single room like prior structures where it was necessary to divide the space by using canvas partitions. There was also a separate sealing room, which did not exist in either the Kirtland or Nauvoo temples.[33]

James Tingen has observed that architect Truman O. Angell Sr. designed the Endowment House "to imply to those progressing through the endowment ceremony that as they moved from room to room they were being raised up and were coming closer to our Father in Heaven." This was accomplished by constructing a step between each room that had to be ascended by participants, as they went from one room to another.[34] The design ensured that those who received their endowments would have complete privacy. This was not available in the Council House, which had offices for federal officials.[35]

Although no Masonic symbols were placed on the structure's plain exterior, such symbols were present in the interior. Lisle Brown has noted that these symbols included "the square, compass, level, and plumb on the garden room walls, the depiction of sun, moon and stars in the same room, and flaming swords over the door in the world room."[36] It was also the first "House of the Lord" to include murals to illustrate the endowment drama.[37]

31. Young, "Spiritual Gifts," *Journal of Discourses* 2:138–39 (December 3, 1854).
32. See *Journal History*, May 5, 1855; Kenney, *Wilford Woodruff's Journal* 4:316. Woodruff wrote, "President Young said He would name it the House of God & when the Temple is built He would call it the Temple of our God."
33. Brown, "'Temple Pro Tempore,'" 65–66.
34. James Dwight Tingen, "The Endowment House, 1855–1889" (Senior History Paper, Brigham Young University, 1974), 11.
35. Brown, "'Temple Pro Tempore,'" 5–8. The instruction room is also referred to as the terrestrial room. Ibid., 44.
36. Ibid., 67.
37. Ibid., 63.

In the Endowment House men and women were endowed and sealed (married) for time and eternity. In 1856 baptisms for the living, for the dead, and for renewal of covenants could be performed when the Endowment House was enlarged to include a font.[38] However, there were no vicarious endowments or marriage sealings, and no children were sealed to their parents, in the structure.[39]

GENTILES AND BACKSLIDERS

The Mormons' initial conflict with federal officials turned out to be an overture for even more rocky relations with non-Mormon officials and soldiers. In 1854 an additional batch of federal officials arrived in the territory followed by Edward Steptoe (1816–1865), a colonel in the United States Army, and three hundred troops. Steptoe was sent to investigate the deaths of John W. Gunnison and his surveying crew, and because of accusations made by the prior federal officials. Steptoe, his soldiers, the federal officials, and the Mormon hierarchy initially maintained cordial relations even though Steptoe knew that President Franklin Pierce (1804–1869), who succeeded Millard Fillmore in March 1853, had already selected him to replace Young as territorial governor. But Steptoe eventually decided to turn down the appointment after the Mormons accused some of his soldiers of taking advantage of Mormon girls.[40]

During this period, the LDS Church was challenged by backsliders who bitterly repeated some of the same sordid tales concerning the endowment. In 1854 Young complained about church members who asked him for permission to receive their endowments and then "go to California, and reveal everything he can, and stir up wickedness, and prepare himself for hell."[41] Three years later the Mormon prophet noted that "giving endowments to a great many proves their overthrow, through revealing things to them which they cannot keep" but rationalized that it served to "qualify them to be

38. Ibid., 18–20.

39. Brigham Young, "The Necessity of the Saints Having the Spirit of Revelation—Faith and Works—the Power of God and of the Devil," *Journal of Discourses*, 3:159 (May 6, 1855); Van Wagoner, *Complete Discourses* 5:1873; *Journal of Discourses* 10:165, 254; 14:124–25; 16:185–189; Roberts, *Comprehensive History* 4:13–15.

40. See Michael W. Homer, "The Federal Bench and Federal Authority: The Rise and Fall of John Fitch Kinney's Early Relationship with the Mormons," *Journal of Mormon History* 13 (1986–87): 89–110; Michael W. Homer, "The Judiciary and the Common Law in Utah Territory, 1850–61," *Dialogue* 21:1 (Spring 1988): 97–108; William MacKinnon, "Sex, Subalterns and Steptoe: Army Behavior, Mormon Rage, and Utah War Anxieties," *Utah Historical Quarterly* 76:3 (Summer 2008): 227–46.

41. Young, "Spiritual Gifts," *Journal of Discourses* 2:144 (December 3, 1854).

devils" since "it takes almost as much knowledge to made a complete devil as it does to fit a man to go into the celestial kingdom of God."[42]

Over the next thirty years these non-Mormons and "jack-Mormons" produced a series of critical books and exposés that reinforced the connection between the endowment house and the illegal practice of plural marriage as well as the oaths of obedience to priesthood authority and vengeance toward the United States. The oath of vengeance, which had been publicized by William Smith, was variously represented as requiring church members to maintain "constant enmity" toward the federal government for failing to avenge the death of Joseph Smith to the more serious charge that it required them to personally avenge the prophet's death.

One of the most disseminated endowment exposés was written by John Hyde Sr., who converted to Mormonism in England in 1848 and immigrated to Utah five years later. In 1856 Hyde was called to serve a mission to the Sandwich (Hawaiian) Islands and received his endowment in the Council House, but by the time he arrived in Honolulu he was already disillusioned and gave a lecture explaining his reasons for withdrawing from the church.[43] Shortly thereafter Hyde published *Mormonism: Its Leaders and Designs* in which he described the various stages of the endowment ritual and, like David Bernard, the famous anti-Mason, justified breaking his oath of secrecy because he believed he was answering a higher call.

Hyde, like the Van Dusens and William Smith, focused on the sensational claim that members were "sworn to cherish constant enmity toward the United States government for not avenging the death of Smith, or righting the persecution of the saints." According to Hyde, this oath required endowed Mormons "to do all that we could toward destroying, tearing down, or overturning that government; to endeavor to baffle its designs and frustrate its intentions; to renounce all allegiance and refuse all submission." He asserted that the "signs, tokens, marks and ideas are plagiarized from masonry," that the purpose of the endowment was "to teach unlimited obedience to Brigham, and treason against the country," and that the ritual was

42. Brigham Young, "Exchange of Feeling and Sentiment Produces Mutual Confidence," *Journal of Discourses* 4:372 (June 28, 1857).

43. Hyde criticized Mormonism in a letter he wrote to *The Polynesian* 13:24 (October 18, 1856) (Honolulu, Hawaii). The following year he published *Mormonism: Its Leaders and Designs* (New York: W. P. Fetridge and Company, 1857), 83–99. Hyde's book was quoted by various travelers, including Jules Remy, who relied on his account of the endowment ceremony. See Kenneth L. Cannon II, "A Strange Encounter: The English Courts and Mormon Polygamy," *BYU Studies* 92 (Winter 1982): 73–83; Michael W. Homer, *On the Way to Somewhere Else: European Sojourners in the Mormon West, 1834–1930* (Spokane, WA: The Arthur H. Clark Company, 2006), 69.

"being constantly amended and corrected."[44] Finally, he noted that W. W. Phelps, the famous anti-Masonic publisher, had a major role in the endowment drama, "which he plays admirably," but he failed to note the irony of Phelps's transition from one who displayed "public abhorance of Masonic ritual" to playing a major role in a restored version of the same ritual.[45]

During this same period Nelson Winch Green wrote *Fifteen Years Among the Mormons*, which was "the narrative of Mrs. Mary Ettie V. Smith," who had withdrawn from the LDS Church, and included her description of the Nauvoo Temple endowment.[46] While Smith insisted that many portions of the ceremony would remain "forever sealed within my own breast by a solemn obligation of secrecy, and must so remain until I can see how their disclosure can contribute the public good," she also repeated rumors concerning the second anointing, which she had not received. Smith claimed that it was "administered without clothing of any kind," and argued that the purpose of the endowment is to "unsex the sexes." She also complained that women are "prostituted under such a system," but whether she meant this literally or metaphorically is unclear.[47] The most ironic portion of Smith's account was her insistence that there was no connection between the Mormon endowment and the rituals of Freemasonry. In fact, she was the first of several Mormon women who were convinced that any connection between the endowment and Freemasonry was superficial or even nonexistent.

Smith noted that "the outside show of some of the regalia and furniture connected with these 'Endowments,' were made to conform with those of Masonry; and Mormons are anxious to have the 'Gentiles' associate all they know of these beastly 'Endowments,' with Masonry, or as being a modified form of it, made eligible to women, as a blind to cover the real objects of this

44. Hyde, *Mormonism: Its Leaders and Designs*, 91–101. Hyde quoted Heber C. Kimball, who said, "We will get it perfect by-and-bye." Brigham Young made essentially the same observation in 1870 when he informed an audience in the tabernacle that "by and by, we shall get them perfect." See Van Wagoner, *Complete Discourses*, 2718 (April 24, 1870), and Brigham Young, "Discourse by President Brigham Young," *Journal of Discourses* 13:330. The Lincoln White House requested copies of Hyde's and Gunnison's books when the president considered Utah's petition for statehood and reviewed candidates for governor. See Mary Jane Woodger, "Abraham Lincoln and the Mormons," in Kenneth L. Alford, ed., *Civil War Saints* (Provo, Utah: Religious Studies Department, Brigham Young University, 2012), 73.
45. Rick Grunder has noted that W. W. Phelps was listed on the title page of *The Anti-Masonic Almanac, for the year of the Christian Era, 1831* as a selling agent and that the almanac was essentially an exposé of a ceremony that bore a number of striking similarities to the endowment. "Within some dozen years," Grunder concludes, "Phelps would go from dramatic public abhorrence of Masonic ritual to dramatic if reverential Masonic-colored worship." Grunder, *Mormon Parallels*, 104.
46. Nelson Winch Green, *Fifteen Years among the Mormons* (New York: H. Dayton, 1859).
47. Ibid., 42, 49, 50, 51.

'Institution.'" Although she acknowledged having "noticed by the public prints, since my arrival in the States, that this was the opinion entertained among those 'Gentiles' supposed to be best informed upon the subject," she vehemently denied any such connection. "This is but a mere blind," she wrote, "and the real object of these mystic forms is no way connected with, or borrowed from Masonry."[48]

TRUE MASONRY

In 1857 President James Buchanan (1791–1868), a Pennsylvania Freemason, sent Col. Albert Sidney Johnston (1802–1862) to Utah with almost one-third of the United States Army under his command, to replace Brigham Young as governor and to reestablish control over the territorial judiciary. Buchanan was motivated, at least in part, by letters that former federal officials who had served in Utah wrote to Washington, claiming that "every Mormon believes that the will of his High Priest is above all human laws, and he is bound by a most solemn oath to obey them in preference to all others."[49] This expedition provoked the first confrontation between Mormons and Freemasons in Utah.

When the Utah Expedition arrived in the Salt Lake Valley in 1858, Alfred Cumming was sworn in as governor and the army established its headquarters at Camp Floyd. From that remote location the military began publishing the *Valley Tan*, which became the territory's first non-Mormon newspaper. The following year twenty-three soldiers, who were Master Masons, petitioned the Grand Lodge of Missouri for permission to organize a lodge under dispensation.[50] On March 6 that grand lodge granted Rocky Mountain Lodge No. 205 a dispensation to organize and open a lodge and within two months the camp commander authorized Rocky Mountain Lodge to construct a building where the lodge would meet. During the first year 162 men joined the lodge that refused to allow Mormon Masons to either join or visit.[51]

48. Ibid., 49–50.
49. Letter from David Burr to Jeremiah Black, n.d. Copy located at the Nebraska Historical Society. See William P. MacKinnon, *At Sword's Point* (Norman, OK: The Arthur H. Clark Company, 2008).
50. For rules governing the organization of a lodge in an area where no grand lodge existed, see Mackey, *The Principles of Masonic Law*, 20–24.
51. Samuel H. Goodwin, *Freemasonry in Utah: Thirty Years of Mt. Moriah Lodge No. 2 F.& A.M., 1866–1896* (Salt Lake City, 1930), 6. The charter of Rocky Mountain Lodge No. 205 was granted on March 6, 1859, received in the spring of 1860, and returned to the Grand Lodge of Missouri in the spring of 1861. See Harold P. Fabian, *Centennial Observance of Freemasonry in Utah* (Salt Lake City, 1959).

During this same period the Mormon hierarchy publicly explained some of the parallels between the endowment and Masonic ritual that they had privately acknowledged for many years. In 1858 Heber C. Kimball insisted that "we have true Masonry" and that "Masonry of today is received from the apostasy which took place in the days of Solomon and David"[52] and emphasized the need for secrecy: "You have received your endowments," he said, "What is it for? To learn you to hold your tongues."[53] Brigham Young made similar statements from the pulpit. "I could preach all about the endowments in public and the world know Nothing about it," the Mormon prophet said. "I could preach all about Masonry & none but a Mason know anything about it." Young noted, after mentioning this link, that "the mane [*sic*] part of Masonry is to keep a secret."[54]

On August 19, 1860, Young told the First Presidency and Quorum of Twelve Apostles that he considered the presence of the United States Army in Utah Territory as a continuing example of the state-sponsored persecution that had begun in Missouri.[55] He warned the brethren that these soldiers and "other Masons" were sent to the territory for the express purpose of murdering him and other leaders of the church.[56] He reminded them that "Joseph & Hyrum were Master Masons and they were put to death by masons or through there [*sic*] instigation and he gave the sign of distress & he was shot by masons while in the act" and that "the people of the United States had sought our destruction and...have worked through the Masonic institution to perfect it."[57] He also expressed his "hope to live to see the day when I can have power to make them do right. They have the blood of the prophets upon their heads & they have god to meet it."[58]

During the same meeting George A. Smith, a Nauvoo Mason and one of Young's counselors, encouraged the church leadership to consider applying for charters to organize Mormon Masonic lodges. Lucius N. Scovil, who succeeded Hyrum Smith as master of Nauvoo Lodge, apparently made this recommendation to Smith, but the apostles ridiculed Scovil because he "thinks so much of masonry that he might join in with them." Smith told

52. *Manuscript History of Brigham Young*, LDS History Library, November 13, 1858.

53. *Journal of Discourses* 5:133 (August 2, 1857).

54. Kenney, *Wilford Woodruff's Journal* 5:418 (January 22, 1860). See also *Journal of Discourses* 4:287–89 (March 25, 1857).

55. Kenney, *Wilford Woodruff's Journal* 5:482–83 (August 19, 1860). See also Furniss, *The Mormon Conflict*, 76, 119–20, 127, 196.

56. Kenney, *Wilford Woodruff's Journal* 5:483.

57. Ibid., 5:482.

58. Kenney, *Wilford Woodruff's Journal*, 5:482–83 (August 19, 1860). Young undoubtedly relied on an unsigned *Times and Seasons* editorial which was published shortly after Smith's death. See "The Murder," *Times and Seasons* 5:13 (July 15, 1844), 584–86.

the group that he did not believe that Scovil would "mingle with our Enemies to the injury of this people," and he continued to recommend that the
church seek at least five charters in England so that it could form a grand
lodge which would "make us independent of all other Grand lodges in the
world."[59]

Young vetoed the idea because he recognized the volatility of the process and undoubtedly understood why his predecessor kept the activities of
Nauvoo Lodge separated from those of the church. He said that "we have
got to look to Lord God of Israel to sustain us & not to any institution
or kingdom or people upon the earth."[60] He concluded that if George A.
Smith's proposal was approved it would be extremely risky because the establishment of a grand lodge by the Mormons "would have a tendency to
bring down all hell upon us as far as they had the power."[61]

During the same year, Jules Remy (who visited Utah for one month in
1855) published *Voyage au pays des Mormons*, which was widely consulted
by travelers who visited Utah and by other writers who were investigating
Mormonism. Remy described Hyde as "a perjured and apostate priest," but
he quoted from his description of the endowment, including his claim that
Mormons "are made to swear to cherish an undying hatred for the government of the United States, because it neither avenged the death of Joseph
Smith nor repaired the outrages and losses suffered by the Saints during
their persecutions; to do all they can to destroy, overturn, and molest this
government; to refuse it all submission and obedience."

Remy (like Gunnison) was not surprised by parallels between the endowment and Masonic ritual and noted that "Mormons carry out freemasonry to a very great extent; that they make a long and serious study of it
under assiduous teachers, who repeat their lessons several times a week." He
concluded that "among the oaths and pass-words which have been added
to the ancient order, they retain for the first grades the words in all masonic
lodges." But, in spite of all these connections, the French traveler remained
convinced "that the masonic lodge of the Mormons is not at all more dangerous than the harmless institution of Freemasonry in other parts of the
world; and we much suspect they have been as greatly misrepresented as
ever the Templars were."[62]

59. Ibid.
60. Ibid., 5:482–83.
61. Ibid., 5:483.
62. Jules Remy, *Voyage au pays des Mormons*, 2 vols. (Paris: E. Dentu, 1860), 2:56–66. In 1861
Remy's book appeared in an English translation. Jules Remy and Julius Brenchley, *A Journey to Great-Salt-Lake City*, 2 vols. (London: W. Jeffs, 1861). For references in the English
edition to the endowment see ibid., 2:65–77. Jules Remy retained Theodule Dévéria (1831–
1871), an Egyptologist who worked in the Egyptian department of the Louvre, to translate
the three facsimiles which were published in "The Book of Abraham." Dévéria concluded

The following year Richard Francis Burton's (1821–1890) book entitled *The City of the Saints* was published describing his three-week visit to Utah Territory the previous year.[63] Burton, a British Mason and a world famous explorer, was very interested in the Endowment House and he made a sketch of that structure, which was published in the book. He recorded that Feramorz Little (1820–1887), who was Brigham Young's nephew, recounted his experiences among the Indians and "compared the Medicine-lodge to a masonic hall, and declared that the so-called Red men had signs and grips like ourselves." Little told him that "the angel of the Lord brought to Mr. Joseph Smith the lost key-words of several degrees, which caused him, when he appeared amongst the brotherhood of Illinois, to 'work right-a-head' of the highest, and to show them their ignorance of the greatest truths and benefits of masonry. The natural result was that their diploma was taken from them by the Grand Lodge, and they are not admitted to a Gentile gathering."[64]

Burton was convinced that the "Saints were at one time good Masons" but that "unhappily they wanted to be better" when they modified the ritual. He lamented that as "heathens without the gate," the Mormons "still cling to their heresy, and declare that other Masonry is, like the Christian faith, founded upon truth, and originally of the eternal Church, but fallen away and far gone in error."[65] He believed that "the ceremonies consist of

---

that the facsimiles were funeral illustrations from "The Book of the Dead," copied by artists who were retained by wealthy Egyptians centuries after Abraham's death to be placed in their sarcophagi to provide them with spells and instructions in order to pass through various gateways in the spirit world. Those who did not have this "Book of the Dead" lacked the proper instructions to navigate into the next world. Remy, *Voyage au pays des Mormons* 1:258, 2:439–467; Remy, *History of the Mormons*, 1:301; 2:536–46. French mission president Louis Bertrand criticized Dévéria's translation and asked, "Who will prove that the rules laid down by Champollion for deciphering the Egyptian glyphs are immutable?" See Louis Bertrand, *Mémoires d'un Mormon* (Paris: E. Detu, 1862), 217. For information concerning Dévéria, see Warren R. Dawson and Eric P. Uphill, *Who Was Who in Egyptology*, 2nd rev. ed. (London: The Egypt Exploration Society, 1972), 85–86. In 1873 T. B. H. Stenhouse discussed Dévéria's study in his potboiler *The Rocky Mountain Saints* and concluded that "many of the Mormons will be staggered by the translation of M. Dévéria, but many more will treat it with indifference," and noted that "the Mormon press has been silent on the opposition of science to inspiration." T. B. H. Stenhouse, *The Rocky Mountain Saints* (New York: D. Appleton & Company, 1873), 519.
63. Burton, *The City of the Saints*.
64. Ibid., 426. For a fuller description of Feramorz Little, see James A. Little, *Biographical Sketch of Feramorz Little* (Salt Lake City: Juvenile Instructor Office, 1890).
65. Burton, *The City of the Saints*, 426. Remy relied on John Hyde's description of the Mormon endowment, and the French author's description was eventually grafted into both the French and Italian editions of Burton's account. See Richard Burton, "Voyage à la Cité des Saints Capitale du Pays des Mormons," *Le Tour du Monde* 2 (1862): 353–400; Richard Burton, *Voyages du Capitaine Burton a la Mecque aux Grands Lacs d'Afrique et chez les Mormons...* (Paris, 1870); and Richard Burton, *I Mormoni e la Città dei Santi* (Milano: Fratelli

some show which in the middle ages, would be called a comedy or mystery,—possibly *Paradise Lost* and *Paradise Regained*—and connect it with the working of a Mason's Lodge" and that Gentiles claimed "the ceremony occupies eleven or twelve hours."[66]

Nevertheless, Burton concluded that Mary Ettie V. Smith's, John Hyde's, and Jules Remy's descriptions of the endowment were suspect, and that "such orgies as they describe could not co-exist with the respectability which is the law of the land." He observed that "every mason knows" that "'the red-hot poker' and other ideas concerning masonic institutions have prevailed when juster disclosures have been rejected. Similarly in Mormonic mystery, it is highly probable that, in consequence of the conscientious reserve of the people upon a subject which it would indelicate to broach, the veriest fancies have taken the deepest root."[67]

During his visit to Utah, Burton published John Taylor's written recollections of the murders of Joseph and Hyrum Smith. Taylor suggested that Willard Richards made a Masonic distress call but he did not mention that either of the Smith brothers did.[68] Thus, it is not surprising that Brigham Young again reminded an audience in the tabernacle shortly after Burton's departure that "Joseph & Hyrum were...put to death by masons or through there [*sic*] instigation and he gave the sign of distress & he was shot by masons while in the act."

Treves, 1875). The word "endowment," in these French and Italian editions, was mistranslated as "admission to the sect," which suggested that the endowment was similar to baptism or confirmation. This mistranslation was probably based on Remy's reference to the endowment as "a species of ordination or initiation for both sexes." Remy, *Voyage au Pays des Mormons* 2:65. The French and Italian editions of Burton's book also contained an engraving, with the caption "The Baptism of Mormons," based on a plate in John C. Bennett's *History of the Saints* which was captioned "Order Lodge." The same engraving was published in the 1879 Italian translation of Baron von Hubner's travel account with the same misleading caption. Alexander Graff von Hubner, *Passeggiata intorno al Mondo* (Milano: Fratelli Treves, 1879), 108–9. The engraving in Bennett's book was similar to illustrations that were published in anti-Masonic almanacs during the 1820s and 1830s which depicted a Mason "receiving his obligation; or the true form of initiating a member to the secret arts and mysteries of Freemasonry." See, e.g., *The New England Anti-Masonic Almanac for...1831*, 1.

66. Burton, *The City of the Saints*, 426, 271. Jan Snoek has suggested similar parallels between Milton's *Paradise Lost* (1667) and the Harodim ritual and argues that French Masons utilized these sources when they created adoptive rituals. Snoek, *Initiating Women in Freemasonry*, 114–20.

67. Burton, *The City of the Saints*, 271. Another historian has quoted a Masonic text written in Russia concerning "Theological Moral Institution[,] A Discussion Concerning Adam's Fall," which he claims was inspired by Milton's *Paradise Lost*. Valentin Boss, *Milton and the Rise of Russian Satanism* (Toronto: University of Toronto Press, 1991), 48–49.

68. Burton, *The City of the Saints* (1861), 625–67; Burton, *The City of the Saints* (1862), 517–47.

The following year Young again emphasized that "Freemasons had sanctioned the Killing of Joseph."[69] After Young made these remarks the Mormon position that Smith used the Masonic distress call to seek the assistance of Freemasons in Carthage Jail just prior to his death was fully institutionalized and has remained (with some exceptions) as the commonly held view to the present time.[70]

69. Van Wagoner, *Complete Discourses* 3:1744 (February 2, 1861).

70. See Whitney, *Life of Heber C. Kimball*, 26–27 ("Joseph, leaping the fatal window, gave the masonic signal of distress. The answer was the roar of his murderers' muskets and the deadly balls that pierced his heart."); "Women's Mass Meeting," *Women's Exponent* 7:13 (December 1, 1878), 98, republished in *Women's Exponent* 10:16 (January 15, 1882), 123, quoted in Jenson, *Latter-day Saint Biographical Encyclopedia*, 1:698 (Zina Diantha Young spoke at a mass meeting called to respond to the "Anti-Polygamy Crusade" and was quoted as follows: "I am a daughter of a master mason! I am the widow of a master mason, who, when leaping from the window of Carthage jail pierced with bullets, made the Masonic sign of distress; but…those signs were not heeded, except by the God of Heaven…. I wish my voice could be heard by the whole brotherhood of masons throughout our proud land. That institution I honor"); and John D. Lee, *Mormonism Unveiled; or the Life and Confessions of the late Mormon Bishop* (St. Louis: N. D. Thompson & Co., 1880), 153. More recently, Richard Bushman concluded that Smith used the Masonic distress call shortly before his death in the Carthage jail. See p. 550. While at least one Mormon educator agrees with Bushman on this issue (Leonard, *Nauvoo*, 397), others have challenged that conclusion. Richard Holzapfel, a history professor at Brigham Young University, argues that the popular interpretation that Smith used the Masonic distress call is "stale, yet sensational" and believes that the gesture instead reminds "one of the Jewish attitude of prayer and the cry of the righteous petitioner in the book of Psalms." Richard Neitzel Holzapfel, "Book Review," *Utah Historical Quarterly* 74:1 (Winter 2006): 86. Similarly, LDS educator Gilbert Scharffs has concluded that "when the Prophet said, just before being assassinated 'O Lord my God,' he was addressing the Lord, awaiting entry into the eternal realm." Gilbert W. Scharffs, *Mormons & Masons* (Orem, UT: Millennial Press, Inc., 2007), 55–60.

Utah Freemasonry

WHEN THE U.S. ARMY left Camp Floyd in 1861 for engagement in the Civil War, the Rocky Mountain Lodge returned its charter to the Grand Lodge of Missouri. Although some Mormon Masons, despite their negative experiences in Illinois, continued to outwardly support the institution of Freemasonry, they did not petition for their own charter.[1] On July 7, 1861, Heber C. Kimball repeated Brigham Young's earlier suggestion that "they gave us a charter for a Masonic Lodge, and then went to work and killed some of the men to whom the charter was given."[2] But Kimball maintained, "I know that I have been true to my country, to my Masonic brethren, and also to my brethren in this Church."[3] Even John Taylor, who was in Carthage Jail when Joseph Smith was murdered, believed that "Freemasonry is one of the strongest binding contracts that exist between man and man, yet Freemasons are mixed up in those different armies, trying to kill each other, and so they have contended against each other for generations past."[4]

Some Mormon Masons were pleased with Young's decision to forego the organization of a lodge system in Utah. Louis Bertrand, a French convert who immigrated to Utah, wrote, "There is not even the shadow of a Masonic Lodge in Utah. As a member of both French and Scottish Freemasonry, it is our opinion that that institution has served its purpose and one would hardly dream of founding a lodge of any rite in Utah."[5]

But the absence of federal troops, and Masonic lodges, in the territory was short-lived. In 1862 Col. Patrick Connor led a group of California Volunteers to Utah and established Camp Douglas in Salt Lake City. This was

1. Goodwin, *Freemasonry in Utah*, 6.
2. Heber C. Kimball, "Early Persecutions—Certain Retribution," *Journal of Discourses* 9:180 (July 7, 1861).
3. Ibid.,9:182.
4. John Taylor, *Journal of Discourses* 10:125–26 (March 1, 1863).
5. L. A. Bertrand, *Memoires d'un Mormon* (Paris: E. Dentu, 1862), 171–72. Hogan mistranslated this quotation from Bertrand as, "It is our opinion that the Endowment is becoming obsolete and one would hardly dream of founding a lodge of any rite in Utah." See Mervin Hogan, "Time and Change," in *1956 Proceedings of the Grand Lodge of Utah*, p. 80.

the third time in eight years that soldiers entered the Salt Lake Valley, and this time they stayed. They were soon followed by non-Mormon merchants, miners, and railroad workers. Connor published the *Union Vedette*, which, like the *Valley Tan*, provided a forum for the non-Mormon population.[6] In 1865 Brigham Young organized a boycott of merchants whom he considered hostile to the Latter-day Saints, and two years later he organized the School of the Prophets as an economic planning tool.[7]

A MASONIC LODGE

When Young created Zion's Cooperative Mercantile Institution (ZCMI) to discourage trade with non-Mormon merchants, he required Mormon shopkeepers to place a sign on their stores that included the slogan "Holiness to the Lord" and a Masonic all-seeing eye. These signs utilizing Masonic symbols to boycott merchants (some of whom were Masons) were criticized by British Mason Chalmers I. Paton who wrote in a London Masonic weekly: "Polygamy is a sin of gross turpitude, which destroys marriage and degrades women. Let the Freemasons on the other side of the Atlantic rise *en masse* and crush this attempt at an unwarranted interference with their symbols, and put in force the already enacted condemnation of a contemptible race."[8]

In November 1865 some of the same merchants whom the Mormons boycotted placed a notice in the *Union Vedette* inviting fellow Masons to meet at the Odd Fellows Hall to organize a Masonic lodge.[9] Several Mormons, perhaps with Young's approval, attended the meeting, but the non-Mormon Masons refused to recognize them as regular Masons when they organized Mount Moriah Lodge.[10] Thereafter the lodge petitioned the Grand Lodge of Nevada for a charter and a dispensation was granted.[11] The

6. Brigham D. Madsen, *Glory Hunter: A Biography of Patrick Edward Connor* (Salt Lake City: University of Utah Press, 1990), 89–120.

7. See Leonard J. Arrington, *Great Basin Kingdom: An Economic History of the Church of Jesus Christ of Latter-day Saints* (Cambridge: Harvard University Press, 1958), 245–51.

8. Chalmers I. Paton, "The Mormons and Masonic Symbols," *The Freemason* (London) 3 (1871): 427.

9. See S. H. Goodwin, *Freemasonry in Utah: Thirty Years of Mt. Moriah Lodge No. 2, F. & A. M. 1866–1896* (Salt Lake City, 1930), 9; Christopher Diehl, "History of Freemasonry in Utah," in Edward W. Tullidge, *The History of Salt Lake City and Its Founders* (Salt Lake City, 1886), Appendix, 15–18; Christopher Diehl, "The Masonic Codes of the Grand Lodge of Utah: A Historical Sketch," in *The Masonic Code of the Most Worshipful Grand Lodge of Free and Accepted Masons* (Davenport, IA: Egbert, Fidlar & Chambers, 1898).

10. See correspondence from Robert Ramsay which appeared in "Freemasonry Among the Mormons," *The Craftsman* 3 (1869): 155–56, and republished in "Freemasonry Among the Mormons," *The Masonic Review* 36 (1872): 280–84. See also "The Mormon Lodge," *The Freemason's Monthly Magazine* 29 (1870): 249–50.

11. See Goodwin, *Freemasonry in Utah*.

dispensation was conditioned upon a pledge that it would not admit Mormons because they were polygamists: "In view of the facts that the laws of the land have declared polygamy a crime, and that the Mormons of Utah Territory have openly and defiantly declared their intention to resist the enforcement of the law whenever the government shall make the attempt, and that polygamy is a moral and social sore which it is the duty of Masonry to discountenance."[12]

The grand lodge's instructions were presumably premised on Freemasonry's "Ancient Landmarks," which required that candidates have strict morals, come well recommended and approved, "obey the moral law," be "a peaceable subject to the civil powers," and not discuss politics or religion in the lodge.[13] The "civil power" prohibited polygamy in 1862 and gentile observers assumed that all Mormons, whether polygamists or not, were in agreement with the church's defiance of this law.[14]

It is surprising that Mount Moriah Lodge objected to this condition even though it is doubtful it planned to admit any Mormons or polygamists. But the lodge stubbornly maintained that the grand lodge could not dictate whom it could admit as members or as visitors. Initially, Mount Moriah Lodge attempted to convince the grand lodge to modify the conditions of the charter by agreeing to accept the charter "as far as polygamists were concerned, but asking [the grand master] to allow [the Utah lodge] our one charity to Masons who neither adhere nor practice it."[15] The grand lodge rejected this request and refused to grant a permanent charter, but it did renew Mount Moriah's dispensation for one additional year.

Afterward, the lodge met and discussed its dilemma: "We accepted it [the renewed dispensation] and by direction of the Lodge, agreed, under our conviction of right and justice, that we could not Masonically exclude a visitor on religious reasons, but would exclude polygamists on general reasons."[16] Despite this explanation the Grand Lodge of Nevada refused to budge and did not grant Mount Moriah Lodge a charter because it

12. *1867 Proceedings of the Grand Lodge of Nevada*, p. 288.
13. See Fred L. Pick and G. Norman Knight, *The Freemasons Pocket Reference Book*, rev. ed. (London: Frederick Mullert, Ltd., 1983), 61–62, 189–90. See also *The Masonic Code*, 38; Knoop and Jones, *The Genesis of Freemasonry*, 176–85; *Constitutions of the Ancient Fraternity of Free and Accepted Masons, under the United Grand Lodge of England* (London: Harrison and Sons, 1884).
14. The practice of polygamy would not necessarily disqualify Mormons from becoming Freemasons in the absence of legal prohibition. From as early as 1723 Muslims, who are allowed by their religion to practice polygamy, were theoretically not precluded from joining Freemasonry. Haffner, *Workman Unashamed*, 124. See also Coil, *Coil's Masonic Encyclopedia*, 518–19.
15. Goodwin, *Freemasonry in Utah: Thirty Years*, 14.
16. Ibid., 15.

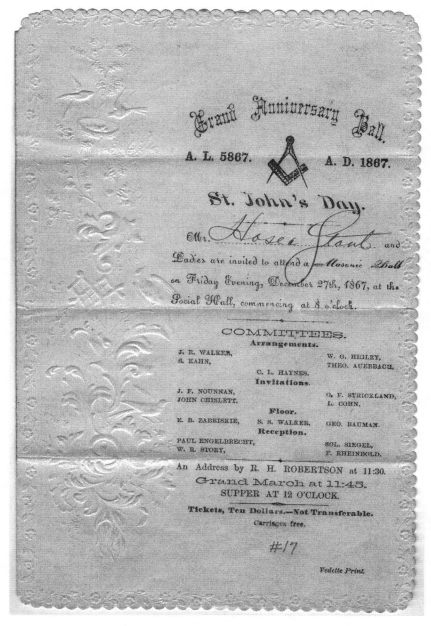

Grand Anniversary Ball.

A. L. 5867.   A. D. 1867.

St. John's Day.

Mr. *Hosea Stout* and Ladies are invited to attend a Masonic Ball on Friday Evening, December 27th, 1867, at the Social Hall, commencing at 8 o'clock.

COMMITTEES.

Arrangements.

J. R. WALKER,   W. G. HIGLEY,
S. KAHN,   THEO. AUERBACH.
              C. L. HAYNES.

Invitations.

J. F. NOUNNAN,   O. F. STRICKLAND,
JOHN CHISLETT.   L. COHN.

Floor.

E. B. ZABRISKIE,   S. S. WALKER,   GEO. BAUMAN.

Reception.

PAUL ENGELBRECHT,   SOL. SIEGEL,
W. R. STORY,   F. RHEINBOLD.

An Address by R. H. ROBERTSON at 11:30.

Grand March at 11:45.

SUPPER AT 12 O'CLOCK.

Tickets, Ten Dollars.—Not Transferable.

Carriages free.

#17

Vedette Print.

Utah Masonic invitation sent to Hosea Stout.
Courtesy Utah State Historical Society.

continued to refuse to accept the restriction. Lacking a charter the lodge was disbanded.

While this dispute was playing out, other Masons (soldiers from Camp Douglas and non-Mormon settlers) organized Wasatch Lodge and obtained a dispensation from the Grand Lodge of Montana.[17] The dispensation did not include any written requirement that the lodge must exclude all Mormons, polygamist or not, as members or visitors, but the grand lodge did require the lodge to change its original name (King Solomon Lodge) to Wasatch Lodge, presumably because Solomon was a polygamist.

Although Wasatch Lodge refused to grant Mormons any Masonic privileges, despite its apparent freedom to do so under its dispensation, it did invite Hosea Stout (a Nauvoo Mason who was the Salt Lake City Attorney) and perhaps other Mormon Masons to a Masonic Ball held at the social hall to celebrate St. John's Day.[18] In 1868 Mount Moriah Lodge received a dispensation from the Grand Lodge of Kansas (ending its dispute with the Grand Lodge of Montana).

WAS HE A POLYGAMIST?

Although some Masons undoubtedly were aware that the Grand Lodge of Illinois had denied charters to the Mormon lodges, and some may have even heard rumors that George A. Smith had requested permission to establish a grand lodge in Utah, the primary reason that Masons gave for excluding Mormon petitioners and visitors was the practice of polygamy.[19] Brigham Young felt so strongly about this snub that he attacked Utah Masonry's rationale for excluding Mormons and reconfirmed his belief that King Solomon had organized the Craft.

Young complained that Mormons "cannot be admitted into their social societies, into their places of gathering at certain times and on certain occasions, because they are afraid of polygamy."[20] He noted, with a tinge of sarcasm, that "they have refused our brethren membership in their lodge, because they were polygamists. Who was the founder of Freemasonry? They can go back as far as Solomon, and there they stop. There is the king who established this high and holy order. Now was he a polygamist, or was he not?"

17. See, generally, Samuel H. Goodwin, *Freemasonry in Utah: The Early Days of Wasatch Lodge No. 1* (Salt Lake City, 1925).

18. The invitation is located in the archives of the Utah State Historical Society. (See figure 26.)

19. Kenney, *Wilford Woodruff's Journal* 5:482–84 (August 19, 1869).

20. Brigham Young, "Discourse by Brigham Young," *Journal of Discourses* 11:327–28 (February 10, 1867); see also *Deseret News* 16:114.

The Mormon prophet noted that if Solomon "did believe in monogamy he did not practice it a great deal for he had seven hundred wives, and that is more than I have; and he had three hundred concubines, of which I have none that I know of." He then told the gathering that if polygamy was "one of the 'relics of barbarism,'" it was also "one of relics of Adam, of Enoch, of Noah, of Abraham, of Isaac, of Jacob, of Moses, David, Solomon, the Prophets, of Jesus, and his Apostles."[21]

Although some Masonic observers questioned the breadth of the restrictions initially imposed by the Grand Lodge of Nevada, others were not sympathetic with Young or his fellow Masons who had been initiated in Nauvoo. Robert Ramsay of Toronto, Canada, wrote that the "Grand Lodge of Nevada erred... in giving a Dispensation, *with special edict attached*" and "in refusing to grant a *Charter* to a Lodge of Masons that, in every particularity, acted up to and abided by the principles of the Fraternity."[22] But the *Mystic Star*, a Masonic publication, noted that "Mormons are regular descendants of the expelled Mormons of Nauvoo" and "it is proper and right to refuse them as visitors."[23]

"For the honor and safety of Masonry," the editorial continued, "we should never receive a petition from any party or sect who array themselves against the common laws of the land; or who repudiate the wholesome relations of domestic life. We would, as a Mason, refuse to recommend the petition of a Mormon, or a member of any sect which blockades the way of its members to becoming Masons, unless the individual would first renounce publicly all affiliation with such a sect or party."[24]

Since Utah Masonry was an exclusive club that denied membership to all Mormons, it is not surprising that members of the Craft were actively involved in many of the legal battles to force the Mormons to eradicate polygamy while at the same time attempting to expand their political and economic base in the territory.[25] Many non-Mormon merchants, which included members of the Craft, had struggled to survive the Mormon boycott and they were quite anxious to reduce their vulnerability.[26]

Robert N. Baskin (1837–1916), a lawyer and member of Mount Moriah Lodge, was one of those who fostered Masonic participation in these

21. *Journal of Discourses* 11:328.
22. See "The Mormon Lodge," *The Freemason's Monthly Magazine* 29 (1870): 249–50.
23. Editorial, "The Mormons," *The Mystic Star* 11:2 (August 1869): 76–77.
24. Ibid., 77. See also "The Mormon Lodge," *The Freemason's Monthly Magazine* 29 (1870): 249–50.
25. Joseph M. Orr, Joseph R. Walker, and Samuel Kahn helped organize the Liberal Party in the Masonic Hall and supported the transition of the *Salt Lake Tribune* from a reform newspaper to an anti-Mormon organ. See Goodwin, *Freemasonry in Utah: The Early Days*, 12.
26. See Jonathan Bliss, *Merchants and Miners in Utah: The Walker Brothers and Their Bank* (Salt Lake City: Western Epics, 1983), 229–78.

battles.[27] In 1867 Baskin became a law partner with Stephen DeWolfe, who was a Mason and the third editor of the *Valley Tan*, the weekly non-Mormon newspaper that was published at Camp Floyd. Baskin and his Masonic brethren were instrumental in the organization of the Liberal Party, which initially met at Masonic Hall and was intended as a counterforce to Mormon political influence. Eventually, however, Utah Masons insisted that only Craft-related functions could be held in its facilities.[28]

Baskin and fellow Mason Reuben Howard Robinson drafted the Cullom Bill, which provided that the federal courts (where justices were appointed by the president of the United States) had exclusive jurisdiction for the prosecution of plural marriages and required that juries be selected by the federal marshal and United States attorneys. Baskin complained that some non-Mormons "became frightened at the threats made by the leading Mormons in a meeting convened by Brigham, and having met in the Masonic hall in Salt Lake City, adopted resolutions protesting against the passage of that bill and forwarded the same to the Mormon delegate, to be used by him to defeat it." Although the Cullom Bill was eventually defeated (it only passed in the House of Representatives and not in the Senate), most of its provisions eventually became law.[29]

DIVINE MASONRY

By the 1870s American Masonry had experienced a miraculous recovery in both membership and prestige. The Craft was once again viewed as an acceptable and even a mainstream institution in part because it had "moderated [its] claims to a special relationship with Christianity, emphasizing instead a vague ethical symbolism." Steven Bullock has noted that this "loosening of the fraternity's tight embrace of Christianity also calmed religious anxieties." During this transition Albert Pike was the guiding force in modifying the Scottish Rite rituals that had previously "promised direct contact with historical and sacred truth" but under the new rituals again "emphasized the fraternity's symbolic aspect."[30]

27. In 1880 Baskin became worshipful master of Mount Moriah Lodge and in 1881 became the grand orator of the grand lodge.
28. See Samuel H. Goodwin, *Freemasonry in Utah: The First Decade of Argenta Lodge, No. 3, and Its First Masters* (Salt Lake City: Committee on Masonic Education and Instruction, Grand Lodge of Utah, 1925), 16–17; Goodwin, *Freemasonry in Utah: Thirty Years*, 37.
29. R. N. Baskin, *Reminiscences of Early Utah* (Salt Lake City, 1914), 56.
30. Bullock, *Revolutionary Brotherhood*, 316–17. Pike, who was mentored by Albert G. Mackey, drafted modifications to the Scottish Rite rituals, which he self-published and which formed the foundation for the revised rituals that have since been utilized. See Arturo de Hoyos, *The Scottish Rite Manual Monitor and Guide*, 2nd ed. (Washington, D.C.:

During this transition Utah Masons continued to enforce their policy prohibiting Mormons from entering their temples either as new initiates or as guests arising from their status as Nauvoo Masons. In 1870 discussions concerning the drafting of an antipolygamy bill were held in the Masonic temple and both the Liberal Party and the Godbeites used the hall for organizational meetings.[31] During that decade some European Masons and Mormon backsliders charged that the Mormon temple ceremony was a form of spurious Freemasonry and that Mormon "rites were taken from Masonry."[32]

In 1871 the Grand Lodge of Colorado granted a charter to Argenta Lodge, which Utah Masons acknowledged was organized to "frustrate the notions of some men, high in power [presumably Mormons] to obtain Dispensations and Charters for Masonic Lodges in Utah, from foreign countries."[33] They wrote that "a young and immature Lodge was in 1871 forcibly torn from the womb as it were of two other Lodges, in order to secure a sufficient number to establish a Grand Lodge, for the avowed purposes of preventing certain persons who were living in open violation of the laws of the land from procuring a Charter to establish a Lodge."[34]

In January 1872 representatives from the three lodges that had been established in Utah met and organized the Grand Lodge of Utah. The grand lodge, which had 124 master masons, adopted a constitution and bylaws that recognized the ancient landmarks of Freemasonry.[35] This development caused a British Mason, who was critical of the American system in which each state could create its own grand lodge, noted that the Grand Lodge of Utah is "absurdly small for such a title; and certainly the rapid increase of late in the number of Grand Lodges is to be deplored."[36] This jurisdictional independence eventually resulted in tensions within American Masonry

---

The Supreme Council, 33°, Southern Jurisdiction, 2009), 23–24; Bullock, *Revolutionary Brotherhood*, 316–19.

31. *Tullidge's Quarterly Magazine* 3 (October 1883): 51, 59.

32. See Robert Wentworth Little, "Mormonism," *The Rosicrucian: A Quarterly Record of the Society's Activities* 14 (Oct. 1871): 168–70; Kenneth R. H. MacKenzie, ed., *The Royal Masonic Cyclopaedia* (London: John Hogg, 1872), 497–98; and A. Woodford Kenning, *Kenning's Masonic Cyclopaedia* (London: Geo. Kenning, 1878), 626. See also Enrico Besana, "Note di viaggio di un Italiano: Le Grandi Praterie Americane e i Mormoni," *Giornale Popolare di Viaggi* 2 (1871): 63; Enrico Besana, "I Mormoni nel 1868," *La Perseveranza*, February 13, 1869, 1.

33. See Samuel H. Goodwin, *Freemasonry in Utah: The First Decade of Argenta Lodge No. 3, and Its First Master* (Salt Lake City, 1925), 8–9.

34. "Report of Committee on Jurisprudence," *1899 Proceedings*, p. 33.

35. *1872 Proceedings of the Masonic Convention and Organization of the Grand Lodge* (Salt Lake City: Tribune Printing and Publishing Co., 1872), 21.

36. A. Woodford, *Kenning's Masonic Cyclopaedia* (London: Geo. Kenning, 1878), 626.

since the new grand lodge continued to follow its unwritten rule prohibiting Mormons from being initiated as Masons and preventing Mormons,
who were already Masons, from visiting Utah lodges.

During the organization of the grand lodge, Worshipful Grand Lecturer Reuben H. Robertson observed that "they guarded well the 'inner
door' and the 'magic power of the mystic brotherhood' increased in this
polygamic community, while none who held his country's authority in defiance or trod its laws beneath their feet entered the portals of our lodges."[37]
The following year Grand Master Obed F. Stickland observed that Utah
Freemasonry "with its secrets and penalties" constituted "a safe depository
where the seeds of progressive human events might find shelter, until the
ground was fitted for the sower to go forth and sow broadcast the main
facts upon which the foundation of all civilized nations now rest; the existence of one God and the universal brotherhood of man." His successor,
Reuben H. Robertson, stated that Freemasonry in Utah "will do much to
correct the wrongs now existing, and to redeem our fair Territory from the
curse of polygamy and its concomitant evils."[38] Finally, Grand Master Louis
Cohn predicted in 1874 that "throughout this extensive Territory, Masonic
Altars will spring into being and supplant the Temples of superstition, and
the humanizing influences of Freemasonry will shine forth as the very counterpart of bigoted Priestcraft."[39]

While Utah Masons were organizing lodges and institutionalizing their
policy that prohibited Mormons from joining their ranks, both Mormons
and non-Mormons continued to acknowledge the connection between
Masonry and Mormonism. John H. Beadle, who published the *Salt Lake
Reporter*, wrote an endowment exposé that claimed (perhaps plagiarizing
Burton) that the endowment was "paraphrased from the Scriptures and
Milton's *Paradise Lost*," "modeled upon the *Mysteries* or *Holy Dramas* of the
Middle Ages," and "extracted from 'Morgan's Free-masonry Exposé.'"[40] But
he also observed that even though he was uncertain "how much of Masonry
proper has survived in the Endowment...the Mormons are pleased to have
the outside world connect the two, and convey the impression that this is
'Celestial Masonry.'"[41]

37. *1872 Proceedings*, 15.
38. See *Proceedings of the First Annual Communication of the Most Worshipful Grand Lodge*
(Salt Lake City: Utah Evening Mining Journal, 1872), 5–6; and *Proceedings of the Utah
Grand Lodge, 1873*, 11.
39. *Proceedings of the Utah Grand Lodge, 1874*, 6.
40. J. H. Beadle, *Life in Utah; or the Mysteries and Crimes of Mormonism* (Philadelphia:
National Publishing, 1870); J. Cecil Alter, *Early Utah Journalism* (Salt Lake City: Utah
Historical Society, 1938), 333.
41. Beadle, *Life in Utah*, 498–99. Beadle's book was published in thirteen separate editions
from 1870 to 1904, was translated into German and Russian, and was liberally quoted

Beadle's description of the endowment's oath of vengeance was an extreme elaboration of prior accounts written by William Smith and John Hyde. He claimed that "initiates take a solemn oath, to avenge his [Joseph Smith's] death; that they will bear eternal hostility to the Government of the United States for the murder of the Prophet; that they renounce all allegiance that they may have held to the Government, and hold themselves absolved from all oaths of fealty, past or future; that they will do all in their power towards the overthrow of that Government, and in event of failure teach their children to pursue that purpose after them."[42]

Thomas Brown Holmes Stenhouse (1825–1882), who was a confidante of Brigham Young and other church leaders before he left the fold, recalled that "Mormon leaders have always asserted that Free-Masonry was a bastard and degenerate representation of the order of the true priesthood." "No other statement than that of the leaders" is necessary, Stenhouse concluded, "to form an estimate of the signs, grips, passwords, rites, and ceremonies of the Endowment House."[43] Similarly Elias Lacy Thomas Harrison (1830–1900), who, like Stenhouse, had aligned himself with the Godbeite schism that was laced with spiritism, noted that charges of plagiarism were oversimplifications. Although he acknowledged that Mormon leaders taught "that there is a sort of divine Masonry among the angels who hold the Priesthood," he criticized the doctrine of detecting spirits of unauthorized beings "by certain grips and secret words," and ridiculed the notion that "such a puny, imperfect thing as a species of Masonry [could be used] by which to keep the evil and pure apart."[44]

GOOD MASONS WOULD REPUDIATE IT

Despite these noted parallels, some prominent women who left Mormonism (like Mary Ettie V. Smith) claimed that the connections between Masonry and Mormonism were bogus, perhaps because they believed it provided the Mormon ritual with greater credibility than it deserved.[45] In

---

during the next two decades by Gentiles and various lapsed Mormons including a notorious English apostate, William Jarman. William Jarman, *U.S.A. Uncle Sam's Abscess or Hell Upon Earth* (Exeter, England: H. Ledoc's Steam Printing Works, 1884), 67–98.

42. Beadle, *Life in Utah*, 497.

43. Stenhouse, *The Rocky Mountain Saints*, 698. But Stenhouse also noted, "In 'The Mormon's Own Book,' by T. W. P. Taylder, 139–47, a singular resemblance is pointed out between the ceremonies in the Eleusinia—a festival among the Cretans—and the mysteries of the Mormon Endowment, as set forth by Van Dusen."

44. *Salt Lake Tribune*, October 8, 1870, 5; reprinted from *Salt Lake Tribune*, September 3, 1870, 4.

45. See Gilbert, "'The Monstrous Regiment,'" 163–64, for an interesting discussion concerning female attitudes toward Freemasonry after the Craft emerged from the anti-Masonic period.

1872 Fanny Stenhouse (1829–1904) wrote *A Lady's Life among the Mormons* in which she admitted, "In justice to the Mormons, I feel bound to state that the accounts which I have frequently read, professing to give a description of the 'Endowments' given in Salt Lake City, are almost altogether exaggerated.... I myself saw nothing indelicate; though I had been led to believe that improper things did take place there, and I was determined not to submit to any thing of the kind."[46]

But two years later she claimed, in her second book, "*Tell it All*," that rumors concerning the Endowment House—namely, that those revealing the secrets of the endowment may have been killed—were not entirely groundless, that she had felt "ashamed and disgusted" by the endowment from the day she received it, and that she felt justified in revealing it because she did not take the vow of secrecy when called upon to do so in the Endowment House.[47] She concluded that although "it has always been commonly reported, and to a great extent believed, that the mysteries of the Endowment House were only a sort of initiation—burlesque, it might be—of the rites of Masonry; but I need hardly say that this statement when examined by the light of facts, is altogether ungrounded and absurd."[48]

Her description of the oath of vengeance in her expanded volume is much less dramatic than Beadle's and she only acknowledged that "we swore that by every means in our power we would seek to avenge the death of Joseph Smith, the Prophet, upon the Gentiles who had caused his murder, and that we would teach our children to do so."[49]

Ann Eliza Webb Young (1844–1925), Brigham Young's estranged wife, weighed in on the topic of Freemasonry in her *Wife No. 19*, confirming that her ex-husband referred to the temple ceremony as "celestial Masonry." But she also mimicked Mary Ettie V. Smith and Fanny Stenhouse when she concluded that it was doubtful if any Masonic connection actually existed. "It is claimed that the mysterious rites were taken from Masonry, and that the Endowments are a direct outgrowth of the secret society," she wrote, but added, "I am very sure all good Masons would repudiate it and its teachings."[50]

46. Mrs. T. B. H. Stenhouse, *Exposé of Polygamy in Utah: A Lady's Life Among the Mormons* (New York: American News, 1872), 95. Fanny's book was published under various titles in at least seventeen printings from 1872 to 1890 and was one of the most popular accounts written by an ex-Mormon during the nineteenth century.
47. Mrs. T. B. H. [Fanny] Stenhouse, *"Tell it All": The Story of a Life's Experience in Mormonism* (Hartford, CT: A. D. Worthington & Co., 1874), 354–55, 356, and 367–68.
48. Stenhouse, *"Tell it All,"* 354.
49. Ibid., 365.
50. Ann Eliza [Webb] Young, *Wife No. 19* (Hartford, CT: Dustin, Gilman & Co., 1875), 371. Young's book was published in at least five variant printings between 1875 and 1908. When

SOLOMON BUILT A TEMPLE FOR GIVING ENDOWMENTS

The most dramatic event demonstrating that the Mormon hierarchy continued to believe there were connections between the Craft and their restored church occurred on January 1, 1877, when Brigham Young attended the dedication of the lower portion of the St. George Temple. The interior of Utah's first temple had canvas partitions that were constructed in the basement to create spaces for the various stages of the endowment. As such, the temple was more reminiscent of the Nauvoo Temple (where the endowment took place in the attic) rather than the Endowment House in which separate and permanent rooms had been constructed that were progressively higher in elevation.[51]

Young had suggested prior to the completion of the temple that when the structure was dedicated, the endowment might be bifurcated into two rituals: one for the Aaronic Priesthood and another for the Melchisedek Priesthood. In 1864 he suggested the practical reason for making such a change: "We can say to a company of brethren you can go and receive the ordinances pertaining to the Aaronic order of Priesthood, and then you can go into the world and preach the Gospel, or do something that will prove whether you will honor that Priesthood before you receive more." But by the time the St. George Temple was dedicated, Young had apparently changed his mind and this modification was never instituted.[52]

Young told the congregation, perhaps alluding to Royal Arch tradition, that Enoch may have "had temples and officiated therein, but we have no account of it," and that "we know that he raised up a people so pure and holy that they were not permitted to remain with the wicked inhabitants of the earth, but were taken to another place." Young alluded to parallels between Solomon's Temple (where he believed the endowment was introduced) and Mormon temples as he had when he dedicated the cornerstone of the Salt Lake Temple twenty-five years earlier. His understanding concerning this

---

Young's book was first published she gave lectures in Cheyenne, Denver, and Washington, D.C. Her manager, J. B. Pond, eventually acted as literary agent for such luminaries as Mark Twain and Arthur Conan Doyle. Pond claimed that Young's lectures were responsible in part for the passage of the Poland Bill of 1874 which increased the federal government's ability to enforce the Anti-Bigamy Act of 1862. J. B. Pond, *Eccentricities of Genius* (New York: G. W. Dillingham Co., 1900), xxi–xxii. But portions of Young's account are so similar to Fanny Stenhouse's experiences that there is reason to suspect that either she, or her publisher, plagiarized portions of Fanny's exposé. Her first-person description of the endowment, which she received when she was a teenager, including the claim that people may have been killed for revealing portions of it, is reminiscent of Stenhouse. She also copied Burton's comparison of the endowment to Milton's *Paradise Lost*. Young, *Wife No. 19*, 357.

51. Brown, "Temple Pro Tempore," 56–57.

52. *Journal of Discourses* 10:308–9 (June 11, 1864).

connection was based on the Old Testament filtered through a Masonic lens. The Mormon prophet proudly told church members that they "were enjoying a privilege that we have no knowledge of any other people enjoying since the days of Adam, that is, to have temple completed, wherein all the ordinances of the house of God can be bestowed on his people."[53] The ordinances that were given in Nauvoo and in the Endowment House (the endowment, the second endowment, marriage sealings, and baptisms for the dead) would be performed in this temple.

Nevertheless, Young taught that the full endowment was not performed in Solomon's Temple, the Kirtland Temple, or the Nauvoo Temple. Young believed that the endowment had not been performed many times, if at all, in Solomon's Temple because the keyword was lost when Hiram Abiff was murdered. He explained that "Solomon built a Temple for the purpose of giving endowments, but from what we can learn from the history of that time they gave very few if any endowments." He relied on the Masonic legend that "one of the high priests [Hiram Abiff] was murdered by wicked and corrupt men, who had already begun to apostatize, because he would not reveal those things pertaining to the Priesthood that were forbidden him to reveal until he came to the proper place." The endowment was not performed in the Kirtland Temple because it "had no basement in it, nor a font, nor preparations to give endowments for the living or the dead."[54]

Finally, the full rituals were not introduced in the Nauvoo Temple, even though Smith restored the keyword that had been lost for centuries, because the Saints had to flee to the Far West. He identified these "full rituals" as those "connecting the chain of the Priesthood from father Adam until now, by sealing children to their parents, being sealed for our forefathers," and noted that "when the ordinances are carried out in the Temples that will be erected, men will be sealed to their fathers, and those who have slept clear up to father Adam. This will be done, because of the chain of the Priesthood being broken upon the earth. The Priesthood has left the people, but in the first place the people left the Priesthood."[55]

Young regretted that he had not been sealed to his father:

If you recollect, you that were in Nauvoo, we were very much hurried in the little time that we spent there after the temple was built.

53. Van Wagoner, *Complete Discourses*, 5:3104, quoting *Journal of Discourses* 18:303–5.
54. Ibid. Despite Young's Masonic background, John Tvedtnes has suggested that he may have been referring to Zachariah (Matthew 23:35; Luke 11:51; 2 Chronicles 24:20). See John A. Tvedtnes, "The Temple Ceremony in Ancient Rites," 18, privately circulated.
55. *Journal of Discourses* 16:185–89. (September 4, 1873).

The mob was there ready to destroy us…. Our time, therefore, was short, and we had no time to attend to this. My father's children, consequently, have not been sealed to him.[56]

But Young rejoiced that the ordinances, which would be introduced in St. George for the first time, included sealings of children to their parents and vicarious work through which the dead would receive their endowments and be sealed to their families.

On April 6, 1877, Young presided over the final dedication of the St. George Temple. During the same month he mentioned connections between Mormon temples and the Temple of Solomon again when he spoke in Richfield, Utah. He noted that the St. George Temple was the first "in which the ordinances for the living and the dead can be performed since the one built by Solomon in the land of Jerusalem, that we have any knowledge of." "The Nephites may have built temples," Young continued, "and in all probability they did, but we have no account of them." Nevertheless he did not believe that the endowment was made available for very long in these prior structures.[57]

Young taught that "in the days of Solomon, in the temple that he built in the land of Jerusalem, there was confusion and bickering and strife, even to murder, and the very man that they looked to give them the keys of life and salvation, they killed because he refused to administer the ordinances to them when they requested it; and whether they got any of them or not, this history does not say anything about." With the death of this "high priest," the keys were lost. But the prophet insisted that in the St. George Temple "we enjoy the privilege of entering into a Temple, built to the name of God, and receiving the ordinances of his House, with all the keys and blessings preparatory to entering the 'lives'; we also enjoy the privilege of administering for our fathers and mothers, our grandfathers and grandmothers, for those who have slept without the gospel."[58] On May 20, 1877, the first endowments for the dead were given in the St. George Temple.

56. Van Wagoner, *Complete Discourses* 5:2998; *Journal of Discourses* 16:185.

57. There were accounts of Book of Mormon temples in II Nephi, 5:16; Jacob 1:17; 2:2; 2:11; Mosiah 1:18; Alma 16:13.

58. *Journal of Discourses* 19:220–21. This work for the dead was not limited to the ancestors of church members. In August 1877 many prominent men, including the signers of the Declaration of Independence and most United States presidents (with the exception of Van Buren and Buchanan) received their endowments. See Kenney, *Wilford Woodruff's Journal* 7:367–69; *Conference Reports*, April 10, 1898, 89–90. On March 19, 1894, Benjamin Franklin and George Washington received their second anointings. Ibid., 9:293. See also Matthias F. Cowley, comp., *Wilford Woodruff, His Life and Labors* (Salt Lake City: Deseret News, 1909), 586–87.

Shortly after the St. George Temple was dedicated, Young attended the dedication of additional temple sites. On April 25 he dedicated a site in Manti, San Pete County, where ground was broken and construction began five days later,[59] and on May 18 Young attended the dedication of a site in Logan where Orson Pratt gave the dedicatory prayer.[60] Thereafter Young became convinced "that it was necessary to have the formula of the endowments written, and he gave directions to have the same put in writing." Prior to that time the church hierarchy had not authorized the ritual to be transcribed. Young undoubtedly believed that prior to his death it was necessary to write a uniform ritual so that disparate rituals would not be performed in the St. George, Manti, Logan and Salt Lake Temples. As part of this process Young gave a lecture at the veil of the St. George Temple while two scribes (L. John Nuttall and J. D. T. McAllister) wrote it all down.[61]

Young asked two of his apostles, Wilford Woodruff (1807–1898) and Brigham Young Jr. (1836–1903), to "write out the ceremony of the endowments from Beginning to End."[62] Woodruff later noted that George Q. Cannon assisted in writing the ritual and that "President Young has been laboring all winter to get up a perfect form of endowments as far as possible. They having been perfected I read them to the Company today."[63] Woodruff wrote that Young told him, "You have before you an ensample to carry on the endowments in all the temples until the coming of the Son of Man."[64]

During this same period Young described an event reminiscent of Masonic legend concerning Enoch's gold plate as well as a Rosicrucian legend concerning the tomb of Christian Rosenkreutz. He recalled that when Joseph Smith and Oliver Cowdery returned some of the gold plates and the urim and thummim to the Hill Cumorah, "the hill opened, and they walked into a cave, in which there was a large and spacious room.... They laid the plates on a table; it was a large table which stood in the room."

59. *Latter-day Saints' Millennial Star*, 39:24 (June 11, 1877). See also Talmage, *The House of the Lord*, 223–32.
60. See Orson Pratt, "Prayer by Orson Pratt," *Journal of Discourses* 19:30–33 (May 18, 1877); Brigham Young, "Remarks by President Brigham Young," *Journal of Discourses* 19: 33–34 (May 18, 1877); and John Taylor, "Remarks by Elder John Taylor," *Journal of Discourses* 19:34–35 (May 18, 1877). See also Talmage, *The House of the Lord*, 216–23.
61. Van Wagoner, *Complete Discourses* 5:3105. See also L. John Nuttall Papers, Special Collections, Lee Library; Kenney, *Wilford Woodruff's Journal* 7:325 (November 1, 1877).
62. Following the completion of the St. George Temple, Young announced that the church would build another temple in Manti, Utah. *Journal of Discourses*, 19:221. Kenney, *Wilford Woodruff's Journal* 7:321–23, 325–27, 337, 340–41 (January 9–March 29, 1877).
63. Kenney, *Wilford Woodruff's Journal* 7:321–23, 325–27, 337, 340–41 (January 9–March 29, 1877).
64. Van Wagoner, *Complete Discourses* 5:3105, quoting *History of the St. George Temple* (1883).

Young stated that there were "many wagon loads" of plates, and that the sword of Laban (which had originally hung on the wall) "was laid upon the table across the gold plates" with the inscription: "This sword will never be sheathed again until the kingdoms of this world become the kingdom of our God and his Christ."[65]

BEFORE OUR SACRED ALTAR

When Brigham Young died in August 1877, many outside observers predicted that without Young's iron-fisted leadership the church would eventually be coerced to abandon polygamy and it would not survive the transition. But Utah Grand Master Joseph M. Orr confirmed, shortly after Young's death, that these developments would not alter Utah Masonry's exclusionary policy, regardless of whether they were polygamists, and anticipated any potential modification in LDS marriage practices by suggesting that Mormonism's past problematic experiences with Freemasonry in Illinois would constitute a valid reason to withhold membership.

In October Orr addressed the annual communication of the grand lodge and said, "We say to the priests of the Latter-day Church, you cannot enter our lodge rooms—you surrender all to an unholy priesthood. You have heretofore sacrificed the sacred obligations of our beloved Order, and we believe you would do the same again. Stand aside; we want none of you. Such a wound as you gave Masonry in Nauvoo is not easily healed, and no Latter-day Saint is, or can become a member of our Order in this jurisdiction."[66]

Shortly thereafter the *Salt Lake Tribune*, a non-Mormon paper founded in 1870, published an endowment exposé. By this time both the Masonic fraternity and Utah's premier non-Mormon newspaper were actively engaged in the national antipolygamy crusade, and there were therefore hints that members of the Craft supported, and perhaps facilitated, the *Tribune's* efforts to "unveil" the temple ceremony.[67] The *Tribune's* exposé published a letter from a self-proclaimed "apostate" who gave a general description of

65. Brigham Young, "Discourse by President Brigham Young," *Journal of Discourses* 19:38 (June 17, 1877). See also Heber C. Kimball, "Emigration—The Saints Warned to Repent or Judgments will come upon them," *Journal of Discourses* 4:105 (September 28, 1856); and Kenney, *Wilford Woodruff's Journal* 6:508–9 (December 11, 1869).

66. *Proceedings of the Grand Lodge, 1877*, 11–12. Masonic publications in Great Britain at this same time also emphasized the Mormon Temple rites. See, for example, Robert Wentworth Little, "Mormonism," *The Rosicrucian: A Quarterly Record of the Society's Activities*, 14 (October 1871): 168–70; MacKenzie, *The Royal Masonic Cyclopaedia*, 497–98; and Kenning, *Kenning's Masonic Cyclopaedia*, 492.

67. Orson F. Whitney, *History of Utah* (Salt Lake City: George Q. Cannon & Sons, 1893), 2:382; Baskin, *Reminiscences of Early Utah*, 98–99.

the various stages in the endowment but which did not provide any detail concerning names, signs, obligations, or penalties.[68]

The following year the *Tribune* published a more detailed exposé written by Caroline Owens Miles, who had abandoned Mormonism after being sealed as a plural wife in the Endowment House. Miles, who used the byline "G.S.R—," revealed the floor plans of the Endowment House and provided a sketch of an apron (decorated with various Masonic symbols) that was worn by the persons, such as W. W. Phelps, who played the role of the devil in the drama.[69]

Despite widespread belief that neither the church nor the practice of polygamy would survive, Utah Masons continued to justify their exclusion of Mormons primarily because of plural marriages. In 1876 John P. Sorenson, a Danish convert to Mormonism who was inactive, was initiated, passed, and raised in Argenta Lodge, and two years later he was chosen to be one of its trustees. In 1879, Sorenson renewed his commitment to the LDS Church and the following month the junior warden of his lodge preferred charges against him. After a trial he was expelled from his lodge.[70]

The charge brought against Sorenson was for gross unmasonic conduct and was premised on the finding that he was in "full fellowship" of the Mormon Church, "whose principles and practices in Utah are in direct violation of the laws of the United States, as well as the laws of morality and common decency." The lodge noted that "he had declared himself an advocate of the principle and practice of polygamy and by so doing had brought Masonry into disrepute." The commission that tried him (John S. Scott, Albert Hagen, J. G. Sutherland, O. A. Palmer, M. K. Harkness, and Moses C. Phillips) voted that Sorenson was guilty of a Masonic offense, but one member of the commission did not believe he should be expelled for being a Mormon.

68. *Salt Lake Tribune*, December 8, 1878, 4.
69. Mrs. G-S-R-, "Lifting the Vail [*sic*]," *Salt Lake Tribune*, September 28, 1879, 4. J. W. Buel, *Mysteries and Miseries of America's Great Cities* (San Francisco, 1883) identified the author as Mrs. Carrie Owen Mills, but her name was actually Caroline Owens Miles. Kate Field, "Polygamy Unveiled," *Woman: A Monthly Magazine* 1 (March 1888): 296–305. See also Chad Flake and Larry W. Draper, *A Mormon Bibliography* (Provo: Religious Studies Center, 2004), 2:233; and Baskin, *Reminiscences of Early Utah*, 98–99. Miles's account was republished at least seven times during the next thirty years. In 1879 two versions of the pamphlet were distributed under the titles *The Mormon Endowment House* (Salt Lake City: Tribune Printing and Publishing Co., 1879) and *Mysteries of the Endowment House* (Salt Lake City, 1879).
70. This episode is reported in Goodwin, *Freemasonry in Utah: The First Decade*, 17–18; Goodwin, *Freemasonry in Utah: Thirty Years*, 37–38; *Proceedings of the Grand Lodge of Utah, 1879*, 31; *First 100 Years of Freemasonry in Utah* (Salt Lake City, 1972), 1:14.

Phillips, the lone dissenter, believed that making church membership a litmus test for disqualification was "a dangerous precedent, as no man should be put on trial as to his religious belief, except he openly declares himself an atheist."[71] Phillips believed it would only be proper to expel Sorenson if "it would be proven that he himself practiced polygamy," and "that the advocacy of a principle is no proof that the one advocating it would practice it."[72]

Despite Phillips's misgivings, the members of the Grand Lodge Committee on Grievance and Appeals (which included Robert N. Baskin, Alexander G. Southerland, and Herbert W. O'Margary) upheld the expulsion. It found that Sorenson's "conduct, in this regard, is not different from, or less reprehensible, than if he had joined some other association organized to commit, foster and protect any other crime, for instance, theft, arson or highway robbery. These crimes stand in the same category with polygamy, and are not less obnoxious to law."[73] They believed that "anyone who joins a conspiracy thereby makes himself an abetter in everything which is afterwards done, in carrying into effect his objects."[74]

Although Sorenson's expulsion was extremely controversial, Utah Masonry's exclusionary policy was still *occasionally* misconstrued. In 1881 Aaron Goodrich, the grand representative of the Grand Lodge of Utah in Minnesota, sent a printed circular to the Grand Lodge of Minnesota in which he incorrectly stated that Utah Masons were "fraternizing with polygamous Mormons and embracing them as Masons before our sacred altar."[75] Because of this and other communications, Utah Masons recognized that "some of our representatives and sister Grand Lodges abroad have misunderstood the grounds upon which we excluded members of the Mormon Church from membership in, or affiliation with any Lodge, within our jurisdiction."[76]

Thus, "in order to prevent any further misunderstanding," the grand master requested Christopher Diehl (1831–1912), the grand secretary, to draft a communication to all the grand lodges in the world explaining why Mormons were excluded from the privileges of Freemasonry in Utah. Diehl reminded his fellow craftsmen that a Freemason must "admit the

71. *Proceedings of the Grand Lodge, 1879*, 31.
72. Goodwin, *Freemasonry in Utah: The First Decade*, 17–18. See also *Proceedings of the Grand Lodge, 1879*, 31.
73. *Proceedings of the Grand Lodge, 1879*, 32.
74. Ibid., 33.
75. Gustin O. Gooding, *History of Utah Masonry* (Salt Lake City: Grand Lodge of Utah, 1972), 14.
76. *Proceedings of the Grand Lodge of Utah, 1882–83*, 18.

Christopher Diehl (1831–1912). Courtesy Grand Lodge of Utah.

theological belief taught on the threshold of our sacred Temple and further, that he must be loyal to the Government under which he lives, and yield a willing obedience to all of its laws."[77] He then noted: "Masons in Utah contend that the latter important prerequisite is wanting in the Mormons, because one of their chief tenets of their Church in Utah is Polygamy which a United States Statute has declared to be a crime, and which all civilized nations considered a relic of barbarism."[78]

Diehl offered no further justifications for excluding Mormons from their lodges. He made no reference to "anti-Masonic" passages in the Book of Mormon, the history of Nauvoo Masonry, or similarities between the Mormon temple ceremony and the Masonic rite. Diehl mailed "a copy to every Grand Lodge throughout the globe. The answers from 9-10ths of the Grand Lodges, written in a half a dozen different languages. [T]he opinion of our sister Grand Lodges is unanimous, and all are with us and will stand by us."[79] Many of the grand lodges published the communication and short responses in their yearly proceedings.

77. *1882–3 Proceedings of the Grand Lodge of Utah* (Salt Lake City: Tribune Printing and Publishing Co., 1883), 24.
78. Ibid.
79. Ibid., 25.

A RESURGENCE OF MASONRY

During the 1880s British Masonic historians organized a research lodge (the Quatuor Coronati Lodge) that deconstructed Masonic history and legends and advanced a revisionist theory concerning Masonic origins. Beginning in 1884 Robert Freke Gould (1836–1915) published *The History of Freemasonry*, which became the foundational work of the "Authentic School of Freemasonry." The Authentic School acknowledged that there was no convincing evidence that there was a connection between Freemasonry and the Temple of Solomon, concluded instead that there was a link between Medieval guilds and speculative Freemasonry, and downplayed any historical religious connections with Christianity.[80]

The school concluded that there were links between operative guilds and speculative masons and that the lodges that organized the first grand lodge in London evolved out of operative guilds, which gradually accepted nonpracticing members who eventually took control of the (merged) lodges. Although the Authentic School's conclusions concerning the relative youth of the Craft (that it could not trace its origins back to Solomon's Temple or to the beginning of time) was relatively noncontroversial, its arguments that eighteenth-century Masons could link their lodges back for more than two hundred years is still being questioned and debated.

Meanwhile, American Masonry's resurgence alarmed Christian leaders who believed that Masonic apologists remained confused about the boundaries between revealed religion and fraternal organizations. Carnes has noted that even the revisionist Albert Pike claimed that "every Masonic temple is a temple of religion; and its teachings are instructions in religion" and that Freemasons, like their predecessors a generation earlier, "did little to allay the fears of the churchmen." Instead, they were intent on "dissolving" Christian sectarianism and believed that "the universal religion of Freemasonry would restore the pristine Christianity of antiquity."[81]

During this same period, Charles Finney and other anti-Masons organized the National Christian Association and attempted to reignite the anti-Masonic movement to tackle Freemasonry which, in their view, was again competing against Christian churches by offering an illegitimate or "counterfeit salvation."[82] In 1882 Thurlow Weed added fuel to this new firefight when he claimed on his deathbed that John Whitney (one of the Masons who was convicted of conspiracy in connection with William Morgan's

---

80. See Robert Freke Gound, *The History of Freemasonry*, 2 vols. (1884–1887). Other proponents of this theory include Douglas Knoop and Gwilyn Peredur Jones who coauthored various books including *The Mediaeval Mason* (1933) and *The Genesis of Freemasonry* (1947).
81. Carnes, *Secret Ritual and Manhood*, 75.
82. Ibid., 72–73.

disappearance) admitted to him more than twenty years earlier that he and four other Masons abducted and killed Morgan by dropping him into the Niagara River bound in chains.[83]

Some American Masons responded to this new onslaught and cross-connected Mormons with anti-Masonry. Rob Morris, the same prominent Freemason who documented Joseph Smith Sr.'s encounter with Eli Bruce, claimed that he had spoken to John Whitney even before Weed and that Whitney told him he and others had bribed Morgan to leave the country and abandon his business partners and family for six hundred dollars. Morris had never mentioned this encounter before, even though he published his *Biography of Eli Bruce* after it took place. He also claimed for the first time that Whitney told him Morgan was "a halfway convert of Joe Smith, the Mormon, and had learned from him to see visions and dream dreams."[84]

William Bryant, who had lived in Ontario County, New York, when Smith organized the LDS Church, made a similar dubious claim during this same period when he wrote that Oliver Cowdery was an anti-Mason and that he had assisted in writing Morgan's *Illustrations of Masonry*. Although Danford Booth, who was born and raised in Manchester, contradicted Bryan and asserted that "Cowdery was a strong Mason,"[85] there is some confusion whether Bryant and Booth were referring to Oliver Cowdery or his brother Lyman.[86]

Since Morgan disappeared in 1826, four years before Smith organized the Mormon Church, the relationship between Morgan and either Smith or Cowdery is fanciful. It is more likely that Morris and Bryant either manufactured or repeated gossip to blacken Morgan's reputation by associating him with Mormonism since some Masons increasingly believed during this period (based on exposés of the Utah endowment) that Smith borrowed generously from Masonic ritual when he introduced the endowment.

During this crossfire, the American Craft continued to experience sustained growth during the 1880s, but the number of Master Masons in Utah only increased from 392 to 486.[87] Nevertheless, Utah Masons continued to be prominent participants in territorial politics and in legal battles to advance Gentile interests in the territory. Baskin lobbied against the various petitions for statehood, pushed for the passage of antipolygamy legislation, prosecuted polygamists, and participated in the disenfranchisement

83. Morris, *William Morgan; or Political Anti-Masonry*, 10–16, quoting an article in the *New York Sun*.
84. Ibid., 196.
85. Vogel, *Early Mormon Documents*, 2:91, 93–94.
86. See *Saints' Herald* (June 1, 1881): 162–63; Vogel, *Early Mormon Documents* 2:91, 93.
87. See, generally, Blaine M. Simons, *One-Hundredth Anniversary of Mt. Moriah Lodge No. 2* (Salt Lake City, 1966).

cases. After the passage of the Edmunds-Tucker Act in 1887, non-Mormons were, for the first time, elected to the territorial legislature and achieved broader participation in the political machinery of local and territorial government.[88]

TEMPLES OF MORMONISM

The Latter-day Saints continued to construct and dedicate new temples even while Utah Freemasons challenged the legitimacy of Mormon polygamy. In 1884 John Taylor dedicated the Logan Temple and four years later Lorenzo Snow dedicated the Manti Temple. Both of these temples had permanent rooms, similar to the design of the Endowment House, in which initiates took steps to a higher elevation as the endowment drama progressed. The church designed all future temples with this feature rather than utilize canvas partitions, as they had in Nauvoo and St. George.[89]

Brigham Young initially stated that there would be no more endowments performed in the Endowment House after the completion of the St. George Temple, because the Lord had only permitted endowments to be performed there "in consequence of our having been driven from our homes, and because of our destitute circumstances."[90] Nevertheless, after the St. George Temple was put into operation the church continued to allow endowments to be performed in the Endowment House (baptisms for the dead ceased), and it was not until after the Logan Temple was completed that they were discontinued in the Salt Lake house.

During this period of temple building, Mormon Church leaders continued to maintain that similarities between the endowment and Masonic ritual could be explained because both rituals had a common connection with the Temple of Solomon, even after the Masonic Authentic School found that Masonry has no historical connections with the Temple of Solomon. In 1884 Helen Mar Kimball Whitney (1828–1896), who was Heber C. Kimball's daughter and one of Joseph Smith's plural wives, defended the practice of plural marriage and testified that the sacred covenants made in the temple were "made to the Great Master Mason, and in His holy sanctuary."[91]

88. Baskin, *Reminiscences of Early Utah*, 32–34, 173, 212. In 1882 Senator George Edmunds wrote in *Harpers* that Mormons continued to "maintain an exclusive political domination." Van Wagoner, *Mormon Polygamy*, 175.
89. See "Discourse of John Taylor," *Journal of Discourses* 25 (May 18, 1884), 176; "Dedication of the Manti Temple," *Latter-day Saints' Millennial Star* 50: 25 (June 18, 1888): 386. See also Brown, "Temple Pro Tempore," 57–59.
90. *Journal of Discourses* 18:264.
91. Helen Mar Whitney, *Why We Practice Plural Marriage* (Salt Lake City: Juvenile Instructor, 1884), 63.

Four years later the *Juvenile Instructor*, a church periodical, published an unsigned article that stated that "although this [Masonic] institution dates its origins many centuries back, it is only a perverted Priesthood stolen from the Temples of the Most High."[92] Even John D. T. McAllister (1827–1910), who was president of the St. George Temple, recorded that Brigham Young "once said that Free Masonary [*sic*] is the corruption of the keys and powers of the Holy Priesthood."[93]

Edward W. Tullidge (1829–1894), who wrote *Women of Mormondom* as a foil to Fanny Stenhouse's *"Tell it All,"* before leaving Mormonism and describing himself as an "apostate," also confirmed that there were parallels between Mormon and Masonic rituals.[94] He wrote that "the Logan Temple is a grand Masonic fabric, reared unto the name of the God of Israel, where endowments are given," and that Joseph Smith became a Freemason because he "understood that the chain of Masonry is the endless chain of brotherhood and priesthood, linking all the worlds."

Tullidge seemed to be tapped into the belief of Nauvoo Masons that Smith "believed that this earth had lost much of its purpose, its light, its keys, and its spirit,—its chief loss being the key of revelation,"[95] and that the "worthy Masonic order" had "preserved among men the divine mysteries." As such, he recognized that the Mormon temples were looked upon as "the *Masonic* embodiment of that 'Polygamic Theocracy.'"[96] The restored endowment, according to Tullidge, consisted of "the Masonic sacred drama of the Fall of Man," and that "a sign, a grip, and a keyword were communicated and impressed upon us, and the third degree of Mormon endowment, or the first degree of the Aaronic priesthood was conferred."[97]

This same type of rhetoric was employed by outsiders who visited the territory and had undoubtedly discussed the endowment with men like Tullidge as well as active church members. Phil Robinson, a British Mason who visited Salt Lake City in 1882, noted that the "rites of the Endowments…[are] generally of the sacred Masonry of Mormonism,"[98] while a

92. *Juvenile Instructor* 21 (March 15, 1886): 91.
93. Devery Anderson, ed., *The Development of LDS Temple Worship, 1846–2000: A Documentary History* (Salt Lake City: Signature Books, 2011), 75– 76, quoting John D. T. McAllister, Temple Minute Book, St. George, Utah, September 3, 1888.
94. See Ronald W. Walker, "Edward Tullidge: Historian of the Mormon Commonwealth," *Journal of Mormon History* 3 (1976): 55–72.
95. Edward W. Tullidge, *Tullidge's Histories, Volume II: Containing the History of All the Northern, Eastern and Western Counties of Utah; Also the Counties of Southern Idaho* (Salt Lake City: Juvenile Instructor, 1889), 425–26.
96. Ibid., 442, 425–65; Edward W. Tullidge, *Life of Joseph, the Prophet* (New York: Tullidge & Crandall, 1878), 391–92.
97. Tullidge, *Tullidge's Histories*, 444–46.
98. Phil Robinson, *Sinners and Saints* (London: Sampson, Law, Marston, Searle & Rivington, 1883), 139.

German journalist named Wilhelm Ritter von Wymetal (using the nom de plume of Wilhelm Wyl), who visited Utah in 1885 to interview men and women who were acquainted with Joseph Smith, claimed that "Mormonism in Utah is to-day nothing but *Joseph's revised or restored Masonry*." Von Wymetal's book, which was published by the *Salt Lake Tribune*, was essentially an anti-Mormon hatchet job. He not only failed to question anyone's credibility, including John C. Bennett, but he even republished Bennett's fanciful account of the "The Nauvoo Seraglio."[99]

OATH TO AVENGE

Hubert H. Bancroft, who wrote with the apparent cooperation of Mormon authorities, was a more credible source when he concluded that the endowment was a "religio-masonic ceremon[y]." Bancroft summarized the contents of the endowment (relying primarily on Fanny Stenhouse's description) including instructions "to avenge the death of Joseph Smith, jun., upon the gentiles who had caused his murder."[100]

This portion of the endowment, which the Van Dusens, John Hyde, and William Smith had previously described, was cited by federal officials as evidence that Mormons were not loyal Americans. Nevertheless, Tullidge labeled the allegation "that an oath is taken against the United States and its Government" as a "direct *lie*," and noted that an oath "to avenge the death of Joseph Smith, the Prophet, upon the Gentiles *who had caused his murder*…must, in its very nature, become obsolete."[101]

Wilford Woodruff, who was sustained as LDS Church president in March 1889, was aware that the "oath to avenge" had become a *cause célèbre* and that the Endowment House, where endowments were no longer being given, had become a symbol for plural marriage. Thus, shortly after Woodruff assumed the mantle of church leader he refused to authorize any additional plural marriages, without his personal blessing, and when he discovered that such marriages continued to be performed he ordered that the Endowment House be demolished.[102]

Several months later eleven Mormon immigrants applied for U.S. citizenship so that they could vote. The Mormons who filed the applications

99. Wilhelm Wyl [Wilhelm Ritter von Wymetal], *Mormon Portraits: Joseph Smith the Prophet, his Family and his Friends* (Salt Lake City: Tribune Printing and Publishing, 1886), 269. (Emphasis in original).

100. Hubert H. Bancroft, *The History of Utah* (San Francisco: The History Company, 1889), 356–57, 358n17. See Anderson and Bergera, *The Nauvoo Endowment Companies*, xix–xxii, for reference to Bancroft's relationship with the LDS hierarchy.

101. Tullidge, *Tullidge's Histories*, 426, 447–49. Emphasis in original. Tullidge also noted that George Q. Cannon was denied a seat in Congress because of this issue.

102. Brown, "Temple Pro Tempore," 51–54.

and the non-Mormons who opposed them were politically motivated since the Mormon People's Party and the Non-Mormon Liberal Party were competing to register voters in their continuing struggle to control the territory.[103] Several "gentiles" objected to these applications because they alleged that at least two of the converts had received their endowments and taken an oath of vengeance.

Utah Federal Judge Thomas J. Anderson presided during a ten-day hearing concerning the Mormon citizenship applications. LeGrand Young, James H. Moyle, and Richard W. Young represented the applicants while Robert Baskin and William Dickson represented the parties who opposed the applications and the interests of the Liberal Party; U.S. Attorney Charles S. Varian represented the government, which also opposed the applicants.

Baskin and Dickson called eleven witnesses who claimed that the oath of vengeance taken during the endowment required endowed Mormons to "avenge the blood of the prophets Joseph and Hyrum Smith upon the Government of the United States, and will enjoin this obligation upon his or her children unto the third and fourth generations." The applicants' lawyers, who also represented the interests of the LDS Church and the People's Party, called fourteen witnesses who denied that the endowment contained any oaths that were disloyal to the United States but refused to describe the oaths they had taken during the endowment.

Mormon witnesses attempted to explain (in very vague terms) that there was no oath taken during the endowment to avenge the death of Joseph Smith that could be construed as disloyal to the United States and that the prayer to avenge the prophet's death was consistent with a passage in the Book of Revelation. These representatives could have, but did not, note that the reference to avenging Joseph Smith's death also had a Masonic parallel.[104] James H. Moyle, who was one of the applicants' lawyers, made the unusual decision to testify that the only reference to avenging the death of Joseph Smith occurred during an address in which instructions were "given that we should pray that God would avenge the blood of his martyred prophets, and that is all." Apostle John Henry Smith (1848–1911) testified that "there was no such oath, or such covenant" and that if there had been he

---

103. James R. Clark, ed., *Messages of the First Presidency of the Church of Jesus Christ of Latter-day Saints* (Salt Lake City: Bookcraft, 1966), 3:171.
104. One Biblical parallel is Revelation 6:9–10. Bernard claimed that the Masonic oath is included in the Elected Knights of Nine Degree where Masons pledge to avenge Hiram Abiff's murder and take vengeance on those who betray the secrets of Freemasonry. Bernard, *Light on Masonry*, 196–99.

would have "repudiated it upon the spot." This testimony was consistent with internal discussions among church officials that took place during the hearings.[105]

Judge Anderson denied the Mormon immigrants' applications for citizenship because "the teachings, practices and aims of the Mormon Church are antagonistic to the government of the United States." He recalled in his opinion that one apostle "testified that all that is said in the endowment ceremonies about avenging the blood of the prophets is said in a lecture in which the ninth and tenth verses of the sixth chapter of Revelation are recited." Although he did not specifically find that an oath of vengeance was taken during the endowment, he did conclude that "the endowment ceremonies are inconsistent with the oath of citizenship."[106]

Wilford Woodruff published a manifesto shortly after Anderson's ruling that reinforced the official Mormon position that "there is nothing in the ceremony of the Endowment, or in any doctrine tenet, obligation or injunction of this Church, either private or public, which is hostile or

105. John Nuttall recorded in his journal that "some thought that the instructions given about praying to the Lord to avenge the blood of the Prophets and referring to the 6th Chap of Revelations of John 9th & 10th verses so as to refute the testimony which has been given today would be proper," and that "Bro. John Henry Smith asked if there would be any objection to his referring to what is written in the Revelations of St. John in regard to payer &c. by way of rebuttal" and that there was no objection. Jedediah S. Rogers, ed., *In the President's Office: The Diaries of L. John Nuttall, 1879–1892* (Salt Lake City: Signature Books, 2007), 387–88 (November 14, 1889). Nuttall also noted that church authorities considered "the propriety of putting further testimony in court more fully explaining the instructions to pray for the avenging the blood of prophets in the Endowments." Ibid., 392 (November 23, 1889). See also Edward Leo Lyman, ed., *Candid Insights of a Mormon Apostle: The Diaries of Abraham H. Cannon, 1889–1895* (Salt Lake City: Signature Books, 2010), 25–27. (Apostle Cannon noted that the church selected witnesses "to disprove this assertion" who were given "instructions in regard to their testimony, no advice being given, however, for them to deceive or tell any untruths.") Also see Heber J. Grant Diary, Church History Library, November 14–December 13, 1889. David H. Cannon gave a consistent description of "the law of retribution" in the St. George Temple. See Temple Minute Book, St. George, February 22, 1912, as cited in Anderson, *The Development of LDS Temple Worship*, 163–64.

106. For contemporary newspaper accounts concerning this hearing, see "The Mormon Case Ended. Judge Anderson to file a written opinion in a week," *New York Times* (November 26, 1889); "Can't Be Made Citizens. The Mormon Applications Promptly Denied," *New York Times* (December 1, 1889); and *Deseret News Weekly*, December 7, 1889, pp. 754–60. Shortly before the Smoot hearings Anderson's clerk published partial transcripts of witness testimony and the court's opinion. See *The Inside of Mormonism: A Judicial Examination of the Endowment Oaths Administered in All the Mormon Temples* (Salt Lake City: Published by the Utah Americans, 1903). Thereafter, the Senate Committee republished the opinion in the record of its proceedings. See *Proceedings before the Committee on Privileges and Elections of the United States Senate* (Washington, D.C.: Government Printing Office, 1904–6), 4:341–61. Finally, Robert Baskin, who was one of the lawyers in the case, published his own account which included partial transcripts. See Baskin, *Reminiscences of Early Utah*, 89–98.

intended to be hostile to the Government of the United States."[107] In October 1890 Woodruff published his more famous "Manifesto," which suggested that the church no longer approved of plural marriages.[108] He later
revealed that he issued that Manifesto because of "laws of the nation against
it and the opposition of sixty millions of people" and because of the possible "loss of all the Temples, and the stopping of all ordinances therein,
both for the living and the dead."[109] The Manifesto led to the organization
of national parties in the territory and the eventual election of Freemason
Robert N. Baskin as mayor of Salt Lake City.[110]

After the October 1890 Manifesto was published, at least two federal
judges approved Mormon immigrants' applications to become citizens.
However, Judge Anderson continued to refuse to grant these petitions
and in one case, which was heard in Beaver, he found that the Manifesto
"does not even advise those members who are now living in polygamy to
stop their polygamist practices and live within the law" and "announces no
change in the doctrine or belief of the church as to the rightfulness of polygamy." As such, he wrote, "I think this manifesto bears on its face conclusive

---

107. Nuttall Diary, 396 (December 2, 1889). The *Deseret News* published the Official Declaration on December 12, 1889. See *Deseret News Weekly* 39: 809–10 (December 21, 1889).
See also Clark, *Messages of the First Presidency* 3:183–87. Joseph Smith III, the first Mormon
prophet's son and the president of the RLDS Church, visited Mormon apostles John Henry
Smith and Wilford Woodruff in Salt Lake City shortly after Anderson issued his ruling. See
Nuttall Diary, 399 (December 11, 1889). Thereafter the RLDS Church, which did not adopt
the temple endowment as a church practice, issued a statement that Brigham Young made
innovations that were inconsistent with the teachings of Joseph Smith but it did not opine
on the legality of the judge's opinion. "The Brighamite Apostasy: Some Mormons Rejoice
at the Utah Decision," *New York Times*, December 29, 1889.

108. Even after the Manifesto was published, the LDS Church did not remove section 132
from the Doctrine and Covenants. In addition, the Manifesto was not published in the
Doctrine and Covenants until the issues of its scope and permanence were finally determined in connection with the second manifesto in 1904, and four years later the "Manifesto" was included in the same book as "an official declaration." See Thomas Alexander,
"Manifesto (1890)," in Arnold K. Garr, Donald Q. Cannon, and Richard Cannon, eds.,
Encyclopedia of Latter-day Saint History (Salt Lake City: Deseret Book, 2001), 699–701. By
including the document which modified a prior revelation, the Mormons adopted a model,
similar to that utilized in the United States Constitution, to publish the original revelation
as well as modifications to the same. In 2013 the church published a new introduction to the
Manifesto which explains that "the Bible and the Book of Mormon teach that monogamy
is God's standard for marriage unless He declares otherwise (see 2 Samuel 12:7–8 and Jacob
2:27, 30)." See Peggy Fletcher Stack, "Scriptures tweaked on race, polygamy," *The Salt Lake
Tribune*, March 2, 2013, pp. A1, A10.

109. *Deseret Weekly News*, November 14, 1891 (reporting a discourse given by Wilford
Woodruff on November 1, 1891, at the Cache State Conference in Logan, Utah).

110. See Baskin, *Reminiscences of Early Utah*. For an analysis of the political landscape during
the territorial period, see Edward Leo Lyman, *Political Deliverance: The Mormon Quest for
Utah Statehood* (Urbana: University of Illinois Press, 1986).

evidence that it was only intended to serve a temporary purpose." Although these reservations were shared by other observers, Anderson ignored the 1889 Manifesto when he found that the 1890 Manifesto did not "advise or order the discontinuance of the disloyal oaths administered in the Endowment House."[111]

Although Utah Masons shared Anderson's reservations concerning the scope of the Manifesto, the grand lodge predicted that "the body politic, that has for forty years misruled our rich and fair Territory and stood in the way of progress will crumble down. On its ruins the body Masonic ought to erect its temple that will stand till time shall be no more. Brothers, our time has come. Let us be up and doing."[112] Such statements, and similar Mormon counter charges made concerning Masonry, poisoned the political waters and had a lasting impact on the twentieth-century debate concerning the relationship between Freemasonry and Mormonism. Even while Masons achieved broader participation in the political process, they continued to resist attempts to modify their exclusionary policy.

111. See "Alien Mormons Excluded from Citizenship, Decision of Judge Anderson, at Beaver, Utah, December 3 [1890]," *Our Day, A Record and Review of Current Reform,* 7:37 (January 1891): 17–20. In the same issue of *Our Day* several religious leaders wrote that the Manifesto "was a political trick" and in an event "simply advice." Ibid., 3–4.
112. *1890 Proceedings of the Grand Lodge of Utah,* 15.

The Last Mormon Masons

DURING THE DYNAMIC developments that pitted Masons against Mormons in Utah Territory, the last Mormon Masons continued to give credence to Masonic legends concerning temple building. Franklin D. Richards observed in 1891 "that Enoch must have had a temple or perhaps several of them, with all necessary equipments, in which to administer the sanctifying ordinances of eternal life, to the people of his great and glorious city." He also wrote that "certain mystic rites which are practiced throughout Christendom claim antiquity with Solomon's temple," which took forty years to construct.[1] He even acknowledged two years later, while speaking at Morgan Stake Conference, that "if a mason talks with you a few minutes and you have anything to say about masonry, he will tell you that his ideas and instructions have come clear down from Solomon's temple."[2]

MASONIC RETICENCE

Despite Richards's continued enthusiasm, most church leaders became increasingly uncomfortable with the connections that had been noted for more than fifty years between Masonic ritual and the Mormon temple. This change in thinking may have been influenced by the findings of Masonry's

---

1. Franklin D. Richards, "About Temples," *Juvenile Instructor* 26 (December 1, 1891), 722–25, reprinted as "The Temple of the Lord," *The Utah Genealogical and Historical Magazine* 11 (October 1920): 147. Ebenezer Robinson (1816–1891), who converted to Mormonism in Kirtland, published his personal history during this same period and claimed that Mormons "had strenuously opposed secret societies such as Freemasons, Knights of Pythias, and all that class of secret societies…but after Dr. [John C.] Bennett came into the church a great change in sentiment seemed to take place, and application was made to the Grand Lodge of Freemasons of the state of Illinois." Ebenezer Robinson, "Items of Personal History of the Editor," *The Return* 2 (June 1890): 287. Robinson joined Freemasonry within a few months after it was organized. He attended Nauvoo Lodge for the first time on May 5, 1842. See Hogan, *The Vital Statistics of Nauvoo Lodge*, 52.
2. Franklin D. Richards, "Temple Manifestations of the Spirit," *Collected Discourses* (Salt Lake City: B.H.S. Publishing, 1989): 3:225 (February 12, 1893).

authentic school, but a more important reason was that the Mormon leadership was weary of being accused by Masons of pilfering their rituals. Tullidge observed that "Mormon apostles and elders, with a becoming repugnance and Masonic reticence quite understandable to members of every Masonic order, have shrank from a public exhibition of the sacred things of their temple."[3]

During his administration LDS Church president John Taylor instructed church architects that they were not required to retain Masonic symbols when making architectural changes during the construction of the Salt Lake Temple.[4] Truman Angell's plans, which were drawn as early as 1854, included squares, compasses, suns, moons, and stars, all-seeing eyes, ritualistic hand grips, and interlaced triangles forming a six-pointed star (known as the seal of Solomon).[5] But the more obvious Masonic symbols (squares and compasses) were eliminated from the temple's exterior.[6]

The temple's interior, which would resemble a sitting room in an earthly mansion, had Tiffany-designed stained-glass windows and ceramic spittoons, as well as a few Masonic symbols including handclasps and an all-seeing eye.[7] The endowment would be presented by live actors who led the initiates from a lecture room to a garden room, world room, and terrestrial room, and through the veil into a celestial room. During this process the initiates would receive instructions concerning four degrees (in connection with the Aaronic and Melchizedek priesthoods) as well as separate grips, passwords, and obligations pertaining to them, and pass through the veil upon the five points of fellowship. These progressive-style ordinance rooms, some of which included hand-painted murals, were similar to rooms in the Endowment House and in the Manti and Logan Temples.[8]

Wilford Woodruff, who succeeded John Taylor, also initiated a significant modification to the design of the Salt Lake Temple by replacing the two flying angels above the central east and west spires (which were designed by Truman Angell) with a fully upright angel to be placed on the

3. Tullidge, *Tullidge's Histories*, 425, 426, 442; Tullidge, *Life of Joseph*, 391–92.
4. See Roberts, "Where are the All-Seeing Eyes?" 26–27.
5. See Andrew, *The Early Temples*, 119–32, 142–45.
6. Talmage, *The House of the Lord*, 247.
7. Brown, "Temple Pro Tempore," 67–68. Gould concluded that Masonic symbols had a much earlier genesis than its rituals. Gould, *History of Freemasonry*, 1:55. Another Mason, Joseph E. Morcombe, noted that it was inevitable that the LDS Church would "borrow from Masonic forms and symbols." Joseph E. Morcombe, "Masonry and Mormonism," *Masonic Standard* 11 (1 Sept. 1906): 6. See also Randy Baker, "A Testimony of Jesus Christ through Geometric Symbolism," April 1992, privately circulated. (Chapter 11, "Masonic Symbols in Mormon Iconography" and Appendix D.)
8. For a description of the rooms, see Talmage, *The House of the Lord*, 181–200, 257–319. For a description of the endowment, see Bancroft, *History of Utah, 1540–1886*, 357–17.

central east spire. Richard Oman has noted that the Nauvoo flying angel was designed "at a time when weather vanes were common features on public buildings." Thereafter "statuary on top of buildings was a familiar custom in the 1860s…exemplified by the figures atop the nation's Capitol in Washington, D.C., and on the Salt Lake City-County Building."[9] In addition, this modification reflected Woodruff's preference that the angel to be placed atop the Salt Lake Temple would represent Moroni, rather than a generic angel surrounded by Masonic and Rosicrucian symbolism, that flew above the Nauvoo Temple.

THE FLYING PROPHET

Nevertheless, Woodruff's decision was rather dramatic when one considers that Thomas Bullock, who had been one of Joseph Smith's scribes, created a banner that he displayed during Pioneer Day parades, which had an image of a flying angel similar to the angel who floated above the Nauvoo Temple except that it had the face of the martyred prophet Joseph. Although some have suggested that Bullock's banner was displayed at the parade as early as 1849, no contemporary accounts mention it until the Salt Lake Pioneer Day parade in 1862 and the Coalville Pioneer Day parade in 1876. Those accounts noted that the banner included the names of the first pioneers who arrived in Salt Lake Valley but they do not identify Smith as the flying angel.[10]

The first contemporary account identifying Smith as the flying angel on Bullock's banner was recorded on July 24, 1880, when Bullock participated in a procession in Salt Lake City that included surviving pioneers in five wagons. Bullock's banner was placed above the first wagon, which carried Wilford Woodruff, Orson Pratt, C. C. Rich, Erastus Snow, Albert Carrington, Joseph Young, John Brown, Thomas Bullock, H. K. Whitney, Aaron Farr, Zebedee Coltrin, T. O. Angell, and Thomas Grover. The *Contributor* noted that Bullock's banner included "the names of all the pioneers and a picture of Joseph Smith, the prophet, in the act of blowing a trumpet."

9. See R. Scott Lloyd, "Another Angel: Moroni Depiction Bespeaks Defining Doctrine of Restoration," *Church News*, September 20, 2008. An example of a flying angel used as a weathervane (circa 1880–1890), which is part of the Jane Katcher Collection of Americana, was displayed at the Fennimore Art Museum in Cooperstown, New York (October 1–December 31, 2011).
10. See "The Twenty-Fourth of July," *Deseret News*, July 30, 1862; and "The Twenty-Fourth in the Country—Coalville," *Deseret News*, August 16, 1876, p. 2. In 1876 when Bullock addressed the parade-goers in Coalville, he "read over the list of Pioneers, stating who were living, and where, and who were reported dead, according to the best information he could get, and requested that if any error was read the people would assist in correcting it." Ibid.

Thomas Bullock banner.
Courtesy H. Michael Marquardt.

The angel on the banner, like the flying angel on the Nauvoo Temple, was dressed in temple clothes, blowing a trumpet with his right hand, and holding a scroll in the left that contained the names of the first company of pioneers to arrive in Salt Lake Valley.[11] It was reminiscent of other artistic renderings that depict famous men's apotheosis in association with flying angels.[12]

After Bullock's death his widow retained the banner in Coalville but the family eventually donated it to the LDS Church. The church eventually utilized Bullock's banner to prepare a copper plate with the names of the original pioneers. This plate was placed on the cornerstone of the

11. "The Twenty-Fourth," *The Contributor* 1:11 (August 1880), 259–60; "The Twenty-Fourth," *Salt Lake Daily Herald*, July 24, 1880, p. 3; "The Pioneer Company. Names of its Members, and its Outfit," *Deseret Evening Press* (July 26, 1888).

12. Napoleon's body was placed under the dome at Les Invalides after it was returned to Paris in 1840 and eventually surrounded by twelve angels including Fame with a trumpet at her side. Similarly, George Washington's image inside the dome of the U.S. Capitol, which was apparently inspired by the apotheosis of Cosimo I in Palazzo Vecchio in Florence, Italy, is surrounded by angels, including Fama. See *Constantino Brumidi, Artist of the Capitol*, 125–39. For a record of second anointing requests (and its suggestion of apotheosis) during the late nineteenth century, see "Guide to the Orson Smith Papers, 1889–1898," MSS 357, Special Collections and Archives, Manuscript Collection, Merrill-Cazier Library, Utah State University. I thank Brad Cole for calling my attention to this collection.

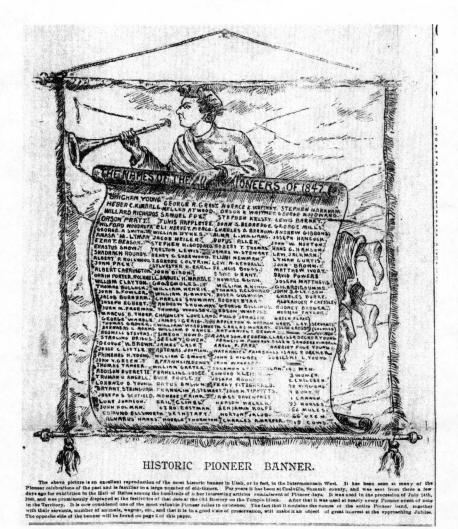

HISTORIC PIONEER BANNER.

Line drawing of Thomas Bullock banner. *Deseret News* June 19, 1897.

Brigham Young Monument on July 24, 1897.[13] Danquart A. Weggeland
(1827–1918), who painted murals for the St. George, Logan, Manti, and Salt
Lake Temples, painted a copy of Bullock's banner and gave it to the Bullock
family.[14]

13. During the same year the *Deseret News* published the image of the angel as well as the
banner's reverse side which contained the inscription: "Names of the Pioneers who left their
winter quarters at Council Bluffs April 11, 1847; Arrived in Great Salt Lake Valley July 24th
95 of whom, returned to Winter Quarters by Oct. 31 of the same year. Without an accident
to any person. Praise ye the Lord." *Deseret News*, June 19, 1897, pp. 1–2.
14. See *Journal History* (March 30, 1897); *Deseret News*, March 30, 1897; *Thomas*

THE UPRIGHT MORONI

Since Woodruff envisioned a different type of angel, he approached Cyrus Dallin (1861–1944), a Utah-born artist who resided in Boston, to design a solid, fully upright, golden angel blowing a trumpet. Dallin initially told Woodruff that he "didn't believe in angels," but the Mormon prophet convinced the artist to speak with his aging mother, who was a pious, believing Mormon, and thereafter the son accepted the commission.[15] Dallin transformed Weeks's unnamed flying angel into a fully upright angel who was identified as Moroni.[16] Although both Weeks's and Dallin's angels wore caps and blew trumpets, Dallin's version did not include any Masonic symbols and was more reminiscent of trumpet-blowing angels located on the exterior of some European churches.[17]

Dallin's primary inspiration may have been the angels that resided above the bell tower of the First Baptist Church in Boston.[18] That church, designed by Henry Hobson Richardson (1838–1886), was built for the Brattle Square Unitarian Society. Frédéric Auguste Bartholdi (1834–1904), a French Freemason who was making plans to construct the Statue of Liberty, designed four carvings representing the four sacraments and four trumpet-playing angels that would be placed on the upper extremities of the bell tower.[19] After Dallin's angel was unveiled on April 6, 1892, and placed upon the highest eastern spire overlooking the grounds surrounding the

---

Bullock—Pioneer, Daughter of Utah Pioneers (Lesson for January 1965), 280; "Thomas Bullock—Pioneer," in *Our Pioneer Heritage* (Salt Lake City: Daughters of Utah Pioneers, 1965), 8:280; Robert C. Mitchell, "DUP Receives Historic Gift," *Deseret News*, October 7, 1965, p. 4F; *1876:Centennial Events and Territorial Activities*, Daughters of Utah Pioneers (Lesson for September 1976), 49–51. Weggeland's copy can be differentiated from Bullock's original (and the image published in the *Deseret News*) since the horn in the original shows part of the interior of the bell whereas the copy does not. Ironically, Weggeland's copy may be closer to William Weeks's design of the flying angel for the Nauvoo Temple since it also did not show the inside of the bell. The Bullock family eventually donated Weggeland's copy to the Daughters of Utah Pioneers Museum in Salt Lake City.
15. See Wendell B. Johnson and Rell G. Francis, *Frontier to Fame: Cyrus E. Dallin, Sculptor* (n.p., n.d.), 69.
16. Talmage later described this angelic figure as "a herald with a trumpet at its lips." See Talmage, *The House of the Lord*, 251.
17. See, e.g., La Chiesa di San Antonio del Portoghesi (1630–1638); Il Palazzo della Consulta (1733–1734) (both in Rome); La Basilica San Antonio (1232–1301) (Padova); the campanile of La Chiesa di Nostra Signora del Suffragio (1866) (Torino).
18. See Maureen Meister, *H. H. Richardson: The Architect, His Peers and Their Era* (Cambridge, MA: Massachusetts Institute of Technology Press, 1999).
19. The First Baptist Church of Boston is located at 110 Commonwealth Avenue. Richardson and Bartholdi apparently met in Paris between 1860 and 1865 and then reconnected in Boston when Richardson was designing the church and Bartholdi was attempting to raise funds for the Statue of Liberty which was dedicated in 1886.

temple, it would eventually become one of Mormonism's most recognized symbols.[20]

One year later Woodruff dedicated the temple and met with the Quorum of the Twelve, and the presidents of the four Utah temples, to complete the process of harmonizing the various versions of the endowment that would be performed in the four Utah temples.[21] Woodruff may have recognized that Freemasons had unsuccessfully attempted to standardize Masonic rituals that were practiced in hundreds of temples and that these rituals remained widely divergent at the end of the nineteenth century. In any case, the Mormon prophet was in a much better position to create a uniform text for the endowment than his Masonic brethren and his successors could continue to modify the uniform version as they deemed appropriate.

When Woodruff commissioned Dallin to create a new image of Moroni, he effectively created a new brand for Mormonism. The trumpet-blowing angel is routinely placed on the tombstones of Mormon soldiers just as crosses are used for Christians and the Star of David is used for Jews. Most significantly, it has been replicated on most modern-day temples and even retrofitted onto completed structures that did not previously feature statuary, including the temples in Provo and Ogden, Utah. When the Nauvoo Temple was reconstructed in 2002, according to the original exterior design, a Dallin-type angel was placed above the spire rather than Weeks's original flying angel. Richard G. Oman notes the irony that "there are figures on buildings in architectural styles that never would have had any sculpture on them except that they're Mormon buildings."[22]

Since the Salt Lake Temple and its trumpet-blowing Moroni have become symbols of Mormonism, it is not surprising that Mormonism's competitors have occasionally utilized these same symbols to counter Mormon exceptionalist claims. In 1909 the Roman Catholic Diocese in Salt Lake City dedicated its own temple, named the Cathedral of the Madeleine, in honor of Mary Magdalene, who has been referred to as the "apostle to the apostles" and has become a symbol of repentance. James Cardinal Gibbons, a long-time critic of Mormonism and its practice of polygamy, presided over the dedication of the cathedral.[23]

20. Moroni's image was later incorporated into the design of the LDS Chapel in Washington, D.C., in 1933 and the Hill Cumorah Monument in 1934. The angel was placed on the spires of the Los Angeles Temple in 1956 and the Washington, D.C., Temple in 1974. The angel on the Los Angeles Temple was designed by Millard F. Malin (1891–1974) holding a trumpet in the right hand and the gold plates in the left, making it even more reminiscent of William Weeks's Nauvoo angel.

21. Kenney, *Wilford Woodruff's Journal* 9:267 (October 17, 1893).

22. See Lloyd, "Another angel."

23. See Gary Topping, *The Story of the Cathedral of the Madeleine* (Salt Lake City: Sagebrush

During the same year Bishop Joseph Glass commissioned an artist to paint two large murals of trumpet-blowing angels, one on each side of the altar, which included passages from Matthew 16:18, reminding the parishioners that St. Peter is the rock of the church, and from Galatians 1:8, warning that "even if we or an angel from heaven should preach a gospel other than the one we preached to you, let him be eternally condemned!" "Of all the scriptural passages he could have chosen," Gary Topping, the archivist of the diocese, notes, "[Glass] chose those that take on the LDS most frontally."[24]

FANTASY ACCOUNTS

The connection between Masons and Mormons continued to be exploited even while their relationship in Utah became increasingly strained. In 1887 Arthur Conan Doyle published his first Sherlock Holmes story, an anti-Mormon melodrama entitled *A Study in Scarlet*. One of the story's villains, Enoch Drebber, the son of a Mormon leader who had close relations with Brigham Young, was found dead in London wearing a gold ring with a Masonic device. Doyle, a Mason himself, may have believed that Mormonism's appropriation of Masonic symbols demonstrated its spurious nature. Young had utilized some of Masonry's symbols, most notably the beehive, and was photographed shortly after arriving in Utah sporting a Masonic pin on his dress shirt.[25]

Press, 2009); Bernice Maher Mooney, *Salt on Earth: The History of the Catholic Diocese of Salt Lake City, 1776–1987* (Salt Lake City: Catholic Diocese of Salt Lake City, 1987).

24. Kristen Mouton, "Catholic-Mormon Ties in Utah: Warming Trend Follows Cold War," *The Salt Lake Tribune*, August 8, 2009, C1, 3. A century later the Most Reverend George H. Niederauer, archbishop of San Francisco, delivered a homily during the celebration of the centennial of the cathedral which may have been intended to highlight a doctrinal difference between Catholics and Mormons. Niederauer noted that, "as spiritual writers have remarked, what we are now, Mary once was, answering God's call here on earth; what Mary is now, we hope and pray to be, fully with God forever." Most Reverend George H. Niederauer, "Homily—Madeleine Cathedral Centennial—Vespers," August 14, 2009. This is a variation of a couplet Wilford Woodruff recorded in his journal in 1856 which he attributed to Brigham Young. Young told him, Woodruff wrote, that "he knew by revelation while in England that there would be an eternal increase in knowledge & as we now are God once was & as he now is we shall be if we continue faithful." Woodruff also recorded that "I told this to Br. Lorenzo Snow." Kenney, *Wilford Woodruff's Journal* 4:439 (August 23, 1856); Van Wagoner, *Complete Discourses*, 1156 (August 23, 1856). Snow later recalled that during the spring of 1840 he formed a couplet—"As man now is, God once was: As God now is, man may become"—that expressed a revelation he received. Eliza R. Snow Smith, *Biography and Family Record of Lorenzo Snow* (Salt Lake City: Deseret News Company, 1884), 46. Gordon B. Hinckley told a reporter in 1997 that "that's more of a couplet than anything else" and that it "gets into some pretty deep theology that we don't know very much about." Don Lattin, "Musings of the Main Mormon," *San Francisco Chronicle*, April 13, 1997.

25. Arthur Conan Doyle, *A Study in Scarlet* (London: Penguin Books, 1988), 125.

Gabriel Jogard (1854–1907), a.k.a. Leo Taxil.
Published in *Les Hommes D'Aujourd'Hui*, No. 71.

But the most dramatic fictional accounts written during this period
were orchestrated by French journalist Gabriel Jogard (1854–1907) using
the pseudonym Léo Taxil. Jogard claimed that Masons and Mormons were
both involved in an international organization whose purpose was to destroy Christianity. He was initiated into the first degree of French Freemasonry in 1881, and wrote extreme anti-Catholic pamphlets before claiming
he was reconverted to Catholicism in 1885.[26] Thereafter he authored anti-
Masonic exposés, perhaps because he realized that the market was much
larger, including revelations (similar to those made by Abbe Barruel and
John Robison) that a Palladium Order, like the Illuminati, had infiltrated
regular Freemasonry, which initiated females and practiced bizarre rituals.[27]

26. Taxil's anti-Catholic hoaxes included *Life of Jesus*, *The Jesuit Son*, and *The Secret Loves
of Pius IX*.
27. Taxil's anti-Masonic works included: *Les Soeurs Maçonnes* (Paris: Letouzey et Ané, 1886);

Beginning in 1892 Jogard enlisted other writers, including Charles Hacks, who published under the pseudonym "Dr. Bataille," to create additional stories that elaborated his hoax. In *Le Diable au XIXe siecle* (which appeared in 240 issues over a thirty-month period), Hacks maintained that Albert Pike, the sovereign grand commander of the Scottish Rite's southern jurisdiction from 1859 until his death in 1891, had founded a secret "Palladism or Luciferian High-Masonry," which also included a Mormon named Phileas Walder.[28] Walder "was no minor character" in these wild tales and was, Hacks claimed, the "real power" behind the Mormon prophet John Taylor (who was also a Palladist), the "connection between Mormonism and Masonry," and the person who introduced the Palladium ritual in France.[29]

Pike eventually appointed Walder's daughter Sophie as a Palladium high priestess and she prevailed in a power struggle with another high priestess (Diana Vaughn) who eventually converted to Catholicism.[30] In 1895 Jogard began a series of stories, which he claimed were written by Vaughn after she converted to Catholicism and which were published over twenty-four months before being published in book form.[31] These stories further elaborated the secret androgynous rituals (reminiscent of Illuminati's "project for a sisterhood") in which both Freemasons and Mormons participated.

Massimo Introvigne has demonstrated that although Jogard's salacious description of female rituals was an elaboration of Barruel's description of the Illuminati's female rituals, his Mormon subplot also relied heavily on French lawyer Joseph Bizouard's descriptions of Mormonism, which were based on Jules Remy's description of the Mormon temple ritual in which males and females participated (which relied on John Hyde's 1857 account)

Les assassinats maçonniques (1889); *Les Mysteres de la Franc-Maçonnerie* (Paris: Letouzey & Ané, ca. 1890); and *Y-a-t-il des Femmes dans la Franc-maçonnerie?* (Paris: H. Noirot, 1891).

28. "Dr. Bataille" [pseud. Charles Hacks], *Le Diable au XIXe siècle*, 2 vols. (Paris: Delhomme et Briguet, 1892 and 1895).

29. For a description of Jogard's career, see Massimo Introvigne, *Enquête sur le satanisme. Satanistes et anti-satanistes du XVIIe siècle à nos jours* (Paris: Dervy, 1997), 143–208; Massimo Introvigne, *Indagine sul satanismo: satanisti e anti-satanisti dal Seicento ai nostri giorni* (Milano: Arnoldo Mondadori, 1994); and Massimo Introvigne, *I Satanisti: Storia, Riti e Miti del Satanismo* (Milano: Sugarco, 2010), 139–300. Umberto Eco discusses Taxil, and apparently relied on Introvigne, in *The Prague Cemetery* (Boston: Houghton Mifflin Harcourt, 2011). See Massimo Introvigne, "C'è complotto e complotto. *Il cimitero di Praga di Umberto Eco*," www.cesnur.org.

30. Dr. Bataille, *Le Diable*, 1:39, 353. Before Hacks joined Jogard in this hoax, he was a doctor in the French merchant navy and had written at least one book entitled *Le Geste*. When he finished his collaboration he became a restaurant owner in Paris and ocassionally gave interviews. See Massimo Introvigne, *I Satanisti* (2010).

31. Diana Vaughan, *Mémoires d'une Ex-Palladiste parfaite initiee, indépendente* (June 1895–June 1897).

SOPHIE WALDER, A L'AGE DE ONZE ANS,

EST PRÉSENTÉE PAR SON PÈRE AUX OFFICIERS DIGNITAIRES DU SUPRÊME CONSEIL DE SUISSE,
SIÉGEANT AU TEMPLE MAÇONNIQUE DE LAUSANNE (1874).

Personnages représentés ci-dessus : 1. — Jules Besançon, souverain commandeur grand-maître.
— 2. Antoine Amberny, lieutenant grand-commandeur. — 3. Jules Duchesne, grand chancelier.
— 4. Louis Ruchonnet, grand orateur. — 5. Eugène Dulon, grand trésorier général. — 6. Henri
Paschoud, grand capitaine des gardes. — 7. Eugène Baud, grand maître des cérémonies. —
8. Philéas Walder, délégué du Suprême Directoire Dogmatique, de Charleston. — 9. Sophie
Walder, louvetonne palladique.

45   LE DIABLE AU XIXᵉ SIÈCLE

Illustration of Phileas and Sophia Walder.
Published in Dr. Bataille, *Le Diable au XIXᵉ siècle* 1:353.

as well as Orestes Brownson's 1862 autobiography.[32] In 1897 Jogard admitted that his religious conversion to Catholicism was feigned and that his tales concerning the Palladium were fraudulent hoaxes that he created to expose the gullibility of anti-Masons.

Thereafter Jogard wrote and published antireligious pamphlets (primarily anti-Catholic) until his death. Despite Jogard's confession, both anti-Mormons and anti-Masons have continued to reference Taxil to support their claims that both Masons and Mormons participated in diabolical rituals of common origin.[33] Nevertheless, the French writers were too provincial to realize that Mormons and Masons could not even get along in Utah, let alone become partners in a worldwide satanic conspiracy.[34]

SECRET SOCIETIES

Although the LDS leadership probably knew nothing about Taxil's baseless charges concerning a worldwide Masonic/Mormon conspiracy, it was increasing reluctant to discuss the more benign connection. As the number of Mormon Masons who had been initiated in Nauvoo was decreasing, there were fewer echoes of Joseph Smith's and Brigham Young's teachings concerning this connection. In 1897 George Q. Cannon, a Mormon apostle who was not a Freemason, noted that while "as a general proposition, it was not considered wise for our brethren to join secret societies," he recognized that "there were men who belonged to the masonic Order, and he did not consider that such membership should interfere with their admission into the Temple or prayer circles."[35]

32. See Massimo Introvigne, "The Devil Makers: Contemporary Evangelical Fundamentalist Anti-Mormonism," *Dialogue: A Journal of Mormon Thought* 27:1 (Spring 1994), 158n14; and Massimo Introvigne, "Old Wine in New Bottles: The Story behind Fundamentalist Anti-Mormonism," *BYU Studies* 35:3 (1995–96), 45–73; Joseph Bizouard, *Des Rapports de l'homme avec le Démon. Essai historique et philosophique* (Paris: Gaume Freres and J. Duprey, 1864); Remy, *Voyage au pays des Mormons*; and Orestes Brownson, *L'esprit frappeur. Scènes du monde invisible* (Paris: H. Casterman, 1862).

33. Subsequent authors have linked Mormonism and Masonry based on this hoax. See Lady Quennborough [Edith Starr Miller], *Occult Theocrasy* [*sic*], 2 vols. (n.p., 1931); John Ankerberg and John Weldon, *Cult Watch* (Eugene, OR: Harvest House Publishers, 1991), 9–54, 93–130; and Ed Decker and Dave Hunt, *The God Makers* (Eugene, OR: Harvest House Publishers, 1984), 116–31. For a discussion of these more recent claims, see Introvigne, "Old Wine in New Bottles," 57–65.

34. For a Masonic response to this episode see Arthur E. Waite, *Devil Worship in France, or the Question of Lucifer: A Record of Things Seen and Heard in the Secret Societies According to the Evidence of Initiates* (London: George Redway, 1896); and Arturo de Hoyos and S. Brent Morris, *Is It True What They Say About Freemasonry? The Methods of Anti-Masons* (Silver Spring, MD: Masonic Service Association of the United States, 1994), 28–45. See also Massimo Introvigne, "The Devil Makers."

35. *Journal History*, April 7, 1897.

Two years later Franklin D. Richards, one of the last surviving Nauvoo Masons, rearticulated Joseph Smith's perspective concerning parallels between Masonic ritual and the endowment. In April 1899 Richards recorded in his diary that he spoke "of some of the circumstances that led up to the Prophet Joseph asking of the Lord & obtaining promise to restore that which was lost indeed to *Restore all things* which enraged the high officials of the Mystic order." Rudger Clawson recorded a more detailed account of Richards's statement: "Joseph, the Prophet, was aware that there were some things about Masonry which had come down from the beginning and he desired to know what they were, hence the lodge. The Masons admitted some keys of knowledge appertaining to Masonry were lost."

According to Clawson, Richards also said that "Joseph enquired of the Lord concerning the matter and He revealed to the Prophet true Masonry, as we have it in our temples. Owing to the superior knowledge Joseph had received, the Masons became jealous and cut off the Mormon Lodge."[36] Richards was apparently interpreting literally the portion of the Masonic ritual in which certain secrets shared by King Solomon, Hiram King of Tyre, and Hiram Abiff "were lost by the murder of Hiram Abiff—a result of his refusal to divulge the secrets—and that certain substituted secrets were adopted 'until time or circumstance should restore the former.'"[37]

Although Bathsheba W. Smith, the wife of Apostle George A. Smith, confirmed during the same year that "Joseph said that Masonry was taken from the priesthood," there were few others with institutional memory who could confirm the endowment's origins.[38] Instead, some church leaders took a different approach and charged that competing organizations (including Freemasonry) were encouraging members to decrease church activity, forego missions, and cease to pay tithing.[39]

On April 12, 1900, the First Presidency and Twelve Apostles discussed "the attitude of the Church in relation to secret societies." The assembled

36. Franklin D. Richards Diary, April 4, 1899, *Minutes of the Apostles of the Church of Jesus Christ of Latter-day Saints, 1894–1899* (Salt Lake City, 2010), 464; Rudger Clawson Diary, April 4, 1899, Rudger Clawson Papers, Special Collections, Marriott Library, University of Utah; reprinted in Stan Larson, ed., *A Ministry of Meetings: The Apostolic Diaries of Rudger Clawson* (Salt Lake City: Signature Books in association with Smith Research Associates, 1993), 42.
37. John Hamill, *The Craft* (Wellingborough, England: Crucible, 1986), 15–16. During the same year Rudyard Kipling, British novelist and Mason, took the opposite view when he concluded that the endowment consisted of "imperfectly comprehended fragments of Freemasonry." Rudyard Kipling, *From Sea to Shining Sea* (New York: Doubleday and McClure Co., 1899), 2:111.
38. Bathsheba W. Smith, Remarks, Salt Lake Temple Sisters' Meeting, Minutes, June 16, 1899, Church History Library, quoted in Anderson and Bergera, *Joseph Smith's Quorum of the Anointed*, 46.
39. "Editor's Table," *Improvement Era* 1 (March 1898): 373–76.

apostles decided that church members "should not have the consent or approval of the Church in connecting themselves with secret societies, and that those who already belong should be encouraged to withdraw as soon as they reasonably can."[40] Although church leaders debated whether the "society of Free Masonry was in some degree excepted, as it was thought that in some instances it might be advisable to join that body," no such exemption was agreed upon. Ironically, Lorenzo Snow, the last surviving Nauvoo Mason in church leadership, was prophet when the church issued a statement that the leadership was "opposed to secret societies" and that those who continued to go into them would be "denied admission to the Temple for ordinance work."[41]

Thereafter, church leaders delivered a flurry of speeches and wrote articles that publicized that the church policy did not make any exception for Freemasonry.[42] "The counsel of the First Presidency of the Church in all cases," they stated, "has been and is against our brethren joining secret organizations for any purpose whatsoever, and that wherever any of them have already joined, they have been and are counseled to withdraw themselves from such organizations."[43] The rationales given to support this new policy included: secret organizations are "snares that are set to entrap our feet and to win our affections from the Kingdom of God";[44] "secret societies are institutions of the evil one"; and that the Book of Mormon condemns such societies.[45] The last rationale is particularly ironic since Joseph Smith joined Freemasonry twelve years after the Book of Mormon was published.

In 1901 Joseph F. Smith and Edward H. Anderson, who were the editors of the church periodical *Improvement Era*, responded to the question, "Why was Joseph Smith the Prophet a Free Mason?"[46] Although their response was arguably consistent with Richards's privately expressed views, it

40. By 1892 a wide range of "secret societies" had been established in Salt Lake City. Thomas G. Alexander and James B. Allen, *Mormons and Gentiles: A History of Salt Lake City* (Boulder, CO: Pruett Publishing Co., 1984), 116. For early references in church discourses to secret societies, see George Q. Cannon, "Secret Combinations," *The Deseret Weekly* (April 7, 1894), 1; "Mormonism vs. Secret Societies," *Salt Lake Tribune* (April 19, 1894), 3; Joseph F. Smith, "Conference Address," *Deseret News* (April 14, 1894), p. 4.
41. Larson, *The Apostolic Diaries of Rudger Clawson*, 154–56 (April 12, 1900).
42. See "Editor's Table," *Improvement Era* 4 (November 1900): 59; 6 (December 1902): 149–52; 6 (February 1903): 150–51, 305–8; 12 (February 1909): 313. In addition, various speakers at general conference also touched on the subject. See *Conference Reports* (April 1900), 30–31 (Marriner W. Merrill); (April 1901), 73 (Joseph F. Smith); (April 1903), 20–21 (C. Kelly). See also Lyman, *The Diaries of Abraham H. Cannon*, 427–28 (December 9, 1893).
43. *Improvement Era* 6 (February 1903): 305, as quoted in Joseph F. Smith, *Gospel Doctrine* (Salt Lake City: Deseret Book Company, 1919), 110.
44. *Conference Report* (April 1901): 72–73, as quoted in Smith, *Gospel Doctrine*, 503.
45. *Conference Report* 4 (Nov. 1900): 59. See also *Provo Enquirer* Nov. 12, 1900; January 13, 1902.
46. "Secret Societies," *Improvement Era* 4 (November 1900): 58.

was also very abstract. They simply referred to the *History of Joseph Smith* in which the Mormon prophet stated on May 1, 1842 (six weeks after he became a Master Mason and three days before he introduced the endowment to the Holy Order), that there were "signs and words by which false spirits and personages may be detected from true, which cannot be revealed to the Elders until the Temple is completed…. There are signs in heaven, earth and hell, the Elders must know them all, to be endowed with power, to finish their work and prevent imposition. The devil knows many signs, but does not know the sign of the Son of Man, or Jesus."[47] The following year Apostle Matthias Cowley (1858–1940) noted during a meeting of the Twelve Apostles that Masonic rituals were "a counterfeit of the true masonry of the Latter-day Saints."[48]

The church hierarchy also became increasingly upset by Masonic claims (after Woodruff released his manifesto) that Joseph Smith had purloined their rituals and that Mormons should therefore be excluded from their lodges even if they were not polygamists. The Utah Masons were absolutely convinced that, despite Wilford Woodruff's manifesto, the LDS Church had not permanently abandoned the practice of polygamy. They noted that the hierarchy had authorized plural marriages after the first manifesto, that the sealings that took place before the manifesto remained valid, and that those men whose wives predeceased them were permitted to marry a second wife in the temple for time and all eternity.[49] This practice proved that, even though the church discontinued the practice of polygamy, it still believed it to be a valid marriage system and that some Mormon men would still be able to have multiple wives in the hereafter.[50]

Nevertheless, when some American Masons criticized Utah Masonry's exclusionary policy (which was originally premised on the practice of polygamy) and encouraged Utah Masons to change the policy or recalibrate the rationale, the Utah Craft would not budge and insisted that the rule was necessary to preserve "true Masonry," which suggests a comparison between Masonic and Mormon rituals. In 1899 the grand lodge received a

47. The reference given by the editors was "Gems from the History of Joseph Smith," in *Compendium of the Doctrine of the Gospel*, 274, which now appears in *History of the Church*, 4:608.
48. Stan Larson, ed., *A Ministry of Meetings: The Apostolic Diaries of Rudger Clawson* (Salt Lake City, in association with Smith Research Associates, 1993), 380.
49. See Paul H. Peterson, "Manifesto of 1890," in *Encyclopedia of Mormonism* 2:852–53.
50. Even when LDS Church leaders denied that they were sealed to multiple living wives in Nauvoo, they acknowledged that they could be sealed to both deceased and living wives. This system is still practiced by the LDS Church today. See *Times and Seasons* (November 15, 1844), 715.

communication from "a representative of the Grand Lodge of Delaware" criticizing Utah Masonry because it did not have "the number of Lodges and membership [as] other jurisdictions."

Christopher Diehl, the Utah grand secretary who had developed Utah's rationale for excluding Mormons because they were law-breaking polygamists, responded to these criticisms by noting that Utah Masonry's slow growth was "due to circumstances over which the Craft have no control." Utah Masons, he wrote, sought to "preserve true Masonry pure and undefiled." Yet Diehl admitted that "there was a time when we all thought a change for the better had to come," but he lamented that "recent occurrences have convinced us that the thought, and if you please, the wish was too previous."[51] During the same year Diehl wrote to the Grand Lodge of New Jersey that "we are proud of our small number of Lodges and membership. The Masons of Utah are true to the core and law-abiding citizens. The celebrated Manifesto has not yet captured us and never will."[52]

In 1904 William H. Upton (d. 1906), a past grand master of the Grand Lodge of Washington, also criticized Utah's exclusionary policy, which prompted Diehl to observe that Upton "touches a subject of which he knows nothing. The pioneers of Utah Masonry knew what they were doing when they taught the Unwritten Law of Utah Masonry, and the present generation has experience enough to teach that law to the next one." He also warned Upton that "he better not mention that subject again; it will do him no good and every line he writes about it is wasted. Utah Masons will stand pat on that line forever and a day."[53]

SANCTIONING POLYGAMY

When the United States Senate's Committee on Privileges and Elections held hearings the following year to determine whether Mormon Apostle Reed Smoot (1862–1941) should be expelled from the Senate, both polygamy and the temple ritual were discussed. The Senate was initially determined to discover whether the Mormon Church continued to sanction plural marriages and whether Smoot was a polygamist, but the senators eventually focused on the contents of the Mormon temple endowment. During the two-year investigation (1904–1906), a number of active and

51. "Report on Correspondence," *1899 Proceedings of the Grand Lodge of Utah*, Appendix, p. 18.
52. Ibid., Appendix, p. 60.
53. "Report on Correspondence," *1904 Proceedings of the Grand Lodge of Utah*, 103–4. See also ibid., 49–50, 87.

inactive Mormons testified concerning the contents of the endowment,[54] while other witnesses argued that any inquiry into the contents of the endowment was offensive and gave ambiguous responses to imprecise and artful questions concerning the ritual.[55]

The committee scheduled hearings concerning the purported oath to avenge the death of Joseph Smith, which was the subject of hearings held before Utah federal judge Thomas J. Anderson in 1889[56] and which was briefly referenced during the Temple Lot Case in the 1890s.[57] Some witnesses testified that the oath of vengeance only required members to pray to God to avenge the blood of the prophets and that endowed Mormons

54. Augustus Lundstrom, Walter Wolf, Hugh Dougall, and Henry Lawrence testified that they had taken an oath of vengeance, while James Talmage and Reed Smoot denied that it existed. See *Smoot Hearings*, 2:79, 148–49, 153, 189, 759, 774; 4:7, 69, 77, 108.

55. Carmon Hardy notes that "some church leaders refused to give any testimony at the hearings, others were caught in their inconsistencies, and several used outright falsehoods. President Joseph F. Smith was one of the latter." Hardy, *Doing the Works of Abraham*, 373.

56. Henry G. McMillan, Judge Anderson's court clerk, published edited transcripts of witness statements and Anderson's opinion, and noted that if Anderson's decision to deny citizenship "to foreigners who are under Endowment House oaths" was valid, then it provided support that Senator Smoot "ought not to be allowed to participate as a legislator…if so counseled by the oligarchy to which he belongs, to help destroy." See *The Inside of Mormonism, A Judicial Examination of the Endowment oaths administered in all the Mormon Temples* (Salt Lake City: Published by the Utah Americans, 1903), 4–5.

57. The Temple Lot Case was an action to quiet title in property located in Jackson County, Missouri, which Joseph Smith designated for the construction of a temple. The Reorganized Church of Jesus Christ of Latter Day Saints (RLDS) initiated the suit and introduced evidence to demonstrate it (and not the LDS Church or the Church of Christ or Hedrickites) was the legal successor to the church which was organized by Joseph Smith and introduced evidence which it argued demonstrated that Brigham Young had created an entirely different church after Smith's death. John Haley, who was a member of the RLDS Church, testified that he had received the LDS temple endowment in Utah and that it included an oath of vengeance against the United States in connection with the death of the Mormon prophet, which was an innovation that took place after Smith's death. *Complainant's Abstract of Pleadings and Evidence* (Lamoni, IA: Herald Publishing House and Bindery, 1893), 454–58. Judge John F. Philips, in his decision in favor of the RLDS Church, found that the LDS Church "has introduced societies of a secret order, and established secret oaths and covenants, contrary to the book of teachings of the old church." See *Decision of Judge John F. Philips*, The Reorganized Church of Jesus Christ of Latter Day Saints *v.* The Church of Christ, et al. (Lamoni, IA: The Reorganized Church of Jesus Christ of Latter Day Saints, n.d.), 39. Judge Philips decision was reversed because the Eighth Circuit Court of Appeals found that the RLDS Church was barred by the doctrine of latches from claiming title to the property. See *The Reorganized Church of Jesus Christ of Latter Day Saints v. The Church of Christ, et. al.*, 70 F. 179 (8th Cir. 1895); and *The Reorganized Church of Jesus Christ of Latter Day Saints v. The Church of Christ, et. al.*, 71 F. 250 (8th Cir. 1895). See also Paul E. Reimann, *The Reorganized Church and Civil Courts* (Salt Lake City: n.p., 1961), 101–87; David L. Clark, *Joseph Bates Noble: Polygamy and the Temple Lot Case* (Salt Lake City: The University of Utah Press, 2009); and R. Jean Addams, *Upon the Temple Lot: The Church of Christ's Quest to Build the House of the Lord* (Independence, MO: John Whitmer Books, 2010).

were not required to take vengeance themselves, while others stated that they believed vengeance would be taken upon the United States or "this generation."[58]

Utah's senior senator George Sutherland (1862–1942), who was descended from Mormons but not a Mormon himself, denied that there was any credible evidence that endowed Mormons took an oath that was hostile to the United States government. Although Sutherland had no firsthand knowledge concerning the endowment ceremony, he argued that Smoot and other Mormon officials, who had testified during the hearings, should be excused for refusing to discuss specific oaths "upon precisely the same theory that a member of the Masonic order or any other secret society would decline if called to testify about the ceremonies of his order."[59]

Some of Sutherland's colleagues agreed that Mormon witnesses were justified when they refused to discuss obligations they had taken in the temple because of these Masonic parallels. Since the Smoot hearings took place during a period when Freemasonry was again experiencing a resurgence—even the president of the United States was a member of the Craft—some senators may have been reluctant to investigate the details concerning the endowment's relationship with Masonic ritual. In fact, according to Carl Badger, Smoot's secretary, President Theodore Roosevelt advised Smoot during the hearings "to have the temple ceremonies abolished; they were foolishness." Badger also observed that "being a Mason he most likely knows something about them."[60]

58. Various witnesses discussed the "Oath of Vengeance" during the Smoot Hearings. *Smoot Hearings*, 2:148, 153, 161, 189, 192, 194; 4:69–71; 1:436–37, 744; 2:759, 762–63, 773–76, 796, 799, 855; 3:71, 279–80, 447–78. Carl Badger (Smoot's secretary) wrote a letter to his wife during the hearings in which he mentioned the oath of vengeance and that Smoot was constrained from explaining "the exact nature of the ceremony." But Badger also admitted that "it is entirely unworthy of us that we should pray for vengeance…but the wrong part is the nature of the penalties…the day will come when they will be no more and when we will be ashamed of them." Rodney J. Badger, *Liahona and Iron Rod: The Biography of Carl A. and Rose J. Badger* (Bountiful, Utah: Family History Publishers, 1985), 242, quoted in Michael Harold Paulos, *The Mormon Church on Trial: Transcripts of the Reed Smoot Hearings* (Salt Lake City: Signature Books, 2007), 337n12.

59. Michael Harold Paulos, "Senator George Sutherland: Reed Smoot's Defender," *Journal of Mormon History* 33:2 (Summer 2007), 107. See also Paulos, *The Mormon Church on Trial*. Sutherland was eventually appointed to the United States Supreme Court by Warren G. Harding, with whom he had served in the U.S. Senate.

60. Carl A. Badger Diary, February 12, 1905, cited in "Minutes of the Apostles of the Church of Jesus Christ of Latter-day Saints, 1900–1909," 307. Roosevelt later wrote a defense of the LDS Church. See Theodore Roosevelt, *Theodore Roosevelt refutes anti-Mormon falsehoods. His testimony as to Mormon character. Advice concerning polygamy. A vigorous arraignment of magazine slanderers* (n.p., ca. 1911). Roosevelt's predecessor (William McKinley) and his successor (William Howard Taft) were also Freemasons.

During the hearings political cartoonists connected the temple (and the angel Moroni) with both plural marriage and the church hierarchy's retention of economic control of the Utah Territory.[61] In addition, former Mormons published exposés repeating claims that the endowment was plagiarized from Masonic ritual,[62] and in 1905 the Grand Lodge of Utah reprinted John Corson Smith's article entitled "Mormonism and its Connection with Freemasonry—1842-3-4—Nauvoo, Illinois" in the *Proceedings of the Grand Lodge of Utah*. The author, a past grand master of the Grand Lodge of Illinois, discussed the history of Mormon Masonry in Illinois and the 1844 grand lodge resolution that declared all Mormon lodges were clandestine.[63]

Although all this information was not listed in the committee's exhibits, it may have influenced its conclusion that a Mormon oath "to avenge the blood of the prophets upon the nation" existed and that Smoot had taken the oath. The committee also determined that "the obligation hereinbefore set forth is an oath of disloyalty to the Government which the rules of the Mormon Church require, or at least encourage, every member of the organization to take." It also determined that "the fact that the first presidency and twelve apostles retain an obligation of that nature in the ceremonies of the church shows that at heart they are hostile to this nation and disloyal to its government."[64] The minority, however, chose not to believe testimony

61. See Michael Harold Paulos and Kenneth L. Cannon II, *Cartoonists and Muckrakers: Selected Media Images of Mormonism during the Progressive Era* (Salt Lake City: Printed by DMT Publishing, 2011), 31, 39. This type of imagery continued thereafter. Ibid., 85–89.

62. The committee reviewed McMillan's exposé as well as the Miles exposé which The *Salt Lake Tribune* republished. William Wolfe, a former professor at Brigham Young Academy in Provo and Brigham Young College in Logan, appeared before the committee and gave a brief description of the endowment. *Salt Lake Tribune*, February 12, 1906, 4. Finally, James H. Wallis Sr., who testified before the committee published a pamphlet, entitled *The Oath of Vengeance*, which used portions of the Miles and Wolfe's testimony, to argue that the ceremony had not changed for almost thirty years. James H. Wallis Sr., *The Oath of Vengeance* (n.p., n.d.).

63. *1905 Proceedings of the Grand Lodge of Utah*, 113–20. The article originally appeared as John Corson Smith, "Mormonism and its Connection with Freemasonry," *The American Tyler* (February 1, 1905). Many fellow craftsmen, particularly from Great Britain, where there were few Mormons, were apparently unaware that polygamy had been abandoned or that Utah Masonry prevented Mormons from joining their lodges. John T. Lawrence, a London Freemason observed [perhaps tongue-in-cheek] that: "We might congratulate the Mormons upon possession of a jurisdiction at all, for the average Brother finds it sufficiently hard work to defend his secrets from one wife, and can only surmise and envy the Masonic steadfastness which keeps half-a-dozen at bay." John T. Lawrence, *Sidelights on Freemasonry* (London: A. Lewis, 1909), 227.

64. *Proceedings before the Committee on Privileges and Elections of the United States Senate* (Washington, D.C.: Government Printing Office, 1904–1906), 4:495–97, hereafter cited as *Smoot Hearings*.

concerning the existence of an oath and determined that Smoot did not take it.[65]

During the Smoot hearings the LDS Church completely abandoned the practice of plural marriage, and those who continued to believe that Mormons were not entitled to become Masons focused their attention on the endowment. Theodore Schroeder (1864–1953), who was originally sympathetic to Mormonism but who bitterly opposed Brigham H. Roberts from taking his seat in the United States House of Representatives,[66] wrote an article in a Masonic publication in which he concluded that "Masonry furnished suggestions for the ground work for the secret endowment ceremony of the Latter-day Saints."[67]

Joseph Morcombe (1859–1942), a prominent Iowa Mason who was well acquainted with the Reorganized Church of Jesus Christ of Latter Day Saints, responded to Schroeder in the same periodical five months later. He challenged Schroeder's premise that Smith had pilfered Masonic rites and noted that the endowment did not replace Masonry in Nauvoo— both rituals continued to perform until the Mormons left Nauvoo—even though the grand lodge revoked its dispensation and refused to charter the Mormon lodges. He also argued that Mormonism's adoption of Masonic symbols "does not prove that Smith intended the endowment to rival Freemasonry."[68]

As the Mormon hierarchy became increasingly sensitive to allegations that Joseph Smith had simply purloined Masonic ritual when he introduced the endowment, it developed a new argument: that Joseph Smith received the entire endowment before he became a Freemason, which was added to previous arguments made during the prior century that Masonry was an apostate form of the ritual practiced in Solomon's Temple; that Joseph Smith restored the same ritual introduced in Solomon's Temple through revelation; and that any similarities between Masonic and Mormon rituals could be explained by their connection with that ritual.

65. *Smoot Hearings* 4: 525–42.

66. When Schroeder arrived in Salt Lake City, he wrote under the pseudonym A. T. Heist, and argued that Utah Masons' attitude toward Mormons was "anti-Mormon idiocy"; he accused the Craft of relying "almost wholly on the evidence of apostates" or the same type of people "who had committed moral perjury by revealing your secrets…as the numerous exposés of Masonry will show." See A. T. Heist [A. T. Schroeder], "Mormon and Mason," *Salt Lake Herald*, Dec. 6, 1891, 3.

67. Theodore Schroeder, "Mormonism and Masonry," *Masonic Standard* 11 (April 7, 1906), 2, republished in *Salt Lake Tribune* (June 24, 1907), 4. The *Tribune* quoted Schroeder as follows: "Masonry furnished the suggestion or groundwork for the secret endowment ceremony of the Latter-day Saints."

68. Joseph E. Morcombe, "Masonry and Mormonism," *Masonic Standard* 11 (September 1, 1906), 6.

In 1909 Matthias Cowley wrote that the fraternity that Joseph Smith sought in Freemasonry "was superseded by a more perfect fraternity found in the vows and covenants which the endowment in the House of God afforded members of the Church."[69] Two years later the LDS First Presidency, in their final reference to the temple legacy, simply concluded that "because of their Masonic characters, the ceremonies of the temple are sacred and not for the public."[70]

After that there were only occasional vague references to the connection. In 1912 James Talmage wrote that during the construction of Solomon's Temple, "Masonry became a profession, and the graded orders therein established have endured until this day."[71] The following year Andrew Jenson (1850–1941), who was Assistant Church Historian, more clearly articulated the temple legacy and seemed convinced that all Masonic mythology was a corruption of primitive revelation. He acknowledged that "if modern Christianity, corrupted as it is today, is a remnant of the true Christianity introduced by our Savior; if the Freemasonry of today is a remnant and corruption of the true signs and tokens of the Priesthood revealed in the days of Solomon, when the Temple of Solomon was built, then it is easy for us to understand and believe that the mythology of the north [presumably Scandinavian legends that Jenson heard as a child] is simply a corruption of the true Jehovah worship."[72]

THOMSON MASONIC FRAUD

While Mormons and Masons continued to develop new justifications for mutually excluding one another, an event that became known as the "Thomson Masonic Fraud" further complicated their troubled relationship. Matthew McBlain Thomson (1854–1932) was born in Scotland where he was initiated into Freemasonry and eventually became master of his lodge. After he converted to Mormonism he demitted from Lodge Newton-on-Ay-St. James No. 125 in 1898 and immigrated to Montpelier, Idaho, where he joined King Solomon Lodge No. 27, which was under the jurisdiction of the Grand Lodge of Idaho.[73]

69. Mathias F. Cowley, *Wilford Woodruff: History of His Life and Labors* (Salt Lake City: Deseret News, 1909), 160.

70. Statement of the First Presidency (Joseph F. Smith, Anthon H. Lund, and John Henry Smith), dated October 15, 1911, appearing in *Deseret News*, November 4, 1911, reprinted in James R. Clark, ed., *Messages of the First Presidency of the Church of Jesus Christ of Latter-day Saints* (Salt Lake City: Bookcraft, 1965–75), 4:250.

71. Talmage, *The House of the Lord*, 7. See also James E. Talmage, "The House of the Lord, Temples, Ancient and Modern," *Improvement Era* 15 (February 1912), 298.

72. Andrew Jenson, *Conference Report* (April 1913), p. 80.

73. See Isaac Blair Evans, *The Thomson Masonic Fraud* (Salt Lake City, 1922); N. R. Parvin,

MATTHEW McBLAIN THOMSON.
Taken from *The Universal Freemason.*

Matthew McBlain Thomson (1854–1932).
Published in Isaac Blair Evans, *The Thompson Masonic Fraud.*

In 1906 Thomson demitted from King Solomon Lodge and the following year he organized the American Masonic Federation, which he later claimed had more than ten thousand members and that it was recognized throughout the world. Thomson, who was undoubtedly aware that Utah Masonry barred its lodge doors against Mormons, formed lodges in Utah under the auspices of the American Masonic Federation and admitted both Mormons and African Americans. By 1912 Thomson had hired men to organize American Masonic Federation lodges and to sell degrees by mail. He promised those who purchased degrees (Craft degrees could cost $550 and the high degrees as much as $200) that they could attend any

Clandestine Masonry, Iowa Masonic Library, n.d.; and Charles C. Hunt, *The American Masonic Federation Case* (New Orleans: Cornerstone Book Publishers, 2008). See also Sharon Haddock, "Masonic Temple a treasure trove of genealogy data," *Deseret News*, May 7, 2010. For a discussion of irregular or clandestine Masonry, see *The Pocket History of Freemasonry*, 326–29.

Masonic lodge located throughout the world. Thomson also published a
Tabloid History of Masonry, a new periodical *The Universal Freemason*, and
eventually dedicated a temple in Salt Lake City. *The Universal Freemason*
challenged the exclusionary policy of the Grand Lodge of Utah. Thomson
argued that Utah Masonry's policy of preventing Mormons from joining
Masonry, or visiting Masonic lodges, was an irregular practice and that the
Grand Lodge was therefore an irregular organization.[74]

Shortly after Thomson organized an American Masonic Federation
lodge in Helper, Utah, the grand secretary of the Grand Lodge of Utah,
Christopher Diehl, wrote a letter to Utah Masons to inform them that
Thompson's lodges were clandestine, spurious, and fraudulent. Dominic
Bergera, who was a member of the federation, wrote a letter to Diehl to
invite him to discuss the matter with Thomson in Helper. Diehl did not
respond but later told Bergera that he refused to meet Thomson because
he was a Mormon, and that: "The organization is all right but...the lodge
could not be cured so long as they had a Mormon for its Grand Master....
[T]hey did accept Catholics [Bergera was a Catholic] in some cases, but...
they absolutely could not meet with a Mormon and that they would not
allow them to visit or to join their lodge."[75]

In 1915, the U.S. Post Office Department began investigating Thomson's
organization. Meanwhile, Thomson received a certificate from Theodor
Reuss that further marginalized his organization from regular Freemasonry.[76] In 1921, U.S. Attorney Isaac Blair Evans (1885–1941), a Freemason
and the son-in-law of LDS Church President Heber J. Grant, prepared the
government's case against Thomson. Charles M. Morris (1882–1947), who
had been the private secretary to Senator Reed Smoot, succeeded Evans and
presented the case to a grand jury, which returned an indictment against
Thompson, Bergera, and others.

The indictment charged that Thomson sold bogus degrees and that
he had misrepresented "the standing and character" of the American Masonic Federation by claiming that his organizations "were and are the only

74. "Scotch Masonry," *The Universal Freemason* 7:1 (July 1914): 2–7. This article quotes ex-
tensively from the work of Joseph E. Morcombe, who wrote about the relationship between
Mormonism and Masonry in *The New Age*, *American Freemason*, and other books on the
history of Freemasonry.
75. Transcript of Record, United States Court of Appeals, Eighth Circuit, *Dominic
Bergera v. United States of America*, 418–20. (hereinafter "Transcript").
76. For a discussion of Reuss and his connection with Aleister Crowley, see Massimo Introvigne, "The Beast and the Prophet: Aleister Crowley's Fascination with Joseph Smith,"
Syzygy: Journal of Alternative Religion and Culture 3:1–2 (Winter/Spring 1994), 141–64;
and Massimo Introvigne, "Between Religion and Magic: The Case of Mormonism," in Michael Fuss, ed., *Rethinking New Religious Movements* (Rome: Pontifical Gregorian University and Research Center on Cultures and Religions, 1998), 81–100.

regular, legitimate and true Scottish Rite bodies in America" and that members of the lodges he organized were recognized by Masonic lodges outside the United States. Thomson was also indicted for using the U.S. mails to distribute his periodical and other books and pamphlets to defraud the public.[77]

Thompson responded that there were no grounds for the charges and that "none of the Grand Lodges other than his own body, have charters from a superior source, and that the so-called regular lodge in Utah was established by an anti-Mormon society. Our lodge is not religious, as is this other body.... Mormons and Catholics belong to our lodge, and these are in good standing. I am a Mormon myself, and I think I am in good standing."[78]

Since Utah's only U.S. district court judge, Tillman D. Johnson, was a Master Mason he had to recuse himself and Judge Martin J. Wade of Iowa was assigned to the case. During the trial, which began in May 1922, Thomson and other witnesses compared the practices of the American Masonic Federation with "regular" Masonic lodges in Utah.

M. E. Wilson, Thomson's attorney, claimed in his opening statement: "There are about 2,000,000 members of the branch of Masonry with which the defendants [Thomson and his associates] are in conflict. But the Universal Masonry practiced by the defendants admits all persons who believe in a supreme being. They draw no religious bars, a distinction which distinguishes the Universal Masons [Thomson's group] from the American organizations with which they are in conflict."[79]

Wilson summarized Thomson's "personal history" and his differences with the Grand Lodge of Idaho, which he claimed was an aristocratic body that denied admission to members of the Mormon Church, among other things, a difference that resulted in Thomson's use of his patent from the Grand Council of Rites of Scotland to begin his propagation of "Universal Masonry."[80] Thomson testified that "after he became a member of King Solomon Lodge of Montpelier, Idaho,...difficulty arose there over degrees he had taken from the Grand Council of Rites of Scotland and over statements by Montpelier Masons that 'Mormons were clandestine Masons,' and that he thereafter took his demit from that lodge and began the formation of

77. *Salt Lake Telegram*, November 23, 1921.
78. Evans, *The Thomson Masonic Fraud*, 149. The quotation originally appeared in the *Salt Lake Telegram* on November 23, 1921, as: "He declared that none of the grand lodges other than his own body have any charters from a superior source and that a lodge was originally established in Utah as an anti-Mormon organization. He said that his organization was not religious and that Mormons and Catholics belong. He said he was a Mormon himself and he thought in good standing."
79. *Salt Lake Telegram*, May 12, 1922.
80. Ibid.

what became the American Masonic Federation."[81] Thomson also claimed that his organization had "charters from a superior source" than "so-called regular lodges in Utah."

The government called Masons from England, Scotland, and the United States who refuted Thomson's testimony and established that Thompson had not received the Scottish Masonic charters under which he claimed to work. The evidence also demonstrated that Thompson did not utilize the proceeds he received from selling degrees for the benefit of the American Masonic Federation. Although Judge Wade later instructed the jury that the case was not a dispute between two Masonic bodies, or alleged Masonic bodies, he did admit evidence concerning the distinction between clandestine and regular masonry.[82] He also instructed the jury that "there is no dispute" that Thomson had "planned to organize and maintain a new organization, claiming for it ancient origin."[83]

The jury unanimously convicted Thomson and his associates, after a two-week trial and two hours of deliberation, on the charge of using the United States mail to defraud. The judge then sentenced the defendants to two years in the federal penitentiary in Leavenworth, Kansas, and fined them each five thousand dollars. Thomson apparently became the prison librarian at Fort Leavenworth Prison while serving his sentence and little is known about him since.[84]

81. *Salt Lake Telegram*, May 13, 1922.
82. "Transcript," 484–86.
83. Ibid., 488.
84. Haddock, "Masonic Temple a treasure trove of genealogy data," p. B1.

An Old Utah Problem

AFTER ALL NAUVOO MASONS in the LDS hierarchy had died, church representatives became increasingly convinced that Joseph Smith received the entire endowment before he became a Freemason. This argument contradicted Masonic claims that the Mormon prophet borrowed portions of the Masonic ritual. In October 1913 Melvin J. Ballard (1873–1939), a Mormon mission president, claimed during LDS conference that Freemasonry was "a fragment of the old truth coming down perhaps from Solomon's Temple of ancient days," but broke with prior church leaders (including Franklin D. Richards) when he maintained that Joseph Smith received the entire endowment while he was still in Ohio.

According to Ballard: "Joseph Smith never knew the first thing of Masonry until years after he received the visit of Elijah, and had delivered to men the Keys of holy priesthood and the ceremonies and ordinances had by us in sacred temples, and had given the endowments to men long before he knew the first thing pertaining to the ordinances and ceremonies of Masonry."[1]

Taking the offense, after Heber J. Grant (1856–1945) became LDS Church president in 1918, the LDS Church continued to develop and institutionalize a thesis concerning the origins of the endowment, which expanded the prior thesis that Masonic rituals were descended from ordinances performed in Solomon's Temple and that Joseph Smith restored the original ritual by revelation.

In 1919 Grant chose Ballard to fill a vacancy in the Council of Twelve, and the new Mormon apostle reconfirmed the same year that "modern Masonry is a fragmentary presentation of the ancient order established by King Solomon from whom it is said to be handed down through the centuries" and that "the temple plan revealed to Joseph Smith...was the perfect Solomonic plan, under which no man was permitted to obtain the secrets of

1. *1913 Conference Reports*, 126.

masonry unless he also held the holy priesthood."[2] But he also claimed, as he had six years earlier, that the "plans for the ordinances to be observed in the Temple built at Nauvoo…were revealed to Joseph Smith…more than a year prior to the time the founder of the Mormon Church became a member of the Masonic Order."

Thereafter, other church officials extrapolated this revised thesis. In 1920 John A. Widtsoe (1872–1952), who would become an apostle the following year, delivered a lecture in which he described the endowment as "the preparatory ordinances; the giving of instructions by lectures and representations; covenants; and, finally, tests of knowledge." Although Widtsoe did not specifically mention Freemasonry, he distinguished between the endowment and corrupted versions of temple worship and suggested that outward symbols (which would include those used by Masons) were not as important as the message.

Widstoe noted that Joseph Smith received the temple endowment and its ritual "by revelation from God," and that it "can best be understood by revelation." Nevertheless, he recognized that the "corruption of [temple] ordinances have been handed down the ages," and criticized "apostates [who] have tried to reveal the ordinances of the House of the Lord." He asserted that temple exposés "have led in all ages to corruptions of temple worship" and that the existence of such exposés through the ages "is a strong evidence of the continuity of temple worship, under the Priesthood, from the days of Adam." He noted that even when these accounts provide "a fairly complete and correct story of the outward forms…they are pitiful failures in making clear the eternal meaning." He also observed that "no man or woman can come out of the temple endowed as he should be unless he has seen, beyond the symbol, the mighty realities for which the symbols stand."[3]

The following year Brigham H. Roberts (1857–1933), a member of the First Council of Seventy, answered an inquiry concerning "the Prophet Joseph Smith's connection with masonry, and its connection with temple ceremonies, and to the endowment rites having been copies from masonry." Roberts maintained that Smith began to receive revelations concerning the endowment in 1835 when he obtained possession of the "Egyptian papyrus

2. *Salt Lake Herald*, December 29, 1919, 5.

3. John A. Widtsoe, "Temple Worship," *The Utah Genealogical and Historical Magazine* 12 (April 1921): 49–64. In July 1921 the same magazine published extracts from speeches given by Brigham Young, as well as other LDS Church authorities, concerning the origins of the endowment. See "Temple and Temple Building," *The Utah Genealogical and Historical Magazine* 12 (July 1921), 113–22. Widtsoe, who was married to Brigham Young's granddaughter, included an extract of Young's discourse given in St. George in 1877 in his *Discourses of Brigham Young*. That discourse contained the markers of Masonic legend including a reference to Enoch's temple and the murder of Hiram Abiff. See John A. Widtsoe, arr., *Discourses of Brigham Young* (Salt Lake City: Deseret Book Company, 1925), 602–3.

manuscript," including facsimile 2 of the Book of Abraham which, according to Smith's translation, made references to "key words" and "the Holy Temple of God." Roberts wrote that these references referred to the "sacred mysteries of our Temple ordinances, and all this from five to seven years before the Prophet's contact with masonry."

Roberts noted that Elias appeared to Smith in the Kirtland Temple and committed "the dispensation of the gospel of Abraham unto the prophet," which would have included the endowment. He also argued that since Smith began publishing the Book of Abraham "about two months before introducing the endowments... [and] must have been at work on the translation of it some months before," that "the Prophet was not at all dependent upon anything he learned in masonry for our endowment ceremonies" and that such ceremonies "resulted from the revelations of God to Joseph Smith, and not from the prophet's incidental and brief connection with Masonry." He therefore concluded that "the evidence, to my mind, is very clear that [Joseph Smith's] knowledge of the endowment ceremonies preceded his contact with Masonry."[4]

Roberts's argument that Smith received the temple endowment independent of his association with Freemasonry is particularly ironic since he believed that Smith's revelations and translations were influenced by his environment. Roberts rejected the Christian fundamentalists' position that there is inerrancy in scripture and argued that Smith did not use a "mechanical process," or a word-for-word transmission from the mouth of God, just as New Testament scholars believe in contextual "dictation" (or "translation") for the New Testament. Roberts believed that this process explained grammatical errors, anachronisms, and familiar phrases (including biblical verses) in the Book of Mormon and in other Mormon scriptures.[5]

4. B. H. Roberts, "Masonry and 'Mormonism,'" *Improvement Era*, 24 (August 1921): 937–39. Roberts challenged the popular notion that Smith had used the Masonic distress call before his death in Carthage. Although he acknowledged that the anonymous author of the *Times and Seasons* editorial (who he believed was Richards, Taylor, or Phelps) asserted that Smith used the Masonic distress call, he claimed he could "form no adequate or positive opinion," but he believed "that not thoughts of deliverance from men and their violence was in the Prophet's mind, but thoughts of God and sacrifice lended in the *martyr-cry* — 'O Lord My God!'" B. H. Roberts, "History of the Mormon Church," *Americana* VI: 7 (July 1911), 695n1; and Roberts, *A Comprehensive History of the Church* 2: 287.
5. Roberts's argument is consistent with Brigham Young's statement that "if the Book of Mormon were now to be rewritten, in many instances it would materially differ from the present translation." "Remarks by President Brigham Young, Bowery, July 13, 1862," *Deseret News* [weekly], August 13, 1862, [49]; *Journal of Discourses* 9:311. Mike Quinn has noted that Young "clearly indicated that the 1830 Book of Mormon substantially reflected Joseph Smith and his times" and that his comments only make sense if Smith's translation of the Book of Mormon "was not a word-for-word translation of the original ancient records." Quinn, *Early Mormonism and the Magic World View*, 193–94.

Sam Henry Goodwin (1862–1951).
Courtesy Grand Lodge of Utah.

Smith's use of Masonic rituals as inspiration for the endowment is consistent with Roberts's thesis of how revelation, and indeed translation, takes place. Smith created a new ritual that contained traces of Freemasonry, which he believed had ancient origins. Smith's interest in the rituals and spirit of Freemasonry would explain similarities, graphic or superficial, between Masonic rites and the endowment regardless of when Masonic rituals originated.

GOODWIN'S REVISED THESIS

During the 1920s Sam Henry Goodwin (1862–1951), a past grand master and chairman of the Grand Lodge Committee on Correspondence, responded to the developing Mormon thesis concerning the origins of the endowment. Goodwin, who was an ordained Congregational pastor and past superintendent of the Congregational Home Missions in Utah, developed additional rationales for excluding Mormons including Mormon doctrines, beliefs, and rituals.

Goodwin realized that Christopher Diehl's original rationale for excluding Mormons (they were polygamists and therefore lawbreakers) had become anachronistic and his rationale for refusing visitation rights to Mormon Masons (they were initiated in Nauvoo) made no sense because those Mormons had all died.[6] Nevertheless, he was also convinced that Utah Masonry's exclusionary policy should be preserved since the Craft continued to thrive as a counterpoint to Mormon domination. From 1890 to 1920 the number of Master Masons in Utah increased more than sevenfold, from 486 in seven lodges to 3,690 in twenty-one lodges. In 1920 alone 669 new Masons, all non-Mormons, were initiated in Utah lodges. As such, Goodwin was prepared to advance new rationales that would support the policy.

In 1921 Goodwin resurrected the issue of Nauvoo Masonry from the grave of Mormon polygamy. He wrote several articles in *The Builder*, a national Masonic magazine, to explain why "Latter-day Saints are not received into Masonic Lodges in Utah, either as visitors or members."[7] Goodwin later published a pamphlet (utilizing material from these articles) entitled *Mormonism and Masonry* in which he discussed the history of the Mormon Masonic lodges in Nauvoo and the symbols and language of the Mormon temple ceremony.

Goodwin quoted directly from temple exposés, written by the Van Dusens and G. S. R.— and including Walter Wolf's testimony during the Smoot hearings. Goodwin mentioned the creation drama, the oaths, grips, signs, penalties, the obligations of sacrifice, chastity and vengeance, and the dialogue that took place when the candidates were taken through the veil upon the five points of fellowship. He also mentioned Edward Tullidge's acknowledgment of Masonic content in the endowment and referred to Melvin Ballard's and John Widtsoe's speeches in which they stated that Masonic ritual was a fragment of the endowment introduced in Solomon's Temple and that the Mormon prophet received the endowment before he became a Mason.[8]

Goodwin also discussed the "significant teachings of Mormonism," which included "absolute obedience to the Priesthood," the discontinued practice of polygamy, belief in continuing revelation, and what he

6. Sam Henry Goodwin moved to Provo, Utah, in 1898 where he became the pastor of the Congregational Church, principal of Proctor Academy, and superintendent of the Congregational Education Society. In 1906 he resigned as pastor but continued as principal, and in 1907 he became a nonresident member of the faculty of the Agricultural College. In 1910 he was appointed as the superintendent of the Congregational Home Missions for Utah. He became master of Story Lodge in 1909 and grand master of the grand lodge in 1912. In 1914 he was appointed chairman of the committee on correspondence of the grand lodge and continued in that capacity for thirty years. He was grand secretary of the grand lodge from 1922 until 1944.

7. Samuel H. Goodwin, "A Study of Mormonism and Its Connection with Mormonism in the Early Forties," *The Builder* 7:2 (February 1921): 36–42, and 7:3 (March 1921): 64–70.

8. S[amuel] H. Goodwin, *Mormonism and Masonry: A Utah Point of View* (Salt Lake City: Sugar House Press, 1921), 20–26.

characterized as the Latter-day Saints' belief in "a plurality of gods." He
noted that the LDS hierarchy discouraged Mormons from joining Masonry
or any other fraternal organization and concluded that "this being true, it
must follow that a member of that organization who would join the fraternity...in direct opposition to the positive declarations of Church officials...
would necessarily be a 'bad' Mormon, and Masons may be excused for seriously doubting if a 'bad Mormon' can be a good Mason."[9]

Based on this background, Goodwin unveiled Utah Masonry's new rationale, one that reflected his religious orientation, for prohibiting Mormons from entering Freemasonry. He argued that there were nine reasons
for excluding Mormons from Masonry even after the abandonment of polygamy. They included (1) "the attitude of the Nauvoo Masons toward Masonic customs and law"; (2) that the endowment was clandestine; (3) that
the Mormon priesthood had "unlimited power of and right to direct and
dictate in all things, temporal and spiritual"; (4) polygamy; (5) the church's
"attitude toward law"; (6) the "inability to answer one question in petition,"
i.e., that he does not believe in the principle of polygamy; (7) "substitution
of 'living oracles' (Priesthood) for the Bible; (8) "male and female deity out
of harmony with that of Anglo-Saxon Masonry"; and (9) that the "L.D.S.
organization holds Masonry to be 'of the evil one' and is opposed to members having connection therewith."[10]

Although Goodwin admitted that polygamy did not "have the importance for the Mason and citizen that it had when Grand Secretary Diehl
sent out his [1882] circular," he still included polygamy and Mormon resis-
tance to antipolygamy laws during the nineteenth century as two of the reasons advanced for excluding Mormons. Goodwin also cited the historical
relationship between Masonry and Mormonism in Nauvoo and the use of
Masonic symbols and language in the Mormon temple ceremony.[11] He believed that close timing between the establishment of the Nauvoo Masonic
Lodge and the introduction of the LDS temple endowment, and similarities between the two rites in published exposés, were persuasive reasons for
excluding all Mormons from Utah Masonry in perpetuity.

The Craft continued to grow while Goodwin was recalibrating Utah
Masonry's exclusionary policy. In 1922, the number of Master Masons in

9. Ibid., 37–38.
10. Ibid.
11. Ibid., 30. Goodwin's claim that Mormonism "borrowed" Masonic symbols is less compelling in light of Masonry's own borrowing of symbols from alchemy, the Kabbalah, Egyptian
rites, astrology, and the Bible. Masonic historian Robert Freke Gould acknowledged that
Masonic symbols had a much earlier genesis than its rituals. Gould, *History of* Freemasonry
1:55. See also Joseph Casla, *Masonic Symbols and their Roots* (London: Freestone Press,
1994).

Utah grew to 4,036, an increase of 348 from the previous year. Freemasonry was also growing outside of Utah where a number of Mormons were joining the Craft. This placed Utah Masonry in an awkward position because some of these Masons were Utah natives who would eventually request permission to visit Utah lodges. In 1923, when Goodwin was elected grand secretary, the grand lodge sent Goodwin's pamphlet to each grand master of the United States, along with a resolution suggesting "the desirability of investigating Utah-born material through Masonic Brethren or Lodges nearest the birthplace or home of such applicants."[12] In 1924 the grand lodge reported that Goodwin's pamphlet had "gone into practically every part of the world,"[13] and that it had also been published by the Masonic Service Association (a quasi-official publisher) as volume 8 of a twenty-volume library of Masonic books.[14]

During the same period, the Utah Grand Lodge determined that Goodwin's new rationales were not merely theoretical and passed a resolution adopting the long-practiced exclusionary policy. The catalyst for the grand lodge's decision occurred when Argenta Lodge initiated a man who was a nominal member of the LDS Church. When one of his lodge brothers found out he filed charges to expel him, a trial was held, the man was found guilty, and he was expelled. But during the 1924 annual communication of the grand lodge, some Masons wondered whether Utah Masonry was justified in denying Mormons the rights and privileges of Freemasonry if their only disqualification was religious pedigree.[15] These Masons objected to the Mormon brother's expulsion and argued that Masonry should not be denied to an individual who "denies real adherence" to Mormonism and "asserts that he is not one of them." W. I. Snyder of Argenta Lodge raised the stakes by proposing a resolution that "a member of the Church of Jesus Christ of Latter-day Saints, commonly called the 'Mormon' Church, is not eligible to become a member of any lodge...in this State."[16]

The resolution was tabled but it was agreed that both the resolution and the expulsion would be discussed at the next annual communication. The following year the jurisprudence committee of the grand lodge ruled that the Argenta Lodge had improperly expelled the Mormon brother, which

12. *1923 Proceedings of the Grand Lodge of Utah*, 65–66. The Grand Lodge of Utah had long favored this procedure. See *1904 Proceedings of the Grand Lodge of Utah*, Appendix, 19. Additional editions of Goodwin's pamphlet were published in 1922, 1924, 1925, and 1927.
13. *1924 Proceedings of the Grand Lodge of Utah*, 25.
14. S. H. Goodwin, *Mormonism and Masonry* (Washington, D.C.: The Masonic Service Association of the United States, 1924). Goodwin's pamphlet was later published as Volume 2 of the *Little Masonic Library* published in 1946. See *Little Masonic Library, Book 2* (Kingsport, TN: Southern Publishers, Inc., 1946).
15. *1924 Proceedings of the Grand Lodge of Utah*, 56–58.
16. Ibid., 82; *1925 Proceedings of the Grand Lodge of Utah*, 48, 65.

resulted in another heated discussion concerning the exclusionary rule. Thereafter, the grand lodge adopted a resolution that amended the *Code of the Grand Lodge of Utah* to prohibit Mormons, including inactive Mormons, from becoming Masons in Utah. Although the Masons of Utah had adhered to this policy since 1866, it was the first time it had reduced it to writing. Thus, it became the only Masonic jurisdiction to adopt written rules precluding members of a named religion from becoming Masons or visiting lodges.

In 1926 Grand Master Benjamin R. Howell made matters worse when he informed the grand lodge that the newly published policy also included members of the Reorganized Church of Jesus Christ of Latter Day Saints (RLDS). This interpretation, which was attached to (but not made a part of) the *Code of the Grand Lodge of Utah*, was also controversial since the RLDS Church had never practiced polygamy, had never constructed temples, and did not have temples or an endowment.[17] Furthermore, RLDS Church president Frederick M. Smith (1874–1946), who was a grandson of Joseph Smith, was a Freemason and later became worshipful master of Orient Lodge 546 (Kansas City, Missouri) in 1934 and served as grand chaplain of the Grand Lodge of Missouri in 1940 and 1942–1945.[18]

The 1925 amendment to the *Code of the Grand Lodge of Utah*, as well as Howell's expansive interpretation, did not sit well with all members of the Craft. Utah governor George H. Dern (1872–1936), a past grand master, was among those who voted against the resolution, and Masons continued to debate the propriety of their unique policy for the next sixty years.[19] The first failed attempt to repeal the amendment occurred in 1927.[20] Nevertheless Utah Masonry continued to grow and by the end of 1927 there were more than five thousand Master Masons in Utah.

During the same year, Goodwin wrote and published a new pamphlet, *Additional Studies in Mormonism and Masonry*.[21] This pamphlet dealt

17. *1926 Proceedings of the Grand Lodge of Utah* (Salt Lake City, 1926), 21, 65–66.
18. See Joseph E. Morcombe, "Religious Tests in Masonic Lodges," *The Masonic World* 18:4 (October 1936): 7.
19. *1925 Proceedings of the Grand Lodge of Utah* (Salt Lake City, 1925), 48, 65. George Henry Dern was born in Nebraska but moved to Utah with his family where he became a successful miner. He was Utah governor (1925–1933) and Franklin D. Roosevelt's first secretary of war (1933–1936). His grandson, Bruce Dern, played the role of Frank Harlow, a Utah fundamentalist Mormon, in the HBO series "Big Love" (aired 2006–2011).
20. *1927 Proceedings of the Grand Lodge of Utah* (Salt Lake City, 1927), 65–66.
21. Samuel H. Goodwin, *Additional Studies in Mormonism and Masonry* (Salt Lake City, 1927). This material was originally published as "Mormonism and Masonry: Anti-Masonry and the Book of Mormon," *The Builder* 10:11 (November 1924): 323–27, and 10:12 (December 1924): 363–67. Goodwin also authored "Mormonism and Masonry: The Story of Their First Contact in New York One Hundred Years Ago," *New York Masonic Outlook* (February 1928): 165–66, 188.

primarily with the Book of Mormon and the anti-Masonic passages that contemporary observers (including Alexander Campbell, Jason Whitman, and Edward Strut Abdy) had identified and discussed. Goodwin noted that these passages, which reflected Smith's own anti-Masonic perspective, were also used by contemporary LDS Church leaders to justify their own opposition to secret societies.

Goodwin noted, for example, that church authorities referred to such societies as "institutions of the evil one," that revelation had "pointed out their origin, character and tendency" and that church members could be excommunicated for joining such groups. He was incredulous that church authorities purported to rely on Smith's anti-Masonry to justify their own prejudice toward the Craft and at the same time argue that Smith later embraced Masonry for fraternal reasons. He concluded that this dilemma had caused "the anxiety of the leaders of the church to lessen the influence of his amazing and perennially troublesome inconsistency.["22]

THE MORMON RESPONSE

While the Utah Grand Lodge formalized its exclusionary policy and adopted Sam Goodwin's new rationales for excluding Mormons from Utah Masonry, the Mormon leadership continued to develop its own thesis to explain parallels between Masonic rituals and the endowment and to counter Goodwin's assertions that Joseph Smith borrowed some of Masonry's rituals. In 1922 John Widtsoe reentered the fray when he informed the Liberty Stake Genealogical Convention that "the statement that the Prophet borrowed the temple idea from some of the several secret societies is the purest rubbish and nonsense." "All that one needs to do," he said, "is to read Church history and to note the time when the Prophet mentions the endowment and hints of coming revelations concerning temple work, to make it quite impossible to believe that any secret order suggested the temple endowment as taught by the Prophet Joseph Smith.["23]

Shortly afterward, Melvin Ballard emphasized that Smith joined Freemasonry because "he needed good friends,["24] and Presiding Bishop Charles W. Nibley again risked upsetting Utah Freemasons when he reminded a Mormon audience that "the prophet Joseph Smith said the time would come when, through secret organizations taking the law into their own hands, not being governed by law of by due process...that the Constitution

22. Goodwin, *Additional Studies in Mormonism and Masonry*, 29–38.
23. John A. Widtsoe, "Fundamentals of Temple Doctrine," *The Utah Genealogical and Historical Magazine* 13:3 (July 1922): 129–30.
24. See, e.g., Melvin J. Ballard, Extract of sermon delivered on January 28, 1922, Brigham Young University, Harold B. Lee Library, Americana.

would, as it were hang by a thread" but that it would be preserved "in consequence of what the Lord has revealed and what this people...will help bring about."[25]

Despite these responses, Heber J. Grant appointed a committee (chaired by Apostle George F. Richards) that recommended revising those portions of the endowment that had been compared with Masonic rituals, including the prayer to avenge the murder of Joseph Smith. This prayer, which was one of the most sensational portions of the endowment discussed during the Smoot hearings, was similar to an oath taken in Freemasonry to avenge the murder of Hiram Abiff, and was considered by some church authorities as "harsh" and inconsistent with Mormon "uprightness and obedience to authority."[26] Because of such concerns, the LDS hierarchy eliminated this prayer along with the language used in connection with penalties.[27]

Several years later James H. Anderson, a member of the general board of the Young Men's Mutual Improvement Association, wrote that "the Masonic Order has rites based on ceremonies in Solomon's Temple," that Masonry was nevertheless a fraternal organization rather than a religious one, and that even though Masons may have symbols that were used in Solomon's Temple which were "part of the religious ritual," it borrowed those symbols and therefore "has no right to complain of the use of that religious ceremony" by others.[28]

During the same year, the *Juvenile Instructor* published the extract from Horace Cummings's journal (which has previously been discussed) that recorded his recollections concerning Joseph Smith's initiation into Freemasonry and his conclusion that Smith understood "many things about the [Masonic] rites that even Masons do not pretend to understand." The *Instructor* apparently believed that Cummings's recollections supported the new LDS position that Smith was already familiar with the endowment ceremony, through revelation, before his initiation into Freemasonry and for that reason he understood Masonic ritual (which was an apostate endowment originally introduced in Solomon's Temple) better than his brethren on the same day he was initiated.[29]

25. Charles W. Nibley, *Conference Reports* (October 1923).

26. Anderson, *The Development of LDS Temple Worship*, 210.

27. St. George Temple Minute Book, June 19, 1924; George F. Richards, Letter to Edward H. Snow, President of the St. George Temple, February 15, 1927, Church History Library. These sources are quoted in David John Buerger, "The Development of the Mormon Endowment Ceremony," *Dialogue: A Journal of Mormon Thought* 20:4 (Winter 1987): 55; Buerger, *The Mysteries of Godliness*, 140; and Anderson, *The Development of LDS Temple Worship*, 218.

28. James H. Anderson, "Temple Ceremonies," *Improvement Era* 32 (October 1929): 971.

29. Horace H. Cummings, "True Stories from My Journal," *Juvenile Instructor* 64 (August 1929): 441. Mervin Hogan concluded that "there is no single known documentation of a

Anthony Woodward Ivins (1852–1934).
Courtesy Utah State Historical Society.

Following this development, President Heber J. Grant asked his counselor and cousin Anthony W. Ivins (1852–1934) to write a book-length response to Goodwin and to summarize the church's new thesis. Before writing his book, Ivins reviewed Albert Mackey's *History of Freemasonry* and became more conversant with Masonic sources than previous twentieth-century LDS commentators.[30] He acknowledged that the LDS Church "advises its members to refrain from identifying themselves with any secret, oath-bound society" and did not complain about Utah Masonry's exclusionary policy. Instead he noted that he wrote his book "primarily to the Masonic fraternity…in a spirit of fairness and reason" to clarify LDS doctrines.[31]

Ivins discussed the origins of the LDS Church and the Book of Mormon and concluded that the church "was not influenced by Masonry, either in its doctrines, organization, or the bringing forth of the Book of Mormon."[32]

---

single specific incidence when Joseph Smith made the alleged impressive interpretations" concerning the origins of Freemasonry and that "when appraising these discourses by the Prophet, his listeners should have borne in mind that he had the advantage of some fifteen years' lead time in his study and command of Masonry." See Hogan, *Mormonism and Masonry*, 278.

30. Ivins also reviewed Albert Pike's *Morals and Dogma*, Joseph E. Morcombe's *History of the Grand Lodge of Iowa*, and John C. Reynolds's *History of the M. W. Grand Lodge of Illinois*.

31. Anthony W. Ivins, *The Relationship of "Mormonism" and Freemasonry* (Salt Lake City: Deseret News Press, 1934), 7–10, 253.

32. Ibid., 89.

He noted that Goodwin had failed to establish "that Joseph Smith, or any one of those who were directly associated with him in the translation and publication of the book ever attended any anti-Masonic meetings, had any knowledge whatever of the ritual of the Masonic fraternity, or participated in the crusade that followed the disappearance of [William] Morgan and consequently could not have made Masonry the basis upon which the [Book of Mormon] was written."[33]

Ivins recognized that Masonic ritual was "intended by symbolical representations to teach the resurrection from death, and the divine dogma of eternal life."[34] He was also aware that the Royal Arch rituals included an Order of High Priesthood, which had been developed by Thomas Smith Webb, but argued that it was "man-made, and of comparatively recent introduction into the ritual of the order."[35] Although Ivins did not claim to be conversant with the specific content of Masonic rituals, he rejected Goodwin's idea that "the ordinances administered in Mormon temples are copied from the ceremonies of Masonry" because Goodwin "fails to indicate the resemblance to the rites of Masonry...and consequently leaves the reader entirely without proof of the resemblances which he states exist."[36]

Ivins noted specific differences between Masonic rituals and those practiced in Mormon temples. He pointed out that women were permitted to participate in LDS temple rituals but also acknowledged that neither women nor "negroes" were ordained to the priesthood.[37] He dismissed Goodwin's claim that Mormons had pilfered Masonic symbols and observed that such symbols had developed an independent meaning, they were no longer in general use and had become obsolete, and "are not seen nor are they referred to in any temple ritual or ordinance."[38]

Although Ivins maintained (like Melvin Ballard) that Joseph Smith joined Freemasonry "to find there the friendship and protection which he so much craved, but which had been denied him outside of his few adherents," he did not explain why Smith would have joined the Craft for that reason when the members of his lodge were Mormons.[39] But Ivins did not adopt Ballard's argument that the prophet was acquainted with the entire endowment prior to his association with Freemasonry. And even though he discussed the various theories concerning the origins of Freemasonry,

33. Ibid., 175–76.
34. Ibid., 13.
35. Ibid., 81–86.
36. Ibid., 10, 89, 251.
37. Ibid., 98–99.
38. Ibid., 90–93.
39. Ibid., 179.

including that its rituals were first performed in Solomon's Temple, he did not conclude that similarities between the two rituals could be explained by common origins.[40]

Instead, he concluded that Smith received the ritual through revelation and that there were obvious differences between the ordinances including baptisms, sealings, and other ordinances for the living and dead that were performed in Mormon temples but not in Masonry. Ivins died before his book was published in 1934, and the LDS First Presidency distributed copies of *The Relationship of "Mormonism" and Freemasonry* gratis to all stake presidents, ward bishops, mission presidents, and faculty members of LDS institutions. During the same year, John A. Widtsoe informed LDS seminary teachers that "we have taken nothing from the Masons any more than we took baptism from the Baptists. Corrupted truth is found everywhere. The temple ordinances were revealed as many other things have been revealed to the Prophet."[41]

The following year, E. Cecil McGavin, an instructor in the LDS Church education system, published his own analysis concerning the relationship between Masonry and Mormonism.[42] The LDS Church did not officially endorse McGavin's book, which was intended to have a more academic approach than Ivins's tome. Nevertheless, he ignored statements made by Nauvoo Masons concerning the Craft and the relationship between the endowment and Masonic ritual. Instead he reinforced the official church position, that Joseph Smith joined Freemasonry to "fraternize with the prominent leaders in the political and religious world," and that he "had a complete knowledge of the Temple ceremony before he became affiliated with the Masons."[43]

He was convinced that all similarities between Masonic ritual and the endowment could be explained because their common source was Solomon's Temple and that Joseph Smith received the endowment through revelation at least a year before becoming a Freemason. He wrote that the Book of Abraham (particularly facsimile 2); Doctrine and Covenants 124 (a revelation received by Joseph Smith on January 19, 1841, concerning the building of the Nauvoo Temple); as well as the Kirtland endowment, all supported

---

40. Ibid., 11–20.
41. Anderson, *The Development of LDS Temple Worship*, 238, quoting John A. Widtsoe, "Answers to Seminary Teachers' Questions, Summer School, 1934," 32–33.
42. E. Cecil McGavin, *"Mormonism" and Masonry* (Salt Lake City: Deseret News Press, 1935). McGavin was a prolific author of faith-promoting books on church doctrine and history. His only controversial book, *The Sex Life of Brigham Young* (New York: Vantage Press, 1963), was published under the pseudonym of Kishkuman Cooper.
43. Ibid., 20, 33.

this conclusion.[44] Nevertheless, he acknowledged that Smith had called upon Freemasons and used the Masonic distress call in Carthage Jail.[45]

Ultimately, the authors of the new LDS doctrine concerning temple rituals believed that the best approach to combat Utah Masonry's new official claim, that the first Mormon prophet utilized Masonic ritual when he created the endowment, was to make a reasoned argument that he received the endowment through revelation before he became a Mason. These authors viewed the Craft from a much different perspective than Nauvoo Masons and were convinced that Smith joined Freemasonry for purely social reasons. Their thesis also seemed consistent with LDS Church policy that discouraged Mormons from affiliating with "any secret, oath-bound society" since such organizations "tend to draw people away from the performance of Church duties."[46]

Nevertheless, Ivins wrote the only quasi-official response to Goodwin, and did not make claims that he could not prove, in particular that Smith received the entire endowment before he became a Freemason, and instead criticized Goodwin for claiming that the Mormon prophet had pilfered their ritual when he was unwilling to publish any portion of the Masonic ritual and compare it with the Mormon endowment. He also challenged Goodwin's Congregational-leaning arguments concerning Mormon beliefs and emphasized that the endowment was materially different from Masonic rituals because it was a product of revelation that trumped any allegations of plagiarism.

FIGHTING DEAD ISSUES

By the time Ivins's book was published, Goodwin's *Mormonism and Masonry* was in its fifth printing, his *Additional Studies in Mormonism and Masonry* was in circulation, and his rationale for excluding Mormons was published in Masonic magazines in the United States, Australia, and South Africa. Nevertheless, some Freemasons insisted that Utah Masonry's exclusionary policy should be abolished. In 1928 Utah governor George H. Dern spoke at the dedication of the new Masonic Temple in Salt Lake City, noting that "the chief battles of our Masonic forbearers in this State were for the eradication of polygamy and Church interference in politics. How well they succeeded, we all know." He noted that Freemasons during the nineteenth century had successfully accomplished their goals: "Polygamy is as dead as slavery, and, in the opinion of many, Church interference in politics

44. Ibid., 33–36, 39, 44.
45. Ibid., 17.
46. Ivins, *The Relationship of "Mormonism" and Freemasonry*, 8.

is no worse in Utah today than it is in many other states. However, eternal vigilance is the price of liberty."[47]

But Dern warned his fellow Masons, "Our present danger is that we will go on fighting dead issues, and neglecting live issues." He suggested a new approach: "Our job is to analyze existing conditions at all times, and shed light in the dark places. Masonry stands for liberty." He did not believe the Craft was doing that job well and reminded his brethren, "We are the enemies of mental slavery, but are prone to scream ourselves black in the face about the poor, deluded member who follows the dictates of churchly authority, and then we go right out and blindly, meekly and supinely follow the dictates of our political party, no matter how corrupt its leadership may be. Is it any more intelligent or any more American to follow a political boss than to follow a religious boss?"[48]

Many American Masons agreed with Dern, including the Grand Lodge of Nevada, which six decades earlier had withheld a charter from Mount Moriah Lodge because the Utah Masons would not agree to exclude all Mormons. In 1929 Grand Master Charles F. Cutts wrote a letter to the secretary of Carson Lodge No. 1, who had inquired whether Mormons could be accepted into the Craft. Cutts informed the lodge that he "found nothing in the Code that prevented any man because of religious convictions, making application to a Masonic Lodge in the jurisdiction."[49]

During the 1930s Utah Masonry, like the Craft in other parts of the country, declined in membership. Fraternal organizations were struggling to remain relevant to a new generation that had developed new interests and was struggling to pay dues during the depression. But the Grand Lodge of Utah, rather than opening its membership to Mormons, produced an expanded version of Goodwin's pamphlets. In 1936 Joseph E. Morcombe, grand historian of the Grand Lodge of Iowa, reentered the debate after the secretary of a Utah lodge told Frederick M. Smith (RLDS Church president, grandson of Joseph Smith and an Iowa Mason) that "if the examining committee had done what it should it would have asked [Smith his] church affiliations, and if [Smith] had told them [he] would have been denied the privilege of fraternal visitation."[50] Morcombe believed that such actions

47. *1928 Proceedings of the Grand Lodge of Utah*, 122.
48. *Ibid.*
49. Gooding, *First Hundred Years of Freemasonry in Utah*, 51–52. See also Ralph A. Herbold, *Mormonism and Masonry* (Los Angeles: Southern California Research Lodge, 1966), 8.
50. Morcombe, "Religious Tests in Masonic Lodges," 7. Morcombe had written two earlier articles entitled "Masonry and Mormonism," in *The New Age Magazine* 2:5 (May 1905): 445–54, and 2:6 (June 1905): 523–30, which examine Masonry and Mormonism in Iowa and Illinois between 1840–1846 and which were later incorporated into his *History of Grand Lodge of Iowa A.F. & A.M.* (n.p.: Grand Lodge of Iowa, 1910): 1:140–73. Morcombe mentioned Calvin H. Rich, RLDS writer and Master Mason, who wrote a pamphlet criticizing

could result in "breaking off all fraternal relations" with Utah Masonry,[51] and that since there were Masons in Iowa, Missouri, and California who were LDS and RLDS, he would expect the policy to become particularly controversial in those states.[52]

NEW TRANSITIONS

After several decades of decline, American Masonry began to grow again during the 1940s. Utah Masonic membership also increased, even though it continued to discourage any rapprochement between Masons and Mormons. In 1945, the year after Sam Goodwin stepped down as grand secretary, there were 4,470 Master Masons in twenty-seven lodges.

That same year Fawn M. Brodie (1915–1981), who was Mormon apostle David O. McKay's niece, wrote a controversial biography of Joseph Smith that discussed the Masonic connections with Mormonism. Brodie was given access to the Church History Library, which contained some of the earliest records concerning Joseph Smith's presidency, including his introduction of the endowment to the Holy Order.

In *No Man Knows My History*, she discussed some of the same issues that Goodwin had highlighted and that continued to create tension between Freemasonry and Mormonism in Utah. Brodie wrote about Book of Mormon passages, which she compared to anti-Masonic rhetoric, and discussed parallels between the endowment and Masonic ritual. She noted that it "may seem surprising that Joseph should have incorporated so much Masonry into the endowment ceremony" and that "his leading men… would have been blind indeed not to see the parallelism between the costuming, grips, passwords, keys, and oaths." Brodie was apparently familiar with some of the primary evidence concerning these parallels and therefore acknowledged that Smith taught the Holy Order that "the Masonic ritual was a corruption of the ancient ritual of Solomon, and that his own was a restoration of the true Hebraic endowment." But she did not quote, or cite any references to, statements made by Joseph Smith, Heber C. Kimball, Brigham Young, or any of their contemporaries who had acknowledged such similarities and parallels.[53]

---

the "intolerance" of the Grand Lodge of Utah and suggesting that its policy should be corrected. Morcombe, "Religious Tests in Masonic Lodges," 8. But Rich also argued that the "ceremonies used in the Mormon temples…are adopted largely, if not altogether, from the Masonic Lodge." Calvin H. Rich, *Some Differences in Faith* (Independence, MO: Herald Publishing House, 1930), 30–31.

51. Morcombe, "Religious Tests in Masonic Lodges," 8.
52. Ibid., 8–9.
53. Brodie, *No Man Knows My History*, 280–82.

Hugh Nibley (1910–2005), a professor of ancient history at Brigham Young University, wrote his first article in Mormon apologetics when he reviewed Brodie's book. He repeated the new LDS thesis that Smith was fully briefed on the complete endowment before he was initiated into Freemasonry. "More than five years before," Nibley wrote in *No, Ma'am, That's Not History*, "Elijah himself had brought the keys to this work 'lest the whole earth be smitten with a curse.'" Following that revelation, even after Smith became a Freemason, "the temples do not change their design or their meaning." Nibley did not discuss the Nauvoo endowment's new content or compare it with the Kirtland endowment and he was apparently not familiar with the primary evidence Brodie had consulted. He therefore challenged her suggestion that the Holy Order recognized similarities between the endowment and Masonic ritual. He asked rhetorically: "'Bald parallels with Masonic rites' the lady finds particularly crude. How did he dare it? Why didn't he disguise it?" He then responded by asserting, "The answer is that to those who know both, the resemblance is not striking at all." Nibley, like Brodie, did not explain who he had in mind when he referred to those who did "know both."[54]

By the end of the 1940s there were 5,807 Master Masons in Utah and there was no pressure to expand the pool of potential Masons. Nevertheless, the debate concerning visitation rights was far more volatile than the positions articulated by Brodie and Nibley, because it pitted Mason against Mason (as it had when RLDS president Frederick M. Smith visited Utah) and threatened the brotherhood of the fraternity. Because of this, Grand Master Ortis C. Skaite, who was a Goodwin protégé, felt compelled in 1949 to clarify Utah Masonry's visitation policy. "Teachings and regulations as would make one ineligible to become a member of a Masonic lodge in Utah," Skaite wrote, "would also make one ineligible to visit a lodge in this jurisdiction even though he might be a Master Mason in good-standing in some other jurisdiction."[55] Skaite's interpretation was slipped into the *Code of the Grand Lodge of Utah*.[56] That same year the grand lodge approved a recommendation by the grand master to republish Goodwin's pamphlet, *Mormonism and Masonry*.

In 1950 Apostle John A. Widtsoe wrote two articles in a series entitled "Evidences and Reconciliations," which were published in the *Improvement*

54. Hugh Nibley, *No, Ma'am, That's Not History* (Salt Lake City: Deseret Book Co., 1945), 17. This pamphlet has been republished in Hugh Nibley, *Tinkling Cymbals and Sounding Brass* (Salt Lake City: Deseret Book Company, and Provo, Utah: Foundation for Ancient Research and Mormon Studies, 1991), 1–52.
55. *1949 Proceedings of the Grand Lodge of Utah* (Salt Lake City, 1949), 30, 71.
56. See *The Code of the Grand Lodge of the Free and Accepted Masons of Utah* (Salt Lake City, 1937), 111 (1949 Standing Resolution).

Era, that further refined the LDS position concerning the origins of the endowment and Joseph Smith's membership in the Craft. Widtsoe wrote in "Whence Came the Temple Endowment?" that "the proposition that the Mormon endowment was built upon secret fraternal rituals cannot be accepted" and that "Joseph Smith received the temple endowment and its ritual, as all else that he promulgated, by revelation from God." He noted that Smith had introduced an endowment in Kirtland and that he announced a new endowment in Nauvoo before he became a Mason. He also claimed that even though some Mormons were "in fraternal circles" that "nowhere can a word be found from these many men indicating that they placed temple work in a class with the ritual of the fraternal orders."[57]

In the second article, entitled "Why Did Joseph Smith Become a Mason?" Widtsoe developed Melvin Ballard's subthesis (which was repeated by Ivins) that Smith was initiated into the Craft to foster "the spirit of brotherhood" and to "lessen the mob persecutions to which the Church had been subjected in Ohio and Missouri." Smith, according to Widtsoe, was "never an active Mason" and "Lodge matters would be left in other hands." Ultimately, however, "Joseph's Masonic membership did not lessen persecution" and "the attempt to win sufficient friends through masonry to stop persecution failed," even though Widtsoe suggested that "no one knows with certainty whether any of them [Masons] took part in the 'Mormon' persecutions."[58]

Widtsoe was the last Mormon apostle to advance the twentieth-century Mormon thesis that included the claim that Joseph Smith received the entire endowment, through revelation, before he became a Freemason. He did not claim (as Joseph Smith's contemporaries believed) that Mormon and Masonic rituals shared a common ancestry with those practiced in the Temple of Solomon, but he did note that no member of the Holy Order "placed temple work in a class with the ritual of the fraternal orders."

Widtsoe did advance the same counterargument against plagiarism (which Ivins discussed in his book), that the similarities between Masonic rituals and the endowment did "not deal with basic matters but rather with the mechanism of the ritual." "The endowment has the promise of eternal growth, of endless blessings," he wrote, while "this is not the ordinary objective of a man-made secret society." Finally, Widtsoe noted that Mormon women were allowed to participate in the endowment (Masons' wives were

57. John A. Widtsoe, "Whence Came the Temple Endowment?" *Improvement Era* 53:2 (February 1950), 94–95.
58. John A. Widtsoe, "Why Did Joseph Smith Become a Mason?" *Improvement Era* 53:9 (September 1950): 694–95.

not) and that the endowment was a sacred ordinance and not a secret ritual like those of secret societies.[59]

AN ARTIFICIAL BARRIER

During the 1950s, when Utah Masonry approached seven thousand members, some Masons began to express greater concern regarding the "Mormon question." Mormons were no longer considered lawbreakers, church members were no longer bitter toward the federal government, and LDS apostle Ezra Taft Benson (whose great-grandfather was a Nauvoo Mason) had been appointed to President Dwight D. Eisenhower's cabinet. In 1954 Grand Orator Calvin A. Behle (1907–1999) delivered a seminal speech to the grand lodge annual communication entitled "Mormonism and Masonry, A Look Today at an Old Utah Problem," in which he attempted to place Utah Masonry's exclusionary policy in historical context. He quoted liberally from passages in Fawn Brodie's book *No Man Knows My History*, relating to anti-Masonic passages in the Book of Mormon, and spoke about the similarities between Masonic ritual and the Mormon temple ceremony.[60]

Behle also addressed Goodwin's rationale for excluding Mormons from the Craft, noting that polygamy was no longer a Mormon practice and that "there is no real possibility, if even desire for its revival." "Today our Fraternity in Utah is practically alone in the official maintenance of our 'Iron Curtain,'" Behle pointed out, "in sharp contrast with conditions before and at the turn of the century. Nor does membership in the Mormon Church stand as a barrier to Masonic membership in states other than our own." Behle noted that "despite considerable official effort to place before our sister jurisdictions our reasons for the barrier in Utah, the plain, hard fact is that our reasoning by and large has simply failed to appeal to our Masonic brethren, in the face of other basic tenets of the Fraternity." He pointed out that "California and Iowa are at least two jurisdictions which have been openly critical of the Utah position. Each of us knows of instances where the rejection of a visiting brother solely upon religious grounds has proven embarrassing, to say the least. Elaboration is hardly necessary."[61]

Behle therefore recommended that the grand lodge "withdraw the blanket prohibition against the visiting Mormon Mason because of L.D.S.

59. Widtsoe, "Whence Came the Temple Endowment?" 94–95.
60. Calvin A. Behle, "Mormonism and Masonry: A Look Today at an Old Utah Problem," *1954 Proceedings of the Grand Lodge of Utah* (Salt Lake City, 1954), 71–82.
61. Ibid., 79.

Church membership per se; and to leave the matter to the sound discretion of the individual Lodge and its members to which the request is made."[62] He also predicted that "eventually Time will bring us an affirmative answer in Utah for the worthy resident member of the dominant Church who may care to apply for a membership in our brotherhood."[63] But he admitted that the time had not yet arrived: "It would seem improvident now to change the principle to which Masons in Utah have adhered for many, many years. With the possible exception of the modification in the case of the individual visiting brother, sound practical reasons still seem to exist for the barrier here between Mormon and Mason."[64]

During this same period Mervin B. Hogan (1906–1998), a Mormon who joined Masonry outside of Utah, began to publish articles concerning the connections between Mormonism and Masonry. He was not openly critical of either institution but clearly suggested that the barrier between the two organizations was artificial.[65] In 1956 he addressed the Utah Grand Lodge and presented a survey of the various charges that had been made concerning the use of Masonic rites in the Mormon temple endowment. He argued that the temple ceremony "cannot be referred to as a 'masonic' ceremony in the sense that that word is used by Masons" and that various alterations that had been made in the ceremony rendered it dissimilar to the Masonic rite.[66]

In 1958 some Utah Masons believed that the time had finally come to "withdraw the blanket prohibition" in favor of the more liberal positions that Behle and Hogan had advocated.[67] The grand lodge debated a resolution that year to amend the *Code of the Grand Lodge of Utah* to allow members of the Church of Jesus Christ of Latter-day Saints to become Masons. Although the resolution was defeated, the grand lodge rejected another resolution that would have codified Grand Master Skaite's 1949 ruling that neither LDS nor RLDS members could visit Utah Masonic temples. The jurisprudence committee noted that under existing procedures "any individual Mason feeling as the proponents of the amendment feel can accomplish the exclusion of any visitor objectionable to him by a simple objection made to the Worshipful Master at the time that application to visit is made.

---

62. Ibid., 79–80.
63. Ibid., 80.
64. Ibid., 81.
65. For a list of Hogan's articles on Mormonism and Masonry, see Hogan, "Mormonism and Freemasonry," 325–26.
66. Mervin B. Hogan, "Time and Change," *1956 Proceedings of the Grand Lodge of Utah* (Salt Lake City, 1956).
67. *1958 Proceedings of the Grand Lodge of Utah* (Salt Lake City, 1958), 70–2, 80, 99–100, 104–5.

It follows that legislation is wholly unnecessary to protect our members from contacts objectionable to them." The grand lodge defeated the resolution and each Utah lodge retained the right to either admit or exclude Mormon visitors.

Beginning in the 1960s both American and Utah Masonry began to experience a downward spiral in membership. Nevertheless, even though Utah Masons had lost some of their political clout the institution was still an important social connection for many non-Mormons. In 1965 the grand lodge debated and rejected another resolution that would have permitted lodges to initiate Mormons.[68] Nevertheless, when Utah Freemasons met in 1966 to celebrate the one hundredth anniversary of the Craft in Utah, some Masons were concerned not only about their exclusionary rule but also about the precipitous decrease in their membership. By 1969 there were 6,315 Master Masons; ten years later the number had dwindled to 5,124.

DEVIATION FROM MASONIC LAW

The LDS Church continued to maintain its own barrier, constructed during Lorenzo Snow's administration, to discourage its members from joining "secret societies." The *Church Handbook* strongly advised leaders that members should not join such organizations, which were "antagonistic to the Church." In 1967 the First Presidency advised that members who had joined such organizations "are counseled to withdraw themselves...as soon as circumstances permit and wisdom dictates." Nevertheless, the primary reason for the policy was apparently the concern of church leaders that such organizations "would cause members to lose interest in Church activities or violate Church standards."[69]

Despite these longstanding instructions, some LDS writers began to acknowledge that there were connections between the endowment and Masonic rituals. In 1958 Hugh Nibley modified the views he had expressed when he reviewed Fawn Brodie's biography of Joseph Smith, by observing that "amongst the first to engage in the Latter-day temple work were many

68. *1965 Proceedings of the Grand Lodge of Utah* (Salt Lake City, 1965). But see Alphonse Cerza, *Anti-Masonry* (Missouri Lodge of Research, 1962), 111–16; and Ralph A. Herbold, "Masonry and Mormonism" (Los Angeles: Southern California Research Lodge, 1966), 8. Ralph Herbold stated that he reviewed the relationship between Mormonism and Masonry in Illinois and concluded, "I respect the decision of Utah in continuing the ban on Mormons in Utah Masonry because of the ever present danger, as they probably see it, of a Mormon domination of Masonry."
69. See Gary James Bergera, comp., *Statements of the LDS First Presidency* (Salt Lake City: Signature Books, 2007), 412–13. This compilation includes extracts from the *Church Handbook* published in 1963, 1976, and 1983, as well as a letter written by Joseph A. Anderson on behalf of the First Presidency on July 25, 1967.

members of the Masons, a society that 'is not, and does not profess to be a religion,' but whose rites present unmistakable parallels to those of the temple."[70] Nibley noted that Joseph Smith had pointed out "a common heritage from what he calls the archaic religion, coming down from Adam in such institutions as Freemasonry, and clearly pointing out their defects as time produced its inevitable corruption."[71]

Nine years later Nibley concluded that the similarities between the endowment and the "broken fragments" of Masonic ritual were purely incidental, because of their common ancestry, and had "nothing to do with salvation." But he also suggested that "Masonic rites and ordinances… have been picked up from various times and you can trace them back…to very early times." Even "the ordinances of Knights Templar and the Hospitalers—two early secret orders imported into Europe at the time of the Crusades," Nibley wrote, "were actually based on Solomon's temple and on work for the dead."[72]

But the most dramatic acknowledgment made by an LDS Church employee concerning the parallels between Masonic ritual and the endowment occurred in 1974 when Reed C. Durham Jr., director of the LDS Institute of Religion at the University of Utah, delivered his presidential address during the annual meeting of the Mormon History Association.[73] Durham concluded that the Mormon temple endowment "had an immediate inspiration from Masonry" and that "most of the things which were developed in the church at Nauvoo were inextricably interwoven with Masonry."

Durham concluded that the connections between Masonic rituals and the endowment were "so apparent and overwhelming that some dependent relationship cannot be denied."[74] He told his audience that there were con-

70. Hugh Nibley, "The Idea of the Temple in History," *Millennial Star* 120 (1958), 247–49, reprinted in Hugh Nibley, *Mormonism and Early Christianity* (Salt Lake City: Deseret Book Company, 1987), 369.
71. Hugh Nibley, "Return to the Temple," in Hugh Nibley, *Temple and Cosmos* (Salt Lake City: Deseret Book Company, 1992), 48.
72. Hugh Nibley, "Apocryphal Writings and Teachings of the Dead Sea Scrolls," in *Temple and Cosmos*, 319–20.
73. Durham's speech has been published at least three times without the author's permission. See Reed C. Durham Jr., "Is There No Help for the Widow's Son?" (Salt Lake City: Research Lodge of Utah F. & A.M., 16 Sept. 1974), 58–73; Reed C. Durham Jr., "Is There No Help for the Widow's Son?" *Mormon Miscellaneous* 1 (Oct. 1975): 11–16; and Reed C. Durham Jr., "Is There No Help for the Widow's Son?" (Nauvoo, IL: Martin Publishing Company, 1980), 15–33. All references to the speech are from the version published by Martin Publishing Company.
74. Durham, "Is There No Help for the Widow's Son?" 18–22. Durham also relied on a holographic letter allegedly written by Joseph Smith to John Hull to support the connection between Masonic ritual and the endowment but it is unlikely that the Mormon prophet wrote the letter.

nections between the signs, tokens, obligations, and penalties of the two rituals, and between the symbolic meanings of the rituals, which were to provide knowledge and keys to return to God's presence. But Durham told his startled audience that there were not only parallels between the endowment and the Craft degrees but also with the *Haut Grades* and even adoptive rites. He discussed the parallels to the Masonic legend of Enoch and said that there were "Masonic overtones" present in the minutes of the Nauvoo Female Relief Society.[75] According to Durham, Smith "accepted Masonry because he generally felt he recognized true ancient mysteries contained therein" and that he "modified, expanded, amplified, or glorified it." Finally, Durham called out Mormon historians for denying the temple legacy "in an ostrich-like fashion, with our heads buried in the traditional sand."[76]

Although Durham undoubtedly recognized that the Mormon Church's official position concerning the temple legacy had changed over the years, he must have been surprised at the response he received after delivering his revisionist contribution to "new Mormon history." He was censured, he no longer participated in the Mormon History Association, and the *Journal of Mormon History* (perhaps at his request) did not publish his address. This extreme reaction suggests that some church leaders still believed that it was improper for an instructor in the church education system to either acknowledge or discuss connections between Freemasonry and Mormonism.[77]

Nevertheless, Durham did not suggest or imply that Smith was not a prophet or that he had simply copied or adapted Masonic ritual when he introduced the endowment. Nevertheless, in his letter of apology, which he attempted to send to every person who heard his speech, he acknowledged that some of his colleagues "questioned my faith in Joseph Smith and the Church." He therefore reconfirmed that he knew that Joseph Smith was a prophet, "that Temple Work, with all its ramifications including Eternal Marriage and the Endowment ceremony is divinely inspired," and that "the

---

75. Durham, "Is There No Help for the Widow's Son?" 18–28. Durham's discussion of female adoptive rituals as models for Joseph Smith's endowment was striking because even those Mormon scholars who recognized Masonic parallels in the endowment had concluded that "the creation and fall narrative, the content of the major covenants, and the washings and anointings have no parallel in Masonry." See, e.g., Buerger, "The Development of the Mormon Temple Endowment Ceremony," 33–76.
76. Durham, "Is There No Help for the Widow's Son?" 22–28.
77. For discussion concerning the slippery slope between reason and faith in a Mormon context, see Clara V. Dobay, "Intellect and Faith: The Controversy over Revisionist Mormon History," *Dialogue: A Journal of Mormon Thought* 27 (Spring 1994): 92, 96; and Launius, "The 'New Social History,'" 109, 123–24.

prime criterion or standard of judgment I am committed to employ as an explanation of any aspect of the Church—either of Joseph Smith and/or the Temple ceremonies—is that of divine revelation."[78]

It is difficult to determine whether Durham's speech had any impact on Utah Masons. Nevertheless, during this same period some Masons were becoming increasingly critical of the Utah practice of excluding Mormons. Mervin Hogan openly challenged the barrier and maintained that "Freemasonry has no incompatibilities as to principles or philosophies with Mormonism" and that the continued exclusion of Mormons was "invalid Masonically and without any justification whatsoever except for unbridled emotional bias and prejudice."

In 1977 Macoy Publishing (which was not an official publisher but whose works were very popular among Masons) substituted Hogan's article "Mormonism and Masonry: The Illinois Episode," in which he criticized Utah Mason, in its *Little Masonic Library*, for Goodwin's *Mormonism and Masonry*, which appeared in the 1946 edition. Macoy's publication of Hogan's article was significant because it demonstrated that many Masons no longer supported the Utah Grand Lodge's exclusionary policy that Goodwin had justified in his publications.[79]

DECLINING MEMBERSHIP AND ATTENDANCE

In fact, most Utah Masons recognized that many American Masons were quite critical of the Utah policy and that membership (which was not available to more than 70 percent of the population) was in sharp decline. In 1981, Grand Orator W. Thuren Odendahl delivered an impassioned speech to the annual communication of the grand lodge in which he acknowledged, "Grand Master after Grand Master [had] express[ed] their concern over Utah's declining membership." He said that "this same concern [was] echoed many times by visiting dignitaries."

Odendahl asked, "How do we reach these brethren to inform them [that] our membership of 6,968 in 1963 has dropped to 5,124 Master Masons at the end of 1979? This loss of 1,844 Masons over a 16 year period represents a loss of 26.5% of our members, which averages out to a loss of approximately 115 members per year. The R.W. Grand Secretary informs me

78. See Reed C. Durham, "To Whom It May Concern," n.d., in Patricia Lyn Scott, James E. Crooks, and Sharon G. Pugsley, "A Kinship of Interest: The Mormon History Association's Membership," *Journal of Mormon History* 18 (Spring 1992): 153, 156.
79. Mervin B. Hogan, "Mormonism and Freemasonry, The Illinois Experience," in *Little Masonic Library* (Richmond, VA: Macoy Publishing and Masonic Supply Co., Inc., 1977), 2:323. For a critical review of Hogan's work, see Kent L. Walgren, "Fast and Loose Freemasonry," *Dialogue: A Journal of Mormon Thought* 18:3 (Fall 1985): 172–76.

our loss for 1980 is 119 members. Should this trend continue for another 13 years, Utah would lose one half of its membership."[80] During this same period some Masonic lodges in Utah began opening their doors to visiting Mormon Masons. The catalyst for this change was the election of a Mormon in 1980 as the grand master of the Grand Lodge of California.

In 1983, the Utah Grand Lodge reconsidered and defeated a motion to amend the code to remove the provision prohibiting Mormons from joining Masonry.[81] But when the resolution was reintroduced the following year, the committee on jurisprudence asked the members of the grand lodge to consider Sam Goodwin's justifications for excluding Mormons that he had outlined in *Mormonism and Masonry* and *Additional Studies in Mormonism and Masonry*.[82]

One of the most important inquiries was whether "the aim of abolishing the Resolution and Decision [was] solely for the purpose of enlarging our membership?" Utah Masonry's exclusionary policy limited the Craft's membership base to less than 30 percent of the state's population. Nevertheless, while as much as 70 percent of Utah was nominally Mormon, a significant number of those were either inactive or had disavowed any allegiance to the LDS Church. But even nominal Mormons were prohibited from joining Freemasonry under the Utah Grand Lodge's bylaws and it was among this class of "Mormons" that some Masons hoped to attract new members if the blanket prohibition was eliminated.

The committee also inquired whether "members of the LDS Church [could] become active and valuable members, thereby strengthening the craft, and at the same time remain loyal to their faith?" This question demonstrated that some Utah Masons were concerned whether active members of the LDS Church could become committed Masons. In other words, did inherent differences exist between Mormonism and Masonry that made it impossible for them to officially associate with one another?

Since Masonry's only "religious" test was that an initiate must "be a believer in the Grand Architect of the Universe," this issue focused on

80. *1981 Proceedings*, 52, "Our Declining Membership and Attendance," February 21, 1981.
81. *1983 Proceedings of the Grand Lodge of Utah* (Salt Lake City, 1983), 61.
82. Ibid. The Grand Lodge was asked to consider seven questions: "Would abolishing the Standing Resolution have any impact on membership, for good or for ill?; Could members of the LDS Church become active and valuable members, thereby strengthening the Craft, and at the same time remain loyal to their faith?; Would such Church members fully respect our Ancient Landmark which prohibits any discussion of religion in a Masonic Lodge?; Would such members apply individual pressure on our devotees to join their Church?; Is the aim of abolishing the Resolution and Decision solely for the purpose of enlarging our membership?; Is there any point in our taking a unilateral action, without any change in the position presently held by the leadership of the LDS Church?; and Are you willing to continue this deviation from Masonic law by retaining this restriction?"

Congregational pastor Goodwin's charge that Mormons believed in the
"plurality of Gods."[83] This was a familiar argument used by many fundamentalist Christian organizations to argue that Mormons were not Christians.
But Masonry did not require candidates to be Christian. Buddhists, Hin-
dus, and members of other religions that believe in plural gods have been
allowed to join Freemasonry for at least two centuries, as long as they are
not atheists or pantheists.[84]

The committee on jurisprudence inquired whether "[LDS] Church
members fully respect our ancient landmark which prohibits any discussion of religion in the Masonic lodge? Would such members apply individual pressure on our devotees to join their Church?" Freemasons insist that
discussions concerning politics or religion cannot take place in the lodge.
The reason for such a prohibition was to prevent the development of a "Masonic theology" and to keep the organization nondenominational. Since
Mormonism has long been recognized, particularly in the United States,
as a missionary church that proselytizes non-Mormons, some Masons were
concerned that if Mormons were allowed to join Masonry they might pressure lodge members to join their church.

The grand lodge also recognized that the Mormon hierarchy had made
strong statements concerning "secret societies" and wondered whether
there was "any point in our taking a unilateral action, without any change
in the position presently held by the leadership of the LDS Church?" Some
members of Utah Masonry were reluctant to amend their code to admit
Mormons without a concomitant change by the LDS Church. The 1983
General Handbook of Instructions for the Mormon Church warned "members strongly not to join any organization that…is secret and oath-bound,"
and further advised "local leaders [to] decide whether Church members
who belong to secret oath-bound organizations may be ordained or advanced in the priesthood or may receive a temple recommend."[85]

While Utah Masons required petitioners to certify that they were not
members of the LDS Church, or that they had withdrawn from the church,
there were few Mormons who tested their own churches' instructions to
refrain from joining "secret societies." But the LDS Church apparently
took no action against members who joined the Masons outside of Utah.[86]

83. *The Masonic Code of the Most Worshipful Grand Lodge of Free and Accepted Masons of
Utah* (Salt Lake City, 1958), 59.
84. Pick and Knight, *The Freemason's Pocket Reference Book*, 139, 280.
85. *General Handbook of Instructions* (Salt Lake City: Church of Jesus Christ of Latter-day
Saints, 1983), 77.
86. See, e.g., Glenn L. Pace, "A Thousand Times," *Ensign* 20:11 (November 1990): 8–10;
Derin Head Rodriguez, "Reaching Out," *Ensign* 22:1 (January 1992): 66–71.

Utah Masons also recognized that other churches, including Presbyterians, Methodists, Lutherans, Anglicans, and, of course, the Roman Catholic Church, had, from time to time, condemned Freemasonry and prohibited their members from joining the Craft.[87]

Perhaps the most significant inquiry was whether Utah Masons were "willing to continue this deviation from Masonic law by retaining this restriction?" Many Masonic observers believed this question was the primary factor that convinced the members of the Grand Lodge of Utah to change their longstanding practice and allow Mormons to visit and join Masonry. Utah Masons had grown weary of their sister lodges' increasing criticisms of this exclusionary rule (despite their continued attempts to explain it) and of being singled out as the only Masonic grand lodge in the world that prohibited members of a named religious faith from becoming Masons.

As the grand lodge's rationales for excluding Mormons became less meaningful, the price it paid for that policy (criticism by fellow Masonic lodges and a narrow membership base) had become too costly. In 1984 the Grand Lodge of Utah voted, following a vigorous debate, to reverse Utah's unique policy of excluding all Mormons from entering their temples at a time when Utah Masonry had fewer members than at any other time since the 1920s.

HAND OVER THEIR HEARTS

Shortly after the grand lodge eliminated its exclusionary policy toward Mormons, the LDS Church modified its own written instructions concerning secret societies. The 1989 edition of the *General Handbook of*

87. In 1983 the Sacred Congregation for the Doctrine of Faith issued a statement that reconfirmed the church's previous position that Roman Catholics who joined Freemasonry could be excommunicated. Cardinal Ratzinger of the Sacred Congregation of the Doctrine of Faith (who became Pope Benedict XVI) published a document, approved by Pope John Paul II, that Catholics who became members of any Masonic organization "cannot receive communion nor any other sacrament" even though a new *Code of Canon Law*, published in 1983, had eliminated Freemasonry from a list of excommunicable offenses. Congregation for the Doctrine of Faith, *Declaratio de Associationibis Massonicis*, of November 26, 1983, in Congregatio pro Doctrina Fidei, *Documenta inde a Concilio Vaticano Secundo expleto edita (1966–2005)* (Vatican City, Libreria Editrice Vaticana 2006), 229. This policy was explained in "Inconciliabilita' tra fede Cristiana e massoneria. Riflessioni a un anno dalla dichiarazione della Congregazione per la Dottrina della Fede," published in *L'Osservatore Romano. Giornale quotidano politico religioso* (the official Vatican newspaper) on February 23, 1985. The Jesuits strongly supported this position in an editorial published in *La Civiltá Cattolica*. Editoriale, "La Chiesa e la Massoneria Oggi," *La Civiltá Cattolica* 4:3393 (November 2, 1991): 217–27. The most recent discussion of the Roman Catholic position is set forth in no. 370 of *Cristianitá* (October–December 2013), the official publication of Alleanza Cattolica.

Instructions removed a provision that discouraged members from joining "any organization that…is secret and oath-bound." Nevertheless, LDS Church spokesman Don LeFevre released a statement three years later that the church "strongly advises its members not to affiliate with organizations that are secret, oath-bound, or would cause them to lose interest in church activities."[88]

Despite the dismantling of Masonic and Mormon barriers to joining the Craft in Utah, Mormons did not join Utah lodges in sufficient numbers to reverse the downward spiral in Utah Masonic membership, which was consistent with a national and even worldwide trend. By December 31, 1990, there were just 3,784 Master Masons in Utah (a decrease since 1979 of 1,340 or 25 percent), and in 2000 there were 2,517 Utah Masons, which represented a further decrease of 1,267 or 33 percent. These decreases were consistent with similar trends in most Masonic organizations, which were also losing membership. In 2012 there were 2,057 Master Masons in Utah, or only slightly more than the number of Mormon Masons who had joined the Craft in Illinois before Joseph Smith was killed.[89] In addition, there were Prince Hall Masons, recognized by the Grand Lodge, and co-Masons (in androgynous lodges) who are not recognized.

Nevertheless, some Mormons who did join the Craft eventually became masters of their lodges and officers in the grand lodge. In 2008 Glen Cook, a Mormon Mason, was installed by the Grand Lodge of Utah as the 137th grand master. This was a significant development and demonstrates that much of the ill will that existed between Mormons and Masons for more than one hundred fifty years had dissipated by the dawn of the twenty-first century.

The dynamic developments in the relations between Masons and Mormons became evident when Gordon B. Hinckley, the fifteenth Mormon prophet, died and his casket was taken from the Salt Lake Tabernacle to the Salt Lake City cemetery. The *Salt Lake Tribune* reported that a "group of Masons gathered on the front steps [of the Masonic Lodge in Salt Lake City]…and stood with their hands over their hearts as the [funeral] cortege

88. *Salt Lake Tribune*, February 17, 1992, D-1, D-2. The 1989 *General Handbook of Instructions* prohibited affiliation with "apostate cults," which it defined as "those that advocate plural marriage." *General Handbook of Instructions* (Salt Lake City: Church of Jesus Christ of Latter-day Saints, 1989), 10–13.
89. Arturo de Hoyas, Brent Morris, and Steven Bullock have noted that American Masonry peaked during the 1960s with 4.2 million members and that forty years later there were only about 2 million. See de Hoyas and Morris, *Freemasonry in Context*, vii; Bullock, "Masons, Masonic History, and Academic Scholarship," xii. For the Utah statistics I am indebted to Lawrence K. Fielden, grand secretary of the Grand Lodge of Utah.

passed."[90] Ironically, these Utah Masons (some of whom were Mormons) honored a non-Mason Mormon prophet while their nineteenth-century predecessors (who were all non-Mormons) failed to show the same respect for Brigham Young, John Taylor, Wilford Woodruff, and Lorenzo Snow who were all Master Masons.

90. Carrie A. Moore, "New Grand Master is First in a Century who is LDS," *Deseret News* (March 29, 2008), E1, E3. The church-owned *Deseret News* incorrectly concluded that Cook was "the first member of The Church of Jesus Christ of Latter-day Saints to be elected grand master in Utah in nearly a century."

14

Legends and Folklore

ERIC FRONER HAS DEMONSTRATED that "racial prejudice was all but universal in antebellum northern society."[1] Most Americans did not believe that African Americans were entitled to become citizens (vote, hold office) or to enter into the same social circles as white citizens. In virtually the entire country African Americans were expected to respect social distinctions that separated the races and many anticipated that they would establish their own settlements in colonies located off shore.

SMITH'S VIEWS ON RACE

When Joseph Smith published his translation of the Chandler papyri in the *Times and Seasons* in 1842, it included the passages he had dictated in 1835 relating to the ineligibility of Ham's descendants to receive the priesthood.[2] When Smith published this translation, the notion that Ham's descendants were cursed was a widespread belief among many Christians[3] and was con-

1. Eric Froner, *Free Soil, Free Labor, Free Men: The Ideology of the Republican Party Before the Civil War* (Oxford: Oxford University Press, 1995), 261. See also Froner, *The Fiery Trial*, 21–24.
2. *Times and Seasons* 3:9 (March 1, 1842):705. Book of Abraham 1:26–27. Book of Abraham 1:1–2:18 was dictated to scribes in November 1835. Book of Abraham 2:19–5:21 and explanations of the facsimiles were dictated in Nauvoo in 1842.
3. See, e.g., Josiah Priest, *Slavery, As it Relates to the Negro, or African Race* (Albany: C. Van Benthuysen, 1843), 134. He asserted that "the first negro of the earth was Ham, a son of Noah" and appealed to the Bible to justify slavery, arguing that Ham was not only cursed with servitude but also with a black skin. The idea that blacks were descended from Ham can be traced to Hebraic literature written between 200 and 600 C.E.; to sixteenth-century English writings; and to seventeenth-century American observers. See Lester Bush, "Mormonism's Negro Doctrine: An Historical Overview," *Dialogue: A Journal of Mormon Thought* 8:1 (Spring 1973), 16, as well as the references he cites in notes 22 and 23; David M. Goldenberg, *The Curse of Ham: Race and Slavery in Early Judaism, Christianity, and Islam* (Princeton: Princeton University Press, 2003); Stephen R. Haynes, *Noah's Curse: The Biblical Justification of American Slavery* (Oxford: Oxford University Press, 2002), in *Brigham Young University Studies* 44:1 (2005): 157–65; and David Brion Davis, *The Problem of*

sistent with Masonry's two-race theory, which prevented *all* African Americans from being initiated, passed, and raised in Masonic temples. Even Nauvoo Lodge, on occasion, blackballed candidates who were described as having a "dark complexion" or "dark skin."[4]

Smith, like many of his contemporaries who were opposed to slavery, believed in a separate-but-equal policy, and stated that he "would confine [African Americans] by strict laws to their own Species," and "put them on national Equalization."[5] He told Orson Hyde, one of his apostles, that if slaveholders joined the church they should "bring their slaves into a free country" and "set them free" and that his policy would be to "Educate them & give them equal Rights."[6] He also predicted that if African Americans could "change their situation with the whites,…they would be like them. They have souls, and are subjects of salvation."[7]

During Smith's presidential campaign he developed an even more nuanced solution to slavery and race relations. In his "Views of the Powers and Policy of the Government of the United States" (written by W. W. Phelps), he called on the nation to "create confidence, restore freedom, break down slavery," and advocated legislation under which slaveholders would be compensated for their slaves by using funds from the sale of public lands. He maintained that the officers of the country "ought to be directed to ameliorate the condition of all, black or white, bond or free; for the best of books says, 'God hath made of one blood all nations of men for to dwell on the face of the earth.'"

The Mormon prophet encouraged the "inhabitants of the slave States [to petition] your legislatures to abolish slavery by the year 1850, or now, and save the abolitionist from reproach and ruin, infamy and shame." Nevertheless, he did not favor federal intervention to accomplish this goal

---

Slavery in Western Culture (Ithaca, NY: Cornell University Press, 1966), 64–65, 217, 316–17, and 451–53. While Noah's curse of Canaan, son of Ham, to be a "servant of servants" implied slavery, it is less clear why it was connected to skin color. Winthrop Jordan notes that "when the story of Ham's curse did become relatively common in the seventeenth century it was used almost entirely as an explanation of color rather than as justification of Negro slavery." See Jordan, *White over Black*, 17–18.

4. "Record of Nauvoo Lodge," June 16, 1842; July 17, 1842. Although the *History of the Church* records that Smith taught the church in Nauvoo that Noah cursed Canaan "by the priesthood which he held…and the curse remains upon the posterity of Canaan until the present day," this entry was not based on a contemporary statement (it was added to the Manuscript History in an addenda book started in October 1854, almost thirteen years after the event described and more than ten years after Smith's death) and may have been based on statements he made in Ohio. See *History of the Church* 4:445–46.

5. *History of the Church* 5:217–18; Hedges, Smith, and Anderson, *Journals* 2:212 (January 2, 1843).

6. Hedges, Smith, and Anderson, *Journals* 2:197 (December 30, 1842).

7. Ibid., 2:212 (January 2, 1843).

since "a hireling pseudo priesthood will plausibly push abolition doctrines and doings, and 'human rights' into Congress and into every other place, where conquest smells of fame, or opposition swells to popularity."

When Smith met Josiah Quincy and Charles Francis Adams, he told them that he "recognized the curse and iniquity of slavery, though he opposed the methods of the Abolitionists" and proposed that the federal government should compensate slaveholders "from the sale of public lands." Quincy compared Smith's comments with those of Ralph Waldo Emerson who later made a similar proposal.[8]

Despite his opposition to slavery, Smith (like most enfranchised white men in Illinois) did not believe that African Americans should be placed on equal political or social footing with whites. African Americans were not allowed to vote in Nauvoo, and on the same day that W. W. Phelps delivered Smith's "Views of the Powers and Policy of the Government of the United States" to an assembly of church leaders, the Mormon prophet and the Nauvoo city court fined two free African Americans for attempting to marry white women.[9] When Smith opened the endowment to women, and introduced a ritual to seal men and women, it added a new complexity to the temple ritual that did not exist when the endowment was introduced in Joseph's first temple.

Nevertheless, during his lifetime there is no evidence that Smith insisted that African men could not be ordained to the Mormon priesthood or participate in the temple.[10] In fact, when he announced that a new temple would be built in Nauvoo, Smith emphasized that it would be open to "all languages, and of every tongue, and of every color."

During the same year the temple's chief cornerstone was laid, Elijah Abel received a renewed certificate as a seventy.[11] He was also a proxy for at least two individuals who were baptized for the dead.[12] In addition, Walker Lewis (1798–1856), another African American who was a member of the Massachusetts General Colored Association, and a past master (1825–1826) and past grand master (1829–1830) in Prince Hall Masonry, was baptized in 1842 (perhaps by Apostle Parley P. Pratt) in Lowell, Massachusetts, and

8. See Josiah Quincy, *Figures of the Past* (Boston: Roberts Brothers, 1883), 397–98.

9. Faulring, *An American Prophet's Record*, 445 (February 8, 1844); *History of the Church* 6:210.

10. Kenney, *Wilford Woodruff's Journal* 2:186–87 (August 10 to September 19, 1842).

11. Nauvoo Seventies License Record 1840–1845, 21, LDS Church History Library. See also Bush, "Mormonism's Negro Doctrine," 11, 52n23; Jenson, *Latter-day Saint Biographical Encyclopedia* 3:577.

12. Susan Easton Black and Harvey Bischoff Black, *Annotated Record of Baptisms for the Dead, 1840–1845, Nauvoo, Hancock County, Illinois* (Provo, UT: Brigham Young University Press, 2002), 1:10.

shortly thereafter he was ordained an elder by William Smith who was the prophet's younger brother.[13]

MASONIC PRACTICES

Shortly after Smith was murdered, the Grand Lodge of Illinois became embroiled in a controversy that may shed some light on the possible connection between the Mormon policy preventing those with African ancestry from entering the temple (which was institutionalized by Smith's successors) and Masonry's exclusionary policy. In the spring of 1845 A. B. Lewis, an African American and Master Mason who did not live in Illinois, was admitted as a visitor in several Chicago lodges.[14] In May one of these lodges, Apollo Lodge No. 32, received petitions from two African American candidates to be initiated as Freemasons.

Within days of receiving these petitions the lodge voted to take no action until it had procured "an expression of the Grand Lodge on the subject."[15] On November 21 Apollo Lodge appointed a committee that reported favorably on the petitions, but when a member of Apollo Lodge, who had attended grand lodge in October, reported that the lodge had not "obtained an expression from the Grand Lodge on the subject," the lodge unanimously passed a resolution that the two petitioners should be allowed to withdraw their petitions for initiation into the lodge.[16]

Despite this decision, Harmony Lodge No. 3 (Jacksonville) passed a resolution on December 2 that stated, in relevant part, that "we cannot recognize *any* individual of the African race as being 'free-born,' as they are, by the constitution and laws of our country, *denied the rights and privileges of citizens*. Neither can we extend to them the hand of fellowship and brotherly love, believing that by so acting…we would be trampling upon all the landmarks of the Institution."[17] Significantly, this resolution stated that all blacks, slave or free, were not "freeborn" as required by the ancient landmarks, and that they were therefore disqualified from becoming freemasons or entering Masonic temples.

The lodge authorized that fifty copies of these resolutions be sent to the other Illinois lodges that generally expressed their support for the general

13. Connell O'Donovan, "The Mormon Priesthood Ban and Elder Q. Walker Lewis: 'An example for his more whiter brethren to follow,'" *The John Whitmer Historical Association Journal* 26 (2006): 47–99.
14. Reynolds, *History of the M. W. Grand Lodge of Illinois*, 382.
15. Ibid., 383.
16. Ibid.
17. Ibid., 365 (emphasis added).

proposition that African Americans should not be allowed into any Masonic lodge in Illinois. Nevertheless, the specific rationale used by each lodge varied greatly. The three lodges located in Chicago (which met together to address this issue), expressed a "desire to respect the feelings and scruples of a portion of the members of the Fraternity, and to continue that harmony which is the strength of our Institution."[18] The belief of Friendship Lodge No. 7 of Dixon, Illinois, was that the admission of blacks would be "in opposition to the fundamental principles of Masonry."[19] St. John's Lodge No. 13 of Peru, Illinois, passed a resolution that "the admission of negroes to such privileges would in our opinion be in *violation of ancient usage*, and that the legal and *other disabilities* under which they labor, *will forever prevent their admission upon equality with others*."[20] St. Clair Lodge No. 24 of Belleville, Illinois, concluded that the "Masonic tie is too sacred, the Union is too close, to admit to the inner chamber of our hearts, *those whose blood the Almighty has by an immutable law declared should never traverse our veins*."[21]

In October 1846 the grand lodge articulated the most striking rationale when it met during its seventh annual communication. It rejected the Chicago lodges' argument "in favor of the rights of negroes to admission, basing their views on the oft-repeated declaration, that whoever is in possession of our universal language is entitled to admission into our halls throughout the habitable globe." It asserted that African Americans were *not* entitled to "mutual reciprocity of all social privileges" and adopted a resolution that lodges must do nothing "that would tend to create social discord and disrupt the political relations of the confederate state." The "Author of all has placed a *distinguishing mark* upon them, clearly indicating that there was a distinctiveness to be kept up; and *it is repulsive to the finest feelings of the heart to think that between them and us there can be a mutual reciprocity of all social privileges*." It concluded with the question, "And why then introduce them into our inner temple, *where the closest connections are inculcated and solemnized?* Other objections might be urged, but your committee deem the above hints sufficient."[22]

In 1851 the Grand Lodge of Illinois passed another resolution that stated categorically that "all subordinate lodges under this jurisdiction be instructed to admit no negro or mulatto, as visitor or otherwise, under any

18. Ibid., 383.
19. Ibid., 368.
20. Ibid., 371 (emphasis added).
21. Ibid., 375 (emphasis added).
22. Ibid., 390 (emphasis added).

circumstances whatever."[23] They believed that African Americans were the descendants of Cain and Ham, that they were inherently not freeborn, and that they were ineligible to enter their temples. This resolution was consistent with those followed in free and slave states and in lodges where there were antislavery and proslavery Masons.[24]

After the Grand Lodge of Illinois passed its second resolution adopting a statewide exclusionary rule, the Grand Lodge of New York published correspondence in which it stated, "It is not proper to initiate in our lodges persons of the negro race; and their exclusion is in accordance with masonic law, and the Ancient Charges and Regulations" and "the Grand Lodge of Iowa adopted a report on foreign correspondence that embodied and endorsed the action of the Grand Lodge of New York." New Hampshire Masons also confirmed that "we should not be willing to admit a negro or mulatto into Masonry." These letters demonstrated that an unwritten policy was followed by virtually all American Masons prohibiting African Americans from joining their lodges or even visiting their temples.[25]

These published rationales, which were previously only discussed in private, confrim that Freemasons denied African Americans access to their temples not only as visitors because of the issue of "exclusive jurisdiction," but that they also believed no blacks were eligible to become Masons because of their ethnic ancestry and because of the ancient landmarks. Nevertheless, most American Freemasons begrudgingly recognized that the United Grand Lodge of London had modified its constitution to provide that Masons must be "freemen" rather than "freeborn" and that men of African descent had been initiated into the Craft in England and in Europe.

In 1854 Robert Morris noted in *American Freemason* that a "negro or mulatto applying for admission as a visitor, may be examined, if he hail from a foreign jurisdiction; but he must not be, if made in an American lodge." As such, Masonic writers carefully distinguished between Freemasons of African descent who were made Masons outside the United States, who could be examined and admitted as visitors, with Prince Hall Masons, who

---

23. For the complete resolution, see *Transactions: The American Lodge of Research Free and Accepted Masons* 4:1, 129–30.

24. Joseph A. Walkes Jr., a Prince Hall Freemason, observed that "American Masons reasoned with [United States Supreme Court Chief Justice] Judge Taney that there are 'slave races,' that black men were by right as well as by law, slaves, and that they could never be participants in the institutions intended for the benefit and happiness of white men. This was the generally accepted sentiment of American Masons, and they knew no 'higher law.'" Joseph A. Walkes Jr., *A Prince Hall Masonic Quiz Book*, rev. ed. (Richmond, VA: Macoy, 1989), 136.

25. George Wingate Chase, *Digest of Masonic Law*, 3rd ed. (New York: Macoy & Sickels, 1864), 211–13; Upton, *Negro Freemasonry*, 34–35.

were not eligible to visit American lodges, and all other African Americans, who were not Freemasons and who were ineligible to become members of a regular white lodge.[26]

BRIGHAM YOUNG'S POLICY

After Brigham Young assumed the mantle of leadership, the church hierarchy embellished Smith's teachings concerning Ham's curse and priesthood eligibility. In April 1845 the *Times and Seasons* published an unsigned article that connected Ham's curse with an apostate priesthood just as George Oliver had connected it with spurious Masonry. The article noted that "Ham had dishonored the holy priesthood" and that "as the priesthood descended from father to son," Noah cursed Ham's offspring: "The descendants of Ham, besides *a black skin which has ever been a curse that has followed an apostate of the holy priesthood,* as well as a black heart, have been servants to both Shem and Japheth, and the abolitionists are trying to make void the curse of God, but it will require more power than man possesses to counteract the decrees of eternal wisdom."[27]

Apostle Orson Hyde taught during the same month that the African race had not been valiant in the pre-existence and was therefore "required to come into the world and take bodies in the cursed lineage of Canaan; and hence the negro or African race."[28] This statement, which was apparently the first time any church leader had connected the curse with the Mormon doctrine of pre-existence, was eventually repudiated by Brigham Young.[29] But neither the *Times and Seasons* nor Orson Hyde mentioned the Book of Abraham or specifically stated that Cain's or Ham's "curse" prevented *all* African Americans from being ordained to the Mormon priesthood or from being endowed in the temple.

In March 1847 Young encountered Warner McCary (ca. 1811–after 1854)—also known as William—who was the son of a white slave owner and an African American woman in Winter Quarters, Nebraska Territory,

26. Chase, *Digest of Masonic Law,* 212–13. See also *Abstract of Proceedings of the Grand Lodge of Massachusetts (1870),* 43–44, which published a June 2, 1846, letter from the grand secretary of New York which stated that "the course of our Grand Lodge, in reference to the African Lodge, is not the result of prejudice, it is only necessary for me to say, that, within the last month, a colored Brother from England has visited, and been kindly received, in one of our city lodges." See also Upton, *Negro Freemasonry,* 149–51.
27. "A Short Chapter on a Long Subject," *Times and Seasons* 6 (April 1, 1845): 857 (emphasis added).
28. Orson Hyde, *Speech of Orson Hyde Delivered before the High Priests Quorum in Nauvoo, April 27th 1845* (Liverpool: Millennial Star, 1845), p. 27. See also Joseph Smith Hyde, *Orson Hyde* (Salt Lake City, 1933), 3, 32; Brodie, *No Man Knows My History,* 174.
29. Kenney, *Wilford Woodruff's Journal* 6:511 (December 25, 1869).

while the Mormons were traveling toward the Great Basin. McCary visited Nauvoo in late 1845 and was converted to Mormonism the following year in Council Bluffs, Iowa, where he may have been ordained to the priesthood. When McCary met Young he claimed that he was half African American and half Native American and that he was the lost son of Choctaw Chief Mushulatubbee. But Young was apparently more interested in McCary's claims that he possessed the power of prophecy and transfiguration than in his racial identity. He told McCary that God had made one flesh from one blood and that the priesthood was not race-based. "It's nothing to do with the blood for [from] one blood has God made all flesh," Young also reportedly said. "We have to repent [to] regain what we [h]av[e] lost—we [h]av[e] one of the best Elders an African [Walker Lewis] in Lowell."[30]

Nevertheless, shortly thereafter Parley P. Pratt, another Mormon apostle who may have baptized Walker Lewis, argued that the Book of Abraham supported the general exclusion of *all* African Americans from being ordained. He told a congregation in April that McCary was a black man with "the blood of Ham in him which linege [*sic*] was cursed as regards the priesthood."[31] The following year McCary was excommunicated from the church, perhaps because he claimed he could take plural wives who included white women, and thereafter marital social considerations in race relations became an explosive new ingredient in the debate concerning whether African Americans were eligible for Mormon priesthood.[32]

30. Church Historian's Office, General Church Minutes, 1839–1877, March 26, 1847, CR 100 318, LDS Church History Library, in *Special Collections from the Archives of the Church of Jesus Christ of Latter-day Saints* (Provo, Utah: Brigham Young University Press, [Dec. 2002]), 1:18. For additional information concerning Warner McCary, see Connell O'Donovan, "Plural Marriage and African Americans: Race, Schism, and the Beginnings of Priesthood and Temple Denial in 1847," to be published by the John Whitmer Historical Association in a collection of essays edited by Newell Bringhurst; Bringhurst, *Saints, Slaves and Blacks: The Changing Place of Black People within Mormonism* (Westport, CT: Greenwood Press, 1981), 85–108; Connell O'Donovan, "The Mormon Priesthood Ban and Elder Q. Walker Lewis: 'An Example for his more whiter brethren to follow,'" *John Whitmer Historical Association Journal* 26 (2006): 82–83; and Connell O'Donovan, "'I Would Confine them to their Own Species': LDS Historical Rhetoric & Praxis Regarding Marriage between Blacks and Whites," Paper Delivered at Sunstone Symposium West (March 28, 2009), Retrieved on January 27, 2013, at: http://www.connellodonovan.com/black_white _marriage.html.
31. Church Historian's Office, General Church Minutes, April 25, 1847, CR 100 138, Box 1, Folder 53, LDS Church History Library, in *Selected Collections from the Archives of the Church of Jesus Christ of Latter-day Saints* (Provo, Utah: Brigham Young University Press [Dec. 2002]), 1:18.
32. In December 1848 McCary was initiated, passed, and raised in Lafayette Lodge No. 41, which was a regular Masonic lodge in Manchester, New Hampshire, apparently because he did not acknowledge his African American heritage but instead claimed to be an American Indian chief. He addressed the Grand Lodge of New Hampshire to seek assistance in forming Masonic Lodges for Indians. See Gerald D. Foss, *Three Centuries of Freemasonry in New*

In May, William Appleby, a Mormon missionary who was serving in Lowell, Massachusetts, wrote in his journal that he encountered Elder Walker Lewis and described him as "a coloured brother" who had been ordained an elder. During this encounter, he became aware that Lewis's son Enoch was married to a white woman and that this was allowed under Massachusetts law. Shortly thereafter Appleby wrote a letter to Brigham Young. "I wish to know if this is the order of God, or tolerated in this Church i.e. to ordain Negroes to the Priesthood and allow amalgamation," he asked. "If it is I desire to Know, as I have Yet got to learn it."

In July Young arrived in the Great Basin, and when he returned to Winter Quarters to reorganize the First Presidency he reviewed Appleby's letter. In December he told members of the Twelve Apostles who were assembled there that amalgamation of the races was wrong and that black men could not be sealed in the temple. He stated that "when they mingle seed it is death to all. If a black man & white woman come to you & demand baptism can you deny them? [T]he law is that their seed cannot be amalgamated. Mulattoes [a]r[e] like mules they cant have children, but if they will be Eunuch for the Kingdom of Heaven's sake they may have a place in the Temple." He also told them that he would have Lewis and his wife killed "if they were far away from the Gentiles."[33]

After Young returned to Great Salt Lake City, he announced to the Twelve Apostles that "the Lord has cursed Cain's seed with blacknes[s]" and that this "prohibited them the priesthood that Abel and his progeny may yet come forward & have their dominion Place and Blessings in their proper relationship with Cain & his race in a world to come."[34] Appleby apparently

Hampshire (Somersworth, NH: New Hampshire Publishing Company, 1972), 502; Daniel J. Littlefield, ed., *The Life of Okah Tubbee* (Lincoln: University of Nebraska Press, 1988), 104. I am indebted to Connell O'Donovan for this information and sources.

33. Minutes of the Quorum of Twelve Apostles, December 3, 1847, 6, Miscellaneous Minutes, Brigham Young Papers, Church History Library. See also Quinn, *Origins of Power*, 478, and Quinn, *Extensions of Power*, 247, 532n145. See also Brigham Young, "The Persecutions of the Saints," *Journal of Discourses* 10:110. ("If the white man who belongs to the chosen seed mixes his blood with the seed of Cain, the penalty, under the law of God, is death on the spot.") Both Newell Bringhurst and Connell O'Donovan have concluded that Walker Lewis's son's marriage to a white woman in Massachusetts strongly influenced Young's decision to exclude African Americans from the Mormon priesthood. Bringhurst, *Saints, Slaves and Blacks*, 98–99; O'Donovan, "The Mormon Priesthood Ban and Elder Q. Walker Lewis," 82–86.

34. Record of the Twelve Apostles in the Handwriting of Wilford Woodruff, February 13, 1849, 12–13, LDS Church History Library. Also in *Journal History* (February 13, 1849), quoted in Bush, "Mormonism's Negro Doctrine," 25. Young made numerous references to the servitude of Cain, Ham, and their descendants before he officially announced that African Americans could not be ordained to the priesthood. See, e.g., Kenney, *Wilford Woodruff's Journal* 4:30 (June 1, 1851); 4:43 (June 29, 1851).

supplemented his journal entry concerning priesthood eligibility following Young's announcement when he wrote that Lewis was ordained "contrary though to the order of the Church or the Law of the Priesthood, as the Descendants of Ham are not entitled to that privilege."[35]

When Young initiated the policy excluding African Americans from priesthood ordination, he did not invoke his predecessor's name but instead stated that "if no other prophet ever spake it before I will say it now in the name of Jesus Christ."[36]

Young institutionalized the policy after he introduced the temple ritual, which was coeducational with males and females in close proximity, and where they were sealed for time and eternity, to the general church membership.[37] Significantly, the full endowment had not been revealed to the general church membership when Elijah Abel was washed and anointed in the male-only initiatory rites that took place in the Kirtland Temple.[38] Although Young and his successors excluded Abel from receiving the Nauvoo endowment, they did not prevent him from functioning in his priesthood office. This suggests that Young's policy had more to do with the coeducational temple endowment and the sealing ordinance than it did a male-only priesthood quorum.[39]

Young believed that Masonic rituals were an apostate version of temple ceremonies practiced in Solomon's Temple, which was restored and introduced to the Holy Order. As such, he may have believed that Masonry's ancient landmarks were remnants of qualifications to enter the temple,

---

35. Journal of William Appleby, May 19, 1847, Church History Library, quoted in Bush, "Mormonism's Negro Doctrine," 56n85. O'Donovan cautions readers about relying on this journal entry to conclude that the "curse" of Ham was used as a rationale to exclude blacks as early as 1847. He notes that this journal entry was apparently not written until the mid-1850s, and that Appleby made an entry twelve days later which referred to a letter to Brigham Young in which he asked whether the ordination of blacks was tolerated in the church. O'Donovan, "The Mormon Priesthood Ban and Elder Q. Walker Lewis," 82–86.

36. Kenney, *Wilford Woodruff's Journal* 4:97–99 (February 5, 1852).

37. Mormon author Vern Swanson has noted that Brigham Young, Heber C. Kimball, Jedediah M. Grant, Orson Hyde, Orson Pratt, Wilford Woodruff, Lorenzo Snow, and Joseph F. Smith taught that Jesus was married. See Vern Grosvenor Swanson, *Dynasty of the Holy Grail: Mormonism's Sacred Bloodline* (Springville, UT: Cedar Fort, 2006), 83, 85. Brigham Young University professors Richard Holzapfel, Andrew Skinner, and Thomas Waymont have acknowledged these teachings, and that there is "no doctrinal reason why Jesus could not have been married and still be the divine Son of God, capable of and willing to atone for the sins of the world." But they note that "many leaders of the [LDS] Church have also cautioned us about speculating on issues that the scriptures have not addressed." Richard Neitzel Holzapfel, Andrew C. Skinner, and Thomas A. Waymont, *What Da Vinci Didn't Know: An LDS Perspective* (Salt Lake City: Deseret Book, 2006), 50.

38. Bush, "Mormonism's Negro Doctrine," 25.

39. O'Donovan has suggested that the catalyst for this policy was Enoch's Lewis' marriage to a white woman. O'Donovan, "The Mormon Priesthood Ban," 47–99.

and that just as Africans were ineligible to enter Solomon's Temple (and its successor Masonic temples), that the policy should be extended to Joseph's temples.[40] Young taught that the Mormon policy was "a law of their existence" because their fathers (presumably Cain and Ham) rejected "the power of the Holy Priesthood, and the law of God." He concluded that "only when the rest of the children [of God] have received their blessings in the Holy Priesthood, then that curse will be removed from the seed of Cain, and they will then come up and possess the priesthood, and receive all the blessings that we are now entitled to."[41]

UTAH'S POLICY

In 1851 Apostle Franklin D. Richards published the Pearl of Great Price, which contained the Book of Abraham as well as portions of Smith's retranslation of the Old Testament, which some authorities cited to justify Mormonism's exclusionary policy.[42] During the same year, Young insisted

40. Ronald K. Esplin argued, before the ban was lifted, that "the doctrine was introduced in Nauvoo and consistently applied in practice at least by 1843." He noted that many, if not most, of Smith's teachings concerning temple-related subjects were private rather than public. The numerous private sessions Smith held with the Twelve and others, especially during 1843–1844, "were the proper forum for the teaching of the 'mysteries of the kingdom' those temple-related teachings that were not to be taught abroad and could not go to the broader membership of the Church until the completion of the temple and the removal of the Church to the relative isolation of the West." Esplin maintained that Young would have had a "private understanding" of Joseph Smith's teaching on this subject even if it was not publicly announced until 1852. But Esplin also acknowledged that the problem in attributing the priesthood policy to Joseph Smith is that "one cannot point to a specific date or place where Joseph Smith taught the principle." Esplin, "Brigham Young and Priesthood Denial," 397–99. See also Klaus J. Hansen, *Mormonism and the American Experience* (Chicago: The University of Chicago Press, 1981), 186–87. Forsberg has expanded Esplin's thesis and concluded that Mormonism's priesthood ban was based on American Masonic policy that excluded blacks from its temples. According to Forsberg, "the debate over whether the priesthood ban was a practice or a doctrine, whether Smith—who ordained a few black men—would approve or disapprove, may indeed be somewhat beside the point. If the Temple is the priesthood, then those who contend for a gentler, kinder Smith on the issue of blacks in priesthood do not have a single leg to balance on." Forsberg, *Equal Rites*, 220–23. See also Michael W. Homer, "'Why then introduce them into our inner temple?'": The Masonic Influence on Mormon Denial of Priesthood Ordination to African American Men," *The John Whitmer Historical Association Journal* 26 (2006): 234–59.
41. Brigham Young, "Delegate Hooper—Beneficial Effects of Polygamy—Final Redemption of Cain," *Journal of Discourses* 11:272 (April 19, 1866). See also Lyman, *The Diaries of Abraham H. Cannon*, 440 (September 30, 1890).
42. The Pearl of Great Price, published in Liverpool in 1851, included the Book of Abraham and its three facsimiles, which revealed that the "king of Egypt was a descendant from the loins of Ham and was a partaker of the blood of the Canaanites by birth," and that Pharaoh was "cursed...as pertaining to the Priesthood." It also included extracts from Enoch's

that "the seed of Ham will be servants until God takes the Curse off from them" and that there "has been a great stir to exalt the Negro & make him equal to the white man but there is a curse upon the head of Cain & all Hell cannot wipe it out & it cannot be taken off until God takes it off."[43]

Shortly thereafter Walker Lewis arrived in Salt Lake City and John Smith (1781–1854) gave him a patriarchal blessing in which he told the African American elder that he was part of the "tribe of Canan [*sic*]."[44] There is no record that Lewis met Young or whether he requested to be endowed, but in January 1852 Young asked the Utah Territorial Legislature, which met at the Council House, to enact legislation that reflected his personal beliefs concerning race and servitude.[45] Thomas Bullock read Young's governor's message, which included some ironic proposals considering his predecessor had urged the Southern states to abolish slavery by 1850.

During his message, Young proposed that Utah Territory adopt a system of indentured servitude that would recognize African American servitude in the territory (as opposed to chattel slavery) and provide a method to compensate slaveholders. He told the legislators that "no property can or should be recognized as existing in slaves, either Indian or African," and that both Native Americans and African Americans could be purchased "into freedom, instead of slavery" in order to be "placed upon an equal footing with the more favored portions of the human race." He argued that "if in return for favors and expense which may have been incurred on their account, service should be considered due" and that legislation was necessary to "provide the suitable regulations under which such indebtedness should be defrayed." This system would improve "the condition of the poor, forlorn, destitute, ignorant savage, or African, as the case may be become ameliorated, and a foundation laid for their advancement in the scale of the useful, exalting existence; useful to themselves, to their nation, and all who shall come within the purview of their influence." Young reminded the legislators that "the seed of cain will inevitably Carry the curse which was placed upon them until the same authority which placed it there, shall see proper to have it removed." As such, "servitude may and should exist, and that too upon those who are naturally designed to occupy the position of

prophecy (dictated by Smith in December 1830) in which "Enoch also beheld the residue of the people which were the sons of Adam, save it were the seed of Cain, for the seed of Cain were black, and had not place among them," and portions of Smith's June 1830 dictation of the visions of Moses ("the Lord set a mark upon Cain, lest any finding him should kill him").
43. Kenney, *Wilford Woodruff's Journal* 4:42–43 (June 29, 1851).
44. O'Donovan, "The Mormon Priesthood Ban and Elder Q. Walker Lewis," 91–92.
45. See Christopher B. Rich Jr., "The True Policy for Utah: Servitude, Slavery, and 'An Act in Relation to Service,'" *Utah Historical Quarterly* 80:1 (Winter 2012): 54–73.

'servant of servants,' yet we should fall in the other extreme, and make them beasts of the field, regarding not the humanity which attaches to the colored race, nor yet elevate them, as some seem disposed to an equality with those whom Nature and Nature's God has indicated to be their masters."[46]

On January 23, Young encouraged a joint session of the territorial legislature to pass a "Bill in relation to African Slavery," but he suggested that the title of the proposed legislation be modified to "An Act in Relation to Manual service."[47] The model for Young's proposed legislation was an Illinois statute that recognized indentured servitude and that was in effect when the Mormons resided in Nauvoo.[48] That law, which was originally adopted in Indiana Territory in 1807 and recognized in Illinois because it was originally part of Indiana before it became a separate territory, allowed slaveholders who resided in the territory to appear before the county clerk where they resided, register their slaves, and execute contracts with their slaves under which they agreed to become indentured to their masters for a specified term.[49]

After Illinois became a state in 1818, its citizens debated and rejected slavery but continued to recognize the practice of indentured servitude. This practice, which was attacked by abolitionists, was a tacit recognition that slaveholders in Illinois retained the right to be compensated for their slaves even when they transferred their residences to free states. As late as 1843 the state supreme court upheld the practice of indentured servitude in *Sarah Borders v. Andrew Borders*. That case was brought by "a woman of color" who had entered into a contract in 1815 for indentured servitude for a period of forty years. She challenged the enforceability of the contract and

46. See "Governor's Message to the Council, and House of Representatives of the Legislature of Utah," *Deseret News* (January 10, 1852), p. 2; Brigham Young, "To the Council and House of Representatives of the Legislature of Utah," in *Journals of the House of Representatives. Council and Joint Sessions of the First Annual and Special Sessions of the Legislative Assembly of the Territory of Utah. Held at Great Salt Lake City 1851 and 1852* (Great Salt Lake City: Brigham H. Young, Printer, 1852), 108–10 (January 5, 1852).
47. "Speech by Governor Young in Joint Session of the Legislature, giving counsel on a Bill in relation to African Slavery, given at Salt Lake City, on Friday, January 23rd, 1852," reported by George D. Watt, Brigham Young Papers, Church History Library, quoted in Collier, *The Teachings of President Brigham Young*, 3:26–29.
48. The United States Constitution recognized the distinction between slavery and servitude. It mentioned "free persons," "Indians," "those bound to service for a term of years," and "three-fifths of all other persons" remaining in the United States. The last reference was a euphemism for African slavery. (U.S. Constitution, Article I, Sec. 2.)
49. John B. Dillon, *A History of Indiana from its Earliest Exploration by Europeans to the close of the Territorial Government in 1816* (Indianapolis: Bingham & Doughty, 1859), 617–19. See also Eric Froner, *The Fiery Trial: Abraham Lincoln and American Slavery* (New York: W. W. Norton, 2010), 7.

the constitutionality and legality of the Illinois law under which such contracts were recognized. The court held that "such contracts and indentures,
made conformably to that act, without fraud or collusion, shall be valid, and
the party held to specific performance."[50]

Young also connected the proposed legislation with his teaching that
African Americans could not receive the Mormon priesthood. He reminded the legislators that since they "believe in the Bible...the ordinances
of God, in the Priesthood and order and decrees of God, we must believe
in Slavery." He told them that even though African Americans could be
baptized, and be confirmed as church members, "they cannot hold the
Priesthood, and inasmuch as they cannot bear any share of the Priesthood,
they cannot bear rule, they cannot bear rule in any place until the curse is
removed from them, they are a 'servant of servants.'" According to Young,
"Such servitude is perfectly reasonable, and strictly according to the Holy
Priesthood." "When the Lord God cursed old Cain," he continued, "He
said, 'Until the last drop of Abel's blood receives the Priesthood, and enjoys
the blessings of the same, Cain shall bear the curse,' then Cain is calculated
to have his share next, and not until then; consequently, I am firm in the
belief that they ought to dwell in servitude."[51]

On February 4, the legislature approved a bill that was captioned "An
Act in Relation to Service." Willard Richards, as president of the council,
and W. W. Phelps, as the speaker of the House of Representatives, forwarded it to Young for his signature. This legislation authorized, like the
Illinois statute, the practice of indentured servitude in the territory if the
masters provided evidence to the probate court "written and satisfactory
evidence that such service or labor is due." The act provided that "persons
coming to this Territory with their servants justly bound to them, arising
from special contract or otherwise, said person or persons shall be entitled
to such service or labor by the laws of this Territory." The act also provided
that the servants' heirs would not be bound "to service for a longer period
than will satisfy the debt due his, her, or their master or masters."

The act also included an antimiscegenation section that provided that
masters who had "sexual or carnal relations" with their "servants of the
African race" would "forfeit all claim to said servant." In addition, the act
provided that any white person who had "sexual intercourse with any of
the African race" could be subject to a fine "not exceeding one thousand

50. *Sarah, alias Sarah Borders v. Andrew Borders*, 5 Ill. 341, 4 Scam. 341 (1843), 345. See also
Nathaniel R. Ricks, *A Peculiar Place for the Peculiar Institution: Slavery and Sovereignty in
Early Territorial Utah* (Master's thesis, Brigham Young University, 2007).
51. Ibid.

dollars, nor less than five hundred" and "imprisonment not exceeding three years." This provision was consistent with statutes in other states and territories as well as with views expressed by Joseph Smith before his death.[52] It was also reminiscent of Brigham Young's strong denunciations of interracial relationships, which began when he was informed about Enoch Lewis's marriage to a white woman.

The act required masters to provide servants "comfortable habitations, clothing, bedding, sufficient food and recreation," as well as to send their servants to school for at least eighteen months between the ages of six and twenty. In exchange the masters were authorized to prudently and humanely punish their servants and to expect faithful labor.[53] Although the provisions of "An Act in Relation to Service" relating to servitude were abrogated in 1862 when the Civil War Congress abolished all slavery in the territories, the antimiscegenation section survived, in modified form, for more than a century.[54]

The legislature also passed "An Act Regulating Elections," which limited voting rights within the territory to "free white male citizens of the Territory of Utah of the age of twenty-one years." Young believed that there was a connection between the "curse" placed on all African Americans and voting rights, and reiterated to the legislature during consideration of this provision that slavery began when Adam and Eve were forced to leave the Garden of Eden because "Eve partook of forbidden fruit and this made a slave of her...and now our old daddy says I believe I will eat of the fruit and become a slave too."[55] According to Young, "Slavery will continue, until there is a people raised up upon the face of the Earth who will contend for righteous principles...operate with every power and faculty given to them to help to establish the Kingdom of God, to overcome the Devil, and drive him from the Earth; then will this curse be removed."[56]

52. See Bringhurst, *Saints, Slaves, and Blacks*, 90.
53. *Acts, Resolutions, and Memorials, Passed by the First Annual, and Special Sessions, of the Legislative Assembly of the Territory of Utah*, 80–82.
54. When Horace Greeley asked Young in 1859 to explain the Mormons' position concerning slavery, the Mormon prophet assured him, "We consider it of divine institution, and not to be abolished until the curse pronounced on Ham shall have been removed from his descendants." Horace Greeley, "Two Hours with Brigham Young," *New York Daily Tribune*, July 13, 1859. Young remained convinced that African Americans would remain the "servant of servants" because of the curse even after Congress abolished all slavery in the territories following the commencement of the Civil War. Brigham Young, "Necessity for Watchfulness," *Journal of Discourses* 10:250 (October 6, 1863).
55. "Speech by Governor Young (expressing his views on slavery) given in Joint Session of the Legislature, at Salt Lake City, Utah Territory, Thursday, February 5, 1852," reported by George D. Watt, Brigham Young Papers, Church History Library. Quoted in Collier, *The Teachings of President Brigham Young* 3:41.
56. Ibid., 3:42.

Young taught that after Cain killed his brother Abel, God cursed Cain and placed a mark on him. "What is this mark?" asked Young. "You will see it on the countenance of every African you ever did see upon the face of the Earth, or ever will see." But Young taught that there were other consequences of the curse. "Now I tell you what I know," Young told the assembled legislators, "the Lord told Cain that he should not receive the blessings of the priesthood nor his seed, until the last of the posterity of Abel had received the Priesthood, until the redemption of the Earth."[57] He also told the legislators that "Negroes are the children of old Cain" and that "they cannot bear rule in the priesthood…until the *times of restitution shall come*" and that anyone who married an African American would similarly be cursed.

Young insisted that if anyone transgressed by "mingling their seed with the seed of Cain," and had their blood shed, that "it would do a great deal toward atoning for the sin."[58] Wilford Woodruff recorded in his journal that Young instructed the legislators that "Any man havin one drop of the seed of Cane [*sic*] in him cannot hold the priesthood & if no other Prophet ever spake it Before I will say it now in the name of Jesus Christ," and that if "any man mingles his seed with the seed of Cane [*sic*] the only way he could get rid of it or have salvation would be to come forward & have his head cut off & spill his Blood upon the ground."[59]

Young taught that this policy was ordained of God and that if he were to change it "the Priesthood is taken from this Church and the Kingdom and God leaves us to our fate."[60] In addition, he stated that "no man can vote for me or my brethren in this Territory who has not the privilege of acting in Church affairs." While he admitted that African Americans "shall have the right of citizenship," he bristled when American abolitionists claimed that citizenship carried with it the same civil rights as other Americans including the right to vote.[61] Young insisted that they "shall not have the right to dictate in Church and State affairs" and that he would never allow African Americans to be "equal with us in all our privileges."[62] According to Wilford Woodruff, he laid down a marker for the legislators: "I will not Consent for the seed of Cane [*sic*] to vote for me or my Brethren,"[63] and after his

---

57. Ibid.
58. Ibid., 3:43–46.
59. Kenney, *Wilford Woodruff's Journal* 4:97–98. Henry Lewis Gates Jr. notes that this "one-drop rule" was contained in "racist laws designed to retain the offspring of a white man and a black female slave as property of the slave's owner." Henry Lewis Gates Jr., *Black in Latin America* (New York: New York University Press, 2011), 10.
60. Collier, *The Teachings of President Brigham Young* 3:46 (February 5, 1852).
61. See ibid., 3:35–40 (February 4, 1852).
62. Ibid., 3:47–48 (February 5, 1852).
63. Kenney, *Wilford Woodruff's Journal* 4:97–98. Young's pointed remarks were never published. The editors of Woodruff's diary (who did not date his notes of Young's remarks)

impassioned speech the legislators approved the act that provided that no nonwhite resident of the territory was entitled to vote.[64]

Two months after the legislation was passed that recognized servitude and prevented African Americans from voting, the church-owned *Deseret News* published an editorial acknowledging the exclusionary policy, which prevented African Americans from holding the priesthood, for the first time. The editorial noted that "the priesthood [has] been restored in this dispensation" through Abraham's descent, and that if Cain's posterity "continue faithful, until Abel's race is satisfied with his blessings, then may the race of Cain receive a fullness of the priesthood, and become satisfied with blessings, and the two become as one again, when Cain has paid the uttermost farthing."[65]

In December 1852, Parley P. Pratt delivered a discourse to a joint session of the second session of the territorial legislature in which he correlated the church's exclusionary policy with the Book of Abraham. The Mormon apostle noted that Smith's translation, which the church republished in 1851, confirmed "that Ham and his race were cursed as it regards Priesthood, but blessed in matters pertaining to the fruits of the Earth and of wisdom." "The Pharaohs and their priests had not the Priesthood," Pratt said, "although they pretended to have received it from Ham, their progenitor. Hence we find a government in Egypt of mere human origin and a priesthood and religion, by law established which worshipped several gods."[66]

concluded that "Governor B Youngs address Before the legislative assembly of the Territory of Utah upon slavery" occurred on February 8, 1852, whereas George D. Watt's notes of Young's speech indicate that it took place on February 5.

64. *Acts, Resolutions, and Memorials* (1852), 104–8. This bill may have been included in "An Act to incorporate Fillmore City, in Millard County," which was voted on the same day. Orson Pratt, who was a member of the Council, voted against this measure "on the ground that colored people were there prohibited from voting." *Journals of the House of Representatives, Council and Joint Sessions of the First Annual and Special Sessions*, 128 (February 5, 1852).

65. See "To the Saints," *Deseret News* (April 3, 1852), p. 2.

66. Kenney, *Wilford Woodruff's Journal*, 4:162–70 (discourse of December 18, 1852, recorded after December 22 entry). Collier maintains that Pratt's speech was actually delivered on December 15. See Collier, *The Teachings of President Brigham Young* 3:157–58. During this same period Gunnison reported that the Mormon hierarchy taught that the "'Negro is cursed as to the priesthood, and must always be a servant wherever his lot is cast.'" Gunnison, *The Mormons*, 1856 ed., 51. After Pratt's discourse church leaders continued to make occasional references to the exclusionary policy in public discourses. See Brigham Young, "The Priesthood and Satan—The Constitution and the Government of the United States—Rights and Policy of the Latter-Day Saints," *Journal of Discourses* 2:184–85 (February 18, 1855); Brigham Young, "Intelligence, Etc.," *Journal of Discourses* 7:290 (October 9, 1859); Brigham Young, "The Persecutions of the Saints—Their Loyalty to the Constitution—The Mormon Battalion—The Laws of God Relative to the African Race," *Journal of Discourses*

During the same session, Young repeated his instructions that servants could be "purchased unto freedom" to serve in the homes of Mormon settlers "thereby obviating the necessity of white servant, who should tread the theater of life and action, in a higher sphere." "Happily for Utah," the governor said, "this question has been wisely left open for the discussion of her citizens, and the law of the last session, so far proves a very salutatory measure, as it has nearly freed the Territory of the colored population; also enabling the people to control, all who see proper to remain, and cast their lot among us."[67]

Several years later, Young reiterated to a congregation assembled in the tabernacle that African Americans could not participate in the Mormon priesthood. "The Lord put a mark on [Cain]," the church president said, "and there are some of his children in this room." He said that only "when all the other children of Adam have had the privilege of receiving the Priesthood, and of coming into the kingdom of God, and of being redeemed from the four corners of the earth, and have received their resurrection from the dead, then it will be time enough to remove the curse from Cain and his posterity."[68]

Meanwhile, Elijah Abel, who had been ordained and endowed in Kirtland, asked Young, while the exclusionary rule was being institutionalized, if he could receive his endowments. Young denied his request but did allow him to continue to function in his priesthood office as a member of the Third Quorum of Seventy. Although this concession may seem inconsistent with Young's policy, it demonstrated that Young considered the priesthood Abel received to be different from the priesthood that Joseph Smith identified with the endowment and was consistent with Young's determination to discourage social integration. Walker Lewis, another African American who was ordained during Smith's lifetime, left Utah (and presumably Mormonism) during this same period and returned to Lowell, Massachusetts, where he remained for the rest of his life.[69]

10: 109–11 (March 8, 1863). Young reiterated, in a speech delivered during the height of the Civil War, that "if the white man who belongs to the chosen seed mixes his blood with the seed of Cain, the penalty, under the law of God, is death on the spot." *Journal of Discourses* 10:110 (March 8, 1863).

67. *Journals of the House of Representatives, Council and Joint Sessions of the Second Annual and Adjourned Sessions of the Legislative Assembly of the Territory of Utah Held at Great Salt Lake City, 1852 and 1853* (Great Salt Lake City: Printed by George Hales, 1853), 132.

68. Brigham Young, "Spiritual Gifts—Hell—The Spirit World—The Elders and the Nations—The Lamanites—The Temple," *Journal of Discourses* 2:138, 142–43 (December 3, 1854).

69. O'Donovan, "The Mormon Priesthood Ban and Elder Q. Walker Lewis," 96–97.

MASONIC JUSTIFICATIONS

While Young was institutionalizing Mormonism's exclusionary policy, some prominent Masonic writers continued to rationalize the Craft's exclusion of African Americans from their temples beyond the standard argument of exclusive jurisdiction. In 1855 Albert Mackey noted that in America, to be considered freeborn, one "must be in the unrestrained enjoyment of his civil and personal liberty, and this too, by the birthright of inheritance, and not by its subsequent acquisition, in consequence of his release from hereditary bondage."[70] George Wingate Chase, another Masonic writer, specifically applied this standard to African Americans: "It is an ancient rule, that candidates for Masonry must be *free-born*. A slave cannot be made a mason. It is established as a general rule, in the United States, that *persons of negro blood* should not be made Masons, even though they may have been *free-born*."[71]

But Chase cautioned that this policy was

> a matter which most Grand Lodges have wisely refrained from legislating upon, as it is at least doubtful whether they can interfere with the right of the individual members of a lodge to select their own members. Within the United States there are no *regular* lodges of negroes, and but few regular Masons among that class, though there are many *irregular* lodges and irregular masons among them. The abstract right of a lodge to initiate a negro, mulatto, Indian, Chinese, or individual of any blood or complexion, cannot be denied. The question of such admission is one of expediency merely, and is wisely left to the conservative judgment of each individual member of the lodge where such persons may apply for admission to the order.[72]

Prince Hall Masons were aware of these anachronistic justifications and they sagely observed that their white brethren were finally acknowledging, for the first time in a public forum, the real rationale for excluding them from their lodges.[73] In 1865 Lewis Hayden, grand master of Prince Hall

70. Mackey, *The Principles of Masonic Law*, 160.
71. Chase, *Digest of Masonic Law*, 211 (emphasis added).
72. Ibid., 211–12. ("No Grand Lodge has authorized subordinates to initiate negroes.")
73. Freemasons held differing views concerning whether exclusive jurisdiction was a valid argument to marginalize Prince Hall Freemasonry. Albert Mackey argued in favor of the "legalistic" nonrecognition of black lodges. Joseph A. Walkes Jr., *Black Square & Compass, 200 Years of Prince Hall Freemasonry* (Richmond, VA: Macoy Publishing & Masonic Supply Co., Inc., 1979), 62n40. But German Masonic historian Joseph G. Findel wrote that Prince Hall Freemasonry was legally constituted before the concept of "the right of jurisdiction" had been created. J. G. Findel, *History of Freemasonry, From its origin to the present day*, 2nd ed. (Philadelphia: J. B. Lippincott & Co., 1869), 357. Even Albert Pike, who served as a

Grand Lodge, addressed a meeting of his grand lodge in Boston and reminded his fellow Masons that Anderson's *Constitutions* required Masons
to be "freeborn (or no bondman)" and that the words "or no bondman"
meant that "the applicant or candidate should, at the time of applying and
when received, be a freeman" and that this "opened the doors of our Lodges
to the good and true men of all colors." He noted that despite this practice,
which was followed in England and Europe, American Masons had instead
utilized the word "freeborn" to exclude all African Americans from Masonic temples.[74]

Hayden observed that one American Mason complained that the
United Grand Lodge of London had changed the word "freeborn" to
"freeman," which constituted "changing an essential feature of the law, or,
in plain terms, removing an indisputable landmark," without recognizing
that Anderson had already substituted the words "or no bondmen" for the
term "free-born."[75] Hayden believed that the Grand Lodge of Illinois and
other grand lodges had publicized the real reasons that American Masons
rejected those of African descent (that they were black and could therefore
not be "freemen"), and compared them to the Masons of Massachusetts,
who had originated the exclusionary policy, had never published it and
"stands to-day with nothing to retract in this respect!" Finally, he prayed
that they "may never lend their aid to any such accursed prejudice, either by
pen or word."[76]

Confederate general, agreed that the concept of exclusive jurisdiction was faulty, and that
"Prince Hall Lodge was as regular a Lodge as any lodge created by competent authority, and
had a perfect right (as other lodges in Europe did) to establish other lodges, making itself
a mother Lodge," but he warned, since he had taken his "obligation to white men, not to
negroes," that "when I have to accept negroes as brothers or leave Masonry, I shall leave it."
Upton, *Negro Freemasonry*, 214–15.

74. Hayden, *Caste among Masons*, 12–17. Both Anderson and Dermott used the same lan-
guage, "freeborn (or no bondmen)," while Benjamin Franklin's first American edition of
Anderson utilized slightly different language ("The Persons admitted Members of a *Lodge*
must be good and true Men, free-born, and of mature and discreet Age, no Bondmen").
See *Anderson's Constitutions of 1738: A Facsimile of the original text with commentaries by
Lewis Edwards and W. J. Hughan* (Bloomington, IL: The Masonic Book Club, 1978), 144;
Dermott, *Ahiman Rezon*, 27; and *The Constitutions of the Free-Masons (Reprint of Anderson's
book by Benjamin Franklin)* (Bloomington, IL: Masonic Book Club, 1975), 49–50.

75. Hayden, *Caste among Masons*, 39–48. Hayden criticized John W. Simons, *A Familiar
Treatise on the Principles and Practice of Masonic Jurisprudence* (New York: Masonic Publishing and Manufacturing Co., 1869), 16. Concerning British Masons recognition of the
right of blacks to become masons, see *Kenning's Cyclopedia of Freemasonry*, 508–9; Kenneth R. H. Mackenzie, *The Royal House Cyclopaedia of History, Rites, Symbols and Biography*
(New York: J. W. Bouton, 1877).

76. Hayden, *Caste among Masons*, 17, 56. Hayden noted that Grand Master Moses deliv-
ered bondmen from Egypt and published the orations that Prince Hall delivered to African
Lodge in 1792 and 1797 in which he discussed Africans' participation in ancient Masonry.
Hayden, *Caste among Masons*, 45, 58–70.

Nevertheless, even after all African Americans were emancipated from slavery, many grand lodges continued to exclude blacks and even passed resolutions that had the effect of prohibiting their lodges from entering into regular correspondence with any grand lodges (even those that were recognized as regular) if they admitted black members. In 1866, the Grand Lodge of North Carolina complained that the Grand Lodge of New York had authorized the organization of black lodges in North Carolina, not realizing that the black lodges being authorized were Prince Hall lodges. The Grand Lodge of New York denied that it had authorized such lodges and recognized that southern grand lodges, for more than half a century, had denounced northern grand lodges, "who admitted blacks into their lodges as visitors, who had been made Masons in foreign countries and by lawful authority."[77]

The Grand Lodge of New York also asserted that the words "free born" meant that the mother must have been free at the time of the birth. "This would, of course, exclude all the negroes of the South who were born into slavery; and this fact should quiet the nerves of our brethren of the North-Carolina committee against having their sensibilities disturbed by being required to take their former slaves into their embraces as brethren, should there ever arise such a preposterous movement as they so credulously attribute to the Grand Lodge of New York."[78]

After the Civil War, the Grand Lodge of Massachusetts continued to maintain that its exclusionary policy, which led to the organization of Prince Hall Masonry, was "simply a question of Grand Lodge jurisdiction, and we can consider it calmly and without prejudice" but that Masonry accepted a man "whatever his religion, his race, or his country."[79] Nevertheless, some grand lodges—mostly in the North—did take the extraordinary step of extending some recognition to Prince Hall Lodges after the Civil War. But when Prince Hall Masons in Missouri claimed in 1871 that they had received some form of recognition from the grand lodges of Missouri, Minnesota, Illinois, Iowa, and other states, a Freemason from Mississippi wrote that it would not happen in his state and he challenged the legitimacy of all black lodges by contending that "the Founder of this negro–so called Masonic colony, if he received any fees" then they were "at the expense of his fellow descendants of Ham."[80]

77. "Negro Lodges," *The Mystic Star: A Monthly Magazine*, 4:6 (June 1866): 162–63.
78. Ibid., 4:6 (June 1866): 163.
79. *Abstract of the Proceedings of the Grand Lodge of Massachusetts (1870)*, 87–88.
80. Walkes, *Black Square & Compass*, 85. In 1870 the grand master of the Grand Lodge of Mississippi wrote that "Negroes are not Masons, but by the laws of Congress, they are voters." Ibid., 81.

THE REVISED AND CANONIZED PEARL OF GREAT PRICE

In 1878, the LDS Church published a new edition of The Pearl of Great Price that included the Book of Abraham and Smith's extrapolations of Enoch's vision and Moses's writings.[81] This edition included some references—that "Cain was called Master Mahan," "the master of this great secret," that Lamech "entered into a covenant with Satan, after the manner of Cain, wherein he became Master Mahan," and that "the seed of Cain were black and had not place among them"—that were not included in the 1851 edition.[82]

In 1880, the LDS leadership made the extraordinary decision to canonize this new edition of The Pearl of Great Price and it became an additional book of sacred scripture. Thereafter, some members of the Mormon hierarchy shrouded the Mormon exclusionary policy with this new scriptural authority and thereby reinforced Young's pronouncement that the policy could not be changed or modified unless a Mormon prophet received a new revelation.

Shortly afterward, Elijah Abel inquired again—this time to John Taylor, the new Mormon prophet—if he could enter the Endowment House. Taylor informed him that he could retain his priesthood office but that he could not receive his endowment.[83] Jane Elizabeth Manning James (1822–1908),

81. The Pearl of Great Price (Salt Lake City: Latter-day Saints' Printing and Publishing Establishment, 1878). In 1879 George Reynolds (1842–1909) published a defense of the Book of Abraham and adopted Louis Bertrand's argument that Egyptology was not proven and that Dévéria's translation could be incorrect. See Reynolds, *The* Book of Abraham. *Its authenticity established as a divine and ancient record. With copious references to ancient and modern authorities* (Salt Lake City: Deseret News Printing and Publishing, 1879); and Bertrand, Mémoires d'un Mormon, 217.
82. The Pearl of Great Price (Salt Lake City, 1878), 11–12, 19. During the same year the Reorganized Church published a revelation of Joseph Smith III, received in 1865, which authorized "ordaining men of the Negro race." See *Reorganized Doctrine and Covenants*, section 116.
83. See Council Meeting Minutes, June 4, 1879; *Journal History of the Church*, Church History Library. In 1879 Zebedee Coltrin told John Taylor, Abraham O. Smoot, Brigham Young Jr., and L. John Nuttall that he and John P. Greene had met with Joseph Smith to inquire whether African Americans could hold the priesthood. He said Smith told them that "the Spirit of the Lord saith the Negro has no right nor cannot hold the Priesthood" and that when Smith learned that Elijah Abel, who had been ordained a Seventy because he worked on the Kirtland Temple, was African American, he dropped him from the quorum. During the same meeting, A. O. Smoot recalled that Warren Parrish, D. W. Patten, and Thomas Marsh, while laboring in the South in 1835 and 1836, refrained from ordaining blacks to the priesthood based on their communications with Joseph Smith. See L. John Nuttall Diary, May 31, 1879, Harold B. Lee Library, Brigham Young University, quoted in William E. Berrett, *The Church and the Negroid People* (Orem, UT, 1960), 9–11. Several days later Joseph F. Smith contradicted Coltrin's recollection because he had seen Abel's Seventy certificate. Minutes of the Quorum of Twelve, June 4, 1879, L. John Nuttall Diary.

another church member of African descent who was a servant in Joseph
Smith's home in Nauvoo, later requested her own endowment (after Abel
died in complete harmony with the church) but she was likewise rebuffed.[84]

Thereafter, LDS Church officials insisted that Joseph Smith introduced
the exclusionary policy, that it was based on the curse of Cain, and that
it could not be modified unless one of Smith's successors received a new
revelation. In 1885 Seventy Brigham H. Roberts relied on the Book of Abraham to suggest that Cain's curse was preserved through Ham's wife and that
Cain's descendants were cursed because "they were not valiant in the great
rebellion in heaven" that "rendered themselves unworthy of the Priesthood
and its powers, and hence it is withheld from them to this day."[85]

Ten years later, Apostle George Q. Cannon told the Twelve Apostles
that Smith introduced the policy, but in 1900 Lorenzo Snow admitted that
he did not know whether Brigham Young's justification for withholding the
priesthood from black members was based on revelation or "what had been
told him by the Prophet Joseph." However, Cannon assured the First Presidency five months later that John Taylor claimed the doctrine was taught
by Joseph Smith. During the same meeting, Cannon "read from the Pearl of
Great Price showing that negroes were debarred [sic] from the priesthood,"
and Apostle Joseph F. Smith (Joseph Smith's nephew) "said that he had
been told that the idea originated with the Prophet Joseph but of course he
could not vouch for it."[86]

Smith claimed eight years later that his uncle stripped Abel of his priesthood as soon as he discovered that he was African American and the First
Presidency and Twelve Apostles voted to confirm the exclusionary policy
and adopted a policy that missionaries "should not take the initiative in
proselytizing among the Negro people, but if Negroes or people tainted
with Negro blood apply for baptism themselves they might be admitted
to Church membership in the understanding that nothing further can be
done for them."[87] Although the LDS First Presidency gradually allowed African Americans to perform some ordinances (but not the endowment) in

84. In 1894 Manning was sealed as a "Servitor" to Joseph Smith. Apostle Joseph F. Smith
acted as proxy for the Mormon prophet. This sealing was revoked the following year but
restored in 1902. See Anderson, *The Development of LDS Temple Worship*, 97–98, nn50–51.
85. B. H. Roberts, "To the Youth of Israel," *Contributor* 6 (May 1885): 296–97.
86. For Cannon's remarks in 1895, see Joseph Fielding Smith, *The Way to Perfection* (Salt
Lake City: Genealogical Society of Utah, 1940), 110–11. Lorenzo Snow's observations are
contained in Council Meeting, March 11, 1900, George Albert Smith Papers, Manuscript
Division, Marriott Library, University of Utah. George Q. Cannon's remarks are recorded
in Council Meeting, August 11, 1900, George Albert Smith Papers, Marriott Library.
87. "Excerpts from the Weekly Council Minutes of the Quorum of Twelve Apostles, Dealing
with the Rights of Negroes in the Church, 1849–1947," Minutes of August 26, 1908, George
Albert Smith Papers, Special Collections, J. Willard Marriott Library, University of Utah.

the temple,[88] the priesthood and endowment ban was retained in part based on the Book of Abraham.[89]

Nevertheless, this rationale was weakened when some non-Mormons challenged the authenticity of the Book of Abraham. In 1912 Utah Episcopal bishop Franklin Spencer Spalding published the statements of eight Egyptologists who concluded that Smith mistranslated a common Egyptian funeral text.[90] The *Deseret News* published responses written by LDS Church authorities, educators, and even a lawyer. These articles, together with one response by Spalding, were later republished in the *Improvement Era*.[91] The authors noted that although Spalding's experts agreed that the writings on Smith's papyri were from the Egyptian Book of the Dead and

88. African Americans were allowed to perform baptisms for the dead soon after the dedication of the Salt Lake Temple. Armand Mauss, "The Fading of the Pharaohs' Curse: The Decline and Fall of the Priesthood Ban against Blacks in the Mormon Church," in Bush and Mauss, *Neither White nor Black*, 186n73. See also Council Meeting, November 10, 1910, George Albert Smith Papers, Marriott Library. ("President [Joseph F.] Smith remarked that he saw no reason why a negro should not be permitted to have access to the baptismal font in the temple to be baptized for the dead, inasmuch as negroes are entitled to become members of the Church by baptism."). George Albert Smith authorized the ordination of a native group in the Philippines ("Negritos") because even though they had black skin they had no known African ancestry. Edward L. Kimball, *Lengthen Your Stride: The Presidency of Spencer W. Kimball* (Salt Lake City: Deseret Book, 2005), 200. David O. McKay made similar decisions concerning white South Africans, Fijians, Australian aborigines, and Egyptians when there was no evidence of African ancestry. Gregory A. Prince and William Robert Wright, *David O. McKay and the Rise of Modern Mormonism* (Salt Lake City: University of Utah Press, 2005), 94. McKay also allowed black men to serve in leadership roles in church auxiliaries and continued to allow black children to participate in proxy baptisms. Prince and Wright, *David O. McKay*, 95. Harold B. Lee approved a policy under which adopted black children could be sealed to their white parents in the temple. Kimball, *Lengthen Your Stride*, 206.

89. See First Presidency Statement (1907), in "George F. Richards Record of Decisions by the Council of the First Presidency and the Twelve Apostles," George Albert Smith Papers, Special Collections, Marriott Library; Joseph Fielding Smith, "The Negro and the Priesthood," *Improvement Era* 27:6 (April 1924): 564–65; Joseph Fielding Smith, *The Way to Perfection* (Salt Lake City: Deseret Book,1931), 42–48, 97–111.

90. Franklin Spencer Spalding, *Joseph Smith, Jr., as a Translator* (Salt Lake City: The Arrow Press, 1912).

91. See B. H. Roberts, "A Plea in Bar of Final Conclusions," *Improvement Era* 16:4 (February 1913): 309–25; J. M. Sjodahl, "The Book of Abraham," *Improvement Era* 16:4 (February 1913), 326–33; Frederick J. Pack, "The Spalding Argument," *Improvement Era* 16:4 (February 1913): 333–41; Junius F. Wells, "Scholars Disagree," *Improvement Era* 16:4 (February 1913): 341–42; John Henry Evans, "Bishop Spalding's Jump in the Logical Process," *Improvement Era* 16:4 (February 1913); Levi Edgar Young, "The Book of the Dead," *Improvement Era* 16:4 (February 1913): 346–48; John A. Widstoe, "Comments on the Spalding Pamphlet," *Improvement Era* 16:5 (March 1913): 454–60; John A. Young, "Scientists Not Always Correct," *Improvement Era* 16:5 (March 1913): 460–66; Orson J. P. Widtsoe, "The Unfair Fairness of Rev. Spalding," *Improvement Era* 16:6 (April 1913): 593–603; N. L. Nelson, "An Open Letter to Bishop Spalding," *Improvement Era* 16:6 (April 1913): 603–10; "Reverend Spalding's Answer to Dr. Widtsoe," *Improvement Era* 16:6 (April 1913): 610–16; "Dr. Widtsoe's Reply

that Smith had therefore mistranslated the document, they could never-theless not agree on the correct translation. The Mormon writers therefore argued, as George Reynolds had almost thirty years earlier, that Egyptology was not perfected and that non-Mormon translators (from Déveria to Spal-ding's experts) had not consulted the actual text of the Book of Abraham but only the facsimiles.

J. E. Homans, a non-Mormon writer, also contributed "scholarly criti-cisms" of Spalding's pamphlet that appeared in both the *Deseret News* and *Improvement Era*. Homans, writing under the nom de plume of Robert C. Webb, PhD, discussed circumstantial evidence that he believed sup-ported Smith's claim that his translation was correct. Twenty years later Deseret News Press published an expanded version of Homans' writings in book format.[92] During this same period, B. H. Roberts acknowledged that Smith's translation was made "confessedly not by scholarship but by inspiration."[93]

In 1931, Apostle Joseph Fielding Smith (Joseph Smith's grandnephew) repeated Orson Hyde's theory,[94] which Brigham Young had rejected,[95] that African Americans would continue to be excluded from the priesthood (and the temple endowment) until all those who were valiant in the pre-existence had an opportunity to accept the priesthood. Only then, accord-ing to Smith, would they be given "some blessings of exaltation, if not the fullness, for their integrity here."[96]

In 1947 David O. McKay (1873–1970), another apostle, opined that the policy was premised on the Book of Abraham,[97] and two years later the LDS First Presidency, which included McKay, released a statement that the

to Rev. Spalding," *Improvement Era* 16:6 (April 1913): 616–19; J. M. Sjodhal, "The Word 'Kolob,'" *Improvement Era* 16:6 (April 1913): 620–23; [See also vol. 16, issues 7–8 (1913)].
92. See Robert C. Webb, "A Critical Examination of the Fac-Similies in the Book of Abra-ham," *Improvement Era* 16:5 (March 1913): 435–54; Robert C. Webb, "Have Joseph Smith's Interpretations Been Discredited?" *Improvement Era* 17:4 (February 1914): 313–51. See also R. C. Webb, *Joseph Smith as a Translator* (Salt Lake City: The Deseret News Press, 1936). See also Brodie, *No Man Knows My History*, 175n.
93. B. H. Roberts, "A Plea in Bar of Final Conclusions," *Improvement Era* 16:4 (February 1913): 325.
94. Orson Hyde, "Speech of Orson Hyde Delivered before the High Priests Quorum in Nauvoo, April 27th 1845" (Liverpool: Millennial Star, 1845), 27.
95. See Kenney, *Wilford Woodruff's Journal* 6:511 (December 25, 1869).
96. Joseph Fielding Smith, *The Way to Perfection* (Salt Lake City: Deseret Book, 1931), 43–44, 102.
97. Correspondence from David O. McKay to Lowell Bennion, November 3, 1947, quoted in Llewelyn R. McKay, comp., *Home Memories of President David O. McKay* (Salt Lake City: Deseret Book Company, 1956), 226–31; also quoted in John J. Stewart, *Mormonism and the Negro* (Salt Lake City: Bookmark, 1960), Historical Supplement entitled *The Church and the Negroid People*, 18–23.

exclusion of African Americans from Mormon priesthood "at the present time" was "a direct commandment of the Lord, on which is founded the doctrine of the Church from the days of its organization."[98]

THE ABANDONMENT OF THE RATIONALES AND POLICY

During the next decade, the LDS hierarchy gradually abandoned the rationales it had advanced to justify the exclusionary policy but still insisted that a revelation was required to modify it. David O. McKay, who became the ninth church president in 1951, initially believed, like many Mormons, that the policy was introduced by Joseph Smith and was supported by scriptural authority. But in 1954 he apparently told Mormon educator Sterling Mc-Murrin (1914–1996), during a private discussion, that "there is not now, and there never has been a doctrine in the Church that the Negroes are under a divine curse." Although McKay's statement was private and was not published until shortly before his death, it is consistent with the church's later refusal to articulate a rationale for the policy[99] even as it continued to insist that a revelation would be necessary to reverse it.[100]

While McKay's notion that the church had not articulated a rational justification for the policy eventually became the church's official position, other Mormon authorities continued to insist that the curse was premised on scriptural authority.[101] Bruce R. McConkie, a member of the Seventy, was the boldest proponent of this thesis in his *Mormon Doctrine*, in which he argued that African Americans were cursed and denied the priesthood and temple blessings because they had not been valiant in the pre-existence.[102]

98. See Statement of the First Presidency (August 17, 1949), as discussed in Bush, "Mormonism's Negro Doctrine," 43–44, Appendix I.
99. Prince and Wright, *David O. McKay*, 79–80. See also Mary Lythgoe Bradford, *Lowell L. Bennion: Teacher, Counselor, Humanitarian* (Salt Lake City: Dialogue Foundation, 1995), 92–94.
100. Prince and Wright, *David O. McKay*, 60–105.
101. See Mark E. Peterson, "Race Problems as They Affect the Church," BYU Speech, August 27, 1954; Joseph Fielding Smith, *Doctrines of Salvation* (Salt Lake City: Bookcraft, 1954–56), 1:66; 2:55.
102. See McConkie, *Mormon Doctrine* [1958], 102, 314, 476–77, 553–54. The following entries were representative of McConkie's perspective: Cain: "the father of the Negroes, and those spirits who are not worthy to receive the priesthood are born through his lineage"; Ham: "Negroes are thus descendants of Ham, who himself also was cursed, apparently for marrying into the forbidden lineage," and that "these descendants cannot hold the priesthood"; Negroes: "those who were less valiant in the pre-existence and who thereby had certain spiritual restrictions imposed upon them during mortality are known to us as the negroes," that "Negroes in this life are denied the priesthood," and that "negroes are not equal with other races"; and races of man: "We know the circumstances under which the

In 1963 the Utah State Legislature repealed an antimiscegenation law that was enacted in 1888 but had roots in the 1852 "Act in Relation to Service," which Brigham Young correlated to his recently announced exclusionary policy.[103] Hugh B. Brown, one of McKay's counselors in the LDS First Presidency, stated publically that the church was considering a change in the exclusionary policy[104] and that it recognized the full civil rights of African Americans.[105] The church released similar statements in 1965 and 1966.[106]

The following year the scriptural foundation of the Book of Abraham, including its references to priesthood, was again challenged after the Metropolitan Museum of Art donated original fragments of the Lebolo papyri to the LDS Church.[107] Hugh Nibley wrote a series of articles in which he acknowledged that the remnants were portions of the Egyptian Book of the Dead but that Smith's "translation" was really a revelation, that there was no need for a manuscript and that whether the Mormon prophet used the *Urim and Thummim* was "totally irrelevant to establishing the bona fides of the Prophet."[108]

---

posterity of Cain (and later of Ham) were cursed with what we call negroid racial characteristics." The 1966 edition included the same entries except for a minor change in "races of men." See McConkie, *Mormon Doctrine*, 108–9, 343, 526–28, 616.

103. Patrick Q. Mason, "The Prohibition of Interracial Marriage in Utah, 1888–1963," *Utah State Historical Quarterly* 76:2 (Spring 2008): 108–31.

104. See *New York Times*, June 7, 1963; *Newsweek*, June 17, 1963.

105. See *Deseret News*, October 6, 1963.

106. See Mauss, *All Abraham's Children*, 229n12.

107. Armand Mauss has noted that "all the experts who studied the papyrus, Mormon and non-Mormon alike, agreed that it seemed to be a common funerary text from an Egyptian period much later than that of Abraham" and that "the text [of the Book of Abraham] bore no resemblance to the writings that Joseph Smith attributed to Abraham," which "set Mormon scholars and apologists to work searching for an alternative explanation for the Book of Abraham." Mauss, *All Abraham's Children*, 239.

108. Nibley wrote a series of articles which were published in the *Improvement Era* beginning in January 1968. See Hugh Nibley, "A New Look at the Pearl of Great Price," *Improvement Era* (January 1968–May 1970); and Nibley, *The Message of the Joseph Smith Papyri*. "Joseph Smith made it perfectly clear," Nibley wrote, "that the vital ingredient in every transmission of ancient or heavenly knowledge is always the Spirit which places his experiences beyond the comprehension and analysis of ordinary mortals.... If it mattereth not by what imponderable method Joseph Smith produced his translations, as long as he came up with the right answers, it matters even less from what particular edition of what particular text he was translating. It is enough at present to know that the Prophet was translating from real books of Abraham, Moses, Enoch, Mosiah and Zenos, whose teachings now reach us in a huge and growing corpus of newly discovered writings." Hugh Nibley, *The Message of the Joseph Smith Papyri*, 54. Nibley also connected the book with the endowment when he noted that it included revelations concerning Abraham's life and teachings, as well as references to "keywords" which harkened back to a more ancient ritual. For additional perspectives, see Klaus Baer, "The Breathing Permit of Hor: A Translation of the Apparent Source of the Book of Abraham," *Dialogue: A Journal of Mormon Thought* 3:3 (Autumn 1968): 109–34; Charles

In 1969 the First Presidency published a statement that Joseph Smith had taught the exclusionary policy but did not reference the Book of Abraham. Instead the statement advanced the notion that the policy was based on "reasons which we believe are known to God, but which he has not fully made known to man." Thereafter, the church never issued any official statement to justify the controversial policy (that African Americans were cursed, that they had wavered in the pre-existence, or that Mormon scripture supported the practice) but it continued to insist that a revelation would be required to change it.[109]

McKay did not receive such a revelation before his death, and some Mormon intellectuals began to challenge both the historical context and religious foundation. In 1970, Stephen Taggart concluded that the policy could be traced to Joseph Smith during the Missouri period when Mormon leaders became sensitive to racial politics,[110] and three years later, Lester Bush published a much more comprehensive and nuanced historical analysis in which he concluded that Brigham Young (not Joseph Smith) instituted the policy primarily because of his racial prejudice.[111]

While neither of McKay's two immediate successors (Joseph Fielding Smith and Harold B. Lee) received a revelation on this subject, the twelfth LDS president became concerned about the practical implications of the policy. In 1975 Spencer W. Kimball (1895–1985) announced that the LDS Church would build a temple in Brazil. Although he later recalled that when he made this decision "he was not thinking in terms of making an adjustment" concerning priesthood eligibility,[112] Armand Mauss has noted

M. Larson, *By His Own Hand: A New Look at the Joseph Smith Papyri* (Grand Rapids: Institute for Religious Research, 1985); Stephen E. Thompson, "Egyptology and the Book of Abraham," *Dialogue: A Journal of Mormon Thought* 28:1 (Spring 1995): 143–60; John Gee, *A Guide to the Joseph Smith Papyri* (Provo: The Foundation for Ancient Research and Mormon Studies, 2000); Robert K. Ritner, "'The Breathing Permit of Hor' Among the Joseph Smith Papyri," *Journal of Near Eastern Studies* 62:3 (September 2003): 161–80; Robert K. Ritner, "The 'Breaching Permit of Hor' Thirty-four Years Later," *Dialogue: A Journal of Mormon Thought* 33:4 (Winter 2000): 97–119; and Edward H. Ashment, "The Facsimiles of the Book of Abraham," *Sunstone* 4 (December 1979): 33.

109. Statement of the First Presidency, December 15, 1969, reprinted in *Church News*, January 10, 1970. This statement was not signed by David O. McKay, who was suffering from bad health, but by his counselors, Hugh B. Brown and N. Eldon Tanner. See also quotation of Hugh B. Brown in *Salt Lake Tribune*, December 25, 1969; and Prince and Wright, *David O. McKay*, 101.

110. Stephen G. Taggart, *Mormonism's Negro Policy: Social and Historical Origins* (Salt Lake City: University of Utah Press, 1970).

111. Bush, "Mormonism's Negro Policy," 11–68.

112. See also Kimball, *Lengthen Your Stride*, 214–24. As early as January 25, 1940, J. Reuben Clark observed that "he was positive that it was impossible with reference to the Brazilians to tell those who have Negro blood and those who do not, and we are baptizing these people into the Church." J. Reuben Clark, Council Meeting, January 25, 1940, George

that "church leaders must have known that this decision would put them in an untenable position if they were to maintain the priesthood restriction, since access to the priesthood is one of the qualifications to the temple rites."[113]

In addition, limited internal dissent may have accelerated the decision to modify the policy. In April 1976 Douglas A. Wallace, a Mormon who lived in Washington and disagreed with the church policy, ordained an African American in a motel swimming pool and later openly protested the church's refusal to ordain blacks during the church's General Conference.[114] In April 1977 Wallace achieved even greater notoriety when a Salt Lake County law enforcement officer who was wounded during General Conference accused church officials of organizing an undercover stakeout to deter Wallace and other protestors.[115]

On June 9, 1978, Kimball announced that he had received a long-awaited revelation that reversed the exclusionary policy and that from that day forward all worthy males could be ordained.[116] But when Kimball made his breathtaking announcement, he did not repudiate the prior policy or the various rationales that had been advanced to justify it and the church emphasized that it continued to discourage mixed-race marriages.[117] Afterward, the Mormon prophet dedicated the São Paolo Temple without concern that church racial policies would complicate or even disrupt temple work in Brazil. The Mormon leadership gradually expanded missionary

---

Albert Smith Papers, Marriott Library. Henry Lewis Gates Jr. notes that there are at least 134 separate categories of black in Brazil. After Brazil abandoned slavery, it encouraged European immigration to mix with those of African descent and "whiten" the population. This concept eventually led to "the idea that Brazil was so racially mixed that it was beyond racism." See Gates, *Black in Latin America*, 16, 45. LeGrand Richards noted after the change in policy that the decision to build a temple in Brazil was one of the factors that was considered by church leadership. See Armand Mauss, "The Fading of the Pharaoh's Curse: The Decline and Fall of the Priesthood Ban against Blacks in the Mormon Church," *Dialogue* 14:3 (1981): 10–45.

113. Mauss, *All Abraham's Children*, 236–37. Mauss concluded that internal pressures ("the missionary imperative" and studies that demonstrated "inadequate scriptural and canonical basis for connecting modern black Africans to an obscure ancient lineage once denied the priesthood") drove the change in policy rather than external pressures.

114. *Salt Lake Tribune*, April 3, 1976.

115. *Salt Lake Tribune*, April 8, 1977; *Salt Lake Tribune*, January 18, 1978.

116. "LDS Church extends Priesthood to all worthy male members," *Deseret News*, June 9, 1978.

117. See announcement and articles published in *Church News*, June 17, 1978, pp. 3–6. See also Marcus H. Martins, *Setting the Record Straight: Blacks & The Mormon Priesthood* (Orem, UT: Millennial Press, 2007). Some critics claimed that the church was pressured by outside forces to change the policy. See Ogden Kraut, *The Holy Priesthood* (Salt Lake City: Pioneer Press, 1995), 2:151–65; Jerald and Sandra Tanner, *Salt Lake Messenger*, July 1978, 7; Jerald and Sandra Tanner, *The Changing World of Mormonism* (Chicago: Moody Press, 1980), 328.

work to South Africa and Zimbabwe and later constructed other temples in South America and Africa.

Just as there was minimal internal pressure to change the exclusionary policy, there was little negative response when the modification was announced. Even Bruce R. McConkie, who had strongly justified the policy, quickly acknowledged that "it doesn't make a particle of difference what anybody ever said about the negro matter before the first day of June this year, 1978."[118] Nevertheless, he didn't modify his *Mormon Doctrine*, which continued to be sold at church-owned Deseret Book, to eliminate the prior justifications for the prior practice, which were retained for more than thirty years after Kimball's revelation.[119]

THE DECLINE OF THE MASONIC POLICY

During this same period, American Freemasons and Utah Freemasons re-evaluated their own discriminatory practices. Many lodges, and in some cases grand lodges, enforced the American Masonic policies that excluded Prince Hall Masons from visiting or men of African descent from joining their lodges. The American Masonic policy, which was counter to the policy of the United Grand Lodge of London, was subjected to even greater internal challenges than the Mormon policy.[120] In addition, since Masons of African American descent who were members of regular lodges were entitled to visit sister lodges, it became increasingly difficult to distinguish between these visitation rights and the inherent right of all African Americans to become Freemasons.

118. Bruce R. McConkie, "All are alike unto God," Speech delivered to CES Religious Educators, August 18, 1978 (Accessed at http://www.speeches.byu.edu).
119. When *Mormon Doctrine* was republished in 1979 the previous entries concerning African Americans were only slightly edited: Cain: "the Lord placed on Cain a mark of a dark skin, and he became the ancestor of the black race"; Ham: "Ham's descendants include the Negroes, who originally were barred from holding the priesthood but have been able to do so since June, 1978"; Negroes: "in all past ages and until recent times in this dispensation, the Lord did not offer the priesthood to the Negroes" with a quotation from the 1978 revelation; races of men: "We know the circumstances under which the posterity of Cain (and later of Ham) were born with the characteristics of the black race." See McConkie, *Mormon Doctrine*, 108–9, 343, 526–28, 616. Eventually the publisher acknowledged that *Mormon Doctrine* was not "Mormon doctrine" ("Nobody Knows: The Untold Story of Black Mormons," Independent Features Project, www.untoldstoryofblackmormons.com, ca. 2009), and in May 2010 Deseret Book announced that *Mormon Doctrine* would no longer be published because of "low sales." See "*Mormon Doctrine* Discontinued," *Sunstone*, no. 159 (June 2010): 70–71.
120. *Negro Masonry. A Committee Report of the M.W. Grand Lodge of F. and A. Masons of Washington.* Reprint from the Proceedings of the Grand Lodge, 1898. This report was written by William Upton in response to an inquiry made by Prince Hall Masons in Washington concerning recognition.

In the wake of the Civil Rights Movement, many lodges began allowing Prince Hall Masons to visit their lodges and recognizing the regularity
of Prince Hall Masonry.[121] But even some of the more enlightened Masons, who advocated that Prince Hall Masonry should be recognized, did
not necessarily favor the admission of African Americans into their own
lodges, and at the turn of the twenty-first century some lodges continued
to exclude African Americans. As late as 2009 at least one grand lodge did
not admit African American men to be initiated into white lodges, and
ten American grand lodges did not recognize the regularity of Prince Hall
Masonry.[122]

Despite the historical parallels between the Masonic and LDS policies,
some Mormon intellectuals have preferred to compare the LDS exclusionary policy with *de facto* practices of other religious organizations rather
than those of Masonry. Armand Mauss noted that "restrictions on access
to the priesthood were not unique to the Mormon Church" and that "it
does not follow that the [Mormon] practice meant Mormons were 'more
racist' than others, either in church matters or secular, civic relations outside the church."[123] Nevertheless, there were important distinctions between
the Mormon policy and the discriminatory practices of other churches. The
primary distinction is that the Mormon practice was a *de jure* policy that
was taught by leaders who claimed that it could not be changed without
heavenly intervention. In addition, the LDS policy was arguably broader
in scope than the practices of other churches since the restriction applied
to *all* male members of African descent while *all worthy white* males were
ordinarily ordained at age twelve.

121. British commentators Fred L. Pick and G. Gordon Knight have noted that "in several
states…there has been dialogue and there have been occasions when, outside their respective lodges, white and negro brethren have been able to co-operate in community projects."
In addition, "The two Grand Lodges of Connecticut have removed all barriers and inter-
visitation is now permitted." Pick and Knight, *The Pocket History of Freemasonry*, 301. In
1997 the United Grand Lodge of England and the Grand Lodge of Utah recognized the
Prince Hall Grand Lodge of Utah. See "Utah Masons OK black fraternity," *Deseret News*
(March 30, 1998). Some black Freemasons claim that Freemasonry can be traced to the earliest period of the Ethiopian and Egyptian dynasties, that it was first practiced by blacks, and
that its rituals are an allegory for their slavery and emancipation. Walkes, *Black Square &
Compass*, 119–20; Mustafa El-Amin, *African-American Freemasons: Why They Should Accept
Al-Islam* (Jersey City, NJ: New Mind Productions, 1990).
122. Mark E. Koltko-Rivera, *Freemasonry: An Introduction* (New York: Penguin, 2011),
97–102.
123. See Mauss, *All Abraham's Children*, 220–21. Mauss recognized "that the traditional
racial doctrines and folklore of Mormonism were [not] free of consequences." Ibid., 221.
See also Armand L. Mauss, *Shifting Borders and a Tattered Cover: Intellectual Journeys of a
Mormon Scholar* (Salt Lake City: University of Utah Press, 2012), 96–115.

APOLOGY AND REPUDIATION

Since 1978, some Mormon intellectuals have urged the church to repudiate the prior practice, acknowledge that it was wrong, and disavow the anachronistic rationales that were advanced to justify such discrimination.[124] While Lester Bush's comprehensive historical analysis concerning the origins of the policy ultimately provided church authorities with a rationale to abandon the exclusionary policy (since he demonstrated that there was no strong evidence that Joseph Smith introduced the policy), it was much more difficult for church officials to repudiate the rationale utilized to justify the policy (Africans were cursed with dark skin and servitude) since Smith believed and taught the same folklore.

As such, the LDS Church remained cautious about making any substantive comments concerning the abandoned exclusionary policy and particularly the rationales some Mormon authorities had articulated to justify it. But in 2012, during Mitt Romney's presidential campaign, the church's hand was forced when Randy Bott, a prominent BYU educator, repeated to a *Washington Post* reporter some of those anachronistic justifications.[125] The LDS Church quickly released a "statement" that repudiated Bott's attempts "to explain the reason for this restriction" and concluded that prior justifications for the policy "should be viewed as speculation and opinion, not doctrine."[126]

The church later released an "official statement" that "it is not known precisely why, how or when this restriction began in the Church, but it has ended." This official statement referred to the church's response to an inquiry made by *The New Republic* several months earlier that maintained that prior explanations "made in the absence of direct revelation…do not represent Church doctrine."[127] The church's statements did not mention

---

124. See, e.g., Larry B. Stammer, "Mormons May Disavow Old View on Blacks," *Los Angeles Times*, 1 (May 18, 1998); "Mormon Plan to Disavow Racist Teachings Jeopardized by Publicity," *Los Angeles Times*, 13 (May 24, 1998). For a discussion of efforts to convince church leaders to repudiate the folklore associated with a "curse," see Mauss, *All Abraham's Children*, 231–66.

125. Jason Horowitz, "The Genesis of a church's stand on race," *The Washington Post* (February 28, 2012) (Accessed at www.washingtonpost.com).

126. "Church Statement Regarding 'Washington Post' Article on Race and the Church," The Church of Jesus Christ of Latter-day Saints, February 29, 2012.

127. "The Church and Race: All Are Alike Unto God," Official Statement of the Church of Jesus Christ of Latter-day Saints, March 1, 2010. (Accessed at www.mormonnewsroom.org). "Has the Mormon Church Truly Left its Race Problems Behind," *The New Republic*, November 15, 2011 (Accessed at www.tnr.com). Some LDS Church leaders have been much more transparent, including Apostle Jeffrey Holland who suggested that his "earlier colleagues'"

Brigham Young's reference to his prophetic mantle when he introduced the practice during the nineteenth century or the First Presidency's 1949 declaration that the policy was based on revelation.

Nevertheless, the church's clarifications did seem to undermine the teachings of Orson Hyde, Joseph Fielding Smith, and Bruce McConkie who connected the practice with the pre-existence (which Brigham Young had previously rejected) as well as Parley Pratt's and Brigham Roberts's conclusions that it was justified by the Book of Abraham. Armand Mauss noted the following year, with apparent disappointment, that "thirty-five years after the end of a racial restriction that has so burdened the church the old racist folklore that came with it has still not been repudiated by the First Presidency."[128] But within six months of Mauss's observation, the LDS Church finally repudiated all prior rationales: "Today the Church disavows the theories advanced in the past that black skin is a sign of divine disfavor or curse, or that it reflects actions in a premortal life; that mixed-race marriages are a sin; or that blacks or people of any other race or ethnicity are inferior in any way to anyone else. Church leaders today unequivocally condemn all racism, past and present in any form."[129]

---

justification for the policy by relying on folklore was "inadequate and/or wrong" and that there "should be no effort to perpetuate those efforts to explain why that 'doctrine' existed." Jeffery Holland Interview, www.pbs.org/mormons/interviews/holland.html.

128. Peggy Fletcher Stack, "35 years later, priesthood ban is gone, but some pain still lingers for black Mormons," *Salt Lake Tribune*, June 11, 2013. Electronic version accessed June 11, 2013, at www.sltrib.com.

129. "Race and Priesthood," posted on December 6, 2013, at www.lds.org. Although the posting noted that Brigham Young (not Joseph Smith) institutionalized the policy, it did not mention that Joseph Smith also taught that blacks were cursed. In addition, while it stated that "the Church disavows that theory advanced in the past" and "unequivocally condemns all racism past and present, in any form," it does not specifically repudiate Brigham Young's institutionalization of the policy.

The Dynamic Relationship

BOTH MASONS AND MORMONS eventually modified or eliminated similar oaths and penalties from their rituals that had linked them and become so controversial. In 1964 the United Grand Lodge of England debated "the barbarous wording of the Penalties, which had already been modified (compulsorily) in Ireland and Scotland." Masonic commentators Pick and Knight have noted that "the penalties had long formed the basis for most of the external attacks on Freemasonry." The United Grand Lodge, following a spirited debate, passed a resolution permitting individual lodges to modify the language.

Despite the fact that most lodges adopted alternate language, the United Grand Lodge debated the same penalties two decades later and voted to require the elimination of "all references to physical penalties...from the obligations taken by candidates in the three degrees, and by a Master-elect at his Installation, but retained elsewhere in the respective ceremonies."[1] In 1990 the LDS hierarchy approved similar revisions to the endowment. The press reported that some temple-goers were extremely pleased that penalties were completely eliminated from the endowment.[2]

Thereafter Mormon scholar Walter E. A. van Beek noted the significance of these changes as constituting a gentle "ousting [of] Masonic influence, which does not have to be at the core of LDS rituals," and that "the whole habitus of the temple services has changed dramatically since the first Nauvoo initiation, which lasted for hours and was interlaced with violin music and square dancing, to the streamlined present-day version on film."

1. Concerning these changes in the Masonic ritual, see Pick and Knight, *The Freemason's Pocket Reference Book*, 134, 145–46; *Emulation Ritual*, 9th ed. (London: Lewis Masonic, 1991), 8–11; and *Deseret News*, February 18, 1987.
2. See "Mormon temple rite gets major revision," *Arizona Republic*, April 28, 1990, A-1, A-14; "LDS Leaders Revise Temple Endowment," *Salt Lake Tribune*, April 29, 1990, 2B; "Mormons Drop Rites Opposed by Women," *New York Times*, May 3, 1990, A1, A17; "Women's Rites, The Mormons modernize a supersecret ceremony," *Time*, May 14, 1990, 67.

But Van Beek also cautioned that "in Mormonism, the authorities discourage speaking about changes in ritual, and temple workers and presidencies are instructed to state that the temple rituals have always been the same and that no major changes have taken place. Historically this is not correct but there is rhyme and reason in the statement."[3] Nevertheless, some Mormon authorities have occasionally discussed the temple ritual in very general terms.[4]

SOLOMON'S TEMPLE

In 1992 Mormon educator Kenneth W. Godfrey summarized the LDS thesis, developed by LDS General Authorities during the 1920s and 1930s, concerning the relationship between Freemasonry and Mormonism. This thesis continues to inform the position of many, if not most, believing church members concerning this dynamic relationship.[5] Godfrey's article, which was published in the *Encyclopedia of Mormonism*, maintained that Smith received the entire temple endowment by revelation before he became a Mason, that he joined Freemasonry primarily for friendship, and that he never actively participated in the Craft.[6]

Godfrey acknowledged that "some Nauvoo Masons thought of the endowment as a restoration of a ritual only imperfectly preserved in Freemasonry" and that "Joseph Smith suggested that the endowment and Freemasonry in part emanated from the same ancient spring," but he did not mention that historians have deconstructed the notion that Masonic rituals can be traced back to Solomon's Temple.

Finally, he argued that resemblances between Masonic and Mormon rituals are "limited to a small proportion of actions and words" and that "where the two rituals share symbolism, the fabric of meanings is different." The Mormon endowment provides a literal gateway to heaven whereas

3. Walter E.A. van Beek, "Meaning and Authority in Mormon Ritual," *International Journal of Mormon Studies* (2010): 31.
4. See Joseph Fielding Smith, *Blood Atonement and the Origin of Plural Marriage* (Salt Lake City: Deseret News Press, 1905), 87, and Boyd K. Packer, *The Holy Temple* (Salt Lake City: Bookcraft, 1980), 191–206.
5. See Peggy Fletcher Stack, "Sacred ceremonies: Latter-day Saints say Temple worship must be experienced to be understood," *Salt Lake Tribune*, March 20, 2009 (electronic version at www.sltrib.com). "Critics claim that some of the temple rites were adapted from Freemasonry, after Smith participated in that fraternal order in Nauvoo, Ill. They point to the common use of symbols such as the all-seeing eye, the fraternal handshake, the compass and the square as evidence of borrowing." Stack quoted LDS Church representatives who "dismiss those claims as overstating the influence of Masonry." See also Gilbert W. Scharffs, *Mormons & Masons* (Orem, UT: Millennial Press, Inc., 2007), 55–60.
6. Kenneth W. Godfrey, "Freemasonry and the Temple," in Ludlow, *Encyclopedia of Mormonism* 2:528–29.

Masonic rituals are "earthbound, pervaded by human legend and hope for something better."[7]

The LDS thesis Godfrey summarized continues to assume that Masonic rituals are remnants of ceremonies celebrated in the Temple of Solomon and that this connection remains a viable explanation for similarities between Masonic rituals and the endowment. This anachronistic portion of the thesis is most likely retained because of Mormonism's reverence for its first prophet and its reluctance to acknowledge that Smith (like many other American Freemasons) was mistaken when he linked Masonic ritual to an endowment actually practiced in Solomon's Temple.

During the twentieth century members of the Quatuor Coronati Research Lodge, including Douglas Knoop and Gwilyn Peredur Jones, continued to publish books, including *The Mediaeval Mason* (1933) and *The Genesis of Freemasonry* (1947), that validated the Authentic School's conclusion that Freemasonry is a relatively young institution and that there was a link between early-modern stonemasons' guilds and even more recent speculative Freemasonry. Some recent Masonic scholars, such as John Hamill, have challenged even that connection.[8]

Today most academic historians recognize the difference between fanciful legends and scholastic history, and even while they continue to debate the development of Freemasonry within the context of its medieval origins, and particularly whether there was a link between operative and speculative Masonry, most Masons no longer believe that the Craft was revealed in the Garden of Eden or that Masonic rituals were practiced in ancient Egypt or even introduced in Solomon's Temple.[9]

MASONIC PARALLELS

The plank of the revised LDS position that is arguably inconsistent with Smith's teachings is the notion that even while there are formulaic similarities including terminology and signs, tokens, and obligations (which readers can confirm by consulting a wide variety of sources), there are no

---

7. Godfrey, "Freemasonry and the Temple," 2:528–29.

8. See Hamill, *The Craft: A History of English Freemasonry*, 17, 19; Snoek, "Researching Freemasonry," 233–34. Snoek argues that the handles of "operative" and "speculative" should be discarded in favor of "Stone masons" and "gentlemen masons." Ibid., 236.

9. Albert G. Mackey observed that "no Masonic writer would now venture to quote [James] Anderson as authority for the history of the Order anterior to the eighteenth century." But he acknowledged that without Freemasonry's "Temple Legend," it "would at once decay and die." Mackey, *Encyclopedia of Freemasonry* 1:57–58; 2:774–75. Arthur E. Waite also recognized that Masonic ritual was of relatively recent origin, but he notes that "antiquity *per se* is not a test of value. I can imagine a Rite created at this day which would be much greater and more eloquent in symbolism than anything that we work and love under the name of Masonry." Waite, *A New Encyclopedia of Freemasonry* 1:427.

substantive parallels between Masonic and Mormon rituals.[10] Hugh Nibley, who crossed swords with Fawn Brodie when she concluded that there were similarities between nineteenth-century anti-Masonic rhetoric and passages in the Book of Mormon, eventually acknowledged that "Masonic rites have a lot in common with ours" and that they "have the same source, if you trace them way back"[11] but that those rituals "have nothing to do with salvation, but consist only of broken fragments."[12] But he acknowledged that "the most consistent thing about histories of Freemasonry by its most eminent historians is the noncommittal position in the important matter of origins."[13]

Similarly, Michael Quinn has concluded that "Freemasonry's minor emphasis on the heavenly outcome of its rituals was a chasm between Freemasonry and the Mormon endowment." He questioned whether anyone in Joseph Smith's generation really believed in the antiquity of the Craft or that any specific signs, symbols, or ceremonies were preserved from antiquity. As such, the chasm was quite large, according to Quinn, since "no Mason at Joseph Smith's time or thereafter defined the central purpose of Masonic rites to be an ascent into heaven."[14]

More recently, Richard Bushman has acknowledged that the Mormon prophet was "intrigued by the Masonic rites" when the Nauvoo Lodge was organized, and that he "turned the materials to his own uses…in the temple endowment." This connection, according to Bushman, explains why a "portion of the temple ritual resembled Masonic rites."[15] Bushman even chose *Rough Stone Rolling* as the subtitle of his book because the first Mormon prophet referred to himself as a rough stone shortly after becoming a Freemason, perhaps because the Entered Apprentice ritual teaches men that they begin their journey as rough stones but become smooth after rolling through life's challenges.[16]

But Bushman argued that the connections between Masonic rituals and the Mormon endowment were superficial because the "Masonic elements

10. See Grunder, *Mormon Parallels*, 956–64.
11. Hugh Nibley, "Apocryphal Writings," in Nibley, *Temple and Cosmos*, 319.
12. Ibid.
13. Hugh Nibley, "One Eternal Round: The Hermetic Version," in Nibley, *Temple and Cosmos*, 419.
14. Quinn, *Early Mormonism and the Magic World View*, 228–29, 234.
15. Bushman, *Rough Stone Rolling*, 449–50.
16. See Bushman, *Rough Stone Rolling*, vi. For references to the Masonic "rough ashlars," see Grunder, *Mormon Parallels*, 435, 958, 1283; and Tobias Churton, *Freemasonry: The Reality* (Hersham, Surrey: Lewis Masonic, 2007), 16, 304. Terryl Givens and Matt Grow have also recently noted that Smith's incorporation of "bits and pieces of Masonic ritual…into the new temple ceremonies" was consistent with his "vision of inspired eclecticism." Terryl L. Givens and Matthew J. Grow, *Parley P. Pratt: The Apostle Paul of Mormonism* (Oxford: Oxford University Press, 2011), 208.

that appeared in the temple endowment were embedded in a distinctive context," that the endowment dramatized "the creation instead of the Temple of Solomon, exaltation instead of fraternity, God and Christ, not the Worshipful Master." Thus, according to Bushman, "Temple covenants bound people to God rather than each other," and "the aim of the endowment was not male fraternity but the exaltation of husbands and wives."[17]

ANCIENT MYSTERIES

Because of the chasm between Mormon and Masonic rituals (and presumably the realization that there is a similar disconnect in comparisons between the endowment and the rituals of Solomon's Temple), LDS writers have argued that there are more ancient sources. Godfrey concluded that "the endowment is more congruous with LDS scriptures (especially the Book of Abraham and Book of Moses) and ancient ritual than with Freemasonry," and that the "Egyptian pyramid texts" are an example of ancient rituals that may have a common remote source with the endowment.[18]

Nibley's work in this area was copious. He contended that the ancient mysteries (which were taught in Egypt before spreading to Greece and Rome) were the real prototypes for the endowment since they promised salvation, exaltation, and apotheosis. His Egyptian thesis was part of a broader argument that Smith's writings (including the Book of Abraham) were the product of direct revelation rather than a literal translation of a primary document.[19] He insisted that the Egyptian and Mormon endowments "have a common origin," that the "ordinances of the Egyptian temple were essentially the same as those performed in ours"[20] and that one could "reconstruct from the *Book of the Dead* most of the temple ordinances."[21]

Likewise, Quinn has concluded that the ancient mysteries were the real source of inspiration for Smith rather than Masonic rituals. He focused on what he identified as "the fundamental characteristics of the ancient

17. Bushman, *Rough Stone Rolling*, 450–51.
18. Godfrey, "Freemasonry and the Temple," 2:528.
19. Hugh Nibley, "The Meaning of the Temple," in Nibley, *Temple and Cosmos*, 27.
20. Ibid., 26.
21. Nibley, "Apocryphal Writings," in Nibley, *Temple and Cosmos*, 320. Nibley noted that secrecy associated with temple rituals has made it more difficult to trace origins. "Scholars are just beginning to realize," Nibley wrote in 1965, "to what extent the early Christians were attracted to the temple, as when the Gospel of Philip says that the Christians are instructed by 'hidden types and images that are behind the veil,' so that 'by these despised symbols we enter into a knowledge of salvation.'" See Hugh Nibley, "Since Cumorah, New Voices from the Dust," *Improvement Era* 68:6 (June 1965): 574, quoting A. Adam, in *Theologische Literaturzeitung* 88 (1963): 101. He believed that the existence of early Christian prayer circles provided additional evidence that Joseph Smith restored an ancient temple ritual. See Hugh Nibley, "The Early Christian Prayer Circle," *Brigham University Studies* 19 (1978): 41–78.

mysteries" in his search for alternative explanations for the origins of the endowment. The "fundamental characteristics" of the ancient mysteries were "revealed by God from the beginning, but distorted through apostasy." The ritual required "worthiness of initiates" who were initiated through "washings and anointings, new name, garment," and "vows of non-disclosure." The ritual included "the lesser and greater rituals," "presentation through drama," "oath of chastity," and "sun and moon." During the ritual "mortals [were] 'exalted' to Godhood," "prophets, priests, and kings," and "God(s) once mortal." Although Quinn recognized that "Masonic rituals shared some similarities with ancient mysteries," he believed that "these [rituals] were not linked to a central concept of heavenly ascent" whereas "the ancient occult mysteries manifest both philosophical and structural kinship with the Mormon endowment."[22]

Finally, William Hamblin wrote that an "early Christian Initiation ritual" has "possible parallels" with the Latter-day Saint temple endowment. The reflections include rituals of baptism and anointing, prayer circles, ritual clothing, handclasps as tokens of recognition, the knowledge of the sacred name of God as necessary for exaltation, symbolization of heavenly ascent, use of a veil, and the notion that mankind can become like God.[23] Ironically, this Mormon search for an ancient source for the endowment is similar to speculations concerning primitive springs for Masonic rituals.[24] Masonic writers traced the Craft back to the ancient mysteries, Old Testament prophets (Enoch, Moses, Noah, and Solomon), the Druids, Rosicrucians, and Knights Templar.[25] Indeed, some very prominent seventeenth-century speculative Freemasons were motivated to join up because they believed they would discover secrets in Masonic rituals that had been preserved from the ancient mysteries. Although they were disappointed when they failed to discover these secrets, subsequent members of the Craft eventually grafted the sought-for hermetic strand into the *haut grades* and claimed that these secrets would empower Masons to work out their own exaltation.

Two centuries later Albert Mackey compared Freemasonry and the ancient mysteries using points of resemblance that included preparation,

22. Quinn, *Early Mormonism and the Magic World View*, 230–34.
23. See William J. Hamblin, "Aspects of Early Christian Initiation Ritual," in John M. Lundquist and Stephen D. Ricks, eds., *By Study and Also by Faith* (Salt Lake City: Deseret Book Company, 1990), 1:211.
24. Albert Mackey noted that William Hutchinson believed that "there is no doubt that our ceremonies and Mysteries were derived from the rites, ceremonies, and institutions of the ancients, and some of them from the remotest ages," Mackey, *The History of Freemasonry* 1:186, quoting Hutchinson, *Spirit of Masonry*, Lecture ii, p. 15, and that George Oliver taught that Spurious Freemasonry was preserved in the pagan mysteries. Mackey, *The History of Freemasonry* 1:187, quoting Oliver, *The History of Initiation*, Lecture I, p. 13, notes.
25. See, e.g., Mackey, *The History of Freemasonry*.

initiation, perfection, secret character, symbols, dramatic form of initiation divided into degrees or steps, and adoption of secret methods of recognition. He noted that Freemasonry and ancient mysteries were "secret societies, that both taught the same doctrine of a future life, and that both made use of symbols and allegories and a dramatic form of instruction" but that "this analogy is the result of natural causes, and by no means infers a descent of the modern form from the ancient institution."[26]

Although Mackey did not believe that there was a direct connection between the ancient mysteries and Freemasonry, he concluded, "These analogies, it must be admitted, are very striking, and if considered merely as coincidences, must be acknowledged to be very singular."[27] He also observed, "It is, however, hardly to be denied that the founders of the Speculative system of Masonry, in forming their ritual, especially the third degree, derived many suggestions as to the form and character of their funeral legend from the rites of the ancient initiations."[28]

Nevertheless, one of the difficulties in pursuing an ancient model for any ritual is that some Egyptologists have concluded that there is not a single "Egyptian religion" and that there is insufficient evidence concerning a myriad of Egyptian rituals to make meaningful comparisons.[29] Toby Wilkinson has noted that ancient Egyptians had a "fondness and talent for theological elaboration" and that the concepts they developed "would echo through later civilization and ultimately shape the Judeo-Christian tradition."[30] Joseph Manning has cautioned that "we can be attracted to ancient lives without thinking that they were just like we are, or forgetting millennia of hard-won social, political and economic development."[31]

FABRIC OF MEANING

Regardless of its origins, Freemasons taught initiates that they could recover what has been lost. The lost word in Masonry's third degree is the ineffable name of God "but the term is used symbolically of Divine Truth."[32] Masonry communicated restored truths to its initiates to lead them from

---

26. Mackey, *The History of Freemasonry* 1:186–88; 192–93, 195.
27. Ibid., 1:197.
28. Ibid., 1:198.
29. Michel Quesnel, "Des mythes sans historie," *L'Actualité religieuse dans le monde*, hors-série n. 1 (mars 1993): 40–42.
30. Toby Wilkinson, *The Rise and Fall of Ancient Egypt* (New York: Random House, 2011), 126, 129.
31. Joseph Manning, "Beyond the Pharaohs," *Wall Street Journal* (March 19, 2011), C1.
32. Michael R. Poll, ed., *Masonic Words and Phrases* (New Orleans: Cornerstone Book Publishers, 2005).

darkness to light and from life on earth without their heavenly parent to life in heaven when they will be reunified with Him.

Catholic scholar Massimo Introvigne cautions that Freemasonry's inclusiveness philosophy, in which all truths are relative, conflicted with Joseph Smith's teaching that one can only be saved by joining the one true church. As such, Introvigne has concluded that "the use of a *language* which is often derived from Freemasonry (and was easily recognizable as such by those 19th-century Americans who were familiar with Freemasonry), does not imply that the *content* transmitted through that language was intrinsically Masonic: in fact, this was not the case."[33]

But Masonic writer Jay Kinney has observed that Masonry provided initiates with "a sparsely furnished organizational shell into which each member could move his own philosophical and spiritual furniture" and that each "initiate has to supply his own content" to find esoteric meaning.[34] The philosophical and spiritual furniture that was placed in some American lodges during Joseph Smith's lifetime was comparable to the Mormon endowment.

Masonic initiates, Salem Town wrote, were taught that they were like Adam in that they were morally blind and must therefore submit to instructions and tests in order to receive increasing illumination. During the third degree a Mason is severely tested, is attacked by enemies, and stares at death before overcoming all temptations.[35] Those who persevered were raised by the five points of fellowship from the grave of darkness to a cradle of light and became a new man. Thereafter, he continued to build his spiritual temple in order to reestablish his presence with God.[36] The rituals of Craft Masonry taught that after death "the Son of Righteousness shall descend, and send forth his angels to collect our ransomed dust; then if we are found worthy, by his pass-word, we shall enter into the celestial lodge above where the Supreme Architect of the Universe presides, where we shall see the King in the beauty of holiness, and with him enter into an endless eternity."[37]

---

33. Massimo Introvigne, *I mormoni. Dal Far West alle Olimpiadi* (Leumann, Torino: Elledici, 2002), 94.
34. Kinney, *The Masonic Myth*, 208–9. David Stevenson has argued that organizations, including the first speculative freemasons, used the organizational framework of operative masons, replete with "secrecy, ideals of loyalty and secret modes of recognition," and have placed within it "their own values...which they could adapt for their own uses." Stevenson, *The Origins of Freemasonry*, 7. Similarly, Mormon writer Joanna Brooks has noted that "English Freemasons adapted the lore of anciency to suit their own ethnic, political and religious sensibilities." Brooks, *American Lazarus*, 124.
35. Town, *A System of Speculative Masonry*, 78–82, 180.
36. Churton, *Freemasonry*, 42–43.
37. Morgan, *Illustrations of Masonry*, 93; Bernard, *Light on Masonry*, 84. For a Masonic oration making reference to this same imagery, see Thomas Cary, *An Oration Pronounced*

The Royal Arch and other high degrees, which were developed after Craft Masonry, were even more esoteric and reminiscent of the endowment and contained language suggesting that enlightenment would lead to exaltation. High priests of the Royal Arch were "exalted" into the Order of High Priesthood and the grand high priest, in his address to the Order of High Priesthood, expressed his hope that the "*chapter* become *beautiful* as the *temple, peaceful* as the *ark*, and *sacred* as its *most holy place.*" He also asked that "you be endowed with every good and perfect gift, while *traveling* the *rugged path* of life, and finally be *admitted within the veil* of heaven to the full enjoyment of life eternal."[38]

Town wrote that the companions of the Royal Arch degrees obtained "a NAME which no man knoweth," discovered "his election to, and his glorified station in, the kingdom of his father," and passed through four veils to be "admitted within the veil of God's presence, where they will become kings and priests before the throne of his glory for ever and ever."[39]

Finally, Town and other Masons in postrevolutionary America believed that Masonry was a "handmaiden to religion" and they interpreted its legends and rituals through a Christian prism.[40] The Masons who advanced this brand of Freemasonry during Joseph Smith's lifetime conflated ancient Masonry with primitive Christianity, teaching that ancient Masonry "was of a sacred and religious nature" and that Masonic rituals provided an important supplement to Christianity's message of salvation and even exaltation.[41]

While Masons did not specifically claim that their ceremonies provided literal keys for admittance into the celestial order, their rituals did contain very lofty language that was suggestive of the promises given in Joseph's Temples. Town believed that the analogy between Freemasonry and Christianity was not partial but complete, that all good Masons must be Christians, and he confidently predicted that as the millennium approached all men would eventually "practice what is now taught within the lodge."[42]

Before the Right Worshipful Master and Brethren of St. Peter's at the Episcopal Church in Newburyport, on the Festival of St. John the Baptist, Celebrated June 24th, 5801 (n.p.: From the Press of Brother Angier March, n.d.): "[W]hen this frail fabric shall be dissolved, and the SUPREME ARCHITECT shall summon his laborers to receive their reward, to the condescending Saviour we will listen for the pass word, which shall admit us to his father's temple, a house not made with hands, eternal in the heavens."

38. Cross, *The True Masonic Chart*, 155.

39. Town, *A System of Speculative Masonry*, 76. See Grunder, *Mormon Parallels*, 1842; and Town, *A System of Speculative Masonry*, 78–82, 180.

40. See Edgar Raymond Johnston, *Masonry Defined: A Liberal Masonic Education, Information Every Mason Should Have* (Kingsport, TN: National Masonic Press, 1930), 256.

41. See Town, *A System of Speculative Masonry*, 37, 83–92, 174, 176, 178–79.

42. Ibid., 78–82, 180.

There were also vivid parallels between the Garden of Eden narratives in some adoptive rituals and the endowment. Although it is debatable whether Smith intended that women would eventually become "priests" in the same sense as men, his inclusion of women in the same ceremony as men was a significant departure from English and American Masonic rituals. While it is also unclear whether Smith would have allowed black men to participate in the Nauvoo endowment (even though at least one African American did participate in the Kirtland endowment), the policy institutionalized by his successor was similar to practices observed in American Freemasonry.

EXACT WORD, PRECISE GESTURE, GENERAL SPIRIT

When Reed Durham delivered his controversial presidential address, he identified some of these Masonic sources that Joseph Smith grabbed onto when he introduced a revised temple endowment to the Holy Order in Nauvoo. Although his conclusions were a radical departure from the twentieth-century LDS position, he remained convinced that Smith's new endowment was based on revelation and inspired. During the intervening forty years, Mormon scholars have increasingly concluded that Smith incorporated the Masonic formula (utilizing a drama, keywords, obligations, penalties, prayer circles, and veils) into the endowment and may have been inspired by even some of Freemasonry's loftier ideas (obtaining illumination in a temple to assist in returning to God's presence) without being drawn into a debate concerning his prophetic powers.

Armand L. Mauss, who recognized that Smith was influenced by his own environment, suggested a more nuanced model for an LDS thesis concerning the dynamic comparisons between Masonry and Mormonism. He observed that although the "most emotional and controversial aspect" of the temple endowment "involves possible borrowings from Masonry," this "should [not] be such a big issue, except to those with a fairly limited understanding of how a prophet gets ideas. Since prophets and religions always arise and are nurtured within a given cultural context, itself evolving, it should not be difficult to understand why even the most original revelations have to be expressed in the idioms of the culture and biography of the revelator."[43]

Similarly, Mormon scholar Wouter van Beek has pointed out that "the kinship between the two initiations [Masonic and Mormon] was clear for most of the participants, who were initiated Masons" but these initiates, "while recognizing the Masonic inspiration...considered the

---

43. Armand L. Mauss, "Culture, Charisma and Change: Reflections on Mormon Temple Worship," *Dialogue: A Journal of Mormon Thought* 20 (Winter 1987): 79–80.

new endowment (still not in the temple) as the 'real thing.'"[44] Van Beek acknowledged that the endowment, like other initiation rites, "derives its authority from its supposedly ancient history, a myth of origin that is generated by the very authority that commands and changes rituals." That tradition, according to van Beek, "is not so much a historical reference but an argument of authority: things are seen as old, and thus have authority."[45]

Rick Grunder has collected the many parallels between those who advocated the Christianization of Freemasonry and Smith's teachings concerning temple.[46] He has concluded, based on the belief of American Masons that their rituals supplemented Christianity's tools for illumination and provided a pathway to reunite them with their Creator, that "the spirit of Masonic temple ceremonies…was, at least ostensibly, parallel to the spirit of the future temple ceremony" and that the parallels between Masonic and Mormon rituals are not only broad but deep and substantive.[47] These correlations, according to Grunder, "demonstrate that Joseph employed [in the endowment ritual] much which seems highly Masonic, both in exact word, in precise gesture, and in general spirit."[48]

The specific parallels between Masonry and Mormonism have inspired a new generation of Mormon scholars to re-evaluate the substance of those connections. They have concluded that the similarities between Masonry and Mormonism are broader than the parallels that are normally discussed, such as Enoch's plate and Joseph Smith's gold plates, anti-Masonic rhetoric and passages in the Book of Mormon, and Masonic rituals and the endowment. Their work demonstrates that there has not been any premature intellectual closure concerning comparisons between Masonry and Mormonism.

Clyde Forsberg has noted traces of Masonry in Smith's first vision and in many of the events that took place in Kirtland.[49] Clair Barrus has highlighted connections between Royal Arch Masonry and Oliver Cowdery's "rod of nature," and Clinton Bartholomew has concluded that there are similarities between Royal Arch cipher and Joseph Smith's "conception of ancient languages." Another scholar, Michael Reed, has analyzed the

44. Walter E. A. Van Beek, "Hierarchies of Holiness: The Mormon Temple in Zoetermeer, The Netherlands," in *Holy Ground: Reinventing Ritual Space in Modern Western Culture*, ed. P. Post and A. Molendijk (Leuven: Peters, 2010), 255–99.
45. Van Beek, "Meaning and Authority in Mormon Ritual," 30–32.
46. Grunder, *Mormon Parallels*, 433, 923, 957, 963, 1841–42.
47. Ibid., 1841.
48. Ibid., 954.
49. Forsberg has argued that there were connections between the architectural design of the Kirtland Temple, as well as the inclusion of women and the exclusion of African Americans from Mormon temple rituals. Forsberg, *Equal Rites*, 89–100, 203–44; Forsberg, "Kirtland through the Christian-Masonic, Neo-Hebraic, Neo-Pagan Looking Glass," 176–205.

connections between those who advocated the "Christianization of Free-masonry" and Smith's introduction of the Mormon endowment.[50]

While some of these connections may be controversial and challenging, they are certainly worthy of further consideration and study and remain relevant in the twenty-first century. The worldwide Mormon population has surpassed fifteen million, and many of these members participate in the Mormon endowment in more than one hundred forty temples (with more announced or under construction) in the Americas, Europe, Asia, Australia, and Africa. The number of Masons in the United States is approximately two million with perhaps another two to three million in the rest of the world. It is therefore ironic that the prediction of some nineteenth-century American Masons that Christians would eventually practice Masonic rituals is more likely within the narrow context of Mormonism than it is in the traditional Christian denominations, which in some cases continue to counsel their members against joining the Craft.

This development is not surprising when one considers that Joseph Smith imported a Masonic-like ritual into his hierarchical church and taught that it was heavenly sanctioned and included keys that literally (not just allegorically) enabled initiates to pass through sentinels into the presence of God. At the same time American Masonry reinvented itself by re-emphasizing its inclusivity, de-emphasizing its Christian connections and no longer claiming ancient origins. The degree to which Smith's new ritual was based on inspiration, as suggested by Mormon scholars, as opposed to his extrapolations of Masonic ritual, as argued by non-Mormons, is ultimately a question of faith.

Nevertheless, while Joseph's temples were not a literal restoration of Solomon's Temple, they are also not a mere pirated copy of Masonic rites. But the first Mormon prophet did use and adapt a Masonic formula and extrapolated some of Masonry's teachings that were developed during the previous one hundred years in England, France, and America. As such, the common aspirations of nineteenth-century Masons and Mormons, to graft Masonic-like rituals into otherwise ritual-less churches, have still long-lasting implications for temple worship as well as for policies concerning gender and race. These aspirations continue to inform Mormons in their continuing quest to receive instructions concerning a pathway to return to God's presence.

50. These authors delivered speeches concerning these connections at the Forty-sixth Annual Conference of the Mormon History Association in St. George, Utah, on May 27, 2011. Clair Barrus, "Oliver Cowdery's Rod of Nature"; Clinton Bartholomew, "Cipher in the Kirtland Snow: The Royal Arch Cipher and Joseph Smith's Conception of Ancient Languages"; and Michael G. Reed, "The Endowment and the 'Christianization of Freemasonry.'"

Chronology

1813   United Grand Lodge of England organized
1815   Elias Boudinot's *The Second Advent* published
1820   Joseph Smith's first vision (first recorded in 1832)
1823   Joseph Smith's vision of Moroni (first recorded in 1832)
1823   George Oliver's *The Antiquities of Free-Masonry* published
1826   John Glazier Stearns's *An Inquiry into the Nature and Tendency of Speculative Free-Masonry* published
1826   William Morgan abducted in Batavia, New York
1826   William Morgan's *Illustrations of Freemasonry* published
1827   Josiah Priest's *View of the Expected Millennium* published
1827   Prince Hall Lodge's Declaration of Independence
1828   First convention of seceding Masons in LeRoy, New York
1828   Joseph Smith dictates a revelation (now Doctrine and Covenants 10) that Satanic conspirators who love darkness more than light were attempting to prevent the publication of the Book of Mormon
1829   David Bernard's *Light on Masonry* (the "anti-Masonic Bible") published
March 1830   Book of Mormon published
April 6, 1830   The Church of Christ organized
December 1830   Joseph Smith revelation concerning temple and endowment
February 1831   Joseph Smith revelation for church to gather in New Jerusalem; Kirtland, Ohio, becomes a way station
June 1831   Joseph Smith and others ordained to high priesthood and endowed with power
July 20, 1831   Revelation concerning a temple in Zion, Missouri
1830–1831   Joseph Smith translates extracts from Book of Enoch and Book of Moses
January 1833   Joseph Smith organizes School of Prophets and introduced washing of face, hands, and feet
May 6, 1834   Joseph Smith revelation concerning House of the Lord in Kirtland
May 1834   Joseph Smith organizes Zion's Camp to redeem Zion
1835   Joseph Smith purchases four mummies with papyri (written in Egyptian hieroglyphics) and translates a portion containing the writings of Abraham
1835   Joseph Smith receives revelations concerning washing of the feet
January 1836   Joseph Smith introduces washing and anointing to high priesthood
March 27, 1836   Kirtland Temple dedicated
May 1839   Joseph Smith settles in Nauvoo, Illinois
December 27, 1839   Illinois Masonic lodges meet in Jacksonville
January 26, 1840   Illinois Masonic lodges meet again in Jacksonville

April 6, 1840 Illinois Masonic lodges reorganize the Illinois Grand Lodge

April 29, 1840 Abraham Jonas installed as Illinois Grand Master

September 1840 John C. Bennett arrives in Nauvoo, Illinois

October 1840 Illinois Grand Lodge holds its first annual communication

January 19, 1841 Joseph Smith receives revelation to build temple in Nauvoo

April 1841 James Adams withdraws from active participation in Freemasonry

June 1841 Mormon Masons seek recommendation from Bodley Lodge No. 1 to organize a Masonic lodge in Nauvoo

October 1841 Illinois Grand Lodge holds its second annual communication

December 29, 1841 Mormon Masons organize Nauvoo Lodge

December 30, 1841 Joseph Smith petitions Nauvoo Lodge for initiation into Freemasonry

January 1842 Nauvoo Lodge holds first communication

January 6, 1842 Joseph Smith records, "The God of heaven has begun to restore the ancient order of his kingdom"

February 3, 1842 Nauvoo Lodge Committee of Investigation reports favorably regarding Joseph Smith petition for initiation

March 1 & 15, 1842 Book of Abraham published in *Times and Seasons*

March 15, 1842 Grand Master Jonas Nauvoo Lodge and Joseph Smith initiated as an Apprentice.

March 17, 1842 Joseph Smith passed (as Fellowcraft) and raised (as Master Mason)

March 17, 1842 Joseph Smith organizes the Nauvoo Female Relief Society

May 3, 1842 Grand Master Jonas sends letter to Master George Miller concerning allegations that had been made against John C. Bennett

May 4–5, 1842 Joseph Smith reveals new endowment to Holy Order

May 7, 1842 George Miller reads Abraham Jonas's communication to the Nauvoo Lodge; Nauvoo Legion holds sham battle attended by Stephen A. Douglas

May 9, 1842 Nauvoo Lodge removes John C. Bennett as secretary; Willard Richards becomes secretary *pro tem*

May 17, 1842 John C. Bennett resigns as church member

May 17, 1842 John C. Bennett resigns as Nauvoo mayor

May 17, 1842 Joseph King responds to Meredith Helm's inquiry concerning John C. Bennett; Joseph Smith instructs James Sloan to accept the resignation of John C. Bennett from church membership "if he desires to do so"

May 19, 1842 Nauvoo City Council passes a resolution tendering thanks to John C. Bennett for his service as mayor; Thomas Grover files charges against Bennett in Nauvoo Lodge

May 26, 1842 John C. Bennett and Joseph Smith attend Nauvoo Lodge;

Bennett apparently addresses the lodge but no vote is taken concerning the charges that have been filed against him

June 2, 1842 Nauvoo Lodge meets but fails to expel John C. Bennett

June 14, 1842 John C. Bennett writes a letter to *The Wasp* defending Joseph Smith against attacks that were published in *Sangamo Journal*

June 16, 1842 John C. Bennett and Joseph Smith attend Nauvoo Lodge; Bennett addresses the lodge concerning the charges that have been brought against him but the lodge takes no action

June 17, 1842 Willard Richards writes a letter to Abraham Jonas explaining the reasons Nauvoo Lodge did not expel John C. Bennett

June 18, 1842 Joseph Smith publically refers to the wickedness of John C. Bennett; Bennett excommunicated from church

June 20, 1842 Willard Richards writes to Abraham Jonas that John C. Bennett has left Nauvoo

June 23, 1842 Joseph Smith writes a letter explaining the Bennett affair

June 24, 1842 Nauvoo Lodge meets and considers evidence against John C. Bennett; Abraham Jonas attends the meeting

June 25, 1842 *The Wasp* publishes Joseph Smith's explanation (written two days earlier) of the Bennett affair

June 27, 1842 John C. Bennett writes his first letter in which he explains his association with Joseph Smith and the Mormons for publication in the *Sangamo Journal*; he alleges that six Mormons (including Joseph Smith) were initiated, passed, and raised before Nauvoo Lodge was installed by the grand master; he repeats this and other claims concerning Nauvoo Lodge's irregularities in letters published on July 15 and July 22

July 8, 1842 John C. Bennett's letter (written on June 27) is published in the *Sangamo Journal*

July 16, 1842 Bodley Lodge No. 1 meets and votes to recommend to Grand Master Jonas that Nauvoo Lodge's dispensation be revoked

July 30, 1842 Abraham Jonas suspends Nauvoo Lodge's dispensation

September 29, 1842 George Miller sends letter to Abraham Jonas in which he claims that Jonas revoked Nauvoo Lodge's dispensation for religious purposes

October 1842 The Illinois Grand Lodge holds its third annual communication; Meredith Helm is elected and installed as grand master; he appoints a committee to investigate Nauvoo Lodge

October 1842 Jonathan Nye and W. B. Warren recommend that Nauvoo Lodge's dispensation be reinstated

November 2, 1842 Abraham Jonas reinstates Nauvoo Lodge's dispensation

November 10, 1842	Nauvoo Lodge meets and elects Hyrum Smith as master
May 28, 1843	Joseph Smith introduces eternal marriage to Holy Order; he is sealed to Emma Smith
June 24, 1843	Hyrum Smith lays the cornerstone of Nauvoo Masonic Temple
September 28, 1843	Joseph Smith introduces "second anointing" to Holy Order
October 1843	The Illinois Grand Lodge holds its fourth annual communication; Alexander Dunlap is elected as grand master; the grand lodge revokes Nauvoo Lodge's dispensation, as well as the dispensations of Helm Lodge, Nye Lodge, and Keokuk Lodge
November 2, 1843	Nauvoo Lodge meets to discuss the grand lodge's revocation of its dispensation; it votes to continue to meet and work as a lodge
January 1844	Grand Master Dunlap sends a letter to Nauvoo Lodge demanding its dispensation, books, and jewels
April 5, 1844	Hyrum Smith dedicates the Nauvoo Masonic Temple
June 27, 1844	Joseph Smith and Hyrum Smith are murdered in Carthage Jail
October 1844	Illinois Grand Lodge holds fifth annual communication; it votes to sever all relations with Nauvoo Lodge, Helm Lodge, and Nye Lodge, declaring that their activities are clandestine and voting to suspend their members from the privileges of Freemasonry
December 19, 1844	Nauvoo Lodge meets; Lucius Scovil is elected master
April 10, 1845	Heber C. Kimball instructs Lucius Scovil to suspend the activities of Nauvoo Lodge
May 14, 1845	Capstone is placed on Nauvoo Temple
October 1845	Illinois Grand Lodge holds sixth annual communication
November 30, 1845	Nauvoo Temple attic (where endowment is to be given) is dedicated
December 1845	Brigham Young introduces first endowments in Nauvoo Temple
January 1846	Nauvoo endowment is introduced to 5,635 men and women
April 30–31, 1846	Nauvoo Temple dedicated
October 1846	Illinois Grand Lodge holds seventh annual communication; it votes to exclude all African Americans from lodges
February 13, 1849	Brigham Young announces that African Americans cannot be ordained to LDS priesthood
February 4, 1852	Utah Territorial Legislature passes legislation in relation to service
December 15, 1852	Parley P. Pratt correlates exclusion of African Americans from the priesthood with the Book of Abraham
1853	Cornerstones for the Salt Lake Temple site are dedicated and the Endowment House is dedicated

1859 Rocky Mountain Lodge No. 205 is organized at Camp
      Floyd
1861 Rocky Mountain Lodge returns its charter to the Grand
      Lodge of Missouri
1865–1866 Mount Moriah Lodge is organized and granted a dispensa-
      tion from Grand Lodge of Nevada
1866 Wasatch Lodge is organized and granted a dispensation
      from Grand Lodge of Montana
1867 Mount Moriah Lodge is disbanded when it is refused a
      charter from the Grand Lodge of Nevada
1868 Mount Moriah Lodge is organized and granted a dispensa-
      tion from the Grand Lodge of Kansas
1871 Argenta Lodge is organized and granted a dispensation
      from the Grand Lodge of Colorado
1872 Three Utah Masonic lodges organize the Grand Lodge of
      Utah
January 1, 1877 St. George Temple is dedicated and thereafter the first
      endowments for the dead are performed there
1877 Brigham Young dies on August 29 in Salt Lake City
1884 Logan Temple is dedicated
1888 Manti Temple is dedicated
1889 Endowment House is demolished; Mormon applica-
      tions for citizenship denied by Federal Judge Thomas
      J. Anderson
1890 Wilford Woodruff issues Manifesto announcing the cessa-
      tion of plural marriage
1892, 1895 "Dr. Bataille" publishes *Le Diable au XIXᵉ Siècle* which
      claimed that Masonry and Mormonism were connected in
      a worldwide conspiracy
1893 Salt Lake Temple is dedicated and the church leadership
      seeks to harmonize the endowment that is performed in
      various temples
1900 LDS Church advises its members not to join secret societies
1904–1905 During the Smoot hearings some witnesses are questioned
      concerning the temple endowment, including the oath of
      vengeance
1919–1930 Heber J. Grant administration develops a new rationale
      concerning the historical connection between Freemasonry
      and Mormonism; during this period the oath of vengeance
      and verbal graphic descriptions of penalties are eliminated
1921–25 Utah Masonry develops new rationales for excluding
      Mormons and adopts a written policy
1922 Matthew McBlain Thomson convicted in mail fraud case
      involving clandestine Masonry

1934 Anthony R. Ivins's *The Relationship of "Mormonism" and Freemasonry* is published

1949 First Presidency states the exclusionary policy based on revelation

1978 Spencer W. Kimball reverses LDS policy excluding men of African descent from being ordained to priesthood and disqualifying them from entering the temple

1984 Utah Masonry reverses its policy excluding Mormons from becoming Masons in Utah or visiting Utah Masonic lodges

1986 The United Grand Lodge (London) votes to require lodges to eliminate penalties from Masonic ritual

1989 LDS Church modifies policy concerning secret societies

1990 LDS Church modifies endowment by eliminating all penalties and the five points of fellowship

1997 Utah Grand Lodge recognizes Prince Hall Grand Lodge of Utah

2008 Utah Grand Lodge elects first Mormon grand master

2013 LDS Church repudiates rationales advanced to exclude men of African descent from being ordained

Selected Bibliography

1783 Francken, Manuscript, Archives of the Supreme Council, 33°, Northern Jurisdiction, Lexington, Massachusetts, published by Kessinger Publishing Company.

1872 Proceedings of the Masonic Convention and Organization of the Grand Lodge. Salt Lake City: Tribune Printing and Publishing Co., 1872.

"A Book of Records. Containing the Proceedings of the Female Relief Society of Nauvoo" (March 17, 1842–March 16, 1844). LDS Church History Library, Salt Lake City, Utah.

Alexander, Thomas G., and James B. Allen. *Mormons and Gentiles: A History of Salt Lake City.* Boulder, CO: Pruett Publishing Co., 1984.

Allyn, Avery. *A Ritual of Freemasonry.* Philadelphia: John Clark, 1831.

Alter, J. Cecil. *Early Utah Journalism.* Salt Lake City: Utah Historical Society, 1938.

Anderson, Devery, ed. *The Development of LDS Temple Worship, 1846–2000: A Documentary History.* Salt Lake City: Signature Books, 2011.

Anderson, Devery S., and Gary James Bergera, eds. *Joseph Smith's Quorum of the Anointed, 1842–1845: A Documentary History.* Salt Lake City: Signature Books, 2005.

———, eds. *The Nauvoo Endowment Companies, 1845–1846: A Documentary History.* Salt Lake City: Signature Books, 2005.

Anderson, James H. "Temple Ceremonies." *Improvement Era* 32 (October 1929): 971.

Anderson's Book of Constitutions of 1738: A Facsimile of the original text with commentaries by Lewis Edwards and W. J. Hughan. Bloomington, IL: The Masonic Book Club, 1978.

Anderson's Constitutions of 1723, with Introduction by Bro. Lionel Vibert. Washington, D.C.: The Masonic Service Association of the United States, 1924.

Andrew, Laurel B. *The Early Temples of the Mormons: The Architecture of the Millennial Kingdom in the American West.* Albany: State University of New York Press, 1978.

Angle, Paul M. *Here I Have Lived: A History of Lincoln's Springfield, 1821–1865.* Chicago: Abraham Lincoln Book Shop, 1971.

Arrington, Leonard J. *Great Basin Kingdom: An Economic History of the Church of Jesus Christ of Latter-day Saints.* Cambridge: Harvard University Press, 1958.

———. "Oliver Cowdery's Kirtland, Ohio, 'Sketch Book.'" *BYU Studies* 12:4 (1972): 410–26.

Bachman, Danel W. "A Study of the Mormon Practice of Plural Marriage before the Death of Joseph Smith." Master's thesis, Purdue University, 1975.

Bancroft, Hubert H. *The History of Utah*. San Francisco: The History Company, 1889.

Barruel, Agustin. *Mémoires pour servir à l'histoire du Jacobinisme*. 5 vols. Hamburg: P. Fauche, 1798–1799.

Baskin, R. N. *Reminiscences of Early Utah*. Salt Lake City, 1914.

Beadle, J. H. *Life in Utah; or the Mysteries and Crimes of Mormonism*. Philadelphia: National Publishing, 1870.

Behle, Calvin A. "Mormonism and Masonry: A Look Today at an Old Utah Problem." *1954 Proceedings of the Grand Lodge of Utah*, 71–82. Salt Lake City, 1954.

Bennett, John C. *The History of the Saints; or, an Exposé of Joe Smith and Mormonism*. Boston: Leland & Whiting, 1842.

Bennett, Richard E., Susan Easton Black, and Donald Q. Cannon. *The Nauvoo Legion in Illinois: A History of the Mormon Militia, 1841–1846*. Norman: The Arthur H. Clark Company, 2010.

Bennion, Marjorie Hopkins. "The Rediscovery of William Weeks' Nauvoo Temple Drawings." *Mormon Historical Studies* 3:1 (Spring 2002): 73–90.

Bergera, Gary James, comp. *Statements of the LDS First Presidency*. Salt Lake City: Signature Books, 2007.

Bernard, David. *Light on Masonry: A Collection of all the Most Important Documents on the subject of Speculative Free Masonry*. Utica, NY: William Williams, 1829.

Bigler, David L. *Forgotten Kingdom: The Mormon Theocracy in the American West, 1847–1896*. Spokane, WA: The Arthur H. Clark Company, 1998.

Bishop, M. Guy. "'What Has Become of Our Fathers?': Baptism for the Dead at Nauvoo." *Dialogue: A Journal of Mormon Thought* 23 (Summer 1990): 85–97.

Black, Susan Easton. "James Adams of Springfield, Illinois: The Link between Abraham Lincoln and Joseph Smith." *Mormon Historical Studies* 10 (Spring 2009): 33–49.

Black, Susan Ward Easton. *Membership of the Church of Jesus Christ of Latter-day Saints*. 58 vols. Provo: Religious Studies Center, Brigham Young University, 1986.

Black, Susan Easton, and Harvey Bischoff Black. *Annotated Record of Baptisms for the Dead, 1840–1845, Nauvoo, Hancock County, Illinois*. 7 vols. Provo, UT: Brigham Young University Press, 2002.

Blanchard, Jonathan. *Scotch Rite Masonry Illustrated*. 2 vols. 1887–1888; reprint ed., Chicago: Ezra A. Cook, 1925.

Bliss, Jonathan. *Merchants and Miners in Utah: The Walker Brothers and Their Bank*. Salt Lake City: Western Epics, 1983.

[Boudinot, Elias]. *The Second Advent, or coming of the Messiah in Glory*. Trenton, NJ: O. Fenton and S. Hutchinson, 1815.

Bradley, Joshua. *Some of the Beauties of Freemasonry; Being Extracts from Publications, Which have Received the Approbation of the Wise and Virtuous of the Fraternity: With Introductory Remarks, Designed to Remove the Various Objections Made Against the Order*. 2nd ed. Albany: G. J. Loomis & Co., 1821.

Bringhurst, Newell G. "An Ambiguous Decision: The Implementation of Mormon Priesthood Denial for the Black Man—A Reexamination." *Utah Historical Quarterly* 46:1 (Winter 1978): 45–64.

———. *Saints, Slaves and Blacks: The Changing Place of Black People within Mormonism.* Westport, CT: Greenwood Press, 1981.

Brodie, Fawn M. *No Man Knows My History: The Life of Joseph Smith the Mormon Prophet.* New York: Alfred A. Knopf, 1945.

Brooke, John L. *The Refiner's Fire: The Making of Mormon Cosmology, 1644–1844.* Cambridge: Cambridge University Press, 1994.

Brooks, Joanna. *American Lazarus: Religion and the Rise of African-American and Native American Literatures.* Oxford: Oxford University Press, 2003.

Brooks, Joanna, and John Saillant, eds. *"Face Zion Forward": First Writers of the Black Atlantic, 1785–1798.* Boston: Northeastern University Press, 2002.

Brown, Lisle G. *Nauvoo Sealings, Adoptions and Anointings: A Comprehensive Register of Persons Receiving LDS Temple Ordinances, 1841–1846.* Salt Lake City: The Smith-Pettit Foundation, 2006.

———. "'Temple Pro Tempore': The Salt Lake City Endowment House," *Journal of Mormon History* 34:4 (Fall 2008): 1–68.

Bruno, Cheryl L. "Keeping a Secret: Freemasonry, Polygamy, and the Nauvoo Relief Society, 1842–44." *The Journal of Mormon History* 39, no. 4 (Fall 2013): 158–81.

Buerger, David John. "The Development of the Mormon Temple Endowment Ceremony." *Dialogue: A Journal of Mormon Thought* 16 (Winter 1987): 33–76.

———. "'The Fullness of the Priesthood': The Second Anointing in Latter-day Saint Theology and Practice." *Dialogue: A Journal of Mormon Thought* 20 (Spring 1983): 10–44.

———. "A Preliminary Approach to Linguistic Aspects of the Anthon Transcript." Unpublished manuscript prepared for a BYU Semester Project, 1978.

Buerger, David John. *The Mysteries of Godliness: A History of Mormon Temple Worship.* San Francisco: Smith Research Associates, 1994.

Bullock, Steven C. "Masons, Masonic History and Academic Scholarship." In de Hoyas and Morris, *Freemasonry in Context: History, Ritual, Controversy,* ix–xiii. Lanham, MD: Lexington Books, 2004.

———. *Revolutionary Brotherhood: Freemasonry and the Transformation of the American Social Order, 1730–1840.* Chapel Hill: University of North Carolina Press, 1996.

Burke, Janet Mackay. "Sociability, Friendship and the Enlightenment among Women Freemasons in Eighteenth-Century France." PhD diss., Arizona State University, 1986.

Burton, Richard F. *The City of the Saints and across the Rocky Mountains to California.* London: Longman, Green, Longman, and Roberts, 1861; New York: Harper & Brothers, Publishers, 1862.

Bush, Lester. "Mormonism's Negro Doctrine: An Historical Overview." *Dialogue: A Journal of Mormon Thought* 8:1 (Spring 1973): 11–68.

Bush, Lester E., Jr., and Armand L. Mauss. *Neither White nor Black: Mormon Scholars Confront the Race Issue in a Universal Church*. Midvale, UT: Signature Books, 1984.

Bushman, Richard L. *Joseph Smith and the Beginnings of Mormonism*. Urbana: University of Illinois Press, 1984.

———. *Joseph Smith: Rough Stone Rolling*. New York: Knopf, 2005.

Calcott, Wellins. *Calcott's Masonry, with Considerate Additions and Improvements*. Philadelphia: Robert DeSilver, 1817.

———. *A Candid Disquisition of the Principles and Practices of the Most Ancient and Honorable Society of Free and Accepted Masons*. With an introduction by Wallace McLeod. Bloomington, IL: The Masonic Book Club, 1989.

Cannon, Donald Q., and Lyndon W. Cook. *Far West Record: Minutes of the Church of Jesus Christ of Latter-day Saints*. Salt Lake City: Deseret Book Company, 1983.

Carlile, Richard. *Manual of Freemasonry, in Three Parts, with an Explanatory Introduction to the Science, and a Free Translation of Some of the Sacred Scripture Names*. London: Wm. Reeves, 1853.

Carnes, Mark C. *Secret Ritual and Manhood in Victorian America*. New Haven, CT: Yale University Press, 1989.

Carr, Harry. *An Analysis and Commentary of Samuel Prichard's* Masonry Dissected 1730. Bloomington, IL.: Masonic Book Club, 1977.

———, ed. *The Early French Exposures*. London: The Quatuor Coronati Lodge No. 2076, 1971.

———. *Three Distinct Knocks and Jachin and Boaz*. Bloomington, IL: Masonic Book Club, 1981.

———. *The Transition from Operative to Speculative Masonry*. N.p.: 1957.

Carr, Robin L. *Freemasonry in Nauvoo*. Bloomington, IL: Masonic Book Club and Illinois Lodge Research, 1989.

Cass, Donn A. *Negro Freemasonry and Segregation An Historical Study of Prejudice Against American Negroes as Freemasons and the Position of Negro Freemasonry in the Masonic Community*. Chicago: Ezra A. Cook Publications, Inc., 1957.

Chase, George Wingate. *Digest of Masonic Law*. 3rd ed. New York: Macoy & Sickels, 1864.

Churton, Tobias. *Freemasonry: The Reality*. Hersham, Surrey: Lewis Masonic, 2007.

City of the Saints in Picture and Story. Salt Lake City: Deseret News, 1906.

Clark, David B. "Sidney Rigdon's Rights of Succession." *Restoration: The Journal of Latter-day Saint History* 6 (April 1987): 8–10.

Clark, James R., ed. *Messages of the First Presidency of the Church of Jesus Christ of Latter-day Saints*. 7 vols. Salt Lake City: Bookcraft, 1966.

Coil, Henry Wilson. *Coil's Masonic Encyclopedia*. New York: Macoy Publishing and Masonic Supply Co., 1961.

———. *Conversations on Freemasonry*. Richmond, VA: Macoy Publishing and Masonic Supply Co., Inc., n.d.

Collier, Fred C. *The Teachings of President Brigham Young.* Vol. 3, 1852–1854. Salt Lake City: Collier's Publishing Co., 1987.

Compton, Todd. *In Sacred Loneliness: The Plural Wives of Joseph Smith.* Salt Lake City: Signature Books, 1997.

Constitutions of the Ancient Fraternity of Free and Accepted Masons, under the United Grand Lodge of England. London: Harrison and Sons, 1884.

Cook, Lyndon W. *William Law: Biographical Essay, Nauvoo Diary, Correspondence, Interview.* Orem, UT: Grandin Book Company, 1994.

———. "William Law, Nauvoo Dissenter." *BYU Studies* 22:1 (Winter 1982): 47–72.

Cowdery, Oliver. "The Outrage in Jackson County, Missouri." *The Evening and the Morning Star* 2:16 (January 1834): 122.

Cross, Jeremy L. *The True Masonic Chart, or Hieroglyphic Monitor.* New Haven, CT: John C. Gray, 1820.

Cross, Whitney R. *The Burned Over District: The Social and Intellectual History of Enthusiastic Religion in Western New York, 1800–1850.* Ithaca: Cornell University Press, 1950.

Cryer, Neville Barker. *The Royal Arch Journey.* Hersham, Surrey: Lewis Masonic, 2009.

Cummings, Horace H. "True Stories from My Journal." *Juvenile Instructor* 64 (August 1929): 441.

Cummings, William O. *A Bibliography of Freemasonry.* New York: Press of Henry Emmerson, 1963.

Daniels, William. *A Correct Account of the Murder of Generals Joseph and Hyrum Smith at Carthage on the 27th day of June, 1844.* Nauvoo, IL: J. Taylor, 1845.

Davidson, Karen Lynn, et al., eds. *The Joseph Smith Papers, Histories, Vol. 1, Joseph Smith Histories, 1832–1844.* Salt Lake City: Church Historian's Press, 2012.

Dawson, Warren R., and Eric P. Uphill. *Who Was Who in Egyptology.* 2nd rev. ed. London: The Egypt Exploration Society, 1972.

de Hoyos, Arturo. *The Cloud of Prejudice: A Study in Anti-Masonry.* Kila, MT: Kessinger Publishing Company, 1993.

———. *Light on Masonry: The History and Rituals of America's Most Important Masonic Exposé.* Washington, D.C.: Scottish Rite Research Society, 2008.

———. *The Scottish Rite Manual Monitor and Guide.* 2nd ed. Washington, DC: The Supreme Council, 33°, Southern Jurisdiction, 2009.

de Hoyos, Arturo, and S. Brent Morris. *Freemasonry in Context: History, Ritual, Controversy.* Lanham, MD: Lexington Books, 2004.

Dermott, Laurence. *Ahiman Rezon.* London, 1756. Facsimile reprint: Bloomington, IL: Masonic Book Club, 1975.

Derr, Jill Mulvay, Janath Russell Cannon, and Maureen Ursenbach Beecher. *Women of Covenant: The Story of the Relief Society.* Salt Lake City: Deseret Book, 1992.

Dobay, Clara V. "Intellect and Faith: The Controversy over Revisionist Mormon History." *Dialogue: A Journal of Mormon Thought* 27 (Spring 1994): 91–105.

Dow, Lorenzo. *Biography and Miscellany.* Norwich, CT: 1834.

Draffen, George. "Prince Hall Freemasonry." *Ars Quatuor Coronatorum* 89 (1976): 70–91.

Duffy, John-Charles. "Clyde Forsberg's *Equal Rites* and the Exoticizing of Mormonism." *Dialogue: A Journal of Mormon Thought* 39:1 (Spring 2006): 4–34.

Dumenil, Lynn. *Freemasonry and American Culture, 1880–1930*. Princeton: Princeton University Press, 1984.

Duncan, Malcolm C. *Masonic Ritual and Monitor; or, Guide to the Three Degrees of the Ancient York Rite, and to the degrees of Mark Master, Dart Master, Most Excellent Master, and the Royal Master*. New York: L. Fitzgerald, 1866.

Durham, Reed C., Jr. "Is There No Help for the Widow's Son?" *Mormon Miscellaneous* 1 (Oct. 1975): 11–16.

Dyer, Colin. *Symbolism in Craft Masonry*. London: Lewis Masonic, 1983.

———. *William Preston and His Work*. London: Lewis Masonic, 1987.

Edwards, Lewis. "Anderson's Book of Constitutions of 1738." In *Anderson's Book of Constitutions of 1738, A Facsimile of the original text with commentaries by Lewis Edwards and W. J. Hughan*. Bloomington, IL: The Masonic Book Club, 1978.

Ehat, Andrew F. "Joseph Smith's Introduction of Temple Ordinances and the 1844 Mormon Succession Question." M.A. thesis, Brigham Young University, 1982.

———. "'They Might Have Known that He Was Not a Fallen Prophet': The Nauvoo Journal of Joseph Fielding." *BYU Studies* 19:2 (Winter 1979): 133–66.

Esplin, Ronald K. "Brigham Young and Priesthood Denials to the Blacks: An Alternative View." *BYU Studies* (Spring 1979): 394–402.

Faulring, Scott H. *An American Prophet's Record: The Diaries and Journals of Joseph Smith*. Salt Lake City: Signature Books in association with Smith Research Associates, 1987.

First 100 Years of Freemasonry in Utah. Vol. 1, 1872–1972. Salt Lake City: Grand Lodge of Utah, 1972.

Flake, Chad J., and Larry W. Draper, comp. *A Mormon Bibliography: 1830–1930*. 2nd ed. Provo, UT: Brigham Young University Religious Studies Department, 2004.

Flynn, John J. "Federalism and Viable State Government—The History of Utah's Constitution." *Utah Law Review* 1966: 311–25.

Ford, Thomas. *A History of Illinois*. Chicago: S. C. Griggs & Co., 1854.

Ford, Worthington Chauncey, ed. *The Writings of George Washington*. New York: G. P. Putnam's Sons, 1893.

Formisano, Ronald P. *American Populist Movements from the Revolution to the 1850s*. Chapel Hill: University of North Carolina Press, 2008.

Formisano, Ronald P., with Kathleen Smith Kutolowski. "Antimasonry and Masonry: The Genesis of Protest, 1826–1827." *American Quarterly* 29 (Summer 1977): 139–65.

Forsberg, Clyde R., Jr. *Equal Rites: The Book of Mormon, Masonry, Gender, and American Culture*. New York: Colombia University Press, 2004.

———. "Kirtland through the Christian-Masonic, Neo-Hebraic, Neo-Pagan

Looking Glass: Architecture, Ritual, Gender, and Race." *The John Whitmer Historical Association Journal* 30 (2010): 176–205.

Foster, Lawrence. *Religion and Sexuality: The Shakers, the Mormons, and the Oneida Community*. Urbana: University of Illinois Press, 1984.

———. *Women, Family, and Utopia: Communal Experiments of the Shakers, the Oneida Community, and the Mormons*. Syracuse, NY: Syracuse University Press, 1991.

Francken, Henry Andrew. *Francken Manuscript, 1783*. Kilo, MT: Kessinger Publishing Company, n.d.

Free Masonry of the Ladies, or the Grand Secret Discovered. London: T. Wilkinson, ca. 1791.

Froner, Eric. *The Fiery Trial: Abraham Lincoln and American Slavery*. New York: W. W. Norton, 2010.

———. *Free Soil, Free Labor, Free Men: The Ideology of the Republican Party Before the Civil War*. Oxford: Oxford University Press, 1995.

Furniss, Norman H. *The Mormon Conflict, 1850–1859*. New Haven: Yale University Press, 1960.

General Handbook of Instructions. Salt Lake City: Church of Jesus Christ of Latter-day Saints, 1983.

Gilbert, R[obert] A. "'The Monstrous Regiment': Women and Freemasonry in the Nineteenth Century." *Ars Quatuor Coronatorum* 115 (2002): 153–82.

Givens, Terryl L. *The Book of Mormon: A Very Short History*. Oxford, Oxford University Press, 2009.

Godfrey, Kenneth W. "Freemasonry and the Temple." In Ludlow, *Encyclopedia of Mormonism* 2:528–29.

———. "Joseph Smith and the Masons." *Journal of the Illinois State Historical Society* 64 (Spring 1971): 79–90.

Goldenberg, David M. *The Curse of Ham: Race and Slavery in Early Judaism, Christianity, and Islam*. Princeton: Princeton University Press, 2003.

Gooding, Gustin O. *History of Utah Masonry*. Salt Lake City: Grand Lodge of Utah, 1972.

Goodman, Paul. *Towards a Christian Republic: Antimasonry and the Great Transition in New England, 1826–1836*. New York: Oxford University Press, 1988.

Goodwin, S. H. *Additional Studies in Mormonism and Masonry*. Salt Lake City: N.p., 1927.

———. *Freemasonry in Utah: The Early Days of Wasatch Lodge No. 1*. Salt Lake City, 1925.

———. *Freemasonry in Utah: The First Decade of Argenta Lodge No. 3, and Its First Master*. Salt Lake City, 1925.

———. *Freemasonry in Utah: Thirty Years of Mt. Moriah Lodge No. 2, F. & A. M. 1866–1896*. Salt Lake City, 1930.

———. *Mormonism and Masonry*. Washington, D.C.: The Masonic Service Association of the United States, 1924.

———. *Mormonism and Masonry: A Utah Point of View*. Salt Lake City: Sugar House Press, 1921.

———. "A Study of Mormonism and Its Connection with Mormonism in the Early Forties." *The Builder* 7:2 (February 1921): 36–42, and 7:3 (March 1921): 64–70.

Gould, Robert F. *Gould History of Freemasonry throughout the World*. 6 vols. New York: Charles Scribner's Sons, 1936.

Green, Nelson Winch. *Fifteen Years among the Mormons*. New York: H. Dayton, 1859.

Grunder, Rick. "More Parallels: A Survey of Little-Known Sources of Mormon History." Unpublished Paper presented at the Sunstone Symposium, Salt Lake City, Utah, September 1987.

———. *Mormon Parallels: A Bibliographic Source*. LaFayette, NY: Rick Grunder Books, 2008.

Guérillot, Claude. *La Genèse du Rite Écossais Ancien et Accepté*. Paris: Guy Trédaniel, 1993.

———. *La Rite de Perfection. Restitution des rituels taduits en anglais et copiés en 1783 par Henry Andrew Francken accompagnée de la tradution des textes statutaires*. Paris: Guy Trédaniel, 1993.

Gunnison, John W. *The Mormons, or Latter-day Saints, in the Valley of the Great Salt Lake*. Philadelphia: Lippincott, Grambo & Co., 1852.

Haffner, Christopher. *Workman Unashamed: The Testimony of a Christian Freemason*. London: Lewis Masonic, 1989.

Hamill, John. *The Craft: A History of English Freemasonry*. Wellingborough, England: Aquarian Press, 1986.

Hamill, John, and R. A. Gilbert. *World Freemasonry: An Illustrated History*. London: Aquarian Press, 1991.

Hamilton, C. Mark. *Nineteenth-Century Mormon Architecture & City Planning*. New York: Oxford University Press, 1995.

Hampshire, Annette P. "Thomas Sharp and Anti-Mormon Sentiment in Illinois, 1842–1845." *Journal of Illinois Historical Society* 72 (May 1979): 84–89.

Hanlon, Mary. *Revelations of Masonry, Made by a Late Member of the Craft, in Four Parts*. New York, 1827.

Hansen, Klaus J. *Quest for Empire: The Political Kingdom of God and the Council of Fifty in Mormon History*. Lansing: Michigan State University Press, 1967.

Hardy, B. Carmon. *Doing the Works of Abraham: Mormon Polygamy, Its Origin, Practice, and Demise*. Norman, OK: The Arthur H. Clark Company, 2007.

———. *Solemn Covenant: The Mormon Polygamous Passage*. Urbana: University of Illinois Press, 1992.

Harris, George W. *"Deposition": A Narrative of the Facts and Circumstances Relating to the Kidnapping and Murder of William Morgan*. Batavia, NY: D. C. Miller, 1827.

Hatch, Trevan G. *Visions, Manifestations and Miracles of the Restoration*. Orem, UT: Granite Publishing, 2008.

Hayden, Lewis. *Caste among Masons: Address before Prince Hall Grand Lodge of Free and Accepted Masons of the State of Massachusetts at the Festival of St. John the Evangelist, December 27, 1865*. 2nd ed. Boston: Printed by Edward S. Coombs & Company, 1866.

Haynes, Stephen R. *Noah's Curse: The Biblical Justification of American Slavery.* Oxford: Oxford University Press, 2002.

Hedges, Andrew H., Alex D. Smith, and Richard Lloyd Anderson, eds. *Journals, Volume 2: December 1841–April 1843.* Salt Lake City: Church Historian's Press, 2011.

Heidle, Alexandra, and Jan A. M. Snoek, eds. *Women's Agency and Rituals in Mixed and Female Masonic Orders.* Leiden: Brill, 2008.

History of the Reorganized Church of Jesus Christ of Latter Day Saints. Independence: Herald House, 1967.

Hogan, Mervin B. "The Confrontation of Grand Master Abraham Jonas and John Cook Bennett at Nauvoo." Self-published.

———. "The Erection and Dedication of the Nauvoo Masonic Temple." Unpublished manuscript, Dec. 27, 1976.

———, ed. *Founding Minutes of Nauvoo Lodge, U.D.* Des Moines: Research Lodge No. 2, 1971.

———. "Freemasonry and the Lynching at Carthage Jail." Self-published.

———. "John Cook Bennett and Pickaway Lodge No. 23." October 12, 1983, 9–10. Self-published.

———. "Mormonism and Freemasonry on the Midwest Frontier." Unpublished manuscript, Salt Lake City, Church History Library.

———. *Mormonism and Masonry: The Illinois Episode.* Salt Lake City: Third Century Graphics, 1980.

———. *The Official Minutes of Nauvoo Lodge.* Des Moines: Research Lodge No. 2, 1974.

———. *The Origin and Growth of Utah Masonry and Its Conflict with Mormonism.* Salt Lake City: Campus Graphics, 1978.

Homer, Michael W. "Masonry and Mormonism in Utah, 1847–1984." *Journal of Mormon History* 18, no. 2 (Fall 1992): 57–96.

———. "'Similarity of Priesthood in Masonry': The Relationship Between Freemasonry and Mormonism." *Dialogue: A Journal of Mormon Thought* 27:3 (Fall 1994): 1–113.

———. "'Why Then Introduce Them into Our Inner Temple?' The Masonic Influence on Mormon Denial of Priesthood Ordination to African American Men." *The John Whitmer Historical Association Journal* 26 (2006): 234–59.

Howard, Richard P. "What Sort of Priesthood for Women at Nauvoo?" *John Whitmer Historical Association Journal* 13 (1993): 20–29.

Howe, E. D. *Mormonism Unvailed.* Painsville, OH: 1834.

Hullinger, Robert N. *Joseph Smith's Response to Skepticism.* Salt Lake City: Signature Books, 1992.

Hutchinson, William. *The Spirit of Masonry.* London, 1775. Reprinted with an introduction by Trevor Stewart. Wellingborough: Aquarian Press, 1987.

Hyde, John, Jr. *Mormonism: Its Leaders and Designs.* New York: W. P. Fetridge and Company, 1857.

Introvigne, Massimo. "The Devil Makers: Contemporary Evangelical Fundamentalist Anti-Mormonism." *Dialogue: A Journal of Mormon Thought* 27:1 (Spring 1994): 165–80.

———. *I mormoni. Dal Far West alle Olimpiadi.* Leumann, Torino: Elledici, 2002.

———. *La Massoneria.* Leumann, Torino: Elledici, 1997.

———. "Old Wine in New Bottles: The Story behind Fundamentalist Anti-Mormonism." *BYU Studies* 35:3 (1995–1996): 45–73.

Irving, Gordon I. "The Law of Adoption: One Phase of the Development of the Mormon Concept of Salvation, 1830–1900." *BYU Studies* 14 (Spring 1974): 291–314.

Iversen, Erik. *The Myth of Egypt and Its Hieroglyphics in European Tradition.* Princeton: Princeton University Press, 1993.

Ivins, Anthony W. *The Relationship of "Mormonism" and Freemasonry.* Salt Lake City: The Deseret News Press, 1934.

Jackson, A. C. F. *English Masonic Exposures 1730–1760.* London: A. Lewis, 1986.

———. *Rose Croix.* London: A. Lewis, 1987.

Jacob, Margaret. *The Origins of Freemasonry: Facts and Fictions.* Philadelphia: University of Pennsylvania Press, 2006.

———. *Strangers Nowhere in the World: The Rise of Cosmopolitanism in Early Modern Europe.* Philadelphia: University of Pennsylvania Press, 2006.

Jacob, Udney Hay. *An extract, from a manuscript entitled The Peacemaker. Or the doctrines of the millennium: being a treatise on religion and jurisprudence. Or a new system of religion and politicks.* Nauvoo, IL: J. Smith, Printer, 1842.

Jennings, Warren A. "Factors in the Destruction of the Mormon Press in Missouri, 1833." *Utah Historical Quarterly* 35 (Winter 1967): 57–76.

Jenson, Andrew. *Latter-day Saint Biographical Encyclopedia.* 4 vols. Salt Lake City: Andrew Jenson Historical Co., 1901–1936.

Jessee, Dean C. "The Early Accounts of Joseph Smith's First Vision." *BYU Studies* 9 (Spring 1969): 275–94.

———. "Joseph Knight's 'Early History of Mormonism.'" *BYU Studies* 17:1 (Autumn 1976): 29–39.

———, ed. *The Papers of Joseph Smith.* 2 vols. Salt Lake City: Deseret Book Company, 1989–1992.

———, ed. *The Personal Writings of Joseph Smith.* Rev. ed. Salt Lake City: Deseret Book; Provo, Utah: Brigham Young University Press, 2002.

Jessee, Dean C., Mark Ashurst-McGee, and Richard L. Jensen, eds. *The Joseph Smith Papers: Journals, Volume 1: 1832–1839.* Salt Lake City: Church Historian's Press, 2008.

Johnson, Paul E. *A Shopkeeper's Millennium: Society and Revivals in Rochester, New York, 1815–1837.* New York: Hill and Wang, 1978.

Johnson, Paul E., and Dean Wilenz. *The Kingdom of Matthias.* New York: Oxford University Press, 1994.

Johnson, Wendell B., and Rell G. Francis. *Frontier to Fame: Cyrus E. Dallin, Sculptor.* N.p., n.d.

Jones, Bernard E. *Freemasons' Book of the Royal Arch.* London: George G. Harrap & Company Ltd., 1957.

———. *Freemasons' Guide and Compendium.* N.p.: Dobby, 1956. Jordan, Winthrop D. *White over Black, American Attitudes toward the Negro, 1550–1812.* Chapel Hill: University of North Carolina Press, 1968.

Journal of Discourses. 26 vols. London: LDS Booksellers Depot, 1854–1886.

Journals of the House of Representatives. Council and Joint Sessions of the First Annual and Special Sessions of the Legislative Assembly of the Territory of Utah. Held at Great Salt Lake City 1851 and 1852. Great Salt Lake City: Brigham H. Young, Printer, 1852.

Kenney, Scott G., ed. *Wilford Woodruff's Journal, 1833–1898.* Typescript, 9 vols. Midvale, Utah: Signature Books, 1983–1985.

Kenning, A. Woodford. *Kenning's Masonic Cyclopaedia.* London: Geo. Kenning, 1878.

Kern, Louis J. *An Ordered Love.* Chapel Hill: University of North Carolina Press, 1981.

Kimball, Edward L. *Lengthen Your Stride: The Presidency of Spencer W. Kimball.* Salt Lake City: Deseret Book, 2005.

Kimball, Sarah M. "Auto-biography." *Woman's Exponent* (September 1, 1883): 51.

Kimball, Stanley B. *Heber C. Kimball: Mormon Patriarch and Pioneer.* Urbana, IL: University of Illinois Press, 1981.

———, ed. *On the Potter's Wheel: The Diaries of Heber C. Kimball.* Salt Lake City: Signature Books in association with Smith Research Associates, 1987.

Kinney, Jay. *The Masonic Myth.* New York: HarperOne, 2009.

Knoop, Douglas, and G. P. Jones. *The Genesis of Freemasonry.* Manchester: Manchester University Press, 1947.

———. *An Introduction to Freemasonry.* Manchester: Manchester University Press, 1937.

Knoop, Douglas, G. P. Jones, and Douglas Hamer. *Early Masonic Pamphlets.* Manchester: Manchester University Press, 1945.

———. *The Genesis of Freemasonry: An Account of the Rise and Development of Freemasonry in Its Operative, Accepted and Early Speculative Phases.* Manchester, UK: Manchester University Press, 1947.

———. *A Short History of Freemasonry to 1730.* Manchester: Manchester University Press, 1940.

———. *The Two Earliest Masonic Manuscripts.* Manchester: Manchester University Press, 1938.

L. John Nuttall Diary. Special Collections, Lee Library, Brigham Young University.

Larson, Stan, ed. *A Ministry of Meetings: The Apostolic Diaries of Rudger Clawson.* Salt Lake City: Signature Books in association with Smith Research Associates, 1993.

Latter-day Saints in Utah. Opinion of Z. Snow, Judge of the Supreme Court of the United States for the Territory of Utah, upon the official course of His Excellency Gov. Brigham Young. Liverpool: F. D. Richards, 1852.

Launius, Roger D. "The 'New Social History' and the 'New Mormon History': Reflection on Recent Trends." *Dialogue: A Journal of Mormon Thought* 27 (Spring 1994): 109–27.

Lee, John D. *Mormonism Unveiled; or the Life and Confessions of the Late Mormon Bishop, John D. Lee.* St. Louis: N. D. Thompson & Co., 1880.

Leonard, Glen M. *Nauvoo: A Place of Peace, A People of Promise.* Salt Lake City: Deseret Book, 2002.

Ludlow, Daniel H., ed. *Encyclopedia of Mormonism.* 4 vols. New York: Macmillan, 1992.

Lyman, Edward Leo, ed. *Candid Insights of a Mormon Apostle: The Diaries of Abraham H. Cannon, 1889–1895.* Salt Lake City: Signature Books in Association with the Smith-Pettit Foundation, 2010.

MacKenzie, Kenneth R. H. *The Royal House Cyclopaedia of History, Rites, Symbols and Biography.* New York: J. W. Bouton, 1877.

———, ed. *The Royal Masonic Cyclopaedia.* London: John Hogg, 1872.

Mackey, Albert G. *An Encyclopaedia of Freemasonry: A New and Revised Edition.* 2 vols. Philadelphia: McClure Publishing Co., 1920.

———. *The History of Freemasonry: Its Legendary Origins.* New York: The Masonic History Company, 1898.

———. *A Lexicon of Freemasonry.* London: Griffin, 1873.

———. *The Principles of Masonic Law: A Treatise of the Constitutional Laws, Usages and Landmarks of Freemasonry.* New York: Jno. W. Leonard & Co., 1856.

MacKinnon, William. *At Sword's Point, Part 1: A Documentary History of the Utah War to 1858.* Norman, OK: The Arthur H. Clark Company, 2008.

———. "'Like Splitting a Man up His Back Bone': The Territorial Dismemberment of Utah, 1850–1896." *Utah Historical Quarterly* 71: 2 (Spring 2003): 100–124.

MacNulty, W. Kirk. *Freemasonry: Symbols, Secrets, Significance.* London: Thames & Hudson, Ltd., 2006.

Macoy, Robert. *General History, Cyclopedia and Dictionary of Freemasonry.* New York: Masonic Publishing Co., 1873.

Madsen, Brigham D. *Glory Hunter: A Biography of Patrick Edward Connor.* Salt Lake City: University of Utah Press, 1990.

Maffly-Kipp, Laurie F. *Setting Down the Sacred Past: African-American Race Histories.* Cambridge: The Belknap Press of Harvard University Press, 2010.

Marquardt, H. Michael, comp. *Early Patriarchal Blessings of the Church of Jesus Christ of Latter-day Saints.* Salt Lake City: The Smith-Pettit Foundation, 2007.

Mason, Patrick Q. "The Prohibition of Interracial Marriage in Utah, 1888–1963." *Utah State Historical Quarterly* 76:2 (Spring 2008): 108–31.

Masonic Code of the Most Worshipful Grand Lodge of Free and Accepted Masons. Davenport, IA: Egbert, Fidlar & Chambers, 1898.

Masonic Code of the Most Worshipful Grand Lodge of Free and Accepted Masons of Utah. Salt Lake City, 1958.

Mauss, Armand L. *All Abraham's Children: Changing Mormon Conceptions of Race and Lineage.* Urbana: University of Illinois Press, 2003.

Mauss, Armand L. "Culture, Charisma and Change: Reflections on Mormon Temple Worship." *Dialogue: A Journal of Mormon Thought* 20 (Winter 1987): 77–83.

McConkie, Bruce R. *Mormon Doctrine.* Salt Lake City: Bookcraft, 1958.

McCullough, David. *1776.* New York: Simon & Schuster Paperbacks, 2005.

McDermott, Don J. "Joseph Smith and the Treasure of Hiram Abiff." *The Cryptic Scholar* (Winter/Spring 1991): 40–50.

McGavin, E. Cecil. *"Mormonism" and Masonry*. Salt Lake City: The Deseret News Press, 1935.

McGregor, Martin I. "A Biographical Sketch of Chevalier Andrew Michael Ramsay, Including a full transcript of his oration of 1737." At http://www.free masons-freemasonry.com/ramsay-biography-oration.html.

McLeod, Wallace. "The Old Charges," in *The Collected "Prestonian Lectures."* Vol. 3. London: Quartuor Coronati Lodge, 1986, 260–90.

———. *The Old Gothic Constitutions*. Bloomington, IL: The Masonic Book Club, 1985.

Meister, Maureen. *H. H. Richardson: The Architect, His Peers and Their Era*. Cambridge, MA: Massachusetts Institute of Technology Press, 1999.

Mock, Stanley Upton. *The Morgan Episode in American Free Masonry*. East Aurora, NY: Roycrofters, 1930.

Morcombe, Joseph E. "Masonry and Mormonism." *The New Age* (May 1905): 445–54; (June 1905): 523–31.

———. "Religious Tests in Masonic Lodges." *The Masonic World* 18:4 (October 1936): 7–12.

Morgan, Dale L. *State of Deseret*. Logan: Utah State University Press and Utah Historical Society, 1987.

[Morgan, William]. *Illustrations of Masonry*. Batavia, NY: 1826.

"Mormon Lodge," *The Freemason's Monthly Magazine* 29 (1870): 249–50.

Morris, Rob. *The Masonic Martyr: The Biography of Eli Bruce*. Louisville, KY: Morris & Konsarrat, 1861.

———. *William Morgan: or Political Anti-Masonry, Its Rise, Growth and Decadence*. New York, 1883.

Morse, Jedediah. *A Sermon, Delivered at the New North Church in Boston*. Boston, 1798.

———. *A Sermon, Exhibiting the Present Dangers, and Consequent Duties of the Citizens of the United States of America*. New York: Printed and Sold by Cornelious Davis, 1799.

———. *A Sermon, Preached at Charlestown, November 29, 1798, on the Anniversary Thanksgiving in Massachusetts*. Boston: Samuel Hall, 1799.

Narrative of the facts and circumstances relating to the Kidnapping of presumed murder of William Morgan. Batavia, NY: Printed by D. C. Miller, Under the Direction of the Committees, 1826.

Newell, Linda King. "Emma Hale Smith and the Polygamy Question." *John Whitmer Historical Association Journal* 4 (1984): 3–15.

Newell, Linda King, and Valeen Tippetts Avery. *Mormon Enigma: Emma Hale Smith, Prophet's Wife, Elect Lady, Polygamy's Eve*. New York: Doubleday, 1984.

———. "'Sweet Counsel and Seas of Tribulation': The Righteous Life of the Women in Kirtland." *BYU Studies* 20, no. 2 (Winter 1980): 151–62.

Nibley, Hugh. *The Message of the Joseph Smith Papyri: An Egyptian Endowment*. Salt Lake City: Deseret Book, 1975.

———. *Mormonism and Early Christianity*. Salt Lake City: Deseret Book Company, 1987.

————. *No, Ma'am, That's Not History*. Salt Lake City: Deseret Book Co., 1945.

————. *Temple and Cosmos*. Salt Lake City: Deseret Book Company, 1992.

Oaks, Dallin H., and Marvin S. Hill. *Carthage Conspiracy: The Trial of the Accused Assassins of Joseph Smith*. Urbana: University of Illinois Press, 1975.

Odierne, James C. *Opinions on Speculative Masonry*. Boston, 1830.

O'Donovan, Connell. "The Mormon Priesthood Ban and Elder Q. Walker Lewis: 'An example for his more whiter brethren to follow.'" *The John Whitmer Historical Association Journal* 26 (2006): 47–99.

[Ogden, John Cosens]. *View of the New-England Illuminati: Who are Indefatigably Engaged in DESTROYING THE RELIGION AND GOVERNMENT OF THE UNITED STATES; Under a Feigned Regard for the Safety—and under an Impious abuse of True Religion*. 2nd ed. Philadelphia: Printed for James Carey, 1799.

Oliver, George. *The Antiquities of Free-Masonry*. London: G. and W. B. Whittaker, 1823.

————. *The Historical Landmarks and other Evidences of Freemasonry Explained in a Series of Practical Lectures*. 2 vols. London, 1845–1846.

Önnerfors, Andreas. "*Maçonnerie des Dames*: The Plans of the Strict Observance to Establish a Female Branch." In Alexandra Heidle and Jan A. M. Snoek, *Women's Agency and Rituals in Mixed and Female Masonic Orders*, 89–113. Leiden: Brill, 2008.

Pascoe, Peggy. "A History of Two Stories." *Dialogue: A Journal of Mormon Thought* 27, no. 2 (Summer 1994): 237–45.

Paton, Chalmers I. "The Mormons and Masonic Symbols." *The Freemason* (London) 3 (1871): 427.

Paulos, Michael Harold. *The Mormon Church on Trial: Transcripts of the Reed Smoot Hearings*. Salt Lake City: Signature Books, 2007.

Payson, Seth. *Proofs of the Real Existence, and Dangerous Tendency, of Illuminism. Containing an Abstract of the Most Interesting Parts of what Dr. Robison and Abbe Barruel have published on this subject; with collateral proofs and general observations…* Charlestown [MA]: Printed by Samuel Etheridge, 1802.

Peterson, Dan. "Notes on 'Gadianton Freemasonry.'" In *Warfare and the Book of Mormon*, edited by Steven D. Ricks and William J. Hamblin, 174–224. Provo, UT: Foundation for Ancient Research and Mormon Studies, 1990.

Peterson, H. Donl. *The Story of the Book of Abraham: Mummies, Manuscripts, and Mormonism*. Salt Lake City: Deseret Book Company, 1995.

Piatigorsky, Alexander. *Who's Afraid of Freemasons?* New York: Barnes and Noble, 2005.

Pick, Fred L., and G. Norman Knight. *The Freemason's Pocket Reference Book*. 3rd rev. ed. London: Frederick Muller, 1983. These reference books have been published in numerous editions and the citations in the text are from later editions.

————. *The Pocket History of Freemasonry*. London: Frederick Mullen Limited, 1965.

Pike, Albert. *The Masonry of Adoption*. N.p.: 1866.

Poll, Michael R., ed. *Masonic Words and Phrases*. New Orleans: Cornerstone
   Book Publishers, 2005.

Pratt, Parley P. *Autobiography of Parley P. Pratt*. 3rd ed. Salt Lake City: Deseret
   Book Company, 1938.

Preston, William. *Illustrations of Masonry*. 11th ed., 1801. Reprinted with an introduction by Colin Dyer. Wellingborough: Aquarian Press, 1985.

Priest, Josiah. *A View of the Expected Christian Millennium*. Albany: Loomis
   Press, 1827.

Prince, Gregory A. *Having Authority: The Origins and Development of Priesthood
   during the Ministry of Joseph Smith*. Independence, MO: Independence Press,
   1993.

———. *Power from on High: The Development of Mormon Priesthood*. Salt Lake
   City: Signature Books, 1995.

Prince, Gregory A., and William Robert Wright. *David O. McKay and the Rise of
   Modern Mormonism*. Salt Lake City: University of Utah Press, 2005.

*Proceedings before the Committee on Privileges and Elections of the United States
   Senate*. 4 vols. Washington, D.C.: Government Printing Office, 1904–1906.

*Proceedings of the Grand Lodge of Illinois, from Its Organization in 1840 to 1850
   Inclusive*. Reprint. Freeport, IL: Journal Print, 1892.

Quaiffe, Milo M. *The Kingdom of Saint James: A Narrative of the Mormons*. New
   Haven, CT: Yale University Press, 1930.

Quincy, Josiah. *Figures of the Past*. Boston: Roberts Brothers, 1883.

Quinn, D. Michael. *Early Mormonism and the Magic World View*. Salt Lake City:
   Signature Books, 1998.

———. "Latter-day Saint Prayer Circles." *BYU Studies* 19 (Fall 1978): 79–105.

———. *The Mormon Hierarchy: Origins of Power*. Salt Lake City: Signature
   Books in association with Smith Research Associates, 1994.

———. "Mormon Women Have Had the Priesthood since 1843." In *Women and
   Authority, Re-emerging Mormon Feminism*, ed. Maxine Hanks, 365–409. Salt
   Lake City: Signature Books, 1992.

Record of Nauvoo Lodge under Dispensation. LDS Church History Library, Salt
   Lake City.

Remy, Jules. *Voyage au pays des Mormons*. 2 vols. Paris: E. Dentu, 1860.

Remy, Jules, and Julius Brenchley. *A Journey to Great-Salt-Lake City*. 2 vols. London: W. Jeffs, 1861.

*Revelation of Free Masonry as Published to the World by a Convention of Seceding
   Masons*. Rochester: The Lewiston Committee, 1828.

Reynolds, John C. *History of the M[ost]. W[orshipful]. Grand Lodge of Illinois,
   Ancient, Free, and Accepted Masons, From the Organization of the first Lodge
   within the limits of the State, up to and including 1850*. Springfield, IL: H. G.
   Reynolds Jr., 1869.

Rich, Paul J. *Chains of Empire: English Public Schools, Masonic Cabalism, Historical Causality, and Imperial Clubdom*. London: Regency Press, 1991.

Richardson, Jabez. *Richardson's Monitor of Freemasonry*. New York: Lawrence
   Fitzgerald, 1860.

Roberts, Allen D. "Where Are the All-Seeing Eyes? The Origin, Use and Decline of Early Mormon Symbolism." *Sunstone* 4 (May–June 1979): 22–37.

Roberts, Allen E. *Freemasonry in American History*. Richmond, VA: Macoy Publishing and Masonic Supply, 1985.

Roberts, B. H. *A Comprehensive History of the Church of Jesus Christ of Latter-day Saints, Century I*. 6 vols. Salt Lake City: Church of Jesus Christ of Latter-day Saints, 1930.

———. *Defense of the Faith and the Saints*. Salt Lake City: Deseret News, 1907.

———. *Life of John Taylor*. Salt Lake City: George Q. Cannon & Sons, 1892.

———. "To the Youth of Israel." *Contributor* 6 (May 1885): 296–97.

Robinson, Phil. *Sinners and Saints*. London: Sampson, Law, Marston, Searle & Rivington, 1883.

Robison, John. *Proofs of a Conspiracy against all the Religions and Governments of Europe carried on in the Secret Meetings of Freemasons, Illuminati and Reading Societies*. 4th ed. London: printed for T. Cadell Jun. and W. Davies and W. Creech, 1798.

Saunders, Richard L., ed. *Dale Morgan on the Mormons: Collected Works, Part 2, 1949–1970*. Norman, OK: The Arthur H. Clark Company, 2013.

Schultz, Edward T. "The Order of High Priesthood." In Stillson, *History of the Ancient and Honorable Fraternity*.

Sharman, Walter. "A look at the Hebraic terms and prayers used in Dermott." *AQC* 105 (1992): 49–68.

Sherwood, H[enry] G. "H. G. Sherwood, 1839–1844." Church History Library, [1854], CR 100 396.

Sheville, John, and James L. Gould. *Guide to the Royal Arch Chapter: A Complete Monitor for Royal Arch Masonry, etc. To Which Are Added Monitorial Instructions in the Holy Order of High Priesthood in Royal Arch Masonry, with the Ceremonies of the Order, by James L. Gould*. New York: Masonic Publishing and Manufacturing Co., 1868.

Shipps, Jan. *Mormonism: The Story of a New Religious Tradition*. Urbana: University of Illinois Press, 1987.

Shook, Charles Augustus. *The True Origin of Mormon Polygamy*. Cincinnati: Standard Publishing Co., 1914.

Smith, Andrew F. *Saintly Scoundrel: The Life and Times of Dr. John Cook Bennett*. Urbana: University of Illinois Press, 1997.

Smith, Ethan. *A Dissertation on the Prophecies Relative to the AntiChrist and the Last Times; Exhibiting the Rise, Character, and Overthrow of the Terrible Power: and a Treatise on the Seven Apocalyptic Vials*. Charlestown [MA]: Samuel T. Armstrong, 1811.

Smith, George. *The Use and Abuse of Free-Masonry*. London, 1783.

Smith, George D., ed. *An Intimate Chronicle: The Journals of William Clayton*. Salt Lake City: Signature Books and Smith Research Associates, 1991.

———. *Nauvoo Polygamy: "…but we called it celestial marriage*. Salt Lake City: Signature Books, 2008.

———. "Nauvoo Roots of Mormon Polygamy, 1841–46: A Preliminary

Demographic Report." *Dialogue: A Journal of Mormon Thought* 27, no. 1 (Spring 1994): 1–72.

Smith, Joseph. "Important Facts Relative to…John C. Bennett." *Times and Seasons* 3:17 (1 July 1842): 839–43.

Smith, Joseph, Jr., et al. *History of the Church of Jesus Christ of Latter-day Saints*. 7 vols. Edited by B. H. Roberts. Salt Lake City: Deseret News Press, 1902–1932.

Smith, Joseph Fielding. *The Way to Perfection*. Salt Lake City: Deseret Book, 1931.

Smith, Lucy Mack. *Biographical Sketches of Joseph Smith, the Prophet, and His Progenitors for Many Generations*. Liverpool: S. W. Richards, 1853.

Snoek, Jan A. M. *Initiating Women in Freemasonry: The Adoptive Rite*. Leiden: Brill, 2012.

———. "Introduction." In Heidle and Snoek, eds., *Women's Agency and Rituals*, 4–7.

———. "Researching Freemasonry: Where Are We?" *Journal for Research into Freemasonry and Fraternalism* 1:2 (2010): 227–48.

Spalding, Franklin Spencer. *Joseph Smith, Jr., as a Translator*. Salt Lake City: The Arrow Press, 1912.

Stauffer, Vernon L. *New England and the Bavarian Illuminati*. New York: Columbia University Press, 1918.

Stavish, Mark. *Freemasonry: Rituals, Symbols and History of the Secret* Society. Woodbury, MN: Llewellyn Publications, 2007.

Stearns, John G. *An Inquiry into the Nature and Tendency of Speculative Free-Masonry*. 2nd ed. Westfield, NY: H. Newcomb, 1828.

Stenhouse, Fanny. *Exposé of Polygamy in Utah: A Lady's Life Among the Mormons*. New York: American News, 1872.

———. *"Tell it All": The Story of a Life's Experience in Mormonism*. Hartford, CT: A. D. Worthington & Co., 1874.

Stenhouse, T. B. H. *The Rocky Mountain Saints*. New York: D. Appleton & Co., 1873.

Stevenson, David. *The First Freemasons: Scotland's Early Lodges and Their Members*. Aberdeen, KS: Aberdeen University Press, 1988.

———. *The Origins of Freemasonry: Scotland's Century, 1590–1710*. Cambridge: Cambridge University Press, 1988.

Stillson, Henry Leonard, ed. *History of the Ancient and Honorable Fraternity of Free and Accepted Masons*. Boston: Fraternity Publishing, 1910.

Stone, William L. *Letters on Masonry and Anti-Masonry, Addressed to the Hon. John Quincy Adams*. New York: O. Halsted, 1832.

Sunderland, La Roy. *Mormonism Exposed and Refuted*. New York: Pieray & Reed, 1838.

Supplementary Report of the Committee Appointed to Ascertain the Fate of Captain William Morgan. Rochester, NY: Printed for the Committee by Edwin Scranton, 1827.

Tabbert, Mark A. *American Freemasons*. New York: New York University Press, 2005.

Taggart, Stephen G. *Mormonism's Negro Policy: Social and Historical Origins*. Salt Lake City: University of Utah Press, 1970.

Talmage, James E. *The House of the Lord*. Salt Lake City: Deseret Book, 1912.

Taysom, Martha. "Is There No Help for the Widow? The Strange Life of Lucinda Pendleton Morgan Harris." Unpublished paper presented at the Mormon History Association, Lamoni, Iowa, May 1993.

Thomas, John. *Sketch of the Rise, Progress, and Dispersion of the Mormons*. London: Arthur Hall & Co., 1848.

Thompson, John E. *The Masons, the Mormons and the Morgan Incident*. Ames: Iowa Research Lodge No. 2 AF&AM, 1984.

Topping, Gary. *The Story of the Cathedral of the Madeleine*. Salt Lake City: Sagebrush Press, 2009.

Town, Salem. *The Probable Origin and Dissemination of Ancient Masonry, Amongst the Various Nations*. N.p.: n.p., 1812.

———. *A System of Speculative Masonry*. Salem, NY: Dodd and Stevenson, 1818. Town's book was published in multiple editions and some citations may reference later printings.

Tucker, Pomeroy. *Origin, Rise, and Progress of Mormonism*. New York: D. Appleton & Co., 1867.

Tullidge, Edward W. *The History of Salt Lake City and Its Founders*. Salt Lake City, 1886.

———. *Life of Joseph, the Prophet*. New York: Tullidge & Crandall, 1878.

———. *Tullidge's Histories, Volume II: Containing the History of All the Northern, Eastern and Western Counties of Utah; Also the Counties of Southern Idaho*. Salt Lake City: Juvenile Instructor, 1889.

———. *The Women of Mormondom*. New York: N.p., 1877.

Turner, Orsamus. *History of the Pioneer Settlement of Phelps and Gorham's Purchase*. Rochester, NY: William Alling, 1851.

Upton, William H. *Negro Freemasonry*. Cambridge, MA: The M. W. Prince Hall Grand Lodge, 1902.

Van Beek, Walter E. A. "Hierarchies of Holiness: The Mormon Temple in Zoetermeer, The Netherlands." In *Holy Ground: Reinventing Ritual Space in Modern Western Culture*, edited by P. Post and A. Molendijk, 255–99. Leuven: Peters, 2010.

———. "Meaning and Authority in Mormon Ritual." *International Journal of Mormon Studies* (2010): 17–40.

Van Dusen, Increase McGee, and Maria Van Dusen. *A Dialogue between Adam and Eve, the Lord and the Devil, called the Endowment*. Albany: Printed by C. Kilmer, 1847.

———. *The Mormon Endowment: A Secret Drama, or Conspiracy, in the Nauvoo-Temple in 1846*. Syracuse, NY: N. M. D. Lathrop, 1847.

Van Noord, Roger. *Assassination of a Michigan King*. Provo, UT: Religious Studies Center, Brigham Young University, 2004.

———. *King of Beaver Island: The Life and Assassination of James Jesse Strang*. Urbana: University of Illinois Press, 1988.

Van Wagoner, Richard S. *The Complete Discourses of Brigham Young*. 5 vols. Salt Lake City: Smith-Pettit Foundation, 2009.

———. *Mormon Polygamy: A History*. 2nd ed. Salt Lake City: Signature Books, 1992.

Vaughn, William Preston. *The Anti-Masonic Party in the United States 1826–1843*. Lexington: University Press of Kentucky, 1983.

Vinton, David. *The Masonic Minstrel*. Dedham, MA: H. Mann and Co., 1816.

Vogel, Dan, ed. *Early Mormon Documents*. 5 vols. Salt Lake City: Signature Books, 1996–2003.

———. "Mormonism's Anti-Masonick Bible." *John Whitmer Historical Association Journal* 9 (1989): 17–30.

Vogel, Dan, and Brent Lee Metcalfe. *American Apocrypha, Essays on the Book of Mormon*. Salt Lake City: Signature Books, 2002.

Waite, Arthur Edward. *A New Encyclopedia of Freemasonry*. 2 vols. London: William Rider and Son, 1921.

———. *The Real History of the Rosicrucians*. London: George Redway, 1887.

Walgren, Kent L. *Freemasonry, Anti-Masonry and Illuminism in the United States, 1734–1850, A Bibliography*. Worcester, MA: American Antiquarian Society, 2003.

———. "James Adams: Early Springfield Mormon and Freemason." *Journal of the Illinois State Historical Society* 75 (Summer 1982): 121–36.

Walker, Ronald W. "Edward Tullidge: Historian of the Mormon Commonwealth." *Journal of Mormon History* 3 (1976): 55–72.

Walkes, Joseph A., Jr. *Black Square & Compass, 200 Years of Prince Hall Freemasonry*. Richmond, VA: Macoy Publishing & Masonic Supply Co., Inc., 1979.

———. *A Prince Hall Masonic Quiz Book*. Rev. ed. Richmond, VA: Macoy, 1989.

Ward, Henry Dana. *The Antimasonic Review and Magazine* 2, no. 10 (October 1830): 293–97.

———. *Free Masonry*. New York, 1828.

Ward, Maurine Carr. "'This Institution is a Good One': The Female Relief Society of Nauvoo, March 17, 1842, to March 16, 1844." *Mormon Historical Studies* 3, no. 2 (Fall 2002): 87–203.

Warvelle, George W. *Observations on the Order of High Priesthood*. 2nd ed. Chicago: J. C. Burmeister, 1915.

Watson, Elden J., comp. *The Orson Pratt's Journals*. Salt Lake City: Compiler, 1975.

Webb, Thomas Smith. *The Freemason's Monitor, or, Illustrations of Masonry*. Albany: Spencer and Webb, 1797, and New York: Southwick and Crooker, 1802.

Weed, Thurlow. *The Facts Stated*. Chicago: National Christian Association, 1882.

———. *Life of Thurlow Weed*. Edited by Harriet A. Weed. Boston: Houghton Miflin and Co., 1883.

Wells, Roy A. *The Rise and Development of Organized Freemasonry*. London: Lewis Masonic, 1986.

———. *Understanding Freemasonry*. London: Lewis Masonic, 1991.

Wheelan, Joseph. *Mr. Adams's Last Crusade*. New York: Public Affairs, 2008.

Whitman, Jason. "The Book of Mormon." *The Unitarian* 1 (January 1, 1834): 47–48.

Whitney, Helen Mar. *Why We Practice Plural Marriage*. Salt Lake City: Juvenile Instructor, 1884.

Whitney, Orson F. *History of Utah*. 4 vols. Salt Lake City: George Q. Cannon & Sons, 1892–1904.

———. *Life of Heber C. Kimball*. Salt Lake City: Published by the Kimball Family, 1888.

Widtsoe, John A. "Fundamentals of Temple Doctrine." *The Utah Genealogical and Historical Magazine* 13:3 (July 1922): 129–30.

———. "Temple Worship." *The Utah Genealogical and Historical Magazine* 12 (April 1921): 49–64.

———. "Whence Came the Temple Endowment?" *Improvement Era* 53:2 (February 1950): 94–95.

———. "Why Did Joseph Smith Become a Mason?" *Improvement Era* 53:9 (September 1950): 694–95.

Wilkinson, Toby. *The Rise and Fall of Ancient Egypt*. New York: Random House, 2011.

Women's Masonry or Masonry by Adoption. Explaining the Making of a Masoness, with the Form and Furniture of the Lodge. The Working of these Lectures, &c. with their Signs, Tokens, &c. Clearly Explained. By a Sister Mason. London: Printed for D. Hookham and D. Steel, 1765.

Wood, Gordon S. *Empire of Liberty: A History of the Early Republic, 1789–1815*. New York: Oxford University Press, 2009.

———. *Revolutionary Characters: What Made the Founders Different*. New York: Penguin Press, 2006.

Yates, Frances A. *The Rosicrucian Enlightenment*. London: Routledge & Kegan Paul, 1972.

Young, Ann Eliza [Webb]. *Wife No. 19*. Hartford, CT: Dustin, Gilman & Co., 1875.

Young, Brigham. "Remarks by President Brigham Young." *Journal of Discourses* 18:303 (January 1, 1877). Liverpool, England: Latter-day Saints' Bookseller's Depot, 1854–1886.

Index